Tower

Historian and biographer Nigel Jones has written acclaimed books on subjects as diverse as Nazi Germany, Patrick Hamilton and Rupert Brooke. A former deputy editor of History Today and BBC History magazines, he has appeared on historical documentaries on BBC TV and radio and writes and reviews widely for national newspapers and periodicals. Nigel is founder-director of www.historicaltrips.com.

He lives near Brighton in East Sussex with his partner and three children.

Praise for Tower

'In writing about the Tower's glory days, Nigel Jones has produced a wonderfully rollicking history of England itself. Told with relish, it should be a godsend to any history teacher who needs to hold the attention of his pupils.'

Christopher Hudson, Daily Mail

'A breezy account of the Tower's past is full of surprises . . . Nigel Jones knows how to tell a tale with just enough detail to make the story work in any period since the 11th century . . . thrilling history.'

Jad Adams, Sunday Telegraph

'Much as I love books on Britain's past, it is a long time since I found one which enthralled me as much as the 400 pages of this volume. Jones tells the colourful story in an equally lively fashion, and the two sections of black and white plates, from the Bayeux Tapestry to the Krays, are well chosen. An epic history – and an epic . . . . okbag

'In the hands of Nig . . . . orary guide, providing the . . . . lling, insight and narrativ . . . . of the Tower.'

Tristram Hunt MP, Sunday Express

'In this jaunty history Nigel Jones seeks to conjure the many characters that have lived, been imprisoned and perished within its walls . . . Jones weaves yarns from the Tower's past into the familiar tapestry of English history. His prose is dashing.'

David Gelber, *Times Literary Supplement*

'This is a riveting, pacy and vivid chronicle of the Tower's turbulent past from the Norman Conquest to the Kray twins. Extensively and soundly researched, it combines a compelling narrative sweep with engaging detail and engrossing anecdotes, and will appeal to serious scholars and interested browsers alike. Given the Tower's rich history, it's an ambitious project, yet it succeeds spectacularly. It's a must for every self-respecting historian's bookshelf. I warmly recommend it.'

Alison Weir, *BBC History Magazine* Book of the Year

'This is the book for you: it is breezy, exciting, and despite much grim subject matter, often humorous. The author demonstrates that the history of the Tower is not only the history of London, but of post-Norman England. *Tower* is as entertaining as it is informative.'

Mike Paterson, *London Historians Blog*

'What Nigel Jones delivers is . . . a complex mixture of history and legend, a virtual primer of English and then British history from William I to Elizabeth II . . . a taut and vivid narrative.'

Brian Morton, *Tablet*

'The biography of a building that has occupied a position of strategic and political importance to English history for more than 900 years. Readers will be impressed by the detailed research revealed . . . [and] the breadth of coverage, but also by the rather novel approach of placing the building at the heart of the story.'

Historical Association.

Tower

Nigel Jones

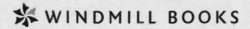 WINDMILL BOOKS

Published by Windmill Books 2012

6 8 10 9 7

Copyright © Nigel Jones 2011

Nigel Jones has asserted his right under the Copyright, Designs and
Patents Act, 1988, to be identified as the author of this work.

This book is a work of non-fiction.

First published in Great Britain in 2011 by Hutchinson

Windmill Books
The Random House Group Limited
20 Vauxhall Bridge Road, London SW1V 2SA

Addresses for companies within The Random House Group Limited can be
found at: www.randomhouse.co.uk/offices.htm

The Random House Group Limited Reg. No. 954009

www.randomhouse.co.uk

A CIP catalogue record for this book
is available from the British Library

ISBN 9780099537656

Typeset in MT Fournier by Palimpsest Book Production Limited,
Falkirk, Stirlingshire
Printed and bound in Great Britain by Clays Ltd, St Ives Plc

Penguin Random House is committed to a sustainable
future for our business, our readers and our planet.
This book is made from Forest Stewardship
Council® certified paper.

ACKNOWLEDGEMENTS

My first appreciations must go to the Constable of the Tower, General Sir Richard Dannatt, and his deputy, Colonel Dick Harrold, and their staff, for making me welcome in their historic domain. The Tower today is a unique village in the heart of London; a close community in which all who work there take an intense and justified pride. Writing its story has been a privilege.

My thanks, too, go to those friends and colleagues who have taken a sympathetic interest in the project and helped it along in various ways: Jad Adams, Barbara Antounyan, David Boyle, Merrie Cave, George Clode, Neil Faulkner, Richard Foreman, John Greenwood, Gerard Greaves, Chris Hale, Mike Ivey, Roger Moorhouse, Dave Musgrove, Paul Lay, Michael Leventhal, Michael Prodger, Jason Webster. Thanks to Helena Bell for finding me a rare 1921 history of the Tower by her ancestor, Walter Bell.

A special thank-you to my former English teacher, Roger Sawyer, the biographer of Roger Casement, for telling me more about Casement's time in the Tower. And thanks, too, to Mark Bicknell for lending me his collection of books about the Overbury case.

Finally, my eternal gratitude to those closest to the project who have lived and sweated it out along with me: my agent and friend Charlie Viney, who has been such a tower of strength, humour and optimism tempered by realism; my patient publisher Caroline Gascoigne, her assistant editor Paulette Hearn and my beloved partner Lally Freeborn and our children.

Thanks to you all.

CONTENTS

PART ONE

CHAPTER ONE

BEGINNINGS

They had been fighting all day, and sheer exhaustion was sapping their strength. The light of the autumn afternoon was fading fast. The grass covering the long slope of Senlac Hill was sodden and greasy with mud and blood, littered with the mangled corpses of the slain, 'soiled with their own gore'. Seven hours of savage combat, as the famed Norman cavalry charged repeatedly uphill, meeting the unbreached dam of the Saxon shield-wall, had taken a grim toll of both armies. They had started the day with roughly equal numbers — seven to eight thousand men each — but a quarter were already dead, and another quarter would follow them to Valhalla before the day was done.

The Normans, after the rough cross-Channel voyage in their open longships, were near despair as their assaults dashed against the rampart of the shield-wall. The English Saxons, dog-tired from their week's forced march from Yorkshire after smashing the last Viking invasion of England at Stamford Bridge, could hardly stand from fatigue. The wall of their inter-locked shields was looking ragged, the gaps torn by the falling dead too wide to be plugged. Only the fierce spirit of their warrior king, Harold, sternly ordering them to close ranks, kept them in their places.

Duke William of Normandy seized the situation at a glance. He had less than two hours left to win a decisive victory and with it the throne of England. If he failed to break the Saxon line by dark, his cause would be lost. Harold would remain king, and William would be lucky to escape ignominiously back across the Channel. Only a massive final effort might yet secure the kingdom. William had already tried a few tricks that day. He had swerved his knights away just as they reached the English front line after a headlong charge. It was a risky manoeuvre — a feigned downhill retreat could easily become a rout. But it had worked. Believing that their enemies were fleeing, some Saxons had broken ranks and chased their enemies down the slippery slope. Once in the open, however, the Norman horsemen had turned on the isolated foot soldiers and cut them down.

Now, William again threw in his cavalry. He flung them at either end of the English line. Simultaneously, William ordered his archers to unleash a storm of arrows at the heart of the Saxon defences: the elite housecarls who guarded Harold with their terrifying five-foot axes. William ordered his bowmen to shoot so that their arrows arched over the shield-wall and fell from the sky, a hard rain on a soft target – the exhausted English rear ranks. A lucky arrow found a spectacular mark: King Harold's eye. Although the faithful housecarls closed ranks for a brave last stand around their stricken king, Saxon morale finally cracked.

Pursued by Norman horsemen, the surviving conscript soldiers of the fyrd fled first. Behind them on the torn ground lay the hacked bodies of England's last Saxon king and his brothers Gyrth and Leofwine. Harold's body was so slashed and battered that only his mistress, Edith Swan-neck, could recognise it by intimate 'certain indications' when she searched the battlefield. Here, on the evening of 14 October 1066, it was Anglo-Saxon England that lay dead along with its king, its bleeding body trampled into the earth. To the victor went the spoils.

Hastings was not the first battle that Duke William had fought – nor would it be the last. Born in 1027/8 as the illegitimate son of Duke Robert 'the Devil' of Normandy by Herleva, a humble tanner's daughter, William learned early that life is an unceasing struggle. Aged eight when his father died in 1035, he was surrounded by plots and assassinations as ambitious nobles vied for the throne. At twenty-three, William won his first victory near Caen against his rebel cousin, Guy of Burgundy. A successful soldier, and a lucky one, William fought off repeated French incursions and steadily expanded his duchy.

His triumphs whetted William's ambitious appetite. He persuaded England's ageing king, the childless Edward the Confessor, to accept his tenuous claim to the English throne. (William's wife Matilda was descended from Alfred the Great, so he was Edward's second cousin, once removed.) Despite having allegedly pledged William his support after being shipwrecked on the Normandy coast, Harold Godwinson, England's leading Saxon nobleman, accepted the crown offered him by the Anglo-Saxon council, the Witan, on Edward's death in January 1066. Incensed, William prepared to back his ambitions by force. He assembled a fleet and an army of Normans, Bretons and French mercenaries, secured the blessing of the Pope, and sailed for the Sussex coast.

Moving slowly, and savagely stamping out sparks of resistance as he went, William took until mid-December to reach Southwark on the south bank of the Thames. He found the wooden London Bridge – the only river crossing – barred against him. Cautiously, he marched west, burning and looting, until at Wallingford he met a submissive Archbishop of Canterbury, Stigand, sent by the Witan to offer him the crown. On Christmas Day 1066, William I was crowned by Stigand in Edward the Confessor's newly built Westminster Abbey.

Outside the abbey, the coronation ceremony was disrupted by angry Londoners loudly opposing their new, foreign-born king. Alarmed, Norman soldiers rushed from the abbey with drawn swords. It was a reminder that their conquest was far from complete. They were a tiny, beleaguered army amidst a hostile, barely cowed populace which bitterly resented these strangers with their weird tongue and alien ways. The Normans had killed the English king and decimated his host, but to enjoy the fruits of victory they realised they must be equally ruthless in repressing Harold's discontented former subjects. And they had a tried and tested method at their disposal: the castle.

Fortified hilltops had been commonplace in England for centuries; as the ramparts and ditches of Dorset's Maiden Castle, dug by the ancient British, attest. The Romans had their fortresses too, as the stones of Hadrian's Wall bear witness. But it was the Normans who patented the 'motte-and-bailey' castle. The idea was simple. Where there was no convenient natural hill, as with a sandcastle, the Normans threw up an artificial mound – the motte – crowned by a wooden tower. They then dug a defensive ditch – the bailey – around its base, using the excavated earth to make an additional encircling rampart, surmounted by a wooden fence. By 1066 the Normans were past masters at the speedy construction of these flat-pack fortresses – they could build one within a week – and their first acts upon landing had been to put up two, at Pevensey and Hastings.

Eventually, the Normans would build some eighty-four motte-and-bailey castles across their newly conquered kingdom. The early ones were sited near their Sussex beachhead – Lewes, Bramber and Arundel – guarding strategic river valleys in case they needed to retreat to the coast in a hurry.

The temporary wooden castles were soon replaced by solid stone, once the Normans felt confident that they were in England for good. The functions of the castle were twofold: as the imposing home and headquarters of the local magnate; and as a refuge for his loyal soldiers, servants and tenants in times of trouble. They were the nodal points of the feudal mesh of occupation that the Normans threw over the conquered kingdom.

William rewarded the knights who had followed and fought alongside him with large parcels of conquered English land – together with the overlordship of the peasants who tilled the soil. Great castles were erected at Dover, Exeter, York, Nottingham, Durham, Lincoln, Huntingdon, Cambridge and Colchester. Norman names – de Warenne, de Lacey, Beauchamp – replaced Saxon ones in the nobility and clergy as a military occupation morphed into a new social structure.

William lavished special care on one castle in particular. His new capital, London, was vulnerable to attack on its eastern, seaward side. It clearly needed the protection that only a great castle could provide. England's earlier military masters, the Romans, had pointed the way. In the fourth century AD, to defend the port-city they called Londinium Augusta, they had thrown up a stout city wall. It ran north–south from today's Bishopsgate down to the Thames before swinging west along the northern bank of the river. Only the foundations of the wall remained by William's time, but it was in the angle of its south-eastern corner, on the site of a former Roman fort named Arx Palatina – erroneously thought by the Normans (and by Shakespeare) to have been put up by Julius Caesar – that William decided to build his super-castle.

The rowdy scenes at his coronation had made it very clear that Norman rule could only be imposed by brute force. As a contemporary French chronicler, William of Poitiers, recorded, 'Certain strongholds were made in the town against the fickleness of the vast and fierce populace.' A fortress to house London's garrison and intimidate its inhabitants – who totalled around 10,000 in 1066 – had to be constructed without delay. Within days of the Christmas coronation, conscripted gangs of Saxon labourers were hacking into the frozen soil. The remains of the Roman city wall served as a temporary barrier on the new fortress's eastern and southern sides. A wide and deep ditch, surmounted by a palisaded rampart, went up on the western and northern sides of the site. A wooden tower was erected within three days in the middle of this rough rectangle. After a decade, however, largely spent in stamping out rebellions in the west and north of his new kingdom, William decided to remake his temporary timber structure in permanent stone.

William had the very man in mind to realise his vision. He envisaged the building of a mighty edifice that would be at once fortress and palace – the last word in state-of-the-art military architecture, as well as an impressive royal residence. A towering, solid structure that would literally set Norman superiority in stone, inducing a Saxon cultural cringe and snuffing out any notion of further resistance to his rule. The master architect that William hand-picked to oversee the project was a talented cleric named Gundulf.

Born in 1024 near Caen, Gundulf, like many medieval bright lads, entered the all-powerful Church. Legend says his decision was prompted by his miraculously surviving a storm during a perilous pilgrimage to Jerusalem in the 1050s. He became a protégé of Lanfranc, the Italian-born prior of the great Benedictine Bec Abbey. Gundulf demonstrated a particular talent for architecture, designing churches and castles. He was an emotional man, given to outbursts of weeping, which won him the disrespectful nickname 'the Wailing Monk'. Nevertheless, when William sacked the Saxon Stigand and chose Lanfranc to succeed him as the first Norman Archbishop of Canterbury in 1070, the new archbishop brought his temperamental clerk with him to Canterbury, where Gundulf supervised extensions to the cathedral.

The castle-building cleric caught the Conqueror's eye, and Gundulf was soon summoned to London. William suggested that Gundulf should crown his architectural career by building in London the greatest castle in all Christendom. Gundulf was reluctant. Ageing and increasingly pious, he told the king that in his time left on earth he wanted to construct an ecclesiastical, rather than a secular, edifice – if possible a cathedral. No problem, William replied. At Rochester, near Canterbury, there already was a cathedral, in ruins since being pillaged in a Viking raid. He offered Gundulf the vacant bishopric and money for the cathedral's restoration – so long as he built the great London castle first. So – doubtless with more tears and fears – Gundulf accepted his commission. In 1077 he became Bishop of Rochester, and the following year – 1078 – work on London's new Tower commenced.

* * *

Gundulf set about his task with vigour. He was fifty-four, old by medieval standards, yet would not only complete both the White Tower and Rochester Cathedral (along with a fine new castle there), but also see out both the Conqueror, and William's son and successor, William Rufus. The White Tower gained its name from the blocks of pale marble-like Caen stone imported from Normandy with which it was constructed – with infill of local coarse Kentish ragstone – and from the coats of gleaming whitewash with which it was eventually plastered. The Tower was a huge structure, the biggest non-ecclesiastical building in England, rising some ninety feet above ground, with four pepperpot turrets, one at each corner. All the turrets were rectangular, with the exception of the north-east one, which was rounded to contain a spiral staircase.

When complete, the White Tower measured 107 feet (33 metres) from east to west, and 118 feet (36.3 metres) from north to south. The massive walls were fifteen-foot thick at their base, tapering to eleven at the top, built on foundations of chalk and flint. An undercroft, or basement, formed the lowest floor of the White Tower, where a well was sunk to supply the inhabitants with water. The cellar vaults were used at first for storing food and drink, as well as arms and armour. A more sinister function was their later use as the Tower's principal torture chambers, the agonised screams of victims muffled by the surrounding earth and stone. The main, middle floor was entered, then as now, on the south side by an exterior wooden staircase, which could be quickly removed in case of siege. This floor was originally the living quarters of the Tower's garrison, and was divided into three vast rooms: a refectory with a great stone fireplace where the soldiers ate and made merry when off duty; a smaller dormitory with another fireplace where they slept; and, in the south-east corner, the beautifully simple Romanesque Chapel of St John, with its twelve huge pillars.

The second floor of the White Tower was reserved for the use of the constable – the Tower's commander appointed by the monarch – for important guests, and eventually for state prisoners of high status. The rooms consisted of a great hall complete with fireplace – used for state banquets – with a minstrels' gallery running around it; and the constable's chamber, a space which served as bedroom, meeting room and living quarters for the Tower's top official. Each floor had latrines with chutes into underground cesspits emptied by the 'night soil men'.

South of the White Tower, a gaggle of smaller buildings sprang up to serve Gundulf's great structure. These, the first of many additions and extensions added to the original keep across the centuries, were temporary structures not designed to last. There were stables, blacksmiths' forges, stores for building materials, chicken coops and pigsties. Before he died, Gundulf oversaw the building of a high curtain wall guarding the Tower on its southern, river side, and the first of many smaller towers girding the great central keep. It is not known exactly when the oldest surviving tower outside the White Tower, the Wardrobe Tower, was built; and the date of the construction of the royal palace south of the White Tower is equally uncertain. It is likely, however, that by the time of Gundulf's death, aged eighty-four, in 1108, a start had been made.

Gundulf had long outlived his original patron. Having finally subdued the English, William the Conqueror was faced with rebellion in his native Normandy by his own oldest son, Robert Curthose. It was on a punitive expedition against the rebellious town of Mantes, in 1087, that the Conqueror, his youthful stockiness run to fat, met his end. Having torched the conquered town with his customary savagery, William was riding through the blazing streets when his horse stepped on a burning ember. The beast bucked violently, throwing William's great gut against the hard iron saddle pommel, and causing devastating internal injuries to his swollen stomach. William took ten days to die in agony. Feared more than loved, when he expired, his remaining followers stripped his bloated corpse and then scarpered. The Conqueror's final indignity came at his funeral, when monks attempted to stuff his carcase into a small sarcophagus. The cadaver split, filling the church with such a noxious stench that mourners fled. It was an inglorious end for the victor of Hastings and the founder of the Tower.

William's second son, Rufus, succeeded him as King William II of England. Rufus was a tyrant who quarrelled violently with the Church, offended his nobles with his extravagance and apparent homosexuality, and oppressed his long-suffering Saxon subjects with punitive taxation. But Rufus, like his father, was an enthusiastic builder. His most lasting legacy was the great Westminster Hall, and he supervised the completion of Gundulf's work at the Tower before his violent and mysterious death by an arrow fired in the New Forest in August 1100.

Henry Beauclerc – so called because, alone among the Conqueror's children, he could read and write – William I's third and youngest son, succeeded Rufus as Henry I. Ruthless, ambitious and astute (he was in the fatal hunting party and may have engineered his brother's death), Henry lost no time in riding to London and claiming the throne. Henry consolidated Norman rule during his long and stable reign – partly by marrying a Saxon wife, Edith, heiress to King Harold's House of Wessex. But although he fathered more bastard children (over twenty, by half a dozen mistresses) than any other English king, like that other later fertile monarch, Charles II, Henry left no legitimate male heir. His only sons by Edith, William and Richard, died when their vessel, the *White Ship*, failed to clear rocks outside Barfleur on a drunken homecoming voyage from Normandy in November 1120.

Henry named his daughter Matilda, widow of the Holy Roman Emperor Henry V, as his heiress. But a female ruler – even an empress – was an unwelcome novelty to the Norman nobility. When Henry died in 1135, the majority of England's barons invited Stephen of Blois, grandson of William the Conqueror by his daughter Adela, to take the throne. Matilda, endowed with her combative family's ferocious genes, refused to accept Stephen's claim to the crown. Aided by her half-brother Robert of Gloucester, she invaded England to assert her right by force of arms.

Stephen's seizure of the throne and Matilda's outraged opposition, condemned England to two decades of sporadic civil war known as 'the Great Anarchy'. Stephen, though a brave and stubborn warrior, lacked the ruthlessness essential in a medieval ruler. He was too weak to eliminate Matilda, yet the prospect of a woman ruler was terrifying enough to his barons to keep him on his increasingly shaky throne. The result was a bloody stalemate in which the over-mighty barons – constantly changing sides – lorded it over their long-suffering serfs as the rival rulers fought like cat and dog.

The more unscrupulous barons, like modern mobsters, imposed a protection tax known as a 'tenserie' on their unlucky tenants. But the extortion provided no protection at all. The *Anglo-Saxon Chronicle* laments, 'When the wretched people had no more to give, they plundered and burned all the villages. Then was corn dear, and flesh and cheese and butter, for there was none in the land. The wretched people perished with hunger; some who had been great men were driven to beggary. Never did a country endure more misery, and men said openly that Christ and His saints slept.'

One of these robber barons was Geoffrey de Mandeville, holder of the office of Constable of the Tower of London, whom his biographer, the Victorian historian J. H. Round, calls, 'the most perfect and typical presentment of the feudal and anarchic spirit that stamps the reign of Stephen'. The office was then a hereditary post, and the first constable, appointed by the Conqueror, had been Geoffrey's grandfather, another Geoffrey de Mandeville – rewarded for his courage at Hastings. The first Geoffrey was succeeded by his son William, and in his turn Geoffrey the younger had taken the post. He had done fealty to Stephen when the new king arrived to secure the capital and the Tower after Henry I's death. A grateful Stephen created Geoffrey 1st Earl of Essex – the first of three holders of that title to enjoy close, but ultimately fatal, connections with the Tower – and rewarded him with land.

Stephen was the first monarch to reside in the Tower, keeping the Whitsuntide festival there in 1140 in the newly built royal palace south of the White Tower. The king hoped that his generosity to Geoffrey would ensure the constable's loyalty as the civil war dragged on. But the unscrupulous Geoffrey took advantage of the chaos to advance his own interests. Given custody of the daughter of King Louis VI of France, Princess Constance, who was betrothed to Stephen's eldest son and heir, Eustace, Geoffrey kept the young girl under virtual house arrest – the first of the Tower's many royal captives – defying Stephen's demands for her release until he had seen who would win the civil war.

In 1141, Stephen was defeated and captured by Matilda's forces at Lincoln and taken in chains to Bristol. Geoffrey deftly changed sides and pledged the Tower's allegiance to Matilda. He demanded in exchange that he should receive yet more land, acquiring in addition the powerful post of sheriff of the counties adjoining London. Matilda also gave him permission to strengthen the Tower's defences. De Mandeville's defensive work came just in time. When Stephen was freed, civil war flared up again and the London Mob – strong supporters of Stephen – chased Matilda from the capital and besieged the Tower. Not only did Geoffrey see them off, he staged a sortie as far as Fulham and abducted the Bishop of London – the king's leading supporter in the capital – as a hostage.

Geoffrey extorted a high price from Stephen for the renewal of his dubious loyalty. He forced the king to grant him yet more land around London, making him the wealthiest magnate in the kingdom. Stephen's patience with the treacherous constable finally ran out in 1142 when he discovered that Geoffrey had secretly renewed contact with Matilda, intending to turn his coat yet again. The king summoned Geoffrey to St Albans in Hertfordshire, arrested him, and forced him to disgorge all his land and castles – including the Tower – before he was freed.

Enraged and embittered, Geoffrey left the court 'like a vicious and riderless horse, kicking and biting' to embark on the final phase of his turbulent career. Imitating Hereward the Wake, the legendary guerrilla leader who had resisted the Norman conquest, he took to the East Anglian Fens around Ely, expelling the monks from Rumsey Abbey in order to use it as his headquarters. Here, the ex-constable lived an outlaw's life for many months, preying on the surrounding countryside. But in 1144, Geoffrey's luck ran out when he was mortally wounded in a skirmish with Stephen's forces at Mildenhall in Suffolk.

Word of Geoffrey's expulsion of the Rumsey monks had reached the Pope himself, who excommunicated him for sacrilege. He was denied a Christian burial, and his body lay in the open 'for the ravens to devour'. His remains were rescued by the Order of the Knights Templar. Grateful to Geoffrey for past services, the Templars clothed his corpse in their robes and brought his body to London's Temple Church off the Strand on the north bank of the Thames – a mile from the Tower where he had held sway for thirteen years. They enclosed the corpse in a lead coffin, but, in obedience to the papal ban, left it unburied between two trees in the churchyard. Here it remained for twenty years before someone took mercy on the old rogue and finally laid Geoffrey to rest before the church's west door. His effigy, clad in Templars' robes, can be seen in the church to this day.

In 1153, after nearly two decades of bloody but inconclusive strife, Stephen and Matilda reached a compromise in the Treaty of Winchester. Depressed by the death that year of his heir Eustace, Stephen disinherited his second son and accepted Matilda's son, Henry – who had already entered the fray on his mother's behalf – as his heir. In return, Stephen would be unmolested for the rest of his reign. Henry did not have long to wait: the following October, 1154, Stephen died at Dover and Henry, England's first Plantagenet king, was proclaimed Henry II.

The year before his death, Stephen had named Richard de Lucy as constable of the Tower in succession to Geoffrey de Mandeville. Henry confirmed the appointment and made de Lucy his Chief Justiciar – the foremost legal officer in the kingdom. Restoring the rule of law and financial stability to England after the bloody chaos of Stephen's reign was Henry's most urgent task, and one he carried out with the driving, restless energy that characterised the Plantagenets. One of the first jobs was to put the neglected Tower into a state fit for its dual role as fortress and palace. These works, early in 1156, were supervised by Henry's most efficient subordinate – his chancellor, friend and future turbulent Archbishop of Canterbury, Thomas Becket. Henry appointed the humbly born Becket to succeed de Lucy as constable of the Tower in 1161. Further works – including giving the chapel in the White Tower a lead roof – were carried out in the 1170s.

In the first written description of the Tower after the improvements, Becket's biographer William Fitzstephen describes the royal palace within the Tower as 'great and strong with encircling walls rising from a deep foundation and built with mortar tempered with the blood of beasts'. The mortar had not literally been mixed with animal blood, and the Tower's use as a zoo still lay some years ahead. This description refers to Roman bricks and tiles which had been pounded into reddish powder to make the mortar. With its contrasting white and red facades, the Tower had become England's keystone.

Brutal and quarrelsome though Henry was – as his notorious ill-judged outburst which led to Becket's murder, and his feuds with his own wife and sons, demonstrate – he was an able and effective ruler. His marriage to the redoubtable Eleanor of Aquitaine added a vast new swathe of French territory to his domains. By the end of Henry's reign in 1189 his Angèvin empire stretched from Ireland to Spain. But things fell apart again after his death, when his glamorous second son and successor, the tall, golden-haired Richard I, called *Coeur de Lion*, abandoned England for the Third Crusade, while Henry's youngest and favourite son, John, proved himself arguably England's worst king. Once again, as under Stephen, local lords flexed their muscles in the absence of any commanding monarch to curb them.

One such magnate was William Longchamp, Bishop of Ely, Richard's chancellor, justiciar and constable of the Tower, who the king had left in virtual charge of the kingdom during his prolonged absence in the Holy Land (Richard spent just ten months of his ten-year reign in England). The French-born Longchamp, as unlike his royal master physically as it was possible to be – he was small, swarthy and crippled – was efficient, but also arrogant and vain.

Longchamp spared no expense in turning the Tower into a stronghold capable of withstanding a prolonged siege. He almost doubled the fortress's size by extending the south curtain wall westwards along the river, and built a new tower, the Bell Tower, at its south-west corner. Beyond this new outer, western ward, Longchamp dug a fresh defensive ditch to the west and north of the castle to make a moat, although this last refinement proved too much for Longchamp's engineers, and for the time being the ditch remained dry. The little cleric also spent £100 equipping the Tower with the latest state-of-the-art military technology: mangonels, giant siege engines that could hurl huge rocks further and faster than existing catapults.

Longchamp's extensions had, however, enraged neighbouring Londoners whose houses he had destroyed and whose land he had grabbed. The chronicler William of Newburgh said of the hated prelate, 'The laity found him more than king, the clergy more than Pope, and both an intolerable tyrant.' There was, therefore, much local support when in 1191 followers of Prince John, attempting to snatch the kingdom from his brother Richard during the king's absence on crusade, laid siege to the Tower. The siege lasted only three days, for Longchamp's moral resolve proved to be rather weaker than his physical defences. He exchanged his clerical garb for the disguise of a woman's dress, limped through the besiegers' lines, and fled to Dover Castle, leaving the Tower in John's hands.

While Richard lived, the quarrelsome, treacherous and avaricious John could never feel secure in his illicitly gained kingdom. In 1192 word arrived that Richard had been arrested in Vienna on his way back from the Holy Land and handed over to the Holy Roman Emperor, Henry VI, to be held in Durnstein Castle on the Danube until a vast ransom of £100,000 was paid by the people of England. Raising this enormous sum crippled the English economy, and left a lasting legacy of resentment among the poor on whom fell the chief burden of paying it.

A Londoner named William Fitzosbert, known as Longbeard, headed popular demands for the financial load to be more equitably spread. A charismatic demagogue, Fitzosbert had a fine line in eschatological, pseudo-religious imagery in his appeals for social revolt. He told one excited meeting, 'I am the saviour of the poor. Do ye, O poor, who have experienced the hardness of rich men's hands, drink from my wells the waters of salvation. And ye may do this joyfully; for the time of your visitation is at hand. I will divide the waters . . . and separate the humble from the haughty and treacherous. I will separate the elect from the reprobate, as light from darkness.' Tradesmen, apprentices and many of the poorer sort flocked to hear Longbeard deliver this intoxicating message, and he attracted a following of thousands to his public orations, thwarting attempts by the Mayor of London to arrest this dangerous rabble-rouser. An ex-Crusader himself, Fitzosbert took his case to King Richard who, released from captivity, was campaigning in Normandy.

After Fitzosbert returned to a London on the verge of civil insurrection, the authorities cracked down hard. The new justiciar and Archbishop of Canterbury, Hubert Walter, sent an armed posse to arrest him. Fitzosbert made the mistake of putting one of Walter's posse to the sword. Panicking, he and his friends sought sanctuary in the spire of St Mary's Church in Bow. Refusing to respect this, the archbishop had a fire lit beneath them and smoked the fugitives out. Half choked, Fitzosbert staggered into the street and was stabbed in the stomach by the son of the man he had murdered. Battered, bleeding, but still alive, he was tied to a horse's tail, and painfully dragged to the Tower, where he was thrown into a dungeon to await his inevitable condemnation. On 6 April 1196 he was again dragged through the streets, this time to Smithfield, a traditional site of butchery, where he was agonisingly stretched between horses, before being hanged along with nine of his followers.

The support that Fitzosbert had attracted among poor Londoners was evident at his execution when the crowd, instead of jeering, watched his suffering in respectful silence, before converging on the scaffold and bearing away the gallows as a sacred relic. The very earth on which the gibbet had stood was carried away in handfuls until a great pit marked the site, while the chains in which Fitzosbert had been hanged were reputed to work miracles. Only after Walter had placed armed guards at the site did popular adulation for the 'martyred' Longbeard die away. But the rebel had inaugurated a tradition of social dissent that would involve the Tower more violently before another two centuries had passed.

In 1199 King Richard I died a lingering death from gangrene after an arrow struck his shoulder while he was besieging the French castle of Chalus. John inherited the kingdom he had coveted for so long. John proved himself a crueller, more grasping, and more untrustworthy king than he had been as a mere prince. After fourteen years of his tyranny, John's barons rebelled in May 1215, entered London, and besieged the Tower. Although the fortress's lieutenant, William of Huntingdon, proved a tougher nut than William Longchamp had been and stubbornly held out, his royal master did not. Within weeks the unpopular king had famously been forced to a humiliating capitulation at Runnymede on the Thames. John put his seal to Magna Carta – the great charter drawn up by the rebel barons which, for the first time in English history, set legal limits to an absolute monarch's arbitrary powers. Only one of the charter's sixty-three clauses specified granting rights and liberties to 'all freemen of the realm and their heirs for ever'; and a second forbade the selling, delay or denial of justice. Most of the other clauses safeguarded the rights and privileges of the barons. It was hardly a great milestone on the road to democracy. But it was a start.

No sooner was the wax hard on his seal, however, than John was trying to persuade his old enemy the Pope to annul the charter. Civil war broke out again, and in 1216 the exasperated barons, terminally tired of their treacherous king, invited the Dauphin of France, Prince Louis, to take John's place on the throne. The leader of the barons who took this radical step, Robert Fitzwalter, had a very personal score to settle with 'Bad King John'.

In 1214, John – a notorious lecher, currently married to his second wife, the teenage Isabella of Angoulcme – had taken a fancy to Robert's eldest daughter, Maud Fitzwalter, known for her beauty as 'Maud the Fair'. Robert, governor of London's second greatest fortress, Baynard's Castle, rejected John's request to make Maud his mistress. Enraged, the king had Maud abducted to the Tower. Here, John imprisoned her in a cage at the top of the circular turret at the north-east corner of the White Tower: the highest point in the fortress. John responded to Robert Fitzwalter's indignant protests with more violence, sending troops to sack Baynard's Castle, and forcing Robert to flee to France with his wife and two remaining children.

Maud remained in her high cage, a cold and lonely prisoner, yet resolute against all John's assaults on her virtue. Neither exposure nor hunger, nor solitary confinement, could break the 'Fair Maid's' resistance. At last, an exasperated John had an egg impregnated with poison. When the egg was presented to Maud the famished girl ate it – and painfully died. Though sources for this story are scanty, it is entirely in keeping with John's malevolent character. Besides, the king had a record when it came to murdering his helpless captives. Apart from killing his nephew Arthur, John kept his niece, Eleanor of Brittany, another 'Fair Maid', imprisoned at Corfe Castle in Dorset until she died. He deliberately starved twenty-two French knights to death in the same fortress. The black legend of 'Bad King John', though questioned by some modern revisionists, accords with the awful facts.

Summoned by the rebel barons to replace their despised king, Prince Louis landed in Kent with a French army in May 1216. The gates of London were opened and he was proclaimed king in old St Paul's Cathedral. As Louis took up residence in the Tower with his small court, John retreated into the East Anglian Fens, where nemesis caught up with him.

The fight was going out of John, who was sick with dysentery. In October 1216, half of his baggage train was lost in the Wash estuary near Wisbech. Along with his crown and coronation regalia, jewels, dozens of gold goblets, silver plate and costly fabrics were swallowed up before the king's horrified eyes in the treacherous tides and quicksands of the Wash. The news was the final straw for John. In a feast of forgetting, the sick king gorged himself on pears and peaches washed down with cider – the very worst diet for a dysentery patient. The next day, afflicted with agonising abdominal cramps, he struggled on by litter through atrocious weather, reaching Newark Castle where, on the night of 18/19 October, he died. Few mourned.

John's death was, however, a body blow to Prince Louis' hopes of power. For John had a legitimate English-born son and heir – nine-year-old Henry of Winchester – who was crowned king in Gloucester a week after his father's death. A strong and capable baron, Earl William Marshal, became regent and set about organising the boy king's forces. London remained loyal to Louis, who doggedly fought on. However, Marshal defeated him at Lincoln and the following year the Dauphin's last hope was destroyed when a French fleet bringing reinforcements was sunk off Sandwich in Kent by an English squadron under Hubert de Burgh. Louis sailed home, and young Henry III became undisputed king of England.

CHAPTER TWO

THE MENAGERIE AND THE MINT

King Henry III is little remembered today and less regarded. But he was not only, after George III, England's second-longest reigning king, he was also the monarch who, after the Conqueror himself, did most to create the Tower of London. Henry grew up under the control of capable men. His first mentor was the great soldier William Marshal. After Marshal's death in 1219, power rested with the next justiciar, Hubert de Burgh. Both men governed wisely during Henry's minority, introducing a sorely needed stability after John's disastrous reign.

Accustomed from his youth to deferring to strong men, Henry never developed his own personality, although he had the obstinacy of the weak, and the arrogance of his Plantagenet genes. He lacked that essential prerequisite of a successful medieval king: the ability to lead an army to victory. Instead, like his later namesake Henry VI, Henry III developed compensating religious and aesthetic interests more suitable to a sensitive cleric than a secular ruler. So, although Henry's reign was a disaster for his kingdom, for the Tower it was a blessing.

Henry adored beautiful things. He loved art and architecture, and spared no expense in richly endowing churches and chantries and filling his palaces with furnishings. He failed to establish a *modus vivendi* with his English barons, preferring to lavish land, titles and cash on foreign favourites, particularly French ones. Naturally, this caused resentment among the English nobility, already grumbling at the king's spendthrift ways. But if the exchequer suffered from Henry's extravagance, the Tower was its beneficiary.

In the 1220s, when Henry was still in his teens, work began on a massive reconstruction and expansion programme at the Tower. The young king had decided to make the fortress a principal royal residence, and the work of transforming it from austere castle to opulent palace went on virtually continuously throughout his fifty-six-year reign. South of the White Tower, Henry also built luxurious private quarters for himself and his French queen, Eleanor, with a great hall between them. Their rooms were connected by a long covered walkway. Yet again, the boundaries of the Tower were hugely expanded. The original Roman city wall, which had formed the Tower's eastward defences, was demolished and replaced by a tall new curtain wall. On the southern, river side of the Tower, the existing curtain wall was strengthened and extended. It was now washed by the Thames and bolstered by new towers: the Salt Tower on the southeast corner; the Lanthorn Tower (so called because it carried a lamp to guide river traffic on the Thames); and the largest tower in the fortress outside the White Tower, the octagonal Wakefield Tower.

Originally called the Blundeville Tower, the Wakefield then acquired the name Record Tower because of its function as the repository of state papers. It got its present name from William of Wakefield, a fourteenth-century royal clerk who acted as archivist of the papers stored there. The Wakefield Tower was conceived and built as part of the royal palace and, along with the neighbouring rectangular Bloody Tower, it is the only surviving part of that structure. The king's private quarters were on the first floor of the Wakefield. Later notorious as the site of the murder of Henry VI, the tiny oratory where Henry was struck down while saying his prayers was originally built by his equally pious predecessor Henry III for his own devotions. The lower floor was the guardroom of the soldiers who protected their king. Just east of the Wakefield was a private watergate from the river for the use of Henry and his guests; while to the west, the vaulted tunnel that visitors walk through under the Bloody Tower today was originally the main watergate entrance to the Tower complex, before the erection of St Thomas's Tower above Traitor's Gate by Henry III's son Edward I.

To the west and north of the Tower, a new curtain wall was raised with a land-gate causeway entrance in the middle of the western section. The encircling wall was crowned with a range of new towers: the Devereux, the Flint, the Bowyer, the Brick, the Martin, the Constable and the Broad Arrow. Beyond the curtain wall, Henry completed Longchamp's work by turning his ditch into a wide moat, skilfully filled with river water by a Flemish expert ditch-digger, one Master John. By the end of Henry's reign, the Tower of London was an impregnable island, surrounded on its western, northern and eastern sides by its moat and bounded on its southern side by the formidable barrier of the Thames. Henry gave the

White Tower a new coat of paint, and behind its sheer new curtain walls it loomed over London more formidably than ever like a great chalk cliff, glimmering and vast.

For all the care and attention lavished on the military fortifications without, and the splendid regal apartments within, the Tower project closest to the devout Henry's heart was the stronghold's new chapel, St Peter ad Vincula (St Peter in Chains – adopted as the Tower's patron saint). This small structure in the north-west corner of the Tower's new Inner Ward – destined to hold the mortal remains of the Tower's most distinguished victims – was originally a parish church lying outside the Tower's walls. The king presented St Peter's with a peal of bells and issued minute and detailed orders for the redecoration of the chapel he had enclosed, reflecting his camp interest in the liturgical elements of religion, including instructions for the figures of saints to be 'newly coloured, all with the best colours . . . also two fair cherubim with cheerful and pleasant countenances to be placed on either side of the great crucifix'. Henry devoted equal care to the existing chapel in the White Tower, the Romanesque St John's, painting its high rounded ceiling a rich shade of red and adding to its simple Norman outlines rood-screens, stained-glass windows and the figures of saints. He endowed it as a chantry, with money for priests and monks to pray perpetually for the souls of the departed. All told, by the end of his reign, Henry's improvements to the Tower had cost the English exchequer a whopping £9,000 (at least £7 million in today's values).

By 1236, although not yet complete, Henry's Tower palace was already a magnificent enough structure to be the setting for the celebration of his marriage at twenty-nine to the raven-haired young beauty Eleanor of Provence, who was just fourteen. The king marked the occasion with a second coronation. Inaugurating a tradition that all monarchs would spend the night before their coronation in the fortress, Henry and Eleanor set out for Westminster Abbey from the Tower amidst the cheers of a capital *en fête* for the occasion: 'London . . . so full of noble gentry and country folk . . . that she could scarcely contain them within her capacious bosom,' wrote a chronicler. 'The streets were delivered from dirt, mud, sticks and everything offensive.' In the Tower itself, Henry lovingly decorated his bride's private chamber with a delicate colour scheme of roses on a white background.

Apart from its two chapels, and his wife's apartments, the luxury-loving Henry splashed out on a new and somewhat eccentric use for his pet palace: the founding of a royal menagerie. Henry's animal collection began in February 1235 when his sister Isabella married the Holy Roman Emperor Frederick II, *'Stupor Mundi'* ('the Wonder of the World'). Frederick was a great patron of the arts and sciences, and generous too. He gave Henry the nearest equivalent in his own zoo to the three lions that adorned the English royal coat of arms: a trio of leopards. Henry decided against sending the leopards to the zoo his great-great-grandfather Henry I had founded at Woodstock in Oxfordshire. Instead he showcased them in his gleaming new Tower of London. Sadly, however, neither William de Botton, the courtier appointed as the leopards' keeper, nor anyone else in England had any experience of tending such exotic beasts, and the animals soon perished. The last reference to a leopard in the royal accounts comes in 1240.

In March that year, however, another big cat arrived at the Tower: a real, royal lion. The royal archives record that one William (probably the same William de Botton who had looked after the leopards), 'the keeper of the King's Lion, [is] to have 14 shillings that he expended in buying chains and other things for the use of the Lion'. In 1251, Henry decided to move all the animals in Henry I's Woodstock menagerie to the Tower. We do not know precisely what species were involved, but references over the years to the zoo at Woodstock mention lions, leopards, lynxes and a camel — so Henry now had a respectable animal collection to show visitors to his proud new palace. Those who came to gawp at them were the Tower's first true tourists. For centuries, the menagerie remained the monarch's private property; and the privileged few allowed in were his favoured friends or the families of Tower employees.

In 1252, the creatures at the Tower were joined by another exotic animal. A polar bear — sent to Henry by King Haakon IV of Norway — arrived, along with a Norwegian keeper. The first ever seen in England, the polar bear attracted enormous public curiosity. When the twopence-a-day allowance provided by the sheriffs of London for its upkeep proved insufficient to meet the beast's appetite, the bear was allowed to fish for free food in the river running past its Tower enclosure. With his usual attention to detail, Henry spelled it out:

> Greetings. We command you that for the keeper of our white bear, lately arrived from Norway . . . ye cause to be had one muzzle and one iron

chain to hold that bear without [outside] the water, [and] one long, strong cord, to hold the same bear fishing or washing himself in the river Thames.

The King at Windsor

Three years later, in 1255, when Londoners had got used to the strange sight of the bear swiping salmon out of the Thames, an even more wondrous beast lumbered into view. Befitting its size and status, the entry of this new addition to the Tower menagerie was slow and stately, attracting enormous crowds en route like the progress of a superstar. Which it was. The first elephant to appear in these islands plodded up the Pilgrim's Way from Canterbury to London led by its keeper, Henricus de Flor. Yet another gift to Henry from a fellow European monarch, Louis IX of France, the elephant made a spectacular entrance to the Tower via a large riverboat. Such was the jumbo's celebrity, that the aged contemporary chronicler, the monk Matthew Paris, was lured from his abbey in St Albans to the Tower to see the new arrival, drawing the elephant in a memorable picture as well as in words: 'The beast is about ten years old, possessing a rough hide rather than fur, has small eyes at the top of his head and eats and drinks with a trunk.'

The sheriffs of London, already too cash strapped to feed the king's polar bear, must have groaned when they saw this enormous arrival. But Henry now commanded Londoners to stump up £22 for the construction of a huge wooden elephant house. He laid down the exact measurements: twenty feet by forty (twelve metres by six). Sadly, despite these spacious surroundings, within two years the elephant died. A huge pit was dug near St Peter's chapel for the gigantic carcass, but the following year, the elephant's remains were disinterred and its bones carted to Westminster Abbey, recently rebuilt and beautified in Gothic glory by Henry. Here the bones were carved into boxes to house the skin, hair, teeth and other relics, allegedly of saints, that were popular icons in medieval Europe. Given the number of reputed saints' bones throughout Christendom, and the high prices such relics fetched, it may well be that the crafty Westminster clerics passed off the elephant's bones themselves as the remains of holy saints. The elephant house did not go to waste either: at least until 1278 it was used to hold some of the Tower's human captives, including scores of the Jews arrested by Henry's son Edward I that year.

It was Edward I who moved the menagerie to its permanent home, a large barbican gateway he built at the west entrance around the appropriately named Lion Tower. Unless let out of their cages to fight or caper in the courtyard, the animals were kept in two rows of cramped cells let into the Lion Tower's walls. From the 1270s on, all those entering or leaving the Tower – including prisoners on their way to execution – made their exits and entrances to the accompaniment of roars, squawks, screeches and growls from the beasts and birds in the monarch's menagerie. Edward I not only kept it supplied with new animals – he brought a lion and a lynx back from a visit to his domains in Gascony in 1288 – he also appointed an official 'Keeper of the King's Lions and Leopards' with accommodation in the Tower. Keepers, members of the royal household, usually held the job for life, though one unfortunate, William Bounde, keeper in Henry IV's reign in 1408, was sacked for complaining that his wages were in arrears. Even when paid on time, those wages were modest: set at sixpence a day, they remained unchanged for more than a century.

Edward's disastrous son and successor, Edward II, was fond of the animals after visiting them as a child. From the limited meat available in medieval London, in 1314 he ordered that the Tower's lion be supplied with a quarter of a sheep per day. In 1392 the zoo's exotica was extended when Richard II was given a camel, while his much-loved wife, Anne of Bohemia, was presented with a pelican, a symbol of piety. In 1436, however, during the reign of Henry V, disaster struck the menagerie when its major attraction – the lions – all died. Whether the big cats perished through neglect, malnutrition or some devastating animal disease, their keeper, one William Kerby, got the blame – and the boot. His successor, Robert Manfeld, presided over a lionless menagerie until 1445, when the pious but inept Henry VI married the feisty French princess, Margaret of Anjou. Margaret's father, the animal-crazy René of Anjou, although impoverished, spent what money he had on maintaining not one but two menageries at his castle of Saumur and his capital, Angers. Seeking to make the homesick teenager feel more at home, an English courtier presented Margaret with the ultimate wedding gift when she married Henry at Hampshire's Titchfield Abbey: a lion.

The treatment of animals in the Middle Ages left much to be desired by today's standards. Even the relatively privileged creatures in the Tower suffered the appalling cruelties routinely inflicted by medieval man in the name of 'sport'. To his credit, King Henry VII vociferously objected after watching two mastiff dogs baiting a lion in the Tower. According to John

Caius's treatise *The English Dogge*, Henry ordered the hounds to be hanged after witnessing the savagery, 'being deeply displeased, and conceiving great disdain, that an ill-favoured rascal cur should with such villainy assault the Lion, the king of all beasts'.

Not all kings, however, were as scrupulous as Henry VII. James I, an unpleasant sadist, became, for all the wrong reasons, of all British monarchs the most enthusiastic patron of the Tower menagerie. James cared not a fig for the creatures' welfare. On the contrary, his chief delight was to watch them tearing each other to bleeding bits. James frequently visited the Tower to slake his bloodlust – even remodelling the Lion Tower in 1603–05 to enhance the spectacle. A double row of cages, complete with trapdoors worked by pulleys, housed the animals, with a courtyard paved in Purbeck stone for them to fight in. The yard had a cistern 'for the Lyons to drink and wasche themselves in'. James even had a thirty-metre wooden viewing platform over the cages constructed for him to watch the fun more closely.

Occasionally, the cruel king was disappointed. In 1604, the year after his accession, James took delivery of a new African lion and ordered two English mastiffs to bait his new king of beasts. To supply them, he turned to the joint Masters of Bears, Bulls and Mastiff Dogs: Edward Alleyn, the famed actor, and his father-in-law Philip Henslowe, another theatrical luminary, who had purchased the post from the previous incumbent as a business sideline. Alleyn owned the Rose Theatre on the south bank of the Thames – neighbour and rival to Shakespeare's Globe. A popular actor–manager in the Admiral's Men theatrical troupe, Alleyn trod the boards at the Rose playing the leads in Christopher Marlowe's great tragedies. But he had a second career as owner of the nearby Hope Theatre, where down-market bear- and bull-baiting shows were staged. These cruel contests, in which specially bred mastiffs and bulldogs were set upon the tethered (and usually toothless) bigger beasts attracted huge crowds and helped Alleyn amass the fortune which he eventually used to found Dulwich College.

On 13 March 1604, James, his Danish queen Anne, and a retinue of bloodthirsty courtiers attended the Lion Tower to watch his new lion take on a trio of Alleyn's fiercest mastiffs:

> [The first dog] straightaway flew to the face of the lion. But the lion shook
> him off, and grasping him fast by the neck, drawing the dog upstairs and
> downstairs. The King, now perceiving the lion greatly exceed the dog in

strength, but nothing in noble heart and courage, caused another dog to be put into the den, who likewise took the lion by the face, and he began to deal with him as with the former; but whilst he held them both under his paws they bit him by the belly, whereat the lion roared so extremely that the earth shook withal; and the next lion ramped and roared as if he would have made rescue . . .

After the third mastiff had been put into the den to battle the lion, the heir to the throne, young Prince Henry, asked for the last dog's life to be spared, and adopted the mastiff as a pet, 'saying that he who has fought with the King of beasts shall never fight with any inferior creature'.

A year later, James was back for more blood sport. This time he watched two live cocks being devoured by a lion and lioness. After this, his blood lust whetted but by no means sated, the king ordered a live lamb to be lowered into the lions' den on a rope. Once more, however, he was cruelly disappointed, for in fulfilment of the biblical prophecy, the lion lay down with the lamb. Or rather, 'the lamb rose up and went towards the lions, who very gently looked upon him and smelled upon him without sign of any further hurt. Then the lamb was softly drawn up again in as good plight as he was set down.' James had to be content with watching another trio of Alleyn's mastiffs being put to the tooth and claw by the lions.

By James's reign, a tradition had grown up linking the fate of the Tower's big cats with the life of the monarch. Lions were sometimes named after the sovereign reigning at their birth, and there was a superstition that if the lion died, its namesake monarch would soon follow. (Since it was a capital offence to foretell the death of the monarch, each demise of a 'royal' lion was probably hushed up, and a younger and healthier animal renamed in its place.) This particular superstition had a long shelf life: as late as 1758, in the reign of George II, the gossipy Lord Chesterfield reported that many of 'the common people' believed that the monarch would die from an attack of gout he was then suffering, since 'one of the oldest lions at the Tower – much about the king's age – died a fortnight ago!'.

In 1599, a Swiss visitor, the chemist Thomas Platter, mentions seeing lions named Edward (after the boy king Edward VI) and Elizabeth after the current monarch, who were both, he assures us, 'more than 100 years old'. In July 1597, a Czech nobleman, the Bohemian Baron Zdenek Waldstein, visited the

Tower and records in his diary seeing 'two great lions and three lionesses, a leopard, a tiger and a huge porcupine'. The same porcupine, a rare beast indeed in Elizabethan England, may have been seen by Shakespeare, since a porcupine is mentioned in *Hamlet*.

By 1622 the Tower menagerie included eleven lions, two leopards, three eagles, two pumas, a tiger and a jackal. The animals owed a debt of gratitude to that stern ruler Oliver Cromwell who, in line with his regime's ban on theatrical performances, put a stop to bear- and bull-baiting. The royal menagerie itself flourished under Cromwell's republic, just as it had under the monarchy. In his book *Londonopolis*(1657) James Howell reports that there were six lions at the Tower, while a Polish visitor, Sebastian Gawrecki, records seeing lions, tigers, lynxes and 'an Indian cat from Virginia' (a cougar?).

In January 1666 another diarist who had only opened his famous journal just ten days previously, made his first of many visits to the Tower menagerie. Samuel Pepys enjoyed viewing an old lion called Crowly, 'who has now grown a very great lion and very tame', so much that, currying favour with his boss at the Navy Office, Lord Sandwich, he returned on 3 May 1662 with Lady Sandwich and her nieces and nephews:

> I took them and all my Ladys to the Tower and showed them the lions and all that was to be shown; and so took them to my house, and there made much of them, and so saw them back to my Lady's.

Pepys was not the only famous Restoration diarist to be associated with the Tower menagerie. His friend John Evelyn also frequently visited – and was much less impressed than his rival, particularly deploring the 'barbarous' baiting of the beasts (reinstated at the Restoration), and unfavourably comparing the cramped cages with the spacious animal enclosures he had seen elsewhere in Europe.

In 1671 the young Surveyor General of the King's Works, the architect and polymath Christopher Wren, took time off from designing the new St Paul's Cathedral to oversee a programme of modernisation at the Tower. This included a new house next to the Lion Tower as a home for the current keeper, Robert Gill. The Gills, an Essex family, had occupied the hereditary post for more than a century since the appointment of Thomas Gill in 1573. The last of the line, Robert's son William Gill, succeeded his father in 1675.

But familiarity with the big beasts did not ensure safety. In 1686 the mistress of William Gill, a Norfolk girl named Mary Jenkinson, showing off to some friends in the lions' den, ventured to stroke one of the creatures' paws:

> Suddenly he catched her by the middle of the arm with his claws and mouth, and most miserably tore her Flesh from the Bone, before he could be unloosed, notwithstanding that they thrust several lighted torches at him.

Sadly, despite the best attention of 'chirurgeons' who amputated Mary's mangled arm, she died.

In 1681 a mysterious malady in the Lion Tower wiped out three lions at a stroke, and the menagerie's population continued to dwindle. To boost the depleted numbers, King James II had several creatures transferred from his private collection in St James's Park to the Tower in 1687. But even though gone, the dead lions were not quite forgotten. Two were stuffed and kept on permanent display. By this date the Tower also housed a collection of 'curiosities' to entertain the public visiting the menagerie. Alongside the stuffed lions, visitors could view a 'unicorn's horn' and even a cloak allegedly lined with a unicorn's fur. In 1699, Ned Ward, writing in *The London Spy*, reported that the stuffed lions were showing their age. After visiting the live lions, 'where the yard smelt as frowzily as a dove-house or a dog-kennel', he encountered the late King Charles II's stuffed lion who 'had no more fierceness in his looks than he had when he was living, than the effigy of his good master [Charles] at Westminster has the presence of the original'. And as for the lion's mate, it 'made such a drooping figure with . . . false entrails, that it brought into my mind the old proverb . . . that a living dog is better than a dead lion'.

By 1704, in the reign of Queen Anne, John Stow's *Survey* listed the Tower menagerie as containing six lions; two leopards (or tigers – Stow is uncertain of the species); three eagles, including a bald eagle; two Swedish owls, one called Hopkins; two mountain cats, 'walking continually backwards and forwards . . . [and] very cruel'; and a jackal. Stow says that the jackal stank so badly that the creature's 'rank smell . . . hath much injured the Health of the man that attends them, and so stuffed up his Head that it affects his speech'.

At the end of the seventeenth century, zoos had become very fashionable, with rival menageries springing up across the country. The Tower authorities became increasingly concerned to protect their profitable monopoly. In 1697 they issued a stern public notice:

> That no person whatsoever (except . . . the Keeper of His Majesty's Lions) do for the future carry abroad, or expose to publick view, for their own private gain, any lions, lionesses, leopards or any other beasts which are *feroe naturae*, as they will answer to the contrary at their peril.

Thanks to the menagerie, by the eighteenth century despite competing rivals, the Tower was beginning to acquire the position it maintains today as the nation's leading tourist magnet. As the eighteenth century wore on and the Enlightenment dawned, the Tower's primary functions were changing. It had begun life as a castle with armoury and arsenal attached; then took on the functions of the kingdom's major royal palace; morphed into the prison, torture chamber and execution site for the state's enemies (real or perceived); now, as times gentled, the fortress's value as a place of entertainment became pre-eminent. Still central among the draws that packed in the punters was the menagerie. In 1741 a charming illustrated children's guide to the zoo listed and pictured the creatures to be seen there, including a lion and lioness called Marco and Phillis with their offspring Nero, a leopard called Will, a panther named Jenny, two tigers, a racoon, a porcupine, an ape, vultures, eagles and an unknown bird of prey called a 'Warwoven'.

The menagerie's growing pre-eminence as a tourist trap – entrance still sixpence, rising to a shilling by the eighteenth century's end – is reflected by the many references to it in English literature. As we have seen, Shakespeare, Pepys and Evelyn visited, as did those great pioneer journalists and pamphleteers Richard Steele and Joseph Addison. Jacobean dramatist John Webster, in his masterpiece *The White Devil*, refers to another menagerie superstition: that if the Tower lions were listless and depressed on Candlemas Day (2 February) and the day was 'fair and bright', then 'Winter will have another flight'. Webster has his character Flamenico say, '. . . the lions in the Tower on Candelemas Day, mourn if the sun shine for fear of the pitiful remainder of winter to come'. Tobias Smollett's novel *Humphrey Clinker* features maidservant Winifred Jenkins visiting the Tower and its 'monstracious' lion with teeth nine inches long; while William Makepeace Thackeray's hero Henry Esmond, in the eponymous novel, visits 'The Tower of London, with the armour and great lions and bears in the moat'.

After Matthew Paris's extraordinary depiction of the Tower's first elephant, probably the most familiar pictorial image of the menagerie is the engraving of a 'tyger' in William Blake's *Songs of Experience* (1794). Blake's depiction is remarkably anatomically accurate for such a fantastical artist, and accompanies the famous poem of the same name. Blake had indeed drawn his 'tyger' from life at the Tower after crossing the Thames from his home in Lambeth to visit the menagerie. Blake was famously unorthodox in his religious views, but a much more mainstream Christian also visited the menagerie for inspiration thirty years before. John Wesley, the founder of Methodism, came there on New Year's Eve 1764. Wesley wished this mission to settle for himself the tricky theological question of whether animals had souls. His method for investigating this was to observe how the lions reacted when music was played by a flautist. The response of the big cats to the flute's toots left Wesley no wiser: 'He began playing near four or five lions; only one of these rose up, came to the front of his den, and seemed to be all attention. Meantime, a tiger leaped over the lion's back, turned and ran under his belly, leaped over him again, and so to and fro incessantly.'

Scientists, as well as writers, artists and theologians, used the menagerie, though one who was inconvenienced by the Tower's resident creatures was the first Astronomer Royal, John Flamsteed. Invited by Charles II to set up an observatory in the White Tower's north-east turret in 1675, Flamsteed, who mapped and identified 3,000 stars, complained that the ubiquitous Tower ravens were depositing their droppings on the lenses of his precious telescopes. Soon afterwards, he decamped to the more salubrious surroundings of the new observatory at Greenwich.

The eminent Scottish surgeon and anatomist, John Hunter ironically, satirised by William Blake in his sole (and unpublished) novel *An Island in the Moon* as the sawbones 'Jack Tearguts' – reached a mutually profitable deal with the menagerie's head keeper John Ellys, who offered the carcasses of his dead animals to Hunter for dissection. Since it was almost impossible for anatomists to acquire human cadavers legally (a situation murderously exploited by the Edinburgh body snatchers Burke and Hare in the next century), Hunter used the Tower's animals for his dissections and for his famous skeleton collection at his homes in London's Leicester

Square and Earls Court. As a result scores of elephants, rhinos, lions, tigers, giraffes and other species all found their posthumous way from the Tower to Hunter's dissecting table in the 1750s – and made their contribution to his pioneering discoveries in the fields of dentistry, respiration, digestion and blood circulation. Hunter's work did much towards dispelling popular superstitions about animals. For example, a popular myth held that ostriches were able to digest iron. In 1751 an ostrich presented to George III by the Bey of Tunis choked to death in the Tower after being fed a large nail. Yet such superstitions died as hard as the unfortunate bird: forty years later, another Tower ostrich died after ingesting no fewer than eighty nails administered by its own keepers.

In those distant days, scientists and artists often worked closely together. Hunter, himself a gifted draughtsman, employed painters to immortalise his animals, including the great equine artist George Stubbs, whom Hunter commissioned to paint an anatomically accurate portrait of a newly arrived Great Indian Rhinoceros at the Tower. India had become a fruitful source of animals for the menagerie after the subcontinent was taken over by the East India Company, which sent many specimens home to the Tower, including elephants and tigers. Sir Edwin Landseer, probably Stubbs's only peer as an animal artist, and a child prodigy, frequently visited the Tower in his youth in the 1820s to sketch the creatures there – particularly the lions, who provided the original inspiration for the four magnificent beasts he eventually sculpted at the foot of Nelson's Column in Trafalgar Square.

Another artist who made the Tower his happy hunting ground, drawing both the menagerie and the Royal Mint, was the caricaturist Thomas Rowlandson. One of his best-known cartoons depicts visitors mingling with apes in the menagerie's 'monkey room', which opened in the 1780s. But after a boy was mauled by an overenthusiastic ape, this early experiment in cross-species communication was abandoned, and the monkeys went back behind bars. The popularity of the menagerie as a leisure attraction fluctuated with its changing animal population. The Napoleonic Wars, when Britain was at times cut off from its far-flung imperial possessions, and the menagerie starved of new blood, was a particularly lean time, coinciding with the long and lacklustre reign as head keeper of the appropriately named Joseph Bullock, who took over in 1801 and held the job for the next two decades. Among the resident creatures when Bullock arrived was a lioness called Miss Fanny Howe, named in honour of Admiral Howe's naval victory over France on 'the Glorious First of June' in 1794 – the lioness having been born in the Tower on the same day.

Besides Miss Fanny, the collection in Bullock's custody catalogued in 1809 also included a black leopardess called Miss Peggy, some tigers, a Barbary panther called Traveller, a hyena, a Mexican wolf, a silver fox, a racoon, a jackal and an eagle. By 1815, when Waterloo brought a final end to Napoleonic strife, the menagerie totalled a few (rather mangy) lions, a panther, a hyena, a tigress, a jackal and a bear. The bear, a famously fierce grizzly from America named Old Martin, presented to King George III by the Hudson's Bay Company, was a favourite with the public, and was treated with respect and care despite his ferocity. Gone were the days two centuries before when a menagerie bear which had killed a child negligently left in its yard in 1609 under James I was 'punished' by being set to fight a lion. Yet again the bloodthirsty James was disappointed when the lion refused to be roused to combat. The king ordered that the chained bear be baited to death by mastiffs instead. The dead child's mother was given a portion of the ticket takings from the bloody spectacle – watched by the entire royal family – as compensation for her loss. By 1822, despite Old Martin's popularity, Bullock's menagerie was down to just two animals – Martin himself and an elephant – and an aviary of birds. It seemed that extinction was nigh.

But at what seemed to be its last gasp, a saviour rode to the rescue in the shape of Alfred Cops, who succeeded the ineffectual Bullock on the latter's death in 1822. Cops was the first (and last) professional zoologist to hold the past of Chief Keeper at the Tower, and he was a man of energy, imagination and compassion for his charges. Already experienced at managing other commercial menageries, Cops set about his new duties with vigour. Not only did he channel resources into new animal acquisitions; he also toured the world himself in search of them. In addition, he applied his rationalist scientific outlook to improving the conditions of the creatures in his care, changing their diet to more nutritious fare, and building a spacious new forty-foot animal house with an aviary attached. As a result of Cops's active approach, six years after his appointment in 1828 the menagerie had improved out of all recognition, boasting a staggering 300 specimens from sixty different species – several born at the Tower, a sure sign of contented creatures.

These included, as well as a wide variety of big cats, wolves, bears, baboons, elephants, kangaroos (a newcomer from the relatively recently discovered continent of Australasia) antelopes, a zebra, and a flock of birds including eagles, vultures, macaws, owls and a pelican. Reptiles, too, were well represented, with alligators, an anaconda, a boa and a rattlesnake. Given the limited space at the Tower, species were crammed uncomfortably close together, living cheek by beak, so to speak – occasionally with fatal results. A hyena snapped off the head of an over-inquisitive secretary bird which incautiously stretched into the malodorous beast's den for a peek. And, in the year that this inventory was drawn up – 1830 – a lion was accidentally let into a cage containing a Bengal tiger and tigress described by a zoo guide as being of 'moody' temperament. A furious three-way catfight ensued, which the keepers were only able to stop after half an hour with the aid of burning torches. The outnumbered and severely mauled lion died later from its wounds.

It is, however, a measure of how much popular taste in entertainment had progressed from the licensed sadism of James I's time to the relative humanity of the Hanoverians, that an event which the Jacobean public would have paid good money to watch now excited a storm of bad publicity. The menagerie's management was widely blamed for their carelessness in inadvertently letting their star big cats fight to the death. Nonetheless, the publicity helped to pull back punters who had drifted away during Bullock's tenure. Business boomed at the Tower's ticket office, encouraged by the wide variety of creatures Cops had secured for a menageric that had regained its place in public affection.

And yet, paradoxically, Cops's success sealed the Tower menagerie's doom. Although Cops was himself keenly aware of the importance of keeping his animals happy, the sheer number of creatures he had squeezed into the Tower's cramped confines offended a public awakening to a new fellow feeling for our furred and feathered friends. (The RSPCA had recently been founded, and an Animal Protection Act giving rudimentary rights to farm and domestic animals had actually reached the statute-book.) In addition, there was mounting pressure from an influential and growing scientific establishment that such zoos should not be for the ignorant gawping of the vulgar multitude, but should have as their primary purpose the scientific study of animal species.

The *coup de grâce* was administered to the menagerie after the appointment in 1826 of the Duke of Wellington as the Tower's constable. The Iron Duke, hero of Waterloo, the man who had beaten Napoleon, and subsequently become prime minister too, was not a man to be trifled with – even by a strong character like Cops. And the duke was determined to close – or at least move – the menagerie and write *finis* to its colourful 600-year-old history. To Wellington's rigidly tidy military mind, the Tower was first and foremost a soldiers' garrison: a vital strongpoint in London's heart that might well be needed again as a fortress should riots and disorder ever threaten to get out of hand. Wellington did not like having to put up with the throngs of rubbernecking tourists who traipsed through the gates every day, getting in the way of his sentries, and gazing open mouthed at his parades. But if he had to endure the vulgar horde, he was damned if he was going to tolerate a herd of noisy, smelly animals and birds on his doorstep howling, screeching and gibbering.

The opening of the London Zoological Society's new Zoological Gardens in Regent's Park in 1828 gave the duke his opportunity for an alternative location; and the near fatal mauling of a keeper, Joseph Croncy, by a leopard in 1830 presented a perfect 'health and safety' excuse for the closure of Cops's beloved collection. Having secured permission from the new king, William IV, and the cooperation of the Zoological Society, Wellington briskly ordered that half the menagerie's inmates – the 150 creatures belonging to the king in the royal collection, including that stubborn survivor Old Martin – be transferred to Regent's Park. In December 1831 the move was made. Cops – as tenacious in his way as the duke kept the Tower menagerie open to show off the remaining creatures that he had personally acquired as his own property, but he was fighting a losing battle against the victor of Waterloo.

Although he halved the entry fee from a shilling to sixpence to compensate visitors for the disappearance of half the animals, Cops knew that he was beaten after two more unfortunate accidents gave the duke his opening to thrust a final bayonet into the menagerie's heart. One Sunday in April 1834 a Canadian timber wolf escaped from its den and loped across the drawbridge towards the Byward Tower, the Tower's main western gateway. A quick-thinking yeoman warder saw the beast approaching and quickly closed the wicket gate, whereupon the wolf seized a terrier belonging to a member of the Tower's garrison, a Sergeant Cropper. The dog, howling in pain and terror, struggled free from the wolf's jaws and fled up the tower's steps and into its master's apartment, hotly pursued by the wolf. Cropper's wife was alone in the apartment with her two young children as dog and wolf bounded in, but the wolf was only interested in finishing his interrupted encounter with the terrier, giving Mrs Cropper a precious few seconds to gather up her offspring and escape, shutting the wolf in as she fled. The beast was recaptured after a heroic struggle by Cops's assistants, but a further incident the following year – in which a monkey bit one of his guardsmen who was taking an illicit short cut through its enclosure – proved the last straw for the duke. A wolf almost devouring a child was one thing, but a monkey taking a chunk out of a guardsman's leg was quite another. He peremptorily told Cops that it was the king's wishes that the Tower menagerie be closed.

On 28 August 1835 the public were admitted to the menagerie for the final time. Between then and October, the last of Cops's creatures were sold to the Zoological Societies of London and Dublin and to fellow collectors, and the empty cages which had housed them were broken up for scrap. Cops clung on grimly to his keeper's house at the Tower (possession of which he had been granted for life, irrespective of the fact that there were no more animals for him to keep). And he still drew his salary of eleven shillings a day, augmenting the allowance by giving animal collectors the benefit of his expert advice and experience. He witnessed the wedding of his eldest daughter Mary to Benjamin Franklin Brown, an American collector who had bought several of his charges, and outlived Old Martin, who survived until 1838 – the year Queen Victoria ascended the throne. Cops lived to see the sad sight of the now redundant Lion Tower demolished in 1852. It must have given him a certain quiet satisfaction, though, to have outlasted his old adversary the Iron Duke, who died the same year. Cops himself passed away soon afterwards, on 21 March 1853. The Tower authorities lost no time in evicting his younger daughter Sarah and her husband from the Keeper's House. The Tower menagerie was history.

In 1248, at almost exactly the same time that the first animals arrived at King Henry III's menagerie, another institution appeared at the Tower that was destined to be almost equally durable: the Royal Mint. Prior to then there had been several regional mints. But from this time on the minting of money became centralised as a royal monopoly: an arcane rite, akin to a craft guild, with its own jealously guarded jargon and customs. Those entrusted with striking the kingdom's coinage in the Tower were a law unto themselves, and although they worshipped at St Peter ad Vincula (and helped to pay for its upkeep), the masters of the mint kept themselves very much to themselves.

Their secrecy and exclusiveness, dictated on security grounds, was helped by the physical location of the mint. It was originally housed in a series of makeshift sheds, but by 1300 a 400-foot-long building was constructed in the narrow canyon between the inner and outer west curtain walls of the Tower. Enclosed on all sides in an area of the Tower which became known as Mint Street, and guarded by a porter appointed by the king 'to keep the gate for all incomings and outgoings and to summon all men required when there was work to do', the 'moneyers' went about their valuable task. Minting money was hot, hard, laborious, noisy and dangerous work. The interior of the mint's workshops were a hellish inferno full of the clash and splash of metal, both hard and molten. A sweaty, smoky, smelly world where hammers clanged deafeningly and glittering, jagged splinters of precious metal and molten droplets flew through the filthy air, causing painful injuries. Few mint workers escaped their service without losing a finger or an eye to their risky craft.

Metal – gold, silver and bronze – was first smelted in crucibles and when liquid, was poured on to stone slabs to cool. It was then beaten out on an anvil with heavy hammers until it became a thin plate. The plates were chopped into smaller sheets called 'blanks' or 'flans', and the blanks were stuck between 'dies' – rounded heavy metal stamps bearing the image of coins. The lower die was called a 'standard', a 'staple' or a 'pile', and the upper die was known as a 'trussel' or a 'puncheon'. A spike or 'tang' on the lower die – or pile – engraved with the obverse side of the coin, was then driven into a solid block of wood, and the blank placed on the engraved coin on the pile's surface. The engraved end of the trussel was then struck sharply with a hammer, thus simultaneously imprinting the impression of the obverse and reverse dies. As well as carrying the images of the reigning monarch and coat of arms, the newly minted coins also usually bore the name or initials of the moneyer – the official responsible for their minting – as an individual hallmark guaranteeing the integrity and quality of the coin, and a primitive precaution against counterfeiters and 'coin clippers', the bane of the mint from medieval to modern times.

Since they bore the image of the anointed monarch – the only picture of their sovereign that the average citizen would see – coins of the realm were accorded a reverence above and beyond their mere monetary worth. Any tampering or forgery was regarded as treason, and punishments for such offences were savage, including mutilation or death. Nonetheless, the greed for gold was so strong that there would always be those avaricious or desperate enough to risk the penalties. The two most common methods of adulterating the coinage were counterfeiting – manufacturing dud coins from base metals such as tin – and 'coin clipping' – trimming the edges of coins and smelting the shaven splinters into gold or silver bullion.

Across the centuries, as the nation's economy grew, so exponentially did the mint. Gradually its workshops crept around the north-west corner of the Tower. Excavations have revealed the presence of a fifteenth-century assay furnace and pots near Legge's Mount, the Tower's north-west bastion. By the sixteenth century, the entire area between the inner and outer curtain walls of the whole Tower was taken up either by the Royal Mint or by the Royal Ordnance Factory and their related activities. Mint Street was now a thriving industrial village within the Tower, as a map of 1701 reveals. It shows separate gold and silver melting houses; milling and assaying houses, and the homes and offices of the mint's officials. The presence of stables suggests that the mills used to drive the mint's machinery were powered by horses rather than by water.

But the physical labour of turning out coins remained exhausting, at least until the belated introduction of machinery in 1662 in the reign of Charles II. The inflation at the end of Henry VIII's reign imposed particular strains on the mint, as it struggled to turn out enough coins to meet the increased demand for a rapidly debasing currency. In 1546, one William Foxley, entrusted with making the mint's melting pots, is recorded as having fallen asleep on the job, and then slept through continuously for fourteen days and fifteen nights, waking 'as if he had slept but one'.

The financial situation had stabilised somewhat by the reign of Henry's daughter Mary. In 1554, as part of her deeply unpopular marriage settlement with King Philip II of Spain, twenty cartloads of Spanish silver in ninety-seven chests, mined in Spain's Latin American colonies, were delivered to the mint. The following year the mint sealed a deal to turn old Spanish silver coins, ryals, into English coinage worth £17,600. At the same time the mint won its first ever foreign contract to mint new Spanish coinage. The coming of the English Civil War in 1642 provided an unwelcome hitch to progress when the then Master of the Mint – a convinced Royalist – absconded to join King Charles I's court at Oxford, taking the mint's dies with him. His flight enabled the cash-strapped Royalists to continue turning out coins without interruption, while those left behind at the Tower mint were forced to come up with hasty substitutes for the stolen dies.

After Parliament's triumph, the Tower mint continued to turn out coins, though obviously without King Charles I's head, which had been lopped for real in 1649. The new ruler, Lord Protector Oliver Cromwell, was happy to have his likeness stamped on coins and commemorative medals instead, but proved as tight-fisted as any king when it came to paying up. The Master of the Mint under Cromwell's Commonwealth, Thomas Simon, found himself £1,700 out of pocket for the coins he had designed. After repeatedly applying to be reimbursed, but only receiving £700, he finally wrote to Cromwell in exasperation, 'I beg you to consider that I and my servants have wrought five years without recompense and that the interest I have to pay for gold and silver eats up my profit.'

Unsurprisingly, Simon was only too delighted to offer his services to Charles II when the monarchy was restored in 1660. But if he was hoping that the poverty-stricken king would match his keen interest in the mint with actual money he was again to be sorely disappointed. While in Dutch exile the king had met an Antwerp goldsmith named Roettier who had loaned the ever cash-strapped monarch money in hope of future prefer-ment. The investment paid off after the Restoration when Charles gave the old goldsmith's three sons jobs at the mint. Charles encouraged the Roettier brothers to compete with Simon in designing the new monarchy's coinage, and chose an elegant one submitted by John Roettier. Nettled, and clearly put on his mettle, Simon dipped into his pocket once again and paid for a coin called the Petition Crown, which he submitted to the king along with an abject note:

Thomas Simon most humbly prays Your Majesty to compare this, his trial piece, with the Dutch, and if more truly drawn and embossed, more grace-fully ordered and more accurately engraven, to relieve [pay] him.

Two years later, and still unpaid, poor Simon became one of thousands of victims of the Great London Plague of 1665.

The ubiquitous Samuel Pepys accompanied King Charles to the mint to inspect new coins struck with his own likeness: 'So we by coach to them and there went up and down all the magazines [workshops] with them; but methought it was but poor discourse and frothy that the King's companions . . . had with him. We saw none of the money; but Mr Slingsby did show the King, and I did see, the stamps of the new money . . . which are very neat and like the King.' The new coinage was the work of an engraver named Blondeau, a Frenchman brought to the mint by Cromwell. Like Simon, Blondeau impartially went to work for the new royal regime and compared Cromwell's warty likeness with the effigies he had made of the new king – doubtless to the latter's advantage.

Pepys was so impressed with the coins and the new-fangled machinery that had struck them – 'So pretty that I did take a note of every part of it' – that he soon returned to the mint to commission Blondeau to engrave a seal for the Admiralty. '. . . and did see some of the finest pieces of work, in embossed work, that ever I did see in my life, for fineness and smallness of the images thereon. Here also did see bars of gold melting, which was a fine sight.' Although Pepys often expressed his pettish disapproval of the King's frivolity, diarist and monarch shared an eye for a pretty woman, and both were captivated by the loveliness of Frances Stewart, a court beauty, one of the few who stoutly refused to become another of Charles's many mistresses. Instead, the king propagated Frances's charms to his subjects by making her the model of Britannia on the country's coins, an image that endured until decimalisation in the 1970s.

The late seventeenth century was a time of transformation for the mint. Not only was machinery – used at other mints elsewhere in Europe since the mid-sixteenth century – finally introduced to replace hand-held hammers, but the greatest scientific mind ever produced by Britain was also brought in to oversee the mint's operations. In 1696 Sir Isaac Newton was appointed Warden of the Mint. The appointment came at a time of crisis both for the mint and for Newton. The prickly Lucasian professor of mathematics at Cambridge University was over fifty – elderly by seventeenth-century standards – and his masterpiece, *Principia Mathematica*, in which he had set out his theory of gravitation and his three laws of motion, was already a decade behind him. His work on the calculus was also largely complete. Never a social animal, the lonely old bachelor was essentially marking time at Cambridge while searching for a new role to occupy a mind still at its peak.

Meanwhile, the nation's treasurer, William Lowndes, was faced with a severe shortage of silver coins – the result of a two-pronged assault on the currency. The first attack was mounted by coin clippers who shaved the old unmilled coins minted before the introduction of machinery. The second prong of the economic assault came from bullion dealers who melted down silver coins into ingots, shipped them abroad where they fetched higher prices than in England, and sold them to buy gold. In September 1695 Lowndes asked the curmudgeonly genius Newton to suggest a solution to the silver shortage.

The economic crisis caused by the silver shortage was acute. The great historian Lord Macaulay suggests that it was more grevious in its effects on ordinary citizens than even the recent political ructions of the Glorious Revolution which had ousted the Catholic King James II and brought his Protestant daughter Mary and her husband William of Orange to the throne in 1689. For, wrote Macaulay, 'when the great instrument of exchange became thoroughly deranged, all trade, all industry were smitten as with a palsy. The evil was felt daily and hourly in almost every place and by almost every class.' The crisis came to a head in 1695, when King William III found that the shortage of ready money – despite the foundation of the Bank of England in 1694 which lent the poverty-stricken government £1.2 million in its first year – was hampering his war against Louis XIV's expansionist, Catholic France.

It did not take Newton's logical mind long to grasp the cause of the crisis – and its cure. Since drastic penalties had not stopped the coin clippers, and the traders who exported silver were only obeying the iron dictates of the market, the practical solution was to make coin clipping unviable and the trade in silver unprofitable. Newton suggested a two-stage remedy. Step one: to recall the entire currency still in circulation. Since silver coins were rapidly disappearing thanks to the activities of the bullion traders this would not be such a gargantuan undertaking as it sounds. The recalled money would then be melted down at the mint and reissued as new machine-made money with milled edges to prevent clipping.

Step two was to deal with the export of silver, and for this Newton proposed changing the intrinsic value of the coins. As the dealers were only exporting the silver because it brought more gold abroad than in England, reducing the amount of silver in each shilling would make foreign gold more expensive when counted in English silver money. Correctly calculated, such a devaluation would make the cross-continental trade in English silver unprofitable at a stroke. Newton's solution was the product of a modern, rational mind. At the dawn of the eighteenth century, the

Age of the Enlightenment, he was weighing and assaying money not according to some mystic value lent by the monarch's head on the coins, but by logic and common sense. Money was worth just what the metal making it up was worth in the marketplace – no more, no less.

In the event, only half of Newton's radical scheme was put into effect. Parliament approved the recall and re-minting of the coinage, but baulked at the proposed devaluation. As a reward for his suggestions, however, a grateful government offered Newton the prestigious – and lucrative – post of Warden, or boss, of the Mint. With almost indecent haste, an equally grateful Newton accepted, packed his bags and books, left his lodgings at Trinity College, Cambridge, in April 1696, and moved into the Warden's House in Mint Street near the Brass Mount bastion at the north-east corner of the Tower.

In reforming the currency, and curbing the coin clippers, Newton found himself up against a mind almost as daring and unorthodox as his own. But that mind belonged to a master criminal. It was a duel of wits as dramatic in its way as the fictional clash between Sherlock Holmes and his arch-enemy Professor Moriarty, the 'Napoleon of crime', and like that titanic struggle, could only end with the death of one of the protagonists. William Chaloner, Newton's adversary, was, like the great scientist, a son of provincial England. Indeed, had he been born a few notches further up the social scale, his talents might have brought him fame and wealth, instead of infamy and an ignominious death on Tyburn tree.

The son of a Warwickshire weaver, born around 1660, the delinquent boy Chaloner was apprenticed by his parents to a Birmingham nail maker. It was here that young William got his first taste of coin counterfeiting by making fake Birmingham groats. But Chaloner had his eye on bigger prizes than mere groats, and around 1680 he walked to London to make his fortune. At the height of the rumbustious reign of the licentious Charles II, Chaloner used the metalworking skills he had picked up in Birmingham to make and sell such items as cheap tin watches for gentlemen and dildoes for the ladies, before graduating to becoming a quack physician and clairvoyant.

Chaloner's quick wits and plausible patter – in vivid contemporary slang his 'tongue pudding' – were deployed to prescribe aphrodisiacs and other love potions for his female clients. In 1684 Chaloner had his first encounter with the Tower when he married a Katharine Atkinson, at the church of St Katharine by the Tower. He continued coining, producing fake French pistoles and English guineas and making an enormous profit in the process. Chaloner's skill as a literal moneymaker was so great that he was soon acknowledged as the 'most accomplished counterfeiter in the kingdom', buying a house in fashionable Knightsbridge and a lifestyle to go with it. He rode around in a carriage with footmen and behaved like a born gentleman about town. Even his future mortal enemy Newton would be impressed, describing Chaloner's transformation from a humble craftsman 'in clothes threadbare, ragged and daubed with colours, turned coiner and in a short time put on the habit of a gentleman'.

In 1696, the year Newton became Warden of the Mint, Chaloner moved up a gear. He bought a house in the quiet Surrey village of Egham and moved in machinery to forge the sophisticated machine-struck coins now being turned out in the mint. The isolated house was deliberately chosen so that the noise of the forging would not attract suspicion, but the new warden was already hot on Chaloner's trail. When he took over at the mint, Newton had conducted a tally of the coinage in circulation. The tally revealed that a staggering one in ten English coins was a fake. If the mass production of forged coins continued at such a rate, the realm's legal tender would be debauched and the nation would face ruin. As the most talented and productive coiner in the kingdom, Chaloner had to be stopped.

It was now that Newton showed a dedication and ruthlessness that surprised anyone who imagined that the shy scientist who had spent most of his life among Cambridge's ivory towers would be lost in the worldly atmosphere of the Tower mint and its sleazy environs. The unworldly scholar began to haunt the beery, smoky inns and sawdust-floored taverns surrounding the Tower – the Dogge was a particular favourite – hunting for clues, witnesses and evidence to nail Chaloner and his counterfeiting gang. By these means, Newton met and successfully suborned John Peers, one of the coiners working with Chaloner at the Egham factory. Newton persuaded Peers to turn king's evidence – and although 'the most accomplished counterfeiter in the kingdom' got away with a short spell in Newgate prison, Thomas Holloway, Chaloner's right-hand man, was convicted and hanged.

Banged up in Newgate prison, Chaloner blamed Newton personally for his plight. 'The Warden of the Mint is a Rogue,' he would tell anyone who listened. It was his turn now to up the ante and challenge Newton on his own ground. Chaloner's method showed a boldness and ingenuity worthy of a higher calling than counterfeiting. In Newgate, Chaloner put his expert knowledge of coins and cash to work, writing a series of pamphlets on monetary policy, and recommending restricting the specialised tools of the coiners' trade to curb their activities. Cheekily, Chaloner was advising the government on how to extricate itself from the financial morass he himself had helped create. It was chutzpah on a grand scale. As historian Thomas Levenson remarks, 'William Chaloner writing on tax policy is a bit like John Gotti weighing in on Social Security, or the Kray brothers offering their thoughts on the National Health Service.' Chaloner's ultimate objective was even bolder: his pamphlets were just the opening shots in a campaign to get himself – crook and jailbird though he was – appointed overseer of the Royal Mint itself by smearing the mint's existing staff – from Newton down – as the real criminals and larceners.

Chaloner charged the moneyers at the mint with a host of crimes: ranging from adulterating the coins they struck, to smuggling dies out of the Tower and selling them to counterfeiters. And Chaloner's campaign got him a long way towards attaining his objective – in fact, into the chamber of the Privy Council, the very heart of government itself. Chaloner was aided by an embittered political patron, Charles Mordaunt, Earl of Monmouth, out of office and keen to supplant the current chancellor, Charles Montague, Earl of Halifax – who was Newton's patron. With Mordaunt's help, Chaloner received a hearing for his accusations against the mint – and his remedies for beating forgers and coiners like himself. The ministers heard him out, but though they did not, as he had hoped, give Chaloner his coveted job in the mint, his 'tongue pudding' was convincing enough for them to order an investigation into security there.

Frustrated, Chaloner upped his game yet again. This time he set his sights on the newly founded Bank of England – he would become the country's first ever master forger of the new-fangled banknote. To a champion counterfeiter like Chaloner, the world's first banknotes – lacking such precautions as today's inbuilt metal strip and complex cross-grained printing – presented few problems. He printed a stock of forged notes, and was ready to pass them into circulation when the bank, alerted by a dud note they had spotted, pounced on Chaloner's printer, who promptly shopped him. Completely undaunted, Chaloner once again played the poacher turning gamekeeper: with barefaced gall he claimed that he had only printed the notes to show up their flaws and how easily they could be forged and duplicated. He helpfully betrayed his own counterfeiting confederates into the bargain. Astonishingly, not only did the bank believe him, but they even gave him a £200 reward for his useful information. Once again, Chaloner had made a monkey of authority.

But one man was determined not to be fooled: Isaac Newton. The new Warden of the Mint had begun his work at the Tower as he meant to go on: in a hurricane of activity. Previously the post had been a sinecure, but Newton was determined to be a hands-on boss. Elbowing aside the mint's incompetent master (or production manager), Thomas Neale, he threw himself into every detail of the production process, from scanning its costs with the gimlet eye of the greatest calculator in the land, to ordering up new furnaces, rolling mills and coining presses to boost the mint's coin-striking capacity from 15,000 to 40,000 coins a day. Under Newton's command, 500 workers laboured for shifts of twenty hours a day except on the Sabbath on the re-coining of a total of £7 million.

The mint became a continuous production line, with a river of silver flowing in at one end of Mint Street in the south-west corner of the fortress, and newly minted coins jingling out of the other end near Newton's house in the north-east corner, all overseen with obsessive interest by the warden himself. By the summer of 1698 the great re-coinage was complete. A triumphant Newton took satisfaction in the knowledge that his theoretical mind had grappled with and conquered a supremely practical problem. As a result, the kingdom had a shiny new currency; economic crisis and social disorder were averted; new money clinked in plump purses once more; the king was able to pay his armies; and production at the mint – which had hit 50,000 coins a day – subsided to less frenetic levels.

Freed from the immediate problem of keeping the kingdom afloat financially, Newton was left with the time and energy to pursue a combined role of detective, magistrate and chief security officer for the mint. Investigating the mysterious disappearance of a set of coining dies from the Tower, instruments which in the hands of William Chaloner could pose a deadly threat to the mint's monopoly of making money, Newton once again embarked on the pursuit of his arch-enemy. To catch his thief, Newton set a gang of lesser criminals on the trail. Starting with two convicted coiners, Peter Cooke and Thomas White, lying under sentence of death in the noisome Newgate jail, Newton began to build a case against

Chaloner. Dangling the possibility of a reprieve before their eyes, the theoretical-physicist-turned-unlikely-criminal-investigator persuaded the coiners to betray their former companion in crime. They admitted that the dies had been stolen from the Tower mint and sold to Chaloner to enable him to make near perfect replicas.

Newton stepped up his inquiry – which was now taking up half his working time and a large part of the mint's budget. The physicist took like a duck to water to the unfamiliar milieu of stinking jails, dung-encrusted back alleys and the dingy inns where coiners gathered. He employed a small army of informers, narks and snoops to gather information about Chaloner and his associates. As a magistrate, he hauled suspects within the intimidating walls of the Tower and interrogated them closely, threatening them with the harsher penalties associated with the grim fortress unless they divulged all they knew.

The scholarly Cambridge scientist had turned into something closely resembling a police state persecutor, pursuing wrongdoers with righteous zeal. Newton's biographer Frank Manuel comments, 'There was an inexhaustible fount of rage in the man, but he appears to have found some release from its burden in these tirades in the Tower. At the mint he could hurt and kill without doing damage to his Puritan conscience. The blood of coiners and clippers nourished him.' Although this goes too far – Newton killed no one, and there is no evidence that he injured them – he later burned the records of his interrogations, and the suspicion remains that he enjoyed the power he wielded over his terrified prisoners.

Apparently unaware of the snares that Newton was patiently setting for him, Chaloner continued his campaign to infiltrate the mint, appearing at the bar of the House of Commons in 1697 to denounce the fraud and forgery he claimed was rife at the Tower, and again brazenly proposing himself as the Hercules who could clear out the Augean Stables in Mint Street if only he were to be given access to it. So impressed with his 'tongue pudding' were the members of the Commons committee investigating the alleged abuses at the mint, that they ordered Newton to arrange an experiment in the Tower at which Chaloner could demonstrate his methods for foiling the coiners. Newton refused. Instead, he appeared before the committee himself, his pockets heavy with coins grooved according to Chaloner's suggestions, to show up the flaws in the master forger's schemes. Chaloner had been rebuffed – but it had been a close-run thing and Newton would not forget it.

The warden's investigation into the dies filched from the mint had run into the sand. But when Chaloner openly accused Newton of incompetence at best, and himself of embezzling from the mint at worst, he made an error that would prove fatal, reviving Newton's dormant enmity against him. Smarting under the public slight that Chaloner's charges of malpractice had inflicted on him personally – he called them 'calumny' and 'libel' – and the idea that MPs would prefer the word of a common criminal to that of the nation's finest mind, Newton plotted his revenge.

A year after he had last been there, in February 1698 a desperate Chaloner – flat broke after the failure of his Egham coining venture – was back before Parliament, this time as a petitioner, pleading that the mint was conspiring against him. He failed, and by that spring was reduced to penury. In an effort to restore his fortunes Chaloner attempted a fresh scam: forging the tickets for a newly established money-raising venture by the treasury, a national lottery. Chaloner was discovered, arrested and confined in the familiar Newgate jail. An implacable Newton took over the prosecution of his case. With a cold, single-minded fury, the warden set about weaving a noose around the neck of the man who had maligned him and his mint. In one non-stop, ten-day session at his house in the Tower Newton took no fewer than 140 witness statements on the case. He left nothing to chance, even inserting stool pigeons – compromised coiners – into Newgate to wheedle incriminating statements from Chaloner. A steady flow of their reports went straight from Newgate to the Tower to join Newton's ever fattening case file.

Feeling the meshes of Newton's net tightening inexorably about him, Chaloner went to pieces. His letters to Newton deteriorated from arrogance, to anxiety, to desperation, to blind panic. One of Newton's spies reported to him that the coiner had gone mad, 'pulling his shirt to pieces and running stark naked at midnight abot. the Ward for half an hour together'. As the shadow of the gallows loomed larger, Chaloner was 'continually raving that the Devil was come for him and such frightful Whimseys'. Newton would have none of it. Suspecting that Chaloner's 'Lunacy' was as genuine as the coins he had turned out, he pressed ahead with constructing a cast-iron case against him.

When the case came to trial at the Old Bailey in March 1699, the court was merciless. After hearing the half-dozen former confederates of Chaloner assembled by Newton testify that he was a master coiner – and had used the missing Tower dies for his work – he was convicted of high treason and sentenced to die on the gallows at Tyburn. Newton studiously ignored a last plea sent from Newgate whose desperation echoes down the years:

> My offending you has brought this upon me . . . Dear Sr. do this mercifull deed O for God's sake if not mine keep me from being murdered. O dear Sr. nobody can save me but you O God my God I shall be murdered unless you save me O I hope God will move your heart with mercy and pitty to do this thing for me.

Newton remained unmoved, and was promoted from warden to the lucrative post of Master of the Mint at the end of the year – presumably as a reward for bringing Chaloner to the gallows.

He remained at the Tower for another quarter of a century, raking in an average of £1,650 a year, considerably more than the scholarly stipend of £100 a year he had earned as a professor at Cambridge. However, the great genius lost an estimated £20,000 of his new-earned wealth in the bursting of the South Sea Bubble in 1720. Even a mind as astute as his, it seems, could not resist the common human frailties of greed and folly. After the crash, Newton, old, disheartened and in failing health, arranged for his niece's husband, William Conduitt, to succeed him as Master of the Mint, and retired from the close confines of the Tower where he had spent so many weary years. Two years later, nearly thirty years after Chaloner had choked his life out on the gallows, Newton followed him into the shades.

CHAPTER THREE

THE CAPTIVES AND THE KINGS

With his eye fixed on his expensive ecclesiastical aesthetics, and his favour lavished on his foreign courtiers, Henry III unsurprisingly became as unpopular with his barons as his father John had been. So long as administration remained in the able hands of his experienced justiciar Hubert de Burgh, the constable of the Tower, a lid was kept on the simmering baronial discontent. But in 1232, a whispering campaign against the ageing chief councillor mounted by envious foreign-born courtiers climaxed in Hubert's sudden dismissal. He was accused of embezzlement, maladministration and other trumped-up offences, was stripped of his lands and offices, and was lucky to escape with his life. Considering Hubert's exemplary service to Henry's father and himself, the king's brutal treatment of his mentor is eloquent testimony to his mean, weak and capricious character.

Blatantly ignoring the sacred rule of holy sanctuary, Henry had Hubert dragged from a chapel in Brentwood, Essex, where he had taken refuge. The fallen nobleman was placed on a 'miserable jade' with his legs tied under the nag's belly and 'ignominiously conveyed to the Tower'. Here, where the constable had so recently commanded, Hubert was clapped in chains and thrown into a dungeon. The old man – he was in his sixties – stayed until pressure from the Church made Henry change tactics. He returned Hubert to the chapel, but placed guards around the building to ensure no food was brought in. Hubert was literally starved out, and a blacksmith summoned to clamp the old warrior back in irons.

The farrier was, however, made of hard metal himself, and refused the cruel job. According to chronicler Matthew Paris he indignantly told Hubert's captors to do their worst: 'Inflict whatever judgment you will on me, for as the Lord liveth I will sooner die any kind of death than put fetters on him. Is not this the faithful and valiant Hubert who hath often preserved England from ruin by foreigners and hath restored England to the English?' Despite the blacksmith's bravery, Hubert was returned to his Tower cell and held in solitary confinement for several months more before Henry relented, pardoned the old man and partially restored him to favour in 1234. However, Hubert never regained his old offices, and died in 1243. Deprived of his wise advice, Henry's reign went rapidly downhill.

Henry's next victim was the Welsh prince, Gruffydd ap Llywelyn. Gruffydd was the eldest son of the mighty Llywelyn ap Iorwerth – Llywelyn the Great – a warrior prince who had wrested control of Gwynedd and Powys (roughly north and mid-Wales) from his uncles. Llywelyn had married Joan, an illegitimate daughter of King John. Unfortunately for Gruffydd, the product of an earlier union, his father disinherited him in favour of his younger half-brother Dafydd, Llywelyn's eldest son by Joan. A discontened Gruffydd was repeatedly imprisoned by his father, spurring him to outright revolt. After Llywelyn's death in 1240, Gruffydd was captured by Dafydd and handed over to Henry III in 1241 as a hostage for the good behaviour of the Welsh.

Lodged in the top storey of the White Tower with his young son Owain, by 1244 Gruffydd could endure his imprisonment no longer. He tried to climb down from his ninety-foot-high prison via a rope of knotted sheets, choosing the feast day of Wales's patron saint, St David, on 1 March, for the escape. He squeezed his considerable bulk on to the White Tower's roof and started descending the sheer south side. But his weight proved too much for his home-made ladder, which broke, flinging him to his doom. The impact drove his head into his chest. Henry punished Gruffydd's warder and ordered his son Owain to be detained 'more straitly'. Gruffydd had two other sons, Dafydd and Llywelyn, who continued the family feud. The winner, Llywelyn ap Gruffydd, would avenge his father by causing Henry's son, King Edward I, more trouble than any other man – with the exceptions of the Scottish warriors William Wallace and Robert the Bruce.

The rest of Henry's long reign was consumed in conflict with his barons, outraged by his arrogance and reckless extravagance. This led to outright civil war even more ruinous than his father's Barons' War had been. Finally losing patience with Henry's rule by petulance out of feebleness, the barons forced him in 1258 to submit to a new Magna Carta – the Provisions of Oxford – which for the first time committed the king to hold regular parliaments and consult his barons in appointing important royal officals. Meanwhile, the rebels made one of their own men, Hugh le Bigod, constable of the Tower. But the barons, led by the king's own brother-in-law, Simon de Montfort, Earl of Leicester, overreached themselves and arrogantly alienated their more moderate supporters, who moved back to the king's side. In February 1461, Henry suddenly struck. Having secretly obtained permission from the Pope to disregard the oaths he had sworn at Oxford, he occupied the Tower.

Henry dismissed Bigod, appointing a loyalist, John Mansel, as constable in his place. Supported by foreign mercenaries, Henry strengthened his hold on London, using the reinforced Tower as his powerbase and his bolthole. For the next few years, the king played cat and mouse with the barons. He would emerge from his fortress, gallop around the country in futile efforts to assert his authority, then retreat into the Tower again. But Henry discovered that the Tower's strength could become a trap. So long as he remained within its walls he was safe. Tying himself down there, however, severely limited his freedom of manoevre, and as opinion once more swung against him, he found himself effectively besieged by the hostile population of his capital.

The weakness of Henry's position was vividly brought home to him in the summer of 1263 when he was shut in the Tower with only his queen, Eleanor of Provence, and its garrison for company. The main royal army under the king's son and heir, Prince Edward, was campaigning in the west against the rebel barons. The baronial leader, Simon de Montfort, had secured Dover and was marching towards London. Henry was willing to make peace. Not so his queen, revolted by any thought of compromise with rebels. She sailed by barge from the Tower up the Thames, aiming to join her son Edward at Windsor.

Eleanor got no further than London Bridge, where a mob of baronial supporters pelted her barge with sticks, stones, rotten eggs and rubbish, forcing her to beat a retreat (after throwing some of the missiles back) with as much dignity as she could muster. Further humiliation awaited her. At the Tower, her terrified husband, fearing that the mob would burst in with her, ungallantly refused to open the fortress gates to readmit her. The queen was finally rescued by the Mayor of London who chivalrously gave her sanctuary in the residence of the Bishop of London at St Paul's.

Three days after this setback, with the Tower unprovisioned for a siege, Henry submitted to a truce and Simon de Montfort's supporter Hugh le Despenser was made constable. Civil war soon broke out again, and Henry was defeated by Simon at Lewes in May 1264. Henry and Edward were made prisoner, and de Montfort became the dictatorial ruler of England. Simon's power lasted barely a year. In 1265, Edward escaped, rallied the royal forces, and in August trapped Simon, le Despenser and their closest supporters at Evesham. The struggle, fought in a summer thunderstorm, was so one-sided that a chronicler called it 'the murder of Evesham, for battle it was none'. Simon was butchered on the battlefield (his corpse was quartered, and his disembodied head mockingly mutilated, with his nose cut off and his genitals nailed to his face in their place) and his surviving supporters slaughtered in Evesham Abbey.

After Simon's death, leadership of the rebel lords devolved on Gilbert de Clare, Earl of Gloucester, known as 'Gilbert the Red' from the colour of his hair and for his fiery personality. In April 1267, taking advantage of the absence of Henry, who was ineffectually grappling with another rebel baron in the Isle of Ely, and of Edward, who was campaigning in the north, Gilbert made a sudden dash from the Welsh Marches for London. The city and the Tower were held by one of the king's favoured foreigners, Cardinal Ottobuono, Italian papal legate in England. The pious king had used him to pronounce penalties – including excommunication – on the clergy who had supported the barons. This had not endeared him to either prelates or the people.

Rebellious Londoners 'without drede of God or of theyr kynge' flocked to Gilbert's banner. Gilbert laid siege to the Tower, using catapults in a vain attempt to break down its massive walls. The mainstay of the garrison were London Jews, who had taken refuge there for fear of a repetition of pogroms carried out by Simon's followers in Leicester, Canterbury and London in 1264, when hundreds had been slaughtered. The Jews, excused the papal ban on usury, had become moneylenders clustered in Cheapside around the road still today called Old Jewry, close to the Tower. Jews were always targets in times of trouble, as killing them freed their Christian debtors from their debts. Meanwhile, the warlike Edward, with an army of 30,000 at his back, stormed south, picked up his father at Cambridge, added reinforcements at Windsor, and by early May was besieging the besiegers.

Henry succeeded in springing Cardinal Ottobueno from the Tower using mercenaries from France who sailed up the Thames to rescue the embattled cleric. But Gilbert's men were well dug in, and the siege continued. The stalemate finally ended after six weeks with another truce, under which Henry agreed to moderate the harsh penalties against those barons who had supported Simon. The Tower was relieved, Gilbert and his supporters were pardoned, and Henry ended his long reign in 1272 in unaccustomed peace and tranquillity.

The new king, Edward I, made a refreshing change from his feeble and unpopular father. Tall, lean, bold, cunning, ruthless when required, an experienced soldier and able administrator, 'Edward Longshanks' was an ideal medieval monarch in the tough mould of William the Conqueror and the first two Henrys. He spent the early years of his reign reducing Wales to obedient submission; and the latter part – with less success – attempting to do the same to Scotland. One quality that Edward I had inherited from his father was Henry III's love of building. Instead of ecclesiastical architecture, however, Edward's tastes were military, and he became the greatest castle builder of his age. He finally squeezed the Welsh into submission by constructing an encircling 'iron ring' of mighty fortresses – Flint, Rhuddlan, Conway, Caernarvon, Beaumaris, Harlech – around the coast of north Wales.

Naturally, the great castle builder added to his father's works at the Tower. By the time Edward's reign ended in 1307 the fortress had essentially assumed the outlines it retains today. Although the interior buildings of the Tower have changed over the centuries, the outline shape that the eighteen-acre site with its twenty towers now shows to the changing world outside its walls is that which Edward bequeathed to his nation.

With the physical damage of Gilbert the Red's nearly successful recent assault still rawly evident, Edward's first priority was to repair the destruction caused by Gilbert's siege engines to the Tower's fabric. In doing so he had to ensure that the Tower was invulnerable to any future attack. He did this by putting as much space between his Tower and the threatening city – with its population now some 80,000 – growing around it by filling in his father's modest moat, and digging a much wider one – more than 100 feet across – of his own. Edward then put up a second outer curtain wall around the whole Tower complex. He next strengthened the western, landward side of the fortress by sealing up the causeway entrance halfway along the western wall and building a new tower – the Beauchamp – where the gateway had been. A single gate, however strong, was vulnerable to a determined assault by battering ram, so the king constructed a triple series of gatehouse towers at the Tower's south-west corner; these remain the entry point through which thousands of tourists still troop daily to enter the Tower.

As we have seen, where today's book- and souvenir shop and café stand, Edward erected the massive barbican entrance gateway, the Lion Tower. Getting past the menagerie's lions and bears would have presented an additional barrier to any besieger. Beyond the great semicircular Lion Tower was a drawbridge, and then a pair of gatehouses with double portcullis, the Middle Tower. Across a bridge traversing the wide new moat was a second drawbridge; and then yet another inner pair of barbican gatehouses with double portcullis, the Byward Tower, giving access to the outer ward courtyard of the Tower itself. Any assailant attempting to rush the Tower would now face a right-angled approach and a series of well-guarded gates, portcullises and bridges protecting the great fortress, probably now the most formidable in all Europe.

Henry III's watergate under the Bloody (then called the Garden) Tower was sealed up and replaced by a portcullis, giving access to the inner ward between the White Tower and the royal palace. Edward adopted the same defensive approach with the Tower's river entrance. In the middle of the southern curtain wall he put up another double tower, St Thomas's Tower, over a wide watergate that became the usual entry point for arriving state prisoners – often hauled straight from the corridors of power in Westminster and Whitehall and rowed downriver by barges to their doom. Because of this sad procession of the mighty fallen, the gateway, its steps covered with green algae from the slapping waters of the Thames, as slippery as the path to power, acquired the sinister name by which it is known to history: Traitor's Gate.

Unlike his father, whose desultory building work at the Tower had remained unfinished at his death, Edward completed his works within ten years: 1275–85. They cost him £21,000, twice what even his free-spending father had lavished. The finished Tower now had the same concentric form of Edward's great Welsh castles. He borrowed this idea from the huge Crusader castles he had seen in the Holy Land. Edward had been away on crusade when his father died in 1272. It says much for his authority that, although he did not return until 1274, no attempt was made in his absence to challenge him, nor – uniquely for any king since the conquest – would any English rebel, rival or baron dare mount such a challenge during his thirty-five-year reign. Edward could be cruel when crossed.

If Edward I had few English foes, he had enemies aplenty in Wales and Scotland. In Henry III's chaotic reign, Llywelyn ap Gruffydd, son of the portly Prince Gruffydd who had died attempting to escape the Tower, had brought much of the principality under his sway, proclaiming himself Prince of Wales in 1258. Llywelyn failed to pay homage to Edward or attend his coronation. The new king's revenge for this insult was slow but sure: starvation. In 1277, Edward seized the Isle of Angelsey, bread basket of Wales, bottling Llywelyn up in Snowdonia's mountains. In 1282, Llywelyn was killed in a skirmish in mid-Wales. His head was hacked off and, adorned with a mocking crown of ivy, sent to decorate the tallest turret on the White Tower. The following year, after his barbaric execution by hanging, drawing and quartering in Shrewsbury, his brother Dafydd, the last hope of the House of Gwynedd for a semi-independent Wales, had his head sent to join his brother's on the very same roof from where their father had made his ill-fated bid for freedom. It was a very visible warning of the dangers of defying England's ferocious new ruler.

For all his tender devotion to his wife Eleanor, Edward I was a vicious and relentless enemy. He was both a 'great' and a 'terrible' king, as his biographer Marc Morris ambiguously titles his life, and as both de Montfort's barons and the Welsh had discovered to their cost. Now it was the turn of England's Jews to suffer his wrath. As we have seen, the Jews were tempting targets for envious popular persecution. In London, the royal protection they enjoyed was exercised by the constable of the Tower, and the fortress gates were often flung open to shelter Jews from rampaging mobs. Tension was especially high during coronations when spending was lavish and debts to Jewish moneylenders soared. There were riots in 1189, during Richard I's enthronement; in 1220 during Henry III's second coronation; and again in 1236, when only the Tower's thick walls stood between London's Jews and their would-be murderers.

But the Jews' sole guarantee of survival – the Crown's protection – depended on the king's fickle favour. And Edward I no longer needed Jewish economic support because he had discovered a new source of loans: Italian bankers from Lombardy. In 1278, as a safety valve to deflect popular discontent during an economic recession, he withdrew some of the Jewish community's special privileges. Two years later, petty persecution turned to a real pogrom in a way horribly prefiguring the turning of the screw against Jews in Nazi Germany. Six hundred members of London's Jewish community were rounded up and herded into the Tower's cells. There were so many that the cells overflowed, and the overspill were crammed into the insalubrious surroundings of the recently vacated elephant house in the menagerie. Half of the arrested Jews were eventually hanged, on a charge of debasing the currency by 'clipping' coins.

The surviving Jews were held as hostages and huge ransoms were demanded from their families to obtain their release. When a judge, Henry de Bray, had the courage to protest against this illegal mass detention, he too was arrested and sent to join what Edward contemptuously called his Jewish 'friends' in the Tower. A distressed de Bray broke away from his guards and, though bound with cords, threw himself into the Thames in a suicide bid, but he was fished out and made to complete his journey to the Tower. Here he tried to beat his brains out against his cell wall, and eventually succeeded in taking his life. De Bray was the Tower's first recorded suicide; he would not be its last. In 1290 Edward took the drastic step of giving Britain's entire Jewish population the stark choice between converting to Christianity or being expelled from the realm altogether. Most stood by their faith and opted to leave. They would not be readmitted until the rule of that unlikely liberal, Oliver Cromwell, three and a half centuries later.

The flail of Edward's rage next fell upon Scotland, earning him yet another nickname: 'Scottorum Malleus', 'Hammer of the Scots'. Edward's heavy-handed involvement in Scottish affairs began in 1290 when he backed John Balliol, one of two rival claimants to the vacant Scottish throne. Edward assumed that a grateful Balliol would be a docile puppet, but the Scots contracted an anti-English agreement with the French – the origins of the 'Auld Alliance'.

Furious, Edward put the luckless inhabitants of the border town of Berwick-upon-Tweed, where Balliol had been chosen king, to the sword. Edward's army smashed the Scots at Dunbar in April 1296, seized Edinburgh, captured Balliol, and compelled him to abdicate. He, along with the Scottish Crown jewels and the Stone of Scone – the rock on which all Scottish kings were crowned – were borne in triumph to London, and Balliol and his son Edward were clapped in the Tower, together with a clutch of Scottish nobles taken prisoner with them.

As a king, Balliol was lodged in some comfort. He and his companions were held for the first six months of their confinement in rooms off the great hall of the White Tower. The records of his captivity tell us that his personal household in the Tower included a chaplain, an assistant chaplain, a tailor, a pantry attendant, a butler, a barber and two chamberlains. Balliol was also allowed the use of two horses stabled in the Tower – with attendant grooms – for exercise riding in the 'Tower liberties' (the quarter of London immediately adjacent to the Tower). He was given a substantial daily allowance of seventeen shillings to maintain this staff. As time went on, Balliol's value as a political prisoner decreased, and he suffered the indignity of being moved to the cramped confines of the Salt Tower – for a time called the Balliol Tower in his memory – and had his allowance slashed. Finally, after two years, his pleas to the Pope to secure his release bore fruit, and until his death in 1314 Balliol was a dependant of the pontiff in France.

The Scottish thistle remained a painful thorn in Edward's side. The ever-dormant fires of Scots nationalism next roared into flaming revolt under the inspired leadership of William Wallace, a charismatic giant with military skills matching his towering physique. Wallace beat an English army at Stirling Bridge in 1297, but was decisively defeated by Edward at Falkirk the following year, and turned guerrilla chieftain. In 1305 Wallace was betrayed by a close companion, Sir John Menteith, in return for a hefty English bribe. The giant knight was captured after a furious struggle in which he broke the back of one assailant and literally brained a second. Wallace was brought to London in chains. Unlike Balliol, the low-born Wallace was not treated with the honours due a king, but as a common rebel and traitor.

Wallace was held at the Tower – since Henry I's reign the official state prison for traitors – before his trial at Westminster Hall. The court did not take long to condemn the warrior rebel, after a show trial in which the great patriot faced his judges standing on a high platform wearing a mocking laurel crown. The savage sentence was spelled out in its full horror, leaving nothing to the imagination:

> You shall be carried from Westminster to the Tower, and from the Tower to Aldgate, and so through the city to the Elms at Smithfield, and for your robberies, homicides and felonies . . . you shall be there hanged and drawn, and as an outlaw beheaded, and afterwards for your burning churches and

relics your heart, liver, lungs and entrails from which your wicked thoughts came shall be burned, and finally, because your sedition, depredations, fire and homicides were not only against the King but against the people of England and Scotland, your head shall be placed on London Bridge in sight both of land and water travellers, and your quarters hung on gibbets at Newcastle, Berwick, Stirling and Perth to the terror of all who pass by.

The same day, Monday 23 August 1305, this fiendish sentence – the standard punishment for treason since the eleventh century – was carried out, and Wallace endured the law's full rigours. First, he was bound to a hurdle fixed to a horse's tail, with his head dangling humiliatingly near the ground. Exposed to the jeers, taunts and filth flung by the braying crowds lining the streets, he made a slow journey to the scaffold, past the stations of the cross decreed in the sentence: Westminster, the Tower, Aldgate and finally Smithfield, where a high scaffold had been erected, the better for the crowds to enjoy this martyrdom. Wallace was first hanged from a gallows, slowly strangling. As the victim involuntarily urinated, defecated and ejaculated, the obscene jeering of the mob reached fever pitch. The executioner, a skilled torturer, slashed through the rope just before death supervened, reviving the insensible victim with a bucket of water. Wallace's genitals were then sliced off and flung into a fire to be burned before his dying eyes. Next, a deep incision was cut in the abdominal wall of the agonised but still living man, and his intestines were slowly drawn out and consigned to the flames. Only when the executioner pushed his bloody hands into the chest cavity and ripped out Wallace's still-beating heart and lungs did merciful death finally ensue.

Even then, though, the butchery was not complete. The corpse was cut into four quarters, each with a limb attached, to be exhibited in the regions where Wallace had dared to rebel. Finally, the patriot's head was hacked off, boiled in salt, and plunged in a preserving pail of pitch, before being spiked on London Bridge. The prolonged martyrdom of William Wallace was finally over, but the legend of 'Braveheart' was born. In the days and weeks following the butchery, more Scottish rebels were brought from the Tower to share Wallace's fate, including the Earl of Atholl, the first nobleman to die for treason since the time of William the Conqueror. But the terror was all in vain. Seven months after Wallace's death a new Scottish champion, Robert the Bruce, was crowned king at Scone. Bruce would avenge Wallace in spectacular style at Bannockburn, and the two

Edwards – Longshanks and his woeful son – would never succeed in subduing Scotland.

The story of the disastrous reign of Edward II – who succeeded his father in 1307 when the old warrior died of bowel cancer, in Cumbria – en route to yet another campaign to bring Scotland to heel, is told in Chapter Thirteen in the context of his nemesis Roger Mortimer's dramatic escape from the Tower. Edward of Caernarvon's awful reign – as so often in the Middle Ages – was sandwiched between those of two mighty and iron-fisted monarchs who brought their realm much needed stability and prosperity: his father, Edward I, and his son, Edward III.

Edward III was no stranger to the Tower himself, having spent large parts of his boyhood there, as a semi-prisoner of his mother Queen Isabella and her lover Mortimer. One of his first acts as king in his own right was to make good the neglect and damage that both fortress and palace had suffered during his father's chaotic reign. In particular he strengthened and heightened the southern curtain wall running along the river, and built a new tower, the Cradle, in its south-east corner to give a private river entrance for the king apart from the often crowded Traitors' Gate under St Thomas's Tower. The Cradle Tower was so called from a lift – the 'cradle' – used to hoist the royal barge from the river.

Edward used the Tower palace as a residence and held his council meetings there. He equipped his rooms with the latest mod cons, including a four-poster bed and hot tubs in which he bathed weekly – an unheard-of luxury to his less hygienically inclined courtiers. Appropriately for a king in awe of Arthurian legend, Edward exalted the spirit of chivalry and founded the Order of the Garter as an exemplar of knightly values. He spared no expense when it came to equipping his court with the very best in costly clothes, tapesteries, regalia and all the trappings of a great king. He augmented the royal menagerie at the Tower with leopards, lions and a bear – and took the creatures on tour to York in 1334, as a status symbol to impress his unsophisticated northern subjects.

At the opening of his reign the Tower's defences left much to be desired. Arriving unannounced one night in December 1340 after a dangerous sea crossing from Flanders, the king was appalled to gain entry to the fortress without being challenged by the sleepy sentries, a dereliction of duty for which the serving but absent constable, Sir Nicholas de la Beche, was sacked and jailed. Edward ordered the sheriffs of London to fork out £40 'to be spent about the Tower of London which is in great need of repair'. As well as his work on the southern wall, and the building of the Cradle Tower, the king reconstructed his own residence, the Garden – later Bloody – Tower, adding a vaulted gateway and a heavy portcullis weighing two tons which needed thirty men to raise and lower it, whose mechanism can be seen to this day.

To oversee this work, Edward appointed a permanent master mason, Henry Yevele, who was paid twelve pence a day for his labours, along with a chief warder, John O'London, whose responsibility was the security of all the drawbridges, gates and portcullises in the fortress. Yevele was the pre-eminent English builder of his generation whose work can still be seen in Westminster Abbey and Westminster Hall, whose superb hammer-beam roof is his monument. In Canterbury Cathedral, Yevele sculpted the magnificent tomb of Edward III's eldest son, Edward the Black Prince. Yevele is also thought to have carved the funeral effigy of Edward III himself, with its lifelike drooping eyelid – a characteristic of the dynasty – and flowing beard. He was a pioneer of the new Perpendicular style of architecture, with its soaring fanned vaulting and flattened arches, and his employment demonstrates Edward's determination to make his kingdom a centre of culture and civilisation equal to any in the world.

It was to the Tower that the young Edward had brought his new French bride, Philippa of Hainault, in 1328. Unlikely though it seems, the Tower proved an ideal honeymoon spot for the teenagers, and Philippa was soon pregnant. Her coronation was brought forward, and on 17 February 1330 she rode in state through cheering crowds from the Tower to Westminster Abbey to prepare for the sacred ceremony next day, wearing a green velvet tunic, a cape of cloth of gold, and a fur wrap to guard her against the chilly winter weather. Soon afterwards, she gave birth in the Tower to her first daughter, Blanche. Although the child soon died – infant mortality in medieval England was high, even in royal circles – the fecund couple went on to produce thirteen more children. Blanche was the second royal birth recorded at the Tower, the first in 1321 being Edward's own sister, known as 'Joan of the Tower', the last child of the ill-matched Edward II and Isabella of France. Queen Isabella's own life in the Tower until the arrival there of Roger Mortimer, the man who became her lover and consort, had been a lonely one during the frequent absences of her homosexual husband. We know that she whiled away her time by reading the romances among the 140 volumes in the Tower's growing library until Mortimer's advent converted her dreams of love and chivalrous knights into reality.

Robert the Bruce's death in 1329 left his son David II as king of Scotland at the tender age of five. He was married to Edward III's younger sister, seven-year-old 'Joan of the Tower' the following year. A child king is an invitation for ambitious adults to plot, and soon Scotland's nobles were squabbling over the spoils of power. Edward III encouraged the regal ambitions of Edward Balliol, son of John Balliol, the Scots king who his grandfather Edward I had imprisoned in the Tower. Supported by the 'disinherited' barons who had lost their lands to Bruce, and stiffened by a company of English archers trained at the Tower, Edward Balliol invaded Scotland by sea in the summer of 1332. He defeated the army of David II at Dupplin Moor, and was crowned king at Scone. Once more, as in Edward I's time, Scotland was divided between a Bruce faction and a Balliol faction. With England under another King Edward backing Balliol, patriotic Scots were bound to side with the Bruce.

In 1346, after King David II had grown to manhood and returned to Scotland to claim his kngdom, the Scots invaded northern England. Their aim was to recover the lands that a grateful Edward Balliol had granted Edward III after the English had helped him defeat David's faction. Two months before the invasion, English longbowmen had shattered the French at Crécy, at the beginning of the conflict that would become the Hundred Years' War, and now that famous victory was repeated over the Scots at Neville's Cross outside Durham. Throughout the wars with Scotland and France the English super-weapon – the devastating longbows which won so many battles – were made and stockpiled in the Tower's armoury. One storekeeper's record noted that before Crécy there were 7,000 bows and a staggering 9 million arrows kept there.

King David – and with him more than fifty Scottish knights and nobles captured at Neville's Cross – was escorted south as prisoners by the triumphant English army. Londoners turned out in force to witness this humbling of Robert the Bruce's son. On 2 January 1347 members of the city's guilds lined the streets, and the constable of the Tower, Sir John Darcy, welcomed King David II – who, though a captive, was mounted on a magnificent black charger – into the fortress at the Lion Tower with all the honours due to a reigning, albeit defeated, monarch.

Edward III himself was not on hand to witness this triumph. After

Crécy, he had besieged the port of Calais – sending to Darcy at the Tower for a supply of giant crossbows from the armoury, to help him reduce the town. The Tower armoury was also where England's first experimental gunpowder munitions were being made. In the year 1346–7 no less than two tons of gunpowder was refined there. Blockaded by land and sea, Calais was starved into submission after a siege lasting almost a year. Famously, the commander of Calais, Jean de Vienne, and half a dozen other leading citizens – or burghers – of Calais emerged exhausted and emaciated, with nooses around their necks to await the pleasure of the king who had promised to hang them all. Only the tearful pleas of his queen, Philippa, moderated Edward's wrath and both the burghers and their town were spared. Calais would remain a treasured English possession for the next two centuries.

De Vienne and the other Calais burghers joined their Auld Alliance allies King David and the Scottish lords as prisoners in the Tower. They endured captivity while the frustratingly long process of raising a large ransom for their release went on. Impoverished Scotland was equally slow to ransom their king after concluding peace with England at the Treaty of Berwick in 1357. Although they agreed to pay 100,000 marks for David's freedom, and the king was immediately released, the sum was never raised in full. One of the Scots lords imprisoned in the Tower with David paid the supreme penalty for crossing Edward. The king had Graham Murdoch, Earl of Menteith, hanged, since the earl had previously paid homage to him and had gone back on his solemn oath. Just as it had not paid to thwart Edward I, so his grandson exacted a harsh price from those who double-crossed him.

No sooner had David been freed, than another reigning king came to the Tower as a prisoner. This was Jean II – known as 'Jean the Good' – the king of France. Jean, along with his third son Philippe, was captured after his defeat at the battle of Poitiers in September 1356 by Edward III's warlike eldest son, Edward the Black Prince. Jean's detention was far from onerous. Feasted in the Black Prince's red silken tent on the battlefield at Poitiers, with the chivalrous prince waiting on him personally, Jean's initial 'prison' in London was the magnificent Thameside palace of the Savoy, home of Edward III's luxury-loving younger son, John of Gaunt, a couple of miles upriver from the Tower.

In stark colour contrast to King David's coal-black courser, King Jean was riding a milk-white steed when he entered the city, whose fountains were said to have run with wine in delighted anticipation of the vast ransom which the French would pay for their king: 300,000 crowns, more than the French kingdom's annual GNP. In the palatial surroundings of the Savoy, the French guests were frequently visited by King Edward and Queen Philippa who made Jean 'Gret feest and chere'. Later he was transferred to Windsor Castle where he was allowed to hawk and hunt; and later still was held at a succession of other castles before arriving at the Tower in 1359.

Records for his first day of captivity in the Tower show that Jean's household were allowed seventy-four loaves, twenty-one gallons of wine, three sheep, one calf, a capon and twelve chickens; together with peppers, ginger, salt, herbs and mustard. The king's amusements during his enforced leisure were necessarily more limited than he had been used to, though he visited the menagerie with young Philippe and generously tipped the keeper. Finally, under the 1360 Treaty of Bretigny, the two royals were released. When King Edward and the Black Prince brought the news to the Tower, Jean showed his gratitude by throwing them a grand banquet in his lodgings. He then returned to France to raise his own ransom. As security, another of Jean's sons, Louis of Anjou, agreed to enter English captivity as a hostage in his father's and brother's place until the ransom was paid. But when, after six months, an impatient Louis escaped from English custody in Calais with the ransom still unpaid, the unfortunate Jean – clearly a man of his word – came back voluntarily as a prisoner to England where he was greeted like a returning hero. He died, still an honoured and unransomed captive, in the familiar surroundings of the Savoy palace in 1364.

The Hundred Years' War, to which the Treaty of Bretigny had brought a temporary truce, resumed in 1369. Edward himself, following the death of the Black Prince and the demise from the Black Death of his beloved Queen Philippa, fell into senility and the clutches of a rapacious mistress, Alice Perrers. The old king died the following year of a stroke. It was a sad end to a fifty-year reign which had seen the consolidation of the English nation. The new king was the Black Prince's ten-year-old son, Richard II.

CHAPTER FOUR

PLAGUE AND PEASANTS

In the summer of 1348 a ship docked at the Channel port of Melcombe Regis in Dorset. In the fleas infesting the fur of the black rats on board were the deadliest plague bacillae that have ever visited mankind. The Black Death emptied towns, wiped out villages, and struck at rich and poor alike, killing the wife and three of the daughters of King Edward III, along with swathes of his poorer subjects. Spreading swiftly inland from that fatal bridgehead in Dorset, the plague reached London by the autumn of the same year. Although the capital, by today's standards, was still tiny – it was possible to walk right across London from the Tower to the city's western wall at Farringdon in half an hour – it was a crowded labyrinth of cheek-by-jowl dwellings; a warren of filthy, mud- and shit-strewn streets, which were an ideal breeding ground for the pestilence.

In a thousand days after that first, fatal landfall, the Black Death wiped out between a third and a half of England's entire population. In London alone one mass burial 'plague pit' north of the Tower accommodated 10,000 victims. Another, at nearby Blackfriars, held 42,000. Although this first blast of the plague had blown itself out by 1350, it was to return in recurrent waves right up to the mid-seventeenth century – the Great London Plague of 1665 in which fifty-eight of the Tower garrison's soldiers died being its last major visitation.

The Black Death left a mixed legacy for the rest of the fourteenth century. With a world population brutally slashed by up to 350 million, labour became a precious commodity. Serfs and peasants, having survived this most perilous of dangers, knew that their time and labour were a prize to be won rather than a right to be demanded by grasping landlords, greedy nobles and arrogant rulers. The reign of young King Richard II coincided with the upsurge of violent protest by his poorer subjects known to history as the Peasants' Revolt.

The revolt erupted in ugly violence like a plague buboe bursting. A cocktail of social ills brewed in the previous reign curdled to bring the pustule to a virulent head. The legacy of the Black Death, combined with the seemingly endless wars in France, had drained manpower away from the land: a labour shortage that the ruling caste vainly attempted to stem with a series of savage laws. The Statute of Labourers of 1351 pegged wages at their 1348 pre-plague levels, despite roaring inflation. Labourers were also commanded to work where and when their lords and masters required. Serfs and villeins who left their lord's land in search of higher wages were threatened with branding, and even giving alms to roaming beggars was banned in a bid to starve the beggars into work. In a desperate effort to raise cash for an exchequer denuded by the cost of the French wars and decreasing productivity, the government slapped tax after tax on a declining population already struggling to survive.

Such was the grim inheritance of the boy king Richard II. A delicate nine-year-old with what the chronicler Richard Holinshed called 'an angelic face' framed by a halo of fair curls, Richard grew into one of those inept kings periodically thrown up by the Plantagenets in marked contrast to their usual run of strong, ruthless warriors. Unlike his fierce father and grandfather, Richard of Bordeaux was a ruler in the mould of Henry III or Edward II – unwarlike, pious, effeminate, and with a strong aesthetic interest. And also like those two ill-starred monarchs, the young king had a streak of stubbornness, coupled with the unwavering conviction that, as God's anointed, he could do no wrong.

Richard's unhappy reign began and ended at the Tower. The day after his grandfather Edward III's death on 22 June 1377 he was taken there in procession, and sequestered until his coronation. Three weeks later, dressed all in white, the divine-looking child king was brought to Westminster Abbey to be crowned. Richard had inherited an inherently unstable and almost bankrupt country from his grandfather. Cash strapped and at a loss, in November 1380 the Royal Council called a parliament to approve a radical new moneymaking scheme. This was a single levy – the poll tax – payable by every English adult, prince or peasant, aged over fifteen, at the same rate: three groats (one shilling). The sum represented a week's wages for a master craftsman, and perhaps a month's hard-earned graft for an agricultural labouring serf.

The commissioners dispatched to the countryside to raise the new tax were bitterly resented and violently resisted. The chief serjeant-at-arms, a thug named John Legge, was reputed to line up young village girls and grope under their skirts to determine whether they were virgins and exempt from the hated tax. Such abuse bred a murderous loathing among the commons. It was the third tax hike in as many years, and rather than pay, many people temporarily vanished from their villages or attacked the tax collectors, who returned to London having only succeeded in raising two thirds of the expected revenue. Foolishly, the council sent them back again in the spring of 1381. This time, grumbling turned into a spontaneous outburst of popular rage the like of which had never been seen in England before.

By June, the temperature in the countryside was as hot as the midsummer sun. A spontaneous tax strike in the villages of northern Essex spread south like wildfire racing through a cornfield, and crossed the Thames into north Kent, where the revolt was coordinated by a popular leader Walter (or Wat) Tyler. Tyler may have been a discharged soldier from the wars in France, and/or a common highway robber. But he was clearly a charismatic, bold and determined character – the first popular revolutionary since 'Longbeard' Fitzosbert had rallied Londoners to the cause of social justice in the reign of Richard I. Tyler turned an inchoate mob of peasants into a focused – if undisciplined – people's army. In early June 1381, some 20,000 strong, Wat's horde converged on Kent's county town of Maidstone.

They ransacked the town jail, releasing its prisoners. One of the freed men, John Ball, was an ordained priest sick of the steadily accumulating wealth and worldly ways of the established Church. Abandoning his parish in York and hitting the road, Ball had become an itinerant preacher of the sort known as Lollards. His proto-Protestant – and to the Church, heretical – doctrines were a potent mix of biblical simplicity – calling for a return to the tenets of poverty and justice preached by Christ – and an explosive social egalitarianism summed up in Ball's oft-repeated couplet:

> *When Adam delved and Eve span*
> *Who was then the gentleman?*

Naturally, this inflammatory question did not go down well with Ball's superiors in the Church, or the civil authorities struggling to keep a lid on simmering social tension. He was repeatedly jailed, and was serving out the latest sentence when Wat Tyler's army arrived at the prison gates.

Ball's wild oratory whipped the peasants on, but they needed little urging. When they arrived at Canterbury, chronicler Jean Froissart tells us, a substantial part of the city's population swelled their ranks: 'And in their going they beat down and robbed houses . . . and had mercy of none.' They ordered the monks at the cathedral to elect a new archbishop, since, they threatened prophetically, the hated current incumbent, Simon Sudbury, was a dead man walking: 'For he . . . is a traitor and will be beheaded for his iniquity.' Ominously, the mob carried out their first executions, decapitating some of Canterbury's wealthier citizens. Moving west towards London, the peasant army arrived at Rochester where they looted the castle built by Gundulf, the Tower's architect; and took the children of the castle's constable, Sir Richard Newton as hostages. Tyler sent Newton ahead with a personal message for King Richard. The ruffian peasant chief demanded that the boy king should meet him in three days' time at Blackheath, a large expanse of common land south-east of the capital.

As Tyler's ragged army trod grimly towards the city from Kent, an even larger peasant army, possibly totalling 50,000 or even 70,000, was simultaneously converging on the capital from Essex. Led by another self-appointed people's tribune, Jack Straw, who harangued his followers from a hay wain on Hampstead Heath which became known as 'Jack Straw's castle', the men of Essex were stirred by the same injustices, and fired up by the same hopes, as the men of Kent. This peasants' pincer movement threw the unprepared royal authorities on to the back foot. The regime's strong man – and chief target of the peasants' wrath – the king's uncle, John of Gaunt, was, fortunately for him, absent on a military mission against the Scots. One of his brothers, Thomas of Woodstock, Earl of Buckingham, was in Wales; while the third royal brother, Edmund of Langley, Earl of Cambridge, was embarking from Plymouth on a military expedition to Spain with the only substantial armed forces available to the administration. As the peasants converged on the fat capital bent on taking it apart, the naked city was defenceless.

Those members of the council still in London sent for King Richard from Windsor Castle, and withdrew with him and his mother Joan, 'the

Fair Maid of Kent', behind the stout walls of the Tower, along with its garrison of around 1,000 men. England's ruling class assembled in the fortress, astonished and fearful at the hurricane of discontent that had so suddenly blown up. The Earls of Kent, Salisbury, Warwick, Arundel, Oxford and Suffolk were there; along with Sir Robert Hales, England's Lord Treasurer; Simon Sudbury, the hated chancellor and Archbishop of Canterbury; John Legge, the loathed serjeant-at-arms and chief enforcer of the poll tax that had sparked the revolt; and William Walworth, a prosperous and hard-nosed London fishmonger who was the city's lord mayor.

On Wednesday 12 June 1381, Tyler's ragtag army arrived at Blackheath and pitched camp. Sir John Newton sailed up the Thames by barge to convey Tyler's message to the king at the Tower. On being admitted to the royal presence, he prostrated himself on the floor and begged Richard's pardon for the insolence of the demands he brought. He asked the king to meet 'the commons of your realm' and hear their grievances. Newton begged the king to give an appeasing answer, for if he did not, the peasants would slaughter his hostage children. On his council's advice, Richard agreed to meet the rebels the next day. A grateful Newton hurried back to Tyler with the good news.

A tense night in the Tower followed. From the battlements, the fearful inhabitants could just make out, in the darkness to the south-east, tiny pinpricks of light from the fires of the rebel host encamped on Blackheath. During the night the elderly Archbishop Sudbury came quaking to the king and surrendered the Great Seal – symbol of his other job, the Chancellorship of England. Word had reached him of the destruction of his see at Canterbury, and now raiding parties of peasants had swarmed into his London palace at Lambeth on the south bank, and systematically vandalised it, tearing tapestries to ribbons and smashing plates while raucously yelling, 'A revel! A revel!'. Sudbury clearly believed that by resigning his secular office he might appease the peasants' fury. But it was too late for such a gesture.

The next day, Thursday 13 June, the feast of Corpus Christi was celebrated by King Richard with a morning Mass. Then the royal party left the Tower in a flotilla of five barges and rowed downriver to the agreed rendezvous. Awaiting their arrival, the peasants, too, had heard a Corpus Christi Mass – a fiery sermon preached by John Ball in which he harped on his favourite egalitarian theme of the yawning chasm between rich and poor.

> They [the rich] are clothed in velvet and camlet furred with grise, and we be vestured with poor cloth. They have their wine, spices and good bread, and we have the dross of the chaff and drink water. They dwell in fair houses, and we have the pain and travail, rain and wind in the fields. And by our labours . . . they keep and maintain their estates. We be called their bondsmen . . . we be beaten . . . and we have no sovereign to whom we may complain, nor that will hear us, nor do us right.

As Ball spoke, their sovereign was on his way to hear their complaints. The court's intention was to disembark between Rotherhithe and Greenwich and walk to Blackheath, but on nearing the river bank they saw the vast and threatening throng gathered there. The royal party understandably hesitated. Froissart reports, 'When they saw the king's barge coming they [the peasants] made such a cry, as though the devils of hell had been among them . . . And when the king and his lords saw the mood of the people even the best assured of them were in dread.' Famished and thirsty in the midsummer heat, with the tempting prize of London lying before them awaiting plunder, the rebels were in no mood to parley with those they blamed for their misery.

With a nervous Sudbury and Hales whispering in either ear – like the archbishop, the treasurer had had his Essex estates trashed by the rebels – Richard stayed on the safety of the river and attempted to address the mob from his barge. In his thin, piping treble the boy king asked for their demands. He was answered by a cacophony of ribald shouts and jeers, from which the clear message emerged that nothing less than the heads of his advisers trembling beside him would satisfy the rebels' thirst for revenge. Thoroughly alarmed, the king's counsellors insisted on turning their barges round and returning to the safety of the Tower as fast as their oars could row them. Following them along the south bank with shouts of 'Treason!', the thwarted peasant army moved west too, in a race which the frantic crew of the barges narrowly won, gratefully regaining the safety of the Tower. Angry, and believing that the king's evil counsellors were stopping Richard from hearing their case, the peasants turned their frustrated fury on the prostrate city before them.

* * *

Reaching London Bridge, they found the drawbridge guarding its southern side barred. Further inflamed, the mob set fire to a nearby Southwark brothel, staffed by Flemish prostitutes and owned by Lord Mayor Walworth. Either this persuaded the guards on the bridge to change their minds, or more probably the bridge gates were opened by sympathisers from within the city. There were plenty of Londoners of the poorer sort, who burned with the same sense of injustice as their country cousins. As the men of Kent swarmed across the bridge and into the city, with blood-chilling yells of 'Burn!' and 'Kill!', their allies from Essex, approaching from Stepney, also gained access through the Aldgate, a few hundred yards north of the Tower. The two peasant armies met and mingled with their allies from within the city, perhaps 100,000 strong: a greater number than the entire population of London.

Fuelled by copious consumption of beer and wine – looted or offered free by terrified tavern owners – the huge mob went mad with the joy of slaughter and destruction. For the first time in its history, London was ruled by an anarchic crowd, intoxicated and metaphorically drunk, too, with their sudden power. Their first target was the princely Savoy palace, riverside home of the hated John of Gaunt. The peasants were adamant that the contents of this all-too-conspicuous symbol of excess should be smashed rather than stolen. One of them, who tried to make off with a plate, was caught and burned alive.

After murdering the guards at the palace gates, the rebel commons took their bloody axes to the great vats and barrels in the Savoy's cellars, releasing a flood of wine. Their next goal was John of Gaunt's treasury. Again, they scorned to steal, and removed the jewels and precious stones, gold plates and silver tableware, only to throw them from the palace's terrace into the Thames. A gorgeous jewel-encrusted padded jacket belonging to the absent duke was draped on a pole as a substitute for the hated tyrant and riddled with arrows. Then it was the turn of the ducal wardrobe to be laid waste. Shimmering silk, rich velvet, furs, plump cushions and ancient tapestries were ripped to shreds, before being piled into a gigantic pyre in the Savoy's great hall and set ablaze. The inferno spread to the rest of the palace and soon the whole building was in flames. Many peasant lives were lost when three unopened barrels were hurled into the flames and exploded with shattering force – the 'yokel band' being unfamiliar with the properties of gunpowder. Scores more looters, over-come with alcohol, were trapped in the cellar when the Savoy's roof collapsed, and slowly asphyxiated under the ruins, their 'cries and lamentations' horrifying all who heard them. By morning, the once proud palace was a smouldering heap of blackened stone, charred timbers and molten metal.

The mob fanned out across the city, searching for new targets. They broke into London's jails and freed the prisoners. As so often, foreign immigrants were singled out for attack. In previous pogroms Jews would have been the chief scapegoats, but since Edward I had expelled them, the peasants turned on Italian Lombards, who had taken over the Jews' moneylending functions, and dozens were slaughtered. Dutch Flemings, resented for their domination of the cloth trade, were another easy target. Thirty-five Flemings, who had sought sanctuary in St Martin-in-Vinery Church, were dragged out and beheaded on a single bloody block. Thirteen more were decapitated outside the St Austin's friary. In all 150 died. A distinguished eyewitness to the savagery, the poet Geoffrey Chaucer – a future custodian of maintenance at the Tower as Clerk of the Kings' Works who, having an apartment over the Aldgate, had seen Jack Straw's Essex men swarm into the city – reported, 'There was a very great massacre of Flemings, and in one heap there were laying about forty headless bodies of persons who had been dragged forth from the churches and their houses; and hardly was there a street in the City in which there were not bodies laying.'

Later, the poet put the savagery he had seen into verse:

> They yelled, as fiends do in hell,
> The ducks cried, as men would him quell, . . .
> The geese, for fear, flew over the trees,
> Out of the hive came the swarms of bees;
> So hideous was the noise, ah Benidicte!
> Certes, he Jack Straw and his men
> Made never shouts half so shrill
> When that they would any Fleming kill . . .

Any citizen who looked remotely prosperous, such as the corrupt banker Sir Richard Lyons, who was killed on sight, was at risk. To be a servant of the state involved in oppressing the poor meant immediate death, as the tax collector Roger Leggett discovered when he was hauled from his house in Southwark and beheaded at Cheapside. The frenzied mob ignored Church sanctuary, prising a terrified Richard Imeworth, hated keeper of the King's Bench prison in Southwark, from the pillar he was desperately clinging to in Westminster Abbey, and slitting his throat.

Knowing that the chief targets of their rage were out of reach with the king in the Tower, the mob took their frustrated fury out on property. The Temple, St John's Hospital at Clerkenwell and ostentatious private houses of the wealthy were all torched because their owners were immured in the Tower. These properties shared the Savoy's fiery fate before the mob, their fury temporarily sated by the orgy of rape, looting, arson and murder, reeled eastwards along the river. Surrounding the Tower, they collapsed on either side of the fortress, throwing themselves down on Tower Hill and St Katherine's Square, screaming taunts, threats and obscenities at the Tower's dumb walls. Inside the fortress, calm amidst his cowering courtiers, was young King Richard. He climbed to the roof of the White Tower to observe the raging fires and the sack of the city by his rebellious subjects.

In the heart of the Tower, the Royal Council spent the short summer night in anxious session. It was split between hawks and doves. The hard-liners, led by London's tough-minded lord mayor, William Walworth, were all for taking the Tower's garrison out on a sortie and scattering their ill-armed besiegers while they were dead to the world. Although the peasants were numerous, Walworth argued, few had weapons, many were too drunk to stand, and the rest would be sleeping off their bloody binge. Even outnumbered by some fifty to one, the Tower's professional soldiers would easily defeat this scum of the earth.

The doves were represented by the old Earl of Salisbury, the council's senior member. He advised the king to appease the mob 'with fine words', and buy time by pretending to grant their requests. Richard, wise beyond his fourteen years, decided to adopt this course. He would ride out to confront the mob – but only to draw them out of London so that the hated ministers, quivering inside the Tower, could escape. Any promises extracted from him under duress would be empty words. The urgent thing was to get the peasant mob out of London, disperse them – then deal with them at leisure.

At daybreak on Friday 14 June, after hearing morning Mass, the king went up to a perch on the Tower's eastern wall. Shouting over the cacophony of yells from the slowly stirring rebel host, he agreed to meet them – so long as they promised to go home afterwards. In the meantime,

added Richard, he was issuing a general pardon 'for all manner of tres-
passes and misprisions and felonies done up to this hour'. To match his
words, Richard flourished a parchment with the promised pardon and
affixed the royal seal to the document in full sight of the mob. A few
minutes later, the great gates of the Tower swung open and the king, with
a knot of his more courageous courtiers, rode out. It was an indisputably
brave thing for the boy to have done – the desperate and still-drunken
mob could have torn him to pieces on the spot. But, miraculously, they
did not.

Awestruck, most of the mob followed the slight figure of the king
as he rode eastwards out of the city to the fields known as Mile End.
The courtiers around Richard were jeered all the way through the city
wall at Aldgate to the open country beyond. But some of Tyler's
followers probably including Wat himself, along with Ball and Straw
– hung back. As the Tower's guards attempted to close the fortress's
heavy gates after readmitting Joan, the queen mother – who had tried
to accompany her son in a wagon, but turned back because of the sheer
press of people in the streets – the peasants swept the sentries aside and
stormed into the fortress. Their hoarse cries of triumph as they insolently
ruffled the hair and tugged the beards of the bewildered sentries echoed
around the ancient walls. For the first time since its construction four
centuries before, London's pre-eminent castle and royal palace was in
hostile hands.

The rebels rampaged through the Tower, smashing locked doors,
helping themselves to food and drink, wrecking and looting as they went.
Then, on the first floor of the White Tower, ignoring the sanctuary of
the church, they burst into the Romanesque splendour of St John's Chapel.
Here they found the most hated men in the kingdom huddled in prayer.
Anticipating their likely fate as they heard the raucous cries of the
approaching mob, Archbishop Simon Sudbury had held a short service,
shriving the sins of his terrified companions. Then the chapel door burst
open, and their ragged enemies, stinking of blood, sweat and drink, were
upon them.

With chilling roars of vengeance, the peasants made good the threats
they had uttered to Sudbury's monks at Canterbury. The archbishop just
had time to gasp the brief prayer *'Omnes sancti orate pro nobis'* ('All the
Holy saints protest us'). Then the old man – along with the equally
detested treasurer Sir John Hales, tax commissioner John Legge, and

William Appleton, personal physician to John of Gaunt – was roughly dragged out of the chapel, borne in savage triumph through the Tower's gates and up the slope of Tower Hill. Luckily for him, the detested John of Gaunt's eldest son and heir, young Henry Bolingbroke, Earl of Derby, and a cousin and almost exact contemporary of King Richard, who was also in the Tower, was hidden by one of his father's retainers, John Ferrour of Southwark – an act of mercy that would have momentous if unintended consequences for the future Henry IV and English history, – and dire ones for Richard himself.

A log was laid on Tower Hill – and the luckless quartet from the chapel became the first of 125 people to be executed in the Tower's shadow over the next 400 years. Archbishop Sudbury was first to suffer. With Christian charity he forgave the amateur executioner before stretching his neck on the block. Nervous and inexperienced, his killer bungled the blow. 'Aha!' cried the stricken archbishop, his hand rising instinctively to the gaping wound on his neck. 'It is the hand of God.' Without waiting for the cleric to remove his hand, the swordsman struck again, severing Sudbury's fingers. Still the archbishop lived, collapsing on the ground. It took a total of eight clumsy strokes delivered to his head, neck and shoulders before death mercifully ensued and the archbishop's head rolled free. Their bloodlust unslaked, the murderers took the mangled head, nailed it inside his clerical mitre, stuck it on a pole and set it up on London Bridge – the traditional display case for traitors' skulls. After watching this horrifying spectacle, Hales, Legge and Appleton were brutally dispatched in their turn.

Meanwhile, similar scenes of horror continued inside the Tower. In the royal palace, the king's bedchamber was vandalised and then, in an inner sanctum, the mob discovered the king's mother: Joan, the first Princess of Wales, once a beauty so alluring that she was known as the Fair Maid of Kent, but now grown so obese that she waddled rather than walked. Reputed to be the damsel whose dropped garter inspired her father-in-law Edward III to found the noblest order of chivalry, Joan at fifty-one, despite her corpulence, was still the embodiment of refinement and female delicacy.

Not that this deterred Wat's army of drunken peasants. They crowded into the chamber where Joan lay in bed surrounded by her terrified and weeping ladies. Tapestries were torn from the walls, coverlets were stripped from the queen mother's bed, and lewd threats were uttered. One of Joan's ladies was raped, and the same fate appeared to await Joan herself. The peasants, however, contented themselves with a few forced snatched kisses. Their beery breath and rough embraces made the queen mother faint away, before they trailed out of the room. For fear that they would return, Joan, still swooning, was disguised in rough commoners' clothes, hustled out of the Tower and into a barge which rowed her upriver to the safety of Baynard's Castle.

Knowing nothing of these bloody events unfolding back at the Tower, Richard spent the day haggling with the peasants, granting demand after demand for an amelioration of their conditions – a freeze on rents, an end to court fines for rent arrears, properly negotiated work contracts – with a show of reluctance, stringing out the negotiations in the hope that the crowds would weary and go home. Finally, some 40,000 rebels – mainly Essex men – turned homewards, some carrying the pardons which the king had granted them. A weary but relieved Richard and his courtiers headed back towards the Tower. They were halfway there when they were met by a herald who blurted out the terrible news of the murders and mayhem that had taken place in their absence. The messenger did not know what had become of the king's mother, but it was clear that the Tower was an unsafe destination. They made instead for the Royal Wardrobe office at Blackfriars which was still in loyal hands.

Arriving there, Richard was relieved to learn that his mother was alive. Hearing the details of her near-death experience, and the confirmation that his senior ministers had been brutally murdered, he hardened his resolve to deal with their murderers in the only language they understood. Having seen that his appeasement had merely led to more bloody anarchy, the young king was now ready to listen to the hard-line William Walworth. Richard's attempts to kill the revolt by kindness had failed, Walworth argued. More concessions would merely whet the rebels' thirst for blood. If they carried on like this, they too would share the fate of the victims at the Tower. It was time for resolute action.

Richard and his courtiers again agreed to parley with Tyler the next day. This time the meeting place was to be Smithfield, the open space north of London where horses were traded and cattle penned and slaughtered.

Smithfield had also witnessed the bloody evisceration of 'traitors' like William Wallace: it was an appropriate setting for the climactic act of violence in the Peasants' Revolt. Saturday 15 June dawned hot and sultry. The king waited until the heat of the day had passed at 5 p.m. before riding out again to meet the mob, pausing en route to say his prayers at Westminster Abbey. He was accompanied by a retinue of around 200 knights, pages and foot soldiers, led by a grimly determined Walworth. Richard, his slight figure disappearing inside a long gown trimmed with ermine, arrived at Smithfield where Tyler and around 20,000 followers awaited him.

Tyler's two days as uncrowned king of London had swelled him to foolish arrogance. In his sweaty pomp he rode up alone to confront Richard. Brandishing a dagger, he grabbed the monarch's hand, insolently addressing him as 'Brother King'. Tyler reeled off a list of new demands, each more outrageous than the last. They included the abolition of all ranks of nobility; the stripping from the former lords of their lands and goods; the confiscation of Church land and property, and the reduction of bishops from princes of the Church to the status of poor, wandering priests like John Ball. It was a redprint for social revolution. In Tyler's primitive communist state, only Richard would be left as titular king, while real power would lie with Wat and his men. Richard replied quietly that all reasonable demands would be granted – providing the peasants now returned to their villages.

There followed a tense pause, as brooding as the torrid afternoon. Tyler demanded a jug of beer. He quaffed a mouthful, before coarsely spitting it on the ground in front of the king – itself an act of unpardonable lese-majesty in the eyes of the horrified courtiers. Then the tension suddenly snapped. Turning to the king's personal page, the peasant leader demanded that he hand over the ceremonial Great Sword of State that he carried, since in future he, Wat Tyler, would be wielding the state's power. Boldly, the page indignantly refused: the sword was the king's property, he declared, and Tyler was not fit to hold it since he was 'only a villein'. Enraged, Tyler stood in his stirrups and, waving his dagger over his head, vowed that he would not eat until he had the page's head on a platter. This was the moment that the lord mayor had been waiting for. Walworth spurred his horse forward.

Shouting that Tyler was a 'stinking wretch', Walworth pushed between the peasant chief and the king. Tyler aimed his dagger at the mayor's chest.

The blow was deflected with a clang, since under his robes Walworth had taken the precaution of donning a breastplate. Now it was his turn to strike. Drawing his short sword, the mayor hit Tyler full in the forehead with the pommel, following up with a slashing blow across the rebel's neck. Dropping his dagger, Tyler reeled back, grabbing instinctively at his bleeding neck. Seizing the moment, another courtier, Sir Ralph Standish, rode up and drove his sword deep into Tyler's guts. Groaning, the peasant lord slid from his horse and collapsed in a bloody heap.

This was the moment of supreme danger for Richard. At the sight of their leader writhing on the ground, the peasants started forward with a collective roar of rage, clearly intent on killing the king and all who rode with him. Richard was equal to the peril. He fearlessly forced his horse forward, piping out, 'Sirs, would you kill your king? I am your rightful captain, and I will be your leader. Let all those who love me, follow me.' Quite alone, Richard rode up to and through the mob, which parted like the biblical Red Sea before the small figure in his royal robe. The king led them north into the open countryside called Clerkenwell Fields, and there, after again promising to pardon their rebellion and address their grievances, he left them – returning to the Tower where Walworth was already rallying a small contingent of troops and frightened Londoners. Returning to Smithfield with this armed following, Walworth's first concern was to ensure that Tyler was dead. To his horror, he learned that the ruffian still lived. Tyler had been taken to the hospital of the nearby Priory of St Bartholemew. Mercilessly, Walworth had the dying man dragged from his bed, taken out to Smithfield, and beheaded.

Miraculously, this bloody climax marked the end of the uprising. Wat Tyler's dream of a peasants' paradise died with him. Without their charismatic leader, the fearsome host of peasants meekly returned to their homes and villages to await the inevitable royal retribution. It was not long in coming. In contrast to his honeyed words and the promises made at Mile End and Smithfield, Richard now proclaimed to the peasants, 'Serfs ye are, and serfs ye shall remain.' Tyler's head replaced that of Sudbury on the spikes topping London Bridge. Some 150 other rebels, including Ball and Straw, were hunted down and paid the full penalty for their revolt. The social order of king, lords and commons which had been so briefly and brutally turned topsy-turvy was restored. But the fallibility of monarchy – in the form of the frail young monarch himself – had been rudely paraded for all to see, and neither peasant nor king would ever forget it.

Sadly, the courage and maturity displayed by Richard in the face of the revolting peasants deserted him on the short journey from adolescence to adulthood. Only seven years separated the uprising from the second great crisis of Richard's reign – the Lords Appellant revolt – but this time the wisdom and bravery that the young king had shown towards his humblest subjects was replaced by purblind arrogance and vicious spite towards his own noble near-equals. Only the king's cunning and deceit remained as his hallmark. And once again, as in the third climactic crisis of the reign – Richard's forced abdication – the crisis played out at the Tower of London.

In 1382, the year after the Peasants' Revolt, Richard married Anne of Bohemia, a daughter of the Holy Roman Emperor Charles. Anne was a gentle, fragile creature described by one observer as 'a little scrap of humanity'. The young couple, despite being married for twelve years, never procreated, and there were rumours that the effete Richard shared the sexual tastes of his great-grandfather Edward II. The couple divided their time between the royal residences at Westminster and Windsor, the palaces of Eltham and Sheen, and the Tower, where Richard spared no expense in refurbishing the royal apartments after the damage caused by the invading peasants.

He installed 105 square feet of expensive stained glass in the Tower's palace, each pane painted with the royal coat of arms and the fleur-de-lys symbol which Edward III had adopted from France after his victory at Crécy. Richard had floor tiles laid depicting heraldic leopards – probably inspired by the animals in the Tower's menagerie – and his own favourite emblem, the white hart, with murals of popinjays worked in gold and vermilion. Certainly, there was more of the arty than the hearty in Richard's kingship.

After the skill he had shown in turning the tables on the peasants, at first there were few to restrain Richard when he began to display the familiar narcissistic qualities of a bad king: from overspending on costly clothes and furniture, to heaping favours on his chosen favourites and ignoring the advice of wiser heads. His own head turned by his success in outwitting the peasants, Richard nurtured furious resentments against his ageing uncles, John of Gaunt, Duke of Lancaster, and Thomas of Woodstock, Duke of Gloucester, who ruled as de facto regents during his minority. The king began to build a younger faction of his own led by Robert de Vere, Earl of Oxford.

By 1386, resentment of this upstart clique had called forth the organised opposition of five senior peers dubbed the Lords Appellant. They included Richard's cousin and contemporary Henry Bolingbroke, Earl of Derby, son of John of Gaunt. The other appellants were the king's uncle, the Duke of Gloucester; Thomas Beauchamp, Earl of Warwick; Thomas Mowbray, Earl of Nottingham, and Richard FitzAlan, Earl of Arundel.

In November 1387 the appellants accused five royal favourites of high treason. Four of them fled in fear of their lives, but the fifth — Robert de Vere — escaped to his own estates in the royalist county of Cheshire, where he gathered an army of 5,000 men. De Vere marched south in mid-December, but the appellants, led by Gloucester and Bolingbroke, trapped him at Radcote Bridge, west of Oxford, on 20 December. Throwing off his armour, de Vere escaped, leaving his adoring king defenceless in London. Richard made for the fortress that had given him sanctuary from the marauding peasants: the Tower. He celebrated Christmas there, while the appellants mustered their forces outside the city, and crowds of hostile Londoners, sensing the royal weakness, gathered on Tower Hill just as the peasants had done in 1381.

In January 1388 Richard was compelled to meet the triumphant Lords Appellant in the newly refurbished throne room of his palace in the Tower. Mistrusting their deceitful monarch, the lords insisted that he send them the Tower's keys ahead of the meeting, lest he try and trap them inside. Eventually, Richard received them in 'a pavilion richly arrayed'. The angry shouts of the crowd outside demanding the dismissal of the hated favourites could be clearly heard even through those thick walls, uncomfortably reminding the king of the humiliating peasant siege he had suffered here seven years before. Richard was again presented with a stark choice: either agree to the appellants' demands or be deposed. As in 1381, he played for time, awaiting the right moment to strike back at his enemies.

Richard's friends paid the price. A special session of parliament convened by Gloucester became known as the 'Merciless Parliament' for the savage sentences meted out to the king's closest associates. The most prominent victims were Sir Robert Tresilian, the king's Chief Justice; and Sir Nicholas Brembre, Lord Mayor of London, who were both executed.

But the one closest to Richard's heart was Sir Simon de Burley, his beloved boyhood tutor who had carried Richard on his shoulders at his coronation. The low-born Burley had excited the nobles' resentment when he was made constable of the great castles of Windsor and Dover as a mark of Richard's favour.

On the orders of Gloucester and Arundel, Burley was executed on Tower Hill. He was the first man to suffer official state execution there, but he would not be the last. Richard never forgot or forgave the judicial murder of his old tutor, carried out in the face of the pleas from his beloved queen, who fell to her knees in front of the 'Merciless Parliament' to beg in vain for a reprieve. Richard's hatred of his enemies grew and festered. When Anne died at the Thameside royal manor of Sheen in 1394, the king, maddened with grief, ordered the palace itself to be totally destroyed. He was still clearly unstable at Anne's funeral in Windsor, and when one of the appellants, the Earl of Arundel, turned up late for the ceremony an enraged Richard struck the nobleman in the face with a staff, drawing blood and defiling the church. It was not a happy omen.

In July 1397, almost a decade after his humiliation at the hands of the Lords Appellant, Richard felt strong enough to take his revenge. He planned his vengeance like a Borgia poisoning, inviting his three chief enemies – his uncle the Duke of Gloucester, and the Earls of Arundel and Warwick – to a feast at the Lord Chancellor's residence on the Strand. Suspicious of Richard's intentions, Gloucester remained at his country estate at Pleshey in Essex, and Arundel also stayed away; but Thomas Beauchamp, Earl of Warwick, trustingly turned up. Richard kindly waited until his guest had eaten his fill before making his move. Men-at-arms burst in and seized the startled peer, hurrying him through the dark riverside garden to the north bank of the Thames where a boat was waiting. He was rowed down to the Tower and lodged in the turret in the middle of the west wall that from henceforward would bear his family name: the Beauchamp Tower.

After his dramatic arrest, Beauchamp saved himself by breaking down 'like a wretched old woman', according to the chronicler Adam of Usk, and incriminating his fellow lords for conspiring against the Crown. Spared death, he nevertheless languished in the Tower for months, and had his lands and titles forfeited. He survived to gloat over Richard's final downfall in 1399.

Beauchamp's fellow appellants were less fortunate. Arundel – who had so infuriated Richard at his wife's funeral – unwisely accepted the king's promise of safe conduct and surrendered. He too was sent straight to the Tower, condemned to death and, on Richard's vindictive special orders, executed at the same spot on Tower Hill where Burley had died. On his way to the scaffold, Arundel called for the cords binding his hands to be loosened, so he could distribute alms to the poor. Such gestures made him a hero to the common folk, who hailed him as a martyr and flocked to the church of the Austin Friars in Broad Street, where the earl's beheaded body was buried. Burley's death was also remembered by the king in the less public vengeance wreaked on his own uncle, the Duke of Gloucester, arrested in person by Richard at his manor of Pleshey. The duke's wife begged her nephew for mercy. Richard appeared to accede to her tearful pleas: 'I will grant him mercy,' he began silkily, before hissing, '. . . in the same measure that he meted out to Burley.'

Thirsty for vengeance though he was, the hostile demonstrations which had followed Arundel's death warned Richard that it would be unwise publicly to kill his own aged uncle. Instead, the fallen royal duke was taken to the Tower and then, in a departure from the norm, secretly smuggled *out* of Traitor's Gate, and shipped over the Channel to Calais. Here he was quietly done to death. Gloucester was apparently asphyxiated between the feather mattresses of his bed, with five heavy thugs lying on top. Piquantly, the man given the task of organising the murder was Thomas Mowbray, Earl of Nottingham, one of the original five Lords Appellant, who had defected to Richard's side and was given this unpleasant task to prove his new allegiance.

Of the original five Lords Appellant, just two were left standing after Richard's savage purge. Mowbray was made Duke of Norfolk as a reward for presiding over Gloucester's murder; while the king's cousin, Henry Bolingbroke, was also given a dukedom – that of Hereford – in a bid to buy his loyalty. But granting such baubles did not mean that Richard had forgotten their earlier disloyalty: once more, he was biding his time. His tactic was to divide the two new dukes, before eliminating them piecemeal. The king let Mowbray know that he, Richard, was planning to relieve Bolingbroke and his ageing father, John of Gaunt, of their titles and lands – possibly even of their lives.

Mowbray passed on this news when he met Bolingbroke out riding. An outraged Bolingbroke promptly stormed off to the king to demand an explanation. Richard summoned Mowbray, who hotly denied saying any such thing. Slyly, the monarch turned the matter over to Parliament who ordered the two dukes to settle their quarrel in a joust. The duel was to take place near Coventry in September 1398, and a large aristocratic audience assembled to watch the dukes, in their gorgeously coloured livery, fight for their lives. But at the very last minute Richard intervened, stopped the contest, and ordered both men to be banished abroad: Bolingbroke for ten years and Mowbray for life. Mowbray departed for Venice, where he died of plague within a year, while Bolingbroke left for Paris.

The following February, 1399, Bolingbroke's father, John of Gaunt, died. Richard seized the chance of appropriating his uncle's lavish Lancastrian property for himself. He declared Bolingbroke's exile permanent and his inheritance forfeit. In June – with Richard absent in Ireland – Bolingbroke landed at Ravenspur in Yorkshire to reclaim his inheritance. The widespread acclaim which greeted his arrival decided him: he would replace Richard on the throne. Two factors swayed him: Richard's evident unpopularity, and the fact that he himself – a grandson of Edward III – was of the blood royal and in his own estimation would make a far better king than the incumbent.

Bolingbroke's tiny army swelled, while that of the absent king dwindled. By the time Richard returned from Ireland in early September, his forces had melted away. He fell into Henry's hands at Conwy Castle in north Wales, and was taken to another of Edward I's great castles at nearby Flint where a promise to abdicate was extracted from him. Shaken by the evident hatred of his subjects – at one point he was pelted with refuse – Richard's morale collapsed and he became, in the words of a biographer, 'a mumbling neurotic . . . sunk in acute melancholia'. In this sad state he was brought to London, and lodged in the White Tower, a prisoner there like the kings of France and Scotland before him. To Richard II, however, belongs the dubious distinction of being the first English monarch to be imprisoned in the Tower.

On 30 September 1399 the Tower witnessed another first: Richard signed an instrument of abdication there – the first English king to do so, and the first to affix his signature rather than the seal (he had given up the royal signet to Henry). The document ran:

I Richard, by the grace of God king of England and of France and lord of Ireland . . . resign all my kingly majesty, dignity and crown . . . And with deed and word I leave off and resign them and go from them for evermore, for I know, acknowledge and deem myself to be, and have been, insufficient, unable and unprofitable, and for my deserts not unworthily to be put down.

That was the public statement, though privately, according to Adam of Usk, one of the wise men brought in by Henry to legitimise the Lancastrian takeover, Richard railed bitterly against his fate, his words reproduced in Shakespeare's *Richard II*:

'My God! A wonderful land is this, and a fickle; which hath exiled, slain, destroyed or ruined so many kings, rulers and great men, and is ever tainted and toileth with strife, and variance and envy.'

The wise men were as rude about Richard publicly as he was about them privately, accepting the abdication because of the king's 'perjuries, sacrileges, unnatural crimes, exactions from his subjects, reduction of his people to slavery, cowardice and weakness of rule'. Within a fortnight, Bolingbroke had himself crowned King Henry IV, riding from the Tower to Westminster Abbey as to the manner born. A bitter Richard remained in the Tower, but as the century turned, in January 1400, a revolt by diehard Ricardian nobles broke out. Henry realised that as long as Richard lived he would be a focus for rebellion. At dead of night, fettered in chains, the fallen king was removed from the Tower and taken to Leeds Castle in Kent before being carried north to Pontefract Castle in Yorkshire. By mid-February, he was dead.

No one knows exactly how Richard met his end. The usual suggestion is that he was deliberately starved to death, though it is possible that he himself went on a hunger strike. The short timescale, however, seems improbably rapid for such a slow means of murder, and the medical historian Dr Clifford Brewer has suggested poisoning – possibly by the death cap fungus (*Amanita phalloides*), which is easily chopped up in food and inflicts lethal damage on liver and kidneys – as a suitable means of non-violent dispatch. Whatever the method, it seems beyond question that Henry ordered his cousin's elimination – and was for ever haunted by guilt for having done so.

CHAPTER FIVE

UNEASY HEADS

So uneasy was the new king about the legitimacy of his usurpation, that he went out of his way to underline his own royal status from the very start. Henry's grandfather, Edward III, had famously founded the most noble order of English chivalry, the Garter. Not to be outdone, at the outset of his reign Henry founded his own order too. Himself unusually hygienic for a medieval monarch – he took a weekly tub – Henry decided to call his new creation the Order of the Bath. On the evening before his coronation, 12 October 1399, the king made forty-six of his family, friends and followers – including his own four sons and the Earl of Arundel, son of the Lord Appellant executed by Richard – the inaugural knights of the new order. Forty-six baths had been lugged into the great hall of the White Tower and placed under individual canopies. The candidate knights then stripped off and stepped into the rapidly cooling water which had laboriously been heated in the Tower's kitchens and poured in by their servants.

As the knights splashed and wallowed, the king entered the hall with a procession of priests and attendants. Approaching each knight in turn, Henry traced the sign of the cross on their wet backs and pronounced:

'You shall honour God above all things; you shall be steadfast in the Faith of Christ; you shall love the King your Sovereign Lord, and him and his right defend with all your power; you shall defend maidens, widows and orphans in their rights, and shall suffer no extortion, as far as you may prevent it; and of as great honour be this Order unto you, as ever it was to any of your progenitors or others.'

Once this first stage of purification had been performed, the king withdrew, and the knights got out of their baths and were vigorously towelled dry by their pages before retiring to rest on forty-six beds. When the

Tower bell rang the curfew, they rose, put on the long brown gowns of monks, and processed next door into St John's Chapel. Here they spent the long and chilly autumn night kneeling in a vigil of prayer and meditation, before rising – their limbs cramped with cold – and placing a lighted candle on the altar with a penny offering. The taper symbolised their spiritual readiness; the coin the token tribute paid to the king who had initiated the order. After donning shining new helmets and gleaming armour, the knights paraded across the yard to the Tower's palace where Henry presented each of them with a shiny sword newly made in the Tower armoury.

By then, the Tower was abuzz with preparations for the coronation. After a hearty breakfast, Henry – who had chosen the day partly because it was the feast day of Edward the Confessor, holiest of English kings, and partly because it was the first anniversary of his last parting from his father as he left England for exile – was magnificently arrayed in robes of cloth of gold. Bareheaded, despite the October rain, he left the Tower on a white horse, before dismounting to walk solemnly through the streets, attended by a retinue of 900 nobles and knights, and gravely acknowledging the acclamation of the crowds while the fountains he passed ran red with wine. The coronation itself included the anointing of the new king with sacred oil said to have been given to St Thomas Becket by the Virgin Mary, and miraculously just discovered in the cellars of the Tower where it had lain for centuries. Whoever was anointed with the oil was said to be destined to regain England's lost lands in France – a feat which proved beyond both Henry himself and his namesake son and grandson, despite being anointed in their turn with Becket's oil.

Behind the celebrations were darker undertones. As the new archbishop, Thomas Arundel, was about to place the crown on Henry's head, he noticed that the monarch's hair was alive with lice – and as Henry prepared to offer the ritual gold coin to God, he dropped it; it rolled away and was never recovered. In a superstitious age such signs were ominous indeed. There was no doubting the new king's popularity in his capital, but among his own class many resented his usurption. Thus, though Henry was able to secure the throne for himself and his son Henry V, the first seeds were already being sown for a dynastic conflict – the Wars of the Roses between York and Lancaster, the two branches of the Plantagenet House – that would tear England apart across the next century.

*   *   *

Plotting against Henry began almost as soon as the coronation oil was dry. The first conspiracy was hatched in mid-December in Westminster Abbey, the building where Henry had been crowned a bare two months before. A group of five Ricardian nobles, known as the Counter-Appellants, and a clutch of discontented clerics, including the disposed Archbishop of Canterbury, laid their unholy scheme. The plotters' plan was a simple one. On Epiphany, 6 January 1400, Henry was to hold a grand tournament at Windsor to which the disloyal lords had been invited. They intended to raise an army, swoop on Windsor and arrest Henry and his four sons, along with the new Archbishop Arundel.

The plot might well have succeeded but one of those at the abbey betrayed it. Once made aware of the conspiracy, Henry acted with characteristic decisiveness. Having sent a warning to Archbishop Arundel, early on the evening of 4 January, accompanied by his young sons, he set out from Windsor on a dramatic ride through the gathering winter dark to London. Avoiding the plotters mustering at Kingston-upon-Thames, he arrived at the city gates at 9 p.m. where he met the lord mayor, riding out to warn him of the revolt. Henry made straight for the Tower, where he spent the night summoning the citizens of London to arms, offering a hefty cash inducement of eighteen pence for a mounted knight and nine pence per archer to join his forces.

By morning Henry had his army assembled with near-miraculous speed. He rode out of the Tower at the head of his men. The overwhelming majority of Londoners were ready to defend the usurping Henry rather than risk a return to Richard's tyranny. In London, a King Richard look-alike, named Richard Maudelyeyn, recruited by the plotters to impersonate the absent king, was hanged with a few followers. And the other plotters were rounded up and executed, two nobles having their severed heads sent to Henry in a basket.

One plotter, Sir Thomas Blount, not being a peer, was denied the privilege of a swift beheading and endured the full horrors of a traitor's death. At Oxford, he was hanged, cut down while still alive, and then revived; his abdomen was slit and his entrails drawn out and burned as he watched the grisly proceedings while seated on a bench. Asked if he wanted a drink, he replied with a magnificent death's door jest, 'No, for I should not know where to put it.' King Henry himself sat in judgement on Blount and several other conspirators. Twenty-six of the Epiphany plotters were executed in all. One who was spared was John Ferrour, the same man who had rescued the teenage Henry when the mob had invaded the Tower at the height of the Peasants' Revolt two decades before. Henry remembered and saved his former saviour.

Although the Epiphany revolt had been comprehensively crushed, it sealed the fate of Richard, whose body, encased in a lead coffin with only the face exposed, was brought from Yorkshire and exhibited at the Tower to prove to doubters that he really was dead. But Henry's troubles were only just beginning. His entire fourteen-year reign was racked by revolts. In September 1400 the discontented Welsh nobleman Owain Glyndwr made Henry pay handsomely for calling him a 'barefoot rascal' and turned a local border dispute with Henry's Marcher henchman Lord Grey of Ruthin into a Welsh national revolt. The rising rumbled on until the end of Henry's reign and elevated Owain into his people's hero.

Alongside Glyndwr's rebellion in Wales, Anglo-Scottish relations proved as troublesome as ever. In March 1406 the heir to the Scottish throne, twelve-year-old Prince James Stewart, was shipwrecked off the east coast of England while en route to France, where he had been sent by his father for his own safety following his elder brother David's assassination. Sadly for the young prince, it was a case of out of the frying pan of lethal Scottish dynastic politics and into the fire of Henry IV's ruthlessness. James was taken hostage by English pirates, and passed from their hands to those of the king. The prince, with his tutor, the Earl of Orkney, was clapped into the Tower to join a fellow Celt: Owain Glyndwr's eldest son, Gruffydd. Young Glyndwr had been taken prisoner after a Welsh defeat at the hands of Prince Henry of Monmouth, displaying the military prowess that would win him immortality at Agincourt as Henry V. After languishing in the Tower for six years, Gruffydd fell victim to one of the recurrent epidemics of bubonic plague that swept the country in the wake of the Black Death.

The news of his son's kidnap so shocked Prince James's father, King Robert III of Scotland, that within weeks of the abduction he was dead of grief. So James acceded to the Scottish throne as King James I while King Henry's prisoner in the Tower. The fact that James was now king did not immediately improve his lot. In Scotland, his uncle, Robert Stewart, Duke of Albany, became regent and showed little inclination to raise the large ransom Henry demanded for his nephew's return. So poor James remained in the Tower for two years until he was moved to Nottingham Castle. Here he stayed a captive for a further sixteen years.

James was kept in the Tower's royal apartments. Henry's accounts show that the constable, Sir Thomas Rempstone, was paid a generous daily six shillings and eight pence for his upkeep, and half as much again for his suite of attendants. James was allowed to pursue his interrupted education, becoming a skilled musician, a practitioner of the arts of war and a proficient poet. James's poetic skills bore fruit when, at the end of his long captivity, he composed *The Kingis Quair* (*The King's Book*), a famous manuscript in the literature of medieval courtly love. The poem, inspired by James's reading of Boethius's fashionable *Consolations of Philosophy* – with its concept of the wheel of fortune which alternately raised its human playthings to the heights of glory, before casting them down to the depths of despair – was a meditation on the circumstances of his own sad captivity:

> The bird, the beast, the fish eke in the sea,
> They live in freedom each one in his kind;
> And I a man, and lacketh liberty;
> What shall I say, what reason may I find,
> That fortune should do so? Thus in my mind
> My case I would argue, but all for nought:
> There was no-one to give my woes a thought

The poet king's verses, also much influenced by Chaucer's *Canterbury Tales* – which, as Chaucer was the Tower's former clerk of works, held pride of place in the Tower library – tells how he was in deep depression over his seemingly endless imprisonment when he saw from his window at the Tower a beautiful girl strolling in the garden below. He decided to marry his muse and eventually did so. This poetic romance was paralleled in James's real life when, late in his imprisonment, he fell in love with Joan Beaufort, King Henry's niece.

Things looked up for James when Henry IV died in 1413. The new king, Henry V, immediately had him brought back from Nottingham to the Tower and took him with him to France on his 1415 Agincourt campaign. However, it was only in 1424, after the death of James's regent uncle Robert, that a ransom of 60,000 marks was finally squeezed from his impoverished Scottish subjects. James was at last freed to wed his Joan in Southwark Cathedral. He bore his bride back to a Scotland he had not seen for nearly two decades. James proved a competent king despite his long absence. But murderous *Macbeth*-style Scottish dynastic politics finally claimed James's life as they had that of his brother. He was assassinated by a rival branch of his own family in 1437.

By the time Henry IV breathed his last in the Jerusalem Chamber of Westminster Abbey on 20 March 1413, he was a prematurely aged wreck, with his power already in the hands of his able eldest son. Henry V, tall and in his prime at twenty-five, proved more than capable of bearing the burden of kingship. On Henry IV's death, he followed the custom established by his father and after riding to the Tower with 'a great rout of lords and knights', according to Adam of Usk, created a new company of Knights of the Bath. That night, on 8/9 April, a huge snowstorm engulfed the country, making the new knights' cold vigil in St John's Chapel even chillier. According to Adam, the snow 'fell upon the hill-country of the realm and smothered men and beasts and homesteads, and drowned out the valleys and the marshes in marvellous wise'. Undeterred, Henry rode out from the Tower to Westminster for his coronation, acclaimed by cheering Londoners in the newly white streets.

Henry's main aim was to bring the Hundred Years' War to a triumphant conclusion. He began preparing an invasion of France almost as soon as he was crowned. In June 1413, he appointed an experienced fletcher, Nicholas Mynot, as the Keeper of the King's Arrows at the Tower armoury. Mynot's task was to replenish the store of longbows and arrows in the fortress, sadly depleted since the golden age of Edward III. The longbow was still the weapon that brought England's formidably trained archers victory on the battlefield, and Henry was determined to use it to its full advantage in the coming campaign.

Mynot was not the only armourer at work in the Tower. William Merssh was the King's Smith at the fortress, and in 1414 took on extra hired hands to make the newfangled cannons that would, in Shakespeare's words, 'afright the air at Agincourt' and eventually replace bows and arrows as the artillery of battle. Merssh's wife Margaret was also a qualified blacksmith who sweated alongside her husband in the Tower's forges. Payments made to Margaret Merssh indicate that she was employed on the more delicate arts of ironmongery – and for that work specially suited to the Tower's function as the chief state prison. One account records that she was paid thirty-five shillings (around £750 in today's values) to make eighteen pairs of fetters and eight pairs of manacles for restraining the Tower's resident captives.

The Tower was the nerve centre where the coming conflict with France was planned. It was to the fortress that London's mayor and aldermen were summoned on 10 March 1415 for a momentous secret meeting at which the king informed them that he had decided to invade France that year, and that he needed money from his wealthy capital to finance the campaign. Henry built up a small invasion fleet to carry his army across the Channel – seven of the ships were moored in the Thames at the Tower's wharf. Authority was also given to the ships' masters to use force to abduct and impress men from the nearby riverside taverns to crew the vessels – the first recorded instance of the notorious press gang in English history. In the spring of 1415 Nicholas Mynot was ordered by an impatient Henry to take on another dozen fletchers at the Tower armoury workshop to step up production of the bows and arrows needed in France. Mynot was also authorised to purchase the necessary extra wood, feathers, wax and silk used in the bowmaker's art.

Mynot's work proved its worth at Agincourt, on 25 October 1415. Here Henry showed himself a warrior king worthy of his ancestors when he defeated a French army up to four times the size of his 'happy few' 9,000 Englishmen. The Tower's bows and arrows and the new cannon ensured the downfall of the French. The slaughter was hideous, with some 6,000 Frenchmen dying for the loss of a mere 150 English slain. Many of the casualties were killed in cold blood on Henry's orders after they had surrendered. Others died of suffocation imprisoned inside their heavy armour when they were unhorsed and entombed under a pile of bodies, fatally funnelled into a narrow gap between two woods. However, some 1,500 French knights and nobles survived to be brought to England to await the ransoms they would fetch for their captors.

The high-ranking captives suffered the indignity of being paraded through the streets of London by a triumphant Henry, before enduring the extra humiliation of sitting through a *Te Deum* thanksgiving for the victory at St Paul's Cathedral. They were then brought to the Tower while the king went on to feast in his palace at Westminster. The most exalted prisoner was the French king's young nephew, Charles, Duke of Orléans. Almost a contemporary of Henry's – he was twenty-four – the young man had already had several brushes with death. His father had been assassinated when he was fourteen and he had seen his mother die of grief, while his first wife – his cousin Isabella, daughter of Charles VI of France – had died in childbirth only three years after their wedding.

At Agincourt, as joint commander of the French army, Charles had barely survived the battle. He was wounded several times and finally buried in his heavy armour under a mound of corpses – from which he had been extracted in the nick of time before asphyxiating. Treated by the king's physicians, he slowly recovered in the White Tower. His younger brother, Jean of Angoulême, was taken prisoner with him, but was held separately from Charles at Groombridge Place in Kent, the home of the knight who had captured him, Sir Richard Waller.

The royal brothers would have more than enough time to recover from the wounds of Agincourt: their imprisonment would last for a quarter of a century. Henry, fearing that they would be viable rivals to his own claims on the French Crown, deliberately set their ransom impossibly high – and gave secret orders that they should never be released. Unaware of this, Charles put his enforced stay in the Tower to good use. Naturally of an artistic rather than a military bent, the duke, like his fellow royal captive James I of Scotland, was an accomplished poet, and composed verse in the fortress: short, delicate roundels on such subjects as the changing seasons and courtly love. At first Charles wrote only in his native French, but as his confinement stretched from months into years, his familiarity with English grew and he began to compose verse in that language too. By the time of his eventual release in 1440 he was more fluent in his captors' tongue than his own.

As with other royal prisoners, although the duke's incarceration was long, it was not particularly rigorous. Unlike those held in the Tower for treason and similar high crimes, his royal wrists never felt the cold bite of Mistress Merssh's manacles. Indeed, he was even allowed to hunt and hawk when he was temporarily taken from the Tower and lodged at various castles around the kingdom: Windsor, Wallingford and Pontefract among them. His writings, however, tell us that he was never reconciled to his loss of liberty, and suffered greatly from homesickness:

Envoi

Paix est tresor qu'on ne peut trop louer:

89

> *Je hais guerre, point ne la doit priser;*
> *Detourbe m'a longstops, soit tort ou droit,*
> *De voire France que mon Coeur amer doit.*

> *(Peace is a treasure one cannot too much praise:*
> *I hate war, which no-one ought to prize;*
> *Right or wrong, it grieved me long,*
> *To see France, to which my sad Heart is bound.)*

He had to wait until after Henry's death before the bulk of his vast ransom of 80,000 *saluts d'or* (worth £50,000 then, perhaps more than £2 million in today's values) was finally raised. Even then, however, he had to sign a bond promising to pay a further 140,000 crowns when his liberty had been achieved. Another large sum was paid to win his brother Jean's freedom.

Charles honoured this debt by marrying a rich third wife (his second spouse, Blanche, having died during his imprisonment). His bride was Mary of Cleves, daughter of the Duke of Burgundy. Mary's enormous dowry enabled Charles to pay his debt to England, but he wrote that he had 'experienced in my English prison such weariness, danger and displeasure that I many times wished I had been slain at the battle where they took me'.

Charles recovered his spirits sufficiently to father a son, who became King Louis XII of France and married Henry VIII's sister Mary.

Henry V capped the Agincourt campaign by capturing his ancestral duchy of Normandy. In 1420 the Treaty of Troyes set the seal on his French conquests. England now controlled all France – including Paris – north of the River Loire, as well as Gascony in the south-west. The Treaty also gave Henry as a prize of war the hand of Catherine of Valois, daughter of King Charles VI of France, along with a handsome dowry. The treaty stipulated that Henry should succeed Charles as king of France in place of Charles's son, the Dauphin Charles – who nonetheless retained effective control of south and central France. Henry's dream of ruling over both England and France seemed so close that he could grasp it.

Henry and Catherine were soon blessed with a son, the future Henry VI, born at Windsor Castle on 6 December 1421. Then, in August of the following year, while besieging the town of Meaux, near Paris, Henry V died aged just thirty-four. His illness was diagnosed as dysentery, which was ravaging his army at the time. As the king's condition was accompanied by 'a bloody flux' and wasting, it is more likely that the fatal disease was the cancer of the bowel that had killed his ancestor Edward I. Whatever the cause, the death of the king at the height of his power was a shattering blow to English hopes of maintaining their newly won French domains. Those hopes now rested with Henry's nine-month-old baby boy.

Less than two months after Henry's demise, Charles VI, the periodically insane French king, followed him into the shadows. Henry VI, the infant king of England, was now in theory monarch of France as well. As he had lain dying, Henry V had made what arrangements he could to secure the future of his Lancastrian dynasty on the thrones of both kingdoms. He appointed one of his brothers, John, Duke of Bedford, to rule as regent over France; and another, Humphrey, Duke of Gloucester, to govern England as Lord Protector to his infant son. Both brothers faced formidable problems: in France half the country did not recognise the foreign baby king, but were loyal to the Dauphin, now Charles VII. In England, a bitter factional power struggle broke out around the royal cradle.

As he grew into manhood it became clear that Henry VI's character was totally unsuited to the taxing demands of medieval kingship. The king was weak, easily dominated and politically inept. Worst of all – like Henry III, Edward II and Richard II before him – he was uninterested in military matters; preferred aesthetic and religious pursuits ('we owe him those masterpieces of English Perpendicular architecture, Eton College and King's College Chapel, Cambridge); and – in stark contrast to his martial father and grandfather – was utterly incapable of leading an army in battle. He was the worst possible ruler to lead his kingdom through the turbulence about to engulf it. At the tender age of eight, Henry was taken to the Tower to spend the traditional night, and anoint thirty new Knights of the Bath, before his coronation. Crowned in London in 1429, and in Paris two years later, Henry grew up under the shadow of English losses as the fortunes of war turned decisively in favour of France.

Stronger characters than Henry filled the vacuum around his throne. Two branches of his Lancastrian dynasty – respectively descended from the first and second wives of Edward III's son John of Gaunt – bid for the vacant seat of power. After John of Bedford's death in 1435, a new faction stepped up to challenge the king's uncle, Lord Protector Humphrey, Duke of Gloucester. The wealthy Beaufort family, led by

Cardinal Henry Beaufort, Bishop of Winchester and Chancellor of England, were descended from John of Gaunt via his mistress and last wife, Katherine Swynford.

For two decades the animosity – bitter as only family rows can be – between Henry Beaufort and Duke Humphrey of Gloucester, paralysed policy and hindered good government. Beaufort, an able administrator, favoured imports of foreign cloth and peace with France. His rival 'Good Duke Humphrey' won huge popularity by advocating a protectionist policy benefiting native English wool producers. Loyal to the glorious memory of his brother Henry V, Humphrey also led the war party dedicated to continuing the conflict with France.

The ding-dong battle between Beaufort and Humphrey almost came to an actual clash of arms when Beaufort garrisoned the Tower against Humphrey and the London mob who backed him; refusing the royal duke entry to the fortress. The release in 1440 of Charles of Orléans from his long imprisonment in the Tower – which Beaufort arranged as a sop to France – was one of many bones of contention between them. In 1441 Beaufort, his power enhanced by being created a cardinal, decided to strike at his old enemy, whose loud protests at his rival's peace policy were becoming a serious nuisance.

Beaufort's chance came with Humphrey's unwise second marriage to his mistress Eleanor of Cobham, a commoner. As Humphrey was heir apparent should his nephew King Henry die childless, Eleanor had the enticing prospect of becoming queen. After having her horoscope cast, she decided to give fate a nudge by melting a wax effigy of Henry in a fire. Discovered, Eleanor and her accomplices were charged with witchcraft, locked in the Tower, and tried before a Church court. Although her clerk, Roger Bolingbroke, was hanged, drawn and quartered – and another associate, Margery Jourdemain, aka 'the witch of Eye', was burned alive – Eleanor escaped the ultimate penalty. Instead, she was required to do public penance, walking barefoot through London for three days, before being confined to a succession of distant castles, ending up at Peel in the Isle of Man, where she died in 1457.

Although Humphrey was not involved in his wife's sorcery, Eleanor's disgrace broke his power. To be married to a witch was social and political death, but soon it resulted in Humphrey's actual death too. First, Humphrey was marginalised, infrequently attending the Royal Council where the Beauforts were pulling the pliable young king's strings. Finally, in 1447, he was arrested and twelve days later it was announced that he had died of a seizure. Inevitably, rumours flew that he had been murdered. Old Henry Beaufort had won his vicious twenty-year feud with Humphrey. But he did not live long to savour it: within weeks he had died too.

Henry Beaufort's political heir, William de la Pole, 1st Duke of Suffolk, was a passionate supporter of peace with France despite – or because of – the fact that both his father and his older brother had died fighting the French. Suffolk himself had been imprisoned in France after surrendering Orléans to Joan of Arc. Released to supervise Henry VI's coronation as king of France, he became closely aligned with the Beauforts. He was given the task of negotiating the young king's unpopular marriage to the French princess, Margaret of Anjou, in 1445. The marriage bargaining was especially delicate because Margaret's father, Duke Rene, pleading poverty, refused to give her a dowry and demanded the two provinces of Maine and Anjou, captured by Henry V, in return for her hand. So desperate were the Beauforts and Suffolk for peace, that these outrageous terms were accepted – although they had to be kept secret for fear of the popular anger they would arouse. Duke Humphrey had sourly described Margaret as 'a Queen not worth ten marks'. But the new queen would soon prove her worth in other ways.

Suffolk, who had succeeded Henry Beaufort as Chancellor of England, continued pursuing peace with France. Suffolk's devious diplomacy incurred popular loathing, as did his manifest corruption. The final nail in his coffin, however, was the humiliating loss of Normandy in 1449. Exasperated by Henry's failure to hand over Maine and Anjou, Charles VII launched a full-scale invasion, of those provinces and of Normandy itself. The French were everywhere victorious. The new head of the Beaufort family, John, 1st Duke of Somerset, who was Lieutenant of France, humiliatingly surrendered Rouen, and by December virtually the whole ancestral homeland of the Plantagenets was lost. The glorious victories of Edward III, the Black Prince, and Henry V were as if they had never been. It was a national humiliation. Somerset returned home in disgrace and committed suicide.

Outraged English opinion demanded a surviving scapegoat; and the hated Suffolk fitted the bill. Oblivious of the gathering storm, Suffolk inflamed popular hostility by marrying his son John to his seven-year-old ward, Lady Margaret Beaufort, a possible claimant to the throne. (Indeed, although she would never rule herself, Margaret would go on to found England's Tudor dynasty.) Suffolk's move was widely seen as furthering his own ambition to be the power behind Henry's shaky throne.

When Parliament reassembled after the Christmas recess on 26 January 1450, hatred against Suffolk was at boiling point. Ignoring the duke's plea that he was the victim of 'Great infamy and defamation', Parliament impeached him and hustled him off to the Tower. Suffolk's plight was summed up in a gloating popular ballad:

> *Now is the fox driven to hole!*
> *Hoo to him, hoo, hoo!*
> *For if he creep out*
> *He will you all undo.*

For a fortnight the duke remained in the 'hole' while the Commons drew up a bill of indictment against him. Suffolk was accused not only of handing over Maine and Anjou to the French, but also of planning a French invasion of England; and plotting to depose Henry VI in favour of his own son John. Suffolk was also charged with having conspired with his French friends to release Charles of Orléans from his long imprisonment in the Tower. The king and queen, who since he had arranged her marriage had regarded Suffolk as her second father, were desperate to save their favourite minister. In March Henry took the case out of the Commons' hands, declaring that he would decide Suffolk's fate. Parliament's defiant response was to add yet more charges to the list, focusing on Suffolk's blatant corruption.

He had, the new indictment stated, 'committed great, outrageous extortions and murders . . . suppressed justice . . . been insatiably covetous . . . embezzled the king's own funds and taxes . . . to the full heavy discomfort of his true subjects'. Suffolk, summoned from his Tower cell, indignantly denied the charges as 'too horrible to speak of . . . utterly false and untrue'. But Parliament was implacably set on destroying the duke. In a final effort to save him by putting him beyond his enemies' reach, Henry sentenced Suffolk to be banished for five years from 1 May 1450.

Freed from the Tower on 18 March, the fallen duke made for his house in St Giles to collect his belongings. But a mob of Londoners, furious that their prey had 'crept out of his hole', broke into the house, and assaulted Suffolk's servants. The duke himself escaped via the back door, fleeing to his Suffolk estates where he lay low until Thursday 30

April – the last day before his appointed exile was to begin. He sailed from Ipswich for Calais, the port which, largely thanks to him, was now England's only possession in northern France. He never arrived. Off Dover, his vessel was intercepted by a flotilla which had been lying in wait, led by a large warship the *Nicholas of the Tower*.

As its name indicates, this ship was usually moored off the Tower's wharf. The current constable of the Tower was Henry Holland, the young Duke of Exeter. He had inherited the office from his father two years before when he was just seventeen. Cruel and rapacious, Exeter was a chip off his father's old block, who was immortalised in the nickname of the fiendish instrument of torture which the old brute had introduced to the Tower's orchestra of terror. The rack, which pulled its victims' limbs on ropes over rollers, stretching, tearing and eventually dislocating them, was dubbed 'The Duke of Exeter's daughter'. Years before, a clairvoyant had told Suffolk that if he could 'escape the danger of the Tower' he would be safe. Having got out of the fortress itself, Suffolk now learned with a sinking feeling the name of the ship to which he was rowed across the choppy Channel waters, and remembered the soothsayer's warning. His fears were confirmed when he was hailed by the ship's master, one Robert Wennington, with the chilling greeting, 'Welcome, traitor!'

Suffolk was detained aboard the *Nicholas* for more than twenty-four hours while a kangaroo court tried him on the articles of impeachment drawn up by Parliament. He was found guilty on all counts. The *Paston Letters*, a chronicle written by an East Anglian gentry family who knew Suffolk well, tell what happened next: 'He was drawn out of the great ship into a boat, and there was an axe and a stock [block], and one of the lewdest of the ship bade him lay down his head.' Then, disdaining the axe, the executioner 'took a rusty sword and smote off his head with half a dozen strokes, and took away his gown of russet, and his doublet of velvet, mailed, and laid his body on the sands of Dover. And some say that his head was set on a pole by it.'

Margaret of Anjou was told of Suffolk's messy end by the duke's widow, Alice Chaucer, granddaughter of the poet Geoffrey Chaucer. The young queen is said to have wept continuously for three days, refusing all food. Then, drying her tears, Margaret vowed vengeance. It was rumoured that Margaret and Henry were determined to wreak revenge for Suffolk's death on the county which had succoured his killers: Kent. Suffolk's closest ally on the Royal Council, the Crown Treasurer, Lord Saye, was said to be planning to depopulate the county, turning peasants and landlords off their land and replanting it as a massive hunting reserve. Kentishmen of every class, including lords and MPs, united against the threat.

By the end of May groups of armed men, assembling across the county to celebrate Whitsun, had formed a rebel army. They had a leader, called Jack Cade. Like Wat Tyler, the Kentish rebel leader of seventy years before, Cade was probably a soldier who had served in France. His aliases included 'Jack Amend-all' and, significantly, 'John Mortimer', which gave a clue as to the real moving spirit behind the revolt. Mortimer was the maternal family name of Richard, Duke of York, the kingdom's wealthiest magnate and an able administrator and soldier. Descended from Edward III via both his parents, he had an arguably better claim to the throne than the Lancastrians who sat on it. This had not mattered under the competent rule of Henry IV and Henry V who were both more than capable of seeing off challenges to the Crown. But now that the sceptre rested in the trembling hand of Henry VI, York began to wonder whether the right Plantagenet ruled. He was the obvious leader of a growing opposition to the corrupt and incompetent government.

By mid-June Cade's army had arrived at Blackheath – where Wat Tyler's rebels had once camped. The court sent emissaries to hear Cade's demands. After these were flatly rejected, a royal army of 20,000 gathered, and Cade retreated into Kent. A force under Sir Humphrey Stafford and his brother William was sent in hot pursuit, while the bulk of the royal army remained in London. Cade sprang an ambush at Sevenoaks on 18 June. After a hard fight, the Stafford brothers were killed, their army routed, and the victorious rebels marched once more against London.

Henry fled his capital to distant Kenilworth Castle in Leicestershire. Before leaving, the king confined the hated and grasping treasurer, Lord Saye, to the Tower as the safest place for him. Once the king had gone, those members of the council remaining in London took refuge there too. Memories of the massacres during the Peasants' Revolt were still fresh among the ruling caste. The rebels' numbers had been swelled by support from Sussex, Surrey and Essex, as what had begun as a little local difficulty grew into a full-scale insurrection.

On 29 June a swaggering Cade, wearing full armour beneath a scarlet cloak, and with the silver spurs of the slain Sir Humphrey Stafford jingling at his heels, was back on Blackheath with a much larger army. By 1 July he had advanced as far as Southwark, opposite the Tower. On 3 July Cade crossed the Thames and entered London. He came as a conqueror, clad in a royal blue velvet gown, carrying a shield studded with gold nails, and with a squire bearing a sword before him as if he were a king.

Cade paused on London Bridge, drew his sword, and slashed through the ropes holding the drawbridge. The capital lay prostrate before him, and to underline the fact he was formally presented with the keys of the city. He proclaimed, 'Now is Mortimer Lord of this city,' before stalking off to be wined and dined by London's aldermen, one of whom carved Cade's meat as if he was his lord. That night Cade returned to his quarters at the White Hart Inn in Southwark, but came back across the bridge the next day with his army at his back. The rebels' mood had turned ugly, and they assembled in front of the Tower demanding the head of Lord Treasurer Saye. The Tower's governor, Lord Thomas Scales, although a grizzled veteran of the Hundred Years' War, thought discretion the better part of valour and tamely turned the hated minister over to the mob.

A terrified Saye was dragged to the Guildhall where he was reunited with his son-in-law William Crowmer, the Sheriff of Kent, who had been taken from the Fleet prison. The two men – with a score of their cronies – were given a summary 'trial' before being marched to Cheapside and beheaded. Cade's rising was degenerating into the bloody chaos of Wat Tyler's revolt. Marking the descent into barbarity, Cade had the heads of Saye and Crowmer impaled on spears and obscenely made to 'kiss'. The heads and the naked, bleeding torsos were then paraded around London before being spiked above London Bridge. Meanwhile, many of Cade's men had begun to loot London. Cade himself, pressed to pay them, extorted money from the city merchants who had hitherto backed him.

That night, after Cade and his leading followers had reeled drunkenly back across London Bridge to the White Hart, a worried delegation of merchants, led by the lord mayor, made their way through the fearful streets to the Tower. They pleaded with the governor, Lord Scales, to act against the spiralling anarchy. Scales agreed and ordered the 1,000-strong Tower garrison under Captain Matthew Gough, a fellow veteran of the fighting in France, to bar the city's gates against the return of Cade's marauding army in the morning.

When Cade and his men realised what was happening, they stormed out of Southwark and a pitched battle ensued on the bridge. Ordinary citizens living in the houses along the bridge were caught up in the fighting; and some were flung screaming into the Thames. The battle raged all night, and Gough was among the forty-two Londoners slain. Cade's men lost 200, and eventually gave way, burning the drawbridge as they retreated. Cade had shot his bolt. On promise of a pardon, he agreed to go home; but as in 1381, the authorities had no intention of keeping their word once the immediate danger had passed.

Cade was declared an outlaw. Deserted by his followers, he fled into the Sussex woods. He was followed by royal puirsuivants, led by Alexander Iden, who had succeeded the murdered Crowmer as Sheriff of Kent. Iden cornered Cade in a garden at Heathfield where he was mortally wounded. Flung into a cart and brought to London, his body was beheaded and quartered. His head was set upon London Bridge, the scene of his last battle, in place of his victims Saye and Crowmer, facing south towards Kent. Cade's quartered corpse was displayed as a grim warning in the various parts of the kingdom where his rebellion had flared and failed.

Royal retribution did not stop there. In a judicial massacre known as 'the harvest of heads' Henry personally presided over the trials and executions of forty-two Kentish rebels. Feeble and pious he may have been, but with Margaret at his side, Henry VI did not lack the bloodthirsty tendencies of his forefathers. But despite the repression, Cade's rebellion, the symptom of the woeful misgovernment of the kingdom under this broken reed of a man, was also a bloody taster of yet more brutal struggles to come.

CHAPTER SIX

ROSES ARE BLOOD RED

In August 1453 Henry VI's always weak mind gave way entirely. He went mad after suffering a 'sudden fright'. The onset of the attack may have been sudden, but in view of his antecedents, was scarcely surprising; Henry's maternal grandfather, Charles VI of France, had also had fits of madness, suffering the awkward delusion that he was made of glass. Though exact diagnosis of Henry's illness is now impossible, this suggests that a gene of mental instability was transmitted through his mother, Catherine de Valois. The attack left Henry in a paralysed stupor – possibly catatonic depression or schizophrenia – unable to move from the chair where he sat. He remained in this sad state for the next eighteen months.

By the time that Henry was struck down, the political situation was rapidly reaching a point where the two factions – the court party and the York party – were so bitterly divided that only violence could resolve the issue. Time after time the rival sides squared up, only for a temporary truce to force the feud underground. Such a moment had come in May 1451 when a member of York's affinity, Nicholas Young, MP for Bristol, moved a petition in the Commons calling for York officially to be made the childless Henry's heir apparent. Young was locked in the Tower for his impertinence.

As the year went on, both sides manoeuvred for advantage, knowing that conflict could not be avoided for ever. Among the most loyal supporters of the king were his young half-brothers, Edmund and Jasper Tudor. Following Henry V's death in 1422, his widow, Catherine de Valois, was left bereft, a lusty young woman in the prime of life. She did not remain single for long. Owen Tudor, a handsome young Welshman of obscure origins, had become her Keeper of the Wardrobe. According to romantic rumour Owen had caught the queen's notice when he stumbled, incapably drunk, into her lap. Intrigued, she spied on him as he swam nude, liked what she saw, and in the late 1420s, secretly married him. Although frowned on by the court, the union between queen and commoner was a happy one, producing six children. Owen was packed back into obscurity after Catherine died in 1437, but his two eldest sons, Edmund and Jasper, inherited their father's charm and won the favour of Henry VI and Queen Margaret.

On 5 January 1453 the Tower was a scene of splendour when the king invested his two half-siblings as earls. Edmund became Earl of Richmond, while Jasper was made Earl of Pembroke. On the chilly winter day, the two new noblemen were grateful to be arrayed in costly furs and gowns of cloth of gold and velvet; along with lands and incomes befitting their new status. The Lancastrian cause was further consolidated during this same Christmas holiday, when Queen Margaret at last fell pregnant. The queen's favourite since Suffolk's murder was the new head of the Beaufort clan, Edmund, 2nd Duke of Somerset – to the extent that he was rumoured to be the father of the son to whom she would give birth in October, after seven years of fruitless marriage to the apparently asexual and puritanical Henry.

Desperate to hide the king's condition, the queen had her lolling, speechless sack of a husband secretly transported to Westminster to await the birth of her baby, which took place on 13 October. She was safely delivered of a healthy boy, whom she named Edward. But when the child was shown to Henry there was no reaction: he briefly glanced at the infant before casting his eyes down again. But now the king's illness could no longer be concealed. Unless he acknowledged Edward as his heir, a regency would have to be declared. A regency council was duly summoned. Finally, the Duke of York made his move.

In December 1453, after York's ally Sir William Oldhall had been appointed Speaker of the House of Commons, and London had filled with armed Yorkist adherents, the Commons impeached Somerset for treason. The same day, he followed the path already trodden by Suffolk to the Tower. Within hours, however, the queen had ordered her favourite's release and Somerset left the fortress for his house at Blackfriars. Word that he was free soon spread, and a crowd of York's supporters besieged his house and ransacked it. The duke barely escaped with his life, fleeing by barge along the river back to the safety of the Tower.

Queen Margaret was desperate to prevent York from being made regent.

On every count – his royal blood, his record as a competent administrator, and his status as the realm's most powerful nobleman – York was qualified to rule in the mad king's stead. But for Margaret, her future and that of her newborn child were at stake. If York once sat in her husband's place, would he ever be shifted? Henry might never recover, his heir was a helpless baby, her chief supporter, Somerset, was in the Tower, and she herself was widely hated. All Margaret had going for her was the support of those nobles – a majority on the council – reluctant to give York regal powers; and her own tenacious will. For months she fought a desperate rearguard battle to get herself or Somerset – whom she had again freed from the Tower – appointed regent. But while many nobles were suspicious of York's dynastic ambition, they did not wish to be ruled by a haughty, imperious foreign woman. In March 1454, York became Protector of the Realm.

York's first act was to send Somerset back to the Tower. Tellingly, when the guards came to arrest him, they found Somerset in the queen's apartments. Although powerless to prevent his detention, the fearless Margaret went out of her way to demonstrate her continuing loyalty to her favourite, even visiting him at the Tower. York packed her off with her son to join Henry in Windsor Castle while he set the dislocated kingdom to rights. Backed by the powerful Neville family, headed by the Earl of Salisbury, whom he made chancellor, and by Salisbury's son, the Earl of Warwick, York made a good start, ruthlessly slashing court expenditure and travelling north to knock the heads of the warring Neville and Percy families together. While in the north, York locked up his unstable young son-in-law, the Duke of Exeter, hereditary constable of the Tower, in Pontefract Castle, as punishment for a revolt that Exeter had joined in Yorkshire the previous year. This, while demonstrating York's admirable impartiality, had the unfortunate effect of turning the duke into a fanatical opponent of his father-in-law's house, and a fierce partisan of the Lancastrians in the coming struggle.

Back at the Tower, Somerset was scheming furiously to regain his freedom and influence. According to a Yorkist newsletter, from his cell Somerset recruited friars and seamen as spies to discover who was loyal to him, and who had strayed into York's camp. The same newsletter claimed that Somerset's henchmen had rented lodgings around the Tower with a view to seizing the fortress.

* * *

Then, on Christmas Day 1454 at Windsor, King Henry, like Rip Van Winkle, awoke from his long stupor. His recovery was as unexpected as the onset of the madness had been the previous year – and as unwelcome to York as it was good news for the court party. As soon as the king showed signs of regaining his senses, his son was again brought to him. This time he expressed delight and wonder, attributing Prince Edward's paternity to the Holy Ghost. It was given out that the king was 'well-amended . . . and in charity with all the world, and he would that all the Lords were so'. But despite the king's pleasure in his own return to health, as historian R. L. Storey remarks, 'If Henry's insanity had been a tragedy, his recovery was a national disaster.'

Henry had emerged from the tunnel of his madness a mere shadow of the already feeble man who had entered it. If he had been weak before, now he was a powerless puppet of whichever faction possessed his person. Pious and unworldly previously, now he appeared utterly lost in his dreams and devotions. Nor was his recovery permanent. The insanity would return periodically for the rest of his sad life, and from henceforth Henry was an empty husk in royal raiment, king in name only and a pathetic cipher to be manipulated at will. On 9 February 1455 Henry was sent before Parliament publicly to demonstrate his recovery. He promptly dismissed York from the protectorate, restoring power to Somerset's cronies. A week later, on 16 February, Somerset himself was released from the Tower and the Duke of Exeter was freed in Pontefract. York grimly concluded that with his enemies back in the saddle and bent on his destruction, only the utmost ruthlessness could save him – and the kingdom.

Early in May, Margaret and Somerset issued, in Henry's name, a summons to all loyal lords to gather at Leicester, in the Lancastrian heartlands, for a great council to reaffirm fidelity to the king and cast the Yorkist lords (who were not invited) into outer darkness.

Hearing of the summons, York, Salisbury and Warwick struck first. They marched south with an army of some 6,000 men and ambushed the outnumbered court party at St Albans, twenty miles north of London. The resulting clash was more of a skirmish than a true battle, but it was savage enough. An appalled Abbot Whethamstede witnessed the slaughter from St Albans Abbey: 'I saw a man fall with his brains beaten out, another with a broken arm, a third with his throat cut and a fourth with a stab wound in the chest, while the whole street was strewn with corpses.'

Arrows flew, one finding its mark in King Henry's neck. As the injured king took refuge in a tanner's cottage to have his wound dressed, his standard bearer abandoned the royal banner and fled. Meanwhile, across St Peter's Street, the Duke of Somerset was making a last stand outside the Castle Inn. Like the doomed Duke of Suffolk, Somerset recalled an encounter with a soothsayer who had foretold that he would die outside a castle. Now he rushed out of the tavern and laid about his enemies, killing four of them before he was struck down with an axe.

Somerset's death ended the struggle. What was significant about St Albans was not the numbers slain – around 100 – but the status of those killed. The victorious Yorkists deliberately slew the leaders of the court party, both in the heat of battle, and in cold blood afterwards. Besides Somerset himself, the head of the Percy clan, Henry the 2nd Duke of Northumberland, was killed; as was Thomas, Lord Clifford, a northern enemy of the Nevilles. After the slaughter, York, Salisbury and Warwick sought out their monarch and knelt in mock submission before him.

York's coup had paid off, placing him and his allies again in pole positions. But the price exacted was high. The blood shed at St Albans opened a corrosive crack in England's ruling elite. The taboo protecting an anointed king had been smashed, and those who had fallen in the battle had left sons and heirs to continue the blood feud. The trio of Yorkist lords now faced a quartet of young Lancastrians, a new generation of hot-blooded young men out for revenge on those who had slain their sires. Twenty-year-old Henry Beaufort, the new Earl of Somerset, had survived St Albans, despite being so severely wounded that he had been carried away in a cart. There was also a new Henry Percy, Earl of Northumberland; and a new Lord Clifford, a brute-tempered nineteen-year-old whose determination to wreak revenge for his father's death was so all consuming that it earned him the nicknames 'Black-faced Clifford' or, more simply, 'the butcher'; and the equally savage-tempered Duke of Exeter.

Inspiring these young bloods, and as savage as any of them, was Queen Margaret herself. Burning to avenge the slaying of Somerset and the humiliations heaped on her husband, she toured the country with her baby son, shoring up Lancastrian support. Henry himself, by contrast, did his best to keep the peace, bringing the rival factions together in London in January 1458 for a peace conference. 25 March was proclaimed a 'Loveday' on which the murderous rivals would parade their new-found amity. In an extraordinary procession, King Henry led his queen and council through the city to St Paul's. Side by side they marched: Salisbury with Somerset; Warwick with Exeter; and – weirdest pairing of all – Queen Margaret squired by the Duke of York with every appearance of chivalrous consideration. It would last barely longer than the echoes of the Mass chanted in the old cathedral. The service was followed by a feast and joust at the Tower. Queen Margaret, seated high on her throne in the tournament stands, was the leading lady as the knights ceremoniously saluted her before thundering down the lists with a lethal intent that they would soon show for real on the battlefield.

Although most Londoners were firmly pro-Yorkist, the Lancastrian-dominated Royal Council used its control of the Tower to stockpile bows and arrows by the thousand at the Royal Armoury there as in the days before Agincourt. The difference was that this time the intended targets were to be fellow Englishmen. The next round in the escalating conflict went to the Lancastrians, who outmanoeuvred the Yorkists and drove their three leaders into exile. A Lancastrian-dominated parliament condemned York, Salisbury and Warwick as traitors and confiscated their estates.

But the Yorkists did not take their attainder lying down. In January 1460 Warwick, the Captain of Calais, raided Sandwich in Kent. The raiders towed away in triumph the fleet that the Lancastrians had been assembling for an attack on Calais. In June, Warwick masterminded another attack. This time, however, he meant to stay. The advance guard was commanded by his diminutive uncle and deputy, William Neville, Lord Fauconberg, Salisbury's younger brother. Fauconberg seized Sandwich and held it as a bridgehead. On 26 June he was reinforced by Salisbury, Warwick and the young Edward, Earl of March, York's eldest son, with 2,000 men. This was an invasion. Gathering men as they went, the Yorkists marched on London.

On 2 July they reached the capital. The city's aldermen admitted them to the city. They paused for a couple of days to amass funds – London's merchants lent them £1,000 – and recruit more men before moving north in search of King Henry who was in the Lancastrian East Midlands. Only one bastion in London held out against the Yorkists: the Tower. Warwick left his aged father, Salisbury, with 2,000 men to besiege the fortress, still held by the equally elderly governor, Thomas, Lord Scales, as it had been during Jack Cade's rebellion.

Scales had taken several Lancastrian magnates – Lords Hungerford, de

Vesci, Lovell and de la Warre, and the Earl of Kendal – together with their ladies and households into the Tower with him for their own safety. There too was Anne, Duchess of Exeter, wife of the absent constable. Anne must have had mixed feelings about the siege since she was the eldest child of the Duke of York, while her unstable husband was a fanatical Lancastrian. Such were the cruel choices forced on divided families by civil war. But old Lord Scales had no doubts where *his* loyalties lay. From the Tower's battlements he opened fire indiscriminately on the streets of Yorkist London with cannon from the Royal Armoury.

Among the weapons in Scales's arsenal was a form of chemical warfare known as 'Greek fire' or 'wildfire', originally developed by the Byzantine empire. A medieval napalm, 'wildfire' was a terrifying cocktail of incendiary chemicals, probably including sulphur and naphtha, sprayed out of siphons. Wildfire burned all those it touched, and stuck to the skins of its unfortunate victims, flaring up even more fiercely if water was thrown over it. This was the first time that the Tower's guns – let alone these horrific flame-throwers – had ever been turned on Londoners, and their fear and rage at Scales's savagery were intense. The old governor was using the brutal methods of warfare he had learned in France, where the English had often used such tactics to terrorise hostile French civilians. It was not, however, what freeborn Londoners expected from their lords and masters and they would have their revenge.

Scales was confident that he could withstand Salisbury's siege until King Henry returned to his capital after trouncing the Yorkist rebels. Salisbury answered Scales's wildfire by placing a battery on the south bank of the Thames at Southwark, and began battering the Tower's southern curtain walls with their balls, 'crazing [cracking] the walls in divers places'. But as the echoes of the rival cannonades boomed out mournfully along the Thames, and Londoners sought shelter from the bombardment, the Lancastrian cause had come to grief on the banks of another river: the Nene at Northampton, where the defection of a treacherous Lancastrian nobleman, Lord Grey, and a sudden downpour which silenced the Lancastrian cannon, helped the Yorkists achieve victory. And vitally, the helpless King Henry, who had sat out the battle in his tent, fell into their hands.

Northampton sealed the fate of the Tower and its stalwart governor. Lord Scales had been holding out for a fortnight, and although he had plenty of weaponry in the Royal Armoury, the large number of Lancastrian ladies he had taken into the fortress meant his food supplies were running low. Moreover, the loud lamentations of the women whenever Salisbury's cannon balls crashed against the Tower's walls was undermining the morale of the garrison. King Henry's arrival in London as a prisoner of his Yorkist captors was the last straw for Scales. He surrendered on 19 July.

Although the terms of the Tower's capitulation stipulated that the Lancastrian lords and ladies within would escape with their lives, lesser members of the garrison had no such guarantees. Warwick, vengeful in victory, sat in judgement at the Guildhall on members of the Duke of Exeter's entourage from the Tower, whom he believed had conspired to assassinate him after the Loveday. They were hanged, drawn and quartered at Tyburn. Nor would Scales escape retribution for the wildfire that he had hosed so indiscriminately over London. The day after surrendering the Tower, he sailed upriver to seek sanctuary in Westminster Abbey. But he was recognised and cornered by Warwick's watermen, who forced him out of his boat and butchered him on the south bank at Southwark. The old warrior's corpse, stripped 'naked as a worm', was left on the steps of the Priory of St Mary Overy (now Southwark Cathedral). Warwick and the Earl of March attended the funeral and gave orders that such violence should cease.

Another temporary truce was called. Under an Act of Accord passed by Parliament, the Duke of York became heir apparent to succeed Henry. This act disinherited little Prince Edward, and there was no way that Queen Margaret would accept it. Indeed, that fierce and feisty woman had, since Northampton, been busy gathering troops in Scotland and the north. She was joined by Somerset, with another Lancastrian army from the south-west. Their combined forces of 20,000 men concentrated at York. The Duke of York could not ignore the threat. Hastily collecting cannon from the Tower, and leaving Warwick to hold London, he marched north with around 5,000 men. The duke was accompanied by the Earl of Salisbury and his second son, eighteen-year-old Edmund, Earl of Rutland. York sent his eldest son, Edward, Earl of March, to raise more men among his tenants in the Welsh Marches. It was a decision which signed his own death warrant − but saved the life of the future king.

Christmas 1460 found York, Salisbury and young Rutland at Sandal Castle, outside Wakefield in west Yorkshire, unaware that the Lancastrians, outnumbering him by some four to one, and led by his bitter enemy

Somerset, were fast approaching from Pontefract. Caught foraging for food and fuel in the open, the Yorkists were overwhelmed. The Lancastrians emerged from woodland hiding places, surrounding them on three sides 'like fish in a net'. Between 1,000 and 2,000 men died in minutes. Among the casualties were York himself and his young son Edmund of Rutland, slaughtered by John 'Black Faced' Lord Clifford who told him, according to Shakespeare, 'By God's blood, your father slew mine [at St Albans] and so will I you, and all your kin.'

Clifford sent Rutland's head to join his father's, which, wearing a paper crown in mockery of his claim to the throne, was set up above Micklegate Bar, one of York's ancient gateways. Here father and son were soon joined by the head of the old Earl of Salisbury who had been caught and executed at Pontefract the day after the battle. The young Lancastrian lords – Somerset, Northumberland, Exeter and Clifford – were avenged for their father's deaths. But their glory would be brief.

The torch of the Yorkist cause had now also passed to younger hands. Warwick was in firm control of London, the Tower, and wretched King Henry. Young Edward of March, the new head of the House of York, six foot three inches of superb masculine charisma, was sweeping through the Welsh Marches gathering men. When he heard the grim news of Wakefield, Edward hardened his heart. Unlike his father, he would make the kingdom his own – and soon.

In his first victory, young Edward swiftly disposed of a Welsh Lancastrian force led by Jasper Tudor, Earl of Pembroke, King Henry's half-brother, at a hamlet called Mortimer's Cross near Hereford. Jasper escaped the field, but his aged father, Owen Tudor, founder of the future Tudor dynasty, was beheaded after the battle. He lamented that 'the head that had once lain on Queen Katherine's lap would now lie on the executioner's stock'. Grotesquely, a local madwoman combed Owen's hair clean of blood before surrounding his severed head with hundreds of candles (it was the feast of Candlemas).

On the morning of Mortimer's Cross, a rare and alarming atmospheric phenomenon – a parhelion – had appeared in the sky as the Yorkists marched to battle. Ice crystals high in the atmosphere refracted sunlight, creating the illusion of three suns to appear, causing consternation among the superstitious soldiers. Edward quickly proclaimed that the three suns represented the Trinity, and was a mark of Heaven favouring their cause. He subsequently adopted the emblem of 'the sunne in splendour' along with the Yorkist white rose as his personal badge. At Mortimer's Cross the son of York first stepped on to the stage on which he would shine until his death two decades later.

Meanwhile, in Yorkshire, an equally indomitable warrior, Queen Margaret, had joined her victorious army after Wakefield, bringing Scottish soldiers with her. The vast host, 30–40,000 strong, marched south along Ermine Street towards London, plundering the estates of York and the Nevilles as they went. The *Croyland Chronicle* compared them to a horde of ravaging locusts. Their approach caused terror in London, where Warwick stripped the Tower armoury of the latest technology of war to use against the invaders – for that was how southerners regarded their northern countrymen, whose dialect was barely comprehensible to them.

Among the array of new military technology from the Tower that Warwick utilised was the fiercesome wildfire that the late Lord Scales had sprayed over London; 'caltrops', an ingenious starfish-shaped steel device fitted with four sharp spikes, one always pointing upwards, designed to deter mounted warriors; twenty-four-foot-long cord nets bristling with nails at every knot which, when spread on the ground, made an insurmountable obstacle for horsemen; huge spike-studded shields called 'palises' which had loopholes to fire through; and cannon firing giant iron-tipped arrows. Warwick's army included Burgundian mercenaries with small cannon fired from the shoulder – an early form of bazooka – to take on the northerners. Londoners volunteered to defend their city, and Warwick soon left London with a host almost rivalling the Lancastrians in size.

Warwick's new military gadgetry did him little good. He reached St Albans, only to be surprised and overwhelmed by the Lancastrians at dawn after a stealthy night march. After a hard day's fighting, Warwick retreated – defeated, but not destroyed. The chief Lancastrian strategist, a mercenary knight named Sir Andrew Trollope, fell victim to the Tower's new technology. He stepped on a caltrop spike, and despite being nailed to the spot, boasted later that he had killed fifteen men who passed him. Queen Margaret vented her customary cruelty on two captured Yorkists, Lord Bonville and Sir Thomas Kyriell; they had stayed behind to guard the captive King Henry, whom Warwick had neglected to take with him in his flight. The poor demented monarch had passed the battle sitting under a tree, singing and laughing in a world of his own. His 'minders' were now brought before Margaret and her son Prince Edward who, though only seven, was showing every sign of having inherited his mother's bloodthirsty temperament. 'Fair son,' said the queen sweetly. 'By what manner of means shall these knights die?' 'Their heads shall be cut off,' piped the little prince – and so the gruesome deed was done. Margaret and Edward were reunited with Henry in Lord Clifford's tent, but the family reunion would be short lived.

Warwick joined forces with Edward while the victorious Lancastrians celebrated their win by pillaging St Albans. Their behaviour terrified Londoners, who feared anarchy if the unruly armed mob were let loose in their prosperous city. Margaret was in a dilemma. On the one hand London was a tempting prize, particularly the Tower, with its plentiful supplies of artillery and military gadgetry. On the other, her army was diminishing as homesick Scots deserted and staggered northwards, loaded with plunder, while the joint forces of Edward and Warwick grew stronger. Playing for time, the city's aldermen barred London's gates against her while they negotiated to save the city from sack.

While Margaret hesitated, Edward struck. He and Warwick entered London on 26 February. Acclaimed by relieved Londoners, Edward's first act was to seize the Tower. The fortress would become his favourite residence – he would enjoy relaxing there with his mistresses and cronies – but there was no time for dalliance now. To secure his position he had decisively to defeat the Lancastrians. He scoured the Tower for every cannon in its arsenal. Lazy and lascivious by nature, Edward could rouse himself to furious activity when occasion demanded, only to lapse into indolence when the crisis had passed. An inspiring military leader – perhaps his greatest qualification as a ruler – like Oliver Cromwell, he never lost a battle.

Now Edward knew what had to be done, and did it with the decision of an experienced ruler rather than the nineteen-year-old youth he was. He formally claimed the Crown on 4 March and no one in London disputed it. The leading Lancastrian lords were retreating north with Henry and Margaret, and given the choice of the two Edwards – the seven-year-old son of Henry and Margaret or this strapping 'sun of York' – Londoners did not have to think twice before deciding the new Edward IV was their man.

Edward issued commissions of array, conscripting every available man between sixteen and sixty, and within days was marching north with an enormous army. Muster rolls indicated that some 36,000 men gathered at

Pontefract Castle where Edward concentrated his command on 27 March. The Lancastrians had an even larger host around York, where around 42,000 were mustered. Most of the available English peerage were here – the majority (nineteen) still on the Lancastrian side, while only eight fought for the Yorkists. It was clear that the coming battle would be a showdown in which fierce family hatreds would run unchecked, and the great dynastic question would be put to the supreme test.

The battle that followed, Towton, was the biggest, longest and bloodiest in English history – surpassing even the first day of the Somme on its casualty list. On Palm Sunday 1461, on a high snow-swept Yorkshire plateau south of York, the great Lancastrian host faced an only slightly smaller Yorkist army. Fought toe to toe without quarter, Towton ended with the Yorkists, led by the charismatic Edward, cracking the Lancastrian line and chasing them into a swollen stream which became a mass of hacked bodies so that the white water ran red for three miles. Many Lancastrian lords died in the slaughter, and the Lancastrian royal family – Henry, Margaret and little Prince Edward – fled from York as news of the disaster reached them.

The bloodbath at Towton was decisive. The Lancastrians were shattered both militarily and politically, as Edward IV's biographer, Charles Ross, noted: 'For most Englishmen, including a majority amongst the barons and gentry, it now became prudent and realistic to acknowledge the authority of the new king.' Edward established his House of York on the throne with the support of most of the country – especially in the south and east. His rule, however, was far from secure. The deposed royal family and their entourage, including the Dukes of Somerset and Exeter, took refuge in Scotland, where they licked their wounds and plotted their next move.

On 26 June the victorious Edward IV formally re-entered London, riding through the streets of the city amidst cheering crowds until he reached the Tower, where the royal apartments in the palace had been refurbished for their new occupant. The next night passed in the traditional pre-coronation vigil, with Edward creating thirty-two new Knights of the Bath, emphasising that although the throne was under new occupation, continuity, rather than radical change, would mark the Yorkist regime. On 28 June, Edward processed amidst more popular acclaim from the Tower to Westminster Abbey for his coronation. Edward's character was a curious mixture of cruelty and conciliation. He could be completely ruthless when acting against his enemies. At the same time, he spared some who he might have eliminated. These even included the man who had led the Lancastrian army at Wakefield – killing his father, brother and uncle in the process – at the second St Albans, and at Towton: Henry Beaufort, Duke of Somerset.

Following Towton, Somerset led resistance to Yorkist rule in Northumbria based on the great castles of Alnwick – seat of the mighty Percy family – Bamburgh and Dunstanburgh on the coast. Repeatedly changing hands, the castles remained a thorn in Edward's side until Somerset surrendered all three of them at the end of 1462, on the understanding that his life would be spared and that he would give his allegiance to Edward. The king was as good as his word. In fact, better. Not only did Edward pardon Somerset, he also bestowed his favour on other members of the Beaufort family. He released Somerset's younger brother, Edmund, from the Tower, where he had been confined since Towton, and gave lavish annuities to his mother and brother-in-law. Somerset himself was literally taken into the king's bed in the Tower. Wonderingly, the chronicler William Gregory reported:

> And the king made full much of him in so much that he lodged with the king in his own bed many nights, and sometimes rode a hunting behind the king, the king having about him not passing six horse[men] at the moat and yet three were the duke's men. The king loved him well, but the duke thought treason under fair cheer and words . . .

The thought of the victorious and the vanquished commanders from the great charnel house of Towton carousing between the same sheets at the Tower may seem strange, but it was common for medieval men to share a bed without there being any sexual implications. Indeed, it seems that Somerset shared Edward's macho heterosexual tastes, and the two men went hunting for woman as well as game. The politics behind Edward's behaviour were clear enough: as the most powerful mainstays of the Lancastrian cause, the Beauforts were well worth winning over. Edward's support base among the nobility was still too narrow for comfort, and the Beauforts' backing would cement his hold on power.

But the pull of Somerset's hereditary Lancastrian loyalties proved stronger than a lads' friendship founded on a mutual taste for the chase. Edward's pampering of Somerset had infuriated his closest allies, such as his chamberlain, Lord William Hastings, and the mighty Warwick. But Edward stuck by his new friend. He took Somerset and 200 men of his affinity north on a peacemaking tour of Yorkshire in the summer of 1463. They halted at Northampton, the town still smarting from its sack in 1461 by Somerset's ravaging Lancastrian army marching from Wakefield. When locals discovered 'the false duke and traitor was so nigh the king's presence', their rage knew no bounds, and only Edward 'with fair speech and great difficulty' saved Somerset from a lynching. The king mollified the mob with a cask of wine, and while they were drinking it he smuggled Somerset to safety, sending him to Chirk Castle in North Wales.

The Northampton lynch mob proved a catalyst for Somerset. After 'ratting' once, now he 're-ratted' and urged local Lancastrians in Wales to rebel and restore Henry VI to the throne. That luckless monarch had been left in the north after Towton by his wife, who had returned to her native France with Prince Edward to drum up support for the Lancastrians. Henry was left with a handful of diehard followers in Bamburgh Castle, where he was joined by Somerset early in 1464. But their forces numbered no more than 500 men – a fraction of the great host smashed at Towton.

King Edward was taking no chances. He knew that the trio of mighty Northumbrian castles, Alnwick, Dunstanburgh and Bamburgh – now again held by Somerset – could provide a springboard for a Lancastrian comeback. So he turned to the Tower's armoury to find the big guns to combat the threat. He plundered the fortress's arsenal of its five great siege guns, called *Edward*, *London*, *Newcastle*, *Dijon* and *Richard Bombardel*. As this formidable battery, commanded by the Earl of Warwick, creaked its slow way north along muddy roads, pulled by ox carts, Warwick's younger brother, John Neville, was sent ahead by the earl.

Neville destroyed Somerset's tiny army in two skirmishes at Hedgeley Moor and Hexham in the spring of 1464. Somerset was captured and unceremoniously beheaded. Edward would not make the mistake of trusting a Beaufort again. Neville was rewarded by being created Earl of Northumberland, the title traditionally held by the Nevilles' great northern rivals, the vanquished Lancastrian Percys. When Warwick arrived with his siege train the garrisons of Alnwick and Dunstanburgh took one look at the Tower's great guns and surrendered on the promise of a free pardon without a shot being fired. Bamburgh proved a tougher nut to crack.

Warwick sent his herald forward to threaten the castle's commander, Sir Ralph Grey:

> If ye deliver not this jewel [Bamburgh], the which the King, our most dread sovereign lord, hath so greatly in favour, seeing it marcheth so nigh his ancient enemies in Scotland, he specially desireth to have it unbroken with ordinance, if ye suffer any great gun [to be] laid unto the wall and be shot, and prejudice the wall, it shall cost you the chieftain's head, and so proceeding for every gun shot to the least head of any person within the said place.

But this dire threat had no effect. Grey, like Somerset, had submitted to Edward after Towton, only to revert to his original Lancastrian allegiance in 1463. He knew that his life was forfeit for this betrayal and grimly fought on. Reluctantly, Warwick gave the order for the Tower's mighty guns to open fire. The great iron cannons *Newcastle* and *London* sent their shot hurtling into Bamburgh's walls. The castle's stonework flew into the sea, while the bronze *Dijon*, a more modern Burgundian weapon, accurately hit Grey's bedchamber, dislodging a chunk of masonry and knocking out the commander. While Grey was out cold, his deputy, Humphrey Neville, agreed to surrender in return for a pardon, and opened the castle gates. The injured Grey was taken to Doncaster and tried before the constable of England, the sadistic John Tiptoft, Earl of Worcester, who ordered his immediate execution.

King Henry vanished for more than a year, leaving behind only a few pathetic belongings, including his crown and a spoon. He was sheltered by loyal northern gentry, shuttling between their homes and sometimes – appropriately for such a pious man – disguised as a monk seeking sanctuary at religious houses. In July 1465 the fugitive king was hiding at Waddington Hall near Clitheroe in Lancashire, the home of the Tempest family, under the care of his former carver and chamberlain, Sir Richard Tunstall. But one member of the family, John Tempest, did not share his relatives' Lancastrian loyalty. Informed by a treacherous monk of the mystery guest at the hall, Tempest organised a posse. When they arrived, a furious struggle ensued. Tunstall held the pursuers off – breaking John Tempest's arm in the process – while Henry, accompanied only by two chaplains and a single squire, made off into nearby Clither Wood. Later that afternoon Henry and his companions were caught crossing the River Ribble by stepping stones, and arrested.

Humiliatingly, Henry, wearing a straw hat in the summer heat, was mounted on a poor thin nag; his feet were bound under the stirrups by leather thongs and, lashed to his saddle with rope, he was brought to London. He was received at Islington by Warwick and led through the city's streets towards the Tower, a placard scrawled with insults around his neck. It was a tragic and frightening return to his capital for the mentally frail fallen monarch. As the forlorn little procession rode through Cheapside, Cornhill and Newgate, ribald crowds of Londoners followed their progress, yelling abuse and hurling refuse and stones at the helpless captive. The saintly Henry heard his wife called a whore, and worse, before the Tower's gates mercifully closed behind him, muffling the hostile jeers. It was to be his home for the last decade of his sad life.

While Henry had been on the run, the kingdom he had lost had enjoyed a brief respite from civil strife. But King Edward lapsed into idle self-indulgence now the pressure was off. His main vices were gluttony – like a Roman patrician he would give himself emetics after a hearty meal, for the pleasure of vomiting and then gorging himself all over again – and lechery. Although his greed made him obese, it was his lust that did Edward the real damage. Both vices were indulged in to the full at the Tower. The king spent more time at his castle palace than any previous monarch. It is a piquant thought that while poor, pious Henry eked out a thin existence as Edward's captive in the Wakefield Tower, reading the Bible and his breviary, praying in his private oratory, eating the frugal meals of a prisoner, and patiently enduring his harsh lot, a few feet away, in the Tower palace, Edward was feasting and fornicating with his mistresses and cronies.

Separated by only a couple of walls, the contrast between the lives of the pathetic fallen king and his sybaritic supplanter was a painful one. Although Henry was allowed visitors – by permission of his jailers – all such contacts were carried out under the watchful eyes of five of Edward's trusties. For company, Henry was permitted a dog and a pet sparrow. For human association, he was allowed around a dozen attendants, including a priest, William Kymberley, who celebrated a daily Mass for him. The captive claimed, probably truthfully, that so long as he was allowed the Sacraments he did not mind the loss of his earthly kingdom. Although occasionally sent wine from Edward's cellars when the king remembered his forlorn prisoner, and granted an allowance of velvet cloth for his gowns and doublets, Henry had never been a drinker or a fashion icon.

Even in the days of his pomp, his simple homespun clothes and old-fashioned square-toed shoes had been mocked by modish courtiers. So Henry stayed in his lonely Tower, as one dull day succeeded another, his thin hands joined in prayer around a guttering candle, resigned to whatever fate more worldly men had in store for him.

Edward's lifestyle at the Tower could not have been more different. Always a lover of luxury, he had his royal rooms sumptuously redecorated; they were aptly known as the 'House of Magnificence'. They were divided into three great chambers: an audience chamber where visitors were entertained and foreign envoys received; an inner privy chamber where private business was conducted; and finally the holy of holies – the royal bedchamber – furnished with pallet beds for the half-dozen squires and gentlemen ushers who serviced the king's most intimate needs: holding the basin in which he washed, the towel with which he dried himself, and the pot into which he pissed. The king's own great tester bed was made and unmade with elaborate ritual, laid with sheets of blanched linen; velvet or satin pillows and bolsters; and an ermine fur counterpane on which holy water was sprinkled before it was used – often for distinctly unholy purposes. Here, behind discreetly drawn bed curtains to ward off the Tower's river chill, the king would spend his nights chastely with favoured male friends, or more energetically with mistresses such as Elizabeth Lucy or Elizabeth Waite, one of whom bore the lusty young king an illegitimate son, Arthur Plantagenet, destined to end his days in the Tower where he may have been conceived – and possibly a daughter, Elizabeth, too.

If Edward had kept his compulsive womanising separate from his dynastic obligations he might have secured the House of York as England's permanent ruling dynasty. But it was not to be. In 1464 he secretly married Elizabeth Woodville, the widow of a Lancastrian knight. Rumour had it that the pretty, blonde young widow had deliberately waylaid the susceptible king by standing under a tree with her young sons, holding one by either hand. The trio made a heart-wrenching picture as she pleaded for his help, and Edward was instantly smitten. However apocryphal this story, the legend well captures Elizabeth's calculating ability to manipulate her royal target. A commoner, a Lancastrian, three years Edward's senior, with a tribe of twelve greedy, grasping siblings in her baggage, Elizabeth had only one thing to recommend her: the randy Edward desperately fancied her. That powerful urge overrode all political objections to the match. Why, then, did Edward not make Elizabeth his mistress as he had so many others? It was said he had wanted to do exactly that, to the extent of holding a dagger to her throat during his rough wooing. But Elizabeth was a cool customer. Like Anne Boleyn in the next century, she held out for a crown. So violent was Edward's lust that he agreed and, despite his continuing infidelity, the union proved lasting and fruitful.

When Edward was forced to reveal his marriage to his shocked council six months later, Warwick in particular was outraged by the union with a penniless widow, whose Lancastrian father he had once insulted for his humble origins. The earl's ire was increased as he had been in the act of negotiating a French royal match for the headstrong young king. Insultingly, after Edward made his stunning announcement, he asked Warwick personally to present the new queen to the council. As the kingdom's richest magnate, Warwick saw himself as the power behind the throne. In his eyes, the House of York was his creation, and, fourteen years Edward's senior, he saw him as a headstrong nephew. Now his exuberant protégé was threatening Warwick's pre-eminence. This was intolerable.

Such were the seeds of Warwick's discontent. Significantly, he refused to attend Elizabeth's coronation after she had spent the traditional pre-ceremony night at the Tower in May 1465. That event was a magnificent affair. The queen, her loveliness enhanced by a satin gown and an array of glittering jewels, was borne by eight noblemen carrying poles from which her carriage was slung, out of her apartment to where six white ponies were waiting to be harnessed to it. In this splendid state she was carried out of the Tower through cheering crowds to Westminster Abbey. The new queen's avaricious relatives made haste to grab the goodies that Elizabeth's royal match had flung their way. Her upstart father, Lord Rivers, was created Lord Treasurer and two of her five brothers were among the fifty new Knights of the Bath dubbed at the Tower in honour of her coronation. In 1467 Warwick absented himself from court altogether in protest at the advancement of the queen's seven sisters, five of whom had made richly rewarding marriages into the peerage, some seizing part-ners who Warwick had marked down for marriage into his own clan.

The earl was also angry at the king's dismissal of his brother George Neville, Archbishop of York, from the post of Chancellor. Most demeaning of all to the Neville family's honour, Warwick's elderly aunt, the wealthy

Dowager Duchess of Norfolk, aged eighty, was hastily wed to the queen's brother John, who was just twenty. A horrified chronicler, sarcastically calling the old duchess 'a slip of a girl', suggested that the Devil himself had arranged the outrageous match. Satanism, in fact, was widely rumoured to be the real reason behind the king's infatuation with Elizabeth. The new upstart queen – in another parallel with Anne Boleyn – was said to be a sorceress who had bewitched the king. By 1469, proud Warwick had had enough and took the decisive step into conspiracy and rebellion.

Warwick had another monarch in mind to place upon the throne that Edward had sullied. The king had two surviving younger brothers. The youngest, Richard, Duke of Gloucester – one day to become England's most notorious king – had, aged seventeen, shown loyalty amounting to hero worship of his glamorous royal brother. The elder, George, Duke of Clarence, was cut from very different cloth. These two would find prominent places in the Tower's pantheon. One would become its greatest villain, the other its most bizarre victim. Clarence, born in 1449, was accurately summed up by Shakespeare as 'false, fleeting, perjured Clarence'. Tall, like his brother, the duke had few other of Edward's regal characteristics. Treacherous, malicious and impulsive, eaten up by envy and ambition, Clarence had foes aplenty, but he was his own worst enemy.

Once Warwick had abandoned dreams of being the king's puppet master and turned to plotting his destruction, he chose Clarence as his cat's paw. As captain of Calais, Warwick strongly favoured a French alliance to drive a wedge between the wily King Louis XI and the Lancastrian exiles planning a comeback from France led by Margaret of Anjou. Edward, dreaming of reigniting the Hundred Years' War, allied himself with France's great rival Burgundy, whose ruler, Duke Charles the Bold, had married his sister Margaret. As the 1460s wore on, there were growing signs that the exiled court of Queen Margaret in France had well-placed sympathisers in England. And Warwick carefully stirred and seasoned the bubbling cauldron of discontent.

In June 1468, a cobbler, John Cornelius, was arrested in Kent as he boarded a ship for France. Cornelius was a Lancastrian courier smuggling letters between Margaret's court and secret Lancastrian cells in England. He was taken to the Tower and in the torture chambers beneath the White Tower the soles of the shoemaker's feet were seared with flaming torches until, in his agony, he began to gasp out his contacts' names. They were a surprisingly high-placed circle, including city merchants, squires and knights. All were hauled into the Tower in their turn and tortured. One of those arrested was another Lancastrian agent, John Hawkins, a servant of Lord John Wenlock, a veteran soldier and former Speaker of the House of Commons who was a strong supporter of Warwick.

Hawkins was stretched on the most fearsome instrument in the Tower's orchestra of pain: the rack. As his agonised screams echoed off the cellar walls with the tautening of the rack's rollers, dragging his limbs from their sockets, Hawkins too named names, and an ever widening circle of covert Lancastrians came under suspicion. Hawkins and Cornelius, both limping from their tortures, were brought before Chief Justice Sir John Markham. The judge, an unusually humane man for that brutal age, refused to admit the Crown's evidence against them as it had clearly been coerced by torture.

The queen's father, Lord Rivers, the new Lord Treasurer, told the king that the uncooperative judge should be fired, to which Edward agreed. Poor Cornelius was then returned to the Tower's torture chambers and still more vicious methods were applied. Red-hot pincers tore chunks of flesh from his body. These extreme measures killed Cornelius before he named more Lancastrian co-conspirators. Frustrated, the authorities continued the wave of arrests and executions into 1469. The moving force behind this reign of terror, from motives of avarice as much as political expediency, was the Woodville family.

Like the Despensers under Edward II, or the Beauforts behind Henry VI, the Woodvilles had become the inspiring instruments of royal tyranny. Idle Edward too easily let his spouse's family have their grasping way. When John Hawkins, again under torture in the Tower, let slip the name of Sir Thomas Cook as a Lancastrian sympathiser, the Woodvilles seized their opportunity. Cook, a wealthy London alderman and former lord mayor, had in his house a costly wall tapestry or arras, woven in gold thread, depicting the siege of Jerusalem. This had been coveted by the queen's mother, Jacquetta, now Duchess of Bedford, who had unsuccessfully offered Cook £800 for it.

When Cook was brought into the Tower for questioning, Jacquetta's husband, Lord Rivers, ordered his men-at-arms to plunder Cook's house. They turned his wife and family into the street and seized the Jerusalem arras, along with several other tapestries, also making off with jewels, plus quantities of gilt and silver plate. Although Hawkins withdrew the accusations against Cook that had been wrung from him under torture, the authorities refused to release the alderman. Indeed, the king stripped him of his office, and grasping Queen Elizabeth got in on her parents' act by demanding – under an obscure old law called 'Queen's Gold' – a cut of £800 in addition to the massive £8,000 fine that Cook had to pay to secure his release from the Tower. He never recovered the goods or the cash that the Woodvilles had stolen, and died in poverty.

One nobleman who never wavered in his loyalty to the fallen House of Lancaster was John de Vere, 13th Earl of Oxford. His fidelity had been cemented in blood in 1462 after his father, the 12th Earl, and elder brother Aubrey, accused of plotting to restore the Lancastrians, were flung into the Tower and, despite their noble status, brutally executed. Father and son were first hanged, before being cut down half choked but still alive, castrated, then forced to watch their genitals burned in the executioners' brazier. Next they were disembowelled while tied to chairs and had their intestines wound out of their abdomens on to a roller. After this gruesome display they were finally beheaded and their pitch-coated heads were spiked on London Bridge.

King Edward clumsily attempted to buy the loyalty of the new Earl of Oxford. He waived the usual attainder that prevented the relatives of traitors from inheriting their titles and estates; released his aged mother from house arrest and pardoned her; and allowed Oxford to take up his family's hereditary office of Lord Chamberlain. Finally, he married Oxford to Warwick's sister, Margaret. The king's actions show that Edward – whatever his other gifts – was no psychologist. Though outwardly conforming – even presiding as chamberlain over Elizabeth Woodville's coronation in 1465 – despite or because of the grim fate of his father and brother, Oxford remained an irreconcilable secret Lancastrian, awaiting his opportunity to strike.

As other Lancastrians were tortured in the Tower, they took cold comfort from the fact that the object of their steadfast loyalty – the shadow of the man who had once been Henry VI – was eking out his existence in the same fortress where they suffered. Late in 1468 there was a fresh wave of arrests. Those held included John Poynings and Richard Alford, accused of contacting the new Duke of Somerset – Edmund, a former prisoner in the Tower – and now a leading light at Queen Margaret's exiled court. Poynings and Alford were tortured before being executed on Tower Hill along with Richard Steeres, a pioneer of tennis in England and former servant of that other great Lancastrian stalwart, the Duke of Exeter. Steeres, like Cornelius, had been caught carrying letters to Queen Margaret. Finally, after the arrests of the heirs of two West Country Lancastrian lords, Sir Thomas Hungerford and Henry Courteney, a bigger fish – the Earl of Oxford himself – landed in the Tower.

After the awful fate dealt to his father and brother there, the young earl must have believed that his last hour had come, and that his next station after his Tower cell would be the scaffold. Instead, miraculously, he was released at Christmas 1468 after just a few weeks. Oxford's stay in the Tower may have been short, but it was not easy. According to a contemporary report he was 'kept in irons' but whether this means that he was merely shackled, or subjected to the excruciating torture of being hanged, by his wrists from iron manacles, we do not know. It seems probable that the pressure was sufficient to open Oxford's lips, for the same letter records that 'he has confessed much' and soon afterwards Hungerford and Courtenay were both hanged, drawn and quartered for treason.

In April 1469, King Edward pardoned Oxford for 'all the offences committed by him'. But having seen the inside of the Tower, and experienced how murderous the Yorkist regime could be, Oxford was not willing to wait on the king's fickle favours. In July, less than three months after his pardon, he was off. At Canterbury he attended a rendezvous of the discontented. There he met Richard, Earl of Warwick; Edward's unruly brother Clarence; Warwick's brother George Neville, Archbishop of York; and Warwick's eldest daughter Isabel, whom the king had banned from marrying Clarence – thereby offending both his brother and Warwick. The high-ranking band of malcontents all had burning grievances against Edward and the Woodvilles. Defying the king, they set sail for Warwick's citadel of Calais bent on vengeance.

There followed a year of complex plots, revolts and battles during which Warwick defied the king by marrying Isabel to Clarence; incited revolts against Edward; invaded England; deposed his protégé the King; executed the patriarch of the hated Woodvilles, the queen's father Lord Rivers; and at one stage had two monarchs – Henry VI in the Tower, and Edward IV at Middleham in Yorkshire – in captivity. This earned him the nickname 'the Kingmaker'. But the Kingmaker still needed a king. Edward turned the tables when a genuine Lancastrian revolt forced Warwick to release him to defeat it. Restored to his kingship, Edward proclaimed Warwick and Clarence rebels and traitors, forcing them to flee to France

Barred from Calais, when Warwick and Clarence finally landed in France they made straight for the court of the scheming Louis XI. The French king, keen to keep England weak and divided, advised Warwick to do the unthinkable: make peace with his arch-enemy, Queen Margaret of Anjou. Warwick saw the sense in combining against the common foe. In August 1470 he met Margaret in Angers Cathedral. The haughty queen kept the proud earl on his knees for a quarter of an hour as he begged forgiveness for his past misdeeds, and talked up the advantages of their unnatural alliance. At last Margaret relented. To seal the deal, it was agreed that Warwick's younger daughter, Anne, should marry Margaret's son Prince Edward. As a sop to the now redundant Clarence, it was decided that he should be heir to the throne should Edward and Anne fail to produce children.

Margaret made clear it would be up to Warwick to do the heavy lifting necessary to prise King Edward from his throne, release her husband Henry VI from the Tower, and smooth the way for her son's belated entry to the city he had not seen since leaving it as an infant seventeen years before. To prepare for his invasion, Warwick repeated the same tactics he had used the previous year. He fomented another Lancastrian revolt in the north to lure Edward from London. Then, in mid-September, with sixty ships fitted out by King Louis, Warwick landed in Devon accompanied by Clarence, Oxford and Jasper Tudor. King Edward had left his wife, Elizabeth Woodville, pregnant with her third royal child, in the palace at the Tower, having had the apartments there expensively refurbished for the birth of what he hoped would be his first son and heir. But the queen had her mind on more than her coming confinement. Well aware of Warwick's bitter hostility to her and her clan, she had the Tower 'full victualled and fortified' against a possible siege; the king having previously taken the precaution of bringing in large cannon from Bristol with extra ammunition to add to the Tower's armoury.

Edward was in York when he heard of Warwick's arrival. Always supremely confident of his own ability, Edward trustingly relied on another Warwick sibling, John Neville, Marquess of Montagu, to hold the north while he hurried south to meet and beat Warwick. However, at Doncaster,

Edward heard alarming news: Montagu had defected to his brother's side and was hastening to arrest Edward. With no time to finish his dinner, Edward fled, accompanied by his youngest brother, Richard, Duke of Gloucester; his bosom friend William Hastings; and the young Lord Anthony Rivers, now head of the Woodville family. The little group rode hell for leather for the Norfolk coast, finding two Dutch ships about to sail home. Edward had no cash to pay for his passage, and gave the skipper a gown trimmed with the fur of pine martens in lieu of a fee. In this bedraggled manner they were put ashore on Burgundian soil. After a decade's reign, Edward IV had lost his kingdom.

The news of her husband's flight reached Queen Elizabeth at the Tower on 1 October. At the same time she heard of the rapid approach of Warwick with some 30,000 men. London was already in a state of high fear after the men of Kent, inspired by Warwick's agents, had attacked the city, targeting, as in the Peasants' Revolt, its large Flemish community. The Flemings, subjects of the Duke of Burgundy who had given shelter to the fallen King Edward, were considered fair game. Shaken by the sudden turn of fortune, and eight months' pregnant, the queen abandoned any idea of defending the Tower. With her mother and two infant daughters she vacated the fortress and – not for the last time in her turbulent life – sought sanctuary at Westminster Abbey.

The next day Warwick's advance guard entered the city. On 3 October the constable of the Tower – the sadistic John Tiptoft, Earl of Worcester – peacefully surrendered the fortress. His gesture did Tiptoft little good. Although Warwick and Clarence had issued a general pardon, Tiptoft, uniquely, was excluded. Guessing what fate awaited him, the constable fled to a forest in the Midlands where he was found hiding in a treetop, and was brought back to the Tower. The cruel constable had incurred particular odium for impaling the bodies of some Warwick supporters on stakes after hanging them, and could have expected no mercy from the earl. The judge was Lord Oxford, whose brother and father Tiptoft had had butchered so gruesomely on Tower Hill. Now Oxford had the sweet revenge of seeing Tiptoft beheaded on the same spot. The constable – a noted classical scholar, despite his brutality – made a bizarre final request to the executioner. He asked that his head should be struck off with three strokes of the axe in honour of the Trinity.

Control of the Tower, and with it, custody of King Henry, had passed to Warwick's lieutenant, Sir Geoffrey Gate. Fearing that too sudden a transformation would tip the king's fragile mind into insanity again, Gate selected a cleric as the most suitable person to break the shocking news to the devout but now institutionalised monarch that he was no longer a prisoner and would be required once again to act out the role of a king. Bishop Wainfleet of Winchester was chosen to bear these tidings, and he, accompanied by London's lord mayor, gently brought Henry out from his gloomy lodgings blinking into the daylight, 'a man amazed, utterly dulled with troubles and adversities'. Neglected during his long incarceration, the king was unwashed, scruffy, smelly and reluctant to resume his royal functions. Or, as the Cambridge chronicler John Warkworth put it, 'Not so worshipfully arrayed, and not so cleanly kept as should seem [befit] such a prince.'

Gate made sure that Henry was given a bath and reclothed in garments suiting his renewed regal status, before moving him into the same freshly decorated apartments in the Tower's palace that Queen Elizabeth had just left. On 5 October, Warwick's brother, Archbishop Neville, arrived at the Tower to greet Henry, and the following day the Kingmaker himself finally entered the city. Warwick went straight to the Tower where, with much bowing and scraping to Henry, as Warkworth tells us, 'he did to him great reverence, and brought him to the palace of Westminster, and so he [Henry] was restored to the crown again'. Another chronicler reported that the king, far from rejoicing in the sudden transformation in his status, was 'as mute as a calf'.

On 13 October Henry was re-crowned in St Paul's Cathedral, with Warwick carrying the king's train, and Lord Oxford bearing his sword before him. Henry was then housed in the suitably clerical surroundings of the Bishop of London's palace, where he did precisely nothing while Warwick ruled his realm.

The Kingmaker was surrounded by enemies – past, present and potential. In addition to the resentful Lancastrians, there were his former Yorkist friends, primarily the exiled Edward. Above all, though, there was Clarence. The treacherous duke had originally allied with Warwick out of ambition, but now, with Henry restored and his son Prince Edward as heir, Clarence's prospects looked poorer than ever. Even before returning from France with Warwick, messages had reached Clarence from his brother, promising forgiveness if he deserted Warwick and reverted to his family allegiance. To get the awkward duke out of the way, Warwick sent Clarence to Dublin as Lieutenant of Ireland. Here, however, in his father's old stamping ground, Yorkist pressure on him increased. His aged mother and his three sisters combined to turn the screw and Clarence succumbed. He agreed to support Edward when the ousted king returned.

Almost as soon as he learned that his wife had given birth to his first son – another Edward – at Westminster, Edward IV made his move. With thirty-six ships, a thousand Yorkists and a small mercenary army provided by his brother-in-law Duke Charles of Burgundy, he left the Dutch port of Flushing. His fleet scattered by storms, Edward landed alone at Ravenspur in Yorkshire – auspiciously the same spot where Henry IV had put ashore seventy-two years before to wrest the throne from Richard II.

Edward made his way south, gathering troops. In the Midlands he linked up with Clarence who had collected 'a considerable army' and announced his defection from Warwick. The Kingmaker was in the forti- fied city of Coventry – a traditional Lancastrian stronghold where he and Oxford had mustered a sizeable army. The earl had left his brother, Archbishop Neville, in charge in London. Fearing that events were again tipping Edward's way, the cleric tried a desperate measure to boost support. He paraded King Henry around the city on horseback. But the gesture backfired. One glance at the wretched king, dressed in an old blue gown, and staring absently around him, served to diminish rather than rally support. Sensing which way the wind was blowing, Archbishop Neville himself put out secret feelers to Edward, offering to surrender the city. But the key to London, as ever, was the Tower. And during the night of 10 April, in a prearranged coup, Yorkist agents seized the fortress. The capital now lay wide open and the next day Edward, accompanied by his brothers Clarence and Richard, entered it at the head of his 7,000-strong army. There was no resistance.

Edward made straight for St Paul's Cathedral where the Archbishop of Canterbury solemnly declared King Henry deposed again – and gave thanks to God for King Edward's return. Before being reunited with his wife, daughters and newborn son at Westminster Abbey, Edward's next port of call was the Bishop of London's palace. Here George Neville fearfully awaited him with his royal charge. King Henry was characteristic- ally mild-mannered in his greeting. 'My cousin of York, you are very welcome,' he declared, adding trustingly, 'I know that my life will not be in danger in your hands.' Edward wasted no time in packing Henry back to his old familiar quarters in the Tower. Henry's feeling on being returned to those secure surroundings – replacing various Yorkist lords who had been held there by Warwick – was probably one of relief.

Henry was soon joined at the Tower – though not in the same rooms – by Queen Elizabeth. For the second time in a few months, the two monarchs changed places. Now it was the queen's turn to move back into the sumptuous apartments of the royal palace, along with her two daughters, baby son, and Edward's aged mother Cecily, the Dowager Duchess of York. The king had sent his family within the Tower's secure walls for their own safety should things go amiss on the battlefield, while he dragged Henry along with his army to be the helpless witness of yet another battle. For the restored king had pressing business: a final settling of accounts with the Earl of Warwick

The decisive battle between the two old comrades-in-arms took place at Barnet, north of London, on Easter Sunday, 14 April 1471. The engagement was fought in thick fog, which created a climate of fear and confusion. When Lord Oxford's livery of the star and rays was mistaken for the sun-in-splendour symbol of King Edward, cries of 'Treason!' swept through the Lancastrian ranks, and the morale of Warwick's army collapsed. The earl and his brother Montagu were killed fleeing the battle, the Duke of Exeter sustained severe wounds, and only Oxford succeeded in getting away. Once again, victory had gone to Edward IV, but he was not yet secure: on the day that Barnet was fought, Queen Margaret and Prince Edward landed at Weymouth.

Buffeted by storms, Margaret had been at sea for an incredible twenty days before her fleet finally limped into port. King Edward now faced the same nightmare that had defeated King Harold in 1066. Having dealt with one enemy at the cost of many casualties, he had to gird himself to face a full-scale cross-Channel invasion of his realm. Edward had barely time to draw breath after Barnet – sending King Henry back to the Tower, dismissing his victorious army, and displaying the naked bodies of his slain enemies, Warwick and Montagu, in their coffins – before he was forced to raise new troops to meet Margaret's threat.

Edward hastily scraped together a small army at Windsor Castle before moving west to confront Margaret. He had to intercept the queen before she crossed the River Severn and reached the Lancastrian heartlands of Wales. The rival armies converged at Tewkesbury, on the Severn. The battle that settled the fate of the House of Lancaster was short but bloody. It ended with a total Yorkist victory, murderous dissent among the Lancastrian commanders – old Lord Wenlock had his brains dashed out by the Duke of Somerset's mace – and a massacre of the surviving Lancastrian leadership, many being dragged from sanctuary in Tewkesbury Abbey to their deaths.

According to rival chroniclers Prince Edward was killed either fleeing from the battlefield, crying vainly to his false brother-in-law Clarence for help, or soon afterwards when he was caught and brought before the king. Edward IV reportedly asked him what he was doing in England, and when the spirited young man replied that he had come to reclaim his inheritance from those who had usurped his father's throne, the king flew into a Plantagenet rage and struck the youth in the face with his steel gauntlet. The blow was the signal for the king's brothers, Richard and Clarence, along with Lord Hastings, to gather round the prince and hack him to death. A similar fate awaited Edmund, Duke of Somerset – the third Beaufort holding that title to die violently in the Lancastrian cause. He was beheaded in Tewkesbury marketplace in front of the vengeful king, along with his brother Sir John Beaufort; the Earl of Devon, and a dozen other Lancastrian knights. This time, Edward was utterly determined to wipe out the rival dynasty once and for all.

Queen Margaret was picked up a few days after the battle and brought before the king. Distraught at the death of her only son, she raged at Edward, before collapsing into passive resignation. All trace of the tigress who had been the terror of the Yorkists for more than fifteen blood-drenched years had gone. Mute with despair, she was placed in a carriage which lurched its way towards London – and to the Tower where her husband was held. But she would never see him again. On 21 May, the same night that Margaret arrived in the fortress, poor, helpless Henry VI, most pathetic of English kings, ended his unhappy earthly existence.

While the fate of the kingdom was decided at Tewkesbury, the Tower had been the centre of military action in its own right. As part of the Lancastrian plan, the Earl of Warwick's nephew, Thomas Neville, a gifted sailor who commanded Warwick's Calais fleet, invaded England. Neville, an illegitimate son of the late Lord Fauconberg, a Yorkist hero of Northampton and Towton, was known as 'the Bastard of Fauconberg'. As a diversion designed to keep Edward in London, the Bastard used the ships and men of the Calais garrison to attack Kent. The diversion was initially successful. With Edward away chasing Margaret to Tewkesbury, what had been anticipated as an in-depth raid turned into a full-scale invasion.

Fauconberg landed unopposed at Sandwich in early May, picking up support from Kentish men always eager to plunder London's riches. The Mayor of Canterbury, Nicholas Faunt, for example, joined him with 200 men. On 4 May, the day Tewkesbury was fought, the Bastard was at Sittingbourne, and on the 12th he appeared at Southwark, styling himself 'Captain and leader of our liege lord Henry's people in Kent' and demanding that King Henry be freed from the Tower and handed over to him. However, emboldened by the news that the Lancastrian cause had been smashed at Tewkesbury, London's lord mayor, John Stokton, refused to admit him.

Reinforced by his fleet, which had sailed round from Sandwich and up the Thames, Fauconberg ferried his men across the river to the north bank and set fire to the alehouses at St Katherine's in the Tower's shadow. When this failed to intimidate the garrison, which was commanded by Lord Anthony Rivers, the queen's brother, Fauconberg decided that harsher persuasion was needed. He opened up with his guns from Southwark, directing a cannonade across the river at the Tower's walls. The terrified inhabitants of the fortress enduring the bombardment included Queen Elizabeth and her children, as well as King Henry. Frightening though the crash and roar of Fauconberg's guns were, he was unable to assault the Tower directly. Even the river banks were largely impervious to the cannon fire as Lord Dudley, the constable of the Tower, had filled huge wine casks with sand and gravel and placed them as bulwarks at vulnerable points to absorb the shot.

Fauconberg, aware that King Edward was fast approaching with his victorious army, knew that time was not on his side. He decided to launch an all-out assault to break into the city. Under the cover of the guns, in a two-pronged attack on 14 May his men rushed London Bridge from the south bank while crossing to the north bank in their boats and attempting to break through Aldgate from the east. The Londoners just managed to drop the gate's portcullis in time, trapping some of the attackers inside the gateway. These unfortunates were swiftly slaughtered. But the fighting raged on until Lord Rivers made a decisive intervention from the Tower at the head of the garrison. Leaving the fortress by an unguarded postern gate, he made a sortie and drove Fauconberg's force as far as Stratford, five miles to the east. As they fled, Fauconberg's men took with them fifty oxen destined to feed the queen's household that they had rustled from their pasture outside the Tower.

On 18 May Fauconberg abandoned his army camped on Blackheath – that traditional gathering ground for Kentish rebels – and, accompanied by the core of his sailors from Calais, rode hard for the coast. At Sandwich, the Calais men reboarded their ships and departed – without their leader. Fauconberg had decided to submit to King Edward. The Bastard still had a powerful bargaining chip – the fifty ships of the Calais fleet that he controlled.

Negotiations began, and on 26 May at Sandwich, Fauconberg handed over his ships to the king's brother Richard, Duke of Gloucester, in exchange for his life. He later accompanied Richard north after Gloucester became the royal lieutenant in that restive region. In September, both Fauconberg and his brother William Neville were accused of treason and executed. The king, with grim gallows humour, had the Bastard's head spiked on London Bridge looking south towards the scene of his rebellion.

Fauconberg's rebellion was the last straw that sealed the fate of Henry in the Tower. Edward had probably decided to kill his helpless rival after the death of the fallen monarch's only son at Tewkesbury anyway, but any last qualms of pity were snuffed out by the chaos that Fauconberg had unleashed in London. Given that the purpose of his attack had been to free Henry from the Tower, it followed that so long as Henry lived he would be the focus for future rebellions. But who could be trusted to carry out such a sacrilegious deed as the murder of an anointed king? The answer stood at Edward's right hand.

Richard, Duke of Gloucester, had been the hero-worshipping loyal sibling ever since his small frame had been strong enough to heft a broadsword. In stark contrast to his other brother, Clarence, Richard had stood by Edward through thick and thin: when he was expelled from his kingdom, in exile, and during his perilous return. Richard had commanded – with competence and courage – wings of his brother's armies at Barnet and Tewkesbury. He was the king's man. Edward's choice was shrewd. Richard was the one person he could trust to carry out his orders without question. He had spotted a streak of ruthlessness in his young brother which echoed – perhaps even surpassed – his own casual cruelty. Blood really was thicker than water.

Summoning Richard, Edward gave him his secret command. He would ride ahead of the main army to London with an advance guard of 1,500 men, secure the Tower, and kill Henry. The murder was to be performed quickly and quietly at dead of night. Richard obeyed. He arrived in a city barely recovered from the pitched battle fought with Fauconberg's men, and roughly took control of the Tower from his sister-in-law Queen Elizabeth and her brother, Lord Rivers. It was Richard's first run-in with the Woodville family which would one day end in murder within these same Tower walls.

On the morning of 21 May, King Edward finally arrived back in his capital after his triumph at Tewkesbury. Like a Roman emperor dragging his captives behind his chariot, he had Queen Margaret, his lifelong enemy and the killer of his father and brother, jolting along in an open cart exposed to the jeers and missiles of the crowds. Her destination was the Tower, but room had to be made for her by getting rid of the current royal prisoner: the husband she had not seen for almost a decade. It was a tragic irony that the royal couple, now within the same fortress, had never been so close since Margaret had sailed from Bamburgh Castle in July 1463, but were now to be parted for ever.

Tuesday 21 May was the feast of the Ascension, and the ever-pious Henry was marking the event with a lone all-night vigil in his private oratory – a tiny chapel set into a niche in the eastern wall in the octagonal Wakefield Tower. As he knelt in prayer, the cold flagstones were hard on his bony, fifty-year-old knees. But he had always accepted pain and discomfort as the lot of a truly Christian king (he wore a hair shirt, alive with lice, next to his flesh). Absorbed in prayer, did he hear the creak of the door as his killer, or killers, entered the chamber? Did the candle flicker and gutter in the sudden draft? Did he look around in terror as the murderer stole up to him, or was he struck down from behind with his eyes still closed, fervently worshipping the God he was about to meet?

The chroniclers are broadly agreed on what happened to Henry. According to John Warkworth, a Lancastrian sympathiser, writing soon after the event, 'And in the same night that King Edward came to London, King Henry, being in ward in prison in the Tower of London, was put to death between eleven and twelve of the clock, being then at the Tower the Duke of Gloucester.' The Burgundian diplomat Philippe de Commines, close to the Yorkists, also accuses Richard of the dreadful deed, charging that Gloucester 'killed poor King Henry with his own hand, or else caused him to be killed in his presence'. John Morton, Bishop of Ely, a loyal servant to both Henry VI and Edward IV in their turn, and later a bitter enemy to Richard, who would also cause him to suffer in the Tower, wrote, 'He [Richard] slew with his own hand King Henry VI as men constantly say.' Polydore Vergil, a court historian under Henry VIII, says it was 'generally believed that Gloucester killed him with a sword'. The London chronicler Robert Fabyan suggests that the murder weapon was a dagger, and a knife reputed to have struck the fatal blow became a revered relic of the martyrdom.

But whichever hand or hands wielded the weapon and whatever weapon was used – and from early twentieth-century forensic examination it seems that Henry's skull was smashed in addition to, or rather instead of, him being stabbed – we know that Gloucester was in charge of the Tower that night. We also know from Richard's later career that he was more than capable of such lethal violence. It is clear, however, that the order for Henry's killing came from the very top. As a loyal sibling, Gloucester would never have carried out such a fateful crime as regicide without King Edward's direct sanction. It seems certain that having disposed of young Prince Edward, the king took the decision in the vivid phrase of a Milanese diplomat to 'crush the seed' of Lancaster once and for all.

Naturally, the Yorkist regime tried to cover up the crime by putting out an official story that the cause of Henry's convenient demise had been 'ire, indignation ... pure displeasure and melancholy' upon being brought the news that his Lancastrian cause was 'utterly despaired of' after Tewkesbury, the death of his son, and the capture of his wife. The dead king's own body silently gave the lie to this fiction when it was displayed the next day at St Paul's. The King's coffin was open and, says Warkworth, blood welled from the wound at the back of his head and dripped on to the pavement when the Duke of Gloucester came to view it – which the superstitious saw as a sure sign of Richard's guilt. When the body was moved to Blackfriars by the Thames for the funeral service before being rowed upriver in a barge to the Benedictine Chertsey Abbey for burial, 'it bled fresh and new' again.

The death of the saintly king caused consternation among his subjects, who had nearly all been raised in the half-century when he had been nominally on the throne. His posthumous bleeding was seen as a miracle, and, according to the *Great Chronicle*, 'the common fame went that the Duke of Gloucester was not all guiltless' of Henry's death. The *Croyland Chronicle* hinted strongly at the same conclusion:

> I shall pass over the discovery of the lifeless body of King Henry in the Tower of London. May God have mercy upon him, and grant sufficient time for repentence to him, whoever he may be, who dared to lay sacrilegious hands on the Lord's Anointed! Let the doer merit the title of tyrant, and the victim be called a glorious martyr.

The king's tomb at Chertsey became a centre of pilgrimage equalling in popularity that of the earlier murdered martyr, Thomas Becket. In 1484, hearing of the miracles reportedly wrought there, after he had become king by dint of more murders, Richard III had his victim's body transferred from Chertsey to the more regal setting of St George's Chapel at Windsor Castle. In November 1910 it was exhumed and examined. The bones of the skull were found to be 'much broken', with brown blood-matted hair still adhering to the fragments – leaving no room for doubt that Henry had met a violent death.

Margaret of Anjou, immured in the Tower, only learned of her husband's death some days later. It was said that her piteous wailing could be heard by people in the streets beyond the moat. The queen was so shell-shocked by the succession of disasters that had befallen her – above all the loss of her only son – that the death of her long-lost husband seemed just another blow in an endless parade of fortune's buffets. She did, however, in a pathetic display of her old fierce spirit, make a strong if unavailing effort to gain custody of her husband's body. Unsuccessful, she lapsed back into a state of deep depression from which nothing could rouse her.

Observing her condition, and realising that she no longer posed a threat, after a few weeks' custody, King Edward decided to release her from the Tower. A second royal death in the fortress would be awkward to explain. Margaret was moved to Windsor Castle, and then, at the end of the year, to Wallingford where she was placed in the care of her old friend the Duchess of Suffolk. She remained in the duchess's household, isolated from the world that had used her so cruelly, until Edward took advantage of a peace treaty with France to ship her back to her native land in 1475.

Here, haunted by her memories, Margaret lived out a twilight existence 'far from the bloody fields of Tewkesbury' as an impoverished pensioner of King Louis XV until her death in August 1482.

The Queen's Lancastrian followers were less lucky. Nicholas Faunt, the mayor of Canterbury who had unwisely joined Fauconberg's insurrection, was brought to the Tower and executed. And Edward's brother-in-law, Henry Holland, Duke of Exeter, the former constable of the Tower, was brought from the sanctuary at Westminster Abbey where he had been recovering from the near-mortal wounds he had sustained at Barnet. Exeter was placed in strict custody in the Tower while his wife, the king's sister Anne, obtained an annulment of their marriage to wed her lover.

Edward's 1475 expedition to France when he disposed of Margaret, also provided a chance to get rid of this other inconvenient survivor from the Lancastrian past. The king brought Exeter over with him to France, but the duke did not complete the return journey. His boat set out from Calais, but on arrival at Dover the duke was missing. 'How he drowned,' remarks Robert Fabyan tactfully, 'the certainty is not known.' Another source is less discreet. Giovanni Pannicharola, Milanese ambassador in Burgundy, was told by Burgundy's Duke Charles the Bold, Edward's brother-in-law, that the king had given direct orders for the duke to be hurled overboard. One more of Edward's old scores was settled.

Another mysterious ducal drowning – that of the Duke of Clarence – was the strangest killing in all the Tower's eventful history, and the fact that it was an official state-sanctioned execution makes the story stranger still. Although Clarence had ostensibly been forgiven for his multiple plots against his brother Edward, his disloyalty was far from forgotten, and the king never fully trusted his wayward sibling again. With the Lancastrian cause extinguished, and Edward's youngest brother, Richard, bound to the king with ties cemented in blood, Clarence became the focus for all those with a grievance against Edward.

Clarence himself, instead of lying low, remained his vexatious, venomous self. His major grievance was the honours granted his loyal younger brother Richard. In particular he resented Richard winning the hand of Anne, younger daughter of Warwick the Kingmaker, the wealthy widow of Prince Edward. After Tewkesbury, Anne had been brought to the Tower with Queen Margaret and immured with her mother-in-law before being released to marry Richard. Clarence – despite or because of the fact that he had married Anne's elder sister Isabel – hated sharing Anne's Neville inheritance with his younger brother and took violent exception to the match. He went as far as abducting Anne and disguising her as a kitchen maid before Richard retrieved and married her.

Clarence's wilfulness was now shading into instability that threatened national security. This time there would be no second chances. In April 1477 Clarence sent a posse to abduct a harmless old woman, Ankarette Twynhoe, on charges of poisoning his wife, Isabel Neville (who had actually died in childbirth). Along with one John Thursby, who was accused of poisoning the duke's son, Ankarette was condemned and hanged. Clarence next turned his paranoia on his brother Edward. The king, he told anyone who would listen, was a warlock ruling by witchcraft. He had used sorcery to cause fog to fall on the battlefield of Barnet, and conjured up the storms that had delayed Margaret of Anjou's invasion. Now, claimed a clearly delusional Clarence, his brother was employing the black arts to kill him slowly, 'consuming [me] in likewise as a candle is consumed by burning'.

King Edward moved to warn Clarence off. On the evidence of John Stacey – an astronomer and fellow of Merton College, Oxford, who had been accused of sorcery and tortured – a member of Clarence's affinity, Thomas Burdet, was implicated in 'imagining' (i.e. attempting to bring about by magic) the deaths of King Edward and his young son Edward, Prince of Wales. Stacey and Burdet were hanged, drawn and quartered at Tyburn.

Foolishly, Clarence ignored this clear shot across his bows. He burst into a meeting of the Privy Council at Westminster with a Lancastrian cleric, John Goddard, and made a voluble protest at the execution of his friend. Edward's patience had run out. Clarence was not only a loose, but an out-of-control cannon, firing in every direction and attracting every malcontent in the land. In July, after being berated by his brother in person, he was taken to the Tower.

Imprisoned in the Bowyer Tower in the fortress's northern ward, Clarence waited for six months before learning his fate. In January 1478, Edward put his signature to a bill of attainder accusing Clarence of the most heinous crimes. He was charged not only with plotting to usurp the throne, but of planning to destroy his brother and the king's children. As the bill described it, 'A much higher, much more malicious, more unnatural and loathely treason than at any time heretofore hath been compassed, comported or conspired'.

Edward threw the book at his treacherous brother, openly charging him with spreading stories that Edward had been born a bastard, and that he, Clarence, was the Duke of York's legitimate son and heir. As a final piece of evidence, Edward had laid his hands on the agreement – carefully preserved by Clarence – made with Margaret of Anjou in 1469 in which Clarence was recognised as heir to Henry VI's son Edward, should he die without issue. The bill was a damning – and deadly – indictment.

Edward summoned Parliament specifically to condemn his brother. He carefully packed both the Commons and the Lords to make sure that the bill passed. A new royal favourite, Henry Stafford, Duke of Buckingham, made the keynote speech in the Lords demanding Clarence's death. The news of his condemnation was brought to Clarence in the Tower. But as a special brotherly favour, he was told, the king was leaving the choice of the method of execution up to him. Either because of his mental instability, or as a last gesture of bravado and contempt, Clarence plumped for the extraordinary exit of being dunked in a butt or pipe of his favourite Malmsey wine. (A pipe would normally contain over 470 litres of the sweet liquor, more than enough to drown even a tall man like Clarence.) The messy and long-drawn-out self-sentence was carried out in the Bowyer Tower on 18 February 1478.

Because of the outlandish nature of Clarence's death, many have assumed that it was a dramatic invention of Shakespeare in *Richard III*. But the Bard was reflecting contemporary sources. The chroniclers Mancini and Commines both unequivocally report the liquid facts, and perhaps most significantly of all, the duke's daughter, Margaret, Duchess of Salisbury – later herself to die violently and bizarrely in the Tower because of her Yorkist blood – wore on a bracelet a tiny silver wine barrel in memory of her father's end. Clarence was buried in Tewkesbury Abbey – the scene of his and his brother's final battle – beside his wife Isabel Neville. Modern examination of the bones also lends support to a death by drowning, since Clarence's skull bears no trace of decapitation – the usual method of execution for high-born traitors.

CHAPTER SEVEN

THE PRINCES, THE PROTECTOR
AND THE PRETENDERS

The House of York had destroyed its deadly rival the House of Lancaster. But in making sure that the beaten enemy was truly dead, it managed to destroy itself. The death of Clarence opened rifts in the ruling family that ultimately brought about its downfall. The old dowager Cicely, Duchess of York, 'proud Cis', had pleaded in vain for the life of her favourite son. She never forgave Edward for the fratricide. And young Richard, Duke of Gloucester, too, it was rumoured, despite his rivalry with Clarence and forgetting for once his slavish loyalty to Edward, had publicly sworn to avenge his brother's death. Richard's rage was focused in particular on the queen and her Woodville brood, whom he darkly suspected of poisoning Edward's mind against Clarence with sorcery. These bitter family rifts would culminate after Edward's death with deadly effect, leading to more dark deeds in the Tower. As the philosopher and lawyer Sir Francis Bacon observed, the Yorks were 'a race often dipped in their own blood'.

In the second half of his truncated reign, Edward IV let himself go. His natural greed and lasciviousness ran riot. Food and fornication continued to be his favourite vices. He fathered ten legitimate children with Elizabeth – one, Richard, Duke of York, born in 1473, a spare to go with his heir Edward, Prince of Wales – and at least half a dozen bastards with a succession of mistresses, mostly casual one-night stands. No woman, it was said, was safe when the king was around, and he didn't much mind whether they were married or maids. Edward's self-indulgence shortened his life. The once magnificent master of the battlefield had, aged just forty, become a corpulent hulk. Even so, few can have expected the sudden end. After boating on the Thames brought on an apparent chill (according to Mancini) or apoplexy (Commines) in March 1483 Edward took to his bed in Westminster. He never rose from it, and after dictating his will, died on 9 April. Edward's premature death was a disaster for England. The king who had vanquished his enemies, restoring stability and solvency, was gone – leaving his kingdom to a twelve-year-old child. A minor on the throne surrounded by ambitious and ruthless men had often proved a recipe for catastrophe in the past, and was to do so once again now.

In his deathbed will, Edward named his surviving brother, Richard, Duke of Gloucester, as protector while his son and heir, the new King Edward V, was a minor. Richard had always shown Edward IV exemplary loyalty, and proved himself an able administrator. As the king's lieutenant in the north, he had been virtual monarch of the region – a competent and courageous soldier. Most of all, he was family. What reason should there be not to trust him to hold the kingdom in stewardship for his own flesh and blood?

Yet Richard had already demonstrated ruthlessness, rapacity and downright sadistic cruelty. Apart from the killing of King Henry and his son, he had imprisoned the Earl of Warwick's widow, Anne (his own mother-in-law), in his castle of Middleham in an effort to get his hands on the extensive Neville estates. The Countess of Warwick was not the only Lancastrian lady to have suffered at his hands. He had also abducted, harried and bullied the elderly dowager Lady Oxford, mother of Lord Oxford, into signing over her estates to him on her deathbed. In the Middle Ages chivalry was usually extended to women of rank, even when they were the wives and widows of enemies. In trusting Richard to treat his widow and children well after he had gone, Edward doomed the House of York.

So who was the thirty-year-old Richard, Duke of Gloucester? In peering through the mists of time at the true face of this remarkable man, we have to clear away first of all the distorting accretions of dust sprinkled over his portrait by Shakespeare, and by so-called 'Tudor propagandists' like Sir Thomas More, who caricatured 'crook-back Dick' as a misshapen villain, born with teeth and shoulder-length hair, who had but to breathe on a flower for it to wilt. Even more misleading are the modern efforts of Ricardian apologists to paint their hero as 'Good King Richard', a near saintly figure, vilely slandered and innocent of the foul crimes of which he is accused. The prime crime, of course, being the murder of his two

Motte-and-Bailey castles were constructed to hold down the Normans' newly-conquered kingdom. This panel from the Bayeux tapestry shows a Norman overseer supervising Saxon slave labourers at Hastings — the scene of their 1066 triumph. The Tower was built by similar men and methods.

Decline and fall: Prince Gruffydd, elder son of Llywelyn Fawr (the Great) Prince of Wales, after three years held hostage in the White Tower, attempted to escape on St David's day — March 1, 1244. His home-made rope of sheets broke, plunging the prince to his death.

Chronicler Matthew Paris drew England's first ever elephant on its arrival at Henry III's Tower Menagerie. Sadly, the great beast soon died.

Burning bright: 'The Tyger' by William Blake from *Songs of Innocence and Experience*. Blake crossed the Thames from his Lambeth home to draw the 'fierce and savage' creature from life at the Tower Menagerie.

James I patronised the Menagerie for all the wrong reasons. Cruel and cowardly, he often visited the Tower to watch the animals there tear each other to pieces.

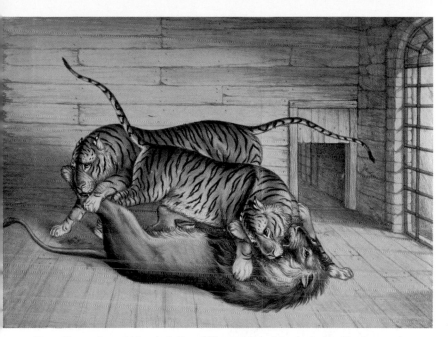

King of beasts: Samuel Maunder's *Extraordinary and Fatal Combat* depicts what happened when a lion and two tigers were accidentally allowed into the same Tower enclosure on December 6, 1830. The animals fought for half an hour before being separated. The lion came off worse in the unequal contest, dying from its injuries.

Newly minted: striking coins at the Royal Mint. A print by Thomas Rowlandson, probably marking the Mint's departure from the Tower in 1811.

King Mob: in June 1381 the Peasants' Revolt saw rebellious rural labourers take control of London, forcing the young Richard II and his court to seek shelter in the Tower. As his Ministers were murdered, the young king bravely ventured out to negotiate with his subjects, but after their leader Wat Tyler was killed, the revolt collapsed.

A medieval French manuscript shows Richard II in the Tower kneeling in homage to his cousin Henry Bolingbroke who has just deposed him and forced his abdication. Richard died mysteriously the following year.

Wounded and taken prisoner at Agincourt in 1415, Charles, Duke of Orleans, was kept in the Tower where he took up poetry. He remained in captivity for a quarter of a century before he was ransomed and returned to France. This illustration to a volume of his verses shows him writing in the White Tower.

Fear and trembling:
a romanticised 19th century
depiction of the Princes in the
Tower awaiting their killers
by French artist, Paul Delaroche.

Anne Boleyn awaits her fate, 1536.
'One hour she is determined to die,
and the next much contrary to that'
reported the Tower's Lieutenant,
Sir William Kingston.

Singular Execution of the Countess of Salisbury in 1541.

Botched job: Margaret, Countess of Salisbury, beheaded on May 27, 1541 at Henry VIII's command on account of her Yorkist blood, is chased by her executioner brandishing an axe.

Delivering pain: the Rack and other instruments of torture used at the Tower.

Cutbert Simson upon the Rack.

The followers of Sir Thomas Wyatt attack the Byward Tower in a bid to seize the fortress in 1554. This Kentish rebellion aimed at preventing the unpopular marriage of Mary I to Philip II of Spain. Wyatt's father and grandfather were both, like him, imprisoned in the Tower. Unlike him, they survived.

Mr W.H.? : Henry Wriothesley, Earl of Southampton – friend, patron and possibly the dedicatee of Shakespeare's sonnets – pictured in the Tower with his cat, Trixie. Imprisoned for his leading role in the Earl of Essex's 1601 rebellion against Elizabeth I, Southampton, unlike Essex, was spared and released on the Queen's death in 1603.

'What shall I do? Where is it?': the bewildered words of the blindfolded Lady Jane Grey as she gropes for her execution block, 1554, romantically, if inaccurately, depicted by Paul Delaroche. (The internal nocturnal scene in fact took place in the Tower's courtyard in broad daylight.)

nephews in the Tower, an atrocity without parallel even in the bloody annals of the English monarchy, combining infanticide, regicide and the slaughter of Richard's blood relatives in one gruesome package. The evidence – both contemporary and more recent – points overwhelmingly to Richard's guilt.

Born on 2 October 1452 at his father's Fotheringhay Castle in Northamptonshire, Richard was a frail child; though not a hunchback, he may have had one shoulder higher than the other, and a withered arm. He overcame any such physical disadvantages to become proficient in the martial qualities expected in a male of his exalted rank. He resembled his father in his slight build and sharp, narrow features rather than his giant elder brothers Edward and Clarence. Brought up largely at Middleham Castle in Yorkshire, owned by the Earl of Warwick, Richard's childhood was overshadowed by the murderous Wars of the Roses. He came into his own after his prominent role in the battles of Barnet and Tewkesbury, and his less publicised part in the killings of Prince Edward and King Henry.

With such a disturbed background, it is not surprising that Richard's character was twisted by his experience of murder, battle, betrayal, treason, exile, and the violent deaths of his nearest and dearest. By the time he reached maturity he had seen his father, two of his brothers, and his childhood guardian, Warwick, killed. The bloody experience of his first eighteen years had hardened and coarsened him, producing a man mistrustful of others and suspicious to the point of paranoia. If childhood circumstances make the man, it is hardly surprising that Richard became a monster.

As soon as he learned of his brother's death, Richard hastened south from York with a retinue of 300 followers. Having set out along the road to usurpation and murder he did not deviate, and one step led inexorably to the next. At first he had allies: the Duke of Buckingham and his brother's closest friend Lord William Hastings. But it speaks volumes for Richard's terrifying character that one, Hastings, was eliminated by the 'protector' within weeks, while the other, Buckingham – Richard's closest confidant in the conspiracy to seize power – turned on his partner in crime to revolt against him.

Buckingham brought 300 men to join Richard at Northampton on his journey south. Their immediate objective was to intercept the young King

Edward V, whose accession had already been proclaimed in London. Edward himself had been at his father's castle at Ludlow in the care of his Woodville uncle, Anthony, Lord Rivers, when news of the king's death arrived. Inexplicably, they had lingered in Ludlow for a fortnight before setting out on the journey to London. The delay would prove fatal.

In the capital, the Woodvilles had taken charge, hastily fixing the new king's coronation for 4 May. The Tower was the vital piece on the chessboard of power. To keep it safely in their hands, just a month before the king's death, the Woodvilles had appointed one of their own, the queen's eldest son, Thomas Grey, Marquess of Dorset, to succeed another, her brother Anthony, Lord Rivers, as constable. The queen's family, justly fearing that the power, titles and wealth they had so greedily acquired would be stripped from them if Richard became protector, intended to circumvent Edward's will, keep Richard from power, and rule using young King Edward V as their puppet. But in Richard the Woodvilles were up against a player even more ruthless and power hungry than themselves.

Richard had an important ally on the Royal Council who distrusted the Woodvilles. William, Lord Hastings, was determined that the will of his dead friend the king should be carried out to the letter. Suspicious that the Woodvilles were keeping Richard in the dark until they had consolidated their power, it was Hastings who sent word to York to inform Richard of his brother's passing. Hastings also insisted that the escort accompanying the young king to London should be limited to 2,000 men, rather than the army which the Woodvilles had wanted. To lull the Woodvilles into a false sense of security while he gathered his forces, Richard wrote to the council, fulsomely proclaiming his loyalty to the new king and his heirs. Then he set off for the south.

After celebrating St George's Day in Ludlow on 23 April, Edward and his uncle Lord Rivers had belatedly left for London the next day with their 'sober company' of 2,000 escorts. When they reached Northampton, Richard had rendezvoused with the Duke of Buckingham north of the town. Sir Richard Grey, the queen's second son, arrived hotfoot from London and urged his uncle Rivers to bring his royal charge to the capital without further delay. They rode on, reaching Stony Stratford, fourteen miles south of Northampton, that night. Here they lodged young King Edward at the Rose and Crown inn, before returning to Northampton to mollify Richard who, with Buckingham, had settled into lodgings in the town.

Continuing his policy of lulling the Woodvilles into a false sense of security, Richard, accompanied by Buckingham, entertained Rivers and Grey to supper that night with every appearance of friendliness. When the two Woodvilles had retired to bed, however, the two dukes stayed up plotting the first of the two coups that would bring Richard to the throne. Having posted their 600 troops on the roads out of town and surrounded the inn where the Woodvilles were sleeping, Richard struck at dawn. He stormed in on the Woodvilles, accusing them of denying him the protectorate and making the king their prisoner. Locking up a stunned Rivers, and taking Grey along as a hostage, Richard and Buckingham then galloped to Stony Stratford and took possession of the boy king.

Since possession is nine tenths of the law, with Edward in his hands Richard had, at a stroke, effectively made himself master of the state. When the dramatic news reached London on the night of 1 May, the ever pragmatic Queen Elizabeth realised that she had lost the power game. She immediately fled to the familiar surroundings of the sanctuary at Westminster Abbey – where she had taken refuge during her husband's exile thirteen years before – along with her daughters and her younger son, the nine-year-old Richard, Duke of York. With the acute political antennae that saw her survive the bloodletting that consumed most of the male members of her extended family, Elizabeth sensed the deadly danger she was in. Assured that Lord Hastings had promised that she had nothing to fear, the queen burst out, 'Ah, woe worth him, for he is one of them that labour to destroy me and my blood.'

Hastings was key in persuading council members that Richard's intentions were honourable, but he was soon to be disabused. In a series of sly steps Richard set about consolidating his power and preparing the next stage of his creeping coup. His first move was to strip his nephew of the advisers and attendants he had grown up with, replacing them with his own trusties. Rivers, Grey and other loyalists were dispatched under guard to Richard's Yorkshire castles – there eventually to be quietly executed without trial. The boy king was understandably distressed at the enforced departure of his familiar friends and relations. He protested his trust in them, and their innocence of the charges of treason that Richard and Buckingham were throwing. All was to no avail: he was reminded in no uncertain terms that he was an ignorant child, and that real power now lay with Richard. Under the protector's silky tones and formal deference lay the barely concealed code of the gangster. In asking to have the honour of escorting Edward to his capital, his captors were making him an offer he could not refuse.

Richard's next move, before he reached London with the king, was to secure the Tower. He knew that if the fortress remained in Woodville hands, it would be a formidable barrier to his seizure of the Crown. He therefore wrote – over Edward's signature – to the aged Archbishop of Canterbury, Thomas Bourchier, demanding that he 'provide for the surety and safeguard of our Tower of London, and the treasure being in the same'. At the same time Richard upbraided another cleric, the Lord Chancellor, Thomas Rotherham, Archbishop of York, for his 'crime' of remaining loyal to the queen, visiting her in her sanctuary, and surrendering to her the Great Seal – the supreme symbol of royal authority. Both men would shortly feel Richard's wrath more keenly.

By the time that Richard and Buckingham entered London with the king, power lay within their grasp. The date was 4 May – the original day set by the Woodvilles for the coronation. This had now been put back to 24 June, but would never take place. As he rode into the capital, Richard had exchanged the black velvet of mourning for his brother, for robes of rich royal blue velvet. The change of clothes was more than symbolic. On 10 May the Great Council met at the Bishop of London's palace. On the agenda was a suitable residence for the new king. Silkily, Buckingham suggested the Tower of London, pointing out that it was where monarchs traditionally spent the night before their coronation. The council agreed, and by 19 May Edward V was in the Tower, and state documents were being issued in his name from the fortress. He would never leave it again.

Richard spent the following weeks quietly preparing the next stage of his coup: the deposition of Edward and securing of the Crown for himself. He moved into Crosby Place, one of London's largest houses, at Bishopsgate, which became the coup HQ. Here he held secret meetings with his clique, including Buckingham, Lord Howard and his son Sir Thomas Howard. The elder Howard was soon to be made Duke of Norfolk as a reward for his support, the founder of a durable family dynasty notable for the safeguarding of its own interests above all else. Also on hand at Crosby Place was a peculiarly nasty trio of 'new men' who had attached themselves to Richard as the surest way of climbing the greasy pole of power. These were the lawyer William Catesby; a political hit man from Yorkshire called Sir Richard Ratcliffe; and Francis, Lord Lovell, a childhood companion of the protector. When Richard became king a popular rhyme neatly encapsulated this unsavoury gang:

> *The Cat, the Rat, and Lovell our dog,*
> *Rule all England under the hog.*

('The hog' is a reference to Richard's personal emblem: the white boar.)

Meanwhile, blithely unaware of the plot thickening at Crosby Place, the council continued to meet at the Tower to plan the coronation. Lord William Hastings, the loyal Lord Chamberlain – newly appointed Master of the Mint at the Tower – was steering the arrangements. Richard used the lawyer Catesby to sound out Hastings – the one man who could conceivably stop his assumption of power – over his attitude to him seizing the Crown. Ever loyal to his dead friend and his son – he had even taken over Edward IV's mistress, Jane Shore, from his late master – Hastings indignantly rejected the idea of supplanting Edward's son and heir. Far too late, he saw where Richard was heading and desperately began to cast around for allies to stop him. But Richard moved first.

On 10 June, the protector wrote to the city council of his power base, York, demanding that they raise and send troops 'to aid and assist us against the queen, her blood adherents and affinity'. He sent his henchman Sir Richard Ratcliffe north with the letters. Ratcliffe also had secret orders to execute the queen's brother Lord Rivers, and her son Sir Richard Grey, along with the other loyalists taken prisoner at Northampton. Preparations for completing the coup now entered their final phase, with Richard summoning council members to a meeting at the Tower the following day, 13 June.

The council assembled early, but it was already light on the midsummer day as they gathered in the council chamber on the top floor of the White Tower to await the arrival of the protector at 9 a.m. Richard had made sure that his chief target, Hastings – sleepy after a strenuous night with his new mistress, Jane Shore – attended the meeting, detailing his minion Sir Thomas Howard to escort the doomed man to the Tower. When Richard entered the room, he was all amiable affability with banter and small talk. Remarking that strawberries were in season, he told John Morton, bishop of Ely, that he had noticed some juicy strawberries growing in the bishop's garden at his house, Ely Place in Holborn, and asked to be given a present of the fruit. Morton assured him that they would be his that very day.

Having metaphorically disarmed the council, Richard excused himself and left the room. A long one and a half hours crept by. The council members transacted some routine business as the morning dragged on. Then, suddenly, Richard was back. This time his mood was dramatically different. According to the later account by Sir Thomas More – who had it directly from an eye witness, Morton – the protector was 'frowning, fretting and gnawing on his lips'. After sitting in glowering silence he abruptly turned to Hastings, blurting out, 'What do men deserve for having plotted the destruction of me, being so near of blood unto the King, and Protector of his Royal person and realm?' Taken aback, Hastings stuttered, 'Certainly, if they have and done so heinously, they are worthy of a heinous punishment.' This was Richard's cue. Leaping to his feet and thumping the table he shouted, 'What? Dost thou serve me with "ifs" and "ands"? I tell thee, they have done it, and that I will make good upon thy body, traitor! I arrest thee!' 'What me, my lord?' gasped an astonished Hastings. 'Yea, thou traitor!' Richard repeated menacingly.

Wildly, Richard swung round, accusing other council members – including the magnate Sir Thomas Stanley and the two trembling clerics, Morton and Archbishop Rotherham, a noted Woodville supporter – of plotting with the queen and Jane Shore (King Edward's former mistress turned Hastings' bedmate) against him. According to More, the charges against the two women – who, as love rivals, were unlikely co-conspirators – featured that old standby of male accusations against women: witchcraft. Richard accused them of using sorcery to wither his arm and stripped his sleeve to demonstrate the deformity. Then, on the protector's prearranged signal, Buckingham and Howard admitted a troop of men-at-arms waiting in readiness outside. Crying, 'Treason!' the guards rushed to arrest Hastings, Stanley, Morton and Rotherham. The two noblemen put up a violent struggle and Stanley, diving under the table, received a bloody head wound before being subdued.

Richard told the helplessly pinioned Hastings that he should confess his sins to a priest at once: 'For by St Paul, I will not to dinner till I see thy head off.' Since dinner was the meal we now call lunch, and it was already nearly noon, Hastings must have known that he faced immediate death. There was no question of due process of law (as a peer Hastings had the right to be tried by Parliament): this was to be murder with no legal niceties. Under Buckingham's supervision, Hastings was dragged from the room, loudly protesting his innocence and pleading for mercy. A priest was summoned from the nearby church of St Peter ad Vincula, who hurriedly shrived Hastings since his killers allowed the doomed man no time for a final confession. Then, on Tower Green, the patch of grass still to be seen in front of the church today, Hastings was forced down with his neck across a rough timber builders' block which happened to be nearby being used for repairs. Without further ado, his head was struck off with a sword: the first and the hastiest of seven executions to take place on the same spot over the next and most bloodstained century of the Tower's history.

Showing a mastery of public relations worthy of a twenty-first-century spin doctor, Richard first sent his agents running through the teeming streets of the city echoing the cries of 'Treason!'. This had the desired effect of thoroughly panicking the population. Then, after enjoying the leisurely dinner he had promised himself after Hastings' head was safely lopped, Richard summoned London's lord mayor and a delegation of leading citizens to the Tower. He issued a proclamation – clearly drawn up before the fatal council meeting at which Hastings' treason had been 'discovered' – explaining that only his drastic action had saved the kingdom from a coup mounted by Hastings in league with the Woodvilles aimed at killing the protector. The proclamation calmed distracted Londoners. The less well-informed were happy that a strong hand guided the ship of state's tiller, while those in the know were stunned into fearful silence. The proclamation was, in fact, the exact reversal of the truth. True, there *had* been a coup – carried out by Richard and Buckingham. And it had completely succeeded.

As for the alleged co-conspirators arrested with Hastings, the two clerics and Stanley were imprisoned in the Tower for a few weeks. Then, scared into silence, they were released after the intercession of the universities of Cambridge (for Archbishop Rotherham) and Oxford (for Bishop Morton) respectively. Richard, pious in his outward religious observance, may well have feared the consequences of striking at the Church. Morton was sent to distant Wales in the custody of Buckingham to keep him out of the way. Here, in Buckingham's Brecon Castle, the cunning prelate began to work on his ambitious jailer to undermine his loyalty to Richard.

With her lover Hastings dead, Jane Shore had no such elevated protection. Charged with plotting with her actual enemy, the queen, she too saw the inside of a Tower cell before she was made to perform a public penance. Wearing only a see-through petticoat and carrying a lighted candle, she walked barefoot from St Paul's Cathedral through the streets of London. But the sight of her, scantily clad and demurely submissive, excited emotions rather different from those expected. Sympathy and outright lust were both expressed, and before long Jane acquired another powerful lover – Richard's own legal advisor, Thomas Lynom – who became her second husband and ushered her into grateful obscurity. She survived Richard's bloody reign and the next, and was still alive – skinny and aged – in Henry VIII's reign.

Richard now turned to his next goal: putting the crown on his own head. To do so, he had first to deny his nephews their rightful inheritance, and obtain physical possession of both the two princes. He already had Edward safely lodged in the Tower, but so long as his brother's heir had a spare – Richard, Duke of York, in Westminster Abbey's sanctuary with his mother the queen – Richard's position was shaky. Now that he had killed the only man who had stood in his way, Richard, his morbid suspicion shading into poisonous paranoia, would vent his fears on innocent children.

On Monday 16 June, with Hastings' blood still staining the grass outside the chamber, the council met again in the White Tower. Richard and Buckingham pressed for the young Duke of York to be removed from his sanctuary. They hid the demand behind a thin cloak of pretended concern for the young boy's welfare, claiming that his brother needed a playmate. With some arm twisting, the council, cowed after witnessing Hastings' fate, agreed to send the Archbishop of Canterbury, old Thomas Bourchier, to Westminster to persuade Queen Elizabeth to give up her second son. One of Richard's hard men, Howard, accompanied the archbishop lest the elderly cleric's persuasions proved ineffective.

Escorted by a menacing company of armed men, Bourchier and Howard confronted the Queen in the abbot's house at Westminster where she tearfully expressed fears for her son's safety outside the sanctuary. But the queen knew that resistance was futile. The presence of Richard's thugs told her that if she did not surrender her son, her own life and that of her daughters might also be in danger. If peaceful persuasion failed, the armed men would storm the sanctuary and take the boy by force. Weeping in despair, the queen eventually yielded. 'Farewell, my own sweet son,' she told the boy. 'God send you good keeping. Let me kiss you once yet ere you go, for God knows when we shall kiss together again.'

Bourchier and Howard took the little duke to the Tower by boat, entering under the dreaded dark shadows of Traitor's Gate beneath St Thomas's Tower. With both male heirs to the throne under his control, Richard now had it all. In terms of raw power, nothing stood between him and the crown but the frail lives of the two boys in his custody. And he was about to deal with that small problem. On the same day that the young Duke of York arrived at the Tower, another Duke Richard – the protector himself – took up residence there.

Symbolically, young King Edward was removed from the royal apartments and confined with his brother to the Garden (now the Bloody) Tower – the small, rectangular gatehouse on the western edge of the palace which, as its name suggests, had its own garden where the boys could play. The princes' uncle moved straight into the vacated royal apartments and began to prepare for another coronation: his own. Before then, however, he had to deny the two princes' legal right to succeed to the throne. And that meant besmirching his own living mother as an adulteress, and branding his dead brother a base-born bastard. Richard did not flinch from the task.

The following Sunday, 22 June, two days before Edward V's now cancelled coronation, a public sermon was preached by a prominent cleric, Dr Ralph Shaw, the brother of London's lord mayor Edmund Shaw, at St Paul's Cross outside the cathedral, on the text 'Bastard slips should not take root'. Such a central location – a fifteenth-century equivalent of a national news broadcast – meant that the sermon was officially inspired by Richard. Heavily underscoring the topical parallel to the biblical theme, Dr Shaw proclaimed that Edward IV's marriage to Elizabeth Woodville had been invalid because the late king had promised marriage to Lady Elizabeth Butler, daughter of the Earl of Shrewsbury. Therefore, he said, the two princes in the Tower – King Edward V and the Duke of York – were both illegitimate 'bastard slips' and barred from succeeding to the throne.

Warming to his theme, the preacher went further. Not only were the two boys illegitimate, but both their father Edward IV, and his brother Clarence (both conveniently dead) were bastards too – the products of an adulterous affair carried out by Richard's mother, 'Proud Cis', the dowager Duchess of York. Although the duchess herself was still alive, there is no record of her feelings about being smeared as a double adulteress by her only surviving son. Dr Shaw concluded his sermon by proclaiming that only the protector was the rightful king.

Right on cue, Richard himself, with Buckingham, proudly rode past the open-air congregation – who, according to Sir Thomas More, 'stood as if turned to stones for wonder of this shameful sermon'. Doubtless the London crowd were left to reflect that Edward and Clarence were abnormally tall for their time, while Richard resembled in his slight build and sharp face, his late father, Richard, Duke of York. Public opinion was being thoroughly prepared for someone other than Edward V to take the crown, and there were no prizes for guessing who that someone would be.

Two days later, Lord Mayor Edmund Shaw, following up his brother's sermon, convened a meeting of leading Londoners at the Guildhall to rubber-stamp Richard's coup. The meeting was packed with Buckingham's affinity. The duke asked the assembled citizens to demand that Richard accept the crown. But this request was met with stony silence, so in desperation Buckingham signalled his retainers, who promptly cast their caps into the air, crying, 'King Richard!' The coup's choreography was proceeding according to plan; the only thing missing was any enthusiasm from Londoners for their new, usurping ruler.

Richard's assumption of power was made formal the next day, 25 June, when a parliamentary delegation led by Buckingham waited on Richard and asked him to take the crown. Their demand was backed by a petition from Parliament castigating the late King Edward for his lax and licentious rule, 'so that no man was sure of his life, land nor livelihood, nor of his wife, daughter nor servant, every good maiden and woman standing in dread to be ravished and defouled'. It seems that Richard felt compelled to spit on his brother's memory, libelling him as the realm's leading rapist, to justify his seizure of power. The next day the protector was formally proclaimed and enthroned in Westminster Hall as King Richard III, while 'Edward Bastard, late called King Edward V' was dethroned.

From then on, things moved quickly. Richard rapidly fixed his coronation for 6 July, and spent the traditional pre-ceremony period in the Tower. Once in the fortress, Richard released the Woodville partisan Archbishop Rotherham of York from the cell where he had languished since Hastings' murder. But Richard's paranoia was as acute as ever. Fearing resistance to his usurpation, he had policed the city with the 6,000 northern soldiers his henchman Ratcliffe had brought from Yorkshire. And he placed Londoners under a 10 p.m. curfew over the three nights that the coronation celebrations lasted, forbidding them either to wear swords or to carry arms. On 4 July, Richard and his queen, Anne Neville – second daughter of Warwick the Kingmaker – were rowed downriver from Westminster to the Tower in a stately barge rather than risking riding through the sullen streets. It was repression not seen since the conquest, and the fact that it was enforced by northerners regarded by Londoners as foreign savages was an unfortunate harbinger of the coming reign.

As if to compensate for the hideous crime he was about to commit, Richard did not stint on the magnificence of his coronation ceremonies. No expense was spared for the two days of pageantry at the Tower that preceded the coronation. On the day itself, the new king wore a doublet and stomacher of blue cloth of gold, embroidered with a pattern of nets and pineapples, and an eight-foot-long gown of purple trimmed with ermine. The queen was similarly splendidly attired in sixteen yards of Venetian lace. The royal pair rode out of the Tower, the king on horseback and the queen in a litter, and, guarded by 4,000 rough northern soldiers, journeyed through largely silent streets to Westminster. Once in the crowded abbey, they divested themselves of their heavy robes in the sweltering summer heat and stood, both naked from the waist up, to be anointed with holy oil before the crowns were placed on their heads by Archbishop Bourchier. But even in his moment of triumph, Richard was not content. A witness observed Richard during the ceremony and was struck by his restless nervousness as he continually looked around and behind him, compulsively biting his lips and – a characteristic and highly significant obsessive gesture – constantly half-drawing his dagger from its sheath and sliding it back. As soon as the coronation was over, Richard left his hostile capital and began a royal progress around his new realm. Left in the Tower were the two princes. Neither was seen alive again.

The only reference to a public sighting of the princes after they were reunited in the Tower on 16 June comes in the *Great Chronicle* which mentioned that 'the children of King Edward' were 'seen shooting [arrows] and playing in the garden of the Tower sundry times'. According to the Italian chronicler Dominic Mancini, who left England immediately after Richard's coronation, by that date they had been deprived of their servants and 'withdrawn to the inner apartments of the Tower proper, and day by day began to be seen more rarely behind the bars and windows'. The reference to the 'inner apartments of the Tower proper' and 'bars' suggests that Richard may have moved the boys from the Garden Tower to the heart of the fortress – the White Tower, traditional prison for royal captives. The *Great Chronicle* states that the boys were now subject to stricter confinement, being 'holden more straight'; and the London chronicler Robert Fabyan confirms that they were under more 'sure keeping'.

Our only detailed guide as to what happened next is Richard's earliest biographer Sir Thomas More, writing in the reign of Henry VIII. More has been damned by Ricardians for writing a piece of mendacious 'Tudor propaganda' as the new dynasty clearly had an interest in blackening their predecessor's name and heaping all possible crimes on Richard's head. The inconvenient fact remains, however, that More was informed by surviving eye witnesses from Richard's reign, principally his old employer John Morton, a cardinal and Archbishop of Canterbury, who had been in the Council Chamber when Hastings was dragged to his death and had himself been confined in the Tower on Richard's orders. A hostile witness certainly, but a witness nonetheless.

Other contemporary chronicles – Mancini, Fabyan, the *Great Chronicle*, the *Croyland Chronicle* and Polydore Vergil – all bear out More's account. And – literally the killer fact – Sir Thomas's version of how the princes met their death was confirmed over a century after More's own execution on 6 July 1535 (ironically the anniversary of Richard's coronation) following his own confinement in the Tower, when in 1674 the skeletons of two boys of the princes' ages when they vanished were discovered – in the exact place and manner that More had described. Given all this, together with Richard's proven paranoid character, his carefully calculated coup, and his ruthless destruction of all those who stood in his way, one would have to be very naive indeed not to believe that he ordered the snuffing out of the princes' lives. Almost all serious modern historians who have studied the facts – principally Michael Hicks, A. J. Pollard, Alison Weir and Desmond Seward – have reached the same conclusion: that Richard *was* guilty of ordering the boys' deaths just as More wrote, and as Shakespeare – admittedly with suitable theatrical embroidery – dramatised.

The dethroned King Edward knew very well what fate lay in store at the hands of his implacable uncle. Told that he was no longer king, and that Richard had taken his throne, More tells us that Edward 'was sore abashed, began to sigh, and said, "Alas, I would my uncle would let me have my life yet, though I lose my Kingdom."' Though the young Duke of York was apparently a bright, healthy and spirited boy, his elder brother was in a pitiful state of physical prostration as well as mental agony. An examination of his presumed skull in the 1930s showed advanced tooth decay which had spread to both jawbones, had become the bone disease osteomyclitis, and must have caused the prince severe pain to add to his mental woes.

Chronic toothache was probably the reason that a royal physician, Dr John Argentine, a friend and informant of Dominic Mancini, was summoned to the Tower to treat Edward. Dr Argentine, the last person apart from their one remaining attendant, the aptly named 'Black Will' Slaughter, and their killers, to see the princes alive, told Mancini that he had found his patient listless and depressed. He added that Edward was going to confession (probably in the White Tower's St John's Chapel) and doing constant penance 'because he believed that death was facing him'. More adds the telling detail that the prince's depression was so deep that he had ceased to wash and take care of himself. He knew his death was fast approaching.

When Richard departed on his royal progress on 20 July he left London, and the Tower, secure in the hands of his loyal henchmen. The newly appointed Lord High Constable – Buckingham – was in overall military command of the capital, while the lieutenant of the Tower itself was Lord Howard. Howard's subordinate – the man charged with the custody of the princes – was the new constable, Sir Robert Brackenbury, a trusted northern retainer of Richard's, who took up his duties on 17 July. Within a month of Brackenbury's appointment, as the king moved west along the Thames Valley and into the Midlands, Richard sent one of his servants, John Green, to the Tower. Green found Brackenbury at his devotions in St John's Chapel. So urgent was the message that Green was bearing that he interrupted the constable's prayers. He told Brackenbury that Richard wanted the princes dead, and asked him to carry out the distasteful duty of killing them.

Brackenbury refused outright, telling Green that he would take no part 'in so mean and bestial a deed'. Richard was furious when Green brought back Brackenbury's negative reply. He received Green in intimate circumstances suiting the unsavoury mission – seated on his close stool at Warwick

Castle – and angrily demanded, in an echo of his ancestor Henry II calling for Thomas Becket's head, 'Ah, whom shall a man trust? Those that I have brought up myself fail me, and at my commandment will do nothing for me.' Richard decided that someone more ruthless than Brackenbury was needed. He turned to Sir James Tyrell, his Keeper of Horse.

Tyrell, a fervent Yorkist, had been knighted for his valour at the battle of Tewkesbury and had been Richard's faithful man ever since. He had already carried out at least two dirty jobs for his master. He had lured the Dowager Duchess of Warwick out of sanctuary and escorted her to Richard's castle at Middleham where she had spent the rest of her life in captivity while Richard stole her vast estates. More recently, he had arrested and guarded Archbishop Rotherham in the Tower on the day of Hastings' execution. Now he was asked to undertake a still more dubious mission in the fortress. It is a macabre coincidence, but nonetheless highly symbolic, that Tyrell shares his surname with the last man accused of killing an English king – Sir Walter Tyrell, the suspected slayer of William Rufus in the New Forest in 1100.

According to More, Richard was so eager for the deed to be done that he went straight from his stool to awaken Tyrell in the middle of the night. Sleepily, Tyrell agreed to take the job, and recruited two hit men to carry out the gruesome task. One was an experienced professional assassin named Miles Forest, 'a fellow', says More, 'flushed in murder beforetime'. The other was John Dighton, one of Tyrell's own burly ostlers, 'a big, broad, strong, square knave'. In August or September, pretending to buy cloth in the capital, Tyrell and his hit men went to London. At the Tower, they persuaded the frightened Brackenbury to turn a blind eye to what was afoot, give them the keys to the Tower for one night, and make sure that the sentries guarding the princes were otherwise engaged. This alone suggests Richard's involvement, since only he or Buckingham would have had the authority to order the guards' removal – and contrary to the efforts of some Ricardians to brand the duke as the killer, Buckingham was absent in Wales, and beginning to regret his support for Richard.

Sometime in September, the killers entered the White Tower at night and stole into the room where the princes slept. Here, says More:

They suddenly lapped them up among the [bed]clothes – so bewrapped them and entangled them, keeping down by force the featherbed and pillows hard into their mouths, that within a while, smothered and stifled, their breath failing, they gave up to God their innocent souls into the joys of Heaven, leaving to the tormentors their bodies dead in the bed.

More's vivid description of the murder is borne out by the earlier *Great Chronicle* which reports, 'Some said they were murdered atween two feather mattresses.' When the two killers were satisfied that their victims' lives were extinct, More goes on:

> [They] laid their bodies naked out upon the bed and fetched Sir James [Tyrell] to see them. Who, upon the sight of them, caused those murderers to bury them at the stairfoot, meetly deep in the ground under a great pile of stones.

Let us fast-forward almost two centuries to 1674, and the remarkable discovery of the mortal remains of the two boys murdered that night. After centuries of neglect, the royal palace in the Tower had fallen into a dangerous state of decay, and in the 1650s, Oliver Cromwell, Lord Protector of England, gave orders for this old relic of royal extravagance to be pulled down. The demolition was started but was still incomplete at the Restoration of Charles II in 1660.

In July 1664, Charles got around to ordering the final destruction of the remaining ruins – including a turret on the south wall of the White Tower which had once enclosed a privy staircase leading into St John's Chapel, reserved for the use of monarchs. Workmen removed the turret and then started to demolish the staircase inside. Burrowing into the rubble around the stair's foundations, some ten feet below ground level, they made a startling discovery: a wooden chest containing two skeletons. The bones were clearly those of children. The taller skeleton, lying on its back, was four foot ten inches tall; the smaller, lying face down on top, was four foot six and a half inches. Those who found them had no doubt that they were looking at the remains of the missing princes.

One anonymous witness wrote, 'This day I . . . saw working men dig out of a stairway in the White Tower the bones of those two Princes who were foully murdered by Richard III. They were small bones of lads in their teens and there were pieces of rag and velvet about them.' The bones were examined by Charles's physician and some distinguished antiquaries. All agreed that they were indeed those of the princes. The bones were placed in a stone coffin and left on display near the builders' rubbish heap.

During this period, souvenir hunters made off with some of them, including tiny finger bones. Other bones made their way, via the collector Elias Ashmole, to his Ashmolean Museum in Oxford, whence they subsequently disappeared. To camouflage these thefts, animal bones were apparently added to the skeletons.

Finally, after four years of this degradation, Charles bestirred himself to give his ancestors a decent burial. In 1678 the bones were taken from the Tower to Westminster Abbey, where they were interred in a tomb urn designed by Sir Christopher Wren, with a Latin inscription identifying them as the lost princes. Fast-forwarding again to 1933, after pressure from Ricardian revisionists who refused to accept their hero's guilt, the abbey authorities agreed to exhume the bones and subject them to a contemporary forensic examination by two experts. Dr Lawrence Tanner combined the roles of physician with that of keeper of Westminster's ancient monuments; and Professor W. Wright was president of the Royal Anatomical Society.

After separating the animal bones from the human remains, they found that the bones were those of two slim young males. The bigger skeleton was that of a youth of twelve to thirteen years old (Edward was two months short of his thirteenth birthday when he vanished in September 1483), and the smaller of between nine and eleven (Richard was ten). In other words, the skeletons were exactly the same age as the boys had been when they disappeared in the Tower – a crushing rebuff to theorists who argued that they had survived there into the reign of Henry VII. The jaw of the bigger skeleton showed evidence of deep-seated dental disease, possibly osteomyelitis, which would have produced pain as well as lassitude and depression – exactly fitting Edward's pitiful state as described by Argentine and Mancini. A red mark on the skull of the older skeleton was thought by the two experts to be a bloodstain caused by ruptured blood vessels consistent with death by stifling. The wisps of velvet that clung to the bones were another clue to the identity of the skeletons, since the material had only been invented in Renaissance Italy in the fourteenth century and was so expensive that it was reserved for royalty and nobility. Tanner and Wright concluded that there were too many coincidences between the forensic evidence and the known facts about the princes for there to be any doubt as to their identity. Despite the earnest efforts of the Ricardian revisionists the mystery of the princes in the Tower was a mystery no more.

*   *   *

Paradoxically, Richard's murder of the princes sealed his own fate. Even in the blood-soaked fifteenth century, the merciless slaughter of such 'inocent babes' caused shock, outrage and disgust. Popular feeling hardened against the usurper king and helped fuel the rebellion by the Duke of Buckingham – previously Richard's closest companion in crime – which broke out soon after the disappearence of the princes. The revolt united the growing number of anti-Ricardians, ranging from Buckingham's own powerful affinity to loyal Yorkists and their former Lancastrian enemies who had never reconciled themselves to Yorkist rule, and now looked to the only surviving Lancastrian claimant to the throne (albeit a very distant one) – the exiled Henry Tudor.

Tudor was the only son of Margaret Beaufort, a sprig of that extensive family descended from Edward III via John of Gaunt and his last wife Katherine Swynford. Henry's father, Edmund Tudor, Earl of Richmond, who died before his birth, was the half-brother of Henry VI on his mother's side, and one of the two sons of Owen Tudor by Catherine de Valois. Henry Tudor had been born to his thirteen-year-old mother on 28 January 1457, two years after the first battle of St Albans had started the Wars of the Roses which he was destined to bring to a close. His birthplace was Pembroke Castle in Wales, homeland of his Tudor forebears. His youth and early manhood was a long story of insecurity, flight, exile and hair's breadth escapes from the bloody fate the accident of his birth had almost guaranteed.

Only with his uncle Henry VI's brief restoration to the throne in 1470 had Tudor got his first taste of a royal court. It is said that on catching sight of his tall and youthful namesake nephew, the simpleton king had cried, 'Truly this is he unto whom both we and our adversaries must yield and give over the dominion.' However apocryphal, this prophecy of the coming House of Tudor did indeed come to pass.

After Edward IV regained his throne in 1471, Henry Tudor's uncle Jasper took the boy with him back into exile in Celtic Brittany where, following the death of Edward, Prince of Wales, at Tewkesbury Henry became the forlorn last hope of the Lancastrian cause. It was, therefore, in Henry's name that Buckingham raised the standard of revolt against Richard in 1483. The revolt was nipped in the bud by Richard III's spy system – and swamped by a nationwide storm and floods. Caught in open country by the deluge, the rebel army melted away and Buckingham himself was beheaded at Salisbury. Henry Tudor – with the luck that attended him throughout his life – narrowly escaped a similar fate. He had sailed from Brittany with a tiny fleet only to be caught in the Channel by the storm. Limping into a West Country port with just two ships, he found the harbour surrounded by Richard's troops. His life until then had taught Henry the habit of caution, and he sent a boat to shore to discover the allegiances of the soldiers, who shouted that they were Buckingham's men. Fortunately Henry's suspicions got the better of his ambition, and, ever mistrustful, he sailed back to Brittany. He would live to fight another day.

The story of Henry Wyatt, a Kentish gentleman and loyal Lancastrian who had supported Buckingham's rebellion, is one of the most extraordinary even in the Tower's over-eventful history, and illustrates the way that the fortress could encompass bewildering switches in fortune, with a tortured prisoner returning to the grim walls later in pomp and glory – and sometimes vice versa. The Wyatts, like other Tudor dynasties – the Dudleys, the Seymours and the Howards, not to mention the Tudors themselves – were to be closely – too closely – associated with the Tower in its bloodiest period over three generations.

Henry Wyatt was born in 1460, and was only twenty-three when he came out for Henry Tudor in Buckingham's rebellion. Confined in the Tower, he was racked in the sadistic King Richard's presence. As he lay agonising, his limbs stretched taut, Richard demanded:

> 'Wyatt, why art thou such a fool? Henry of Richmond is a beggarly pretender; forsake him and become mine. Thou servest him for moonshine on water.'

When such entreaties had no effect on the stubborn Lancastrian, King Richard, in a rage, had Wyatt:

> confined in a low and narrow cell, where he had not clothes sufficient to warm him and was a-hungered. A cat came into the cell, he caressed her for company, laid her in his bosom and won her love. And so she came to him every day and brought him a pigeon when she could catch one.

Wyatt, according to this charming family legend, persuaded his gaoler to cook the pigeons – a diet which kept him alive during the two long years of his imprisonment. When, in August 1485, Henry Tudor triumphantly rode into London after slaying Richard at Bosworth, one of his first acts was to free the faithful Wyatt. His loyalty was amply rewarded. Wyatt prospered mightily under the Tudors, and was created a Knight of the Bath at the traditional eve-of-coronation ceremony at the Tower when Henry VIII came to the throne – and eventually rose to be the king's treasurer. Wyatt was evidently a financial wizard, since Henry VII – notoriously mean himself – made him both custodian of his Crown jewels and keeper of the Royal Mint at the Tower, in which office Wyatt oversaw an entire recoinage of the realm.

Wyatt acquired Allington Castle in Kent and rebuilt it on Tudor lines before dying at the advanced sixteenth-century age of eighty. The grandeur and comfort of his old age were a very long way from his starved youth in the Tower. His son and heir, the poet Thomas Wyatt, had less happy associations with the fortress. A confidant and possible lover of Queen Anne Boleyn, he was imprisoned in the Tower and saw the unhappy queen walking to her execution from his cell window, commemorating the event in mournful verse. He was fortunate to escape the same fate himself. Thomas Wyatt's son, Thomas the younger, was not so lucky.

Thomas junior's first brush with the Tower was relatively innocuous: he was briefly confined there with his bosom friend Thomas Howard, Earl of Surrey, after a drunken escapade in which the aristocratic blades had amused themselves by breaking the windows of sleeping Londoners. In 1554, however, he was back – this time having led a full-scale rebellion in his traditionally restive native county of Kent. The revolt was aimed against Mary Tudor's coming marriage to King Philip II of Spain. Wyatt, having accompanied his father on a diplomatic mission to Spain, had a horror of the Inquisition and the merciless methods of Spanish Catholicism. Soon after his revolt was crushed he was led out of his cell to Tower Hill and executed. Three successive generations of the same family suffering in the Tower is an unenviable record – equalled, but not surpassed, by the Dudley family.

The snuffing out of Buckingham's abortive rebellion had not ended the threat to Richard III's rule. The man he loftily misspelled as 'Henry Tydder' lived still, an ever present threat. Knowing that Henry would attempt another invasion, Richard sent agents to try to abduct him in Brittany. Forewarned, Henry narrowly escaped by fleeing into neighbouring France where he began to collect mercenaries for his second bid for the throne.

In the closing months of Richard's reign it must have seemed to him as if God was smiting him for murdering the little princes. Firstly, his own only son Prince Edward wasted away and died, probably of tuberculosis. Richard was apparently devastated by grief; and his son's death made his own hold on power even shakier, since there was now no heir to the throne. Then Queen Anne died in March 1485. It says much for Richard's reputation that it was widely believed that he had had her poisoned – to clear the way for him to marry his own niece, Edward IV's daughter Elizabeth of York.

By the early summer of 1485, Richard's invasion fears were at fever pitch. He imported gunsmiths from Flanders to the Tower's armoury to make 'Serpentines' – the latest state-of-the-art cannon, long, thin and mounted on a pivot to increase their range and flexibility in firing their four-pound shot. Not knowing where Henry was to land, Richard moved to Nottingham in the Midlands so he could rapidly march to any corner of the kingdom. His proclamations of treason against 'Tydder' took on an increasingly hysterical tone. Finally, in August 1485, the news that he had dreaded reached Richard: Henry Tudor had landed at Milford Haven in his native south Wales. With a minuscule army of French mercenaries he was on the march.

Richard III only discovered the true depths of his unpopularity when his allies deserted him as he confronted Henry's outnumbered army near Bosworth in Leicestershire on 22 August 1485. The battle should have been a walkover for the king, but a large force led by Lord Stanley and his brother Sir William Stanley, on whom the king had been relying, deserted at the crucial moment and joined Henry. Richard, screaming, 'Treason!' rather than Shakespeare's 'My kingdom for a horse!', was cut down in the Midlands mud.

The battered and bleeding little corpse was slung unceremoniously across a horse's back and Richard's own herald, trailing his white boar banner, was forced to lead his late master's body back to Leicester, where he was hastily buried. On the battlefield, a servant of Henry Tudor's mother Margaret Beaufort found the gold coronet that had surmounted Richard's helmet lying in a hawthorn bush and took it to his master, Lord Stanley. Hastily making up for his late intervention on the winning side, Stanley placed it on Henry's head, shouting, 'King Henry! King Henry!' Few realised it at the time, but a new dynasty was born at that moment and the wars which had blighted and bled England for as long as almost anyone could remember were almost over.

Almost – but not quite. No usurper could be completely confident, and just as Henry Tudor's ancestor and namesake Henry IV spent his reign foiling plots and putting down revolts, so Henry VII's hold on his newly acquired throne was decidedly shaky. Margaret, Duchess of Burgundy, the sister of Edward IV and Richard III, was behind numerous Yorkist plots to regain the throne. Since almost all the genuine Yorkist heirs were dead or jailed, Margaret was obliged to support pretenders. The only living Yorkist with a genuine claim was young Edward, Earl of Warwick, teenage son of the union between the unlamented Duke of Clarence, and Isabel, daughter of Warwick the Kingmaker. Richard III had taken the precaution of locking the lad up in Yorkshire, and after Bosworth Henry VII had him brought to the Tower and kept under strict guard. Either because he had barely known freedom or because of a genetic weakness, young Warwick had the feeble mental fragility of a previous Tower incumbent – Henry VI – and hardly posed a serious threat to the throne.

Although King Henry could not afford to let this blighted Yorkist sprig flourish, he treated another flower of the Yorkist line more kindly. Elizabeth of York, eldest daughter of Edward IV and Elizabeth Woodville, had been betrothed to Henry during Buckingham's rebellion, and when he arrived in London after Bosworth, Henry fulfilled his pledge to wed her. First, though, he had to convert the impromptu crowning on the battlefield into a formal coronation. Tall, dark, and though not handsome, of suitable regal manner, Henry was determined to stamp his mark on his kingdom by luxuriously lavish celebrations to impress on his subjects that their new king was here to stay.

Though notoriously mean, Henry spared no expense for his coronation. He knew that appearances mattered. He spent his pre-coronation night at the Tower, creating a dozen new Knights of the Bath, with the ritual baths heated in the dungeons beneath the White Tower 'as of old time hath been accustomed'. And it was to the Tower that the court returned after processing through the city to the formal coronation in Westminster Abbey. The new king hosted a banquet in the Tower palace's great hall, at which that great Lancastrian survivor the Earl of Oxford – participant in so many losing battles, but whose strategy had at last triumphed at Bosworth – set the crown on the new monarch's head.

Henry lost no more time in wedding Elizabeth of York, which he did on 18 January 1486. His wedding gift to his bride was a strangely appropriate present to a woman destined to die in the Tower – the volume of verse written by the Duke of Orléans in the long years after Agincourt when the French nobleman had been a prisoner in the fortress, patiently awaiting ransom. Exactly nine months after the wedding, the comely Elizabeth – her face is said to be the model for the queen on packs of playing cards – gave birth to the first of their seven children, Prince Arthur. The pregnancy delayed the queen's own coronation, which took place amidst great pomp and splendour in November of the following year.

The Tower was once again the scene of elaborate ceremonies surrounding the event, which Henry intended as the final sealing of the union between the savagely sundered Houses of York and Lancaster in his own new Tudor dynasty. He had a new Tudor rose – a blend of the red and white flowers of the rival feuding families – designed to symbolise the fresh beginning. Henry's public devotion to his queen was not all show. He genuinely adored his Yorkist bride. On the morning of her coronation the queen was brought upriver from the palace at Greenwich in a fleet of barges 'freshly furnished with banners and streamers of silk'. The king waited on the Tower's wharf to receive her and the royal couple spent the traditional pre-coronation night in the Tower. The next day Elizabeth, tall, beautiful, and dressed in rich gold and damask, with an ermine cloak over which her golden hair, under a golden crown, cascaded, was carried to Westminster Abbey in a litter, also festooned with cloth of gold and damask. Mean he might have been, but Henry was determined to demonstrate that the Tudors were monarchs by right as well as conquest.

There were many who disputed that right. Six months before Elizabeth's coronation, in the very last battle of the Wars of the Roses, Henry was forced to confront an armed challenge to his Crown. The moving spirits behind the revolt were Margaret of Burgundy and John de la Pole, Earl of Lincoln. Ironically, Lincoln was the grandson of the Duke of Suffolk, the Lancastrian stalwart whose murder at sea in 1450 had sparked the whole bloody cycle of the Roses wars. Suffolk's son, John de la Pole, had switched allegiance to the Yorkists, and had married Elizabeth, sister of Edward IV and Richard III – thus endowing his eleven children with a dribble of Yorkist royal blood. Lincoln and his numerous siblings therefore had their own ambitions for the Crown. He had been encouraged by Richard III, who had recognised his nephew as heir to the throne after the death of his own son.

Early in 1487, a Yorkist priest in Oxford, Richard Symonds, identified a bright pupil of his, a baker's boy named Lambert Simnel, as a suitable stand-in for the simpleton Earl of Warwick imprisoned in the Tower. Wiping the flour from Simnel's face, Symonds coached him in his new role, spreading stories that Warwick had escaped. The priest brought his pretender to Dublin – a Yorkist hotbed – where Simnel was recognised as Warwick by the powerful Fitzgerald clan, who sent the good news to Burgundy that a viable Yorkist claimant had appeared.

Margaret of Burgundy, ever eager to make mischief for the Lancastrians, supplied 2,000 hired mercenaries under Martin Schwartz, a German soldier of fortune, and money to pay them. Two leaders of the exiled Yorkists, Lincoln and Viscount Lovell (Richard's former henchman 'Lovell our dog'), sailed to Dublin to lead the expedition against Henry's England. Henry, learning of Simnel's pretensions, fetched the real Warwick out of his Tower cell and paraded him through London's streets. But the Yorkists had their candidate and intended to go through with the masquerade. Simnel was crowned in Dublin as King Edward VI and coins were minted in his name.

In June 1487, the Yorkists, with Schwartz's 2,000 mercenaries and 6,000 enthusiastic but ill-trained Irish 'kerns', and their protégé 'King Edward VI' aka Simnel in tow, landed in Lancashire. Henry dealt decisively with the Yorkist pretender. The royal army met the Yorkists near the village of Stoke in the East Midlands. The last army of the White Rose was trounced. Lincoln and Schwartz were killed, Lovell disappeared, and Lambert Simnel fell from his brief royal status to resume his culinary duties – as a scullion in the royal kitchens, where he allegedly invented the simnel cake.

There would be no such mercy for the next Yorkist pretender. Four years after Simnel's royal dreams were smothered at Stoke, another Yorkist pretender appeared in Ireland. The delicately handsome youth called himself Richard, Duke of York, and claimed to be the younger of the two princes who had disappeared in the Tower in 1483. He was actually probably Perkin Warbeck, the son of a Flemish boatman. Resembling the young Edward IV, he may indeed have been one of that libertine king's innumerable bastards, but could also even have been the illegitimate son of Margaret of Burgundy herself by a cardinal. Warbeck, whoever he really was, well served the purposes of his alleged aunt, Margaret of Burgundy, tireless fount of all Yorkist plots against Henry Tudor. Margaret received Perkin at her court, coached him in royal ways, and officially recognised him as her missing nephew. He was also recognised by King Charles VII of France, and the new Holy Roman Emperor, Maximilian, who had a common interest in keeping England weak and war-torn. Warbeck spent his young manhood trailing around the courts of Europe to stake his claim as the new 'White Rose of York' before making his debut in the British Isles in 1491.

Like that of his predecessor Simnel, the chosen first venue for Warbeck's tour was Ireland. Failing to arouse much enthusiasm in Cork, he appeared off Kent in 1495 with a small fleet provided by Margaret. An advance guard sent ashore without Warbeck was rapidly rounded up. The eighty prisoners were taken to the Tower 'railed in ropes like horses drawing a cart' and executed on Tower Hill. The pretender himself sailed back to Ireland, and then to Scotland where he received a more friendly reception from King James IV – as keen to make trouble for England as his Continental cousins. James funded Warbeck's enterprise, and even furnished the self-proclaimed 'King Richard IV' with an aristocratic wife: Lady Katherine Gordon, daughter of the Earl of Huntley.

The Scottish–Yorkist invasion was stopped in Northumbria. Once again Warbeck returned to Ireland, before in October 1497 arriving in Cornwall, where a rebellion had broken out against Henry's rapacious taxation. Warbeck placed himself at the head of a rebel army of 6,000 but proved militarily inept, deserting his men at Taunton, and fleeing to the sanctuary of Beaulieu Abbey in Hampshire where he fell into Henry's hands. Taken to the Tower, Warbeck was provisionally released and even received at court, where a curious Henry questioned him closely about his mysterious origins. Warbeck took advantage of the lenient conditions of his captivity to attempt an escape. Henry punished him by exposing him to the insults and brickbats of the London mob, and then humiliatingly forced him to make a public confession of his imposture in the presence of his wife (who had borne him two children). Warbeck was then returned to the Tower. He remained in close captivity there for two years in a cell adjacent to Warwick. The wily Henry allowed the two young men to associate and walk around the Tower's walls together. Evidently, he was giving them enough rope to hang themselves.

The king's hand was finally forced by the impending marriage of his elder son, Prince Arthur, to Katherine of Aragon, daughter of King Ferdinand and Queen Isabella of Spain. Ferdinand informed Henry that the marriage was off unless the Yorkist threat to his throne was removed once and for all. He was not prepared to entrust his daughter to a here-today, gone-tomorrow monarch. Henry – who never let sentiment stand in the way of realpolitik – acted with ruthless efficiency to wipe out the Yorkist threat. In 1499 both Warbeck and his new friend Warwick were accused of plotting to murder the constable of the Tower, Sir John Digby, escape from the fortress, and for good measure set fire to the Tower as they left. They were also charged with having bribed a warder to assist their unlikely schemes.

There could be only one verdict for such capital crimes: death. Poor Warwick, who had spent fourteen years as Henry's prisoner merely on account of his Yorkist blood, was so simple minded that, as a spectator at his trial remarked, 'He could not discern a goose from a capon.' Tried before that reliable Lancastrian hit man Lord Oxford, he was condemned and beheaded on Tower Hill.

Warbeck, despite his royal pretensions, was punished as a commoner. Humiliatingly conveyed from the Tower to Tyburn on a hurdle, he was hanged with the warder he had supposedly tried to bribe. Yet again he read out a confession that he had been a pretender all along. Henry also took the chance to eliminate another rival of dubious loyalty. Sir William Stanley, who had saved the day at Bosworth by dramatically throwing his weight behind Henry at the crucial moment, was accused of having backed Warbeck's bid for the Crown. In fact, Stanley, the Lord Chamberlain, had merely said that if Warbeck truly was Richard of York, he would be obliged to support him. Such careless talk was enough to cost him his life. He was imprisoned in the White Tower before an appointment with the headsman on Tower Hill.

The murder of Warwick – for murder it was – was not well received in the country at large. Popular pity for the unfortunate young man ran high. After his death it was rumoured that he had pronounced a dying curse on the House of Tudor, prophesying that from then on no male member of the dynasty would grow to manhood. Whether apocryphal or not, the prophecy would come true.

There was just one loose thread left for Henry to tie before he could be completely confident that the throne was his. Sir James Tyrell, Richard III's henchman who had organised the elimination of the princes in the Tower in 1483 had, as an efficient administrator, been pardoned by Henry and confirmed as governor of Guisnes Castle outside Calais. But Tyrell secretly remained true to his Yorkist roots. In 1501 he came out for the next Yorkist claimant: Edmund de la Pole, Earl of Suffolk, younger brother of the Earl of Lincoln whose bid for the throne using Lambert Simnel had ended so bloodily at Stoke. Suffolk fled into exile at Guisnes where Tyrell gave him shelter. Henry grimly laid siege to the castle, lured Tyrell out and had him brought to the Tower, the scene of his great crime, and tortured – with hideous irony in the dungeons under the White Tower. Tormented beyond endurance, Tyrell blurted out the truth about his role in the deaths of the princes – and was duly executed. The princes were avenged.

CHAPTER EIGHT

THE KING'S GREAT MATTER

As the sixteenth century opened, King Henry VII, at last secure on his hard-acquired throne, celebrated the beginning of the Tudor age at the Tower with that traditional mark of confidence in the stability and continuity of a ruling dynasty: a royal wedding. The bridegroom was Prince Arthur, at fifteen the first fruit of the reunion between the sundered Houses of Lancaster and York, and the bride, the shy and demure sixteen-year-old Princess Katherine of Aragon, daughter of King Ferdinand and Queen Isabella of Spain.

In October 1501 King Henry and Queen Elizabeth moved into the Tower's palace to prepare for the nuptial festivities. The Tower's tilting yard was the scene of daily jousts, and its great hall echoed nightly to the carousing of lavish banquets and dances. Henry was the last monarch to treat the Tower as a home. He embellished the royal apartments, adding a gallery to the Cradle Tower, and converting the nearby Lanthorn Tower into an adjunct of the royal palace, complete with a bedchamber and privy closet. He spent much time at the palace and his personal bodyguard – the Yeomen of the Guard, in their scarlet Tudor liveries – were direct ancestors of the Yeoman Warders who are the proud custodians of the Tower today.

Henry's eventual abandonment of his beloved palace marked the start of the Tower's decline from glittering royal pleasure dome to gloomy decay, and its sinister sixteenth-century role as the site of torment and martyrdom for Protestants and priests in turn; and the last station of condemned queens and nobles on their way to execution. This transformation in the Tower's fortunes was speeded by two tragic personal bereavements. In 1502, just five months after his wedding so hopefully feasted at the Tower, Prince Arthur died at Ludlow Castle, probably from tuberculosis. The following year, in February 1503, nine days after giving birth in the Tower to a daughter, Katherine, Queen Elizabeth herself, now in her late thirties, died there, probably from puerperal fever – just yards from the spot where her two brothers had been murdered and where their undiscovered bodies still lay. The baby Katherine died a few days later.

Henry's triple bereavement hit him hard. He gave orders for Elizabeth's body to be embalmed 'with gums, balms, spices, sweet wine and wax' and on Sunday 12 February, the corpse was borne from the royal palace to St John's Chapel in the White Tower which had been hung in black mourning silk and crêpe. For three days, surrounded by 500 tall candles, the queen's body lay in state while priests chanted the prayers for the dead. The body was then taken in solemn state and buried in Westminster Abbey. After these disasters Henry, never the happiest of men, became ever more morose, miserly and miserable. He never remarried, and though Arthur's widowed teenage bride Katherine was betrothed to his second son and heir, the tall, clever, athletic and strapping Henry, the king himself moped his life away, eventually succumbing to the same disease which had killed his eldest son – tuberculosis – in April 1509.

The next king, whoever he had been, would have seemed an improvement on grim and grasping Henry, but the fact that the eighteen-year-old Henry VIII appeared a Renaissance man personified only added to the general joy at his accession. Not yet showing the gross obesity of his maturity, young Henry had the imposing height and physique of his grandfather Edward IV. The golden-haired youth radiated a confidence and learning beyond his years. Originally intended for the Church, he was well versed in theology; he was also fluent in Latin and French, enjoyed swordplay and jousting, could sing and dance well, played a variety of instruments, and even composed music and songs. Flattering foreign diplomats compared him with the sun and moon in their swooning first reports on the glamorous new king.

Within hours of succeeding to the Crown, however, Henry made a dramatic move that, while popular with his subjects, demonstrated his ruthless savagery that would become more and more apparent as his sensibility coarsened and his cruelty increased. The leading lights in his father's council were the lawyers Edmund Dudley and Sir Richard Empson. The late king had used their legal skills to squeeze cash from his subjects. By such dubious methods as charging wealthy people with imaginary crimes, then dropping the proceedings on reception of a hefty bribe, they had diverted the vast sum of almost £5 million into their master's coffers.

Such extortions had not made them popular, and when Empson and Dudley realised that Henry was on his deathbed they had gathered their few friends around them to discuss their future. It was to be short. The day after Henry wheezed his last, the new king, en route by barge to the Tower for the traditional pre-coronation ceremonies, gave orders for the immediate arrest of the two hated ministers. They were flung into the Tower's cells. Unable to kill his victims for merely doing their jobs too zealously, Henry trumped up a capital charge. Using the excuse of the gatherings at their houses as his father lay dying, Henry accused the pair of having treasonably attempted to block his accession and assassinate him.

After an unsuccessful attempt to escape from the Tower, Dudley tried to worm his way back into royal favour by writing a treatise in his Tower cell, *The Tree of Commonwealth*. This early example of the considerable body of literature produced in the fortress hovered between shameless fawning – it was dedicated to Henry – and sound, pragmatic advice. It extolled the benefits of monarchy, counselled the king to rule firmly, but advised him to temper justice with mercy. All Dudley's literary labour was in vain. After sixteen months of imprisonment the stone-hearted monarch had him and Empson executed in August 1510. Nor would Dudley be the last member of his family to suffer imprisonment and execution at the Tower. Astonishingly, both his son John, Duke of Northumberland, and his grandson Lord Guildford Dudley, would share his fate at the hands of Henry's daughter, Queen Mary, for their abortive attempt to place Guildford's wife Lady Jane Grey – another Tower victim – on the throne.

Among the survival skills Henry VIII had inherited from his father was a healthy fear of reviving the ruinous Roses wars. This meant that anyone representing the dormant hopes of the House of York had to be neutralised or eliminated. William de la Pole, a scion of the family named as heirs by Richard III, spent a record thirty-eight years until his death imprisoned in the Tower solely because of his Yorkist blood. Even so, he was more fortunate than his elder brother Edmund, Earl of Suffolk, who had fled into exile near Calais to be sheltered by Sir James Tyrell, killer of the little princes. Returned to England, Edmund spent the best part of a decade locked up with his brother in the Tower. But Henry decided to do away with this relic of the Yorkist cause before departing on his first visit abroad as king. Almost casually, Henry gave orders for de la Pole to be beheaded on Tower Hill in April 1513.

As was customary for a new reign, Henry had had the Tower refurbished for the joint coronation of himself and Katherine, marking the event with four decorative 'caps' – still there today – on the corner turrets of the White Tower; and having the halls of the royal palace hung with the Tudor colours of red, white and green. He arrayed a battery of modern cannon on the Tower's riverside wharf to boom out a salute to his greater glory. On 22 June, the eve of the coronation, Henry created twenty-six Knights of the Bath; mostly his own cronies and contemporaries, who were ritually purified, bathed and shaved according to the ancient custom before serving the king at dinner and spending the pre-coronation night in prayer in St John's Chapel.

As the royal couple rode from the Tower to Westminster the following day, fountains and conduits spurted free wine for Londoners to toast the health of the newly wed monarchs. Henry rode bare-headed, his golden hair glowing in the summer sun, clad in a scarlet velvet robe and a gold tunic set with diamonds, rubies, pearls and emeralds. Behind him the queen sat in a litter drawn by two white palfreys. Katherine herself, 'beautiful and godly to behold', was dressed in white satin with her dark hair hanging loose down her back, surmounted by a gold coronet spangled with precious stones.

Alas, the union which had begun in such shining splendour was not destined to prosper. Katherine – five years older than her youthful husband – gave birth to children who either were stillborn or died soon after their births. The only surviving child, born in 1516, Mary, was a girl rather than the longed-for male heir. As Henry had one healthy son, Henry Fitzroy, with his mistress Bessie Blount, he knew that any fault in fertility did not lie with him, and professed to believe that his marriage was cursed by God. He pointed to a verse in Leviticus in the Old Testament forbidding a man to lie with his dead brother's wife. By 1525, Katherine's childbearing days were done, and her husband began to look elsewhere. To secure the all-important continuation of his house, he decided, he would have to put Katherine aside and marry again.

Henry's desire for divorce became urgent when the king's lust was added to reasons of state. Around 1526 Henry became deeply infatuated with

Anne Boleyn, a raven-haired, dark-eyed, sharp-featured teenager whose high intelligence and cheeky vivacity whetted the king's desire. The king had already made Anne's elder sister, Mary, his mistress and assumed that Anne would fill the same position in her turn. Anne, however, played for higher stakes. A confident and calculating young woman whose education in the Netherlands and France had steeped her in the advanced ideas of the Protestant Reformation, Anne was not overawed by her royal suitor, whom she had known from an early age both at court – where she became a maid of honour to the queen – and during Henry's visits to the Boleyn family home at Hever Castle in Kent.

Encouraged by her ambitious father, Thomas Boleyn, and by her maternal uncle Thomas Howard, Duke of Norfolk, Anne set her sights on becoming queen. As her besotted childhood friend and Kentish neighbour, the poet Sir Thomas Wyatt – who would share her imprisonment in the Tower – wrote:

> There is written her fair neck about
> Noli me tangere; *for Caesar's I am*
> *And wild for to hold though I seem tame.*

The long political dominance of Henry's chief minister, Cardinal Thomas Wolsey, ended with his failure to secure an increasingly impatient Henry a marriage annulment from Rome. He fell in 1529 (he would have died in the Tower had he not died en route there at Leicester Abbey instead), paving the way for the rise of his former secretary, Thomas Cromwell. A humbly born man like Wolsey, Cromwell rose to the top by hard work and administrative ability. It was he who restored the royal coffers by dissolving England's monasteries and taking the accumulated wealth of the Church into the Crown's hands (as well as his own).

If Thomas Cromwell managed the political side of the king's 'great matter' – as his search for a way out of the marriage was discreetly known – with ruthless ease, it was Thomas Cranmer who masterminded the theology of the English Reformation. Cranmer first came to prominence as one of the radical Cambridge theologians who drank in the bold new Protestant doctrines preached in Germany by Martin Luther. Rising to be chaplain to Anne Boleyn, Cranmer commended himself to Henry by suggesting that the king should ask English churchmen rather than Rome whether he could divorce Katherine and marry Anne. Tired of the Pope's endless prevarications, Henry delightedly exclaimed, 'He hath the right sow by the ear,' and followed Cranmer's advice. He would do the same for the rest of his reign.

Between them, Cromwell and Cranmer carried through a very English Reformation. The king replaced the Pope as head of an English Church still broadly Catholic in its rituals. And the monasteries and other houses of religion were dissolved and had their assets seized by the state. By 1532, as Parliament began to levy the first fines and penalties on a Church reluctant to acknowledge Henry as its supreme head, Sir Thomas More resigned as Lord Chancellor, proving that his Catholic conscience was stronger than his worldly ambition. In January 1533 Cranmer secretly married Henry to Anne, who was already pregnant with the future Elizabeth I. In April Cranmer presided over a Church court that pronounced Henry's marriage to Katherine null and void, and a fortnight later Anne was taken to the Tower for the traditional vigil preceding her coronation. More snubbed the king by refusing his personal invitation (and a £20 bribe to buy himself new clothes) to attend the event.

Henry spared no expense in his lavish display of pride in his new wife. Cocking a snook at those who rejected Anne as an adventuress and harlot, he ostentatiously greeted his pregnant bride with a smacking public kiss when she arrived at the Tower's wharf by barge from Greenwich for her coronation at Whitsun 1533. That night the usual score of Knights of the Bath were created and knelt in homage before the new queen. The following day, the coronation procession from the Tower to Westminster rivalled in magnificence anything that even that well-trodden route had ever seen.

Through streets lined at Henry's command with silk banners, gorgeous tapestries and hangings of crimson and cloth of gold, Anne rode in a carriage decked in damask. The queen was seated beneath a golden awning tinkling with bells, and wore a scarlet coronation robe glittering with jewels. Her slender neck, destined to be severed in just three years, was decorated with a necklace of pearls, 'each larger than big chick-peas and diamonds of great value'. Her mane of black hair which had so enchanted Henry had been unpinned and fell about her hips. The fountains ran red with free wine and the coronation parade was headed by foreign ambassadors from France and Venice (the Spanish ambassador, like More, had boycotted the event) along with England's great and good, including the Archbishops of Canterbury and York, London's lord mayor and most of the peerage. It was an impressive display of Henry's power to bend a reluctant populace to his will. But how capricious that will was to prove, the new queen would shortly discover.

Almost exactly a year later, on 17 April 1534, the Tower would play host to a very different guest. The king's patience with Thomas More's refusal to take the oath acknowledging him as Supreme Head of the Church – now required of every subject – had finally run out. Henry – urged on by a vengeful Anne – ordered his fallen servant taken to the Tower. He was conveyed by river from his Chelsea home by Thomas Cromwell's nephew Richard. More's fallen status was brought dramatically home to him when, on arriving at the Tower, he was asked to give up the heavy gold chain bearing the Tudor rose that he wore so proudly in his famous Holbein portrait. He was also required to surrender his costly fur gown as a 'fee' to the grasping boatman.

More was confined to the ground floor of the Bell Tower, a high vaulted chamber just inside the Tower's main gateway, and the conditions of his imprisonment were not severe to begin with – although he had to write his first letters with a piece of charcoal until he was given pen and ink. The king evidently still hoped that a taste of the Tower would bring More to heel. He was allowed to keep his illiterate servant John Wood, although Wood was ordered to report any treasonable remarks made by his master. As a distinguished state prisoner More was permitted to enjoy the 'liberties' of the Tower, taking a daily stroll in the fortress's gardens. More importantly to him, he was also allowed to attend Mass daily in the Tower's chapel, and receive visits from his family, including his favourite daughter Margaret, who urged him to swear the oath as she and the rest of the family had all done. But More's stubborn – or saintly – streak remained firm. Though tempted, he refused to yield.

More's initial confinement may not have been cruel, by the Tower's grim standards, but it was certainly austere. His cell was about nineteen feet across, with walls thirteen feet thick, illuminated by a few slit windows. The hard earth floor was strewn with rushes and the prisoner slept on a thin straw pallet bed. A rough wooden table and chair completed the sparse furnishings. Situated only a few yards from the river, the Bell Tower was particularly susceptible to damp; and although More had the walls hung with straw mats to counter the chill and used a small brick stove, the cold was penetrating, even in the spring and summer. The gloomy atmosphere, with water constantly dripping down the dank walls and the slit windows providing the only light, apart from a guttering tallow candle, hit More's health hard. An old man at fifty-seven, he complained of chest aches and leg cramps. His hair and the beard which he refused to cut turned white. Tormented by such bodily pains, he suffered far worse from the pangs of a tortured conscience.

More spent long sleepless nights wrestling with insomnia partly prompted by guilt over the suffering he was bringing on his family. His letters from the Tower are among the most moving documents ever penned from the fortress. Always of a sado-masochistic temperament, More habitually wore a hair shirt crawling with lice to mortify his flesh; and as Lord Chancellor had delighted both in witnessing the torture of Protestant heretics, and in getting his daughter to flog him, allegedly for spiritual purposes. Now, as he flagellated himself in his cell, his imagination dwelt on the tortures awaiting him in the Tower's dungeons if he persisted in his obstinacy. He found, he wrote, 'my fleshe much more shrinkinge from payne and from death, than me thought it the part of a faithfull Christian man'. Nonetheless he strove to comfort his family, bidding them, 'Make you all merry in the hope of heaven.'

More put the tedious hours to literary and spiritual use, writing a devotional meditation on the Passion of Christ and, tellingly, *A Dialogue of Comfort Against Tribulation*. The tone of the *Dialogue* is a martyr's resigned fortitude. As he meditates on the 'four last things' – death, judgement, heaven and hell – More concludes that only one final task remains to him: to make a good end of his life, forsaking earthly ties and temptations, and resigning himself to the infinite mercy of God.

The authorities left More under no illusion as to his fate, making him watch a group of four Carthusian monks who had also refused to swear the oath going to their deaths from the Tower – where they had been held in fetters making it impossible for them to lie down or move – in May 1535. More's only reaction was regret that he had not followed the religious vocation himself. Watching the Carthusians leaving the Tower en route to Tyburn, More remarked to his daughter Margaret that they went to their deaths 'as cheerfully as bridegrooms to their marriage'.

More knew that his own earthly journey was nearing its end and claimed to be glad of it. He told a fellow Tower prisoner, Dr Nicholas Wilson, a priest who had been chaplain to the king, 'I have since I came to the Tower looked once or twice to have given up my ghost before this, and in good faith mine heart waxed the lighter in hope thereof.' The devout Wilson was not made of the same stern stuff as More, since he finally submitted to the oath in 1537 after three years in the Tower.

A few days after he had watched the monks going so cheerfully to their doom, More was summoned to a meeting of the Privy Council held in the Tower under Thomas Cromwell's chairmanship. Still trying to break his resistance with kindness, they invited More – a former councillor – to sit with them. Stiffly aloof, he stood to give one of the greatest speeches in defence of the individual human conscience ever delivered, in words that rang to the Tower's ancient rafters:

> 'I am the king's true, faithful subject . . . and daily pray for his Highness and all the realm. I do nobody harm. I say none harm. I think none harm, but wish everybody good. And if this be not enough to keep a man alive, in good faith I long not to live. And I am dying already, and I have since I came here, been several times in the case that I thought to die within one hour, and I thank our Lord I was never sorry for it but rather sorry when the pang had passed. And therefore my poor body is at the king's pleasure. Would God my death might do him some good.'

The presence near More of another prisoner jailed on the same charge of refusing the oath gave him great comfort. John Fisher, the aged Bishop of Rochester, had been confessor to the king's grandmother, Margaret Beaufort, but neither this connection nor his eighty years mollified Henry's wrath when Fisher became the only English bishop to refuse the oath. A straight-talking Yorkshireman, Fisher scorned, unlike More, to take refuge in hair-splitting legalese. Fisher occupied the cell above More in the Bell Tower, but his imprisonment was even harsher than More's, since the old man shivered on a thin straw mattress on the cold floor with no other furnishing. Often deprived of food for a day at a time, he suffered bitterly in the harsh winter of 1534–5, writing pathetically to Cromwell:

> I have neither shirt nor suit, nor yett other clothes . . . but that be ragged and rent so shamefully. Notwithstanding I might easily suffer that, if they would keep my body warm. But my diet also, God knoweth how slender it is at any tymes, and now in mine age my stomach may not away but

with a few kinds of meats, which if I want [lack] I decay forthwith and
fall into coughs and diseases.

Fisher's fate – and probably that of More, too – was sealed when the new
Pope, Paul III, hearing of his suffering, made him a cardinal. An enraged
Henry vowed furiously that he would send Fisher's head to Rome for its
red hat. At dawn on 22 June 1535, the lieutenant of the Tower, Sir Edward
Walsingham, climbed the wooden staircase that connected his luxurious
lodgings with Fisher's spartan cell. He told the old bishop that he was to
die that day. Fisher begged for a few more hours' rest 'by reason of my
great weakness and infirmity' and Walsingham promised to return at 9
a.m. At the appointed hour, helped by an attendant, Fisher dressed for
the last time and walked unaided beneath the arch of the Bloody Tower
and along the causeway to the Bulwark Gateway, where he collapsed and
apologised for being too weak to go further – and for being unable to
give his escorts their customary tip, on account of having 'nothing left'.

The old man faced his end with dignity and quiet courage, asking the
crowd on Tower Hill to help him with their prayers so that he did not
weaken in his allegiance to his Catholic faith as he received his 'stroke
of death'. After the axe fell, people marvelled that Fisher's emaciated
body could produce such fountains of blood, but the way his remains
were treated after his head was struck off reflected no credit on his killers.
His corpse was stripped, impaled on spears, and flung into a common
grave at the nearby church of All Hallows by the Tower – only to be
dug up a fortnight later and reburied within the Tower walls at St Peter
ad Vincula.

By then More, too, lay under the shadow of death. After another confron-
tation with the council in which all Cromwell's subtlety had failed to draw
an incriminating denial of the king's spiritual authority from More, harsher
pressure was applied: he was denied the use of the books and writing
materials that had sustained him in the Tower for more than a year.
Withdrawing such a privilege from a man whose whole life had been
devoted to letters was tantamount to stepping on More's oxygen tube. It
was also the means by which his long travail in the Tower was ended.
The man who came to More's cell to take away his books was a former
protégé of his, an unscrupulous lawyer named Sir Richard Rich who,
insatiably ambitious, had risen to be Solicitor General.

Rich had already used his black arts in interrogating Fisher to provoke the old cleric into making fatally damaging admissions. Now, as he supervised the strapping up and packing into a sack of More's books by two lesser officials, Sir Richard Southwell and William Palmer, Rich engaged his former mentor in seemingly casual conversation. Devastated by the loss of his spiritual food, a despairing More pulled the blinds against the strong summer light streaming through the slit windows into his cell and sat despondently in darkness. When Rich asked him why, More replied, 'Now that the goods and implements are taken away the shop must be closed.' More apparently let down his guard as Rich continued to badger him. According to Rich's account – which was used in the indictment that finally sent More to the scaffold – the two lawyers engaged in legal banter, batting forth absurd scenarios. What if Parliament made Rich king – would More accept that? Marry, More batted back, what if Parliament declared that God was not God, what would Rich say then?

Rich then posed another question and, fatally, More answered it. Parliament had voted to accept the king as Supreme Head of the Church. If, as More said, he accepted Parliament's decisions, why did he not accept this one? More agreed that Parliament had passed the Act of Supremacy. But, he added, 'Most foreign countries do not accept the same,' meaning that that particular law was against the universal law of Christendom. This was treason. Rich wrote a memo of his conversation for his master Cromwell who used it to frame More. The amoral Rich was easily induced to 'sex up' his conversation with More to have Sir Thomas specifically deny Henry's right to head the Church – a piece of perjury which More scornfully rejected at his trial in Westminster Hall. Was it likely, he asked, that he would entrust not just his life but his immortal soul to a rogue like Rich whom he had always despised as a liar? Although Southwell and Palmer both declined to back Rich up, claiming that they had been too far away to hear the fatal conversation, Rich's perjured word was enough. More was condemned to death.

More welcomed his martyrdom and used his last speech to caution his judges that they too stood near death. He was confident of going to heaven, he said, but warned his judges that he would only meet them 'merrily' there if they renounced their impious heresy and returned to the old faith. An axe turned towards him as a mark of condemnation, More then returned to the Tower by river. The Tower's constable, Sir William Kingston, a gnarled old soldier, had come to know and love More during his long detention and burst into tears when they disembarked at the fortress. More comforted him. They would, he assured Kingston, 'meet merrily' in heaven thereafter. On the Tower's wharf there was an affecting scene as More's children, led by his favourite daughter Margaret, pushed through the thicket of spearmen guarding him to tearfully embrace their father. That night – again reduced to writing in charcoal – More penned his last letter to Margaret. Sending her his hair shirt and a final blessing, More told Margaret that he 'longed to go to God'.

At dawn on Thursday, 6 July 1535, Sir Thomas Pope, a former friend and privy councillor, was sent to tell More that he would die that day. More thanked him for his 'good tidings' and asked him to pass greetings to the king who was killing him, together with his thanks for letting him live long enough in the Tower to reconcile himself to God. More was, he told Pope, beholden to Henry for 'ridding me out of the miseries of this wretched world. And therefore will I not fail earnestly to pray for his grace, both here and in another world.'

In readiness for making a grand exit, More donned his finest clothes. But when Pope pointed out that the executioner got to keep his victim's clothing as part of his fee, More swapped the costly garments for a simple grey smock belonging to his faithful servant, John Wood. To make sure that the headsman made a clean cut, though, he generously tipped him with a gold angel coin. In the clear light of the summer morning, More trod steadily up the gentle slope of Tower Hill, clutching a small red cross. When he reached the scaffold, he saw that the wooden structure was old and tottering. He turned to the Tower's lieutenant, Sir Edward Walsingham, and spoke a magnificent exit jest: 'I pray you, Master Lieutenant, see me safe up, and for my coming down let me shift for myself.'

More slowly mounted the creaking structure and was greeted at the top by the executioner who knelt to ask his forgiveness. The prisoner graciously granted it and briefly addressed the crowd gathered below. (Henry, fearing the power of More's eloquence, had sent him a message commanding him not to say much. More, as ever an obedient servant of the Crown, obeyed.) He blessed the crowd, and affirmed that he died a good Catholic and a faithful servant of the king, adding significantly, 'but God's servant first'. Then, only pausing to ask the executioner to strike straight, he tied a linen bandage around his own eyes with a steady hand and lay full length, stretching his neck out over the low block. He carefully lifted his beard clear, remarking that it should not be cut as it had not committed treason. Then the axe fell.

Less than a year after More's head had replaced that of his fellow martyr John Fisher on the spikes of London Bridge, the woman who had been their nemesis fell too. The capricious Henry had already tired of Anne well before More's head was taken off, and when the news of the execution was brought to him at Greenwich as he was playing dice, he turned to the queen and viciously hissed, 'It is because of you that the honestest man in my kingdom is dead,' before stalking angrily away. Henry's disdain for Anne was compounded of several factors: the familiar psychological pattern of long pent-up lust turning sour as soon as it is satisfied; resentment of the time and trouble Anne's reluctance to become his mistress had caused; guilt over the deaths of More and the other martyrs; annoyance at the queen's headstrong, arrogant and domineering behaviour; and the fact that he was already involved with the woman who would succeed Anne in his affections – a demure maid of honour to the queen called Jane Seymour.

But the most pressing reason of state behind the king's brutal decision to rid himself of the woman for whom he had changed the kingdom's religion was her failure to produce a male heir. After giving birth to the Lady Elizabeth in 1533, she had rapidly conceived again – only to suffer a miscarriage in March 1534. Anne miscarried again in 1535, just after hearing that the king had been hurt in a jousting fall; and in January 1536, following another shock – the death of her old rival Katherine of Aragon – she gave birth to a stillborn premature male child. At that, Henry finally gave up. 'You shall have no more sons from *me*,' he pointedly told her.

Anne had no shortage of enemies at court. Ever since Henry had first conceived his passion for her, wagging tongues had accused Anne of sorcery, spreading stories that the queen had such infallible signs of a witch as six fingers on one hand. The Catholic faction loyal to Katherine, encouraged by the imperial ambassador, Eustace Chapuys, worked tirelessly for her downfall. Henry – his paranoia, possibly exacerbated by his chronic endocrinal condition, Cushing's syndrome – ever increasing, eagerly jumped to the conclusion that his union with Anne, as with Katherine, was a sin against God, cursed by the lack of a live male heir. And once again he reached for the same solution as before: finding a new bride among his queen's ladies.

Henry's rage against the woman he had once lusted after could only be slaked with blood. His loyal servant, Thomas Cromwell, constructed a case against Anne. Her unpopularity, the rumours that she was a witch and her reputation as a teasing flirt with a circle of adoring young men combined to give Cromwell the weapons to ensure Anne's destruction. With a wolf's nose for the weakest animal in her pack, he picked on Mark Smeaton, a low-born musician favoured by Anne for his skill at the lute and virginals.

Smeaton, an effeminate, timid youth, was an unlikely candidate for the role Cromwell had cast him for – that of Anne's lover – but he would serve as the instrument to bring her down. On 30 April 1536 the unsuspecting musician was invited to dinner at Cromwell's riverside London town house in Stepney, just east of the Tower. Bursting with pride at this unexpected favour from the kingdom's most prominent statesman, Smeaton arrived, only to be immediately arrested. Preliminary torture was applied in Cromwell's presence. It did not take much to break the young man's will. A knotted rope was wound round his skull and steadily tightened with a stick as Cromwell's voice penetrated through the fog of pain.

Under the intolerable pressure – his eyes felt as though they were being forced out of their sockets and his skull seemed like an eggshell about to be crushed – Smeaton crumbled. Ready to say anything to stop the agony, he confessed that he had been the queen's lover, along with more elevated courtiers in her circle. Perhaps hoping that the sheer number would demonstrate the absurdity of the charges, he agreed to every name that Cromwell spat at him: Henry Norris, yes; William Brereton, yes; Francis Weston also. Thomas Wyatt, too, and Richard Page, and not forgetting the queen's own brother George Boleyn, Lord Rochford, with whom, said Smeaton, she had committed incest.

By the time that Smeaton, bruised, battered, his head ringing and aching, and scared out of his wits, was locked into an attic room in Cromwell's house for the night, he had accused half a dozen men closest to the queen of being her lovers. The charges were almost certainly lies, but that was beside the point – Cromwell had enough evidence to rid Henry of his inconvenient queen. Cleverly, he ensured that the men he accused all had reputations for sexual laxity. The atmosphere of flirtatiousness and the air of sin that hung around the queen's circle like a bad odour lent Cromwell's charges some credence. It is significant, however, that the only man who actually admitted them was the only one who was subjected to torture (and doubtless to promises of lenient treatment if he told his tormentors what they wanted to hear): young Smeaton. As aristocrats, the other accused were not subjected to the Tower's grosser forms of pressure – a privilege not enjoyed by the humbly born musician.

By 1 May, Smeaton was in the Tower, fettered by iron manacles in an underground dungeon. Henry was at Greenwich watching a tournament when Cromwell's report reached him. Anne was with him, although by now the royal pair were barely on speaking terms. Immediately, without bothering to bid his wife a final farewell, the king summoned a knot of courtiers, including Sir Henry Norris. Riding through the spring countryside which then separated Greenwich from London, Henry told Norris that he was accused of adultery with the queen – an act of treason punishable by death.

Norris indignantly denied the charge, and protested the innocence of the queen too. With the jousting they had witnessed fresh in his mind, he offered to face the king in a trial by tournament to establish his innocence. Henry dispatched him to the Tower instead. There he was joined by Sir Francis Weston, one of those dubbed a Knight of the Bath at the Tower ceremony honouring Anne's coronation. The party was completed by William Brereton, a wealthy Cheshire landowner, and by the queen's brother, George Boleyn, Lord Rochford, accused of incest with his sister. Although married – his wife Jane would play a dishonourable part in the downfall of Henry's fifth wife, Katherine Howard – Boleyn was said to be both a fornicator and a sodomite, and thus was another easy target for Cromwell's malice. Perhaps Boleyn's biggest crime in the king's eyes, however, was to have heard Anne's complaints about Henry's inadequate performance in bed. Two more gentlemen in Anne's circle, also accused of adultery by Smeaton, Sir Richard Page and the poet Thomas Wyatt, were hauled in for questioning but then released. The four remaining accused stoutly denied the charges but were detained in the Martin Tower in the north-east corner of the fortress's inner ward.

The next day, 2 May 1536, nemesis knocked for Anne. It came in the shape of a four-man delegation from the Privy Council, headed by Cromwell and her own uncle, Thomas Howard, 2nd Duke of Norfolk, as she ate dinner at Greenwich. When she learned of what she was accused from Norfolk's lips, Anne hotly protested her innocence.

She was the king's faithful wife, she said, and only he had touched her body. To Norfolk, a vile crawler who would undergo any abasement to keep his power and privileges, the sacrifice of a close family member was barely a minor embarrassment. Without giving Anne the opportunity to change her clothes, he had her hustled into a barge, which retraced her coronation journey and delivered her to the same Tower that had been the scene of her triumph three short years before.

With dreadful irony, she was received by the same constable who had been her deferential host on that occasion – Sir William Kingston. Then, he had been all smiles, bows and flowery compliments. Now, he was cold, formal and grimly correct. Nervously, Anne asked if she was to be sent to a dungeon, to which Kingston replied, 'No, Madam, to the lodging that you lay in at your coronation.' Detaining Anne in the palace rooms where she had stayed at the height of her glory was itself, of course, an act of psychological cruelty.

Deprived of her usual ladies, and with the closest members of her male coterie also in the Tower, as Anne was escorted under the arch of the Bloody Tower she came close to despair, flinging herself on the ground and calling on God to bear witness to her innocence. She was under round-the-clock surveillance by a quartet of women – including her aunt, Lady Boleyn, and the constable's wife Lady Kingston – under orders to report her most casual remarks. As her dire position sank in, Anne alternated between bouts of weeping and fits of laughter. One remark in her distracted talk, 'Oh, Norris, hast thou betrayed me?', was twisted by Cromwell when reported to him as a confession that she had slept with Norris. More likely, it was in reaction to the lie that Norfolk had told her when she was detained in an effort to unnerve her: that both Norris and Smeaton had confessed their guilt. This was true of Smeaton, but never of Norris, who maintained his and the queen's innocence until the end.

Anne recovered some composure and wrote to her husband from the lodgings of the lieutenant where she was transferred while the palace was made ready for her trial. Her letter, headed, 'From my doleful prison in the Tower', was a dignified plea, not for mercy (she knew Henry well enough to realise that that quality was in short supply) but for justice. Expecting to die, she pleaded with him not to involve wholly innocent men in her ruin. Most of all she was anxious to shield their daughter Elizabeth from his wrath. Anne begged Henry not to let 'that unworthy stain of a disloyal heart towards your good Grace ever cast so foul a blot on me, or on the infant Princess, your daughter'.

Henry, however, could not wait to rid himself of the wife he now hated.

So hasty was the preparation of the indictment against Anne and her co-accused, that of the twenty counts of adultery, she had cast-iron alibis for twelve. Ignoring such inconsistencies, the authorities pressed ahead with the trials with indecent speed. On 12 May, Norris, Weston, Brereton and Smeaton were taken from the Tower to Westminster Hall for their trial. The jury was presided over by none other than Thomas Boleyn, Earl of Wiltshire, the father of Anne and George. This disgusting man was even more eager than the Duke of Norfolk to distance himself from his own flesh and blood. All the accused save Smeaton continued indignantly to deny the charges. Their obvious innocence availed them nothing, and the patently rigged verdicts of 'Guilty' by the hand-picked jury were duly passed. The unfortunate quartet were all condemned to be beheaded on Tower Hill.

Anne and George, thanks to their high status, and also for fear that there would be popular demonstrations of sympathy, were tried within the Tower – in the great hall of the royal palace. The Duke of Norfolk presided, along with twenty-six other peers (the repulsive Thomas Boleyn's eager offer to serve was politely refused). Anne, dressed in a black velvet gown over a kirtle of crimson brocade, a simple cap with a black and white feather on her famous raven-black hair, entered the hall, the eyes of 2,000 spectators upon her. Accompanied by her 'minders' Sir William and Lady Kingston, she was escorted to a chair on a raised dais covered with purple velvet in the middle of the room. She bore herself well under the fearful circumstances, one witness noting, 'She made an entry as though she were going to a great triumph and sat down with elegance.'

Impassively, she listened as Cromwell listed the monstrous charges. In addition to her adultery, she was also supposed to have supplied poison to Norris which had killed her predecessor, Queen Katherine, and was intended to kill Princess Mary and the king's illegitimate son Henry Fitzroy, Duke of Richmond, too. There were no witnesses to this or to the supposed 'adultery'; because neither offence had ever been committed. The only thing she had ever given Norris, said Anne, were a few trinkets from her jewel box. She also owned up to dancing with her own brother, but fiercely denied charges that they had exchanged 'French' kisses. Perhaps the most judicious verdict on this farce was pronounced by an eye witness, London's lord mayor, who as a magistrate had witnessed many trials. He remarked, 'I could not see anything in the proceedings against her, but that they were resolved to make an occasion to get rid of her.'

Despite the lack of evidence, the kangaroo court, whose verdict had been decided in advance – Henry had told Jane Seymour that morning that Anne would be condemned – lost no time in returning a unanimous vote of 'Guilty'. Only Anne's sometime suitor, the Earl of Northumberland, after casting his ballot in line with the other twenty-five judges, was overcome by remorse and collapsed. After he was removed to lie at an open window, the Duke of Norfolk, weeping copious crocodile tears, passed the terrible sentence on his niece: 'Thou hast deserved death and thy judgment is this: That thou shalt be burned here within the Tower of London on the Green, else to have thy head smitten off as the King's pleasure shall be further known.'

As the savage sentence was pronounced, an inhuman shriek split the silence. Mrs Orchard, Anne's childhood nurse, was led wailing from the court. Anne herself retained her icy composure. Calmly she addressed her judges:

> 'I think you know well the reason why you have condemned me to be other than that which led you to this judgment. My only sin against the King has been my jealousy and lack of humility. But I am prepared to die. What I regret most deeply is that men who were innocent and loyal to the king must lose their lives because of me.'

As she was led from the court by the ever attendant Kingstons, her face was deathly pale beneath her now dishevelled hair.

Economically, the same court and jury sat for the trial of George Boleyn which followed immediately. Lord Rochford shared his sister's fiery spirit, and during his initial interrogations had defended himself with such wit and conviction that those who heard him bet each other odds of ten to one that he would be acquitted. They underestimated Henry's vindictiveness. George Boleyn had apparently spread rumours of the increasingly obese Henry's near-impotence with his sister. Reports so sensitive were not referred to in open court, but were written down and shown to the accused before George, too, was condemned to death.

Anne still hoped against hope for a reprieve – according to Kingston offering to enter a nunnery if it would save her. But the only concession Henry made was to commute her sentence to beheading rather than burning, the traditional punishment for a witch. Granting this 'mercy' was probably his intention all along, but it was offered to Anne as an inducement by Thomas Cranmer, Archbishop of Canterbury, when he visited her in the Tower the day after her trial. Cranmer – who sympathised with Anne as a fellow reformer – told her that in exchange for her agreement that her marriage to Henry had been invalid because the king had been the lover of her elder sister Mary, she would be offered the swift death of decapitation. She consented to this diplomatic discretion – thereby giving Cranmer convenient grounds to annul her marriage the next day, without the huge embarrassment of declaring Henry's marriage to Katherine legal after all.

Having agreed to this face-saving deal, Anne was told that she would die four days later, on 19 May – the first ever English queen to be executed. In a mood of fatalistic resignation, the doomed woman – like Smeaton an accomplished player of the lute – put her feelings into a sad song:

> *Oh death rock me asleep*
> *Bring on my quiet rest,*
> *Let pass my very guiltless ghost*
> *Out of my careful breast.*
> *Ring out the doleful knell,*
> *Let its sound my death tell;*
> *For I must die,*
> *There is no remedy,*
> *For now I die.*

So resigned was Anne to her fate that Kingston wrote that his prisoner 'hath much pleasure and joy in death'. In fact, it was not dying that Anne minded, so much as the false accusations she would take to the grave. In a cell elsewhere in the Tower, George Boleyn was also taking leave of the music-making that had been his joy:

> *Farewell my lute, this is the last*
> *Labour that thou and I shall waste,*
> *For ended is that we began,*
> *Now is the song both sung and past,*
> *My lute be still, for I have done.*

The king's chief concern was to dispose of both Boleyns as cleanly and covertly as possible. He wanted to ensure that there would be no public demonstrations, no embarrassing speeches from the scaffold, and no long-drawn-out messy deaths. In keeping with his desire to get things over as discreetly as possible, he commuted George's sentence from hanging to beheading; and confirmed that Anne would be executed by a swordsman weilding a two-handed broadsword, rather than the usual headsman hacking with an axe. Finding no one in the kingdom with the necessary lethal skills, Henry had sent for a French swordsman from St Omer with a reputation for performing quick, clean decapitations. This is further evidence that the queen's trial was rigged in advance, since the swordsman had been summoned to London even before she had appeared in court.

Anne's five alleged lovers were executed together on Tower Hill early on Wednesday 17 May. In a piece of refined cruelty, a reluctant queen was brought to the window of her room in the Lieutenant's Lodgings to see them cross the great courtyard on their way to their deaths. The men were brought from separate cells in the Martin and Beauchamp Towers, and were also watched from his cell in the Bell Tower by Thomas Wyatt, who had only just learned that he was to be reprieved. The poet remembered the moment in doggerel verse when he wrote:

> *The Bell tower showed me such sight*
> *That in my head sticks day and night;*
> *There did I lean out of a grate . . .*

George Boleyn was the first to die. He, like the others, trod a careful course in his last words to the crowd. Had the prisoners publicly denied the charges they would have been stopped from speaking by the watchful attendant sheriff, and their families might have suffered after their deaths. So, without explicitly admitting anything, they accepted that they deserved to die for their general sins rather than for the specific adultery for which they were condemned. Boleyn came closest to displaying his scorn for Henry when he exhorted the watching crowd not to place their 'trust in states and kings but only in God'. He added that he himself had never offended the king, despite the sinful life that he had led. The queen's brother then knelt in the straw around the block, and the executioner severed his head with a single blow.

Norris was next to mount the scaffold, followed by Weston, Brereton and finally the luckless Mark Smeaton. Norris, as he had done when first arrested, spoke up for the queen's innocence – thus, by implication, asserting his own. Weston also admitted he had committed 'abominations' and beseeched the witnesses to learn by his fate.

Brereton bewailed the wretched sinfulness of his life (he had been guilty of extortion from the tenants of his Welsh estates) but hinted that he was guiltless of the sin for which he was dying, by repeating, 'If ye judge, judge the best,' before kneeling at the block. Finally Smeaton, the only one to have admitted adultery, albeit under torture, climbed on to a scaffold by now slippery with the blood of the others. The poor musician merely declared that he was being justly punished for his misdeeds. 'Masters,' he added, 'I pray you all pray for me for I have deserved the death.'

The busy William Kingston hurried back to the Tower, as a cart piled high with the butchered bodies rumbled back for their burial in the churchyard of St Peter ad Vincula. He told Anne to prepare for her death the next day – 18 May. Anne anxiously questioned the constable on what the doomed men had said. She was dismayed that Smeaton had failed to retract his allegation of adultery, expressing the belief that his soul was already being punished in hell for his dishonesty. By contrast, she said, George Boleyn and the others were already with Christ in heaven where she herself soon hoped to appear.

Anne did not get much sleep on what she thought would be her last night on earth. Her mind was full of the ordeal she would have to endure in the morning, a prospect she was unable to forget since the Tower was loud with hammering and sawing as a scaffold was constructed on the green on the north side of the White Tower for the event. (The site of the scaffold at the Tower today outside the Church of St Peter is a nineteenth-century mistake. Recently discovered documents relating to the execution of the Earl of Essex for rebelling against Anne's daughter Elizabeth I confirm that the scaffold was sited between the White Tower and a derelict house of ordnance part of the Tower armoury – today occupied by the Waterloo Barracks.)

During that night, mainly spent on her knees in prayer, Anne received a final visit from Cranmer. The archbishop heard her confession and gave her the Sacraments. Even her sworn enemy, the imperial ambassador Eustace Chapuys, who habitually called her 'the Concubine', was impressed by the cool courage displayed by the queen, and wrote, 'No person ever showed a greater willingness to die.' Chapuys added that he had personally heard from Lady Kingston that 'before and after receiving the Sacrament, [the Concubine] affirmed . . . on the damnation of her soul, that she had never offended with her body against the King'. Since Anne died believing in heaven and hell, this final affirmation of her innocence as she stood on death's threshold weighs heavily in favour of her innocence. It is unlikely that she would have endangered her immortal soul by dying with a lie on her lips.

Anne was to have died at 9 a.m., but the execution was delayed until noon by Cromwell who ordered Kingston to clear the Tower of all unauthorised persons. Anne sent for the constable, now moved to pity by her long-drawn-out ordeal, and complained of the delay. On being assured by Kingston that she would feel only a quick and 'subtle' pain, Anne circled her neck with her hands and laughingly remarked that she had a 'very little neck' and that she hoped the executioner would be as skilled as his reputation suggested. But agonisingly, for reasons unknown, the execution was then delayed yet again – to 9 a.m. the following day, 19 May. Yet another sleepless night followed for the anguished woman. Her mood of gallows humour persisted, for she jested grimly with her attendants that after her death she would be nicknamed 'Queen Anne Lackhead'. She also, via Lady Kingston, sent a message to Princess Mary, begging her forgiveness for any wrongs she had done her and adding that these were the only sins that lay on her conscience.

Two hours before the time appointed for her death, Anne heard a dawn Mass said by her almoner, John Skip, and, after again receiving the Sacrament, managed to get down some breakfast. At 8 a.m. the dread figure of William Kingston, like the Grim Reaper himself, once more darkened her door. With her black hair coiled under a cap, leaving her narrow neck exposed, Anne dressed in a gown of dark damask, with a white collar trimmed with ermine and a scarlet kirtle (a colour traditionally symbolising martyrdom). She sternly encouraged the nervous constable to pull himself together and do his duty, 'for I have been long prepared'. Then, accompanied by Kingston who slipped a purse of £20 into her hand to 'tip' the executioner and distribute alms, and also by John Skip and four unidentified young ladies, all weeping softly, she left the lieutenant's lodging.

According to Sir Francis Bacon, before stepping into the bright spring sunshine Anne murmured to an attendant that she had one last message for the man responsible for her death:

> Commend me to His Majesty and tell him that he hath ever been constant in his career of advancing me. From a private gentlewoman he made me a marchionesss; from a marchioness to a queen; and now he hath left no higher degree of honour, he gives my innocence the crown of martyrdom as a saint in Heaven.

Apocryphal as the story may be – and the terrified attendant would certainly have been too fearful actually to pass the message on to Henry – it has the authentic ring of Anne Boleyn: proud, teasing, defiant and arrogant. She had the last word.

A gasp, speedily hushed, went up from the crowd as the doomed woman appeared. Among those assembled to watch her die were her uncle, the Duke of Norfolk; his son, the Earl of Surrey; and Thomas Cromwell. All three were not to know – though as courtiers in the murderous court of Henry VIII they might well have guessed – that they too would enter the Tower as the king's prisoners before ten years were out. And two of the three would share Anne's fate at the headsman's hands.

It took several minutes for the little procession, watched by 1,000 spectators, and guarded by 200 Yeoman Warders, to cross the courtyard and reach the scaffold steps. Anne distributed alms to the crowd, glancing behind her to ensure that her ladies were still with her. The scaffold was draped in black crêpe and strewn with straw. Among the officials standing on it was the French executioner, who, as a foreigner, was not clad in the black suit and mask of the English state executioner. It was, therefore, not until Anne had climbed the four or five steps on to the low structure that the executioner – speaking French, a language Anne knew well identified himself, and, as was traditional, knelt to beg his victim's forgiveness.

Anne asked Kingston's leave to say a few words to the crowd. In a quiet voice that gathered strength as she spoke, she said:

> Good Christian people, I am come hither to die, according to the law, for by the law I am judged to die, and therefore I will speak nothing against it. But I pray God save the King and send him long to reign over you. For a gentler nor a more merciful prince was there never; and to me he was

ever a good, a gentle and sovereign lord. And if any person will meddle of my cause I require them to judge the best. And thus I take leave of the world and of you all, and I heartily desire you all to pray for me.

With these gentle, dignified, if slightly ambiguous words, Anne removed her headdress and collar, handed them to one of her ladies, and knelt in the straw. Her eyes closed and her lips moved in a final prayer as behind her the executioner picked up the heavy sword in both hands.

To Christ I commend my soul. Jesu accept my soul.

The sword, flashing in the sun, swept through the air. The king's great matter was finally over.

CHAPTER NINE

THE HENRICIAN TERROR

No sooner were Anne's head and body bundled unceremoniously into a narrow chest built to store arrows for the Tower's armoury and carried off to St Peter ad Vincula for burial near the men accused of being her lovers, than Henry married her supplanter, Jane Seymour. But Anne's execution seems to have unleashed dark forces in the king's character which were to cost many more lives in the final, bloody decade of Henry's reign.

Charles Dickens succinctly summed up Henry as 'a blot of blood and grease on the pages of English history' and this seems a fair judgement. Henry had more English people executed than any other monarch. His victims ranged from priests, monks, friars and ordinary folk who resisted his war on the Church to Protestant heretics; from the highest in the land – men as different as More and Cromwell – to his own nearest and once dearest – his second and fifth wives, Anne Boleyn and Katherine Howard. The Tower was often choking with crowds of those imprisoned at the king's whim, and it is from Henry's reign that it first acquired the sinister reputation of jail, torture chamber and scaffold that stickily clings to its walls to this day.

Anne's execution was the watershed marking the transformation of Henry from the admired, learned and powerful Renaissance prince of his early years, to the Henry familiar to us today: gross, obese, cruel, paranoid. Modern medical opinion ascribes the most likely cause of these changes to Henry suffering from a chronic condition – most probably Cushing's syndrome. For centuries it was thought that Henry's irrational rages, his moon-faced features, the unexplained sores and ulcers on his legs and nose, and the onset of his abnormal obesity which saw his chest and abdominal mass balloon to some fifty-three inches, were the result of syphilis. However, the fact that neither his wives nor his children were infected rules this diagnosis out. Cushing's syndrome is the condition that best fits Henry's known symptoms – possibly exacerbated by brain and leg injuries caused by frequent falls while jousting in his youth before his ulcers and weight made this pastime impossible.

Henry's health problems and his diminishing libido became an acute crisis of state during the last decade of his reign, as competing Catholic conservative and radical Protestant factions battled for power – their principle weapons the unfortunate women whom Henry made his queens. After the piously Catholic Katherine of Aragon, the short reign of the reform-minded Anne Boleyn coincided with Henry's dissolution of the monasteries masterminded by Thomas Cromwell. When he perceived that the king's affections had shifted, Cromwell was happy to engineer Anne's downfall to make room for Henry to marry Jane Seymour, an orthodox Catholic.

However, in October 1537, Jane, a fortnight after giving birth to Henry's longed-for male heir, Prince Edward, contracted puerperal sepsis and died. Cromwell, charged with finding a replacement, produced, as wife number four, a Lutheran princesss from the small statelet of Cleves in north-west Germany. Hans Holbein, the German-born court painter, was dispatched to Cleves and returned with a flattering portrait. But the reality, when Anne of Cleves arrived in 1540, did not meet Henry's eager expectations. He may not have called her a 'Flanders mare' but privately poor Anne was called far worse, and Cromwell had his ears boxed for bringing the mismatch about.

Catholic conservatives at court, who had long hated Cromwell for being a base-born upstart, and for having ruthlessly pillaged the houses of religion to fill the king's empty coffers, saw their chance to bring the hated minister down. They dangled yet another young woman before Henry's porcine features as a temptation he would not resist. The chosen victim was eighteen-year-old Katherine Howard, like her cousin Anne Boleyn a niece of the Duke of Norfolk who led the anti-Cromwell faction at court. The times were propitious for the conservatives to strike. Norfolk had recently put down a dangerous religious rising directed against Cromwell's spoilation of the religious houses: the Pilgrimage of Grace.

The Pilgrimage of Grace broke out in Lincolnshire in October 1536, five months after Anne Boleyn's death. The revolt, supported by the ancient aristocratic families who had long held sway in the north – the Percys, the Nevilles, the Dacres and the Darcys – although suppressed in Lincolnshire, spread to Yorkshire, Lancashire and Cumbria. The uprisings were triggered by Cromwell's assault on the monasteries which were the mainstay of the social and economic fabric of northern life. The great Yorkshire abbeys – Fountains, Jervaulx, Rievaulx and Byland – were forcibly closed, along with scores of smaller houses, their clergy turned out and their goods and lands confiscated or sold. Stirred by secret funds and encouragement from the imperial ambassador, Chapuys, the northern peasants, led by their lords and priests, rose under the banner of the five wounds of Christ, demanding Cromwell's head, a return to Rome, a revival of tradition, and the reversal of the Henrician Reformation.

To the Tudors, rebellion was the one unforgivable sin, and Henry was determined to wreak a terrible revenge on the rebels. He was, however, cunning enough to string them along with false promises of pardon until their formidable armies dissolved, and he was able to punish them at leisure. The Pilgrimage of Grace was the most serious threat to the Crown between the Peasants' Revolt and the Civil War of the 1640s. With considerable cunning, Henry put the Duke of Norfolk, a Catholic and a known enemy of Cromwell, in charge of negotiating with the rebels whose army had seized Pontefract Castle, traditional key to the north.

The Tower played its part in the suppression of the revolt, with a fleet of ten warships laden with guns and ammunition from the armoury being sent north in November to reinforce the royal forces. The ships left the Tower's wharf after an attempt to dispatch the ordnance by land under Cromwell's nephew Richard Cromwell had literally bogged down in the autumn mud. Soon afterwards, Marmaduke Neville, the first of the pilgrimage's leaders to be held at the Tower, arrived in the fortress after being arrested trying to spread the revolt into East Anglia. He would not leave it alive. Equally doomed were two members of the powerful Percy family, the Nevilles' old rivals, Sir Ingram and Sir Thomas Percy, who made the mistake of believing the blandishments of Henry and Norfolk, came south voluntarily, and were promptly thrown in the Tower. They would only leave its walls to be executed. Many other leading 'pilgrims' were given 'safe conducts' to London, only to be arrested and sent to the Tower, whose cells were soon bursting with northern rebels.

The pilgrimage's two principal leaders, the honourable one-eyed Yorkshire squire Robert Aske, and Lord Darcy, who had surrendered Pontefract Castle to the rebels before joining their cause, were among the most tragic victims of Henry's bloodlust. Aske, a moderate man who had met the king at Christmas 1536 and been commended for persuading his fellow rebels to disband, suffered for naively trusting Henry's honeyed words. He too was flung in the Tower.

After tasting the Tower's rigours for a month, Aske's spirit began to crack. He wrote pathetically to those who had jailed him:

> I most humbly beseech you all to be good unto me . . . for unless the King's highness and my Lord Privy seal [Cromwell] shall be merciful and gracious unto me I am not able to live, for none of my friends will do nothing for me, and I have need to have a pair of hose, a doublet of fustian, a shirt (for I have but one shirt here) and a pair of shoes. I beseech you heartily that I may know your mind herein and how I shall be ordered that I may trust to the same for the love of God.

Aske's appeal went unheard, and his family – as was normal with prisoners in the Tower – bore the cost of his imprisonment there which, austere though it was, was still set at six shillings and eight pence per week. Aske was eventually hanged in chains from the walls of York Castle, along with hundreds of lesser rebels who were hunted down and suffered similar fates.

Old Lord Tom Darcy's incarceration was easier since as a peer he had privileges denied to commoners like Aske. His Tower expenses were set at twenty shillings a week. Darcy had no doubt who was the chief villain responsible, boldly penning a direct attack on the king's minister:

> Cromwell it is thou that art the very original and chief causer of all this rebellion and mischief, and art likewise causer of the apprehension of us that be noblemen and doe daily earnestly travail to bring us to our end and to strike off our heads, and I trust that or thou die, though thou wouldst procure all the noblemen's heads within the realm to be stricken off, yet there shall one head remain that shall strike off thy head.

Both of Darcy's grim prophecies were fulfilled. His own head was struck off on Tower Hill in June 1537, and spiked on London Bridge. Viciously, Henry denied the old man's last request – to be buried next to his wife – and his body was contemptuously tipped into a common burial pit near the scaffold. In an act of particular spite Henry posthumously stripped Darcy of his Garter knighthood, awarding it to the dead man's mortal enemy Cromwell. But Darcy, as he had foretold, would be avenged: Cromwell's head would soon join his, grinning from London Bridge.

* * *

Buoyed by his triumph over the Pilgrimage of Grace, Norfolk and his Catholic faction felt strong enough to move against the hated Cromwell. It was he and his heretic friends who had caused the rebellion, they whispered to Henry – and destroying him would head off any similar revolts in the future. The king, still irritated by Cromwell having saddled him with his unwanted German bride, was ready to listen. Cromwell attempted to deflect the gathering storm to other victims. The pilgrimage, he argued, had been an attempt to restart the Wars of the Roses, setting north against south, and with the old feudal families who had fought then – the Percys and the Nevilles – again coming out against the Crown. Above all, urged Cromwell, it was high time to exterminate the last descendants of the House of York, for as long as such potential royal rivals lived, the Tudors could never sit securely on their thrones.

The chief target in Cromwell's sights was Reginald Pole, grandson of Edward IV's brother George, Duke of Clarence, and of Warwick the Kingmaker's daughter Isabel. Pole had become a churchman, an ardent opponent of Anne Boleyn and the Protestant reformers. At the height of the marriage crisis he fled to Rome where he became the de facto leader of exiled English Catholics. Created a cardinal, Pole orchestrated foreign Catholic support for the Pilgrimage of Grace, even while his two brothers, Henry and Geoffrey, served with the royal forces. Cromwell employed secret agents in failed attempts to abduct or assassinate him.

In August 1538 the king, prompted by Cromwell, arrested Reginald's younger brother Sir Geoffrey Pole. Geoffrey was flung into one of the Tower's darkest, filthiest and dampest cells and kept there for two demoralising months. Detained in permanent semi-darkness; lonely, cold and hungry; threatened with the rack and repeatedly interrogated by the thuggish William FitzWilliam, Earl of Southampton, one of the king's 'enforcers', it is little wonder that Geoffrey's will weakened. After the first of his seven interrogations, Geoffrey tried to take his own life by stabbing himself in the chest. Mercilessly, the authorities then piled on the pressure by confronting him with his wife, Constance, who, observing that he was approaching breaking point, warned other family members that her husband was about to implicate them in treason. In late October Geoffrey finally cracked, accusing members of his own family and other friends with Yorkist blood of treasonous talk against the Tudors.

As soon as he had the confession, Cromwell acted. He had Geoffrey's brother Henry Pole, Lord Montagu, arrested, along with Henry Courtenay,

Marquess of Exeter, another aristocrat with Yorkist blood. Not content with sending the two Henrys to the Tower, Cromwell locked up their wives and children with them. Montagu and Exeter were tried for high treason and conspiring with the exiled Cardinal Pole, but the only pieces of evidence produced against them were that the former had once compared life in Henrician England to that in a gaol; and that Exeter had condemned 'these knaves which rule about the king' and said that he hoped to live to see 'a merry world one day'. Such words in Henry's England were enough to cost a man his life. The two noblemen were beheaded on Tower Hill on 9 December. Geoffrey, guilt-stricken for betraying his brother, was freed by a contemptuous government to wander, isolated and miserable, until his death.

This effusion of Yorkist blood was not enough to slake Henry's thirst for more. The two dead men's sons, Henry Pole and Edward Courtenay, remained as captives in the Tower where little Henry Pole, distant heir to the Yorkist claim to the throne, literally rotted away. He was so strictly confined and ill-fed that he stopped growing and died a year later. Edward Courtenay survived there for fifteen years until he was released in 1553 by Henry's daughter Queen Mary. That, however, was not destined to be the end of the young man's acquaintence with the Tower.

Even more unforgivable than Henry's cruelty towards these innocent boys was his treatment of young Henry's grandmother, the matriarch of the Pole clan, Margaret Plantagenet, Duchess of Salisbury. This blameless old lady (she was sixty-eight at the time of her hideous death) was the daughter of George, Duke of Clarence – whose bizarre death in the Tower she commemorated by wearing a tiny silver barrel on a bracelet – and the granddaughter of Warwick the Kingmaker. Margaret had been honoured as a fellow royal by Henry in his youth. But when her son Reginald came out against the king's divorce and remarriage, and Margaret herself remained loyal to Queen Katherine and her daughter Mary, Henry turned against her with a vengeance.

Cross-examined at length across two whole days like her son Geoffrey, by the fearsome Earl of Southampton, the canny old woman gave nothing away, stoutly denying that she had had contact with her exiled son. Even after being taken to Cowdray, Southampton's Sussex home, and held there for almost a year she did not talk. In frustrated respect, Southampton reported to Cromwell: 'We may call her a strong and constant man rather than a woman.'

Finally, in the autumn of 1539, the countess made her final journey – from Cowdray to the Tower. Despite her sex, her age, and her royal blood, Margaret and her two female maidservants were sadistically refused any change of clothing. So harsh was her treatment that even her jailer, Thomas Philips, was moved to write to Cromwell protesting against the conditions in which the countess and her gentlewomen were held: '[She] maketh great moan for that she wanteth necessary apparel both for to change and also to keep her warm.' Henry was in no mood for mercy. In 1541, after an attempt to reignite the Pilgrimage of Grace, Henry belatedly decided to visit the disaffected north. Before departing, he issued an order to kill all state prisoners held in the overcrowded Tower – including the aged and ailing Margaret.

The hasty decision to dispose of the last Yorkist having been made, no delays were allowed. The execution order was issued so suddenly that there was no time to summon the official headsman, and the grisly work was left to an amateur. Early in the morning of 27 May 1541, Countess Margaret was roused from sleep and told to prepare for death. After Anne Boleyn, she would be the second royal person to die on Tower Green – within a few yards of where her father Clarence had also died – on a bright spring morning. Margaret walked calmly to the block at 7 a.m. There had been no time to build a scaffold and only a scattering of straw surrounded the spot. Arriving at the site north of the White Tower where Anne had died, the old countess asked the witnesses to pray for the king, queen and royal children, especially the Lady Mary whom she had known as a child.

Before she had finished, she was brutally interrupted and told to lay her head on the block. At that point, Margaret seems to have lost her self-control and tried to run away, shrieking that she was no traitor and did not deserve a traitor's death. The poor old lady was caught and pinioned down on the block. But the young lad drafted in to carry out the execution, understandably unnerved, botched the job. His trembling hands hacked ineffectually with the axe at the screaming woman, reducing her head and neck to a bloody pulp, before death mercifully intervened.

Cromwell himself had not survived to see this horrific shambles. A year before, though newly created Earl of Essex, he had finally fallen victim to Henry's displeasure and his Catholic enemies' hatred. His fall was as sudden as it was final. Arriving at Westminster Palace for a routine meeting of the Privy Council on 10 June 1540, Cromwell, carrying a bundle of state papers, was taking his usual place at the head of the table when he was suddenly interrupted by his arch-enemy, the Duke of Norfolk.

'Cromwell! Do not sit there! That is no place for you! Traitors do not sit among gentlemen!'

Numbly, as though knowing that his days of power would end like this, Cromwell replied in a low voice, 'I am not a traitor.' At that moment, by a prearranged signal, the captain of the guard, Sir Anthony Wingfield, strode into the room with half a dozen burly guardsmen at his back, and seized the minister by his arm, announcing, 'I arrest you.' Cromwell knew this drill: he had presided over the arrest of too many 'traitors' to have any illusions about the fate awaiting him. Nonetheless, he went through the motions of denial, demanding to be allowed to speak to the king. When this was refused, in impotent rage he threw his cap to the floor, teeth grinding and eyes starting from his head in fury. Reading the hatred in the cold eyes of the council, he demanded, 'Is this a just reward for all my services? On your consciences I ask you, am I a traitor?'

Like a pack of hounds long denied their prey, the council turned as one man on Cromwell, spitting suppressed hatred. 'Traitor!' they chorused. Some moved physically to attack the man whose upstart power they had feared for so long. Wingfield, mindful of the strict rule that no blood should be shed in a royal palace (except for the Tower, of course), had the fallen minister hustled away. A boat was waiting to row Cromwell to the Tower.

Courageously, only Thomas Cranmer stood by his fallen friend as others scrambled to distance themselves. The archbishop wrote to Henry praising Cromwell's 'wisdom, diligence, faithfulness and experience'. It was to no avail. Henry was determined to have his faithful servant's blood. Within two hours of Cromwell's arrest, the king sent his thugs to take possession of Cromwell's palatial London residence, Austin Friars, stripping it of gold and silver plate and other treasure worth £15,000 in sixteenth-century values – perhaps as much as £10 million today. The loot went straight into Henry's coffers. On the principle of killing two birds with one stone, property that Cromwell had confiscated during the dissolution of the monasteries – the large Southover Priory at Lewes in Sussex, for example – went to Henry's discarded queen, Anne of Cleves, as her reward for quietly accepting a quickie divorce. Cromwell's scores of servants were paid off with their master's less expensive clothes and other articles.

Meanwhile, in the Tower, Cromwell wrote long grovelling letters to the king protesting his innocence, 'prostrate at your most excellent majesty's feet'. One ended abjectly, 'Written with the most quaking hand and the most sorrowful heart of your most sorrowful subject and most humble servant and prisoner, this Saturday at your [Tower] of London.' Bizarrely, Cromwell forgot to write the dread word 'Tower' (a Freudian slip), as if by omitting the name of the fortress he could somehow avoid the doom there to which he had sent so many. Cromwell's enemies were working hard to relieve him of his head as soon as possible. The parliamentary bill of attainder against the 'most false and corrupt traitor' accused him not only of using his high offices to line his own nest, but also of spreading 'detestable heresy' under the cloak of dissolving the monasteries.

It was not, however, for his corruption, nor for his heresy, that Thomas Cromwell died, but for displeasing the king in that area of Henry's life which always loomed so large: his marriages. The king dispatched three minions to the Tower to extract from Cromwell the last valuable service that he would perform for the master who was about to become his murderer. To secure the dissolution of his marriage to Anne of Cleves, Henry needed written evidence from Cromwell that he, the king, had been displeased with his royal bride from their first meeting, and that he had consequently refrained from having sex with her on his wedding night. Cromwell did as he was bid.

On 30 June he penned another long letter from the Tower setting out in embarrassing detail all the disobliging comments the king had made to him about the 'Flanders mare'. Cromwell wrote in cold legalese, signing off that he was ready to 'take the death' when God and Henry pleased. But a desperate scrawled postscript to the letter tore off the mask, revealing the naked terror beneath: 'Most gracious prince, I cry for mercy, mercy, mercy. Thomas Cromwell.'

Although Henry had Cromwell's plea read to him three times, he remained unmoved. On 9 July Cromwell's testimony that the king had found poor Anne repulsive at first sight helped persuade the country's senior clergy to grant Henry the dissolution of his fourth marriage. Cromwell's death followed swiftly On 28 July, after a hearty breakfast, he emerged blinking into the summer sunshine from the same lieutenant's lodging where Anne Boleyn had been held, to walk the well-trodden path up Tower Hill to the scaffold. He had been stripped of his recently granted Earldom of Essex and as plain commoner 'Master Cromwell' he was denied a private death within the Tower's walls.

Cromwell did not die alone. As an extra humilation he was executed alongside a mentally disturbed peer, Lord Walter Hungerford, sentenced to die for sodomy, for raping his own daughter, and for paying necromancers to predict the king's death. As the two men walked up the hill between hundreds of grim-faced halberdiers, Cromwell tried to calm the deranged peer, who was gibbering with fear. Calmly, the fallen statesman told Hungerford that if he sincerely repented his sins, he would be forgiven through the mercy of Christ. 'Therefore,' he concluded cheerfully, 'though the breakfast we are going to be sharp, yet, trusting in the mercy of the Lord, we shall have a joyful dinner.'

It is not known whether Hungerford took comfort from these words, but Cromwell's fortitude remained steady. Reaching the scaffold, he addressed the crowd, confessing that he was a sinner – but affirming that he died in the Catholic faith, rebutting stories that he was a Lutheran heretic. He attributed his own downfall to his pride, and described the man who had ordered his death as 'one of the best kings in the world', asking people to pray for the king and his son Edward, 'that goodly imp'. Then he knelt in the straw for a last prayer, asking both friends and enemies – his foes Norfolk and Chapuys had come to gloat at his downfall – to pray for him.

Spotting a familiar face in the crowd, Cromwell recognised Sir Thomas Wyatt, a fellow reformer implicated in the fall of Anne Boleyn. Wyatt, though imprisoned in the Tower, had miraculously survived and been released on the intervention of Henry's new love, Katherine Howard. Now the kindly poet was one of the few who wept openly to see Cromwell die. Cromwell told him to dry his eyes. 'Gentle Wyatt, goodbye. Pray for me and do not weep. For, if I were no more guilty than you when they took you I should not be in this pass.' Finally, with a plea to the young executioner to cut his head off with a single stroke, Cromwell submitted to the headsman.

The executioner, a Spaniard named Gurrea – did not oblige. He made a bloody mess of Cromwell's decapitation, hacking and sawing at his head and thick neck amidst the loud protests of the crowd, especially Hungerford who knew he was about to undergo the same butchery. Finally, however, the awful ordeal was over and the heads of Cromwell and Hungerford, parboiled to preserve them, were spiked on London Bridge. Cromwell's body joined that of his victim Anne Boleyn in the chapel of St Peter ad Vincula. That very day, a heartless Henry married his fifth wife: Lady Katherine Howard.

Katherine Howard, for obvious reasons, has often been compared to her cousin and predecessor, Anne Boleyn. But the two women who died at their royal husband's hands, though close relations, were very different. Where Anne had been intelligent, learned, sophisticated, spiteful and well-travelled, Katherine was virtually illiterate, unintellectual, naive, kind-hearted and had never left England. The daughter of Lord Edmund Howard, younger brother of the Duke of Norfolk, she had been born in the early 1520s. Her mother had died early and her education had been neglected.

By puberty, however, it was clear that though small, Katherine had a pretty face and an impishly cheerful, sunny personality. Her ruthless Howard relations cynically brought her to court as bait to catch the monstrous royal fish, and bring Henry under the influence of their family faction. The plan worked only too well. Henry, bloated and old before his time, with his stinking, ulcerated leg, was unlikely to appeal to his spirited, sexy teenage bride. Henry, however, fell for her with senescent, dribbling lust. He called Katherine his 'Rose without a thorn' and showered her with gifts – economically including jewels that had belonged to his dead former wives – without wondering whether the lusty girl could be expected to return the feelings of a rotting hulk of flesh.

In his mood of sentimental adoration, Henry indulged Katherine's requests to free Wyatt from the Tower, and send Margaret of Salisbury the clothes she had pathetically requested to keep her warm in her chilly Tower cell. As a result of Katherine's kindly intervention, the queen's own tailor was ordered to send Margaret furred satin nightgowns and petticoats, a worsted kirtle, four pairs of tights and shoes, and a pair of slippers. But the king's indulgence of his 'rose' would not last long.

Katherine's sexuality had already flowered, and unknown to the king, younger and lustier lovers than he had already had their ways with her. After her mother's death, Katherine had been sent to the household of her grandmother, the Dowager Duchess of Norfolk, in Lambeth, south London. The duchess was often absent at court, and the atmosphere in the house, crowded with fun-loving young people, was morally lax, even licentious.

Katherine's music teacher, Henry Manox, was the first to enjoy her favours. Although full sex may not have occurred, it certainly did with the man who succeeded Manox in her bed – a certain Francis Dereham. Relations with Dereham were brought to a sudden end when Katherine's family brought her to court and trailed her before the king. But once she became queen, reminders of her recent past appeared, and, exercising a form of moral blackmail, demanded positions at court. Manox returned like a bad penny, followed by Dereham himself, who turned up at Pontefract Castle in August 1541 while the king was on a northern progress with his bride.

When Katherine appointed her ex-lover as her private secretary, a puzzled Henry asked why the unqualified youth should receive preferment. Embarrassed, Katherine pretended that she was giving the young man a job as a favour to her grandmother, the dowager duchess. The besotted Henry accepted this lame explanation, but Katherine's cover-up of her past could not last long. While the royal couple were on their leisurely progress, the leader of the Protestant reformers in London, Archbishop Thomas Cranmer, was handed the weapon to destroy Katherine and discredit her family.

Cranmer was approached by a fellow Protestant, John Lascelles, who revealed that his sister, Mary Hall, had information that would incriminate the new queen. Though not a vindictive man, Cranmer was aware that unless he moved against the Howards, his own position as the realm's leading Protestant reformer would be in severe danger and he might well follow his friend Cromwell to the block. Mary Hall, another former member of the jolly Lambeth household, told Cranmer the details of Katherine's dalliances with Manox and Dereham, claiming she had taken Dereham to her bed more than a hundred times. The girls at Lambeth shared a dormitory, and Katherine's friends were left in little doubt about what had gone on after Dereham, dressed only in doublet and hose, had climbed between her sheets. Cranmer set out the allegations in a letter to Henry just as the king and Katherine arrived back at Hampton Court Palace after their northern progress.

Ironically, Henry was attending a special service of thanksgiving for his happy union with Katherine in the palace's Chapel Royal when Cranmer dropped his bombshell. The archbishop quietly left his letter beside the king and glided out without a word. Henry's first reaction – horrified disbelief – was rapidly replaced by a determination to establish the truth. Summoning Cranmer, a humiliated Henry ordered his friend to dig out the whole dirty story and 'not to desist until he had got to the bottom of the [chamber] pot'. Meanwhile, Katherine was placed under house arrest in her apartments. He would never set eyes on his 'rose' again. Their marriage had lasted for just fourteen months.

During her progress, with naivety amounting to stupidity, Katherine had compounded her innocent teenage dalliances (before she had met Henry) with actual adultery. Her partner was Thomas Culpeper, a distant cousin on her mother Joyce Culpeper's side. Culpeper had been one of the many hopefuls who had flocked to the new queen's court jockeying for the favour of the foolish girl. Young Thomas became a particular favourite of the king, but he too was arrested. Unlike Katherine, he, along with Manox and Dereham, went straight into the Tower.

Katherine was dancing with her ladies when a group of grim-faced guards burst in to tell her that 'the time for dancing was over'. The distraught queen raced along the corridor to the door of the Chapel Royal, screaming desperately. Remorselessly, she was caught and dragged back whence she had come. (Her shrieking ghost is said to haunt the corridor to this day.) She would neither eat nor drink, nor sleep, and spent hours helplessly weeping. Her only companion was hardly encouraging. Jane Boleyn, Lady Rochford, her Lady of the Bedchamber, was the widow of the ill-fated George Boleyn, brother of Queen Anne Boleyn. Jane's evidence at her husband's trial for incest with his sister had helped put both Boleyns' heads on the block. Now, her foolish conniving at her mistress's adultery would send both her and Katherine to the scaffold. Knowing the peril they were in, the two women repeatedly threw themselves into each other's arms, sobbing with despair and fear.

Jane Rochford had acted as Katherine's go-between with Culpeper, running messages between them, ensuring that the coast was clear before their clandestine adulterous meetings, and smuggling the queen's lover in and out of her apartments. All this was revealed as Cranmer doggedly pursued his inquiries. By 6 November he reported to the Privy Council, presided over by Henry, that Katherine had indeed enjoyed premarital sex with Manox and Dereham. Moreover, added the archbishop, he believed that worse revelations were to come. 'She betrayed you in thought,' he told Henry ominously, 'and if she had an opportunity would have betrayed you in deed.' At this, self-pity overwhelmed Henry. He wept openly in front of his embarrassed councillors. Then hiding his shame, the cuckolded king took refuge in his secluded palace at Oatlands, near Weybridge, bidding Cranmer continue his investigation. For the first time, the archbishop confronted Katherine directly. He found the queen 'in such lamentation and heaviness as I never saw no creature'. So distressed was Katherine, often screaming in panic, that Cranmer was unable to get any sense out of her at first. Eventually, after seeing a letter from Henry in which he promised to show mercy so long as she made a full confession, she calmed down somewhat.

Katherine was persuaded to pen a confession to Henry in which, excusing herself because of 'my youth, my ignorance, my frailness', she admitted having allowed Manox to 'touch the secret parts of my body'. Dereham 'by many persuasions procured me to his vicious purpose' and 'used me in such sort as a man doth his wife, many and sundry times'. The confession might have saved Katherine's life since it only admitted to sexual misconduct before her marriage. Fatally, however, it made no mention of Culpeper. On 11 November, while the king considered how best to punish her 'abominable behaviour', Katherine, stripped of the finery and jewels her doting husband had lavished on her, left Hampton Court by river for Syon Park further downstream at Brentford. She was separated from Lady Rochford whose barge was bound for a more sinister destination further downstream: the Tower.

It was to the Tower – and its rigorous interrogation methods – that Cranmer looked to find the evidence to condemn Katherine and her family faction which posed such a deadly threat to him personally and the future of reformed religion. The first to be questioned there by experienced interrogations from the Privy Council led by Sir Henry Wriothesley was Katherine's earliest suitor, Henry Manox. While admitting touching her private parts, Manox strenuously denied having had full sex with Katherine, whose affections, he alleged, had been transferred to Dereham.

The council homed in on Lady Rochford – newly arrived at the Tower – as the queen's abetter in her adultery with Culpeper. Their suspicions were confirmed by the discovery among Culpeper's papers of a damning letter which the queen had stupidly sent her swain, and which Culpeper had failed to destroy. The letter confessed that 'it maketh my heart die . . . that I cannot always be in your company', and concluded, 'Yours as long as life endures. Katherine.'

When Lady Rochford herself was summoned before the council, she tried to save her skin by throwing all the blame on Katherine. Jane Rochford readily admitted her mistress's adultery with Culpeper, and further confessed that she had kept guard during their illicit trysts. Culpeper himself was next. He candidly confessed that he had fallen in love with the queen, and had striven hard to overcome his cousin's resistance to his amorous advances. Although – knowing the dire penalties – he denied adultery, it was obvious that more than sweet nothings had passed between them.

The council now had enough evidence for a charge of adultery with Culpeper to be brought against the queen. All they needed for the case to be closed was Katherine's own confession. Cranmer and Wriothesley journeyed upriver to Syon to confront her. But the distraught Katherine desperately persisted in her denials. Nonetheless, the council considered their case watertight enough to tell Henry that his thornless rose had pricked him most intimately. Katherine was stripped of the title of Queen on 22 November. Her ruthless family, desperate to distance themselves from the wreckage, had already abandoned her. The Duke of Norfolk declared that he wished to see his niece burned.

The queen's downfall made waves that would drown the Howards. Norfolk's mother, the Dowager Duchess of Norfolk, was held responsible for the lax regime at her Lambeth house which had allowed Katherine's dalliances with Manox and Dereham. Despite feigning illness, the duchess was arrested and ferried to the Tower. Here, in the chilly dankness of late November, she fell genuinely ill and was in bed when interrogated by the council's investigators.

The council threw the book at Culpeper and Dereham. They were accused of treason and, together with Katherine – described as a 'common harlot' – of having led 'an abominable, base, carnal, voluptuous and licentious life'. Culpeper was charged with having had 'criminal intercourse' with the ex-queen after her marriage; and Jane Rochford with abetting the affair. Dereham was charged with becoming Katherine's secretary in order to continue their illicit liaision, and concealing his unofficial engagement to Katherine so that she could marry the king. After a trial presided over by the Duke of Norfolk, both Culpeper and Dereham were condemned and sentenced to be hanged, drawn and quartered at Tyburn.

But the law wasn't finished with Dereham yet. Because he continued to proclaim his innocence (while Culpeper changed his plea to 'Guilty' during the trial) and because he was not, unlike Culpeper, of noble blood, the Tower's rougher methods were brought to bear. On 6 December, Dereham, doubtless trembling with terror, was brought into the torture chambers in the cellars beneath the White Tower and shown the instruments for inflicting indescribable pain. Then, under the personal supervision of the sadistic Solicitor General, Richard Rich – the same man who had tricked Thomas More into making his fatal confession – the torture began. We do not know exactly which methods were employed to loosen Dereham's tongue. We do know that 'the Breaks', a crude but effective dental device for breaking teeth, were employed on a friend of his, William Damport, in a bid to get him to implicate Dereham, so he may have suffered the Breaks too. One source suggests that his fingernails were torn out with tongs. Or – most excruciating of all – he may have suffered the rack. Rich, as we know from the well-documented case of the Protestant martyr Anne Askew, did not scruple to operate the rack himself, and if he used it on Dereham, the young man's resistance would have been short.

The torment achieved its purpose: a full confession was wrung from the wretched youth. He admitted canvassing the possibility of Henry's early death with Katherine; agreed that he and everyone else at Lambeth had regarded them as betrothed; and wrote that they had regularly enjoyed sex, 'kissing and hanging by their bellies like a pair of sparrows'. Another, and far less pleasurable, form of hanging now awaited Dereham. On 10 December he and Culpeper paid the agonising penalty for their forbidden pleasures. Drawn to Tyburn from the Tower, Culpeper, as a nobleman, was granted the swift end of decapitation. Dereham's already tortured body suffered the additional agony of hanging, emasculation and disembowelment.

Katherine herself lingered on for a few more weeks while Parliament passed an act of attainder against her and Lady Rochford. The teenage queen, reported to be 'plumper and prettier than ever', now seemed resigned to her fate; Katherine requested only that she should die swiftly and in private. The king was happy to oblige. Although the rest of the Howard clan – including the old dowager duchess – were stripped of their cash and property, they were spared death and eventually released from the Tower. The ignoble, grovelling Duke of

Norfolk himself – as a special humiliation – was sent to Syon to inform his niece that the king had mercifully granted her request, and that she would die in the Tower, in the same way and place as her cousin Anne Boleyn.

On Friday 10 February the lords of the Privy Council went to Syon to conduct Katherine to the Tower. Facing the dreadful reality of her imminent fate, the girl's courage failed. She had to be dragged and hustled to the three waiting boats. Accompanied by four ladies who would attend her in the Tower and by four burly oarsmen, and dressed in a black velvet gown against the river's wintry chill, the ex-queen, travelling in the middle boat of the little convoy, passed under London Bridge. Mercifully, since her barge was enclosed, she was spared the sight of her lovers' heads decomposing on the spikes above her.

Sir John Gage, who had recently replaced Sir William Kingston as constable of the Tower, was waiting at Traitor's Gate to meet Katherine and escort her to her rooms in the Lieutenant's Lodgings – the same lodgings where her cousin Anne had stayed prior to her execution. Gage was perturbed by his young charge's condition, reporting to the council that she 'wept, cried and tormented herself miserably and without ceasing'. At least Katherine was spared the weeks of waiting in the Tower that her cousin had endured – she only spent a weekend in the fortress, since her execution was fixed for Monday 13 February.

Katherine passed much of that weekend in prayer. She made her last confession to John Longland, Bishop of Lincoln, regretting her youthful follies but swearing that she had not abused her sovereign lord's bed. On the Sunday night, Katherine made a strange request to Gage. She asked that the execution block be brought to her chamber so that she could practise placing her neck across it in readiness for the morning's ordeal. Gage had the gruesome object taken to Katherine's room for the grim dress rehearsal.

Monday morning dawned dank and misty. It was an early start for the members of the Privy Council who had been summoned as official witnesses to the execution. They arrived by river and, dressed in fur-lined gowns against the cold, took their places on the wooden benches surrounding the black-draped scaffold to the north of the White Tower. It was the same structure on which Anne Boleyn had died, as if Henry had left it standing with the knowledge that he would kill another queen there some day. A group of more humble spectators, with connections to the condemned woman, were allowed in through the Tower's landward entrance to see the spectacle. One of these, a confectioner named Otwell Johnson, who had supplied dainties and sweetmeats to the queen, left us the only eye-witness account of the proceedings, in a letter written soon afterwards to his brother.

At 7 a.m., Gage rapped on the door of Katherine's chamber. The victim was ready to be offered up. Dressed in black velvet, with a cloak covering her gown, Katherine and her ladies were led down to the Inner Ward and around the corner of the White Tower to the scaffold. The spectators were not as numerous as the crowd which had seen Anne Boleyn die, and watched in silence as the tiny figure mounted the scaffold and tipped the masked headsman who knelt to ask her forgiveness. Katherine's speech from the scaffold, as noted by Johnson, was equally traditional. She had finally mastered her fears and met death with dignity.

In Johnson's account, there is no mention of the legend that Katherine said that she died a queen, but would rather have died 'the wife of Thomas Culpeper'. Instead, he said, she made a conventional affirmation that her death was a just punishment for her 'heinous offences' against God and the king. She concluded by asking people to pray for Henry – and for herself – before allowing her ladies to bandage her eyes and shut out the light for the last time. She knelt in the straw and laid her head on the block as she had practised the night before. The executioner severed her neck with a single stroke, holding it up by her auburn hair with the cry, 'Behold the head of a traitor!'

As Katherine's head and body were bundled up in a black shroud by her weeping ladies, ready to be taken away for burial next to her cousin Anne in St Peter's chapel, Lady Rochford was brought to the scaffold in her turn. When Katherine's blood was sluiced away with buckets of water, and fresh straw strewn, the grim ritual was repeated for the woman who had helped condemn her. Jane Rochford too admitted her offences and declared her death to be just and merited. She too exhorted her audience to treat her death as an awful example and amend their own sins. She too knelt in the damp straw and received her death in a single stroke. Otwell Johnson was mightily impressed by the grace shown by the two women in death. 'Their souls are with God,' he told his brother. 'For they made the most Godly and Christian end that ever was heard tell of (I think) since the world's creation.'

One of those who had watched Katherine Howard's end – as he had observed that of his other cousin, Anne Boleyn – was the Duke of Norfolk's son and heir, Henry Howard, Earl of Surrey. He was the great white hope of his ambitious, grasping family. Dashing, daring, good-looking, impetuous – a man who combined love of the arts with the talents of a warrior – Surrey was a gifted poet who reputedly introduced the sonnet form from the Italian into English verse. A crony and drinking buddy of his fellow poet Sir Thomas Wyatt, Surrey shared the driving ambition that was his dynasty's defining characteristic. Unlike his despicable father, however, he lacked the sycophantic skills necessary to survive in Henry's murderous court. And his recklessness would finally bring the old duke to the Tower – and himself to the scaffold.

The downfall of Katherine Howard dealt a severe blow to the Howard family's hopes of controlling the king and the succession. It had not, however, utterly destroyed them. The final years of Henry's reign were dominated by the see-saw struggle between the radical Protestants and conservative Catholics, led politically by Norfolk, and theologically by Stephen Gardiner, the hard-line Bishop of Winchester, a cleric with a nose like a buzzard's beak, and a penchant for burning heretics whenever he could smell them out.

The Protestants, under the guidance of the deceptively mild-mannered Thomas Cranmer, Archbishop of Canterbury, included a cluster of thrusting new men who, while not particularly devout themselves, were happy to ride the wave of the Reformation to propel themselves into power. The reformers included the uncles of Henry's heir, Prince Edward, brothers of the late queen, Jane Seymour: Edward Seymour, Earl of Hertford, and his even more ambitious younger brother Thomas Seymour. Allied with the Seymours was John Dudley, Lord Lisle, son of Edmund Dudley, the grasping finance minister whose execution had been one of the first acts of Henry's reign; and the king's fixer, Sir Anthony Denny, a secretary of state who controlled access to the monarch.

The balance of power on the council between Catholic conservatives and Protestant reformers was held by men like Thomas Wriothesley and Richard Rich – ambitious, time-serving opportunists, who while officially orthodox Catholics, were happy to swing with whichever wind was blowing, so long as it kept them in wealth and power. Unlike Norfolk, Surrey, the Seymours and Dudley, these men's visits to the Tower were confined to their official duties as interrogators and torturers, and they both died in their beds and kept their heads.

The two rival factions waged a constant proxy war on each other by making martyrs out of the fervent followers of their faiths from lower social stations. Their hope was that these humble folk would implicate their co-religionists in more influential positions. The Tower was thus often crowded with prisoners whose only crime was too loud a proclamation of their faith, or those who had stubbornly clung to doctrines that had passed out of favour. During the king's divorce from Katherine of Aragon, the dissolution of the monasteries, and the Pilgrimage of Grace, the full weight of official persecution had fallen heaviest on Catholic monks, friars and priests. After the fall of Cromwell, it was Protestant heretics who suffered torture and death – often the agonising deaths of burning at the stake. And even after the execution of Katherine Howard and the decline of her family, it took the death of the king and the advent of his staunchly Protestant young son, Edward VI, before the wind shifted definitely towards reform once more.

Though he had displaced the Pope as head of the Church and dissolved the religious houses, Henry remained a doctrinal conservative. Even after the reformers on the council, taking a leaf from the Howards' book, had succeeded in engineering Henry's sixth marriage in 1543 – to one of their number, Thomas Seymour's mistress, a Cumbrian widow named Catherine Parr – Protestants continued to be persecuted, although the kindly Catherine did what she could to ameliorate their suffering. One martyr she was unable to save was a fellow north country gentlewoman, Anne Askew.

Askew, a feisty young woman in her early twenties, was a sixteenth-century proto-feminist, who had embraced Protestant doctrines and been thrown out of her Lincolnshire home by her husband, Thomas Kyme, for her hot gospelling. Coming to London, she had drawn unwelcome attention by her Protestant preaching. In the chauvinist eyes of the Church, to quote Samuel Johnson, witnessing a woman preacher was like seeing a dog walking on its hind legs. 'It is not done well, but you are surprised to see it done at all.' Being a Protestant was bad enough, but being a young and beautiful woman preacher was a near obscene sacrilege.

Askew was repeatedly arrested, sent back to her husband, and, when she returned to London, put in the Tower on charges of heresy. Specifically, she had denied the 'Real Presence' – the Catholic dogma that the consecrated wafers and wine consumed during Mass miraculously constituted the actual body and blood of Christ. Anne held that 'God made man, but that man can make God I never yet read'. Hearing rumours that this bold Protestant had contacts with the court circle surrounding the new queen, the council's Catholics resolved to extract such incriminating information from Anne by force. In this way, they could bring down their reforming rivals along with their royal patron. They decided to do what had never been done before – to torture a woman in the Tower.

The dirty work was entrusted to the kingdom's highest-ranking legal officials, the Lord Chancellor, Sir Thomas Wriothesley, and his sidekick, the Solicitor General, Sir Richard Rich, assisted by the Chancellor of the Exchequer, Sir John Baker. Anne, in the brief interval between her torture and her barbaric execution, was able to write and smuggle out of the Tower her own vivid testimony of Tudor torture. Brought from her cell to the gloomy cellars beneath the White Tower on 29 June 1546, she was confronted by her high-ranking inquisitors, who bombarded her with questions about her links with Queen Catherine's court – including comforts she had received in the Tower from the wives of the leading council reformers, Sir Anthony Denny and Edward Seymour, Earl of Hertford.

Frustrated by her non-committal answers, Wriothesley and Rich sent for the Tower's lieutenant, Sir Anthony Knyvett, who was normally responsible for operating the rack on recalcitrant captives. Pointing out that it was unheard of to torture a woman, a distinctly unhappy Knyvett was overawed by his superiors, and ordered Anne – dressed only in a skimpy shift – to be roped to the fearful torture machine. Knyvett told his torturers to go easy on their victim, inflicting 'just a pinch' as a taster of the terrible torments that the rack could deliver. When this mild introduction failed to persuade Anne to be more forthcoming, Wriothesley and Rich ordered Knyvett to use the rack to its fullest extent. The lieutenant refused.

At that, the two officials shouldered the sweating torturers aside, and throwing off their expensive gowns, flung themselves on the machine's cranks. The rack's rollers revolved, and its creaking ropes tautened, lifting Anne's straining body from the wooden frame of the machine into the air, as her limbs were agonisingly drawn from their sockets. Her desperate screams rent the room, penetrating the White Tower's ancient walls and the muffling earth itself, until she was heard by Lady Knyvett and her daughter, who were strolling in the Tower's garden. Anne's mind must have been a red mist of pain as her muscles tore and her sinews cracked, but still the questions kept coming.

She wrote a few days later, 'Because I confessed no ladies and gentle-women to be of my opinion, they kept me [on the rack] a long time. And because I lay still and did not cry [again] my Lord Chancellor [Wriothesley] and Master Rich took pains to rack me with their own hands till I was nigh dead.' We cannot exclude the strong possibility that Wriothesley and Rich were exceeding their usual official duties because they obtained sexual satisfaction in sadistically torturing a near naked and attractive young woman. At any rate, it was at this point that Knyvett protested again and insisted that the torment be halted.

The ropes relaxed, Anne was untied, and collapsed, fainting, on the cold floor. They threw a bucket of water over her and then Wriothesley stretched himself beside her and for two hours grilled her, in her words, 'with many flattering words, persuading me to leave my opinion. But my Lord God gave me grace to persevere and will do – I hope – to the very end.' That end was not long in coming. A fortnight after her ordeal, Anne was carried – the rack had left her unable to walk – to Smithfield, the traditional site for the incineration of heretics. Here she was placed astride a stool chained to the stake and faggots were piled around her. As a last gesture of mercy before the fire was lit, her executioners hung a small bag of gunpowder around her neck, which exploded and killed her as the flames licked around her. Burned alongside Anne was John Lascelles, the Protestant who had first brought news of Katherine Howard's adultery to Archbishop Cranmer. The Howards were taking a belated revenge.

The torture and burning of Anne Askew was more than the elimination of an uppity heretic woman. It was part of a Catholic conspiracy aimed at destroying the queen herself and ending the hold of the reformers on the now clearly moribund Henry. In early July 1546, between Anne's torture session in the Tower and her execution at Smithfield, Henry was persuaded to sign a warrant for the arrest of his sixth wife. Terrified, and only too mindful of the fates of Anne Boleyn and Katherine Howard before her, Catherine threw herself on Henry's mercy and played the role of what she called 'a poor silly woman' unable to form judgements on matters of religion and eager to defer in this, as in all things, to her husband. Somewhat lamely, she suggested that she had only discussed her Protestant opinions with Henry as a way of distracting his attention from his mounting maladies.

Magnanimously, Henry forgave the queen, but forgot to tell Wriothesley – who had been tasked with arresting Catherine and escorting her to the Tower – of his change of heart. The next night the king was sitting with the soothing woman he called 'Sweet Kate' when the Lord Chancellor entered with forty halberdiers and tramped menacingly towards the queen, whose heart must have leapt in fear.

Enraged, Henry heaved his great bulk from the throne and boxed the hapless official's ears, calling him a 'knave and fool'. Sent on his way, Wriothesley's humiliation marked the moment when the tide turned against the Catholic faction.

Deftly, the reformers Anthony Denny and John Dudley had eased themselves into key positions on the council and managed to exclude Bishop Gardiner from court altogether – Dudley even cuffing the cleric in the face as a mark of his contempt. Then it was the turn of the Howards. The family's weakest link was not the old Duke of Norfolk – who over a lifetime of grovelling had honed his survival skills to a fine art – but his impetuous son, the Earl of Surrey.

This troubled and troublesome young man had got into hot water a number of times. He was a notorious drunken brawler: a noble yob as well as a social snob. His rowdy exploits included duelling and a drunken binge in which he and his fellow poet Sir Thomas Wyatt had fired pebbles from crossbows, breaking the windows of respectable London citizens and disrupting the trade of prostitutes touting for business in London's red-light district of Southwark. Such behaviour had landed Surrey in prison more than once, but his contrition, often expressed in verse, had soon got him out again. He was a particular favourite of the king, who called him a 'foolish, proud boy'. Surrey's luck had held – until now.

His violent ways had, however, made a mortal enemy of one of the men who now dominated the council – Edward Seymour, Earl of Hertford. The feud had started when Surrey had struck Seymour in the face for suggesting that this scion of a traditionalist Catholic family sympathised with the Pilgrimage of Grace rebellion. Surrey had found himself in the Fleet prison, and although soon out again, he and Seymour remained at daggers drawn.

The rivalry came to a head in December 1546 in the final crisis of Henry's reign. Knowing that the monarch was dying, the Seymours played on the king's fears surrounding the succession and his precious Tudor line. They suggested that the Howards wanted to place the robust young Surrey on the throne in place of Henry's son, the sickly Prince Edward. As evidence of this intention, they whispered, Surrey – who was indeed descended from royalty via both his parents – had had a coat of arms drawn up in which King Edward the Confessor's arms had been quartered with his own. This little piece of heraldic snobbery would now be Surrey's death warrant.

Surrey was discreetly arrested by Sir Anthony Wingfield, the same captain of the guard who had carried out the detention of Cromwell. Knowing of Surrey's violent temper, Wingfield tricked him. Pretending that he had a request for Surrey to relay to his father, the Duke of Norfolk, Wingfield led the earl to a quiet corridor in the Palace of Westminster where a dozen burly halberdiers pounced and bundled him into a boat. After initial interrogation at Ely Place, Wriothesley's house in Holborn, Surrey was taken to the Tower on Sunday 12 December. As he was led through the gawping crowds, his father, the Duke of Norfolk, joined him. Stripped of the Order of the Garter and his badge of office, the white staff of the Lord Treasurer, the seventy-three-year-old duke was almost apoplectic with indignation to find himself in the dread place where he had sent so many others. Sychophantically he told anyone who would listen that he was the king's most loyal subject.

Such 'loyalty' cut no ice with the monstrous king when the succession of his dearly conceived son was at stake. His first act on getting the Howards safely in the Tower was to strip their estates. Commissioners were sent on a dawn raid to the Howard lands in East Anglia where anything transportable – tapestries, clothing, gold and silver plate – was catalogued, strapped into chests and heaved onto carts for transfer to the royal coffers. Even the duke's mistress, Elizabeth Holland, was stripped of gold buttons, pearl necklaces and the very rings from her fingers, before being interrogated on any treasonable pillow talk that the duke had indulged in.

At the Tower, once lodged in Constable Sir John Gage's chambers, Norfolk put quill to paper and penned a grovelling appeal to his master. Protesting that a 'great enemy' must have been telling lies about him, Norfolk demonstrated his usual crawling ignominy. He offered to dump his faith if that would save his skin, telling Henry, 'I shall stick to whatever laws you make' and claiming that he would rather shed twenty lives than give the Pope 'any power in this realm'.

In a stream of letters to the king and council, Norfolk plumbed the very dregs of degradation as he listed those unfortunates who he had hounded to their deaths – not least members of his own family – as proof of his own limitless loyalty. Over at St Thomas's Tower, where Surrey was being held, the young poet adopted a more literary style of protest, writing verse letters inveighing against the false friends who had landed him in his plight:

> It was a friendly foe, by shadow of good will
> Mine old . . . dear friend, my guide that trapped me;
> Where I was wont to fetch the cure of all my care,
> And in his bosom hide my secret zeal to God.

As aristocrats, the Howards had an easier time in the Tower than most state prisoners. The accounts of the lieutenant, Sir Anthony Knyvett, give a glimpse of the luxuries available to the VIP prisoners. They record that Norfolk spent the vast sum of £210 (almost £60,000 today) on comforts – including coal and candles – for himself and his attendants during the first two months of his detention. Surrey slept on a feather bed with two pillows, a pair of fustian blankets and a quilt. Five fine tapestries were hung on his cell walls to keep out the river's clammy chill, and a coal fire was kept constantly blazing. When not penning pretty verses to his friends, the young poet passed his time in writing free translations of the Psalms, a suitably spiritual endeavour for a man about to make the journey into eternity.

Surrey's mind was not yet entirely fixed on the hereafter, however. As the gravity of his situation dawned on him, he made a desperate attempt to escape. He was aided by his manservant, Martin, one of two attendants he was allowed in the Tower. Martin smuggled a dagger in to his master, hidden in his breeches. He was instructed to descend to nearby St Katherine's dock, hire a boat and await his earl, who hoped to be with him by midnight. Surrey had carefully observed his chambers, which had been refurbished for the coronation of Anne Boleyn – when the latest mod con, a latrine, had been installed.

Surrey had noted that the waste shaft running down from the privy emptied directly into the river beneath – except at low tide. After dark, it would, he worked out, be possible for a thin man such as himself to squeeze into this evil-smelling exit, clamber down inside it, drop unseen into the soft sludge below, rejoin Martin and sail away to freedom. He would use the dagger, if necessary, to kill the two warders posted to keep an eye on him.

When the long winter evening drew in, the earl put his plan into action. He complained of feeling ill, and said he would turn in for an early night. The guards reassured him that they would not disturb him before midnight. Doubtless relieved of being spared the need to kill them, Surrey later crept from his bed and checked that the river was low. Shortly before midnight, he removed the latrine lid and saw that there was only about two feet of water at the bottom of the shaft. He scrambled in and began to climb down the slippery, smelly tube.

But he had left it just a little too late. At that moment, the guards returned and saw at once that his bed was empty. Storming into the closet, one warder reached down and grabbed the earl by the arm, hauling him back into the room. The other guard shouted for help, and more warders ran to their aid, restrained the struggling Surrey, and shackled his feet with manacles. Outside the Tower, hearing the hue and cry, Martin made himself scarce – along with the money that his master had given him to hire the boat.

On 13 January, a cold winter's day, Surrey, elegantly dressed in a satin cloak trimmed with rabbit's fur lent him by the compassionate Knyvett, was led from the Tower to the Guildhall for his trial. The day before, his treacherous father had put the cherry on the cake of his son's fate by signing a confession of high treason that implicated Surrey in the quartering of the royal arms. Since there was no argument that Surrey had commissioned the arms in question, and since the king had pronounced this to be treason, the duke's confession was tantamount to signing his own son's death warrant, and there was little for the jury to argue over. Yet when the inevitable 'Guilty' verdict was returned, and an axe's blade was turned towards Surrey, the proud earl could not resist one last, indignant outburst. 'Of what have you found me guilty?' he demanded. 'Surely you will find no law that justifies you, but I know the king wants to get rid of the noble blood around him and to employ none but low people.'

Despite this public outburst, so typical of Surrey's fiercely snobbish but fearless spirit, Henry rescinded the savage sentence of hanging, drawing and quartering at Tyburn, and substituted decapitation on Tower Hill. A week after his trial Surrey was led from his cell and climbed the slope to the scaffold. Among the papers left in his cell was a poem of stoic resignation, coupled with an irrepressible cry of rage against the 'wretches' who had laid him low. It began:

> These storms are past, these clouds are over blown
> And humble cheer great rigour hath repressed;
> For the default is set a pain foreknown,
> And patience graft in a determined breast.

And ended:

> But when my glass presented unto me
> The cureless wound that bleedeth day and night
> To think alas such hap [luck] should granted be
> Unto a wretch that hath no heart to fight
> To spill that blood that hath so oft been shed
> For Britain's sake, alas, and now is dead.

A week after Surrey's execution, on 27 January, the act of attainder against his father passed, clearing the way for Norfolk to follow his son to the block. It only needed the king to sign for the headsman's axe to fall. But it never did, for at two o'clock on the frosty morning of 28 January King Henry himself drew his last breath. Thomas Cranmer, perhaps the closest this monster of selfishness could come to calling a friend, had been summoned to offer the king his last spiritual solace. Meanwhile, Sir Anthony Denny and the other reformers, eager to get their hands on the levers of power, impatiently paced the gallery outside the death chamber. The archbishop, called from his home in Lambeth Palace in the middle of the night, hastened across the river to Whitehall Palace and found the dying king beyond speech. When Cranmer asked him if he died in grace, he pressed his hand. So passed England's Stalin, a murderous monster who had raised his kingdom to great power status in Europe, but at the cost of despoiling its cultural heritage in the religious houses, and the needless sacrifice of a river of innocent blood.

CHAPTER TEN

TUDOR CHILDREN

Spared from death by his murderous master's demise, the Duke of Norfolk nevertheless remained incarcerated in the Tower for six more years – though in more comfortable circumstances than most of his fellow 'guests'. The despicable old rogue thus survived the reign of the fiercely Protestant Edward VI while the boy king and his ministers instituted a thorough-going religious Reformation which overturned the ancient Catholic rituals that Norfolk and his cohorts had striven to uphold.

The Edwardian Reformation was more drastic than anything seen between his father Henry's break with Rome and Cromwell's Puritan Commonwealth. This Calvinist purge saw the abolition of the Latin Mass, which was replaced by Holy Communion in the English tongue; Cranmer's Book of Common Prayer, a masterpiece of limpid English prose, was made compulsory; elaborate altars, rood-screens, stained glass and other regalia were replaced by plain walls, tables and glass. The Tower itself did not escape this hurricane of change: the priests at both St John's Chapel and St Peter ad Vincula were replaced by Protestant chaplains.

King Edward was no stranger to the Tower. He had known the fortress literally from the cradle. The cannons installed there by his father had roared 2,000 shots to celebrate his birth, and as a child he had often visited the fortress when its palace was being expensively refurbished. Henry VIII's contribution to the Tower's military architecture had been the construction of mounts to support his heavy artillery: Legge's Mount at the Tower's north-west corner, and Brass Mount at its north-east. Many of the Tower's cannons had actually been made there, and the Royal Ordnance Factory, housed close to the Royal Mint, meant that the west and northern parts of the fortress were a busy industrial plant – with billowing clouds of smoke and steam, the deafening clang of metal, and sizzling shards of hot flying iron.

Henry's addition to the Tower's civil architecture was a tidying up of the higgledy-piggledy medieval building work. He reroofed the chapel of St Peter ad Vincula after a fire early in his reign. Today's chestnut-wood roof is Henry's work, along with the chapel's elegant arches and windows. Henry certainly ensured that his two wives and the various ministers executed by his command had a fine resting place. As the great nineteenth-century historian Thomas Babington Macaulay wrote of St Peter's:

> There is no sadder spot on earth . . . Death is there associated, not as in Westminster Abbey and St Paul's, with genius and virtue . . . but with whatever is darkest in human nature and human destiny, with the savage triumph of implacable enemies, with the inconstancy, the ingratitude, the cowardice of friends, with all the miseries of former greatness and of blighted fame.

The typically Tudor black and white half-timbered houses seen to the left of the Bloody Tower as visitors pass into the Tower's Inner Ward, were also built by Henry and were used to provide comfortable modern lodgings for the lieutenant and for his highest-ranking prisoners. Increasingly, it was to such small, easily heated wood-panelled rooms that the Tower's resident inhabitants were drawn and the great echoing halls of the palace – despite Henry's refurbishments – gradually fell into disuse and decay, to be finally demolished a century later by Oliver Cromwell and Charles II.

So it was to a gleaming and spruced-up Tower that ten-year-old King Edward VI rode on the last day of January 1547, three days after his fearsome father's death. Beside him rode his uncle Edward Seymour, Earl of Hertford, his presence a visible sign that he was the real power in the land. They were met at the Lion Gate by Constable Gage and Archbishop Cranmer. The boy king and his retinue were escorted to the Tower's palace, its walls 'richly hung and garnished with cloth of Arras and cloth of Estate'. The great halls were so crowded with jostling courtiers, all jockeying for power and influence in the new regime, that the Tower's limited accommodation overflowed and many were forced to seek lodgings elsewhere.

King and court remained in the Tower for a fortnight while

preparations were made for Henry's funeral at Windsor – he had asked to lie next to Edward's mother, Jane Seymour – and the coronation. Behind the scenes, frantic politicking was in progress. Edward Seymour assumed the title of Protector – in effect regent – during his nephew's minority, and his fellow council members needed to be cajoled, and if necessary bribed or threatened, to agree. To grease the wheels, a wholesale award of peerages was announced coinciding with the coronation. Seymour himself became Duke of Somerset; his future rival John Dudley was named Earl of Warwick, while Thomas Wriothesley became Earl of Southampton. Peerages went too to Wriothesley's fellow Tower torturer, Sir Richard Rich, and to Edward Seymour's younger brother Sir Thomas who also became Lord High Admiral. Thomas Seymour, after an indecent interval of barely a couple of months, married Henry VIII's very merry widow, Catherine Parr, who had been his mistress when Henry's greedy eyes had first fallen upon her.

On 19 February, in the traditional pre-coronation ceremony, Edward created forty new Knights of the Bath at the Tower. The next day, resplendent in white velvet, and dripping with diamonds, rubies and pearls, the boy king rode out on a white horse caparisoned in crimson satin and beaded with pearls to meet his people. Their cheers of delight were doubtless tinged with relief that the reign of his grim old father was finally over. The elaborate coronation was shortened and adapted to a monarch of Edward's tender years, and special acts, like an acrobat sliding down a cable from the steeple of St Paul's Cathedral, were laid on to amuse him. Even so, the fragile thin boy appeared understandably fatigued – and his pale and wan features betrayed the early presence of the tuberculosis that would kill him.

Somerset and his fellow reformers were well aware that their lives hung on the frail thread of Edward's failing health. The succession was a problem. Under Henry VIII's will, the crown would pass, in the event of the boy's death, to his elder half-sister, Princess Mary, the staunchly Catholic daughter of Katharine of Aragon; and then, if Mary died childless, to his other half-sister, the moderately Protestant Lady Elizabeth, daughter of Anne Boleyn. Edward, a pious and highly learned boy, had embraced extreme evangelical Protestantism with all the fervour of youth. So long as he lived, the Reformation sweeping through the kingdom would continue. But how long would that be?

Somerset's position as protector was undermined by the reckless behaviour of his younger brother, Thomas Seymour. Wild and ambitious, Thomas had demanded the guardianship of the young king as the price for supporting his brother as Protector. Bought off instead with a peerage and the Admiralty, he still attempted to gain access to Edward as often as he could. His insensate ambition even extended to wanting to marry one of the royal princesses, Mary or Elizabeth – he did not much mind which. His wife, the dowager Queen Catherine Parr, was Elizabeth's guardian, and by marrying her before Henry's corpse was cold, Seymour was in constant close proximity to the pubertal princess. Catherine herself seems to have been so bedazzled by Seymour's glamour that she was blind to his intrigues.

Elizabeth was not the only royal child in Catherine's household. As Seymour and the quickly pregnant Catherine Parr started to enjoy married life, he became the guardian of Lady Jane Grey, eleven-year-old eldest daughter of Henry Grey, Duke of Suffolk, and his Duchess, Frances – the daughter of Henry VIII's younger sister Mary. Fatally for Jane's future, royal blood ran thickly in her veins since she was also descended from Queen Elizabeth Woodville by her first husband, Sir John Grey, and her second, Edward IV.

Like her second cousin Elizabeth, Jane from her earliest years was a formidable scholar, perhaps the most learned child in Europe. Partly to escape her cruelly neglectful parents, Jane sought solace in her books. Like King Edward, she was a fervent Protestant who could best any Catholic priest in theological argument. During his wife's pregnancy, however, it was not to the pious and decidedly blue-stockinged Jane that bold Thomas Seymour laid siege – but to the lively redhead Elizabeth, at fourteen a nubile and far from shy teenager. A bare-legged Seymour would steal into Elizabeth's room in their Chelsea town house for games of slap and tickle so lively that it was difficult to tell where boisterous horseplay ended and erotic foreplay began. Amidst Elizabeth's shrieks and blushes Seymour would strip off the bedclothes, exposing her half-naked body. These were dangerous games indeed, and he would pay dearly for them.

Thomas Seymour's relations with his elder brother were anything but fraternal. With the resentment often felt by a younger brother for his elder sibling, the younger Seymour deeply resented his brother's power, and control over the king. At first, Somerset tolerated his brother's outrageous behaviour. Gradually, however, as Seymour increased his influence over

Edward by telling him that the protector was keeping him short of cash and making him 'a beggarly king', and even supplying the boy with regular pocket money himself, Somerset's irritation turned to alarm.

That alarm became downright panic when, in August 1548, Catherine Parr gave birth to a girl, Mary – and within a week was dead from puerperal fever. The bereaved Seymour was now free to further his political career by marital intrigues. He toyed again with marrying Princess Elizabeth, who had grown so infatuated with him that a jealous Catherine had had her transferred from her household. Alternatively, Seymour meditated marrying his ward Jane Grey to his nephew King Edward. Finally, however, it was Seymour's own insane impetuosity which brought him down.

Seymour attempted to get physical possession of a monarch he feared was being deliberately kept out of his reach. Early on the morning of 16 January 1549, with two servants at his side and a pistol in his hand, he broke into Edward's privy garden at Westminster and attempted to gain access to the king's bedroom itself. As he struggled with the key, Edward's pet spaniel bit him, and an enraged Seymour shot the dog dead. The commotion alerted the royal guard who rushed in shouting, 'Murder!' Fortunately, the only murder victim was the faithful hound, and Seymour – feebly protesting that he had merely been testing the efficiency of royal security – was hustled away to the Tower.

Seymour's moment of madness brought his house of cards down about his ears. As his attempted abduction was investigated, gossip about his familiarity with Princess Elizabeth spread. The princess herself was questioned, and her maid Kat Ashley was hauled into the Tower for more rigorous interrogation. Under the pressure, Mistress Ashley made a full confession, testifying that Seymour had seen Elizabeth near naked; that he had slapped her buttocks, and that the couple had been caught embracing by the late Queen Catherine. It was more than enough to condemn Seymour, who was accused of thirty-three charges, including treason.

Because Seymour was the king's uncle and had been the husband of a queen, the entire Privy Council waited on him at the Tower to read the charge sheet. True to his proud and arrogant nature, Seymour refused to answer them. A bill of attainder with an automatic death sentence was hastily drawn up and signed – in a shaky hand – by his brother, the Protector. As he waited for death Seymour himself put pen to paper. Like his equally proud predecessor, the Earl of Surrey, he turned to poetry to express his last thoughts:

> *Forgetting God to love a King*
> *Hath been my rod, or else nothing*
> *In this frail life, being a blast*
> *Of care and strife till it be past;*
> *Yet God did call me in my pride*
> *Lest I should fall and from him slide*
> *For whom he loves he must correct*
> *That they may be of his elect.*
> *Then death hast thee, thou shalt me gain*
> *Immortality with Him to reign.*
> *Lord! Send the King in years as Noye*
> *In governing this realm in joy*
> *And after this frail life such grace*
> *That in thy bliss he may find place.*

Deprived of writing materials, Seymour ingeniously devised his own means of communicating. Fashioning a pen from metal buttons and wires pulled from his own tunic, he manufactured a secret ink 'so craftily and with such workmanship as the like hath not been seen'. He used these to write two letters – to the Princesses Mary and Elizabeth – urging them to overthrow their brother and liberate him. He sewed the letters into the soles of his velvet slippers, ordering his servants to deliver them. But the slipper missives were discovered and read by the council – and with that the last possibility of reprieve vanished. Elizabeth herself lost no time in distancing herself from the man who had been her first love. Told of his execution she coldly but accurately remarked, 'This day died a man of much wit and very little judgement.'

Seymour was beheaded on Tower Hill on 19 March. Few details survive of his last moments, but according to the later Protestant martyr Bishop Hugh Latimer, he died 'dangerously, irksomely, horribly'. The preacher added that he was a man 'furthest from the fear of God that ever I knew or heard of in England'. Latimer's testimony is suspect, however, for at the time he uttered it, he was in the pay of Somerset, who had ordered him to blacken his brother's reputation to deflect attention from his own growing unpopularity. Despite separating himself from his unruly sibling, however, Somerset fulfilled the prophecy being whispered in the streets, that 'the fall of one brother would be the overthrow of the other'. Within a few years, Edward Seymour would be treading in his brother's footsteps along the melancholy path from the Tower to the scaffold.

Somerset's fall was brought about by a combination of economic and religious discontent, and the machinations of a man, John Dudley, who proved a more ruthless operator than he in the worst Tudor tradition. 1549 became a year of revolt as the kingdom's woes came to a violent head. Somerset was ill-placed to deal with the crisis as his reputation had been fatally undermined by his brother's fate. Damned by family association with such a man, Somerset was also damned by his part in his brother's death, with one woman telling him to his face that Thomas's blood 'cried against thee unto God from the very ground'.

The religious Reformation had got out of hand, with liberty becoming licence. Ordinary folk were confused and offended by the sudden ending of ancient traditions – candles being withdrawn from the festival of Candlemas, for instance – and with the introduction of Cranmer's unfamiliar English Book of Common Prayer. Their bewilderment was exacerbated by landlords racking up rents to cope with rampant inflation, and enclosing land which had been common for centuries. Instead of taking a firm line with the discontent, Somerset let things drift.

In the summer of 1549 the pressure cooker exploded. A Whit Sunday protest against Cranmer's new prayer book in the Devonshire village of Sampford Courtenay became a fully fledged rebellion that crackled across Devon and Cornwall like a raging brush fire. Two officials sent to enforce the government's new religious edicts were murdered by mobs, and encouraged by their priests, a rebel army besieged and seized Exeter. Ominously, the rebels adopted as their emblem the five wounds of Christ – the same symbol used by the Pilgrimage of Grace in Henry VIII's reign.

While Somerset dithered, the council sent an armed force to confront the rebels, but by the time they arrived in the West Country, a fresh revolt – centred on economic, rather than religious, grievances – had broken out in East Anglia. Peasant labourers tore down the fences that local landowners had thrown up to enclose their estates, preventing the landless poor from grazing their animals or growing crops. One of the landowners targeted, Robert Kett, unexpectedly joined the protesters and swiftly became the revolt's leader. Kett planted himself under an oak on Mousehold

Heath outside Norwich, the second largest city in England, and laid down the law as his followers tore down enclosures across the county.

The two rebellions threatened a pincer movement on London from east and west. The Privy Council unanimously blamed the Protector for the unrest. Although Somerset attempted to crack down on both outbreaks, he would not be forgiven by his fellow grandees for his radical reforms and weakness in countenancing a revolt that looked alarmingly like an egalitarian social revolution. In the late summer, Lord Russell, commander of the government forces, retook Exeter and in three pitched battles, finally smashed the prayer book rebellion. More than 3,000 rebels died, and hundreds more were executed in subsequent reprisals.

Simultaneously, Kett's rebellion was also snuffed out. The Privy Council's hard man, John Dudley, Earl of Warwick, rode to Norfolk with a large army, stiffened by seasoned Swiss mercenaries. A battle took place in Norwich and on Mousehold Heath, which destroyed Kett's untrained peasant army. Dudley allowed most of Kett's followers to return to their hovels. A few ringleaders, however, were hanged from Kett's oak tree, and Kett himself and his brother William were taken to the Tower. There they were tried and sentenced to death before being carted back to Norwich for the ghastly final act: like Robert Aske, leader of the Pilgrimage of Grace, both suffered the slow torture of being hanged in chains.

The twin revolts spelled the death of Somerset, too. Within a few weeks he was deposed by John Dudley, whose prompt response to rebellion had contrasted so painfully with Somerset's dithering. Recent research, however, has revealed suspicious links between Kett's revolt and Dudley, the man who apparently quashed it so firmly. One of Dudley's Privy Council cronies, Sir Richard Southwell, was channelling government cash intended for the suppression of the rebellion to the rebels themselves. Moreover, Southwell visited Kett during his brief incarceration in the Tower, and was himself later confined to the Tower for financial malpractice. Finally, in his will, Southwell left £40 to Kett's son, who was in his service. It seems possible, if not likely, that Dudley, using Southwell as his go-between, was manipulating the rebellion to discredit and dispose of his rival Somerset. His involvement may also explain his relative leniency to the rebels.

In October 1549, Dudley gathered the majority of the council in London and secured the Tower against an attempt to take it by Somerset, who was holding the king at Windsor Castle. ('Methinks this is a prison,' the astute boy told his uncle.) As his support drained away, Somerset was reduced to pathetically begging his former colleagues to spare his life. Arrested at Windsor by the ubiquitous Sir Anthony Wingfield, captain of the guard, he was taken to the Tower. The king, who was fond of his Protestant uncle, was informed that he was ill. The deception, however, would not last long.

The few Catholics on the council, led by Thomas Wriothesley, Earl of Southampton, thought that the duke's downfall meant that the Reformation would be stopped in its tracks. When, however, at young King Edward's insistence, Dudley gave orders for the reforms to proceed at full steam – with bonfires being made of Catholic relics in marketplaces across the country – the Catholics decided that he was as bad as Somerset and must suffer the same fate. Wriothesley went to the Tower in December to interrogate the former Protector, hoping that he would incriminate Dudley, taking with him his fellow councillors the Earl of Arundel and William Paulet.

Somerset told his interrogators that if he was guilty of treason, then so was Dudley. This was music to Wriothesley's ears. On their way out of the Tower he told his companions, 'I thought ever we should find them [Somerset and Dudley] traitors both, and both worthy to die on my advice.' Arundel agreed that Dudley should join Somerset in the Tower. But Paulet wisely kept his counsel. He went straight to Dudley and warned him of Wriothesley's plot. At the next council meeting, held in Dudley's house in Holborn as the earl was either ill or feigning sickness, Wriothesley demanded that Somerset be executed for his 'many treasons'. Knowing that his was the next name on Wriothesley's little list, Dudley sprang out of his bed 'with a warlike visage', laid his hand on his sword, and snarled at Wriothesley, 'My lord, you seek his blood and he that seeketh his blood would have mine also.' Dudley summoned the guard and had Wriothesley confined to his nearby house. His co-conspirator Arundel was also placed under house arrest, and deprived of office. Sore and seeking revenge, he became an embittered enemy of Dudley. For Wriothesley, losing office was a death sentence. He died – possibly by suicide – in July 1550.

Having secured supremacy in the council, Dudley dished out the usual round of peerages and posts to reward supporters. Paulet, who had revealed Wriothesley's plot, became the Earl of Wiltshire; Russell, who had vanquished the prayer book rebellion, became Earl of Bedford; while Northampton – who had been less successful at putting down Kett's rebellion – became Lord Great Chamberlain. Sir Anthony Wingfield at last reaped a reward for all the high-profile arrests he had carried out as captain of the guard, being promoted to Comptroller. Somerset's secretary, Sir Thomas Smith, who was sharing his master's imprisonment in the Tower, made a cynical comment in verse on Dudley's honours list.

> *This day made new Duke, Marquis or Baron*
> *Yet may the axe stand near the door*
> *Every thing is not ended as it is begun*
> *God will have the stroke, either after or before.*

King Edward pressed for his uncle's release from the Tower. This accorded with Dudley's plans, since he saw the humbled ex-protector as a useful firewall to deflect criticism from his own policies. In early February 1550 Somerset was bailed for the hefty sum of £10,000 and formally pardoned – though he was kept under house arrest at Syon Park for the time being. Somerset did not stay out in the cold for long. In April he was received by the king and dined with his supplanter Dudley, and the following month he was taken back on the council, his misrule seemingly forgiven if not forgotten.

Somerset's brief spell in the Tower appeared to have made him a humbler and wiser man. He had read improving Protestant tracts finding therein 'great comfort . . . which hath much relieved the grief of our mind'. At first the reconciliation between the former friends seemed permanent. The seal was set on their amity by the wedding, in June 1550, between Somerset's daughter Anne and Dudley's son Lord Lisle – though it was noted that Somerset was not present to give his daughter away.

But Somerset could not resist returning to politicking for position and power. His tactics were to seek a reconciliation with his old Catholic enemies. He visited the ultra-Catholic Bishop Stephen Gardiner in the Tower, seeking his agreement to recognise Cranmer's prayer book. Tired of the Tower, the hard-line Gardiner, somewhat surprisingly, agreed. But when told of Gardiner's submission Dudley insisted that he make a full confession of his errors, and returned with Somerset to the Tower to hear them. An indignant

Gardiner refused, declaring he would rather take a dip in the polluted sewer that was the Thames, and stayed inside.

In early October 1551, exactly two years after Somerset's first fall from grace, a defector from his camp, Sir Thomas Palmer, told Dudley that Somerset was planning to ignite a popular revolt against his rule. The 'Good Duke' had always enjoyed great popularity among the common people, and Dudley found Palmer's tale both credible and convenient. Among those named by Palmer as plotters was Sir Miles Partridge, who was to raise the city of London apprentices, using them to seize and hold the Tower. As in an efficient modern police state, Somerset and his followers were rounded up in a single morning. The 'Good Duke' himself was the first to be arrested at Westminster. Along with two of his sons, he was taken back to the Tower. By the end of the week a dozen of the duke's closest associates – including his beautiful but unpopular second wife, Anne Stanhope, and the Earl of Arundel – had joined him there.

Although noblemen like Somerset and Arundel were spared torture, the council authorised its use on lesser conspirators. After some were locked in a room at the Tower without food or water, confessions soon spilled out. Somerset was personally interrogated by Dudley. On the basis of the evidence extracted, Somerset was accused of attempting to abduct Dudley and seize the Tower, together with 'the treasure, jewels and munitions of war therein contained'; and of inciting rebellion among the common people. He was rowed upriver from the Tower at 5 a.m. to Westminster Hall for the trial, for fear that his popularity might lead to a rescue attempt. Shouts of 'God save the Duke!' from the crowds milling outside penetrated the hall and may have influenced the jury, which, astonishingly for a state trial, cleared Somerset of treason. He was, however, convicted of attending unauthorised assemblies.

The mixed verdict caused confusion among Somerset's supporters. Most assumed that he had been completely cleared and lustily cheered his expected release. To pacify them, Dudley promised to pardon the duke, telling him, 'I will do my best that your life may be spared.' Dudley's duplicity in pretending to pardon the 'Good Duke' while privately contriving his death weighed heavily on his conscience. Two years later, facing his own execution, he admitted that 'fraudulently procuring . . . [Somerset's] unjust death' was the sin for which he was most sorry.

The demonstrations in Somerset's favour had unnerved Dudley. Again, he visited his rival in the Tower, apparently undecided as to whether to execute or spare him again. Christmas passed with the country in frozen suspension as to its political future. Finally, Dudley resolved to execute Somerset before demands for his reprieve overwhelmed him. One factor in his decision was the resolution of King Edward himself. The boy had been persuaded by the evidence that his uncle was a traitor and commanded that 'the law take its course', signing the duke's death warrant without a qualm. Historians have often portrayed Edward as a helpless puppet of Dudley, but the reverse seems to have been the case. The young king was determined to rule in his own right. He was prepared to go against his entire council to get his way. Now he ordered the execution of his own, once beloved, uncle without turning a hair. Edward was, after all, a true Tudor.

On the evening of 21 January a royal messenger brought Somerset in the Tower the letter from Edward that he had been dreading. It notified him that his nephew had agreed to his execution the following morning. Somerset took the news philosophically. Reaching for the book of devotions he had been keeping in the Tower he wrote calmly:

> *Fear of the Lord is the beginning of wisdom.*
> *Put thy trust in the Lord with all thine heart.*
> *Be not wise in thine own conceit, but fear the*
> *Lord and flee from evil.*
>
> *From the tower, the day before my death. E. Somerset.*

Around eight o'clock the following day, Somerset paced the melancholy path up Tower Hill in his brother's footsteps. Hoping to fool the duke's many friends, Dudley had announced that the execution would take place at noon, but the ploy failed: an enormous crowd lined the route, many murmuring their sympathy as the 'Good Duke' made his final journey. Reaching the scaffold, Somerset knelt and raised his hands in prayer. Facing east towards the rising sun he addressed the crowd. He said that he accepted his death and thanked God that he had been granted time to prepare for it. He affirmed that he did not regret the religious reforms that he had pushed through, and wished them to be pushed further still as the alternative to a 'worse plague'.

At that point a single loud thunderclap split the silence, leaving Somerset dumbfounded and the crowd amazed. Some hurled themselves into the

Tower's moat in fear. Many thought it an act of God to prevent the execution. Somerset silenced the murmuring crowd, asking them to pray for the king. When they responded with cries and whispers, he begged the people to be silent lest they disturb his final moments on earth. He then read out his confession from a scroll, shook hands with the witnesses on the scaffold, tipped the executioner who gently removed his gown and ruff, and without more ado knelt at the block. His head was severed by a single stroke, at which a great groan of disapproval went up from the crowd, many darting forward to soak their kerchiefs in the 'Good Duke's' spurting blood.

Edward coolly recorded the event in his journal: 'The Duke of Somerset had his head cut off on Tower Hill between eight and nine o'clock this morning.'

Like Macbeth after Duncan's death, having achieved supreme power by reluctantly eliminating the man who stood in his path, Dudley began to feel that he was 'stepped in blood so far that returning were as tedious as go o'er'. Somerset's eldest son John died in the Tower of unknown causes, but the smaller fry of the conspiracy survived to be beheaded and hanged a month after their master. Noted for his unusual leniency earlier in his career, now that he had the power, Dudley began to exhibit all the hallmarks of a tyrant. Even light-hearted comments about the regime were visited by savage penalties such as ear cropping. Other malefactors had their ears nailed to the pillory. Elizabeth Huggons, a servant of Somerset, was sent to the Tower for commenting that Dudley deserved to die more than the late duke. Depression and ill health – including stomach ulcers, a sure sign of stress – plagued Dudley, who talked openly of desiring death.

He was not the only one to fall sick. As the New Year of 1553 opened, King Edward took to his bed with an ominously persistent cough. The illness could not be shaken away, and by May the king was coughing up blood and mucus. The tuberculosis bacillae, triggered by an attack of measles the previous April, were firmly lodged in the king's lungs and he was clearly dying. Realising that he could not recover, Edward's thoughts – and those of his Privy Council – turned to the succession.

Edward's bigoted Protestantism revolted at the thought of his equally bigoted Catholic half-sister Mary succeeding him and undoing the Reformation. And although his younger half-sister Elizabeth, who was next in line after Mary, was a Protestant, she was also a daughter of the condemned 'concubine' Anne Boleyn, and therefore a bastard. Edward decided to exclude both his half-sisters from the succession. Writing in the bedchamber of Greenwich Palace that had become his sickroom, Edward drew up a 'Device for the succession'. Disinheriting his siblings, this document declared that the succession would pass down the line started by Henry VIII's youngest sister, Mary, to her daughter Frances, and then to her firmly Protestant daughters Jane, Catherine and Mary Grey, and thence to their male heirs.

The king deciding this was one thing; persuading the Privy Council and Parliament to enact it was quite another. John Dudley, Duke of Northumberland, was naturally the strongest supporter of the scheme since, as the chief driving force behind the continuing Protestant Reformation, he would have everything to lose if Mary inherited the crown. Jane Grey, a slip of a girl, might, he thought, be easier to manipulate than the tough-minded Edward. To ensure that the kingdom stayed in his hands, Dudley hastily arranged for his youngest surviving son, Lord Guildford Dudley, a handsome seventeen-year-old, to marry Lady Jane.

To make assurance doubly sure, Northumberland also arranged for the son of one of his closest allies, Lord Herbert, Earl of Pembroke, to marry Jane's younger sister Catherine Grey. At first Edward hoped to live long enough to see Lady Jane produce a son, but, with his stomach and feet swelling, he realised his time was fast running out. He therefore altered the 'Device' to give Jane herself the crown. For Edward, nothing was more important than keeping Catholicism and Princess Mary at bay. Although desperately sick, he browbeat his reluctant council into allowing Jane to be his heir. Naturally, in a male world, the blissfully ignorant Jane herself was not told that she was about to become queen.

By July, it was clear that the king was about to die. His fingernails and hair were falling out and his extremities were turning gangrenous. Although they had Jane under their control in Chelsea, the council failed to lay hands on the rival claimant, Princess Mary, who was living at Hunsdon near Ware, just twenty miles from London. The Duke of Northumberland fatally underestimated Mary, who, another true Tudor, was determined to claim the crown when her half-brother died. This long-expected event occurred on the evening of 9 July at Greenwich.

Immediately, Jane was moved to Syon Park on the river, where Northumberland and the council's other leading lords attended her the next day, knelt before her, broke the shattering news that the king had died – and named her as his heiress. Flabbergasted, Jane protested that Mary was the rightful queen. When the councillors insisted that Edward had excluded Mary and that it was her dynastic and religious duty to take the crown, Jane reacted with a storm of weeping. Her parents, the Duke and Duchess of Suffolk, having failed to pacify her, her new husband, Lord Guildford Dudley, was brought in who, with 'prayers and caresses', managed to calm his bride. Bullied and cajoled by her parents, the government and her husband, Jane eventually agreed to accept the unwanted crown. The following day, 11 July, as heralds proclaimed her accession to a muted reception in London, Jane was rowed downriver to the Tower. The fortress would become in rapid succession her palace, her prison, her scaffold – and her tomb.

Dressed in a white headdress and a green velvet gown embroidered with gold, with wide sleeves and a train borne by her mother, Jane landed at the Tower's steps and ceremoniously entered under the Byward Tower. She was a tiny creature who disguised her small stature by wearing 'stilts' (built-up cork heels) beneath her dress. Beside her walked the tall and attentive figure of her young husband, resplendent in white and silver. A pretty girl with auburn hair, hazel eyes, dark eyebrows, freckles, red lips and sparkling teeth, Jane was no one's fool, and was as regal and insistent on her dignity as a queen – or 'Jane the Quene' as she signed herself as she had been stubborn in refusing the job at first. She too was a true Tudor.

Conducted to the great hall of the old royal palace, Jane was seated on the throne amidst much ceremony. Among the precious stones and treasures brought out of the Tower's jewel house by the Lord Treasurer, the Marquess of Winchester (formerly William Paulet, the man who had betrayed Wriothesley's plot to Dudley), was the crown itself. Taken aback, Jane declined to try it on, but her indignation turned to fury when Winchester told her that another one would be made for her husband 'King Guildford'. Jane declared that she might make her husband a duke, but never a king. Tudor women disliked sharing power with anyone.

Faced with her obduracy, Guildford did what any petulant adolescent might do: he fetched his mother. The Duchess of Northumberland scolded Jane like a schoolgirl, and when the queen remained defiant, declared that her son would not sleep with her and ordered him to return to Syon. Again, Jane put her tiny foot down. She summoned the Earls of Arundel and Pembroke and commanded them to stop her husband from leaving the Tower. His place, she said, was at her side. A sulky Guildford obeyed his wife rather than his mother and stayed. He would not leave the Tower alive. The ancient fortress, as so often, for the next fortnight became the fulcrum of power where the nation's future governance was decided.

While the new queen was unexpectedly asserting her new authority inside the Tower, outside its walls the people were displaying a very different reaction. The reading of the accession proclamation had received a decidedly cool reception. Gilbert Potter, landlord of a London tavern, grumbled that 'the lady Mary hath the better title' when he heard it read at Cheapside, and was hauled away to have his ears chopped off 'to the root' for his temerity. Meanwhile, Northumberland had belatedly sent two of his sons, John and Robert Dudley, in search of Mary. With a posse of 300 horsemen, the Dudley brothers arrived at Hunsdon, only to find their bird had flown. Mary had secretly received word that Edward was dying from a sympathetic spy at the deathbed – probably the Earl of Arundel – and had fled into East Anglia, where the Dudley name was still reviled for the crushing of Kett's rebellion in 1549.

Reaching Kenninghall, at the heart of the Catholic Howard estates, Mary sent a messenger, Thomas Hungate, to the council at the Tower, with a letter proudly asserting her claim to the crown and her right to rule. It was 'strange', she added acidly, that the council had not seen fit to inform her of her brother's demise, but now that he was dead, she expected their loyal support. In a classic case of shooting a messenger, the elderly Hungate was contemptuously told by Northumberland that at his age he should have known better than to bring such insolent tidings – and flung into a dungeon.

It was dawning on the duke that Mary was a dangerous – indeed deadly – obstacle to his plans. His duchess, with a woman's intuition of disaster, reacted to Hungate's message by bursting into tears. Nonetheless, the council sent back a robust reply to Mary, signed by all twenty-three members, indignantly denying her claims, and calling on her to cease her 'vexation' and be 'quiet and obedient'. At the same time, the council took the menace posed by Mary seriously enough to issue a propagandist proclamation in Jane's name reminding the people that Mary was merely a 'bastard daughter to our great uncle Henry the eighth of famous memory'.

Meeting in almost continuous session, the council also took the decision to send an armed force into East Anglia and bring the vexatious Lady Mary back to the Tower where she could be safely kept under lock and key. The Duke of Suffolk, Jane's father, was selected for the task, but behind the scenes his wife – a close friend of Mary – was hedging her bets, ostensibly backing her daughter Jane, whilst trying to keep channels open to Mary. As a result of his wife's entreaties Suffolk declined the task, pleading ill health, and it devolved upon Northumberland himself, with his experience of quelling a previous East Anglian revolt.

Northumberland was reluctant to go. He felt his safest place was in the Tower beside the throne. There was no telling what the council would get up to behind his back. But since no one else seemed willing, he had no alternative. 'Well, since ye think it good, I and mine will go,' he told them, eyeing his fellow councillors suspiciously. 'Not doubting of your fidelity to the Queen's majesty, which I leave in your custody.' Before leaving, he demanded that each member of the council reaffirm their loyalty to Queen Jane. Apparently reassured, he murmured, 'Pray God it be so. Let us go into dinner.' After the meal, he left London with some 600 horsemen and 2,000 foot soldiers, backed up by brass cannons supplied from the Tower's armoury. He noted gloomily as they rode north through the city that though crowds assembled to watch them go, none had wished them 'God-speed'.

On Saturday 14 July Northumberland's force reached Cambridge, having rendezvoused with his sons John and Robert, and stopped en route to burn Swanston Hall, where Mary had stayed while flying from Hunsdon to Kenninghall. Meanwhile, Mary herself had not been idle. Seemingly spontaneously, men had flooded in from across East Anglia in her support, so that Kenninghall proved too small to hold them all. On the 13th she moved to Framlingham in Suffolk, the region's largest castle. All over the country reports came in of towns refusing the council's order to proclaim Queen Jane – and declaring for Mary instead.

In the Tower, the departure of Northumberland, the power behind Jane's shaky throne, had given Mary's secret sympathisers the signal to come out openly in her support. The Lord Treasurer, William Paulet, Marquess of Winchester, was a particularly flimsy reed – or rather, a willow, the bendy tree that he compared himself to when asked how he had survived the dizzying religious changes of the century, during which he embraced no fewer than five faiths, from Catholicism to Puritan Calvinism. Winchester, Pembroke and other peers attempted to flee from the Tower, but were prevented from leaving by Suffolk, the queen's father. The fortress's great gates were then locked fast, and its keys delivered to Jane's personal keeping.

It was time for the Earl of Arundel to take a delayed revenge on the man he now called a 'thirster of blood' and 'the Tyrant'. Northumberland had imprisoned Arundel for a year in the Tower and fined him the equivalent of £3 million for his part in Somerset's plots. Now, with typical Howard treachery, it was Arundel's turn to plunge the dagger between the duke's shoulder blades. He arranged for a special council meeting outside the Tower at Baynard's Castle. Unconvincingly denying that he was motivated by personal malice, Arundel told his fellow councillors that Northumberland was trying to become 'Lord of this land' in place of the 'rightful, lawful' successor, Mary, who 'shone with goodness', and at whose hands they could expect 'mercy and mild government' – a spectacular misjudgement of the woman who was arguably the cruellest Tudor of all.

As soon as Arundel sat down, the hotheaded Earl of Pembroke – hitherto Northumberland's most loyal ally – sprang to his feet, smacked his sword and vowed melodramatically, 'If my Lord of Arundel's persuasions cannot prevail with you, either this sword shall make Mary Queen, or I will lose my life.' Pembroke almost outdid Winchester in his inconstancy. Although he had recently married his son Henry to Jane's younger sister Catherine, after deserting the Greys he had the marriage annulled and threw little Catherine out of the house.

The desertion of these leading councillors was decisive. To a man, the rest of the council switched sides. Totally reversing their actions of only a few days before, they hastily arranged for heralds to proclaim Mary as queen at Cheapside and other central London locations. In contrast to the sullen silence that had greeted the proclamation of Queen Jane, the announcement was received with wild rejoicing by Londoners. Caps and coins were flung in the air, bonfires were lit in celebration, toasts were drunk to the new queen, and a solemn Catholic *Te Deum* was sung at St Paul's.

At the Tower, as noise of the celebrations faintly penetrated the thick walls, a heavy-hearted Duke of Suffolk entered the room where his daughter sat at supper and broke the news that her reign of nine days was at an end, and that she must accept Mary as queen. His daughter tartly replied that this was better advice than his original order to take the crown had been. The duke tore down the cloth of estate, symbolising the majesty of monarchy, that hung above her head. Finally, he crept out of the Tower, and proclaimed Mary as queen on Tower Hill, before slinking off into the gathering summer twilight. Back in the Tower, poor Jane, deserted by those who had fawned upon her, was left alone. Doubtless she wished that she could go home too. But that mercy would not be granted to her. Instead, the Yeomen Guards escorted her from the royal palace to the Lieutenant's Lodgings. In the space of an hour, the queen had become the prisoner.

At 5 p.m. in Cambridge on the same day, Northumberland, too, threw in the towel. Or rather, threw his cap in the air as he proclaimed Mary queen in the marketplace. His eyes, though, betrayed his real feelings as he staggered, weeping, back to his lodgings. He was accosted by an onlooker who asked him his plans. Mary, Northumberland replied, was a 'merciful woman' whom he would petition for pardon. 'Be assured you will never escape death,' replied the prophetic stranger, 'for if she would save you, they that now rule will kill you.'

News of her triumph reached Mary at Framlingham on 20 July as she returned to the castle from inspecting the army that had rallied to her in the little Suffolk town. The bringer of the good tidings – together with a grovelling letter signed by the whole Royal Council – was the Earl of Arundel, the main instigator of the council's change of heart. Mary tasked him with the doubtless sweet duty of arresting his old enemy, Northumberland, in Cambridge. Ten days later, Northumberland returned to the capital in Arundel's custody. As they rode towards the Tower, an army of 4,000 men was needed to protect the fallen duke from the wrath of the crowds who yelled, 'Death to the traitors and God save the Queen!' At Bishopsgate, a figure waving a sword, with dirty bandages hiding the bloody stumps of his freshly severed ears, accosted Northumberland.

It was Gilbert Potter, the innkeeper who had been the sole Londoner with the courage to openly dispute Jane's right to the throne. Now that the fickle crowd had followed him, he had his say again. 'Behold the free tongue of an honest citizen, as you have disfigured the head of an innocent man by the mutilation of his ears, so shall you be dragged to the punishment due to treason, according to your deserts!' he roared. Stung by the words, and perhaps scared also, Northumberland turned to Arundel, demanding to know why 'this impudent fellow' was allowed to 'afflict him' before any charges had been brought against him. 'Be of good courage,' Arundel answered. 'Although I cannot stop the tongues of men accusing you, yet I will stop their hands from hurting you.'

As they rode over Tower Hill, women waved kerchiefs stained brown with the blood of the 'Good Duke' Somerset shed at that spot. It was a sombre reminder to Northumberland that he would soon share his rival's fate. Once in the Tower, Northumberland was taken to its grimmest location – the 'Bloody' Tower. He was separated from his five sons. Henry, John, Ambrose, Robert and Guildford Dudley – who had all loyally joined their father's attempt to make Jane queen – were kept together across the Inner Ward in the Beauchamp Tower, where John whiled away the long hours by carving an elaborate rendition of the Dudley coat of arms, the bear and ragged staff, into the stone wall, where it can still be seen today.

Mary herself reached her new capital on 3 August, after a slow but triumphant progress from Framlingham. Mounted on a palfrey, guarded by 1,000 soldiers, and gorgeously arrayed in purple velvet encrusted with gold and pearls, the new queen also headed for the Tower. Her reception was very different from Northumberland's. She could barely force her horse through the cheering throngs, whose hoarse hurrahs competed with the frantic ringing of church bells and the blasts of trumpets.

Arriving at the Tower, Mary was greeted by a small line of gentlemen and one lady, all kneeling uncomfortably on the hard ground. Blinking in the summer sunshine after years in the Tower's shadows were the old Duke of Norfolk – the great survivor from Henry VIII's reign who had been incarcerated there since just before the old monster's death – and two Catholic prelates, Bishops Stephen Gardiner of Winchester and Edmund Bonner of London. These elderly men were joined by one young man, who, despite his youth, had been immured in the Tower for longer than any of them. Edward Courtenay, shortly to be made 1st Earl of Devon, had been held there for fifteen years since 1538 solely because he was the great-grandson of Edward IV, and the last Yorkist claimant to the throne. Anne Stanhope, the Duchess of Somerset, held in the fortress since her husband's execution, completed the line-up. Mary smiled at them all fondly, and kissed each in turn. 'These are my prisoners,' she said proudly, freeing them.

* * *

Mary's first duty was to arrange the funeral of her dead half-brother. The boy king was buried in Westminster Abbey in a Protestant service presided over by Cranmer. The queen stayed away, attending a Catholic Requiem Mass at St John's Chapel in the White Tower instead. Elsewhere in the Tower, Lady Jane Grey, the tiny figure at the centre of the recent storm, wrote a long letter to Mary from the Lieutenant's Lodgings explaining her part in the proceedings. She freely admitted her fault in allowing herself to be persuaded to take the crown – but denied that either ambition or malice towards Mary had prompted her action. 'No one can say either that I sought it [the throne] as my own, or that I was pleased with it.' At first, Mary was inclined to believe Jane's honest protestations of innocence and pardon her. But her advisers – in particular Simon Renard, the imperial ambassador in London – persuaded her that Jane free would inevitably become a magnet for opposition, and an alternative queen once Mary's popularity waned. So Jane stayed in the Tower – her fate suspended.

There was, however, no chance of clemency for Northumberland and his closest associates. Tried at Westminster Hall on 18 August along with his son John and the Marquess of Northampton, brother of Queen Catherine Parr, Northumberland exonerated Jane Grey, affirming that she had only claimed the crown 'by enticement and force'. For himself, he could only plead that his 'treason' had consisted in following the commands of the late King Edward – a course, he pointed out, which all the lords trying him had followed too. If he were guilty, so were they. Brushing this aside, the court – once again presided over, as in the treason trials of Henry VIII's day, by the vicious old Duke of Norfolk – sentenced Northumberland, Northampton and the younger John Dudley to death.

Their deaths – along with those of three of their lesser henchmen – were fixed for Monday 21 August. But as he prepared to walk to the scaffold that morning, Northumberland grasped at a final straw. Urgently, he told his guards of a last request – he wished to hear a Catholic Mass in the Tower before he died. This was a propaganda coup that Mary's new Catholic regime could not afford to pass up. For the driver of the Edwardian Reformation to convert to the old faith in the hour of his death was little short of miraculous. Even if it meant postponing his execution for twenty-four hours, the opportunity must be grasped.

A Mass was swiftly arranged in St Peter ad Vincula. Northumberland attended, along with the associates due to die with him. Just before he received the host, Northumberland told the congregation that Catholicism was 'the very right and true way'. He and they, he added, had been seduced from 'true religion these sixteen years past' (i.e. since Henry VIII's break with Rome), 'by the false and erroneous preaching of the new preachers'. He himself regretted, he concluded, having 'pulled down the Mass' and was grateful that his power to do further wrong had been halted.

Whether Northumberland's renunciation of the Protestant religion and sudden conversion to Catholicism was genuine, expedient – in the hope of saving his own life and those of his family and friends or at least preserving his children's inheritance – or, as seems most likely of all, merely desperate cannot be said with certainty. He would, however, have died with more dignity if he had stuck to the cause for which he had hazarded everything. In this respect the girl he had treated as his puppet – Jane herself, who watched from her window overlooking the Inner Ward as Northumberland demeaned himself at the chapel – set a more steadfast example of courage and fidelity than the man who had exploited her.

That night, his last on earth, Northumberland doggedly fought on for his life. The grovelling letter he wrote from the Bloody Tower to his old enemy Arundel, pleading for him to intercede with the queen, gives a measure of his desperation:

> Alas my good lord, is my crime so heinous as no redemption but my blood can wash away the spots thereof? An old proverb there is, and that most true, that a live dog is better than a dead lion. Oh, that it would please her good Grace to give me life, yea the life of a dog, that I might but live and kiss her feet. Once your fellow and loving companion, but now worthy of no name but wretchedness and misery. J.D.

By the next morning, Northumberland had given up any slight hopes of a last-minute reprieve. As he mounted the scaffold on Tower Hill, almost exactly forty-three years after his father Edmund had died at the same bloody spot, he threw off his sand-coloured cloak, leant casually on the rail and addressed the crowd. He had been an 'evil liver', he confessed, who had been led astray by those Protestant pastors who had persuaded him to renounce the 'Catholic faith and the true doctrine of Christ'. He blamed the nation's turning away from Rome for all the 'misery, sedition, division and rebellion' that had troubled England ever since. Finally, as was customary, he thanked the monarch who was putting him to death for her 'mercy' in giving him the 'time and respect' to repent. Then, with a final prayer and a recital of the psalm *De Profundis,* he submitted to the executioner, who deftly removed his doublet and handed him a kerchief blindfold. Northumberland knelt at the block and lost his head in one blow.

The two men who died with him, Sir Thomas Palmer, whose defection from Somerset's camp had been instrumental in bringing the 'Good Duke' down, and Sir John Gates, former captain of King Edward's guard, offered contrasting studies in bravado and meekness in their last moments. Gates had been sought out by Northumberland that morning when they had attended their final Mass in the Tower, and exchanged mutual forgiveness, though both blamed each other for their predicament. Gates, with a soldier's courage, refused a blindfold. A decision he may have regretted when the headsman botched his job and took three blows to decapitate him.

Palmer, by contrast, swaggered on to a scaffold already slippery with blood, cheerfully roaring, 'Good morrow!' to the crowd. He told them that he had had a vision of Christ sitting at God's right hand while in 'a little dark corner in yon Tower'; and his cheeriness was prompted by the knowledge that he was bound for heaven that very day. In contrast to the turncoat Northumberland, he said he died in the Protestant faith, and was happy to leave a vain world in which he had found 'nothing but ambition, flattery, foolishness, vainglory, pride, discord, slander, boasting, hatred and malice'. Death was not to be feared, he affirmed: 'Not even the bloody axe itself shall make me afraid.' Greeting the executioner, Palmer jested, 'Come on, good fellow, art thou he that must do the deed? I forgive thee with all my heart.' Laying his neck in the slot on the block, he joked that it fitted perfectly, said a last prayer and, like Northumberland, lost his head in a single stroke. The three bodies were carted back to the Tower and buried at St Peter's where they had worshipped less than an hour before.

We have an unusually detailed account of Jane Grey's time in the Tower, thanks to Rowland Lee, an official of the Royal Mint who had access to her. Lee seems to have developed a crush on the spirited young ex-queen, and his pen portrait of her vividly conveys her personality. A week after Northumberland's demise Lee dined with Jane and found her still regal, but full of praise for Mary's 'mercy'. She was indignant at Northumberland for abandoning the Protestant faith so easily. 'As his life was wicked and full of dissimulation – so was his end thereafter.' Jane promised that if and when she was in the same position she would not renounce her faith so lightly. She was as good as her word.

While in the Tower, as a noblewoman of royal blood, Jane was permitted to retain four attendants: two ladies, a manservant and her former nurse. The government paid a generous ninety shillings a week for her keep, plus twenty shillings for each of her servants. She was allowed liberty to stroll and enjoy the late summer in the gardens, as well as to read the books of her choice. Her companions in the Tower included the Protestant prelates Thomas Cranmer and Hugh Latimer, who took the places of the Catholic Bishops Gardiner and Bonner. Jane was not, however, permitted to meet her husband Guildford Dudley, who remained confined with his brothers in the Beauchamp Tower. A distant glimpse of Guildford as he stretched his long legs on the tower's lead roof was the most that Jane was permitted.

Meanwhile the reaction against the Protestant Reformation was in full swing. Altars, vestments and other Catholic regalia were restored to the Tower's two chapels. Jane displayed an icy fury at the backsliding of a minister, Dr Harding, once the Protestant chaplain to the Grey family who, a true Vicar of Bray, had prudently renounced his 'heresy' and returned to Rome. From the Tower, she wrote a stinging letter to him deploring that he, once the 'lively member of Christ' had become 'the stinking and filthy kennel of Satan'. From a 'stout Christian soldier' he had become a 'cowardly runaway' and a 'white-livered milksop'.

In late September, the customary coronation preparations for Queen Mary began at the Tower. She was accompanied by her half-sister Eizabeth, now a fiery redhead of twenty. Mary eyed Anne Boleyn's daughter with grave suspicion. Not only did she regard her as a bastard of the woman who had displaced her mother; she was also a Protestant heretic. Mary strove dutifully to convert her heir apparent to Catholic orthodoxy, but the wily Elizabeth, while outwardly conforming to Catholic rites, would not be moved. She was sent into the country while her half-sister tried fruitlessly to find a way of excluding her from the succession.

Meanwhile, Mary attempted to solve the succession problem by producing an heir herself – with the most unsuitable and unpopular bridegroom she could find, none other than Philip II of Spain, son and heir of the Emperor Charles V. News of the marriage sparked outrage among English patriots who felt it would mean subservience to a foreign tyranny. Mary, half-Spanish herself, failed to understand the resentment even after a dead dog, dressed in Catholic vestments, was thrown into her own presence chamber.

On 13 November, Lady Jane Grey went on trial at London's Guildhall with her husband Guildford and two other Dudley brothers, Henry and Ambrose. Arraigned alongside them was Thomas Cranmer. The spiritual father of the English Reformation had been replaced as Archbishop of Canterbury by Cardinal Reginald Pole – the arch-Catholic scion of the Yorkist dynasty whom Henry VIII and Cromwell had tried in vain to kill, and who had returned in triumph from decades of exile in Rome. All the prisoners were dressed in black – the colour of penitence and mourning though Jane's repentance was tempered by her holding a prayer book – a symbol of her Protestant faith. The inevitable death sentences were passed – in Jane's case by burning, the automatic punishment for a woman convicted of treason. Few thought, however, that she would suffer such a fiery fate, as it was rumoured that Mary was minded to pardon her altogether.

The queen's mind was changed by a popular revolt against her marriage to Philip. The revolt's leaders included Edward Courtenay, Earl of Devon, who, although having been freed by Mary from the Tower where he had spent most of his life was disappointed not to have married her himself. Instead, the plotters intended him to be rewarded with Elizabeth's hand. Fatally for Jane, her father Henry Grey, Earl of Suffolk, also joined the plot; as did Sir Thomas Wyatt, a Kentish squire whose father, the poet Sir Thomas Wyatt, and grandfather Henry, had all seen the inside of the Tower.

Wyatt was the only conspirator to get his rebellion off the ground. Though confined to Kent, it proved the most potent threat to Tudor rule since the Pilgrimage of Grace. The plan was for a coordinated rising in different parts of the country on Palm Sunday, 18 March 1554. Courtenay was to raise his native Devon; Jane's father was to rise in the Midlands; another landowner, Sir James Croft, would raise the Welsh Marches; and Wyatt would lead the revolt in Kent – with their four armies converging on the capital. But in January the government learned about the rising from the loose tongue of one of the rebels, Sir Peter Carew. Bishop Gardiner quizzed Courtenay – his companion as a fellow Tower prisoner for several years – and the truth tumbled out.

All the plotters, apart from Wyatt, scattered in panic. Suffolk was arrested hiding in the woods after an abortive attempt to seize Coventry. Wyatt, however, had more luck in Kent. Wyatt's own tenants were joined by a militia company of London-trained bands tasked by Mary to arrest him, who defected to the rebels. The octogenarian Duke of Norfolk, sent by Mary to repress the revolt, retreated before the rebel advance.

Having taken Rochester, Wyatt's 3,000-strong rebel force pushed on to Dartford, intending to seize London and the queen, and forcibly prevent the marriage. Mary refused advice to retreat into the Tower, and remained defiantly at Westminster. Then, in a foretaste of her half-sister Elizabeth's speech defying the Armada at Tilbury, the queen went to the Guildhall, proclaimed herself her 'father's daughter and her kingdom's wife' and appealed to Londoners to resist the rebels. The speech worked wonders. The crowds cheered Mary and vowed to die in her defence.

Two days later, Wyatt's little army reached Southwark to find London Bridge barred against them. While his followers looted and torched Bishop Gardiner's palace and shot dead a Tower boatman on the river, Wyatt dithered for three days before marching west, crossing the Thames at Kingston, and doubling back into the city from the west. But Mary's resolution had united London against the rebels. Her popularity grew when it was reported that she had refused to order the Tower's great guns to open fire on the rebels across the river, lest innocent civilians in Southwark be harmed. Wyatt's diminishing force made its way into the heart of London through a Fleet Street lined with sullen, silent citizens, only to find the city gates at Ludgate barred. Turning back, Wyatt's army was overwhelmed by royal forces at Temple Bar in a short and sharp fight which left forty dead. Wyatt himself, clad in full armour, was captured and brought to the Tower, whose cells rapidly filled with his followers. After a frightening fortnight, the revolt was crushed. Now followed the retribution.

Mary's marriage and Wyatt's rebellion spelled the death of Jane Grey. Mary was finally persuaded that so long as Jane lived, her throne was under permanent threat. Moreover, Jane's father and uncles had been among the would-be rebel leaders, despite having pledged their undying loyalty to the queen only a fortnight before. Such brazen betrayal could merit only death. To underline the point, Bishop Gardiner demanded in his Lenten sermon that for the safety of the commonwealth it was necessary that the 'rotten and hurtful' rebel members should be 'cut off and consumed'. Without more ado, Mary signed the death warrants of Jane and Guildford, but commuted Jane's sentence of burning to beheading.

Suffolk joined his daughter in the Tower. Although father and daughter were not permitted to meet, Jane and Guildford Dudley managed to write encouraging messages to him concealed in a battered old prayer book kept for the use of prisoners. Guildford's touching inscription read:

Your loving and obedient son wisheth unto your grace long life in this world, with as much joy and comfort as I wish to myself, and in the world to come life everlasting. Your humble son to the death, G. Dudley.

The book was then passed to Jane who wrote with a more cold eyed realism than Guildford's hopes for 'long life in this world'. She knew they were all destined for martyrs' deaths:

The Lord comfort your grace, and that in His Word wherein all creatures only are to be comforted. And though it has pleased God to take away two of your children, yet think not, I most humbly beseech your grace, that you have lost them, but that . . . we, by losing this mortal life, have won an immortal life.

Your grace's humble daughter Jane Dudley.

Mary remained reluctant to execute Jane while she persisted in her Protestant 'heresy'. She had decided what to do with her cousin's little body, but was still trying to save her soul. The queen sent her chaplain, Abbot John Feckenham, to the Tower to try to persuade Jane to renounce her faith. Feckenham was an ideal choice. An ex-Benedictine monk, he was a warm, jovial, fatherly figure with a persuasive tongue. Moreover, he had himself been sent to the Tower by Archbishop Cranmer in Edward's reign for resisting the Protestant Reformation.

While there, Feckenham had been visited by King Edward's Protestant tutor, the Cambridge scholar John Cheke. The learned Cheke had fruitlessly tried to persuade him of the truth of Protestantism. At the end of Jane's nine-day reign, Feckenham was freed, and Cheke himself arrested and put in the Tower. Cheke, a timid man, was released on condition that he went into exile. However, later during Mary's reign he was abducted in Brussels on the orders of Philip of Spain, brought back to England and once again put in the Tower. In one of the ironical turns of fortune of the English Reformation, he was again visited there by his old sparring partner Feckenham. Terrified of being burned as a heretic, Cheke apparently succumbed to Feckenham's honeyed words and agreed to convert to Catholicism – but the shock of the experience proved too much, and he died in 1557.

When the wheel of religious fortune turned once again and Catholic Mary was succeeded by Protestant Elizabeth, poor Feckenham was yet again arrested and sent to the Tower. He spent fourteen years there and in other prisons before being bailed to live in the Fens, where he became beloved because of his charity to the poor. His stubborn refusal to renounce his papist faith, however, saw him constantly jailed until he finally died in prison at Wisbech after a quarter of a century's sporadic confinement. This was the kindly man repeatedly received by Jane in the Tower as she waited for death. At first Jane told the priest that she wanted to prepare for death rather than debate religion. Soon, however, the disputatious sixteen-year-old found she could not resist an intellectual wrestle with such a worthy opponent as Feckenham. Jane argued that her current dire situation – far from representing, as Feckenham believed, just punishment – was a divine test of her faith and 'a manifest Declaration of God's favour to me'. Jane warned Feckenham that he was bound for hell if he persisted in his 'error'. He returned to Mary, vainly begging a pardon for the spirited girl.

Jane spent her last night, 8 February, writing letters to her family. To her father, who would soon follow her to the block, she offered the comfort that she would be exchanging the earthly crown that she had so briefly worn for a heavenly one – and she looked forward to meeting him there. To her nearest sister Katherine, she sent a New Testament:

> A book, which, though it be not outwardly trimmed with gold, yet inwardly it is of more worth than precious stones. It will teach you to live. It will learn you to die. Deny the world, defy the devil, despise the flesh.

Jane herself had so far left worldly ties behind that she refused her husband's request for a farewell meeting, writing that such a tryst could only 'increase their misery and pain', and it was better to put it off until they would 'meet shortly elsewhere and live bound by indissoluble ties'. At dawn, the sounds of hammering from the White Tower told Jane that her scaffold was being erected – her royal blood ensuring that she would enjoy the 'privilege' of a private beheading within the Tower. The disturbance did not break her inner serenity, nor did the sight of her husband being led out of the Beauchamp Tower to death on Tower Hill. Jane calmly watched him leave from her window in the Lieutenant's Lodgings. Although he had cried like a child when told his sentence, Guildford Dudley died bravely. Having refused the services of a Catholic priest, his head was severed by a single stroke. Faithfully and courageously, Jane was still at her window when the cart carrying her husband's body, its head wrapped in a bloody cloth, returned to the Tower for burial. She seemed, wrote an onlooker, 'nothing at all abashed' by the gruesome sight. Then it was her turn.

Escorted by the Tower's lieutenant, Sir John Bridges, and wearing the same black dress and clutching the same prayer book that she had held at her trial, Jane descended the stairs and followed the route to the scaffold trodden by Anne Boleyn and Katherine Howard before her. The execution scene is imprinted on our minds, thanks to the nineteenth-century French romantic painter Paul Delaroche. His depiction (1834) accurately shows a blindfolded Jane struggling to locate the block and being gently helped to find it – but almost everything else in it is false. Jane is depicted dressed in virginal white rather than funereal black. The dark background suggests an interior location at midnight rather than the Tower's Inner Ward on a crisp winter morning. Altogether, as Jane's biographer Leanda de Lisle remarks, the painting, an undeniably powerful image, 'has all the erotic overtones of a virgin sacrifice'. Jane's moment of blind helplessness falsely pins her down as a victim rather than the determined, opinionated and brave young woman that she was.

Jane's demeanour on the scaffold was as self-possessed as the rest of her short life. In her final speech she regretted allowing herself to be made queen. Then, repeating a phrase she had used in her last letter to her father, she dramatically mimed washing her hands, declaring, 'I do wash my hands thereof in innocence, before God, and the face of you, good Christian people, this day.' She had agreed to the presence of her Catholic intellectual sparring partner Feckenham, and turning to him, asked whether she should recite the psalm 'Have Mercy on me O God'. That done, she distributed a few last gifts. Her prayer book went to her host Lieutenant Bridges, inscribed:

> Good master Lieutenant, Live still to die, that by death you may purchase eternal life. For, as the Preacher says, there is a time to be born, and a

time to die; and the day of death is better than the day of our birth. Yours, as the lord knows, as a friend, Jane Dudley.

This done, Jane began to remove her outer garments and the executioner stepped up to assist. Jane sharply refused and sought the help of her two lady assistants. After asking the executioner to dispatch her quickly, she tied the blindfold around her eyes with her own hands. As the world plunged into blackness for a moment she panicked. Groping blindly for the block she cried, 'What shall I do? Where is it?' like a suddenly abandoned child. Helpful hands guided her, and, calm again, she spoke her last words: 'Lord, into thy hands I commend my spirit.' The axe fell.

Jane's execution had done nothing to rid Mary of the succession problem. So long as another stubborn, rebellious and craftier Protestant girl – her half-sister Elizabeth – lived, and so long as Mary laboured fruitlessly under the perennial Tudor curse of an inability to produce a legitimate heir herself, then the Catholic restoration remained in peril. The malign influence of her Spanish and clerical advisers, and her growing despair about her failure to produce children, combined to embitter her and drive her towards becoming the familiar 'Bloody Mary': a cruel and bigoted tyrant, a bishop burner and slayer of her own people who, as a result, increasingly turned against her.

A few days after Jane's death, Mary sent a posse of 250 horsemen to Ashridge, the country house in the Chiltern Hills where Elizabeth had been kept since the coronation. Wyatt had cleared her of any knowledge of his rising, even resisting the Tower's torturers to insist on her innocence. But it was clear that it had been the rebel intention to place Elizabeth on the throne of a Protestant England. The posse's mission was to bring Elizabeth captive to the capital. They arrived late at night when the princess was in bed. Despite being informed that she was ill, the leaders of the troops forced their way into her bedroom, telling her that the queen had ordered her brought to London dead or alive.

Early next morning, with Elizabeth in a litter, they set out. At her imperious insistence, they travelled slowly, reaching London almost a week later. Elizabeth was already demonstrating her penchant for procrastination that served her so well in later life. Indignantly protesting her innocence, she was examined by the council in Whitehall Palace, who, try as they might, could extract no damning admissions from her. She wrote to Mary, 'protesting before God' that she had never 'practised, concealed, nor consented to anything that might be prejudicial to your person in any way, or dangerous to the state by any means'. But she was refused permission to see her half-sister and after a fortnight, was told that she was going to the Tower.

The fortress's sinister reputation as death's waiting room was already well established, and with the example of her mother, her paramour Thomas Seymour, and most recently Jane Grey before her, Elizabeth cannot be blamed for taking the terrible news as her death warrant. Few of her royal blood who entered the Tower as prisoners left it alive again. She furiously protested at being sent to 'a place more wonted for a false traitor than a true subject'. But her lamentations were in vain, and on Palm Sunday, 18 March 1554, a barge took her from Whitehall's wharf to the Tower.

It was a cold, cheerless, grey day, and the princess's mood matched the weather. Her spirits were further depressed when she saw Traitor's Gate, the entrance that for so many – including her mother – had meant a final exit from the earth. Rain had swollen the river, and making the excuse that she did not want to get her feet wet, she refused to leave the boat. Her escort, the 'willowy' old Marquess of Winchester, drily replied that she had no choice.

Finally, and very reluctantly, Elizabeth gave way, declaring, 'Here landeth as true a subject, being a prisoner, as ever landed at these steps, and before thee O God, I speak it, having none other friends than thee.' Then she sat down on the sopping stones, angrily arguing that as she was no traitor she would not go through the dreaded gate. Lieutenant Bridges, the man who had just seen Jane Grey to her death, pointed out that if she continued to sit in the river she would catch her death of cold. At last, calling on 'all good friends and fellows to witness that she was no traitor but the queen's true subject', Elizabeth reluctantly followed the lieutenant through the gate.

The princess was housed, not in the relative comfort of the Lieutenant's Lodgings where Jane had lately lived, but in the upper chamber of the Bell Tower – the same spartan accommodation where Bishop John Fisher had suffered, above the cell where Sir Thomas More had languished. At first her only privilege was to be allowed to walk for exercise along the rooftops – the leads – between the Bell and Beauchamp Towers, where the surviving Dudley boys were still held. One of them, Robert Dudley, whom she had known since childhood, would become the love of her largely loveless life. From her walkway, still known as 'Princess Elizabeth's Walk', she was relieved to see the scaffold used for Jane's execution being dismantled. She hoped it meant that the attempt to implicate her in Wyatt's rising had finally failed.

Mary, however, still intensely suspicious of her half-sister, told the Tower authorities to keep a strict eye on her. The constable, Sir John Gage, ordered a particular watch kept on the food that she, a privileged prisoner, had sent in from outside the fortress. Elizabeth only received her victuals after they had been minutely examined by the Tower's staff: a humiliating procedure that infuriated the haughty princess. Her complaints redoubled when she noticed that her guards were helping themselves to the choicest food before it reached her, to supplement their own meagre rations. The strong-willed Elizabeth was so insistent – threatening to report the pilfering to the queen – that she won her point. From then on the food was delivered to her own servants, who arranged to cook it in the lieutenant's kitchens before serving it to their royal mistress.

As spring advanced, Elizabeth was allowed to walk in the Tower's Privy Garden. The fortress's other inmates were strictly forbidden to speak to her or even look at her. When a five-year-old son of a warder innocently presented her with a sprig of flowers, he was reprimanded and the bouquet instantly confiscated and torn to pieces lest it contain a hidden message. Elizabeth's fellow prisoners included scores of Protestants brought into the fortress to repent of their 'heresy' or suffer the consequences. The week after her arrival, the Church of England's top trio of reformers, headed by the aged Thomas Cranmer, with Hugh Latimer, Bishop of Worcester, and Nicholas Ridley, Bishop of London, were brought in. The Tower was so crowded that the three prelates had to share a cramped cell.

On 11 April, the overcrowding was slightly relieved when Sir Thomas Wyatt left the fortress to die on Tower Hill. From the scaffold he exonerated Elizabeth from all blame for his rising. A hundred of Wyatt's rebels died with their leader – half of them hanged in London on a single day. Jane Grey's father, Henry, Earl of Suffolk, was executed a few days after his daughter. The four surviving Dudley brothers – John, Ambrose, Henry and Robert – were luckier. They were detained until the autumn, then released – although John, the eldest, only survived for a fortnight, his death doubtless hastened by his confinement in the Tower, while Henry would die fighting in defence of Calais in Mary's lost French wars.

Amidst this orgy of state violence, Elizabeth had a very clear idea of the fate she would suffer if she made a single slip during her continual examinations by privy councillors and the ruthless Bishop Gardiner, who was quite determined to see her die. Far more guileful than Jane Grey, however, Elizabeth outwitted them all. Her confidence in her own cleverness is well expressed by the taunting couplet she is reputed to have scratched on a glass pane with a diamond ring:

Much suspected by me – nothing proved can be.

On 19 May, after two and a half months in the Tower, Elizabeth was freed. She left, as she had come, by water, travelling first to Richmond Palace – where she would die half a century later – then on to the rural seclusion of the palace at Woodstock in Oxfordshire. When next she returned to the Tower, she would be queen.

CHAPTER ELEVEN

FALLEN FAVOURITES

The release from the Tower of Elizabeth and the Dudley brothers, along with genuine conspirators such as Edward Courtenay, Earl of Devon, was less the result of the Marian government adopting a policy of mercy, than a panicky attempt to win back lost public approval, disgusted both by Mary's Spanish marriage and by the mass incineration of Protestants. During his brief stays in England after marrying Mary, Philip of Spain steered well clear of the Tower, only briefly visiting the fortress three times, and never staying there overnight. Mary, by contrast, spent the autumn and winter of 1555–6 there, hoping against hope that her absentee husband had made her pregnant.

These hopes turned to ashes – the ashes of more than 300 Protestants burned at the stake by Mary for refusing to renounce their heresy, a policy that has irredeemably blackened her name in history. Foremost among the martyrs were Cranmer, Latimer and Ridley – who went to the flames at Oxford after ten months in the Tower. Latimer prophesied at the stake that they were lighting a Protestant flame in England that would not be extinguished. Scores of ordinary men and women suffered similarly for the 'crime' of refusing to conform to the new Catholic orthodoxy. Mary's bitter cruelty was fuelled by her failure to become pregnant – despite numerous wish-induced false alarms – and by her growing realisation that her husband was merely using her and her kingdom as an instrument of Spanish foreign policy. Mary obediently converted Spanish silver to coins at the Tower mint; supplied the Tower's ordnance and ships to fight Philip's campaigns against France; and filled her court with Spanish priests and monks. Her only reward was to lose Calais – England's sole remaining possession in France – causing her famous lament that after her death the word 'Calais' would be found carved on her heart.

That death, in November 1558 – followed within hours by that of her chief spiritual adviser Cardinal Reginald Pole – was caused by uterine cancer, which Mary, pathetically, had mistaken for pregnancy. The news of her half-sister's demise and her succession was brought to Elizabeth at Hatfield House, just north of London. Any sorrow at her sibling's passing was short-lived, and a grateful nation joined in frantic rejoicing that a new ruler was on the throne with the promise of a future un-brightened by flames consuming human flesh.

Elizabeth arrived at the Tower on 28 November, after negotiating her way through London streets thronged with crowds cheering themselves hoarse. It was a very different entry from her last stay in the fortress. Although she knew that she would have to go through the formal coronation ceremonies at the Tower as custom and tradition dictated, Elizabeth – for very understandable reasons – was not anxious to prolong her time in the prison-palace that stood in her mind only for suffering, danger and death. Elizabeth's long reign, in fact, marks a defining watershed in the Tower's history – when its royal functions began to decline, and its image became indelibly associated with its darker role as prison and torture chamber to the elite. After Elizabeth, no monarch would ever reside there or treat the Tower as home again.

For the first week of Elizabeth's reign, however, the Tower was the powerhouse where the future course of policy was set. Meeting constantly with her council in the palace's great hall, the new queen, with her chief adviser William Cecil, later Lord Burghley, at her side, laid down her law. She turned her back on her sister's policy, proclaiming that England would once again become a Protestant nation. Surviving Protestant clerics, like her Archbishop of Canterbury, Matthew Parker, were reappointed to posts newly vacated by their Catholic counterparts like Bishops Bonner and Gardiner. Elizabeth's brand of the faith, however, would not be the extreme evangelism of her half-brother Edward. A moderate, middle-of-the-road Anglicanism, eschewing fundamentalist Calvinism on the Left and fanatical Catholicism on the Right, would be the order of the day. Elizabeth said that she had no wish to 'make windows into men's souls'. Sincere religious belief – so long as it did not threaten the security of the state – would not be punished by the fires of Smithfield.

It did not take long for these pious intentions to ram into the hard rocks of realpolitik. Elizabeth's brother-in-law, Philip – who had now succeeded his father Charles V as Holy Roman Emperor and King of Spain – resented Elizabeth both for her Protestantism and for her patriotism, which threatened Spain's place as the Western world's pre-eminent power. Elizabeth's reign would be dominated by a growing conflict with Spain and Catholic Europe, which, waged by land and sea, became an affair of state as England's Catholic community were torn between their duty as subjects of the queen and their fidelity to their faith. After the Pope excommunicated Elizabeth for heresy, declaring that it was the duty of good Catholics to kill her, they inevitably were seen by an increasingly repressive state, as the malevolent enemy within: a fifth column of treacherous subversives who must convert, conform – or be crushed.

Elizabeth's prime purpose was to ensure her own place on the throne. Like her father, she took any threat to the Crown personally. Historians are divided as to whether Elizabeth's reluctance to marry was because she was unable to wed the real love of her life, Robert Dudley, her former companion in misery at the Tower; or because she refused to share power with any spouse. (Even Mary, devoted to her husband Philip, had refused his demand to be crowned king at her side.) Early in her reign, Elizabeth's concerns about marriage, fertility and her royal rights became focused on the tiny figure of Catherine Grey.

Catherine was the younger sister of Jane Grey, with the same Royal blood as her executed sibling. Just before Jane's reign, when her sister had wed Lord Guildford Dudley, Catherine had been married to Henry Herbert, Earl of Pembroke, son and heir of Northumberland's chief lieutenant, as part of Northumberland's machinations to make himself the power behind Jane's throne. After the collapse of Jane's reign, Herbert, at his repentant father's urgent command, wasted no time in having the now inconvenient marriage to a traitor's sister annulled on the grounds of non-consummation. Poor Catherine, her father and sister executed as traitors, was brutally cast adrift.

Elizabeth took pity on the jilted girl and made her a lady-in-waiting. But when Catherine made the mistake of falling for Edward 'Ned' Seymour, Earl of Hertford – handsome son and namesake of Edward VI's fallen Lord Protector Somerset – the queen suddenly remembered that as great-granddaughter of her father Henry VIII, Catherine had a claim to the throne. Worse, in 1561 it emerged that Catherine and Seymour – who himself had a smidgen of royal blood via his mother's descent from Edward III – had secretly married the previous year in the presence of a priest with Ned's sister Jane as their sole witness. Worse still: Catherine was now pregnant.

Fearing the queen's wrath, Catherine confided her secret to Robert Dudley, who promptly informed his royal mistress. Elizabeth, in a pattern that would become increasingly familiar, went almost mad with rage. Catherine was instantly arrested and taken to the Tower where – with savage irony – she was lodged in the Bell Tower, the grim prison where Elizabeth herself had been housed a few short years before. Seymour was in France when the secret came out. Ordered home by a furious Elizabeth, he was clapped in a cell in the White Tower – cruelly kept in strict seclusion from his wife, who was about to give birth.

Catherine was safely delivered of a boy on 24 September. The baby was baptised with his father's name in St Peter ad Vincula, the very place where the headless corpses of the infant's aunt, grandfather and great-uncle were decomposing. The two lieutenants of the Tower during Mary's reign, Sir John Bridges, followed by his brother Thomas, were loyal Catholics dismissed by Elizabeth. They had been replaced by Sir Edward Warner, a Protestant who had held the post during Edward VI's reign. Warner was under strict instructions from Elizabeth to keep the Seymours apart, but either through kindness or negligence, or bribery, he allowed Ned Seymour to make at least one conjugal visit to his spouse – which resulted in Catherine becoming pregnant again.

In February 1563 she gave birth to a second son, Thomas, at the Tower, who was also baptised at St Peter's. When Elizabeth heard of this fresh act of insolence, her rage was titanic. Warner was summarily sacked and imprisoned in one of his own Tower cells and Seymour fined the vast sum of £15,000. One of the couple's problems was that they were unable to prove that they were married. Seymour had entrusted the marriage certificate to Catherine before leaving for France – but she had since lost the document. Their only witness, Seymour's sister Jane, had inconveniently died, and the priest who had conducted the ceremony was too frightened of the queen's wrath to come forward. (He owned up thirty years later after Elizabeth was safely dead.)

Although the conditions of Catherine's imprisonment were not harsh, as a surviving inventory of her comfortable furnishings proves, she, like her sister Jane before her, was now permitted only tantalising distant glimpses of her imprisoned husband in the Tower. Her furnishings included a bed with a down bolster, tapestries, curtains, Turkish carpets and a velvet-covered chair in crimson and gold, embroidered with the royal coat of arms. As some compensation for the lack of her husband, she was allowed a pet dog and a monkey. In the summer of 1563, an outbreak of plague in London caused the couple to be moved to the country – but they were still kept segregated.

In a bitter January in 1568, depressed after her continual requests to be reunited with her husband had been refused by the vindictive Elizabeth, Catherine, living at Cockfield in Suffolk, succumbed to tuberculosis probably incubated in the damp Tower. Her husband eventually married again. But he never forgot his Catherine and after Elizabeth's death, when the priest who had wed them finally came forward, the union was at last recognised as legitimate and the unfortunate couple's elder son inherited his family titles. By an astonishing coincidence, Edward and Catherine's grandson, William Seymour, would also infuriate an irate monarch by marrying too close to the throne – and would also be confined to the Tower for his pains. As we shall see, he would not tamely accept that fate.

Queen Elizabeth's aversion to her courtiers marrying, or still worse having babies, only increased as it became clear that she would neither wed nor give birth herself. As she passionately lamented when informed that Mary, Queen of Scots had given birth to James Stuart, the infant who would eventually succeed her on the English throne, 'The Queen of Scots is lighter of a fair son – but I am of barren stock.' It made things still worse when the miscreants who sought a sexual or family life outside Elizabeth's jealous orbit were themselves her former favourites. The pre-eminent case is that of a man who, perhaps more than any other figure in its long history, is most tragically associated with the Tower – Sir Walter Ralegh.

Ralegh epitomises in one extraordinary life, the great explosion of adventurous achievement that was Elizabethan England. Soldier, sailor, scientist, statesman, courtier, explorer, poet, plotter, philosopher, historian – Ralegh was all these and more. His second, lengthy imprisonment in the Tower was the major milestone in his life – producing children, herbal remedies, and his *History of the World*, a landmark in English literature. But who was this superman? And why did he outrage not one but two monarchs, to the point where the Tower was thought to be the only place fit to hold his fiery spirit?

Ralegh was quintessentially a Devon man. He was born in 1552 into the county's Protestant seagoing squirarchy who provided the 'Sea Dogs' of Elizabeth's reign: Francis Drake, Humphrey Gilbert, John Hawkins and Richard Grenville were all kin, and Ralegh shared their assumptions and aspirations. After Oxford, Ralegh spent years as a volunteer mercenary fighting in the French Wars of Religion and in Ireland. By the time he arrived at Elizabeth's court around 1581, he was a ruthless buccaneer who had seen much of the darker side of life.

The perfumed elegance of the Elizabethan court masked a ceaseless struggle for power every bit as brutal as the atrocities Ralegh had witnessed on the battlefield. To survive and prosper Ralegh had to capture the capricious monarch's fickle favour. Related to Kat Ashley, Elizabeth's childhood nurse, Ralegh had a flying start in gaining the queen's attention. Fortunately he also had those qualities that Elizabeth appreciated in a man. Good-looking, supremely masculine, Ralegh had brains and brawn – swapping poetic tags with this most literate of female rulers.

Most of all, he had charm. That fleeting quality is seen in the legend that he spread his cloak across a puddle to keep Elizabeth's feet dry. Such attention-seeking tactics rapidly achieved their purpose. By early 1583 he was the queen's favourite – deferred to even by her chief minister, Lord Burghley.

Appointed captain of the queen's Yeoman Guard, who supplied the Tower's garrison, Ralegh was at the peak of his power in the 1580s. To extensive Irish estates were added a London town home, Durham House off the Strand; and the substantial country estate of Sherborne Castle in Dorset. An MP for Devon and Cornwall, Ralegh's many political and economic interests there made him the virtual uncrowned king of the West Country; and he was in charge of defending its coastline against the Spanish Armada in 1588. Ralegh also drew income from a monopoly of Cornwall's tin mines and his investments in voyages to the developing Americas. A keen coloniser, Ralegh was involved in the first tentative attempts to found settlements in Virginia, where he famously grew and imported tobacco and potatoes. Then, in 1592, his world collapsed.

Naturally this warrior with culture cut a swathe through the hearts of the queen's ladies. According to the antiquary John Aubrey, Ralegh's wooing style was rough but effective:

> He loved a wench well and one time getting up one of the maids-of-honour up against a tree in a wood . . . who seemed at first boarding to be something fearful of her honour and modest, she cried 'Sweet Sir Walter, what do you ask me? Will you undo me? Nay, sweet Sir Walter!' At last, as the danger and the pleasure at the same time grew higher, she cried in ecstasy 'Swisser, Swatter! Swisser, Swatter!' She proved with child . . .

If there is any truth in Aubrey's tale, the lady could well be Elizabeth 'Bess' Throckmorton, the woman who would be Ralegh's wife and lifelong love – and the cause of his first great fall. Born into a distinguished Tudor family, Bess, a dozen years younger than the forty-year-old Ralegh, fell pregnant by him, and in 1590 he secretly married her. The pregnancy was temporarily hidden from the queen, as Bess left court for her confinement in March 1592. She gave birth to a boy named Damerai, and, leaving him in the country, returned to court.

When gossip brought news of the marriage and birth to the queen's ears, she erupted in fury. Ralegh attempted to flee on a long voyage, but contrary winds prevented his departure. In August 1592, as a feline courtier, Sir Edward Stafford, wrote to fellow courtier Anthony Bacon, 'If you have anything to do with Sir Walter Ralegh, or any love to make to Mistress Throckmorton you may speak to them tomorrow at the Tower.'

The Raleghs – along with their baby – were arrested and taken to the dread fortress. Ralegh was immured away from his wife and child in the Brick Tower. The queen's drastic action was not entirely motivated by jealousy, however. The fact that Bess had drops of royal blood in her veins; that another rising favourite, Robert Devereux, the young Earl of Essex, had stood godfather to the Raleghs' baby; and the Raleghs' foolishly snobbish boasts to friends that the child was 'a Plantagenet' rang dynastic alarm bells in the queen's Tudor ears, ever alert to rival claims on her crown.

Ralegh's first bout in the Tower was short. He used his enforced leisure and his literary gifts to try to write his way out. His initial effort was a self-pitying sonnet – a verse form recently imported from Italy – on the frugal conditions of his captivity.

> *My body in the walls captived*
> *Feels not the wounds of spiteful envy,*
> *But my thrilled mind, of liberty deprived,*
> *Fast fettered in her ancient memory,*
> *Does naught behold but sorrow's dying face.*
> *Such prison erst was so delightful*
> *As it desired no other dwelling place;*
> *But time's effects and destinies despiteful*
> *Have changed both my keeper and my fare.*
> *Love's fire, and beauty's light I then had store;*
> *But now close kept, as captives wonted are,*

That food, that heat, that light I find no more.
Despair bolts up my doors, and I alone
Speak to dead walls, but those hear not my moan.

An early practitioner of Disraeli's dictum that 'everyone loves flattery, and when it comes to royalty you must lay it on with a trowel', Ralegh next wrote a lengthy ode to his angry sovereign, calling it *Book of the Ocean to Cynthia*. The title was a pun on Elizabeth's familiar pet name for Ralegh – 'Water' – and 'Cynthia' – his polite name for her. A mixture of self-pity, pleading and his hallmark arrogance, the poem was addressed to the queen in twelve sections, one for each year they had known one another.

Ralegh's effusion hit heights of absurdity and plumbed lows of self-abasement:

Such force her angel-like appearance had
To master distance, time or cruelty,
Such art to grieve, and after to make glad,
Such fear in love, such love in majesty.

He had almost completed it, when, on 15 September, a month after his imprisonment began, he was suddenly freed. It was not Elizabeth's melting heart that caused this unexpected deliverance, but a more basic emotion: greed. A Portuguese galleon, the *Madre de Dios*, loaded with spices, herbs, ebony, ivory, jewels, silks, silver and gold had been hijacked by an English privateering expedition to the Caribbean that Ralegh had organised and funded. (This was the voyage that Ralegh had planned to take to escape the Queen's wrath.) The vessel had been brought to Dartmouth in Devon, and furious squabbling had broken out over the spoils. There was only one man, advised the head of England's navy, Sir John Hawkins, who could sort out the problem: Ralegh himself.

Momentarily forgetting her rage, the avaricious queen ordered Ralegh's release. But as he distributed the booty – reserving the lion's share for himself – his wife Bess remained in the Tower. In October an outbreak of plague reached the fortress. The Tower's moat was a stinking open sewer, filled with offal, excrement and the foul outpourings of the warren of streets surrounding London's castle. Such a cesspit was a breeding ground for pestilence, and little Damerai Ralegh died. In December the queen finally relented and released the bereaved Bess a few days before Christmas.

Though free, the Raleghs were not restored to favour. They retired to their country estate, Sherborne in Dorset, where Ralegh built a fine new residence in a fashionable style. A volcano of energy, he then organised an expedition to the Amazon in search of the mythical city of gold, El Dorado; helped capture the Spanish port of Cadiz, where he was wounded and lamed for life; and at his London town house dabbled in dangerous debates about God, the Devil, atheism and heaven and hell with a private circle of intimates – including the playwright Christopher Marlowe – that became known as the School of Night. Though Ralegh intrigued constantly to regain his place at court, and partially succeeded, he never recaptured his former pre-eminent place in the queen's affections.

Ralegh's place in Elizabeth's heart was usurped by a young man almost as charismatic as himself. Robert Devereux, 2nd Earl of Essex, born in 1566, was as handsome as Ralegh, as rich as Ralegh, as bold as Ralegh and at least as arrogant as the man dubbed 'the Great Lucifer'. Moreover, unlike Ralegh, he was born into the highest of aristocratic court circles, being the stepson of Elizabeth's long-term favourite, Robert Dudley, Earl of Leicester, via Leicester's third wife Lettice. Essex cemented his place in the queen's charmed circle by his marriage to Frances Walsingham, widow of the archetypal Elizabethan gallant gentleman Sir Philip Sidney, and daughter of Sir Francis Walsingham, Elizabeth's renowned spymaster.

Essex consequently rose even more rapidly than Ralegh in the queen's favour, becoming her Master of the Horse, and after Leicester's death in 1588, stepping neatly into his stepfather's shoes as a new 'sweet Robin': her closest confidant. The young blade and the queen thirty years his senior gamed together, hunted together and of course flirted together. Elizabeth was an ageing woman by this time, her lead-painted white face raddled and cracked; her fiery red hair replaced by wigs to cover her baldness. But her conceit had only increased with the years, and courtiers who wanted to get on were expected to prolong the myth of 'Gloriana': the ever youthful, ever beautiful object of love and devotion. At first Essex was prepared to flatter with a fervour putting even Ralegh to shame.

In 1596, Ralegh suffered the humiliation of having Essex put over his head to command the expedition which took Cadiz and burned a Spanish fleet, with Ralegh serving as his deputy. The closeness that had seen Essex act as godfather to Ralegh's first child had been replaced by a jealous mistrust curdling into mutual hatred. Ralegh resented Essex for having taken his place in the queen's heart; while Essex became convinced that Ralegh was conspiring with Robert Cecil – who had replaced his father Lord Burghley as Elizabeth's senior statesman – to destroy him. But Essex needed no extra enemies; he was, as Francis Bacon would point out at his trial, his own most dangerous foe.

Elizabeth was determined to quell a grumbling guerrilla war led by the Irish nobleman, Hugh O'Neill, Earl of Tyrone, against rapacious English colonisation. In 1599 Essex was given command of a large army, with orders to crush the revolt. But instead of 'bringing rebellion broached on his sword' as Shakespeare flatteringly wrote of him in *Henry V*, Essex negotiated a truce with Tyrone, before rushing back to England after only six months' absence to explain his actions to a furious Elizabeth.

Deliberately defying the queen's orders to stay at his Irish post, Essex, sweaty and mud spattered, stormed unannounced through the queen's privy chamber into her bedchamber. It was early and he caught the old lady at her toilette. Bald and wrinkled as she was, denuded of the powders, potions, wigs and stays she used to prop up the illusion of youth, it was a cruel revelation of the Goddess Gloriana's mortality. Icily, Elizabeth refused to listen to Essex's excuses and his furious denunciations of his enemies. He was placed under arrest. Kept sequestered from his family, Essex's disgrace can be judged from the fact that Elizabeth denied him permission to write to his wife after she had given birth to a baby girl. Only when Essex sank into what appeared a terminal decline did the queen allow him home.

Brooding on his wrongs in Essex House, his luxurious riverside home on London's Strand, Essex plunged deeper into the mire. Believing that Cecil and Ralegh had poisoned the queen's mind against him, he took the final, fatal step into treason. Cursing the queen as 'crooked in her mind as she is in her carcass', he gathered a wild assortment of malcontents: unemployed former officers who had served under him, Catholic conspirators, and Puritan preachers. He sent messages to King James VI in Scotland appealing for aid to overthrow Elizabeth. The messages were intercepted by Cecil's secret service as he allowed Essex to stretch his neck further on the block awaiting him. He was only too obliging.

On the morning of Sunday 8 February 1601, Essex assembled a small army in the courtyard of Essex House. His chief lieutenant was the dandified Henry Wriothesley, Earl of Southampton. The grandson of the Henry

Wriothesley who had been Henry VIII's chief enforcer and Tower torturer, young Southampton was a thug who also appreciated the arts. A close friend and patron of Shakespeare, and the dedicatee of the Bard's poems *Venus and Adonis* and *The Rape of Lucrece*, Southampton has been plausibly suggested as the mysterious 'Mr W. H.' to whom Shakespeare's sonnets are dedicated. The Bard and his patron may have enjoyed a homosexual affair. Southampton was certainly reported to have had a gay relationship with a fellow officer in Ireland, where he served Essex as captain of the cavalry. It was probably Southampton who suggested bribing Shakespeare's Lord Chamberlain's Company to revive *Richard II*, with its theme of the overthrow of a tyrannical monarch, to put Londoners in the mood to back Essex's revolt. Although the cast were innocent of any prior knowledge, the play was indeed staged at the Globe Theatre on Saturday 7 February: the eve of the rebellion.

The government, learning what was afoot, sent a Privy Council delegation to dissuade the rebels. For their pains they were locked in a room in Essex House. Then Essex's 300 braves, with the earl at their head, sallied into the streets and headed east to capture the Tower. As he galloped along Essex yelled to bemused onlookers that there was a court plot to kill him. But Cecil had already proclaimed Essex a traitor and rebel, and no one joined him as he headed up Fleet Street to Ludgate. Surrounded, as Wyatt had been in the same streets half a century before, Essex and his men defended themselves with their swords, and in the melee several men were killed.

Essex and Southampton cut their way through to the river, found a boat, and rowed back to Essex House. They barricaded themselves in, refusing to surrender until guns were brought from the Tower armoury and fired a warning cannonade. At last, the earls bowed to the inevitable and gave up. The confused rebellion had lasted less than twelve hours. Soon, in the dead of night, Essex and Southampton were back on the river – this time being rowed downstream to the Tower. On arrival at Traitor's Gate, Essex was taken to his new quarters: the tower in the north-west corner of the fortress behind St Peter ad Vincula that ever since has been called the Devereux Tower in honour of Essex's family name. Southampton's first thought was for his wife, and in a hurried note he told her of the failure of their revolt:

Sweet hart I doute not but you shall heare ere my letter come to you of the misfortune of your frendes, bee not to[o] apprehensive of it, for gods will must be donn, & what is allotted to us by destiny cannot bee avoyded . . .

The queen had had a narrow escape. London was placed under martial law and Lord Thomas Howard was made constable of the Tower, charged with guarding the two earls. Eighty of Essex's followers were examined at the Tower – none too gently – to provide the necessary evidence, and on 19 February the earls were rowed to Westminster Hall to stand trial.

Tried by their peers, the earls sat within a square of benches surrounded by their judges. Essex was dignified in black, while Southampton wore a gown with long sleeves in which his trembling hands were concealed. In an eloquently vicious speech, the chief prosecutor, Attorney-General Sir Edward Coke, called attention to the earl's black garb, saying that if he had succeeded he would have worn 'a gown of blood'. 'It hath pleased God,' Coke concluded, 'that he who sought to be Robert the First of England should be Robert the last of his earldom.' Essex replied that Coke's eloquence was 'the trade and talent of those who value themselves upon their skill in pleading inocent men out of their lives'. The trial was full of high drama. At one point, the tiny, hunchbacked figure of Robert Cecil appeared to deny Essex's claim that he had plotted to put the Infanta of Spain on England's throne. At another, Southampton claimed unconvincingly that he had tried to talk Essex out of their enterprise.

At last, as the wintry shadows gathered in the ancient hall, and candles were lit, the lords called for food, beer and baccy. The French ambassador, Monsieur de Boissise, wrote scornfully:

> For while the Earl and the Council were pleading, my Lords guzzled as if they had not eaten for a fortnight, smoking also plenty of tobacco. Then they went into a room to give their voices; and there, stupid with eating and drunk with smoking, they condemned the two Earls.

Once back in the Tower, Essex refused to see his wife or children. Under the evil influence of the Revd Abdy Ashton, a Puritan preacher spying for the government, he wrote a four-page statement naming co-conspirators, including his own sister.

Although Essex claimed to have done with the 'baubles' of this world and to have his eyes firmly fixed on eternity, a tale about his last days in the Tower suggests that he still had hopes of the queen's mercy. The story goes that a besotted Elizabeth had once given Essex a ring, telling him that if he ever returned it, whatever his crime, he would be forgiven. Essex decided that the time had surely now come. Wrenching the ring from his finger and leaning out of the Devereux Tower, Essex entrusted his ring to a passing pageboy. He ordered the lad to take it to Lady Scrope, a female admirer of his at court, and via her to give it to the queen. The boy sped off on his mission. But instead of presenting the ring to Lady Scrope, he gave it to her sister, Lady Nottingham, wife of Lord Charles Howard, the Tower constable and one of Essex's worst enemies. Lady Nottingham kept the ring and the secret to herself. Two years later, when both Lady Nottingham and the queen were near death, she told all to Elizabeth. The monarch cried in anguish, 'God may forgive you – but I never can.'

Essex's execution was fixed for Ash Wednesday, 25 February 1601. Elizabeth, fearing a violent popular reaction to the killing of the celebrity earl, had decreed that he be privately beheaded within the Tower's walls. Essex would be the last person – and the only man (unless we count the messy deaths of the Duke of Clarence and Lord Hastings) – to be executed inside the fortress until a series of German spies were shot there in the two world wars. Elizabeth had ordered two executioners to attend, lest, as she explained, 'should one faint the other may perform it'.

Informed that he would die the next morning, Essex told his guards that for all his former wealth he would be unable to tip them: 'For I have nothing left save that which I must pay to the Queen in the morning.' The earl spent his last night on his knees praying. They came for him at 7 a.m. It was a wet and chilly winter morning, and Essex wore a black felt hat, and a black velvet cloak over a black satin suit. He walked through the drizzle accompanied by several Puritan preachers. The earl mounted the scaffold on the same spot when Anne Boleyn, Katherine Howard and Jane Grey had died.

Essex must have looked askance at his hated rival Ralegh, who, with grim satisfaction, was present in his capacity as captain of the Yeoman Guard. Ralegh had written a vicious letter to Cecil warning him not to reprieve Essex: 'If you take it for good counsel to relent towards this tyrant, you will repent when it shall be too late.' Now, after some in the crowd protested at his tasteless presence, Ralegh withdrew from the scaffold to the White Tower, where he watched from a window; although the story that he callously puffed a pipe of his imported tobacco as Essex died may be a malicious rumour.

Raising his voice against the wind and rain, Essex told the crowd that he had been justly tried and condemned; and rightfully 'spewed out of the realm'. His sins, he said, were more numerous than the hairs on his head. 'I have bestowed my youth in wantonness, lust, and uncleanness. I have been puffed up with pride, vanity and love of this wicked world's pleasures.' He protested, however, that he had never intended to harm the queen. Nor, he added, with a sly dig at Ralegh's supposed atheism, had he ever disbelieved in God. His greatest regret, Essex concluded, was that men had died for his pride and ambition. Now he would atone. He asked those present to pray for and forgive him – as he 'forgave the whole world'.

He was ready. From force of habit, he called for his manservant Williams to help him disrobe. But Williams was not there. Hair plastered against his wet skin by the rain, Essex had to remove his cloak and ruff himself, then unbutton his black doublet to reveal a splash of colour – his waistcoat, soon to be spattered with his own blood, was bright scarlet. Refusing a blindfold, he lay flat on the wet straw as psalms and prayers were intoned, before he flung out his arms and called on the headsman to strike home. But the man botched his job. The first blow of the slippery axe bit into the earl's shoulder. The second also went astray. Only with the third stroke was that proud head off and in the executioner's hands as he held it by the hair and asked the crowd to behold the head of a traitor.

Southampton's obsequious conduct in court, and the intervention of Robert Cecil on his behalf, were enough to win him a reprieve – though he stayed in the Tower for the two years that Elizabeth had left to reign. The earl was comfortably lodged in an apartment at the east end of the Tower's royal palace. Here he had a sitting room and bedchamber with mullioned windows rather than bars. The queen was merciful to the young dandy, allowing Southampton's mother to visit her errant son. Elizabeth also allowed him medicines for his frequent chills and fevers which were exacerbated by the unsalubrious Thames and the Tower's filthy moat.

Southampton had companions in his captivity. He had one attendant, Captain Hart, who grumbled that he was a prisoner too. More welcome than the grouchy Hart was Southampton's pet, a faithful black and white cat, which, Tower legend alleged, had made its way to his quarters via the chimney. The cat featured in a famous portrait that Southampton had painted of himself after his imprisonment. An inset shows a picture of the Tower itself with the defiant Latin tag '*In vinculis invictus*' ('In chains unbowed').

CHAPTER TWELVE

PAPISTS, PLOTS AND POISONS

Despite the rivalry of Ralegh and Essex, real power in Elizabethan England was in the hands of less glamorous figures who had never boarded a Spanish galleon, sunk in an Irish bog, sought for El Dorado, or singed the King of Spain's beard, but who controlled the destinies of the kingdom from behind the scenes. These were her secretaries of state William Cecil, Lord Burghley, and after him his hunchbacked second son Robert Cecil, who equalled and perhaps surpassed his father in guile, ruthlessness and his dedication to maintain England as a Protestant power. The Cecils were sustained by the queen's lifelong companion Robert Dudley, Earl of Leicester, and by the creator and master of her secret service, the austere Sir Francis Walsingham.

This quartet were responsible for resisting the twin threats of Spanish invasion from without and Catholic conspiracy to kill the queen from within. So long as Mary Stuart, Queen of Scots, lived – especially after her Scottish subjects kicked her out and she fled to England in 1568 – she would pose an intolerable threat to a Protestant England. As a succession of plots were uncovered by Walsingham's spies, so the cells of the Tower filled with genuine Catholic conspirators, compromised Catholic noblemen, innocent Catholic citizens and hunted Catholic priests. Elizabeth's promise not to 'make windows into men's souls' was forgotten in the interests of the state's survival.

The first serious threat came in 1569, the year after Mary's arrival in England. At first given considerable freedom, she was able to communicate with her supporters and encourage their treasonable plans. A plot was hatched among the traditionally Catholic northern nobility to rise against Elizabeth in her favour. The plotters planned for Mary to marry Thomas Howard, 4th Duke of Norfolk. The duke was the son of the Earl of

Surrey, the last victim of Henry VIII's reign to be executed at the Tower. As Elizabeth's Lord Lieutenant of the north, the 4th duke had been deputed to receive Mary. Thrice widowed, yet still under thirty, Norfolk had fallen in love with her, signalling his willingness to reign at her side in Elizabeth's place.

The duke's hopes of marrying Mary were encouraged by his sister, Jane Howard, wife of the Earl of Westmoreland, one of the two leaders of the coming revolt. Thomas Percy, 7th Earl of Northumberland, and Charles Neville, 6th Earl of Westmoreland, were the hereditary heads of the north's ancient aristocratic dynasties. They were both Catholics attracted by the prospect of a new Catholic Queen Mary to champion their religion. Norfolk – though nominally a Protestant – allowed himself to be drawn into the plot.

The rebels captured Durham, whose ancient cathedral echoed to the Mass for the first time in years. However, resolute action by the queen and council nipped the Northern rising in the bud. The rebel troops melted away as they moved south; the two earls fled to Scotland; and Norfolk, found cowering on his East Anglian estates, was thrown into the Tower. Elizabeth gave him the same comfortable quarters at the east end of the royal palace that Southampton would occupy, so Norfolk could stretch his legs in the palace's long gallery. Elizabeth rather liked the handsome duke, despite his weakness and overt ambition. Norfolk's friends at court quietly pleaded his case, and kept him informed of developments via messages on black paper, dropped into the dark corners of his privy, and letters rolled into tubes and inserted through a hole bored in his wall. Although interrogated personally by William Cecil, Norfolk managed to avoid incriminating himself.

Francis Walsingham, however, had eyes and ear everywhere, and the spymaster's patience was soon amply rewarded. In 1570, encouraged by the Pope's bull *Regenis in Excelsis* releasing Catholics from their duty to Elizabeth and calling for her overthrow or death, Roberto Ridolfi, a Florentine banker based in London, lent his name to a new plot. The queen was to be assassinated; a Spanish army would descend on England from the Netherlands; and Mary would marry Norfolk and reign over a Catholic country once again.

Meanwhile, Norfolk was freed from the Tower but was still under strict surveillance. He foolishly let Ridolfi inveigle him into his plot and thus put his neck upon the block that Walsingham had set up. In September

1571, a Catholic courier, Charles Bailly – under scrutiny since a spell in the Tower the previous year – was caught at Dover carrying letters detailing Spanish support for the plot. After the discovery of coded letters from Norfolk to Mary's more suspect friends, the duke was re-arrested. This time there were to be no palace privileges. Norfolk was lodged in the place with the most evil reputation of all: the Bloody Tower.

Three other towers – the Salt, the Coldharbour and the Beauchamp – filled with the duke's co-conspirators. Although Norfolk, as a nobleman, was spared torture, Bailly was racked, and in excruciating pain, revealed the key to the ciphers he had been carrying, and the names of the other plotters. Their plans included a scheme to seize the Tower in Mary's name, and this alone was enough to convict the duke of treason in January 1572. Urged on by Walsingham and Cecil, the reluctant queen put her signature to the duke's death warrant four times – only to cancel it each time. The effect of this cruel psychological torture on the duke over six agonising months can only be imagined. To be repeatedly told to prepare for an imminent death – and just as repeatedly reprieved – was a refined torment worse than the rack. Finally, however, there was no reprieve. Norfolk was beheaded on Tower Hill in June 1572.

He died courageously, with the executioner severing his head 'with singular dexterity'. Norfolk's was the first head to fall there there for a dozen years, and a new scaffold had to be constructed to replace the rotten old one.

One of the two earls who had led the Northern Rising – Thomas Percy, Earl of Northumberland – was sold to the English by the Scots, and beheaded at York. His co-leader, Charles Neville, Earl of Westmoreland, lived out a life in exile on a Spanish pension. He never saw his wife, Jane Howard, or his four children again. Thomas Percy's younger brother Henry, the new Earl of Northumberland, despite having shown no previous disloyalty – indeed he had fought for the government against the Northern Rising – took up his dead brother's cause as soon as he inherited his title. Twice he was put in the Tower, and twice he persuaded the authorities to let him out again. But it would not be third time lucky for the foolhardy peer.

In 1584 another Catholic plot was discovered. It took its name from Francis Throckmorton, a cousin of Walter Ralegh's wife Bess. The details were the mixture as before: a cross-Channel invasion in support of an

English Catholic rising aimed at deposing Elizabeth and putting Mary in her place. Northumberland, freed from the Tower, held a plotters' meeting at one of his country houses, Petworth, in Sussex. Word of this reached the government, and two plotters, Throckmorton and William Shelley, were arrested, taken to the Tower and racked.

At first Throckmorton was confident that he could withstand the rack's rigours. He wrote a coded message to friends on a playing card pledging to die a thousand deaths before he would betray them. The spirit was undoubtedly willing, but the flesh strained and the sinews snapped – and soon Throckmorton and Shelley were naming names, places and dates. Armed with their confessions, the authorities had Northumberland arrested again in December 1584. He was interrogated, though not tortured, denying all knowledge of the plot. Eventually, Throckmorton was executed, but the problem of Northumberland remained.

On 21 June 1585, the problem was solved. Northumberland was found shot dead in his Tower cell – a pistol loaded with three balls had been discharged through his heart. An inquest jury brought in a hasty verdict of suicide, but pamphlets were printed across Europe accusing the government of murder. Sir Walter Ralegh later alleged that one of his court rivals, Sir Christopher Hatton, had ordered the killing on behalf of the Privy Council, using the Tower's ardently Protestant lieutenant, Sir Owen Hopton, as the murderer. At length, the rumours forced the government to mount an inquiry – which confirmed the suicide verdict. This is unconvincing. Northumberland was buried in the Tower's chapel, St Peter ad Vincula, which, had he been a genuine suicide, would not have been allowed. The weight of the admittedly scanty evidence points to murder for reasons of state. At all events, the earl was yet another victim in a lengthening list of mysterious deaths at the Tower.

The fortresss claimed its victims in various ways. The son of the executed Duke of Norfolk, Philip Fitzalan, Earl of Arundel, was imprisoned there in 1585, apparently for little more than his Catholic faith. Chiselled into the wall of his cell in the Beauchamp Tower, he added his name with a flourish to those of the Dudleys and several of his own co-religionists who had been previous inmates. He even carved the date: 22 June 1587, two years after Northumberland's mysterious death, and a year before the Spanish Armada arrived. A pious and gentle man, Arundel lived a monastic life during his decade in the Tower, giving away much of the money he received for his own maintenance to the poor, and subsisting on a frugal diet.

In 1588, Arundel's wife bribed a warder to leave a door open so that a Catholic priest, imprisoned in the nearby Bell Tower, could steal along the walkway once used by Elizabeth for exercise and say Mass in his cell. When the government heard that the Mass had been to pray for the success of the Armada, the priest was tortured into confessing. Arundel was then tried for treason and condemned to death – though the sentence was never carried out. Instead, in 1595, the earl caught dysentery – a condition exacerbated by his poor diet. Knowing that he was dying, he petitioned the queen to be able to see his wife and child before he expired. She replied that if he renounced his religion he would be released. Arundel scornfully refused, saying he wished he had more lives that he could sacrifice for his faith – and duly died. Buried in St Peter ad Vincula, he was later exhumed and beatified, and now lies in the Howard family's chapel in the Sussex town from which he took his title, yet another martyr to the religious intolerance that disfigured the Tudor century.

In 1587 came the Babington Plot, the most important of all the Catholic conspiracies aimed at eliminating Elizabeth and substituting Mary. The plot was carefully manipulated by Walsingham's spies to make a trap to destroy Mary, 'this devilish woman' as Walsingham called her. Throughout the 1580s, the twin threats of Spanish invasion and Catholic subversion grew – and so did the government's efforts to counter them. Walsingham had agents in every European capital; the ports were closely watched; suspect travellers were questioned; and Catholic houses harbouring Jesuit missionary priests were repeatedly raided.

One such priest was the saintly scholar Edmund Campion, who, after his capture in 1581, suffered the torments of the tiny Tower cell known as 'Little Ease' – a niche in a wall in the White Tower's cellars designed so it was impossible for the inmate to stand or lie down, the crouched position adopted causing agonising cramps. This having failed to teach Campion the error of his ways, he was racked three times. His arms were so badly dislocated that he was unable to raise them at his trial and execution.

A Jesuit who evaded Walsingham's bloodhounds for eight years before he was caught was the poet–priest Father Robert Southwell. Holed up in the country homes of Catholic recusants, he wrote devotional verse such as *The Burning Babe*. In 1592, however, Southwell fell into the merciless hands of Richard Topcliffe, the queen's notoriously sadistic persecutor-in-chief of fugitive Catholics. Tortured in the private chamber that Topcliffe kept for the purpose in his London house, Southwell was then thrust into a tiny dungeon known as 'Limbo' in the Gatehouse prison at Westminster. When he was found crawling with lice, his father petitioned that he be tried and executed immediately as the gentleman he was rather than endure further suffering.

The authorities transferred the poet–priest to the Tower, where he was de-loused and allowed new clothes and books. The government's 'humanity', however, had a purpose: to make Southwell talk. During his three years in the Tower he endured no fewer then ten sessions of torture. His sole consolations were his faith and his poetry:

> *O life! What lets thee from a quick decease?*
> *O death! What draws thee from a present prey?*
> *My feast is done, my soul would be at ease,*
> *My grace is said: O death! Come take away.*
>
> *Thus still I die, yet still do I revive,*
> *My living death by dying life is fed;*
> *Grace more than nature keeps my heart alive,*
> *Whose idle hopes and vain desires are dead*

Southwell's desire for death was granted in 1595 when he was executed.

A young graduate of the exiled English Catholic colleges at Douai, Rheims and Rome that were turning out these missionaries was Gilbert Gifford, described as a beardless boy. Gifford was intercepted by Walsingham's men on arriving at the Sussex port of Rye in December 1585. He was carrying letters in cipher destined for Mary Stuart from the Scots queen's chief agents in France, Thomas Morgan and Charles Paget. (It is a tribute to the English spy chief's fearsome thoroughness that both Morgan and Paget are suspected by some historians of having been double agents working for Walsingham, despite their ostensible loyalty to Mary.) Gifford and his letters were sent on to London to be examined by Walsingham and his chief code breaker and forger, Thomas Phelippes.

The spymasters saw at once that they had been handed the instrument to destroy Mary. On pain of torture and death, Gifford was persuaded to become a double agent working for Walsingham. He would proceed as planned to Chartley, the Staffordshire country house where Mary was held in increasingly close confinement by her rigidly Puritan keeper, Sir Amyas Paulet. Here, Gifford would open a channel of communications via an ingenious method that Walsingham's backroom boy Phelippes had worked out after visiting the moated house. Weekly deliveries of keg beer were made to Chartley from the nearby town of Burton, and the empty barrels were picked up by the same brewer. The secret letters would be hidden inside the barrels' bungs, and Gifford would be the postman. In this way, Mary's covert correspondence could be monitored and doctored by the secret service, in order to secure the damning evidence that would send her to the block.

Gifford was a witting – and apparently willing – agent luring Mary to her doom, delivering her first letter from Morgan in almost a year. But the man whose letters finally ensured her – and his own – destruction was a starry-eyed young Catholic gentleman utterly devoted to the captive queen. Anthony Babington had met Mary while serving as a boy page to the Earl of Shrewsbury, the Scots queen's first guardian after her arrival from Scotland. Babington had fallen under her spell, and vowed to be the knight errant who would spring her from her prison. In the meantime he hid Catholic priests – including Campion – and ferried them around his native Midlands.

Travelling to France, Babington contacted Mary's agents and offered to smuggle letters to her giving details of a new Catholic rising and her rescue. Back in London, he recruited a group of like-minded young Catholic gentlemen for a desperate double enterprise: to rescue Mary and to kidnap or kill Elizabeth. Revealing letters began to flow in and out of Chartley via the barrel-bung post. Mary was cautious, but after eighteen years of captivity she was growing desperate. Thomas Phelippes, running Gifford and his post for Walsingham, carefully forged additions to the letters 'sexing them up' to implicate Mary in treason. Plotting Mary's escape was one thing – Elizabeth would hardly consent to her death on those grounds alone – but giving her approval to a Spanish invasion and her cousin's killing would be her death warrant. Walsingham authorised Phelippes to manufacture the evidence.

Their forgeries were superfluous. In her next letter, a six-and-a-half-page effusion, Mary fitted her own neck to the block. The letter agreed to all Babington's plans: the rising, her rescue, a Spanish invasion and – crucially – the murder of Elizabeth, even advising Babington on how to get away after the deed. Walsingham's master forger was so confident that, after deciphering the self-incriminating letter, Phelippes sketched a gallows on the envelope before sending it on to his boss. In the late summer of 1586, armed with this damning evidence, Walsingham swooped. Babington and his fourteen young confederates were rounded up in London, along with their spiritual counsellor, the Catholic priest John Ballard, who went under the pseudonym 'Captain Fortescue'. They joined their co-religionists in the Tower.

There was no mercy for the fanatical young idealists who had vowed to kill their queen. Elizabeth, who had naturally taken a personal interest in the unfolding conspiracy to murder her, ordered that the full gruesome medieval ritual of hanging, drawing and quartering should be carried out, in order 'for more terror' to be struck in the hearts of anyone tempted to emulate Babington. The plotters were executed in two groups in September. Tied to hurdles in the Tower, they were drawn to Holborn where the bloody and barbaric ritual was enacted. The slow deaths of Babington and his friends by strangulation, castration and final evisceration of their entrails and hearts so shocked even the hardened Tudor crowd, that when the second group were executed the following day, they were allowed to dangle on ropes until they were dead before the posthumous butchery began.

One of the men who died so horribly with Babington was Chideock Tichborne, a young Hampshire gentleman. On the eve of his bloody execution he wrote a poignant and tragic poetic farewell to his wife Agnes and a world he had hardly begun to know – probably the greatest, and certainly the saddest, work of literature of the many penned in the Tower:

> My prime of youth is but a frost of cares,
> My feast of joy is but a dish of pain,
> My crop of corn is but a field of tares
> And all my good is but vain hope of gain;
> The day is past, and yet I saw no sun,
> And now I live, and now my life is done.
>
> My tale is heard and yet it was not told,
> My fruit is fall'n and yet my leaves are green
> My youth is spent and yet I am not old,

I saw the world and yet I was not seen;
My thread is cut and yet it is not spun,
And now I live, and now my life is done.

I sought my death and found it in my womb,
I looked for life and saw it was a shade,
I trod the earth and knew it was my tomb,
And now I die, and now I was but made;
My glass is full, and now my glass is run,
And now I live, and now my life is done.

The executon of the Babington plotters was but the starter to the main meal as far as Walsingham was concerned. He and Burghley were set upon Mary's death, despite prolonged dithering on Elizabeth's part. Mary's trial and execution at Fotheringhay Castle, without the queen's authorisation, followed in February 1587. Elizabeth threw a tantrum when told of her treacherous cousin's demise, and sent one of the responsible officials to the Tower. She even briefly dismissed the faithful Burghley from court. She could not, however, afford to sulk for long: 1588 was the year of the Spanish Armada, and all Elizabeth's and England's energies went towards repelling it.

By 1603, it was clear that Elizabeth's long reign was drawing to a close. The old lady spent long periods staring silently into space, her finger in her mouth, idly twirling a ring – perhaps the ring that had belonged to Essex – and dreaming of the past. Those around her began to make discreet arrangements for the future. Robert Cecil had already established contact with the heir apparent, Mary Stuart's Scottish son James VI, in Edinburgh. Of rival claimants to the Crown, one, the Infanta Isabella of Spain, was daughter of the hated Philip of Spain. The other, Arbella Stuart, was suspected of Catholicism – and was an unmarried woman. England had had more than enough of single and infertile female rulers. James, though son of the Catholic martyr Mary, had been brought up as a Protestant, and, while interested in the thornier questions of theology, showed few signs of converting to Catholicism – despite the fact that his Danish-born queen, Anne, had done so. In addition, the Scottish king, though homosexual, had fathered three children by Anne – Henry, Charles and Elizabeth – so the Stuart succession was secure.

James was an oddball, which, considering his upbringing, was hardly surprising. His mother had narrowly escaped murder when he was still in her womb. While he was an infant, his father had been murdered and his mother, after outraging public opinion by marrying the murderer, had been chased into exile. He had never seen her again. James had grown up a helpless puppet of Scottish political and religious factions, in constant danger of abduction and assassination. The man who had emerged from this singularly disturbed background was himself singularly disturbed. Understandably neurotic about his own security, he wore stab-proof padded jackets and breeches, slept in a cocoon of mattresses, forbade his courtiers to carry knives or swords, and was averse to violence. On the other hand, he had a strongly sadistic streak. As we have seen, he frequently visited the Tower menagerie to watch animals tearing each other to shreds. He adored hunting, and stayed in the saddle for hours, urinating and excreting on the hoof rather than dismounting. When a stag was killed, he delighted in the peculiar practice of plunging his spindly legs into the beast's hot and bloody entrails.

James's personal hygiene was poor. He rarely washed, his many phobias including a terror of water. His only concession to cleanliness was to wipe his fingers with a damp rag, and his courtiers claimed they could tell what the king had eaten by observing the stains adorning his clothes. He disguised his appalling stench by drenching himself with perfume. His ingrained dirt had darkened his skin to a velvety texture. James had goggle eyes and a tongue too big for his mouth, which lolled out when he slobbered over his male favourites' necks, while his hands rummaged in their breeches. An unlikely intellectual, who wrote tracts against witchcraft and Ralegh's tobacco, James lived up to his reputation as 'the wisest fool in Christendom' since his lack of common sense and cowardly, vindictive character make him one of Britain's most unattractive monarchs.

This was the thirty-seven-year-old man who in March 1603 was brought the long-expected news that Elizabeth had died in the palace of Richmond, and that he was now King James I of England, the first Stuart monarch, and the first joint king of the feuding nations of England and Scotland. James's accession initially pleased English Catholics, who optimistically looked forward to more tolerance than they had enjoyed under Elizabeth's harsh repression. They were to be deeply disappointed. But the initial losers in the change of dynasty were the quintessential old Elizabethans who had gloried at fighting Spain on land and sea. No one was likelier to rub James on the raw than that ageing essence of Elizabethan swagger: Sir Walter Ralegh.

When Ralegh hastened to welcome the new king as he journeyed south, he was greeted coldly. 'I have heard rawly of you, mon,' spat the monarch in his strong Scots dialect, punning on the old warrior's name. James's dislike of Ralegh had been kindled during his feud with Essex, with whom the king had been in correspondence. His mind thoroughly poisoned, James stripped Ralegh of his job as captain of the guard, and turned him out of his London residence, Durham House. Later, he confiscated Ralegh's country estate, Sherborne Castle, telling him, 'I mun have it for Carr' — Robert Carr being the gay king's current boyfriend.

Ralegh was further tainted by his suspected involvement in two plots against the new Jacobean regime. The so-called Main Plot ran alongside the Bye Plot, a hare-brained venture dreamed up by two Catholic priests to capture James and force him to announce toleration of their religion. Ralegh's friend Henry Brooke, Lord Cobham, and his brother became involved and were arrested. Ralegh was detained in July 1603 after his friend had falsely incriminated him. Outraged at finding himself back in the Tower accused of connection with a Catholic plot, and despairing of gaining the favour of the hostile king, Ralegh wrote grovelling letters to anyone he could think of who had the king's ear. When these had no effect, in a fit of uncharacteristic self-pity Ralegh made a hysterical attempt at suicide by stabbing himself in the chest with a table knife, causing a superficial wound. On recovering, Ralegh changed tactics. His wails of innocence were replaced by a successful effort to charm the Tower's lieutenant, Sir John Peyton. When Robert Cecil discovered what was afoot, he sacked Peyton, compensating him with one of Ralegh's old jobs as governor of Jersey.

Ralegh was tried for treason at Winchester, for London was in the grip of one of its periodic plague outbreaks. Ralegh's part in the downfall of Essex, the people's hero, had made him wildly unpopular with the London public and on his way to the trial his coach was pelted with clay pipes — for his role as the chief importer of tobacco, and the high prices he charged for the noxious 'sot-weed', were also resented. The lynch mob grew so menacing that, in the words of a witness, it was 'hob or nob whether he should have been brought alive through such multitudes of unruly people as did exclaim against him'. In acute danger of death, Ralegh responded loftily, 'Dogs always bark at what they know not.'

Ralegh retained his sangfroid at his trial, responding to a vindictive tirade from the Attorney General, Sir Edward Coke, who called him a 'monster . . . the most vile and execrable traitor that ever lived [with] an English face but a Spanish heart!' by quietly replying, 'You speak indiscreetly, barbarously and uncivilly.' Convicted solely on his former friend Lord Cobham's patently false evidence, and sentenced to death, Ralegh was taken back to the Bloody Tower to await his execution.

In imminent expectation of death, during a sleepless night, he wrote a moving final farewell to Bess:

Remember your poore child for his father's sake, that chose you and loved you in his happiest tymes. Get those letters (if it be possible) which I writt to the Lords, wherein I sued for my life, but God knoweth it was for you and yours that I desired it, but it is true that I disdayne myself for begging it. And knowe it (deare wife) that your sonne is the child of a true man, and who, in his own respect, despiseth Death, and all his misshapen and oglie formes.

I cannot wright much. God knows how hardlie I stole this tyme, when all sleep; and it is tyme to separate my thoughts from the world. Begg my dead body, which living was denied you . . . I can wright noe more. Tyme and death call me awaye . . .

Yours that was; but now my owne, W. Ralegh.

To add to Ralegh's anguish, Cobham himself, after being subjected to a mock execution by the sadistic James, got off with a sentence of imprisonment. Cobham was given privileged accommodation in the Tower's Lieutenant's Lodgings. As Ralegh paced the short section of the wall outside his tower (still known as 'Ralegh's Walk') waiting for death it must have galled him to see the man who had put him there living as the new lieutenant's guest. As it turned out, Ralegh would wait a full thirteen years for the axe to finally fall. The reprieve was thanks to one of his chief court enemies, Robert Cecil, who had always secretly hated the swaggering, cocksure sea dog, even though he had often allied with Ralegh – such as when they had combined against their mutual enemy, Essex. Now Cecil yielded to the desperate pleas of Bess Ralegh, his sister-in-law, and showed mercy.

The Bloody Tower, where Ralegh lived in two rooms on the upper floor, was a damp, cramped and miserable setting for the once wealthy and magnificent Ralegh. He was fifty-two now, elderly by seventeenth-century standards, and racked by frequent fevers. His old wounds troubled him, forcing him to lean heavily on a cane. The winter of 1603–4 was very cold, the walls ran with water, and the plague still raged, claiming victims within the Tower's walls. Ralegh had a few comforts. His everyday needs were met by a servant, Dean, while a young man, John Talbot, doubled as his secretary and as tutor to Ralegh's son Wat, who, aged eleven, was preparing for university. A waterman, Owen, brought beer to the captive, as the polluted water in the Tower was undrinkable.

Ralegh's chief consolations were the faithful Bess and Wat, who were allowed unrestricted access to him, virtually sharing his imprisonment. Another son, Carew, conceived in the Tower, was born to Bess Ralegh in 1605 at the house on Tower Hill that she had rented. Sustained by his family's support, Ralegh rallied, and began work on the most sustained and massive piece of literature written in the Tower: a complete *History of the World*.

A true Renaissance man, Ralegh's life as a statesman and man of action had hitherto obscured his achievements as a writer and scholar, but restricted to the Tower's tiny world, he was forced to focus on his literary gifts. The result was an explosion of intellectual productivity. Apart from the massive *History*, political tracts, poems, philosophical essays and letters poured from his quill. In addition, by exercising his charms on the new lieutenant, Sir George Harvey, who had replaced Peyton, Ralegh procured the use of a wooden shed in the lieutenant's garden – where he cultivated his own herb garden. The hut was no ordinary potting shed. When Bloody Mary had crowded the Tower with Protestant prisoners, it had done duty as the cell where Bishop Hugh Latimer, a notable Protestant martyr, had been imprisoned; and more recently it had become a chicken coop.

Ralegh converted the hen hut into a laboratory for scientific and alchemical experiments, equipping it with retorts and copper tubing. In one experiment, he succeeded in extracting the salt from seawater and turned it into fresh water; in another, he invented a method for curing his beloved tobacco. All the while he developed yet more skills to add to his protean achievements: those of physician and herbalist. Always a self-healer who rarely consulted doctors, with the help of the herbs in his garden, some grown from cuttings he had brought back from the Amazon, Ralegh produced potions which became popular folk remedies in high society. The wife of the French ambassador, for example, seeing Ralegh gardening while on a visit to the Tower menagerie, successfully asked him to boil up and send her a bottle of his 'Guinea balsam'. Another of Ralegh's concoctions, a reviving cordial of strawberry water for relieving faintness, also proved popular with the ladies. The most celebrated of all his medicines, however, was a 'Great Cordial' – an elixir, probably containing quinine from the Americas, which he claimed could heal almost every ailment. Ralegh's inquiring mind, though tethered, was now freed from worldly ambition and was inquiring still.

And now that he was a victim, his infamous pride humbled in adversity, Ralegh's previously dire popularity took an astonishing upwards turn. Sympathetic crowds gathered on the Tower wharf to see the tall and stately Elizabethan hero as he limped along 'Ralegh's Walk'. They cheered him on his way, to which Ralegh responded with a grave bow. Court ladies, susceptible as ever to his charisma, flocked to visit him. A trip to see Ralegh in the Tower became part of the social round for London's glitterati. The visitors he entertained ranged from a group of Indians he had brought from the Amazon (who rented a house on Tower Hill to be near him), to the astronomer and scientist Thomas Harriot, and Ralegh's sea captain Lawrence Keymis – both faithful friends who had accompanied him to the Amazon and did not desert him now. The playwright and poet Ben Jonson, who would write a preface to Ralegh's *History*, was also among his regular guests. Ralegh's relationship with Jonson – a fervent Catholic, a brawling thug (he was imprisoned for killing an actor in a duel), and a literary genius – illustrates the breadth of his world, despite its narrow physical confines, and its eclecticism. The last embers of the astounding Elizabethan Renaissance were still burning brightly in the confines of the Bloody Tower.

Curious about this man whom her husband so hated, but who was the talk of the town, James's Catholic wife Anne of Denmark, and her brilliantly attractive eldest son, Prince Henry – who had inherited all his father's intellectual gifts, but none of his defects of physique and character – also visited Ralegh. The old charmer strained every sinew to dazzle the prince, doubtless hoping that the firmly Protestant youngster would restore Ralegh to his rightful position. Henry duly fell under Ralegh's spell, saying of his new hero, 'Only my father would cage such a bird.' Henry's contempt for his cruel and cowardly father became ever more blatant. When James took a reluctant prince to see one of his gruesome animal fights at the Tower's menagerie, Henry was sickened by the spectacle of three mastiffs being dispatched by a lion in quick succession. He asked his father to stop the slaughter, but James decreed that 'such a bonny battle' must be fought to a finish. Eventually, the compassionate Henry begged Edward Alleyn, the theatrical entrepreneur who staged the baiting, to take one surviving mauled mastiff home, heal his wounds and 'make much of him'.

Ralegh's relationship with Prince Henry – who was the same age as his son Wat – soon transcended mercenary motives. Indeed, so frequent were the young prince's hero-worshipping trips to see the star of the Bloody Tower – and so intense their discussions on exploration, seamanship, the Americas, religion and statecraft – that the sinister tower became a cross between a schoolroom and the nucleus of an alternative court. Early in their friendship Ralegh built the prince a model ship, and together they planned future voyages to the Americas that they would undertake when the 'caged bird' was free.

It was as a result of his relationship with the Prince of Wales that Ralegh conceived the huge project of writing his vast world *History*. On one level it can be seen as the record of Ralegh's role as unofficial tutor to the very bright heir to the throne. But Ralegh's global *History*, beginning at the Creation, was no dully didactic chronology, but rather a massive literary, philosophical and religious epic whose theme was the justification of God's ways to mankind. As such, it convincingly refuted rumours that Ralegh was a secret atheist. And in its insistence on a universal moral law, it is a worthy precursor of Kant. Chronologically, the first volume of the *History*'s 1,364 folio pages got no further than 168 BC, but Ralegh was not shy of working in contemporary events such as the tactics used to repel the Armada, and reminiscences of his own youthful campaigns in France, when discussing ancient wars. He also used biblical and classical times as a transparent camouflage for his own often rueful reflections on kingship, justice and religion:

> The judgments of God are for ever unchangeable, neyther is hee wearied by the long process of time, and won to give his blessing in one age to that which he hath cursed in another.

If the *History* has heroes, it is the great warriors of the ancient world, Alexander and Hannibal, whom Ralegh clearly perceives as forerunners of himself. Apart from its intrinsic interest as perhaps the greatest work ever to emerge from a prison cell, and its testimony to its author's phenomenal industry and erudition, Ralegh's *History* is a masterpiece of English prose written in the language's springtime – the English of Shakespeare,

Marlowe, Jonson; and of the King James Bible. Despite its size and length, the book's success was immediate. It went into ten editions – twice as many as Shakespeare's plays – and its influence during and after the author's lifetime was enormous. Its reflections on kingship, and its insistence that God trumped the authority of earthly rulers, were seized upon later in the seventeenth century by Roundhead radicals – including those Tower inmates the Leveller John Lilburne, and the pamphleteer William Prynne – who threw down and beheaded the son of the man who had persecuted Ralegh. Praised by the Protestant Parliamentary poets John Milton and Andrew Marvell, it was given by Oliver Cromwell himself to his own son. The liberal philosopher John Locke thought that if any gentleman wanted to improve his education he should read Ralegh's book; and the great nineteenth century historian, Lord Acton, though he described Ralegh as a 'villainous adventurer', declared that he nonetheless 'venerated' him for the *History*.

Predictably, though, one voice dissented from the chorus of praise: that of King James himself. James was astute enough to see that Ralegh's attacks on ancient tyrants were lightly coded criticisms of himself. Spluttering that the book was 'too saucy in its censuring of Princes', the man who believed that he held his throne by divine right tried in vain to ban the book. He rightly read passages like this brutally accurate description of his ancestor Henry VIII as a reflection on his own fitness to rule: 'If all the pictures and patterns of a merciless Prince were lost to the worlde, they might all again be painted to the life out of the story of this king.' James's opinion of the author was not improved by the fact that, at the time when he was negotiating with Spain to win a Spanish bride for Prince Henry, Ralegh, doubtless with the approval of the saucy prince, boldly but tactlessly wrote not one but two tracts denouncing the idea of marriage with his old foe.

Although he had planned his *History* in three volumes, Ralegh only completed the first. He had written twenty pages of the second volume when a curious incident stopped him in his tracks. Working in his study one day, Ralegh was distracted by a loud noise, and going to his window found a violent fight in progress among a group of workmen who had been carrying out some routine building maintenance. As Ralegh watched, one of the men was fatally injured. His curiosity aroused, Ralegh attempted to discover the cause of the deadly quarrel, but inquire as he might, he could never get a satisfactory answer. That was when he laid down his pen and burned the first pages of the second volume. For, he reasoned, if he could not establish the truth about an event he had witnessed with his own eyes, how could he possibly write with authority about battles, rulers and happenings in faraway lands he had never visited, among peoples he knew of only from other – and most likely unreliable – writers? It was a sadly inconclusive end to one of the century's great works.

For all his intense intellectual activity, Ralegh's restless spirit found imprisonment intolerable. His frustration at having his wings so cruelly clipped is poignantly expressed in the desperate lines he wrote to his friend-turned-enemy Robert Cecil:

> I cannot think myself to have bin an enemy, or such a viper, but that this great downfall of mine, this shame, loss and sorrow, may seem to your Lordship's heart and soul a sufficient punishment and revenge. And, if there is nothing of so many years' love and familiarity to lay in the other scale. O my God! How have my thoughts betrayed me in your Lordship's nature, compassion and piety. For to die in perpetual prison I did not think that your Lordship could have wished to your strongest and most malicious enemies.

Cecil's heart remained unmelted. He did, however, ensure that Bess Ralegh was not reduced to dire poverty because of her husband's misfortune. Despite his own entreaties and Prince Henry's pleas to his father to release his friend, Ralegh remained in the Tower. He was there to witness the two great crises which shook the Jacobean kingdom, both of which were played out in the fortress: the Gunpowder Plot and the murder of Sir Thomas Overbury.

It did not take long for the embattled English Catholic community to realise that the fond hopes they had placed in King James for a lifting of the punitive penalties they had suffered under Elizabeth, and which had driven many of them into poverty, exile, or both, were misplaced. Raised in the unforgiving world of the Calvinist Scottish Presbyterian Kirk, James had even separated the young Prince Henry from his mother when Anne converted to Catholicism, for fear that the prince would be contaminated by her faith. Although James took abject steps to seek peace with Spain, this was not through any sympathy for Catholicism, but merely because he was broke and mean, and hated war. The harsh anti-Papist laws of Elizabeth, with their stiff fines for non-attendance at Anglican Communion, and the ban on publicly celebrating the Mass, were reaffirmed. In rage and despair, some hotheaded young Catholics turned to plot what one of them, Guy Fawkes, called 'a desperate remedy for a desperate disease'.

The moving spirit in the Gunpowder Plot was not its fall guy, Fawkes, but its initiator, Sir Robert Catesby. Descended from Richard III's thuggish lawyer William Catesby, Robert came from a Midlands Catholic gentry family. He had a streak of reckless extremism, and supported Essex's wild rebellion – for which he was fined. Deeply disappointed by James's failure to restore or even relieve Catholicism, in 1604 Catesby again turned to treason. He recruited a dozen fellow Catholic gentlemen – all, except Fawkes and his own servant Thomas Bates, related to him by blood or marriage – plus a couple of priests to give his plot their spiritual blessing. Then he outlined his scheme. The plot was an inhumanly audacious act of random mass terror like 9/11. The plan was to blow up the Houses of Parliament during the state opening by the king and Prince Henry on 5 November 1605 – a day when the entire English ruling caste, king, Lords and Commons, would assemble in a single building. Catesby planned to lay a gunpowder charge beneath them large enough to destroy everyone in the Palace of Westminster. After half a century's apostasy, England would be literally blown back to Rome.

The plotters rented a coal cellar directly under the Palace of Westminster and filled it with barrels of gunpowder, reinforced by hundreds of metal bars to make the giant explosion even more deadly. The lethal load was stowed neatly away, camouflaged by bundles of firewood. Fawkes, a fanatical, red-headed giant who had proved his devotion to his faith by fighting for years in the Spanish army in the Netherlands, thereby acquiring his extensive knowledge of explosives, was placed in charge of the store-room awaiting the fateful day.

As November neared, with their preparations complete, the plotters had time to consider the moral implications of their plan. There would be fellow Catholics, including friends and relations, among the assembled parliamentarians. Was it really right, they asked themselves – and their spirtual counsellors, the Jesuit priests Fathers Garnet and Greenaway – to destroy their co-religionists along with the heretics? The priests reassured them that saving the soul of the nation outweighed the loss of a few individual lives, but doubts lingered. One plotter, Francis Tresham, was particularly concerned about his brother-in-law Lord Monteagle, a Catholic peer due to attend the state opening.

Ten days before the event, someone – probably Tresham – apparently sent Monteagle an anonymous warning not to attend. The cryptic letter, delivered to a servant while the peer sat at supper at his home in Hoxton, advised him to skip the state opening as 'they shall receive a terrible blow this Parliament, and yet they shall not see who hurts them'. This fairly transparent warning was passed to Robert Cecil by Monteagle, and from Cecil to King James. Paranoid about assassination, James ordered a thorough search of the parliamentary cellars.

Getting wind of the betrayal, Catesby and his chief lieutenant Tom Wintour taxed Tresham with having written the warning, but he hotly denied it. After a week with no apparent action from the authorities, Catesby breathed again. No one had disturbed their cellar, and it looked as though the government had ignored Monteagle's warning. They decided to go ahead as planned. All the plotters except Tresham and Fawkes left London for the country where they planned to launch a Catholic revolt as soon as Parliament blew up.

On the afternoon of 4 November, the cellars were searched. Fawkes was found guarding the plotters' chamber. He claimed to be 'John Johnson', the servant of plotter Thomas Percy. 'Johnson' calmly unlocked the cellar for the searchers' inspection. They made a casual examination of the firewood without finding the lethal material beneath. A relieved Fawkes watched them troop away.

When the searchers reported to James that evening, however, they described 'Johnson' as 'a very bad and desperate fellow . . . up to no good'. James's ears pricked up. He ordered a second search that night, beefed up with soldiers. Just before midnight the searchers again found Fawkes/Johnson, still guarding the cellar door. They delved deeper into the piled firewood, and soon uncovered the thirty-five barrels of gunpowder with the lethal iron bars. The Gunpowder Plot had misfired.

A body search of 'Johnson' revealed several incriminating items, including a length of slow-burning match cord, a touchwood to light it, and a watch. Fawkes also carried a lantern, still to this day in Oxford's Ashmolean Museum. He was marched off to Whitehall to be personally examined by the king. Questioned by James in the royal bedchamber, Fawkes readily admitted intending to blow up Parliament. His only regret, he said, was in not having blasted those he called, with no deference to his sovereign's nationality, 'all the Scotch beggars back to their native mountains'. He stoutly refused, however, to name his co-conspirators.

Realising that they would get no more that night from the tough ex-soldier, the king ordered Fawkes to be taken straight to the Tower. James admitted finding Fawkes quite admirable. The miscreant had shown, he said, 'a Roman resolution' when under fierce cross questioning. Once at the Tower, Fawkes was thrust into the cramped niche cell Little Ease where his co-religionist Edmund Campion had suffered in the previous reign.

After an extremely uncomfortable night, the sleepless Fawkes was dragged to the Lieutenant's Lodgings to be questioned anew. Three months before, Sir George Harvey, the second lieutenant whom Walter Ralegh had succeeded in charming, had been removed for his laxity, and replaced by a much tougher nut, Sir William Wade – or Waad. The son of another government servant Amigal Wade (who made an early voyage to America in 1536, and from whom the tennis player Virginia Wade's family are descended), William Wade was employed by the Tudor and Jacobean state as a brutal fixer – a man to send for if a dirty job needed doing.

A former member of Walsingham's intelligence service, and therefore a gnarled veteran of statecraft's sharper end, sixty-year-old Wade had first crossed swords with Ralegh when he had acted as gaoler at Sir Walter's treason trial in Winchester. He was the obvious choice when a hard man was needed to succeed the kindly Harvey. But Wade had only just started on the pleasurable job of making Ralegh's life a misery by restricting his use of the garden laboratory and other petty cruelties (Ralegh referred to him simply as 'that beast Wade!') when his attention was diverted by the Gunpowder Plot. A skilled and ruthless interrogator who did not scruple to use torture, Wade confronted Fawkes in his own Tower apartment.

King James, whose personal interest in the plot must have been heightened by the knowledge that his own father, Lord Darnley, had been murdered in Edinburgh after his house had been ripped apart by a massive explosion, had appointed a high-powered commission of peers, headed by Robert Cecil, to investigate the conspiracy. The king had even drawn up a list of questions for Fawkes, aimed at linking him to the Papacy, the Jesuits, or a foreign power. But if Fawkes remained obstinately tight-lipped, James specifically authorised the use of 'the gentler tortures' at first, to be followed by harsher methods, a command that the learned king disguised in Latin – '*et sic per gradus ad ima tenditur*' ('and so by degrees proceeding to the worst') – before concluding, 'And so God speed your good work.'

By the 'gentler tortures' the king meant the manacles, the breaks and the thumbscrew. And by 'the worst' he had the rack in mind. The Tower possessed the only working example of this fearsome bed of pain to be found in England. It is probable that Guy followed his co-religionist Edmund Campion's path in being subjected to the manacles at first, but the strong and determined man – literally a tough Guy – held out against his tormentors. It was with mingled respect and pleasure then, that William Wade warned his prisoner to brace himself for the worst – and led him to the dark chamber beneath the White Tower where the rack was located.

Guy Fawkes had been arrested around midnight on 4/5 November. For two days and nights he held out against the escalating persuasions of his captors – blandishments, threats, 'Little Ease', the manacles – before he was broken by the rack and started to talk sometime on 7 November. Perhaps he judged that enough time had elapsed for his co-conspirators to make their escape. Or perhaps he simply, like other mortal men and women, cracked under the weight of the agonising pain that the rack delivered. Fawkes is thought to have withstood the rack for longer than anyone else on record. A total of two and a half hours is sometimes mentioned. By that time, the sinews and ligaments in his arms and legs would have been stretched and torn, and his wrists and ankles, chafed by ropes attaching them to the rack's rollers, were blistered and bloody.

A mute but graphic testimony to Fawkes's suffering is seen if the signatures he put to two confessions are compared. The name beneath the first statement, before his torture, is written as 'Guido Fawkes' in a script as bold as its owner's character. But the faint scrawl under the transcript of the answers he gave to Wade on the rack is horribly changed. They must have put the pen between his numb fingers as all he could manage is a faint, weak and disjointed 'Guido . . .'. That done, and the names of his fellow plotters secured, Fawkes was carried back to Little Ease, to subsist on a meagre diet of barley bread and stagnant water from the Tower's rank moat.

Meanwhile, outside the Tower, the conspiracy was not unfolding according to Catesby's plan. Catesby and his closest companions had travelled to Holbeche House, a stronghold of Midlands Catholicism in

Staffordshire. They had taken with them a cartload of extra gunpowder left over from their stock, as munitions for the planned Catholic rising. One plotter, Sir Everard Digby, told Catesby that he had around fifty men prepared to rise. Digby left to round up his little army while Catesby unwisely spread the gunpowder – soaked by the November rain – in front of a blazing fire to dry. A spark ignited the powder, and a sheet of flame badly burned some of the half-dozen plotters left with Catesby.

In despair, three plotters – Robert Wintour, Hugh Owen and Stephen Littleton – fled into the night, while Catesby, Tom Wintour, Thomas and Kit Wright, Ambrose Rookwood, John Grant and Thomas Percy grimly awaited their fate. The next morning, 8 November, the house was surrounded by a government posse led by the Sheriff of Worcester. Catesby and the others refused to surrender and were all shot dead, or were wounded and taken prisoner. These included John Grant who had been blinded in the gunpowder blast – hoist by his own petard. 'Stand by me, Mr Tom,' said Catesby to Wintour, 'and we will die together.' But it was another Tom, Percy, who died with his chief: they were killed by the same musket ball. The plot leader, in his dying moments, kissed an icon of the Virgin Mary – symbol of the faith for which he had sacrificed his own and many other lives.

Over the next days and weeks, the surviving plotters were rounded up. Only Hugh Owen managed to find his way abroad. The others were taken to the Tower along with two Jesuit priests – Fathers Garnet and Oldcorne – who had sustained them. As they were brought in, each conspirator was given the same treatment meted out to Fawkes: over three long weeks they were manacled and racked, and in between torture sessions supervised by Wade, were kept barely alive on a diet of stale bread and stinking water. Francis Tresham, suspected of betraying the plot to Lord Monteagle, died in the Tower – either from one of the diseases rampant in the fortress, or as the result of torture. Monteagle himself was awarded an annual pension of £700 for divulging his co-religionists' plans to the authorities.

Apart from the crudity of the rack, Wade had subtler means of ferreting out the priests' secrets. A veteran Papist hunter, Wade knew how well the Jesuits were trained in evasive answers – the technique known as 'equivocation' – and he adopted similar tricks. He treated the priests with relative kindness, visiting them in their cells and endeavouring to break down their defences with cosy chats. Wade confided that he was considering converting to Catholicism himself, and moved Gerard and Oldcorne into comfortable adjoining cells in which they could communicate through a hatch. The cell was fitted with the seventeenth-century equivalent of an electronic listening bug: a hole drilled through the wall by which the crafty old lieutenant overheard the priests' whispered conversations. Realising that Wade now knew all about his involvement, Garnet confessed to having foreknowledge of the plot – but hid behind the priestly vow of silence to explain why he had not seen fit to inform the authorities of the fiery end awaiting them.

The conspirators remained astonishingly defiant despite their desperate plight. Fired by their faith, none expressed regret for their actions. Even the kindly Everard Digby said that of the hundreds of Parliamentarians whose lives they had intended to terminate he did not think there were 'three worth saving'. In January 1606 the eight surviving core plotters – Guy Fawkes, Thomas and Robert Wintour, Ambrose Rookwood, John Grant, Sir Everard Digby, Robert Keyes and Thomas Bates – went on trial in Westminster Hall, herded together in a dock designed to resemble a scaffold. King James covertly watched proceedings from a hidden vantage point. The evidence was overwhelming, the prosecution by the bloodthirsty Attorney General Sir Edward Coke terrifying, and the jury of peers – containing two Catholic lords lest the government be accused of religious discrimination – took little time in convicting, and passing the prescribed savage sentence for treason of hanging, drawing and quartering.

The eight were executed in two batches of four on successive days. Digby, Robert Wintour, John Grant and Thomas Bates were the first to die, on Thursday 30 January. Three were dragged upside down on wicker hurdles from the Tower to St Paul's Churchyard, while Bates, the common servant, who had not been held in the Tower, was brought from the Gatehouse prison. English class distinctions held firm even in this extremity. Digby had spent his last night at the Tower writing letters of love to his wife and sons. He had also composed a farewell poem in which his undimmed faith was expressed:

Who's that which knocks? Oh stay, my Lord, I come.

Digby was the first to mount the scaffold. Hanged and cut down alive, he was castrated and disembowelled. Then, according to Sir Francis Bacon, who witnessed the scene, as the doughty Digby's still beating heart was plucked out of his chest, the executioner cried the traditional formula, 'Behold the heart of a traitor!' to which Digby, in his last moment of consciousness, managed to mouth the magnificent response, 'Thou liest!' Robert Wintour next went quietly to his death, followed by John Grant who, blinded by the blazing gunpowder at Holbeche House, also remained defiant to the last, insisting that what he had done had been right in the sight of God. Thomas Bates was the only plotter to express penitence. He had acted, he said, out of love and duty for his master Catesby; but now he prayed for forgiveness and mercy.

The next day, it was the turn of Tom Wintour, Ambrose Rookwood, Robert Keyes and – last but not least – Guy Fawkes. Symbolically, their deaths would take place at the Old Palace Yard, outside the Palace of Westminster – the very building that, had their plot succeeded, would have been blown apart by their powder. Tom Wintour died hard, being cut down and messily eviscerated after hanging for only a 'swing or two of the halter'. Ambrose Rookwood had his eyes closed in prayer as his hurdle was bumped along from the Tower. He opened them on arrival at Westminster to behold the face of his lovely young wife. 'Pray for me!' he cried, and when she promised to do so, urging him to be of good courage, he calmly submitted to the hangman, and appeared unconscious when he was cut down and chopped up.

Robert Keyes, the third man to die, went 'stoutly' up the ladder, and then, once the noose was around his neck leapt into space, hoping that he would thus break his neck and be spared further torment. Sadly, the rope broke and, still alive, he was picked up and carried to the chopping block. Finally, it was Fawkes's turn. By now, the scaffold was swimming in blood, but Guido appeared undismayed. His powerful frame broken by the rack, his arms and legs almost useless, he had to be helped up the ladder by the hangman. He cheated his tormentors by jumping off the gallows and succeeded in breaking his neck. Mercifully, the ritual disembowelling was performed on his lifeless corpse.

Father Henry Garnet, the plotters' chief spiritual confessor, despite slippery equivocations finally went to his death in St Paul's Churchyard too. As he left the Tower he told the man who cooked his meals there, 'Farewell, good friend Tom: this day I will save thee a labour to provide my dinner.' William Wade was so proud of his work in searching out the plot's secrets that he had a plaque put up in the room in his lodgings where he had interrogated Fawkes and where it can still be seen:

To Almighty God, guardian arrester and avenger, who has punished this great and incredible conspiracy against our most merciful lord the King . . . [which was] moved by the treasonable hope of overthrowing the Kingdom . . . [by] the Jesuits of perfidious and serpent like ungodliness, with others equally insane, were suddenly, wonderfully and divinely detected, at the very moment when ruin was impending, on the fifth day of November in the year of grace 1605.

The Gunpowder Plot set back Catholicism in England for more than two centuries. It terrified loyal Protestants, convincing them that if they relaxed anti-Papist laws they would all be murdered in their beds by scheming Jesuits. Following 'Bloody' Mary's burnings and the Spanish Armada, the plot entrenched a vision of Catholicism as an essentially alien intrusion in the body politic. Unfairly, it made criminals out of loyal Catholics whose only crime was their faith. They would suffer because of what Wade correctly called their co-religionists' 'insanity'.

One such man was Henry Percy, 9th Earl of Northumberland, whose father, the 8th Earl, had died so mysteriously in the Tower – by either murder or suicide – during his third bout of imprisonment as a suspected Catholic conspirator. The 9th Earl was also strongly suspected of being a crypto-Catholic, as were most members of his ancient family. Percy's chief interest, however, lay in science and the occult – dangerously heterodox pursuits which won him the nickname 'the Wizard Earl'. The dividing line between alchemy and chemistry, at the dawn of the seventeenth century, was still a blurred one. His great wealth allowed Percy to fund his scientific experiments, and his circle included such free spirits in the arts and sciences as the magus John Dee, playwright Christopher Marlowe, astronomer Thomas Harriot, and – of course – Walter Ralegh. Meetings of the discussion circle known as 'the School of Night' were reputed to have taken place at the Wizard Earl's London home, Syon Park.

Neither Percy's wealth and social position nor his non-dogmatic nature saved him from persecution after the Gunpowder Plot. He was first cousin to Tom Percy who had died with Catesby at Holbeche House, and the earl had employed his cousin as a steward to collect rents from his estates. It was suspected that some of this cash had funded the plot, as Percy had rented the cellar where the powder had been stored. The cousins had even dined together at Syon Park on the eve of the plot's discovery. This was more than enough to indict the earl, who was convicted in the Star Chamber court of 'misprision' – i.e. foreknowledge – of treason.

Though he escaped the supreme penalty, the earl's punishment was severe enough. He was condemned to perpetual imprisonment and fined a massive £30,000 (perhaps £4 million in today's values). He was destined to remain in the Tower for even longer than his friend Ralegh – languishing there for sixteen years. Life in the fortress, though, was not entirely uncongenial for the Wizard Earl who, mildly deaf, was of a reclusive disposition anyway.

A highly privileged prisoner, the earl took over the Martin Tower – the future home of the Crown jewels – as his private apartments-cum-library and laboratory, where he experimented, among other things, on turning stale alcohol into drinkable whisky. For relaxation he built a bowling alley. He had his own cook, and paid Wade £100 annually to keep him in the comfort to which he was accustomed. The gruff old lieutenant was further softened by presents of rubies for his daughter, given by the Wizard Earl's wife, who, like Bess Ralegh, rented a nearby house on Tower Hill. Like his friend Ralegh, the earl turned his time in the Tower to good literary account, writing a volume in 1609 of wise advice to his son and heir, Lord Percy, who sometimes stayed with him in the Tower.

The earl and Ralegh swapped books on Machiavelli and Tasso; on warfare, astronomy, astrology and the exploration of the Americas; and held court to a stream of distinguished scholarly visitors. The arrival in the Tower of this congenial fellow spirit was welcome news for Ralegh. The two captives' shared interest in such subjects as maths, navigation, astronomy and chemistry must have eased the passing of many weary Tower nights. Despite his huge fine, Northumberland was still rich enough to pay pensions to a trio of mathematicians – Thomas Hariot, Thomas Hughes and Walter Warner – whom he called his 'Three Magi'; and the presence of such powerful minds made the Tower's atmosphere at the time akin to a university college. Hariot even voluntarily took up residence in the Tower so that he could be close to his two detained patrons. From the Tower he corresponded with the great German astronomer Johannes Kepler on the properties of rainbows.

In May 1612, the death of Robert Cecil, ennobled by James as Lord Salisbury, was welcomed by Ralegh with a bitter epitaph, as he regarded the clever little crook-backed minister as a former friend who had betrayed him. But with Cecil's death the Jacobean court plunged towards corrupt decadence; and the kingdom, without his guiding hand on the tiller, sailed ever closer to Ralegh's old enemy Spain. Far more important than Cecil's passing, however, was the sudden demise that autumn of Ralegh's patron and pupil, Prince Henry.

The prince, a keen swimmer, unwisely took a dip in the Thames one hot day. The seventeenth-century river was more or less an open sewer, and Henry contracted typhoid fever from the toxic water. In the last extremity of his illness, his mother insisted – against her husband's wishes – that a phial of Ralegh's 'Great Cordial' should be brought from the Tower and administered to the prince, who was already in a coma. Ralegh's elixir was poured between the prince's lips and for a minute a miracle seemed to happen. The unconscious boy opened his eyes, sat up and spoke. But it was a false rally. Henry lapsed back into his coma and died on 6 November. With him perished Ralegh's last hope of early release – and much of the spirit seemed to flicker out of the old warrior.

The deaths of Cecil and Henry left a gaping vacuum at the heart of James's kingdom. The space was inadequately filled by the gay king's favourite, Robert Carr. A handsome fellow Scot, whom the besotted king created Viscount Rochester, Carr was little more than a pretty face. He was a political nincompoop, utterly unable to perfom the various jobs the king bestowed on him. He depended almost entirely on his closest friend, Sir Thomas Overbury, an ambitious and intelligent young courtier who had steered Carr's career since the young Scot had first attracted James's attention by dramatically breaking a leg at a tournament in front of the royal box.

His curiosity aroused, James visited Carr as he recovered, and interest soon turned into besotted lust. Carr was entrusted with the sort of state business that Cecil had once handled, but, too incompetent to master it, he thrust the paperwork in Overbury's direction. Overbury thus became, by default, the king's chief minister at one remove, and Queen Anne summed up the situation admirably if cattily when she observed that 'Carr ruled her husband and Overbury ruled Carr'. Such influence made the proud and arrogant Overbury many enemies.

Carr soon became the lust object of another important player. This time his admirer was not an ugly, middle-aged male, but a young, beautiful and utterly ruthless woman. Frances Howard, Countess of Essex, was yet another sprig of the infamous Howard dynasty. As a fourteen-year-old, she had been married to the thirteen-year-old son of the executed Earl of Essex, but the couple had been separated after the ceremony and young Essex had been sent on a prolonged European tour. On his return, he failed to consummate his marriage. It is unclear whose fault this was. Essex's second wife also complained of his impotence, but he protested that he was capable of sex with other women, and even demonstrated his prowess to doubting friends by lifting his nightshirt to exhibit a powerful erection.

There is no doubt, however, about Frances's reluctance to grant her husband his conjugal rights. She used every excuse, from illness to absence, to keep him from her bed, and when they were alone, he complained, she dampened his ardour with a stream of abuse. To extinguish any remaining desire, it was said, she employed necromancers to make waxen images of the unfortunate Essex. These effigies' outsize genitalia would be melted, or transfixed with pins. Frances's reluctance to copulate with her husband became desperate when, around 1610, she fell violently in lust, if not love, with the king's catamite, Robert Carr.

At first, wishing to keep his friend happy, Thomas Overbury encouraged the dalliance. A gifted writer, among his other talents, Overbury even penned the love letters that Carr sent to Frances. When it dawned on him that the couple wanted to marry, however, Overbury reverted to violent opposition, as he could see himself losing his hold over his feeble friend, who would become a creature of the Howard clan.

The head of the Howard family at this time was Frances's great uncle, Henry Howard, Earl of Northampton. Younger brother of the 4th Duke of Norfolk executed by Elizabeth, and second son of the Earl of Surrey whose execution had been ordered on his deathbed by Henry VIII, Northampton had all his life been a closet Catholic. His family's record of treason and suspicion of his secret faith had kept him away from the power he craved throughout Elizabeth's reign, but he had carefully cultivated contacts with James, and with the king's accession, at last came into his own. Northampton became the kingdom's second minister after Cecil. He was a schemer and deceiver without rival. His long years in the cold had embittered him, and he was determined to rule James via his great-niece and her empty-headed husband-to-be Carr. As Overbury stood in his way, Overbury had to go.

Overbury's opposition to the match had hit frantic heights. He wrote a best-selling tract, *The Wife*, proving why Frances would be an unsuitable spouse to his friend. The former friends had a furious public row when Overbury called Frances a 'whore'. On hearing of this, the ruthless young woman and her evil old great-uncle concocted a scheme to dispose of Overbury – permanently. It is uncertain whether the dim-witted Carr was yet privy to their murderous plans, but he was certainly ready for his friend to be consigned to the Tower for a while. The plotters needed to have Overbury off the scene when Frances applied for an annulment of her marriage to Essex on grounds of his impotency.

In April 1513, the king offered Overbury – who had been a diplomat – two foreign ambassadorships, one to distant Moscow. Overbury indignantly refused both. He was instantly, and much to his amazement, rowed off to the Tower on charges of 'disobedience' and lodged in the ground floor of the Bloody Tower, becoming Sir Walter Ralegh's neighbour. Meanwhile the conspiracy to destroy him got into gear. The Howards' first step was to procure an annulment of Frances's marriage to Essex. Despite the doubts of the bishops who sat on a special commission to decide the issue, Frances swore blind that she was still *virgo intacta*. Midwives who examined the heavily veiled woman claiming to be Frances agreed – though there were strong rumours that a virginal stand-in had been substituted. While the commission deliberated, at the Tower, the second stage of the plot was initiated.

The slow poisoning of Sir Thomas Overbury is the most macabre murder case in the Tower's history. It is one of John Webster's Jacobean dramas made putrid flesh: full of sexual jealousy, revenge, intrigue, the occult and murderous sadism. The Howards knew that Sir William Wade, though a tough and cruel lieutenant, was also an honest man who did things by the book. There was no hope of inveigling him into a scheme to illicitly kill one of his charges, so he had to be removed. Using as an excuse Wade's failure to prevent the temporary escape of Arbella Stuart from the Tower (*see* Chapter Thirteen, 'Great Escapes') Wade was fired and replaced by Sir Gervase Elwes, a lawyer and tool of the Howards to whom he paid a hefty £2,000 'thank-you' for his preferment. It was not money well spent, as it would cost Elwes his life.

Frances Howard had her poisons – and her poisoners – ready. Her chief accomplice was her friend and confidante Mrs Anne Turner, a young widow, who had, as a sideline to her other interests as a brothel madam, caterer and poisoner, developed a combined starch and yellow dye which, thanks to her contacts at court (her brother was the king's falconer), had made stiff yellow ruffs and sleeves extremely fashionable. Mrs Turner, in turn, employed a pox-ridden city apothecary, James Franklin, to make up the poisons to kill Overbury. The final step was to get Richard Weston, a servant of Mrs Turner, appointed as Overbury's keeper in the Tower. His job would be to administer the poisons. Overbury did not yet know it, but he was now entirely at the mercy of his merciless enemies.

The conspirators moved cautiously and with devilish cunning. They even made Overbury complicit in his own death by suggesting that if he took small doses of poison – purgatives known as 'vomits' – and made himself ill, the king would look more sympathetically on his abject pleas to be released. Naively, Overbury went along with the plan, unaware that real, deadly, poisons were also being fed to him. On 6 May Mrs Turner passed a phial of green and yellow poison called *rosalgar* (red arsenic) to Weston, who was met by Sir Gervase Elwes as he carried the suspicious-looking substance to the Bloody Tower in one hand while bearing a bowl of Overbury's supper soup in the other. 'Shall I give it to him now?' asked the warder. Elwes, either feigning innocence or genuinely ignorant, asked him what was in the bottle. 'As if you did not know, sir,' snorted Weston, going into the tower. 'They will have me give it to him, first or last.'

Three days later, on 9 May, Weston mixed the arsenic into Overbury's evening broth. The poor prisoner spent the rest of the night excreting, vomiting and retching. Weston demanded his reward from Mrs Turner, but was told he would only get it when Overbury was safely dead. 'Perfect your work, and you shall have your hire,' she said. Overbury continued to sicken, and three weeks later wrote to Carr, pleading for his former friend to use his influence with the king to get him out, and complaining of his illness. The favourite responded sympathetically, saying the time for his release was not yet right but as soon as possible he would 'hasten your delivery'. In hindsight, that phrase has a very sinister ring. With the letter, Carr enclosed a white powder which he claimed would help Overbury's sickness. The trusting man took it – and grew much worse, excreting sixty stools in one night.

Although the conspirators prevented his family and friends from seeing him, Overbury was attended by teams of doctors – some probably in the poisoners' pay – who assured the patient that sickness and lassitude were part of a prisoner's lot in the Tower. Among the doctors he consulted was King James's personal physician, the celebrated Swiss Huguenot Sir Theodore de Mayerne. A piteous letter from Overbury describes his symptoms after a visit from Mayerne:

This morning, notwithstanding my fasting till yesterday, I find a great heat continues in all my body, and the same desire of drink and loathing of meat etc. I was let blood Wednesday 10 o'clock, yet today, Friday, my heat slackens not, the same loathing of meat, having eaten not a bit since Thursday sennight [fortnight] to this hour, and the same vomiting yesternight. About 8 o'clock after Mr Mayerns was gone I fainted.

On 1 July Weston administered another dose of arsenic, again mixing it into Overbury's food, cooked in Elwes' own kitchen. Three weeks later, ringing the poison changes, Weston took delivery of a dose of deadly mercury sublimate, a highly toxic metal compound often used to treat syphilis, which the poxed Dr Franklin had made up. The poison was sprinkled over tarts and jellies which Overbury had requested as delicious dainties. His suspicions beginning to stir, when Overbury left some of the delicacies untouched they quickly became black and furred.

By now, the previously strong and healthy thirty-two-year-old had become a wasted shadow of his former self. His tormented body, encrusted with sores, along with poisoned plasters, had erupted in a mass of boils and blisters, causing his callous killers to refer to him mockingly as 'the Scab'. Yet still Overbury obstinately refused to die, and as long as he lived he was a deadly danger to the Howards. He knew too many of the dirtiest secrets of the spectacularly corrupt Jacobean regime, and, increasingly frustrated by his inability to plead his way out of the Tower, was threatening to spill some very messy beans.

His threat of blackmail sealed Overbury's fate. With the annulment of Frances's marriage to Essex still not granted, any statement from the dangerous and by now desperate prisoner could throw a spanner into the Howards' plans. In September Elwes was ordered to move his dangerous charge to a dark dungeon with no windows, making it impossible for Overbury to communicate with the outside world. Here the final blow was dealt.

The 'medicines' prescribed for Overbury by Mayerne were prepared by his brother-in-law, an elderly Huguenot apothecary, Paul de Lobell, who lived conveniently close to the Tower in Lime Street. De Lobell used a young apprentice, William Reeve, to run the physic to the Tower. Reeve was paid a huge bribe of £20 by Mrs Turner to add a fatal dose of

Franklin's mercury sublimate to a clyster, or enema, which Weston gave to the doomed man, remaining with him throughout a pain-wracked night on 14/15 September. In extreme agony, Overbury finally expired at dawn.

As soon as Weston reported the death, the Howards rushed to bury the evidence. Northampton wrote to their agent Elwes:

> Noble Lieutenant, if the knave's body be foul, bury it presently [i.e. immediately]: I'll stand between you and harm. But if it will abide the view, send for Lidcote [Sir John Lidcote was Overbury's loyal brother-in-law] and let him see it to satisfy the damned crew. When you come to me, bring this letter again with you, or else burn it.

Elwes obediently did as he was ordered, and Overbury's already decomposing corpse was buried at St Peter ad Vinoula before sundown on the same day. Northampton, who had rushed to the Tower to make sure his bidding was done, reported to Carr with sadistic satisfaction:

> He stank intolerably, in so much as he was cast into a coffin with a loose sheet over him. God is good in cutting off ill instruments from off the factious crew. If he had come forth they would have made use of him. Thus sweet lord, wishing you all increase of happiness and honour, I end. Your Lordship's, more than any man. Henry Northampton.

Perhaps to explain why the dead man had been dosed with mercury, the Howards spread the story that he had died of 'the pox' – or syphilis, a disease often treated with mercury – but gossip about the murder could not be buried as quickly as the body. Too many people were in the know, and the Howards had too many enemies, for the secret to stay hidden for ever. For the moment, they enjoyed their triumph. A fortnight after Overbury's death, the commission at last annulled Frances's marriage, and she promptly wed her lover in London's Chapel Royal amidst scenes of great magnificence. Ben Jonson penned a masque to celebrate the nuptials, and John Donne wrote an ode. The king, rejoicing in his catamite's happiness, made Carr Earl of Somerset, and, though up to his goggle eyes in debt, managed to find £10,000 as a wedding present, and covered the bride in jewels. Frances herself, her face a picture of childlike innocence, and her fair hair tumbling over her shoulders as a sign of her unsullied virginity, walked up the aisle on the arm of her proud great-uncle, and fellow murderer, the Earl of Northampton. The impression of wide-eyed innocence was rather spoiled by Frances's scandalously low-cut neckline which, in a first for fashionable court weddings, stopped only just short of her nipples.

Within months, however, it had all gone horribly wrong. Northampton died in June 1615, thereby escaping the fate that was about to overtake his co-conspirators. In the interim, an aggrieved William Wade, still smarting over his sudden dismissal from the Tower's lieutenancy, had been quietly gathering information from his ex-employees there. The skilled interrogator had assembled a dossier of damning statements, all pointing to the murder of Overbury and a high-level cover-up. Wade took his evidence to the newly appointed Secretary of State, Sir Ralph Winwood, who initiated an inquiry.

Circumstances now conspired to make it convenient to revisit the Overbury case. Northampton's death had left the Howard faction leaderless, and their pro-Catholic, pro-Spanish policy vulnerable. Moreover, the king had fallen out of love with Carr, and in love with another handsome young man, George Villiers, who had been pushed before the king by the anti-Howard Protestant faction. If the plot to kill Overbury can be seen as a Catholic conspiracy – both Northampton and the murderous Mrs Turner were Catholics – then the uncovering of the murder was a Protestant reaction. The main discoverers, Wade and Winwood, were devout Protestants, as was Sir Edward Coke, the Lord Chief Justice who presided over the Overbury trials, and Villiers was as much a Protestant puppet as Carr had been a Catholic one.

The lesser lights in the plot were picked off first. Under ferocious questioning Elwes cracked, admitting that Overbury had been poisoned. Elwes was hanged at his own request on Tower Hill, outside the fortress he had misgoverned. He interrupted his speech from the scaffold to implore a friend in the crowd to give up gambling – Elwes' own great vice. Mrs Turner was hanged at Tyburn, mockingly dressed in the yellow ruff and sleeves she had made so popular. In her honour, the hangman was also arrayed in yellow. At her trial she had tearfully pleaded that she had only fallen into Frances Howard's clutches after her husband's death had left her penniless and unable to feed her children. But there was too much evidence of her own dabbling in witchcraft for her guilt to be doubted. Her judges branded her 'a whore, a bawd, a sorcerer, a witch, a papist, a felon and a murderer'.

Overbury's actual murderer, the warder Weston – who had been paid £180 by the countess for all his trouble – expressed the fear before his execution that the authorities had made a 'net to catch little birds, and let the great ones go'. How right he was. The poxed apothecary, Franklin, was the fourth conspirator to suffer the extreme penalty. The evidence against him included a list of the full cocktail of poisons fed to Overbury. These included mercury sublimate; aqua fortis, a corrosive liquid made by distilling purified nitre with calcined vitriol (sulphuric acid); red and white arsenic; potash; powdered diamonds; crushed spiders; and another poison derived from insects, the irritant known as cantharides, or Spanish fly, which was added to an onion sauce with two partridges sent to Overbury from the court. Fed this sort of toxic diet, it's a wonder that Overbury survived for six days, let alone the six months that he did hold out. Instead, according to a letter sent by Elwes to Frances Howard:

> Madam, the Scab [Overbury] is like the Fox, the more he is cursed, the better he fareth . . . Sir Thomas never eat White Salt but there was White arsenick put into it: once he desired Pig and Mrs Turner put into it *Lapis Costitus* [potash].

Finally, it was the turn of the 'Great Birds'. The evidence produced at the trials of the lesser conspirators by a gloating Attorney General, Sir Francis Bacon, had left no doubt as to the late Earl of Northampton's guilt, and that of the Carrs, newly ennobled as the Earl and Countess of Somerset. They were charged with poisoning Overbury and tried before the House of Lords in May 1616. Frances, pale and trembling, was supported in the dock by Sir George More, who had succeeded the executed Elwes as lieutenant of the Tower. More was the father-in-law of the poet and churchman John Donne, who had composed verses celebrating the Carrs' wedding. Since the evidence was overwhelming, the unhappy couple were quickly found guilty and sentenced to death. Frances had taken the precaution of becoming pregnant, so knew that she would not hang immediately as the law forbade the execution of pregnant women. She gave birth to a daughter, Anne, in the Tower.

As an extra refinement, Frances was lodged in the same cell in the Bloody Tower where her victim Overbury had suffered so cruelly. Realising this, she gave way to a fit of hysterics. Ralegh himself had recently been temporarily released, and the Carrs were allowed to cohabit in the Bloody Tower in adjoining chambers with a communicating door. Still officially under sentence of death, they were given considerable freedom, and the countess furnished her room with costly crimson velvet, and had three maids waiting upon her. Carr continued to wear the jewels and insignia that James had heaped upon him, and paid social calls to the imprisoned 'Wizard Earl' Northumberland in the Martin Tower.

It may have been the weight of accumulated strain and guilt over Overbury, or just the discovery in the Tower's cramped confines that a little love goes a very long way, but soon the earl and countess discovered that they could not stand each other. The silence of the Bloody Tower was split by screaming rows, and before long the pair were cohabiting no more. By the time they were freed from the Tower – though kept under house arrest in the country – they were no longer on speaking or even screaming terms, and lived at opposite ends of their large Oxfordshire home. James finally pardoned the evil pair a few months before his own death in 1624. Frances died a painful death from cancer in 1632. Carr survived in obscurity until 1645.

It is still not clear how much James himself knew of the killing of Thomas Overbury. Though undoubtedly jealous of Overbury's hold over Carr, and happy to see him in the Tower, it is unlikely – but not impossible – that he approved his slow murder. However, it was probably Carr's knowledge of his sovereign's secrets that lay behind James's decision to pardon him. James had a dread of poisons and witchcraft, and though his personal physician, Dr Mayerne, treated Overbury, there is no evidence that the elderly Huguenot had been involved in the murder. On the other hand, James's court was spectacularly corrupt and decadent, ruled by James's perverse passions, and such was the toxic atmosphere there that the king was darkly suspected of having poisoned his own son Henry. Poison, literal or metaphorical, was the lifeblood of James's court, and the Overbury murder its representative crime.

The ill wind of the Overbury scandal at least blew one Tower resident a little good – or so it seemed at first. Sir Walter Ralegh, who had been physically near the crime scene as Overbury's neighbour in the Bloody Tower, had long bombarded the king and court with petitions for his release on the grounds that he could mount another expedition to the Amazon and bring back the untold wealth of El Dorado. James had never listened to these wild claims, but with his huge debts mounting, and the anti-Spanish Puritan Winwood as Secretary of State, he decided in desperation to release the hated old man from his long captivity and give him a chance both to redeem himself and to enrich the Crown. Ralegh was under no illusion that it was greed, rather than compassion, that motivated this meanest of monarchs.

In March 1616, Ralegh had his first taste of freedom in more than a decade. He was provisionally released from the Tower – albeit under surveillance – on condition that he mounted his gold-digging expedition.

Ralegh found a London much changed since his Tudor heyday. Nevertheless, helped by his son Wat, he worked with the energy of a man twenty years younger to build and equip a new ship, hopefully named the *Destiny*, to lead the fleet that would accomplish his dream. It took him time to finish the ship and recruit trusted men, led by his old skipper Lawrence Keymis – the faithful friend who had accompanied him up the Orinoco River half a lifetime before in 1595 and who now got his old job back. A year after leaving the Tower, Ralegh's expedition was ready. He set sail from Plymouth in March 1617.

Ralegh's last adventure was a disaster from the start. Repeatedly blown back into the ports of his beloved Devon by contrary winds, he discharged fifty seamen as incompetent or insubordinate; and only in August did he finally get away. Putting in to the Canary Islands, Ralegh stopped one of his headstrong captains who wanted to plunder a Spanish ship. Ralegh was under strict instructions from James to avoid a clash with Spain. The aggrieved skipper returned to England and spread the lie that Ralegh had been the aggressor. En route across the Atlantic, the little fleet was stricken with fever, and some fifty sailors died, including Ralegh's faithful secretary, John Talbot, who had made a fair copy of the *History* in the Tower. Ralegh himself went down with the disease, keeping to his cabin for four weeks.

Too ill to accompany his son Wat and the main party down the Orinoco to find El Dorado – or at least a goldmine that could be profitably plundered – Ralegh kicked his heels on the island of Trinidad anxiously awaiting news. When it came it was the worst. Against orders, the expedition had attacked a Spanish settlement, and the headstrong Wat had been shot dead leading the charge. Desperate to retrieve something from the disaster, Captain Keymis had sent Ralegh's cousin George Ralegh blundering further into the jungle on the wild-goose chase after what young Wat had truthfully perceived as fools' gold. Apart from a couple of looted ingots, they returned empty-handed.

Failure was complete and unmitigated, and now disgrace and death stared Ralegh in the face. Paralysed by the catastrophe, the indomitable spirit which had survived the Tower was utterly broken. He knew that in England he would face the wrath of the king, the scorn of his enemies – and the block. With a heavy heart, he steeled himself to break the news of their bereavement to Bess.

> I was loath to write because I know not how to comforte you. And God knows I never knewe what sorrowe meant till nowe . . . Comfort your hart (dear Bess) I shall sorrowe for us both; and I shall sorrowe the lesse because I have not long to sorrowe, because not long to live . . . My braynes are broken, and it is a torment for me to write, and espetially of Miserie . . . The Lord bless you, and comfort you, that you may beare patientlie the death of your valiant Sonne.

Ralegh's cup of 'sorrowe' ran over after two of his captains turned pirate and left the fleet, while the faithful Keymis, blaming himself for the disaster and mortified by Ralegh's cold reception – 'You have undone me by your obstinate folly' – retired to his cabin and shot himself. The ball being deflected by a rib, he finished the job with a dagger. Ralegh briefly considered turning privateer in the service of France, but he knew that to evade his tragic fate would look like cowardice. Bereaved, broken-hearted and with a mutinous crew, he sailed for home. On 21 June 1618 the *Destiny* docked again at Plymouth.

News of his disaster had preceded Ralegh. Totally under the influence of the Spanish ambassador, Gondomar, the king had denounced Ralegh's alleged aggression against Spain, abjectly promising Gondomar that he would send Ralegh to Madrid in chains – but this was a step too far for even his craven council to swallow. In Ralegh's absence, the Puritan secretary, Ralph Winwood, had died and the faction favouring a Spanish alliance was once again in the ascendant. Public opinion, however, in striking contrast to 1603, was wildly in favour of the last Elizabethan sea dog – a living example of the glory days of the Armada when England's monarch had not acted as a servile Spanish lapdog.

For several weeks Ralegh remained in Plymouth. Bess urged him to escape to France, enlisting one of Ralegh's old captains, Samuel King, and a ship to make the attempt. Twice Ralegh actually set off in a dinghy – and twice he returned. Finally, a treacherous kinsman, Sir Lewis Stukeley, arrested him and conveyed him towards London. At Salisbury, hearing that James was about to arrive on a royal progress, Ralegh staged a humiliating fake illness to try to grab the king's attention – rolling naked on the floor roaring, and getting a physician to rub irritants into his skin to produce sores. He also wrote an abject *Apology* to explain the Orinoco debacle. This theatrical demonstration failed. The king refused either to see him or to read his *Apology*.

Ralegh arrived in London where he was tricked into making another escape bid on a French ship, which was betrayed by Stukeley. This allowed the authorities to activate the death sentence imposed back in 1603. For the third and final time, the gates of the Tower crashed shut behind him. Lodged in the Brick Tower – his former quarters in the Bloody Tower were now occupied by the murderous Carrs – Ralegh finally resigned himself to his fate. Queen Anne pleaded for her old friend, but her influence over her homosexual husband was nil.

One of the despairing notes that a friendly jailer, Edward Wilson, smuggled out of the Tower for Ralegh complained that he was 'sick and weak and in perpetual pain and unrest'. The old man, nearing seventy now, was broken, and when he left the Tower for the last time to appear before his judges at Westminster, his hair was white and matted, and he was, as Attorney General Sir Henry Yelverton noted, 'a man to be pitied. He hath been a star at which the world hath gazed. But stars may fall, nay they must fall when they trouble the sphere wherein they abide.'

The cowardly James was extinguishing the last and brightest star in the Elizabethan firmament on the orders of England's enemy – Spain. It was a national humiliation and hugely unpopular with the public who, barely a decade after they had tried to lynch Ralegh, would now have liked to rescue the hero from a despised king's hands. Fearing just such an attempt, the authorities rushed to execute him on 29 October, the day after his sentence. He spent his last night, not in the Tower, but in the Gatehouse of Westminster Abbey, close to the Palace Yard where the scaffold had been erected. Even in his last extremity, Ralegh still had enough spirit to play to the gallery – tossing his hat to a bald man, saying that he would need it no more, and asking another bystander if he knew of a plaster to re-affix a severed head. A visiting kinsman, Francis Thynne of Longleat, worried that such jests would detract from his dignity on the scaffold. 'Do not grudge my last mirth in this world,' Ralegh replied. 'When I come to the sad parting you will see me grave enough.'

The saddest parting of all, later that evening, was from Bess, his companion through so much misfortune. As she left him at midnight she confided that she had been given permission to bury his body. 'It is well, dear Bess,' he answered sadly, 'that thou mayst despose of that dead which thou hadst not always the disposing of when alive.' Bess Ralegh was faithful to her husband after death, burying his body and keeping his embalmed head with her in a velvet bag until the day she died at the great age of eighty-two. Left alone, Ralegh reworked an old poem he had written for Bess in their springtime and inscribed it in a family bible. It made an excellent epitaph for an explorer on his final journey:

> Even such is Time, which takes in trust
> Our youth, our joys, and all we have,
> And pays us but with age and dust,
> Who in the dark and silent grave
> When we have wandered all our ways
> Shuts up the story of our days.
> And from which earth and grave and dust
> The Lord shall raise me up I trust.

These moving lines are proof enough that if Ralegh had ever toyed with atheism, such doubts were now behind him. He was dying a Christian, reconciled with God and the world – a fact which seemed to disappoint the Dean of Westminster, Dr Robert Tounson, when he came to offer him Holy Communion and spiritual consolation. Ralegh rose from his knees, reported Tounson, 'very cheerful and merry' and even ate a hearty breakfast and smoked a pipeful of his own tobacco. He dressed like an actor donning a costume for a famous last performance: satin doublet, black velvet waistcoat, grey silk stockings, black taffeta breeches and a large black velvet coat. His hair was now carefully combed.

Ralegh's last morning was a bright, dry and crisp autumn day. Refusing to tarry by a fire lest he be seen to shiver as he climbed the scaffold, Ralegh stepped out to greet the crowd – remarking how pleased he was to see them all in broad daylight. The spectators around the scaffold were astounded by his calm demeanour. Even his enemies, who had come to gloat and scoff, conceded that these were the last moments of a brave man – and a great soul. Eagerly accepting a glass of sherry, and speaking from pre-prepared notes, he said he would not keep people waiting long as he expected to be meeting Christ in his Kingdom within fifteen minutes.

He forgave those such as Stukeley who had betrayed him 'as I hope to be forgiven' and he pointed out that he had returned voluntarily from South America, refuting whispers that he had been disloyal. He denied hounding Essex to his death, pointing out that his own troubles had begun with his rival's death. Lastly, he reviewed his own long career 'as a seafaring man, a soldier and a courtier' – and, he might have added, as the Tower of London's most distinguished prisoner. Finally, declaring that he died a member of the Church of England who hoped to be saved and have his sins washed away by the 'precious blood and merits of our Saviour Christ', he said goodbye as he departed on his final voyage: 'I have a long journey to take and must bid the company farewell.'

Turning to the executioner, Ralegh removed his outer clothes and asked to see the hidden axe. Checking that the blade was well whetted he joked, 'This is a sharp medicine – but it is a sure cure for all diseases.' In an echo of Ralegh's most famous gesture, the executioner spread his own cloak out for the condemned man to kneel on. As he knelt, some pedant asked whether he wanted to face east, as was customary. Ralegh, as ever, was scornful of custom. 'So the heart be right,' he observed, 'it is no matter which way the head lieth.' Refusing a blindfold, he told the headsman that since he was not afraid of the axe, he would not fear the axe's shadow. Clearly disconcerted, the man hesitated, and Ralegh's last words were an irritated order, as though he was commanding a reluctant soldier in battle: 'What dost thou fear? Strike, man, strike!'

The executioner struck. But it took a second blow before Ralegh's head fell. Overcome with emotion, the headsman lifted the dripping object, but omitted the traditional cry of, 'Behold the head of a traitor.' The crowd watched in stunned silence. Then a single voice spoke for them all. 'We have not another such head to be cut off!'

PART TWO

CHAPTER THIRTEEN

GREAT ESCAPES

The attempted flight of the Earl of Surrey vividly shows that the Tower of London, seemingly so solid and impermeable, was vulnerable to determined and well-planned escapes. The Tower's thick walls and stout turrets look far from fragile. Guarded and watched, protected by a wide moat, it seems both impregnable to foes trying to enter from the outside and impenetrable to those trying to get out. Yet, remarkably, no fewer than thirty-seven prisoners have succeeded in escaping – some only temporarily – from the Tower. They ranged in social class from humble foot soldiers to earls and lords, and their breakouts began soon after the White Tower was completed, and continued until the eighteenth century when the Tower ceased to be used regularly to hold state prisoners. Tower security did not seem to improve across nearly ten centuries.

Ranulf Flambard would have flourished in any age, but his special talents were ideally suited to the robber-baron world of early Norman England. Flambard was the loyal servant of one of England's most ruthless and rapacious monarchs, William II, 'Rufus' or 'the Red', a tribute to either his carroty hair or his choleric complexion. Rufus was determined to outdo even his father, William the Conqueror, in severity towards his English subjects who, forty years after Hastings, he still saw as hostile, potentially rebellious serfs to be exploited by their Norman overlords until every last drop of sweat had been wrung from them. Flambard was happy to assist.

Flambard was born in Normandy and followed his father into the Church. A bright boy with a domineering personality, in the Conqueror's chancery he proved adept at squeezing revenues from the English. He was one of the chief compilers of William's *Domesday Book* – the vast audit of the country's economic value – which lists young Ranulf as holding land in several counties. By the time the Conqueror died in 1087, he was chaplain to Maurice, Bishop of London, and keeper of the royal seal.

William I's patrimony was split between his three sons. The eldest, Robert Curthose, inherited Normandy. The second born, William Rufus, received England, while the youngest, Henry, got hard cash. Flambard chose to serve Rufus, the new king of England. Already holding a prebend (church stipend or salary) in the wealthy diocese of Salisbury, Ranulf acquired similar church sinecures, demonstrating the acquisitive habits that became his hallmark, refusing to replace church canons when they died and continuing to draw their stipends himself.

No mean extortionist himself, Rufus admired Flambard's ruthlessness, and the cleric rose to become chief treasurer, justiciar (lawmaker) and chaplain to Rufus's licentious court. Flambard effectively ran the country during Rufus's absences, and he brought his creative accounting methods to bear on his new responsibilities. Tasked with raising the *fyrd* – the ancient Saxon militia – for Rufus's campaigns against his brother Robert in Normandy, Ranulf assembled archers and swordsmen, relieved each man of the ten shillings his native village had given him for his keep – and discharged them all. After creaming off a generous commission for himself, he used the remaining cash to raise mercenaries to fight the king's war. Another ingenious money-making wheeze was to extort a tax – known as a 'relief' – from the unfortunate sixteen abbeys and bishoprics he administered. Of Flambard's rule a chronicler truly said, 'He skinned the rich, ground down the poor, and swept other men's inheritances into his net.'

In 1099 Flambard became Bishop of Durham. Rumour alleged that he had paid a hefty bribe of £1,000 to secure his mitre. 'All justice slept – money was the Lord,' a chronicler recorded. But this flinty-hearted exploiter of the poor was also one of the great builders of early medieval England. As well as constructing Durham Cathedral, Flambard threw London's first stone bridge across the Thames and was responsible for erecting Westminster Hall. He also put up the first curtain wall around the White Tower of London – a structure with which he was about to become uncomfortably familiar.

On 2 August 1100, Rufus died a famous death in the New Forest. Pierced through the chest by an arrow fired – in malice or by mishap – as the sun set on a burning summer day, the king lay on the forest floor all night while his killer, Sir Walter Tyrell, and other courtiers scattered to nearby ports. A passing charcoal burner named Purvis slung Rufus's corpse on his cart and carried it to Winchester Cathedral, where it rests to this day. Flambard was one of the few to mourn his dead monarch. Rufus's brother Henry wasted no time claiming the Crown. Henry moved to win approval from his new subjects by punishing the hated Flambard, and a fortnight after Rufus's death, he was seized, charged with embezzlement and immured behind the gleaming new white walls of the Tower that, by a hideous irony, he himself had constructed. He was the first recorded state prisoner jailed in the fortress.

Flambard stayed almost six months in the Tower before achieving another record: the first state prisoner there became the Tower's first successful escaper. As a wealthy prince of the Church, he had been allowed to retain his servants, and his meals were brought in. Access to the outside world allowed him to organise his exit. On the night of 2/3 February 1101 Flambard threw a lavish banquet for his jailers. The wine, paid for from the bishop's deep pockets, flowed freely, and the turnkeys were soon the worse for wear. Taking advantage of their befuddlement, Flambard slipped away to an antechamber where a rope, sent in previously inside a barrel of oysters, lay coiled. Fastening it securely, Flambard squeezed his bulk through the narrow window, slipped down the rope, and, climbing his own curtain wall, found a prearranged horse which carried him to a waiting ship on the river.

Doubtless gold had greased Flambard's path to freedom, and the constable of the Tower, Geoffrey de Mandeville, may have been in on the plot. King Henry himself might even have covertly allowed the able administrator to get away. This theory is given weight by the haste with which the king made his peace with Flambard. Taking refuge with Duke Robert in Normandy, the errant bishop helped Robert invade England only six months after his dramatic escape. A temporary truce between the warring brothers was signed at Alton in Hampshire which Flambard probably helped arrange. Under its terms he was formally forgiven by Henry and restored to the See of Durham.

In 1105 warfare between the brothers resumed and in September 1106 Henry decisively defeated Robert at Tinchebray in Normandy. Flambard transferred his loyalty to the winner, retired from politics and settled in Durham where he completed work on the cathedral and Durham Castle. He died in September 1128 and was buried in the chapter house at Durham. His tomb was opened in 1874 by the ever-inquisitive Victorians. Flambard's skeleton revealed that he had been five foot nine tall. His bishop's crozier and signet ring had been buried with him.

Like Flambard, the second state prisoner to escape the Tower was also de facto ruler of England during the reign of an incompetent, unpopular king. Unlike Flambard, however, Roger Mortimer's time in the Tower marked the beginning, not the end, of his dictatorial power. Mortimer was a Marcher lord, with huge estates along the lawless borders of Wales. Born at his family's Herefordshire seat, Wigmore Castle, on 25 April 1287, Roger's evident ability won him the regard of the ageing Edward I. Young Mortimer became a boon companion of Edward, Prince of Wales, the man he was destined to supplant and – probably – murder. Superficially the two young men were similar: tall, handsome and lusty. Mortimer fathered a dozen children in as many years; Edward, despite his homosexual dalliances, sired two sons and two daughters legitimately and had one bastard son. Though bold and muscular like his father 'Longshanks', the first Prince of Wales lacked the steel which Mortimer was so soon to display. Young Edward was drawn to 'effeminate' pursuits such as music and the decorative arts, and offended conservative courtiers by such lowly behaviour as harnessing himself to a peasant's plough, or plying the oars of a rowing boat.

But after succeeding his father in 1307, it was Prince Edward's unconventional sexuality which hastened his downfall. In 1312 he lost his first gay favourite, Piers Gaveston, murdered by barons whom Gaveston had gone out of his way to mock. An outraged but powerless Edward bided his time and brooded on his revenge. Roger Mortimer remained loyal. But his once close companionship with the king withered in the face of the monarch's ineptitude, until finally dissolving in total disillusion.

By 1318 Edward's doting gaze had fallen on a new favourite, with all Gaveston's ambition but none of his charm. Hugh Despenser was a man whose greed and guile knew no bounds. Roger Mortimer was an ancestral foe of the Despensers. His grandfather had killed Hugh's grandfather at the battle of Evesham, and young Despenser had not forgotten the ancient feud, vowing to destroy Mortimer. After a long absence fighting Edward's wars in Ireland, on returning to England Mortimer was horrified to find how far the king had fallen under Despenser's thumb. The ruthless new favourite flouted law, custom and human decency in amassing goods, land and property. He specialised in intimidating women as he cheated, robbed and bullied his way to become the richest magnate in the kingdom. Once again, the barons combined to curb an overreaching royal favourite. The Marcher lords – Mortimer among them – led the revolt. Again Edward backed down, agreeing to exile Despenser and his equally rapacious namesake father.

Once the Despensers were out of the way, however, the barons squabbled over the spoils that the fallen favourites had left behind. Edward exploited these divisions, and within two years had re-established his untrammelled power. He recalled the Despensers from banishment, defeating his enemies, and wreaked vengeance with a string of hangings and beheadings. More than a dozen peers and hundreds of their humbler followers perished in a terror marking the beginning of a true royal tyranny. Mortimer surrendered to the king at Shrewsbury in January 1322. In front of the gloating Despensers, he was humiliated, stripped of his land – including his beloved birthplace, Wigmore Castle – and left with only the clothes he stood up in. He was consigned to the Tower while Edward and the Despensers travelled north to extinguish the last embers of the barons' revolt.

Mortimer languished in the Tower for three months before the king's thoughts returned to him. In the interim Edward had destroyed his enemies at the battle of Boroughbridge in Yorkshire. There was now no barrier to the despotic power of the Despensers, and Mortimer's future looked short. In July, he was taken from the Tower to Westminster Hall, tried for his recent rebellion and condemned to death. Surprisingly, the king, perhaps mindful of their youthful companionship, commuted the sentence to life imprisonment. For now, Hugh Despenser was deprived of his prey.

The reprieve was brief. In the twelve months that followed, Despenser spared no effort in adding to his already bulging portfolio of property and riches, mostly acquired illegally. The king was wax in his hot hands, granting every gift and title demanded. Finally, the vengeful tyrant demanded the best prize of all: Roger Mortimer's head. But Despenser had made an enemy more dangerous than Roger, helpless in his Tower cell. He had reckoned without Edward's long-neglected queen, Isabella, who would soon live up to her nickname 'the She-wolf of France'.

The daughter of Philip IV of France – named 'the Fair' for his blond good looks, which she would inherit – Isabella had married Edward in 1308, when she was twelve. They wed in Boulogne-sur-Mer and the young queen immediately received a clear indication of her new husband's sexual priorities when, arriving at Dover, she and the French nobles accompanying her witnessed a long and loving embrace between Edward and Piers Gaveston. Further shocks were in store at the wedding feast in Westminster Hall when Gaveston shamelessly appeared in the costly finery which Isabella's father had bestowed on his new son-in-law as wedding gifts. Horrified by the insult, the French nobles stormed out. This pattern continued throughout the reign, and although the royal couple succeeded in producing four children, Edward's sexual preferences became obvious to his comely young wife, and her resentment festered.

We do not know exactly when Isabella and Mortimer first met, but as a prominent nobleman Roger was a familiar figure to Isabella by the time he was confined in the Tower in 1322. Isabella gave birth to her youngest child, Joan of the Tower, there in 1321. While pregnant with Joan, Isabella had openly signalled her growing displeasure with her husband by adding her voice to the chorus demanding that the hated Hugh Despenser be banished. His return from exile turned her disillusion into outright disgust.

That revulsion was reinforced when, in 1322, Edward and Despenser fled from Robert the Bruce's marauding Scottish army, leaving the queen marooned at Tynemouth Abbey. Only by luck did she escape by sea, losing two of her ladies-in-waiting in the process. Her hatred of her husband now hardened into a determination to exact revenge for the serial humiliations she had suffered at his hands. Mortimer's presence in the Tower gave Isabella an ally – and, possibly, more. It is quite likely that her pity for Mortimer's plight turned now into a physical passion. It seems certain that they met covertly in the Tower and plotted. The result was that Isabella intervened on Roger's behalf against their common enemy. In February 1323 she protested to the king that Roger's loyal wife Joan and his aged mother were being subjected to royal harassment. The liaision that would bring her and Mortimer to supreme power was first forged at the Tower that foggy February.

Mortimer was not a man to submit patiently to incarceration in the White Tower. Like Flambard, he had, even in his reduced state, the means to persuade his jailers to do his bidding. This included smuggling messages to the world outside, and bringing replies back to his cell. But royal spies intercepted some of Roger's letters to a network of nobles and clerics across the country. An ally of Roger's, Lord Berkeley, under torture supervised by Edward and Despenser, blurted out his knowledge of Mortimer's scheming. Armed with this evidence, Despenser again insisted that Mortimer was too dangerous to be allowed to live. Edward was persuaded, and Mortimer's death was set for early August 1323.

Warning of the king's lethal intentions was brought to Mortimer in the Tower by Isabella. He knew that he had to act quickly. On 1 August under the cover of celebrations marking the feast day of St Peter ad Vincula, the Tower's patron saint, Roger put his escape plan into effect. His jailers gathered in the main hall of the White Tower for a banquet to honour their saint. Wine flowed and caution and sobriety were thrown to the winds. But one high-placed guest at the long trestle tables watched the hilarity with a coldly sober eye. Gerard d'Alspaye, second-in-command to the Tower's lieutenant, Stephen de Segrave, was the insider who had ferried Mortimer's letters in and out of the fortress. Now he would be the key to unlock his prison. Given free run of the Tower's cellars and kitchens, d'Alspaye had discreetly added sleeping draughts to the drinks and watched as de Segrave slumped unconscious, along with most of his men.

D'Alspaye slipped from the room, picked up a concealed crowbar and a couple of coiled rope ladders, and hurried to the cell which Mortimer shared with a confederate, Richard de Monmouth. D'Alspaye went to work with the crowbar on the old mortar until one of the great stones was prised out. On his side of the wall, Mortimer was also working with improvised tools to dig out a hole in the masonry which he had loosened in advance. Breathing a prayer to St Peter – along with a promise to build the saint a dedicated chapel at Ludlow in his native Marches if the prayer was granted – he and de Monmouth sweated desperately in the hot summer night to heave the stones free. Both knew that their lives depended on their speed.

At last a ragged hole was made big enough for the two men to squeeze through and they quickly crept downstairs, out of the White Tower, and into the kitchen of the adjoining royal palace to the south. The chief cook, also in on the plot, showed them their means of escape: up a wide chimney kept cold and empty for the purpose. They clambered up the sooty interior and found themselves on the kitchen roof under the wide, starry summer sky. D'Alspaye's rope ladders now came into their own. Such ladders had been successfully used by Bruce's Scots to capture castles and had been copied in England. Feverishly, they slung a ladder, with a grappling iron attached, over the high Inner Ward wall and heaved themselves over. A final barrier faced them – the Tower's outer curtain wall. Using their second ladder, they flung it over the wall, scaled it, and found themselves splashing along the marshy north bank of the Thames.

A prearranged boat was waiting in the shadows, and the two escapees were rowed downriver to Greenwich, where, guarded by four of Mortimer's liegemen, two horses were saddled and ready. Avoiding the Dover road, the most obvious route for a cross-Channel escape, the fugitives rode south-west to Portchester in Hampshire, where they took ship for France. As he sucked the sea air into his lungs, Mortimer now had one implacable purpose. God had freed him for a reason: to avenge himself on the tyrant king who had locked him in the Tower. Nothing would distract him from that goal.

When informed that Mortimer had escaped, Edward's rage was murderous. The hapless Segrave was sacked and replaced as Tower lieutenant by Walter de Stapledon, Bishop of Exeter and one of Edward's most slavish supporters. Mortimer was proclaimed a rebel, outlaw and traitor. A fresh wave of persecution swept the land which saw Roger's friends and family deprived of their estates. Darkly suspecting the queen of involvement in the getaway, Despenser persuaded the king to strip Isabella of her property and slash her personal living expenses to the bone. With Roger living under the protection of Isabella's brother, King Charles IV of France, the queen's fellow countrymen fell under suspicion as a potential fifth column. All French citizens living in England were arrested, including thirty members of Isabella's own household staff. The final cruel indignity to the slighted queen was to remove Isabella's children from her care and to place them under the control of Hugh Despenser's wife. Three of Roger Mortimer's sons were locked in the Tower in place of their father. Mortimer's daughters were immured in priories, while his wife Joan was imprisoned and given just one mark a day to feed herself and her five servants.

In March 1325, Edward made a fatal mistake. Increasingly isolated, fearful of a French invasion, he sent Isabella to France to negotiate peace with her brother Charles. Once free from her husband's control, Isabella was determined that she would only return to England to liberate it from Edward's tyranny. She succeeded in her peace mission, and in May a treaty was agreed. A clause of the treaty stipulated that Edward should personally pay homage to Charles. Instead, Edward sent his own son and heir, Prince Edward, to pay homage in his place. This was his second fatal error.

The caged bird sings: frontispiece of Sir Walter Ralegh's *History of the World* (1614) written in the Bloody Tower during his long imprisonment. Further volumes were planned, but abandoned.

THE

HISTORIE OF

THE VVORLD.

IN FIVE BOOKES.

1 *Entreating of the Beginning and first Ages of the same from the Creation vnto Abraham.*
2 *Of the Times from the Birth of Abraham, to the destruction of the Temple of Salomon.*
3 *From the destruction of Ierusalem, to the time of Philip of Macedon.*
4 *From the Reigne of Philip of Macedon, to the establishing of that Kingdome, in the Race of Antigonus.*
5 *From the settled rule of Alexanders successors in the East, vntill the Romans (prevailing ouer all) made Conquest of Asia and Macedon.*

By Sir WALTER RALEGH, Knight.

River of blood.
the gateway beneath the Bloody Tower showing Traitor's Gate and the river beyond. This 19th century engraving of the most notorious of the Tower's score of towers shows the vaulting inserted under Edward III in 1360-61 by Henry Yevele.

Gunpowder guys: a contemporary Dutch print of the Gunpowder plotters in 1605 shows Guy Fawkes (third from right) and, on his right, the plot's leader Robert Catesby.

The Wizard Earl: Henry Percy, 9th Earl of Northumberland, as depicted by Anthony van Dyck. Nicknamed for his fondness for scientific experiments, the Earl converted the Martin Tower into a lab during his long incarceration for suspected involvement in the Gunpowder plot.

Yeomen of England: the Tower's Yeoman Warders or 'Beefeaters' in their Tudor costumes on their way to search the cellars beneath Parliament. Now a picturesque ceremony, the ritual recalls the arrest here of Guy Fawkes while guarding the Gunpowder intended to blow up King and Parliament.

Wicked lady. Frances Howard, Countess of Somerset, was the moving spirit behind the slow poisoning of Sir Robert Overbury in 1614, an infamous Tower crime which led to her own imprisonment in the fortress.

Restored: the Tower in 1660, the year of Charles II's restoration. Engraving by Wenceslaus Hollar.

Bloody, bold and resolute:
'Colonel' Thomas Blood, the arch rogue
who stole the Crown jewels from the Tower
in May 1671: but was the heist an inside job?

Getaway:
Blood and his gang make
their escape with the loot.

Bloodproof?
The Crown jewels as they
appear today. Under armed
guard and behind bullet proof
glass, security is hopefully
tighter than in Blood's time.

Charles II in his coronation
regalia, showing the Crown,
orb and sceptre that Blood stole.

Heads you lose:
after the bungled execution of the
Duke of Monmouth following the
bloody failure of his rebellion in 1685,
his head was re-attached to his body
so his handsome face could be
immortalised in paint – possibly by
court artist Sir Godfrey Kneller.
Monmouth's peaceful features betray
little hint of his agonising death.

Cross dresser:
the bold and resourceful Lady Winifred Nithsdale escorts her disguised husband from his condemned cell in the Tower under the noses of his guards on the eve of his execution in February 1716. The Jacobite aristocrats spent the rest of their lives, poor but safe, in Rome.

Ugly old head:
Simon Fraser, Lord Lovat, as engraved by William Hogarth en route south from Scotland after his arrest for taking part in the '45 – Bonnie Prince Charlie's 1745-46 Jacobite rebellion. Despite being in his 80th year, Lovat tried in vain to save his own skin by sacrificing his son. His 'ugly old head' came off on Tower Hill in May 1747 – the last execution there.

"Breaking into the Strong room, in the "Jewel Tower" and "Removal" of the Regalia, on the night of the Fire, Oct. 30, 1841"

Smash and grab: in stark contrast to Blood, Metropolitan Police Superintendent Pierse smashed the glass and grabbed the Crown jewels – for entirely laudable reasons. Pierse was saving the jewels from the devastating Tower fire of 1841, and when he emerged his clothes were smouldering. George Cruickshank visited the scene to record his feat the next day.

Brave man or spy?
German Naval officer Carl Hans Lody, shot by firing squad in November 1914, was the first person executed inside the Tower since the Earl of Essex in 1601. Lody asked the officer in charge. 'I suppose you will not shake the hand of a German spy?' The man gallantly replied: 'No, but I will shake the hand of a brave man'. Lody's compatriot, and fellow spy Josef Jacobs, was the last person (to date) executed in the Tower when he was shot there in the Second World War.

Hero or traitor?
Ireland's Sir Roger Casement
on trial for his life in May
1916. Arrested after landing
from a U-boat, Casement
twice tried to commit suicide
while detained in the Tower.
He survived to be hanged
in August 1916.

Bad boys:
twins Reggie and Ronnie
Kray began their notorious
criminal careers by absconding from the Tower where
they were detained in the
garrison's guard room in
the Wellington Barracks
for repeatedly deserting
from National Service
in the Army. The Army
finally tired of their antics,
and discharged them.

With her son safely at her side, Isabella openly proclaimed contemptuous defiance of her husband. The man leading the delegation accompanying young Prince Edward to France was the new lieutenant of the Tower, Bishop Walter de Stapledon. The bishop humiliated the queen in front of the French court by demanding that she return home with him to her husband. The 'She-wolf' turned on the cleric in fury: 'Someone has come between my husband and me, trying to break this [marriage] bond. I protest that I will not return until this intruder is removed, but, discarding my marriage garment, shall assume the weeds of widowhood and mourning until I am avenged on this Pharisee.' There were no prizes for guessing that the 'Pharisee' was Despenser.

Once de Stapledon had been sent packing, Isabella united her fortunes with those of Roger Mortimer to overthrow the tyranny of Edward and the Despensers. By Christmas, the lovers were openly living together and plotting their return. It was no small matter in medieval Europe for a queen to spurn an anointed king and live in adultery with another man. It is a measure of the strength of Isabella's character, her hatred for Edward, and her love for Mortimer that she was prepared to trample this taboo.

Roger went to the court of Count William I of Hainault (the modern Netherlands) to prepare their invasion of England, while Isabella stayed in France, raising men and money. Count William agreed to subsidise the enterprise, and provide the ships, in return for a pledge that his daughter Philippa would marry young Prince Edward. Meanwhile, a plot by Hugh Despenser to murder the lovers was foiled when a ship containing barrels of silver to bribe French courtiers to murder Mortimer was intercepted and the Despensers' treasure diverted to Hainault to fund Mortimer's overthrow of their despotism.

By September 1326 Mortimer had gathered an invasion armada of almost 100 ships with a small army of 1,500 mercenary soldiers off Rotterdam. On 21 September, Isabella and Mortimer embarked and a week later landed at the mouth of the River Orwell in Suffolk. Edward awaited their arrival at the Tower. At first, he was not unduly worried. Against the tiny invasion force, he had a notional army of 50,000. Thanks to the Despensers' extortions, the Royal Exchequer was full of cash to pay the troops. But, as Edward and the Despensers discovered, no money could buy the loyalty they had wantonly squandered. The soldiers they summoned ignored the call. Instead of the king, their allegiance went to Isabella. As Isabella and

Mortimer's growing army moved towards Oxford, Edward and Despenser abandoned the Tower and fled west, making for Despenser's lands in south Wales. The Tower's lieutenant, the hated Bishop Walter de Stapledon, was caught seeking sanctuary in St Paul's Cathedral, and had his head sawn off with a bread knife.

By the time Edward and Despenser arrived in Wales, royal authority had melted away. Riding with a handful of retainers, they were caught near Neath on 16 November, arrested and separated. Despenser was taken to Hereford where the triumphant queen was waiting. Knowing he could expect no mercy from the 'She-wolf' Despenser tried to starve himself to death, but Isabella was implacable. On 24 November, Hugh and two followers were paraded before an immense crowd who hooted and jeered the fallen tyrant. Crowned with mocking nettles, the doomed man was pulled from his horse, stripped naked and had biblical verses denouncing ambition and evil scrawled on his emaciated flesh. Led into the market square where a vengeful Mortimer and Isabella sat, Despenser listened while his many sins were listed. Judged a traitor and thief, he was condemned to the terrible punishment of being hanged, drawn and quartered.

Dragged by four horses to one of his own castles, Despenser was tied to an enormous fifty-foot ladder and hoisted high above his castle walls. The executioner clambered up a parallel ladder and set about his grisly task. First, the condemned man's genitals were sliced off and flung into a bonfire at the foot of the ladder. Then the executioner plunged his knife into Hugh's abdomen and cut out his guts, throwing the entrails into the fire. Finally, Despenser's chest was ripped open and his heart followed the other organs into the flames. The despot was then quartered and his head sent to London for display, while his limbs and torso were dispatched to the four corners of the kingdon he had tyrannised. York, Newcastle, Dover and Bristol – the city where his own father had earlier been executed – all received a hunk of flesh. It was a horrible but fitting end for a monstrous tyrant. We can be sure that Isabella and Roger had enjoyed the show.

King Edward II's fate, in contrast to his favourite's very public end, was private and masked in mystery. The deposed monarch was shuttled from castle to castle between Kenilworth, Corfe and Berkeley near Gloucester. In January 1327, at Kenilworth, Edward had publicly agreed to abdicate.

But with the Despensers dead, popular sympathy for the deposed monarch returned, and there were several serious attempts to rescue him from his cell. His frustrated jailers had tried without success to kill him by putting him in a dungeon filled with stagnant water and decaying animal cadavers, while shaving him with ditch water.

Mortimer apparently now decided that such methods were too slow, and gave orders to kill the stubborn king as quickly and unobtrusively as possible. According to legend, Edward was either suffocated in his cell or suffered the exquisite agony of having a red-hot copper rod inserted through a horn into his rectum and twisted in his bowels while he was pinioned under a table or mattress. It has been suggested that this fiendish, agonising means of dispatching the king was either to conceal the crime by leaving no exterior marks on the corpse, or as a symbolic punishment for Edward's homosexuality, or both. It has also been plausibly proposed by medieval historian Ian Mortimer that Edward did *not* die in Berkeley, but survived his supposed death by some fourteen years as a wandering hermit after he had been successfully sprung from the castle. Whatever the truth, Edward's reign effectively ended with his abdication in January 1327, even if his life did not.

Roger Mortimer's life now entered its final act. Effectively dictator of the kingdom, he was, as lover of the queen regent, also guardian of the teenage monarch, Edward III. Mortimer's position was not enviable, since many noblemen did not relish submitting to another tyrant. Young Edward's feelings about the man who had probably murdered his father, usurping his place in his mother's bed, are also unlikely to have been friendly. In addition, Mortimer treated the king with arrogant disrespect.

At a tournament held at his seat, Wigmore Castle, in the summer of 1329, Roger played the part of King Arthur in a pageant – having himself crowned before the young king. Power appears to have gone to Mortimer's head, and he began to act in a way that, ironically, mirrored the tyrannical behaviour of the man he had deposed: Hugh Despenser. Mortimer styled himself Earl of March, overlord of his native region, and acquired large estates, oppressing those who opposed him. His most unforgivable deed was to implicate Edmund, Earl of Kent, younger brother of Edward II, in a plot to free the imprisoned monarch. Mortimer personally oversaw the earl's trial and decapitation. In the words of his namesake biographer Ian Mortimer, 'He had grown too mighty . . . Despenser's brutal tyranny had been reborn.' Or, as Roger's own son Geoffrey told him, Mortimer had morphed from chivalrous knight into the 'King of Folly'.

Nemesis swiftly followed. In October 1330, at Nottingham Castle, a band of nobles, led by their young king, now almost eighteen, stole into the castle at night via a tunnel in the sandstone rock on which the fortress stood. After a brief brawl, Mortimer was arrested. Edward ignored his mother's plea to 'spare the gentle Mortimer' and Roger was returned to the familiar surroundings of the Tower. This time, there would be no escape.

Edward III gave orders that Mortimer, his son Geoffrey, and his chief henchman Simon Bereford should be literally walled up in the Tower. Their cell's door and windows were filled in with masonry and mortar, and the room was placed under the round-the-clock guard of six serjeants-at-arms supervised by two knights of the royal household. To make security doubly sure, Edward himself moved into the room next door. The Mortimers and Bereford, kept alive on bread and water, spent a miserable month incarcerated inside their dark and chilly prison.

Then, laden with heavy chains, Roger was taken to Westminster Hall to be tried for treason. He was gagged to prevent him from speaking, and rapidly condemned to death. Returned to the Tower, on 29 November he was placed on an ox hide and bumped painfully along the uneven roads between the Tower and the gallows at Tyburn. Battered but alive, he made a short speech to the crowd confessing the injustice of his execution of the Earl of Kent. He was then hanged. The king was more merciful to his mother, who ended her days comfortably enough in 1358 – nearly three decades after the ignominious execution of her lover and partner in power.

Sir John Oldcastle is best known today as the model for Shakespeare's uproarious Sir John Falstaff. Early versions of *Henry IV* Parts 1 and 2 featured a character called Sir John Oldcastle, though when the play was printed in 1598, the surname 'Falstaff' had been substituted. In truth, the real historical Oldcastle – lean, hard and courageous – bore no resemblance to Shakespeare's cowardly, vainglorious 'fat knight', and there was little to laugh about in Oldcastle's life and tragic death. He did, however, have one thing in common with his fictional counterpart: he was a bosom companion of young Prince Hal, later England's quintessential hero monarch Henry V, forever associated with his famous victory at Agincourt in 1415.

Both men hailed from the same small corner of the world. Henry was born in 1387 in Monmouth — a quarter of a century before his father Henry Bolingbroke seized the throne from Richard II to become Henry IV. Oldcastle was born between 1360 and 1378 at Almeley in nearby Herefordshire, the son and heir of Sir Richard Oldcastle. John Oldcastle served in Henry IV's campaigns against the Scots and the Welsh rebellion of Owain Glyndwr, when he first met Prince Henry. In 1408 Oldcastle leapt upwards from country knight to landed aristocracy when he married Joan, 4th Baroness Cobham. The couple were hardly novices in the marriage stakes. Joan was Oldcastle's third wife, and he was her fourth husband. The new Lord Cobham's home was the resplendent Cooling Castle on the Kentish marshes, and through his marriage Oldcastle acquired broad acres in five counties: Kent, Norfolk, Northamptonshire, Wiltshire and his native Herefordshire. An MP, praised by the new king as 'one of my most trustworthy soldiers', Oldcastle had arrived. But he placed everything in jeopardy by espousing new, dangerously radical, religious ideas.

Oldcastle was entranced by the novel doctrines dubbed as 'Lollardy' (the term comes from the Dutch word for 'mumbling'), an insulting epithet eventually proudly adopted by the preachers of the 'New Light'. The Lollards were the early-morning stars of the Reformation, taking their inspiration from the English reformer John Wycliffe's teaching. They sympathised with the poor, and criticised the rampant corruption of the Church; believing that devout laymen could preach the Gospels as well as any priest. Lollards denied the necessity of a hierarchical clergy, founding their faith firmly on the Scriptures studied in Wycliffe's first English Bible. As 'premature Protestants' they were fiercely persecuted as heretics.

Oldcastle emerged as a promoter of Lollard ideas in 1410 when churches on his Kentish estate were put under a Church interdict for allowing unlicensed preachers. The chief persecutor was Thomas Arundel, Archbishop of Canterbury. When the archbishop heard that Oldcastle had put up Lollard preachers in Cooling Castle as his house guests, he complained to the king. Henry confronted his friend at Windsor Castle. Speaking with an old soldier's bluntness, Oldcastle pledged that his life and fortune were at the king's disposal — but not his sincere private beliefs. Oldcastle withdrew to Cooling in disgrace. In fifteenth-century Europe, once the word 'heresy' was heard, reason retreated and the hangman approached.

Or rather, the flames drew near. Another bone of contention between Oldcastle and Arundel was Sir John's objection to a new law which the archbishop had adopted from the Spanish Inquisition: allowing heretics to be burned at the stake. Oldcastle objected to the barbaric foreign import, and Arundel duly noted another charge against the king's mentor. His chance to strike Oldcastle down finally came when a spy reported that a heretical book belonging to Sir John had been seized at a Paternoster Row bookshop. This time the king stood aside. The law would take its terrible course.

Arundel summoned Oldcastle to appear before an ecclesiastical court. From behind Cooling's battlements, Oldcastle defied him. Arundel procured a royal writ from the king that the old soldier could not disobey. He was taken under guard to the Tower, and handed over to the lieutenant, Sir Robert Morley. The lieutenant treated his prisoner with respect and lodged him in the Beauchamp Tower, then the most comfortable accommodation in the fortress. (Afterwards, the tower was alternatively named 'Cobham Tower' in Oldcastle's honour.) Here he was visited by friars and priests who vainly attempted to argue him out of his stubbornly held heretical opinions.

On 23 September 1413 Oldcastle was taken from the Tower to the church court in an old Dominican convent on Ludgate Hill, with his bitter foe, Arundel, presiding. The jury was composed of Augustinian canons and Carmelite friars. Oldcastle, the denouncer of monkish abuses, was now on trial for his life before a jury of monks. He made a 'confession of faith' declaring that he believed in the Sacraments of the Church, but holding out against the adoration of images of the Virgin or the saints – which, he said, was heathen idolatry. He also denied the 'Real Presence' – that the body and blood of Christ were present in Holy Communion. This was the Protestant programme as laid out by Luther a century later. But the time for such bold ideas had not yet come. Horror-struck, one juror denounced Oldcastle for 'flat heresy' and on 25 September he was sentenced to die at the stake.

On hearing the sentence, Oldcastle replied:

> Ye judge the body, which is but a wretched thing, yet am I certain and sure that ye can do no harm to my soul. He who created that, will of His

own mercy and promise save it. As to these articles [his opinions] I will stand to them, even to the very death – by the grace of my eternal God.

Despite his brave defiance, Sir John seemed bound for the flames. Once again, however, the king came to his old friend's rescue. He granted him a forty-day stay of execution, hoping that he would recant. The Church spread false rumours that this was indeed what the 'good Lord Cobham' had done.

To counter their spin, Oldcastle had a rebuttal smuggled out from the Tower and pasted up around the city by Lollard friends. But Oldcastle's heroic accomplices were prepared to do even more and on 29 September 1416 they struck. The court records for 1416 at the subsequent trial in Newgate Gaol of Oldcastle's chief rescuer, a fur dealer and parchment maker named William Fisher, take up the tale:

> William Fyssher . . . of London . . . together with other traitors . . . whose names are unknown, did go privily to the Tower, and break into that prison and falsely and traitorously withdraw the said John Oldcastle therefrom, and take him from thence to his own dwelling house, in the parish of St Sepulchre in Smithfield, and did falsely and traitorously harbour him in that said dwelling-house, knowing that he was a traitor and there did keep the said John Oldcastle in secret until the Wednesday next after the Feast of our Lord's Epiphany [6 January]. Upon which Wednesday the aforesaid William; together with the said John Oldcastle and other traitors, these conspiring and imagining how to slay our said Lord the King, and also the brothers and heirs of the same Lord the King and to destroy and disinherit other nobles of the realm of England, and to make the aforesaid John Oldcastle regent of the realm, on the same Wednesday, armed and arrayed in warlike guise falsely and traitorously, against his allegiance, did arise, and from thence and then and there did proceed towards a certain great field in the parish of St Giles, there to carry out and finally fulfil his false, nefarious and traitorous purpose.

Oldcastle had gone too far. Private religious opinions were one thing; treason and open rebellion quite another. The suspicion must be that Sir John's escape from the Tower (like Flambard's dramatic exit three centuries previously) had inside help, possibly from the king himself. Why else did no one bother to properly search Oldcastle's own town house in Smithfield during the three months he had been 'harboured' there? But if Henry had been prepared to overlook Oldcastle's stubborn adherence to his Lollard principles for the sentimental sake of their old friendship, he could not turn a blind eye to armed revolt.

The Lollards' plan was apparently to seize the king and his brothers during a Twelfth Night mumming feast at Eltham, when, disguised as revellers, Lollards would infiltrate the festivities. But the plot was betrayed to Henry by a carpenter. The king, at his best in a crisis, moved fast. Taking his brothers and Archbishop Arundel with him, he left the party at Eltham and galloped hard for London. Once in the capital, he ordered the city gates to be closed and guarded, and stationed armed retainers, emblazoned with white crosses as their recognition sign, in woods around the Lollards' rendezvous point in St Giles' Fields. As they gathered, the ambush was sprung. The king and his guards fell on the rebels, and in a short but sharp fight, some were killed and the rest captured. Among those arrested was William Fisher who would be hanged at Tyburn, his head spiked as a traitor on London Bridge.

Oldcastle managed to escape again. He spent the next four years flitting from one hiding place to another, in Kent, Hertfordshire and Yorkshire. Once, warned of a raid on his hiding place in a humble peasant's cottage in St Albans, he evaded his pursuers by seconds, in his haste leaving religious books behind. They were found to have the pictures of the saints carefully defaced in accordance with Oldcastle's Lollard beliefs. Finally, he made his way back to Herefordshire, his childhood home.

But Oldcastle was not a man to disappear quietly from history. Courageous, foolhardy, a fighter to the last, he continued to conspire from his rural backwater. Finally, in November 1417, his long escape came to an end. Hiding out with fellow Lollards in a woodland glade still known as 'Cobham's Garden' on Pant-mawr farm, Broniarth, in mid-Wales, he arranged to meet a local landowner, Edward, Lord Charleton of Powys. Charleton decided to betray the old rebel, and arrived at the meeting with a band of armed retainers. There was a brief fight, ending only when Oldcastle was 'sore wounded ere he would be taken'. He was secured and carried to London on a litter. There is some bitter satisfaction in the knowledge that the treacherous Welsh peer who betrayed him died of natural causes before he could claim his thirty pieces of silver – the 1,000-mark reward on Oldcastle's head.

There were to be no more narrow escapes. Like Mortimer, Oldcastle was returned to the Tower from which he had once fled, and condemned twice over. He was already a convicted heretic, and now he was a traitor too. As such he was to be doubly punished: burned as a heretic, hanged as a traitor. On 14 December 1417 he was taken from the Tower to St Giles' Fields, the scene of the abortive Lollard plot in 1414. Here he was hanged over a burning pyre which eventually consumed both the gallant Sir John and the gallows he dangled from. Oldcastle died as steadfastly as he had lived – a premature Protestant martyr whose courage was only matched by his indiscretion. He deserves better than the caricature of Shakespeare's buffoonish portrayal. Sir John Oldcastle was composed of the stuff of which true heroes are made.

Heroes and martyrs are not the exclusive property of any single denomination. In the great divide that opened in England in 1534 when Henry VIII broke with Rome, there were to be plentiful martyrs on both sides of the doctrinal schism. One prisoner of the Tower who managed to avoid an agonising death at the hands of a state which some 150 years after Oldcastle's death had finally become Protestant, yet suffered a prolonged, painful martyrdom nonetheless, was the Jesuit priest Father John Gerard.

Like Oldcastle, Gerard, a big man physically and morally, was born with the martyrdom gene. By a huge irony, his grandfather, Thomas Gerrard, rector of All Hallows, Cheapside, was an early Protestant in the reign of Henry VIII. Thomas Gerrard was one of a group of Lutherans burned for heresy in Smithfield on 30 July 1540. John Gerard's father, also called Thomas, was by contrast militantly Catholic and also suffered for his faith. He was imprisoned in the Tower for plotting to free Mary, Queen of Scots, as part of the Catholic Rising of the North against Elizabeth I in 1569.

Born in 1564, John Gerard was five years old at the time of his father's arrest. Thomas Gerard was freed in 1573, and returned to his country estate at Bryn in Lancashire. John went up to Exeter College, Oxford aged twelve. Traditionalist Oxford was a hotbed of Catholicism, and so persuasive was the boy Gerard that he converted one of his tutors to the old faith. In 1577 he was sent down for refusing to attend an Anglican service, and successfully applied for a licence to continue his studies in Europe.

For three years he studied at the English College at Douai in the Spanish Netherlands. The college had been founded in 1568 by William Allen, an exiled Oxford academic on a mission to overthrow Queen Elizabeth and return England to the Roman faith. Allen's college trained scores of young English exiles as 'seminary priests' and returned them secretly to their native land. Allen fell under the potent influence of the Jesuits, the shock troops of the Counter-Reformation. Founded by the Spanish knight Ignatius Loyola in 1540, the Jesuits had a formidable (to their friends) or frightening (to their foes) reputation for semi-military discipline, doctrinal rigour, cunning guile and an austerely fanatical devotion to their faith.

Gerard decided to become a Jesuit priest but after unwisely returning to England, he was arrested and spent a year inside London's fetid Marshalsea jail. The Marshalsea was bursting with fellow Catholics. In May 1584, one of them, the young Derbyshire squire Anthony Babington – later notorious for his plot to kill Elizabeth and put Mary, Queen of Scots on the throne – stood bail for Gerard, who immediately fled to France. Gerard was a young man in a hurry. He persuaded the Pope himself, Pius V, to grant him special dispensation to be ordained a Jesuit priest below the statutory age. Finally, on 15 August 1588, in the week that the Spanish Armada was defeated and dispersed, twenty-four-year-old Gerard was admitted to the priesthood along with another English Jesuit, Edward Oldcorne. A month and a half later, on 28 October, the two young men stood together on a Norfolk beach just south of Cromer. Their mission to reclaim their homeland had begun.

Gerard spent the next eight years living the hunted life of a priest on the run. His unquenchable faith helped him survive. A big, jovial bear of a man, he did not *look* like a priest. Dressed as an English gentleman he looked the part because he *was* the part. Moving from recusant house to house, he evaded the ever-eager armies of licensed 'pursuivants' – posses authorised to hunt down fugitive priests. It was a brutal cat-and-mouse game. Since the Armada, Catholics (like Western Communists in the Cold War) had become not just followers of an alien ideology but potential traitors – enemies within who, at any moment, could rise up to kill the queen and murder good Protestants in their beds.

Gerard's autobiography reads like a memoir of an SOE agent in occupied Europe during the Second World War. There is the same mistrust: could the servant bringing the priest meals betray the presence of a mysterious stranger in the house? The same all-pervasive fear of detection and arrest. The same hurried secret meetings in supposedly safe houses. The same false names and identities. Instead of concealed radio sets and weapons there are the hidden vestments, chalices and other telltale forbidden objects for conducting Mass. And there are the same artfully concealed hiding places.

Most of the 'priest holes' which litter the old Catholic houses of rural England were the work of one remarkable man: Nicholas Owen. Born in the early 1560s to a poor but devoutly Catholic Oxford family, little Owen – he may have been a dwarf, and he was certainly very small, a handicap he turned to advantage when constructing his priest holes – was a genius of carpentry. He knew how to create seamless joints invisible to the untrained eye; how to conceal a hide in a room with typically Tudor wooden panelling; how to build a staircase with a hidden chamber beneath.

Beginning in 1588, the fateful Armada year, for seventeen years Owen faithfully carried out his self-appointed task as hide builder to England's embattled Catholics, often working with Gerard who said:

> I verily think that no man can be said to have done more good of all those who laboured in the English vineyard. He was the immediate occasion of saving many hundreds of persons, both ecclesiastical and secular.

Owen passed from one house to another – linked beads along the rosary of Catholic homes in sore need of spiritual comfort – constructing his priest holes. Always working alone – for reasons of security – and often at night, Owen created scores of hiding places in ingenious locations. Many times he would build several priest holes per house, so artfully concealed that some may remain undiscovered to this day.

Eventually, in 1594, the Elizabethan state caught up with Gerard. Betrayed by John Frank, a trusted servant in an Essex house owned by a recusant family called Wiseman, Gerard had the narrowest of escapes from a persistent posse of pursuivants who surrounded the house at dawn on Easter Monday. They practically demolished the house around him. Sustained only by a jar of quince jelly, he successfully withstood a five-day 'siege' in one of Owen's tiny hides without betraying his presence. After recovering from the ordeal, he and Owen – known to intimates as 'Big John' and 'Little John' – were smuggled to a safe town house in Holborn owned by the Wisemans.

Innocently, the family matriarch, Mrs Wiseman, sent the treacherous John Frank to Holborn with a letter for Gerard. The servant delivered his message late on 23 April, and then hurried off to alert the authorities.

Two hours later, Gerard and Owen were woken by a thunderous midnight knocking. There were no priest holes to hide in, and their bedchamber had only one door. As Owen hastily burned Mrs Wiseman's incriminating letter, the pursuivants burst into the room. Gerard and Owen were prisoners.

Taken to the Counter prison in London's Poultry, they were separated, and the questioning began. An obvious gentleman, Gerard was treated gently at first, though Owen was more roughly handled. Gerard stoutly denied his real identity until proofs – provided by Frank – were presented to him. He continued to shield the Wisemans from suspicion, thereby saving their lives. At this point, Gerard was confronted with Elizabethan England's torturer-in-chief, Richard Topcliffe. This man, MP for Old Sarum, was chief persecutor of England's embattled Catholics. He enjoyed the queen's trust, and received official permission to set up a private torture chamber in his Westminster home. Topcliffe was terrifying enough to make the strongest captive quail. 'I am Topcliffe!' the persecutor announced as he entered Gerard's cell. Slapping his sword on a table for dramatic effect, he added menacingly, 'No doubt you have heard people talking about me.' But Gerard was not intimidated. 'His acting was lost on me,' he recalled. 'I was not in the least frightened.' In fact, claimed Gerard, to show his defiance he was 'deliberately rude' to his tormentor. To put extra pressure on the priest, both Owen and Richard Fulwood – Gerard's servant, hauled in by the relentless Topcliffe in another raid – were tortured using the manacles, a simple but fiendishly effective device introduced into the English penal system by Topcliffe himself.

The manacles or gauntlets consisted of a pair of handcuffs, jointed in the middle like a horse's bit. The victim was suspended by his wrists from a hook high on the wall while standing on wooden blocks. The blocks were then removed, leaving the unfortunate prisoner dangling, suspended from his pinioned wrists. According to Gerard, both Owen and Fulwood were subjected to this agonising torture for a full three hours.

After more than two months of fruitless questioning in the Counter prison – 'Only my priesthood could be proved against me,' commented Gerard tersely – his fellow Catholics managed to bribe a senior legal official to get Gerard transferred to the milder regime of the Clink jail. The Clink was a prison in the maze of alleys on the south bank of the Thames close to where the Globe theatre was packing in the groundlings to see Shakespeare's new plays. Gerard said of the transfer that it was 'a translation from Purgatory to Paradise'. The Clink was crammed with Catholics, who by bribery and blackmail had forced their jailers to give them the free run of the prison. They were thus able to plot and communicate with their co-religionists in the outside world without interference. Gerard was even able to arrange safe houses for fellow priests newly arrived from Europe while in the Clink.

But such liberty would not last. In April 1597 the authorities belatedly woke up to the fact that Gerard was continuing his conspiratorial work despite having been in their custody for three years. Once again, he had been betrayed. The agent of his downfall was probably a fellow Catholic priest and Clink inmate, Robert Barwise. Gerard was promptly sent to the tender mercies of the Tower of London's torturers.

Gerard was immured in the Salt Tower, on the south-eastern corner of the fortress's Inner Ward. Daylight revealed the evidence of fellow Catholics who had been lodged in the same grim chamber. Prominent on the wall was carved the name 'HENRY WALPOLE' – still clearly visible to Tower visitors today. The man who had laboriously chiselled out his signature was a fellow Jesuit priest who had spent more than a year in the Tower being tortured by Topcliffe, before being taken to York and hanged in 1595. Putting Gerard in the martyr's old cell was probably intended as psychological torture, but the robust priest took it more positively. Merely seeing Walpole's name, he said, had given him comfort to be in 'a place sanctified by this great and holy martyr'.

The day after arriving in the Tower, Gerard's own moment of martyrdom arrived as he was led out to face his torturers. The reception committee waiting in the gloomy cellar of the White Tower, a windowless vault lit only by flickering torches, was a high-powered one, befitting Gerard's status as a renegade member of the ruling caste. In the chair was Sir Edward Coke, Attorney General and legal pinnacle of the Elizabethan state. Coke was accompanied by Sir Thomas Fleming, the Solicitor General; Sir Richard Berkeley, the Tower's lieutenant; Sir William Wade or Waad, the notoriously cruel future Tower lieutenant and privy councillor; and last, but not least, the MP, lawyer, philosopher, scientist and writer, the ambitious Sir Francis Bacon.

After a preliminary interrogation, in which his inquisitors attempted in vain to get Gerard to name his correspondents from the Clink, the panel applied the next turn of the screw: they showed him the Privy Council's warrant authorising them to torture him. Then, preceded by jailers with lighted candles, they led him into the dim inner recess of the torture chamber itself. Here he was shown the dreaded manacles. As Gerard remained steadfast, the torture began. The manacles were clamped around his wrists and fixed to an iron staple high up on a wooden post. Then the wooden steps that Gerard was standing on were removed. To his tormentors' consternation, the priest was so tall that his toes still touched the ground, obliging them to scrabble in the dirt of the earthen floor until they had dug a pit so that he could dangle free, his heavy weight hanging agonisingly from his pinioned wrists.

Asked again to confess, Gerard found himself unable to speak even if he had wanted to:

> I could hardly utter the words, such a gripping pain came over me. It was worst in my chest and belly, my hands and arms. All the blood in my body seemed to rush up into my arms and hands and I thought that blood was oozing out from the ends of my fingers and the pores of my skin. But it was only a sensation caused by my flesh swelling above the irons holding them.

Fighting down a natural urge to tell the torturers what they wanted to know and end his suffering, Gerard remained obdurate. The lawyers and politicians left him to the care of the turnkeys and he blacked out. The steps were replaced and he recovered consciousness and began to pray. Hearing this, the jailers removed the steps again and the whole painful process was repeated eight or nine times across an endless afternoon.

At five o'clock the Tower's bell rang out. This signalled the end of their shift and knocking-off time for the torturers, who freed Gerard and half dragged, half carried the fainting man back to his cell. The next day, he was taken back to the torture chamber for more of the same treatment. This time, however, his wrists were so swollen by the previous day's torments that the manacles would barely fit around the bruised skin. Hung up as before, he fainted again and at first could not be revived. The lieutenant, Sir Richard Berkeley, was summoned by the alarmed turnkeys, and Gerard came to on a bench with warm water being dribbled down his throat and nostrils – a sixteenth-century version of waterboarding. The torture session continued, but Berkeley appeared uncomfortable, and after an hour he had the punishment halted.

The lieutenant's revulsion at Gerard's suffering is thought to have been the reason for Berkeley's resignation a few weeks later. In the meantime, Gerard was again returned to his cell in the Salt Tower and the increasingly sympathetic care of his gaoler, a man named Bonner. Berkeley himself, guilt-stricken at the priest's treatment, wrote to Elizabeth's chief minister, Robert Cecil, petitioning for Gerard, 'ill and weak' as he was, to be allowed out of his cell occasionally to 'take the air on a wall near his prison'. Berkeley added compassionately, 'The man needs physic [medicine].' Berkeley was not the only official to feel uncomfortable at Gerard's suffering. Bacon, too, had declined to be present for the second day's torture. The polymath was not to know that he was himself destined to see the inside of the Tower several years later after being charged with bribery and corruption.

Gerard was in a lamentable state. His wrists remained monstrously swollen, and his arms and shoulders felt as though they had been dislocated. Unable to dress or feed himself, he depended on Bonner's charity to survive. It took three weeks before some movement began to return to Gerard's arms. By this time, a relationship had developed between the priest and his turnkey that would eventually open Gerard's path to freedom. Day by day he increased his influence over the susceptible Bonner. The intimate bond that had blossomed between them as the warder cut up Gerard's food, shaved him and helped him to dress and undress would pay the ultimate dividend for the Jesuit. For his first favour to his prisoner Bonner promised to obtain money from Gerard's friends at the Clink. The cash would be used in part to bribe him to win Gerard more solid favours.

Bonner used some of the money to buy his charge a bag of oranges. Exercising his still-stiff hands and fingers, Gerard fashioned a rosary from the peel. But instead of drinking the juice he squeezed it into a jar. Then, using a home-made toothpick as a pen, Gerard wrote a message to his friends in the Clink in the invisible ink of the orange juice, which became briefly visible when the paper was heated. He scrawled a few innocuous lines in charcoal across the secret letter as cover to allay suspicion, and, using Bonner as his postman, sent the missive, together with the peel rosary, to the Clink. By this means, the ever-resourceful and indomitable Gerard had once again established a secure, if fragile, channel of communication to his Catholic comrades outside the Tower's walls.

At last, motivated by money as well as sympathy, Bonner became Gerard's trusted ally and agent. It says much for the Jesuit's powers of persuasion that he was able to turn the victim of his blackmail into an accomplice without incurring the warder's resentment. Like British PoWs in wartime Germany who inveigled the 'Goons' guarding them into a small transgression, using this hold to demand ever greater favours, Gerard gradually reversed their roles and turned his jailer into his prisoner.

Meanwhile, plans were afoot to effect Gerard's escape. The priest and his allies outside the Tower – including Nicholas Owen who had meanwhile been freed – laid their schemes carefully. As a first step, some six months into his imprisonment in the Tower, Gerard made contact, by signalling in mime language, with a fellow Catholic prisoner. John Arden, a Northamptonshire recusant, had been held in the Cradle Tower under sentence of death for ten years for an alleged plot against the queen's life. His cell lay some thirty yards from Gerard's eyrie in the Salt Tower. The Cradle Tower was a small and seemingly insignificant structure, but, crucially, it lay in the south curtain wall of the Tower's Outer Ward, overlooking the Thames.

Using his hold over Bonner, Gerard strengthened his links with Arden. His first message was written in juice on a wrapper around an orange. Not understanding Gerard's mime signals, Arden threw it in his cell fire. Then Gerard persuaded – and paid – Bonner to take his messages in clear. Finally he prevailed upon him to let him go across to the Cradle Tower under cover of darkness, and spend several hours with Arden, praying and delivering spiritual comfort. Gradually, these nocturnal visits became a regular occurrence. As a long-term prisoner, Arden had been allowed visits from his wife, who regularly brought in a covered basket of provisions which, after so many years, the guards now rarely bothered to search. Mrs Arden smuggled in the holy objects needed for the two men to celebrate Mass, and then something of more immediate and worldly value to them: a long length of cord.

Gerard selected the evening of 3 October 1597 for the breakout. Careful preparations had been made, both inside the Tower and without, where a getaway boat was waiting on the river. Bonner escorted Gerard across to the Cradle Tower and – not being privy to the escape plot – locked him in. As soon as he had departed, Gerard and Arden set to work. They managed to break the bolt on the cell door that led to the tower's roof. As the main Tower bell chimed midnight, the two men were on the roof looking out over the river. They saw their escape boat rowed by John Lillie, one of Gerard's old cellmates from the Clink, and Gerard's faithful servant Richard Fulwood (who had himself escaped from prison the previous year) – with Gerard's old warder from the Clink at the tiller manoeuvring towards the shore.

Then, disaster struck. A resident in one of the houses along the Tower wharf, noticing the unusual sight of a boat mooring at midnight, emerged and questioned the three boatmen. To mollify the inquisitive man, the trio cast off again. But now the river tide had begun to turn. Borne by its irresistible force, the little boat drifted away from the bank. The two would-be escapers watched helplessly from the Tower's battlements as the current carried away their hopes of rescue. A new crisis now arose which nearly turned disappointment into complete catastrophe. The gathering tide swept the boat up and pinned it against one of the piles of London Bridge, threatening to capsize the frail craft at any moment.

Horrified, Arden and Gerard heard the desperate cries of the men caught in the mill-race. Crowds with lanterns gathered along the banks and on the bridge to watch as other boats surrounded the stricken craft, not daring to approach too closely lest they be sucked into the same vortex. Fortunately, a sea-going ship strong enough to resist the tide appeared, and the men were hauled to safety. Relieved, but still deeply disappointed, Arden and Gerard returned to the cell they had hoped to quit for ever. In the morning Gerard was heartened to receive a letter from Lillie interpreting the rescue as a sign from God that their escape had merely been postponed. With his help they would succeed next time.

At midnight on the next night, 4/5 October, Arden and Gerard were once again in place on top of the battlements. Again they watched, hearts in mouths, as the little boat moored at the wharf. Lillie and Fulwood, carrying a stout rope, emerged and fastened it to a towpath stake. Gerard threw down the cord which Mrs Arden had smuggled in to them, with a small iron ball attached to carry it over the moat. Fulwood tied the rope to the cord and Gerard hauled it up to the roof where he secured it to a heavy cannon.

Arden was first to slide down. But the rope, which was by no means taut, sagged under his weight and began to flap about as Gerard added his considerable bulk to it and began his descent. Gerard started to spin helplessly like a giant top around the loosening rope. Suspended a few feet over the black water of the moat, he clung on for dear life. Now, the agonising toll wreaked by the torturers' manacles on his arms and shoulders began to tell, and Gerard started to feel desperately tired as he inched out into space. He prayed fervently for salvation, and his prayers were answered. Somehow, he summoned up the last reserve of his ebbing strength and dragged himself along the slackening rope. But reaching the wall separating the moat from the wharf, Gerard found that even divine aid could not get him over, and he dangled helplessly on the rope's end with his feet brushing the top of the wall. John Lillie scrambled up and bodily heaved Gerard over. Both men collapsed in a gasping heap on the cobbles of the wharf.

They struggled to their boat and rowed away as silently as they could. Putting ashore before light as far away from the Tower as they could go, Lillie took responsibility for hiding Arden, while Gerard's servant Fulwood resumed his old role with his master. At a prearranged safe house in Spitalfields, another old friend was waiting with fresh horses: Nicholas Owen. The reunited travelling companions were soon on the road again – riding west towards the village of Uxbridge, near today's Heathrow airport, where Henry Garnet was waiting to receive them. John Gerard would never see the inside of a prison cell again. Arden, too, after his decade in the Tower, managed to evade the long arm of the Elizabethan state.

It says much for Gerard that he had not made his successful escape without caring for the fate of the man who, however unwittingly, had made it all possible: Warder Bonner. The priest had left behind three letters: one to the new lieutenant of the Tower, Sir John Peyton, who had recently replaced the squeamish Berkeley. The letter exonerated Bonner from any knowledge of, or responsibility for, his escape. A second letter went to the Privy Council, justifying his breakout and similarly exonerating both Bonner and Peyton. The third letter went to Bonner himself and was dispatched by special messenger to catch the jailer at home before he left for the Tower. Gerard explained what he had done; warned Bonner against reporting for work; and offered him a lifetime annuity of 200 florins to stay away from London and lie low in a Catholic safe house. Wisely, Bonner took this advice, and used Gerard's money to make a new life for himself and his family. He died in 1602 after converting to Catholicism.

With undiminished faith and courage, Gerard resumed his mission to England's Catholic community until the discovery of the Gunpowder Plot made the country too hot to hold even his fiery spirit. He left England disguised as a Spanish diplomat in May 1606. Little Nicholas Owen, hide builder extraordinaire, was far less fortunate. Arrested with Edward Oldcorne, the priest who had arrived in England with Gerard, Owen died under torture in the Tower. Oldcorne was executed at Tyburn. His eyeball flew out as his head was severed and is preserved as a sacred relic to this day. John Gerard lived on in Rome, dying, aged seventy-three, on 27 July 1637. He had more than earned his peaceful end.

Of all the thirty-seven men and women who succeeded in escaping the Tower, only one managed the feat twice, and very nearly succeeded a third time. In 1598, one year after Gerard and Arden's escape, Edmund Nevill finally bid farewell to the Tower where he had been incarcerated – on and off – for thirteen long years.

Edmund was a scion of the powerful northern Neville family; he fell on hard times after his cousin, Charles Neville, 6th Earl of Westmorland, co-led the Catholic Northern Rising in 1569. As an ex-soldier of fortune who had – suspiciously – served with the Spanish army in their vicious war against the Protestant Dutch, Nevill was a marked man. Amidst the increasing paranoia of late Elizabethan England, he was suspected of conspiring in the Catholic cause. In 1584 Nevill was approached by William Parry, a Welsh Catholic MP notorious for his garrulous instability. Parry tried to inveigle Edmund into a fantastic plot to assassinate Elizabeth. Suspecting that Parry was an agent provocateur, Nevill informed the authorities of the Welshman's plan.

Parry was arrested, taken to the Tower and executed in March 1585. Nevill did not share his fate, but the authorities decided that, while no danger to the state, this potential troublemaker was best kept in custody. So he lingered in a kind of limbo in the Tower, as the days stretched into weeks, the weeks into months, then into years. But Edmund Nevill was a patient man, and a resourceful one. Once he realised that his imprisonment could last indefinitely, he decided to escape. He had been given fairly free rein in the Tower, and was frequently allowed out of his cell in St Thomas's Tower above Traitor's Gate to exercise. He built up an intimate knowledge of the fortress's geography, and during his wanderings picked up various odds and ends, including scraps of metal which he fashioned into that traditional escaper's tool: a file.

Working methodically and quietly night after night, Nevill sawed through the bars of his cell window. Choosing a moonless night for his escape, he silently squeezed through and jumped down to the ground. Only the Tower's outer curtain wall stood between him and freedom. He had studied its masonry and selected a point where the stonework was rough and offered handholds. The old soldier was an athletic man, and he sprang lithely over the wall before sliding quietly into the stagnant and slimy moat and swimming across. Dripping, stinking, but exultant, he emerged on the other side. Edmund Nevill was free.

It was morning before he was missed. Immediately a hue and cry was raised and travellers leaving London were stopped and searched. But Nevill was already clear of the city and heading for the coast. Some 6 miles from the capital he was forced by hunger to stop at a village shop for food and drink. Here he was overtaken by a horseman from London who had heard of the escape. Nevill's wet clothes, encrusted with the moat's malodorous mud, betrayed him. He was arrested and returned to the Tower.

Back in his old cell, Edmund was shackled with heavy leg irons during the day, and as an extra punishment, a wooden block replaced the pillow on his bed. More months and years passed, and the vigilance of his jailers inevitably relaxed with time. In 1588 Edmund successfully applied for his wife Jane to be allowed to visit him, and in September 1590, his former privilege of having the 'libertie of the Tower' was restored.

Edmund had either kept his old file or made a new one, and once more set to work on an escape plan. He also had a rope that his wife had smuggled into his cell. Again, he chose a dark night to effect his exit. Scrambling silently out of his cell window after removing the bars he had previously filed through, again he crossed to the curtain wall and hurled his rope, with a grappling hook attached, to the top and heaved himself up. So far, his luck had held. But it was about to run out.

He had intended using the rope to descend the wall, but to his horror, found it much too short. He would have to jump into the moat with an unpleasantly loud splash, shattering the quiet of the night. The sentries inside the Tower heard the splash, and went out to investigate as Edmund desperately struck out for the far bank. He hit the other side ahead of the pursuing guards. Quick as a flash, he adopted the guise of an indignant member of the public chasing an escapee, and set off in hot pursuit of his imaginary quarry with loud cries of 'Stop!' But long confinement and his soggy clothes slowed Edmund down. He was brought to the ground by a fleet-footed turnkey. His second escape had been foiled.

Back in his cell, heavily shackled as before, Edmund rethought his tactics. He recognised that subtler methods would be needed if he was to be lucky a third time. Patient as ever, he formulated a new plan and began to work towards its fulfilment in 1596. His first step, as with Gerard, was to trick his jailer, Henry Frewen. He adopted the habit, every time Frewen entered his cell, of sitting, silent and motionless, against his cell window. Over weeks, Frewen grew used to seeing his prisoner brooding over his fate, and hardly gave Edmund a second glance. Using material and straw that he had laboriously collected, Edmund made a dummy mannequin, roughly his own size. He dressed it in his clothes, sat it in his usual window seat, leaning forward as if lost in thought, and, as a final touch, masked the model by draping his velvet cloak around its shoulders.

Then he put the next stage of his plan into operation. His deceptively simple idea was to change his identity from Edmund Nevill, Tower political prisoner, to Edmund Nevill, jobbing Tower blacksmith. He had carefully carved a set of farrier's tools in wood, smearing them with polish to give a dark metallic sheen, and had sewn a blacksmith's apron from strips of leather and cloth. Hanging his fake 'tools' from a belt, he rolled up his sleeves, rubbed dirt, dust and polish into his face and forearms as if he had come straight from his forge, and waited for Frewen's familiar steps climbing the steep spiral staircase to his door.

As he heard the approaching turnkey, Edmund hid in an alcove behind the cell door. The keys rattled, the bolts shot, and the door swung open, hiding Edmund, as the warder entered carrying his food. As Frewen, half-aware of Edmund's familiar figure in the window, moved across the cell, the real Edmund tiptoed nimbly around the open door and darted down the stairs. Once in the open air, he began to stroll towards the main Tower gateway as casually as he could. Freedom must have again seemed so close that Edmund only had to seize it.

A woman suddenly appeared, nosily quizzing the 'blacksmith' as to his identity and business. As Edmund started to stutter an explanation, a breathless Frewen appeared in the doorway. The dummy had not fooled him for long and Edmund's ruse had been discovered. Sadly, the serial escaper was returned to his cell. Now, however, an end was at last in sight. Perhaps recognising that whatever danger Edmund had once posed to the state had long passed, in 1598 the authorities released him after thirteen years' incarceration. He left England with his wife and their seven children, and spent the rest of his life doggedly – but unsuccessfully – pursuing his claim to be recognised as the successor of his cousin Charles as 7th Earl of Westmorland.

Despite acknowledging the validity of Edmund's claim, the mean-spirited James I refused to grant it, and Edmund remained in exile until his death in Brussels in 1640, forty-two years after gaining his freedom from the Tower. We can still admire his dauntless spirit today – and in person, in the shape of his magnificent effigy, kneeling opposite his faithful wife Jane, surrounded by their three sons and four daughters. The monument, which stands in the twelfth-century parish church of St Mary Magdalene in East Ham in London's east end, reads:

IN MEMORIA SACRUM

In memory of The Right Honourable EDMOND NEVILL Lord Latimer, Earl of Westmorland, and Dam Jane his wife with the memorials of their seven children. Which Edmond was lineally descended from the honorable blood of Kings and princes in ye line of ye 7th Earl of Westmorland of the name of Nevill.

The story of two royal lovers star-crossed in a way that Romeo and Juliet could not have imagined is one of the Tower's most tragic tales. Lady Arbella Stuart and her husband William Seymour might have known that their match would end in tears if they had studied the bloody history of their own respective families more closely. But we can salute their courage in attempting to escape the chains that genes, history and a poisonously vile king wrapped around them.

The couple had much in common, including ties of blood. They were both Tudors, being directly descended from sisters of Henry VIII. Arbella was the great-granddaughter of Henry's elder sister Margaret, Queen of Scotland; William was the great-great-grandson of Henry's younger sister Mary, Duchess of Suffolk. Bloodshed and violence had blighted both their family lines. Arbella was also the niece of Mary, Queen of Scots and her husband Henry Darnley. Thus, fatally for her future, she was first cousin to that ill-starred couple's son, King James. Arbella's grandmother, Margaret Douglas, had also been flung in the Tower by her own uncle, Henry VIII, when the old tyrant had found out about her unsuitable love affair with Lord Thomas Howard – who, unforgiven by the king, had died there of jail fever in 1537.

The closer that young lovers were to the throne in Tudor and Jacobean England, the more their passion could bring them to the Tower – and the grave. William's paternal great-grandfather, Edward Seymour, Duke of Somerset – Protector of England under his nephew, the boy king Edward VI – had been imprisoned in the Tower and executed on Tower Hill; while his maternal grandmother, Lady Catherine Grey, had been imprisoned in the Tower by Queen Elizabeth for her temerity in marrying his grandfather, Ned Seymour, and what was worse, falling pregnant. Both grandparents, as we have seen, had been jailed in the Tower – never meeting again after they had unwisely conceived a second child in the fortress. Undaunted by the unfortunate example of his grandparents, William Seymour was also to aim high for love, only to fall and yet rise again.

Born in 1575, and orphaned as a young child, Arbella had been brought up by a quintessential Elizabethan great lady, Elizabeth Talbot, Countess of Shrewsbury, known as 'Bess of Hardwick', her domineering maternal grandmother. Escaping from Bess's tyranny in 1603 when her cousin James succeeded Queen Elizabeth on the English throne, the plain and sickly Arbella came to court hoping that the king would help her make a good marriage. However, the king's mind was poisoned by rumours that she could become an alternate candidate for the English throne. Marriage negotiations with various candidates came to nothing, and in 1510 a desperate and now ageing Arbella (she was thirty-four, ancient for a royal bride) married twenty-two-year-old William Seymour, a man she barely knew, at dead of night in Greenwich Palace. When he found out a fortnight later, King James flew into a furious rage, and ordered the newly-weds' immediate arrest for daring to marry without his permission. William was flung into the Tower, while Arbella was placed under house arrest across the Thames in Lambeth.

At first William was comfortably housed in the lodgings of the Tower lieutenant, Sir William Wade. However, the hard-faced lieutenant made an uncongenial host, and William was soon removed to St Thomas's Tower. Seymour's room had windows overlooking the river on one side, and on the other over the short raised walkway from the Bloody Tower known as Ralegh's Walk, where the redoubtable Elizabethan adventurer – the Tower's most distinguished current resident – stretched his legs during his long confinement.

To make his quarters homelier, Seymour borrowed furniture, costly tapestries, silver plate, candlesticks and fine linen from Arbella's house; and was loaned a substantial sum by his grandfather, the Earl of Hertford. William's marriage with the semi-royal Arbella had given him credit with local tradesmen who loaned him cash and goods to make his spartan cell comfortable. And he was also given the 'Libertie of the Tower' – that precious freedom to wander at will within the fortress's precincts. Like Edmund Nevill, he would put his liberty to good use.

Poor Arbella, always mentally frail, was driven to the brink of madness by the enforced separation from her new husband. She wrote pathetic, distracted pleas to the hard-hearted king, begging to be forgiven and reunited with William. Almost a year passed with no response. Then, driven by desperation, Arbella got her servants to row her across the river to St Thomas's Tower, and, standing on the wharf, spoke to Seymour through his cell window. The king got to hear of the clandestine meeting and was vexed to renewed fury. He ordered Arbella north in the care of the Bishop of Durham. The sick woman got no further than Highgate before an onset of alarming symptoms, including the purple-coloured urine typical of the 'royal malady' porphyria, halted her progress. Her physician, Dr Moundford, told an enraged James that she could not physically go further, and she was taken to a Parson Adams's house in Barnet to recuperate.

At this point, Arbella's fabulously wealthy aunt, Mary Talbot, Countess of Shrewsbury, like some fairy godmother, took an ostensibly benevolent interest in her niece's desperate situation. The countess was cut from the same tough cloth as her mother, Bess of Hardwick. Possibly genuinely motivated by pity for the young couple, but more probably hoping to advance herself using them as her instruments, she came to the rescue. After failing in her own attempt to obtain a pardon for the miscreants from the malevolent king, she resolved to spirit both Arbella and Seymour out of the country beyond James's reach.

The countess set in motion a complex escape plan costing thousands of pounds. A French ship and crew were hired; officials were bribed; and clandestine meetings set up to ensure that everyone involved – especially the two principals – knew exactly what they had to do. But there were fundamental flaws in the countess's over-elaborate scheme. Too many people were in the know: no fewer than nine of the couple's servants and attendants were involved in the double escape, plus a score of sailors and watermen. And fatally, there was no provision for a fallback Plan B should Arbella and William fail to meet at their agreed rendezvous. Inevitably, given that so many things could go wrong, something did.

All began well. On Monday 3 June 1611, Arbella told her Barnet hostess, Mrs Adams, that she intended to go out in disguise that night to meet her husband, returning early in the morning. Spurred by sympathy for the romantic assignation, Mrs Adams helped Arbella don her drag: a man's doublet and a long peruke wig, topped off with a black slouch hat; with showy long red-topped yellow boots, a cloak and a rapier sword. Accompanied by a servant, William Markham, Arbella set off for 'a sorry inn' where she was to pick up horses hired by Hugh Crompton, another servant.

The ostler holding the horses noted the bizarre appearance of the 'gentleman' mounting the gelding. Observing Arbella as she awkwardly sat astride the beast (she would previously only have ridden a ladylike side-saddle), the man doubted out loud whether they would make it to London. Undaunted, Arbella wobbled off with Crompton and Markham riding beside her. After a fourteen-mile cross-country journey they arrived in time for the six o'clock rendezvous at a riverside tavern in Blackwall where she was due to meet William. Here, as arranged, were two of William's servants, Edward Reeves and Edward Kirton, along with Arbella's lady-in-waiting Ann Bradshaw. The little group settled down to wait for William to appear.

Back at the Tower, the plan had started to unravel. Seymour had carefully studied the comings and goings of tradesmen visiting the fortress. He had noted that a certain carter delivered hay and firewood each evening, departing immediately after calling at his last stop, St Thomas's Tower. The cart would remain outside the tower's west door for five minutes. Here, William decided, was his best chance. If he could swap places with the carter, he would be able to drive out himself under the Byward and Middle Towers – and the noses of their guards – to freedom.

William's barber, Thomas Batten, contacted the carter. Money changed hands. That night, along with his usual change of fine clean clothes, Batten brought some unusually rough garments to his master – the carter's homespun apparel – and a horsewhip. All seemed ready. But on the evening set for the escape, for reasons unknown, the carter did not appear. Boiling with frustration, William peered from his window as the hazy June dusk gathered. One hour went by. Then two. Then, just when all seemed lost, the cart slowly creaked into view.

Dressed in the carter's coarse clothes, Seymour tore down the same spiral stairs that Edmund Nevill had descended twelve years before. He cautiously opened the door at the tower's foot. The carter heard him and casually strolled round to let the tail of the cart down and rummage among his hay bales. In a single stride, William took the man's place on the driving platform. He cracked his whip and urged the plodding carthorse out towards the Byward Tower. Behind him the carter flattened himself under the hay. The sentries at the Byward and Middle Towers, used to its daily visits, barely gave the departing cart – or its driver – a glance as it clattered under the arches. Once outside, William steered the cart sharp left, down to the wharf and the river. At a spot called the Iron Gate – where Tower Bridge stands today – he halted. A trusted friend, Edward Rodney, was still waiting with a boat. Running two hours late as he was, William wasted no time for farewells to the carter, but dashed down the steps and jumped aboard.

When they reached the inn at Blackwall where they were supposed to meet Arbella and her party, the reception committee were nowhere to be seen. Tragically, they had only missed each other by minutes. Arbella had lingered at the inn as long as she dared. But after waiting with steadily diminishing hope for two hours, at eight o' clock – about the time her husband was casting off from the Iron Gate – her attendants had persuaded her that unless they continued downriver the tide would turn and all would be lost. In two boats, the little party rowed downstream to Leigh in Essex in the gathering darkness. Arbella was wrapped in her voluminous velvet coat against the river's chill. En route they passed the lighted windows of Greenwich Palace, where the year before Arbella had married William, and where the king was now in residence, blissfully unaware of this fresh defiance. When he found out, his rage would know no bounds.

Ironically, the agent of discovery was to be William's own beloved younger brother, Francis. At eight o'clock the next morning, Francis Seymour received a letter from Edward Rodney, telling him not to expect to see his brother again for some time. His suspicions aroused, the young man sped to the Tower and compelled the barber Thomas Batten to open the door of William's cell. It was empty, William having quit the fortress twelve and a half hours previously. Desperate to cover his own back, Francis told the Tower's lieutenant, Sir William Wade, of the breakout. Wade hastened to Greenwich to inform the king.

An enraged James issued a proclamation inveighing against Arbella and William's 'divers great and heynous offences'; and naming 'divers Lewd persons' who had assisted their escape. Anyone who aided the runaways, the king said darkly, did so at their peril, and anyone apprehending them, he added, would have the reward of knowing that their action would please their monarch: 'Wee would take [it] as an acceptable service.'

While this notice was being posted in the London streets, and search parties were combing the capital, the two fugitives were tossing uncomfortably in separate boats as their tragi-comedy of errors continued. Having reached, with great difficulty and delay, the waiting French ship lying off Leigh, Arbella and her party found they had missed the tide to carry them away from England. Later, William and Rodney also arrived at Leigh. Seeing no sign of the French ship, they rowed out to a collier, the *Charles*, whose master, a Captain Seerson, proved willing, for a hefty fee of £40, to delay collecting his coals from Newcastle, and ferry the fugitives to Calais instead.

As they sailed out along the Thames estuary on the Tuesday morning tide, William and Rodney spotted a French ship heave to. Suspecting that this was the ship that had collected Arbella, they asked Seerson to anchor and row over to the foreign ship to investigate. Apparently afraid of being abandoned if the vessel was not the right one, they themselves stayed on the *Charles*. Seerson obediently boarded the French ship. While there he saw a woman sitting on a hatch: this was almost certainly either Arbella herself or Miss Bradshaw, but contact was not established. Anxious not to lose his fat fee, Seerson returned to the *Charles* and told William and Rodney that the French ship was not the one they sought. The collier skipper's avarice had snapped the last, tenuous thread binding William and Arbella together. They would never meet again.

The *Charles* continued her cross-Channel voyage. Contrary winds first blew her north along the Essex coast to Harwich, then eastwards away from Calais. Only after four days of fearful winds, on the evening of 8 June, did they arrive off Ostend. Groggy from seasickness, William and Rodney struggled ashore, expecting to meet Arbella. But she was in an entirely different place: she had replaced her husband in the Tower.

* * *

Inevitably, word of the mysterious strangers who had so urgently sought a cross-Channel passage at Leigh had spread, reaching the ears of the local naval commander Admiral Sir William Monson. He sent the fast pinnace *Adventure*, skippered by Captain Griffin Cockett, in pursuit. Cockett spotted Arbella's ship, which, buffeted by the same winds which had delayed William, was wallowing in heavy seas off Calais. The French coast was only a mile away, but tantalisingly out of reach. Cockett soon overtook the slower ship. Thirteen musket shots whistling through his sails and rigging persuaded the French captain, Tassin Corve, to heave to, and a dejected Arbella and her accomplices were arrested. Within sight of safety, her desperate bid for freedom with the husband she adored had finally failed.

James's vengeance on the cousin who had defied him was vicious and extended to all those who had – knowingly or unwittingly – helped in her attempt. Everyone with the remotest connection to the conspiracy – even the innocent wigmaker who had made Arbella's peruke – was rounded up and jailed. Those held ranged from Arbella's physician, Dr Moundford, and the hapless Mrs Adams, to the humble boatmen who had rowed her down the Thames. Also detained were the two captains, Corve and Seerson, and even the priest who had officiated at the couple's marriage. Arbella's servants Crompton and Markham were questioned at the Tower – and Markham was even racked to loosen his tongue. Arbella herself, along with her scheming aunt Mary, Countess of Shrewsbury, who had organised the whole affair, were also flung in the Tower. The huge sum of cash – £3,000 – that Arbella had raised to fund her new life abroad was confiscated. Closely confined to a cell in the Bell Tower, she literally pined away. She refused to eat, the symptoms of porphyria reappeared, and in 1615, sick and lonely, she died in the Tower.

The husband she had hardly known did not mourn his bride for long. Any threat to James's lineage had died with Arbella, and in 1616 William was forgiven. He returned to England and made a more acceptable second marriage – to Frances Devereux, daughter of Elizabeth I's favourite, Robert, Earl of Essex, the last person to be beheaded within the Tower walls in 1601. William, made Marquess of Hertford, sired seven children with Frances, and found more favour with James's son, Charles I, than he had with his father.

He was made tutor to the Prince of Wales, the future Charles II, and in the Civil War, took a prominent – if largely unsuccessful – military role as commander of Royalist forces in the west. William was among the chosen companions allowed to attend King Charles I before his execution in 1649. He made his peace with the victorious Parliamentarians, however, and sat out Cromwell's rule in comfortable country retirement. William lived to witness the Restoration, dying in 1661 aged seventy-two. The year he died, Charles II granted his old tutor his executed great-grandfather's title and William was buried, loaded with years and honours, as the 2nd Duke of Somerset. That summer night when he fled the Tower in a common carter's clothes must have seemed a very long time ago. But he had not forgotten his tragic first wife. Seymour's will requested that he be buried alongside her in Westminster Abbey. That wish was not fulfilled: instead William lies with his second wife Frances and other members of the Seymour family in the eleventh-century church of St Mary the Virgin in the Wiltshire village of Bledwyn Magna.

The twenty years of Civil War, Commonwealth, Protectorate and Restoration between 1640 and 1660 were as turbulent for the Tower as for the rest of the country. Many famous prisoners passed in and out of its walls. Security was often lax, and as well as the escapes described here, others exited by such crude means as sawing the doors off their cells. The changing cast list of its prisoners fluctuated with the turning fortunes of war, and the destinies of two prominent inmates who managed to escape the Tower faithfully reflected the era's topsy-turvy politics. One was a faithful Royalist; the other a loyal Roundhead.

Lord Arthur Capel of Hadham Hall in Essex, from his long ringletted locks to his pointed Van Dyck beard, was the very image of a Cavalier. In the Second Civil War of 1648, when Royalists rose in Capel's native Essex, he was prominent among the Cavaliers who grimly held the county town of Colchester against a two-month siege by Thomas, Lord Fairfax, commander of the New Model Army.

By then, both sides had been hardened by four years of bitter war, and little quarter was asked or given. When Colchester was starved into surrender at the end of August, after the population had been reduced to eating horses, cats, dogs and – according to rumour – their own children, even the moderate Fairfax was in an unforgiving mood. The two commanders of the Royalist garrison, Sir Charles Lucas and Sir George Lisle, were shot by firing squad. But Fairfax was more merciful to his fellow peers among the Cavaliers than the men whom he called common 'soldiers of fortune'. Both Lord Capel and Lord Norwich were packed off to the Tower to await Parliament's pleasure.

Capel was visited by his loyal wife Elizabeth and at least some of their five sons and four daughters (like his fellow Tower escapers Edmund Nevill and William Seymour, he was remarkably fecund). He was urged to escape by his family and friends, who suggested that he should swim the moat. When Capel objected that he was a non-swimmer, it occurred to someone that this might not be necessary. Since milord was so tall, he could wade across instead.

His friends circled the moat, looking for a spot where the murky water might be fordable. Eventually they found a place where accumulated filth provided a narrow causeway of sludge. Ropes and a grappling iron were smuggled into Capel's cell between the Lieutenant's Lodgings and the Beauchamp Tower. The bars on his cell window were carefully loosened in advance of the attempt, and on a particularly dark, foggy autumn night late in 1649, he wrapped one rope around his torso, fixed the other end securely, and slid down into the shadows. He used the second rope with the grappling iron to climb the curtain wall, and worked his way along the battlements until he reached the place where the moat was apparently shallow.

Securing his rope to the battlements with the iron, Capel slid down it and fearlessly slipped into the icy water. He was rewarded when his feet touched bottom and the water was at chest level. But as he stepped out, his feet sinking into the oozy slime, the water level rose alarmingly until it was lapping his beard. At the same time, he was becoming disorientated in the mist. For all his courage as a soldier, Capel began to feel the panic of the non-swimmer out of his depth. Then, miraculously, the water level fell again. He found his footing and once more began to step forward. A few more paces, and he reached the slimy, reeking ooze of the far bank. His friends saw him and rushed to his rescue.

Frozen and filthy, Capel was helped by willing hands to a waiting coach, and within an hour was bathed, dry and secure in a Royalist safe house in the nearby Temple. The hue and cry raised for him was formidable. To lose such a prominent Royalist prize was an unendurable humiliation for the Roundheads. Royalist houses in the city were raided and searched, and after a couple of days the friends sheltering Capel decided to move him south of the river until the frenzy had died down. It was a fatal mistake.

He was taken at dead of night to Temple Steps where a hired boat rowed him across the Thames to Lambeth Marsh. But his great height was a giveaway, and the suspicious boatman heard one of his companions address Capel as 'my Lord'. Greedy for the reward which had been placed on the nobleman's head, the waterman landed them safely before pocketing his ferryman's fee. He then – at a discreet distance – followed the group to their destination, noted the address, and hurried off to inform the authorities and claim his twenty pieces of silver – for £20 was the reward for Capel's recapture.

Capel was rearrested and returned to the Tower. His master the king was on trial for his life after he too had fled captivity and been recaptured. Capel had letters smuggled out of the Tower urging his friends to rescue the king – another black mark against him which came to Parliament's attention. After Charles's execution at the end of January, Parliament was not in a merciful mood, and Capel was condemned to share the monarch's fate. Capel was highly regarded for his nobility and devotion to his chosen cause. When his loyal wife Elizabeth petitioned for his life, it took a speech by Oliver Cromwell himself to confirm the death sentence by a mere three votes. Capel's very qualities of courage, industry and resolution, argued Cromwell, would always make him 'a thorn in the side' of Parliament if they allowed him to live.

On 9 March 1649 Capel was brought to the block in New Palace Yard, Westminster. He walked to the scaffold through Westminster Hall 'saluting his friends with a serene and undaunted countenance'. On the eve of his execution he had written movingly to his wife, 'I shall leave thee my dear children; in them I live with thee; and leave thee to the protection of a most gracious God.' He was accompanied to the scaffold by the Bishop of Winchester, Dr Morley, who described the parting from his 'most dear lady' as 'the saddest spectacle I ever beheld'. Capel told his seventeen-year-old son, another Arthur, not to seek revenge for his death, and in a passionate speech to the crowd who had gathered to see him die, told them his only crime had been obedience to his lawful sovereign. He concluded by calling on them to give their allegiance to the new King Charles II, 'a prince endowed with all those virtues which could make a nation happy'.

Missing the executioner among the crowd on the scaffold he asked, 'Where is the gentleman?' and when Richard Brandon, the headsman, came forward to ask the customary forgiveness from his victim, Capel replied, 'I forgive thee from my soul,' and gave him a £5 tip to perform his work well. Brandon duly struck off Capel's head with one stroke – as he had cleanly executed the king a few weeks previously – and Capel's body was borne back to his Essex home for burial. Brandon himself died later that year, some said from remorse. The boatman who had betrayed Capel, it was said, 'became the scorn and contempt of everybody, and lived afterwards in shame and misery'.

At the Restoration of Charles II, the king made young Arthur Capel the Earl of Essex – like William Seymour, Capel senior had been a tutor to the young prince during the Civil War. Lady Elizabeth Capel had died early that year and was buried with her husband in St Cecilia's Church in Little Hadham.

John Lambert was one of the most attractive and able figures to emerge from the Civil War. Next to Fairfax and Cromwell himself, Lambert was the Parliamentarian officer arguably most endowed with military gifts, and his political skills exceeded those of the often clumsy protector, though in the end he found himself on the wrong side of history as public opinion reacted against the grim years of Puritan military rule.

Born into the Yorkshire gentry, Lambert learned his soldiering skills from his fellow Yorkshireman, Thomas Fairfax. Still under thirty when the war ended, Lambert transferred his loyalty to Cromwell, and was his trusted lieutenant in the great victories over the Scots and Royalists at Preston, Dunbar and Worcester. Popular in the army, and a moderate Republican in politics, Lambert seemed set fair to succeed Cromwell as Lord Protector, but he fell out with his chief for political as well as personal reasons. Handsome, vain and self-important, Lambert made little secret of his ambitions to succeed Cromwell, and was instrumental in blocking Oliver's acceptance of Parliament's offer of the crown: a slight which the Lord Protector never forgave.

Cromwell took his revenge in 1658, and Lambert was briskly removed from his posts in Parliament and the army – though compensated with a generous pension – shortly before the Lord Protector's death. Lambert retired with his wife Frances and children to his house in Wimbledon, but re-emerged on to the political stage after the fall of Cromwell's son Richard is 1659. One of the ruling Council of State, Lambert attempted to impose a new military dictatorship. But the zeitgeist had turned decisively against military rule, and was increasingly flowing towards a Royalist restoration.

After crushing Booth's Royalist revolt near Manchester in 1659, Lambert was comprehensively outmanoeuvred by the secretly Royalist General Monck, deserted by the troops who had once adored him, and finally, in January 1660, as a result of Monck's machinations, sent to the Tower by Parliament – who resented Lambert for having once dissolved it in the high-handed Cromwellian style. Without the attractive figurehead of Lambert to lead it, Republican resistance to Monck's Royalism faded away, and by April the Restoration was a done deal: Charles II would return from his long exile the next month.

Brooding in his cell in St Thomas's Tower – where Nevill and William Seymour had been confined before him – Lambert resolved to prevent this 'happy return' at the eleventh hour. Aided by Republican sympathisers, he plotted his escape with his customary military skill. A rope – woven from silk by 'a lady' for a £100 fee – was smuggled into the general's cell, and on the overcast evening of 10 April, at about 8 p.m., Lambert left his cell by the window, whose bars had been pre-loosened. Handkerchiefs wrapped round his hands to prevent friction burns, he slithered down the rope, scaled the curtain wall, and, avoiding the sentries on the wharf, met up with half a dozen old Cromwellians waiting to receive him on the river with a hired barge.

Behind him in his cell bed, Lambert had left an extra precaution against early discovery – his bed maker, a girl named Joan, whom the handsome general had charmed into assisting his getaway. Joan, her features hidden under Lambert's woollen nightcap, and her voice muffled by the bed curtains, had gruffly acknowledged the jailer's cheery 'Goodnight, my Lord' when the turnkey did his rounds and locked 'Lambert' in for the night. The escape was not discovered, nor the alarm raised, until the same warder returned in the morning, and, to his dumbfounded astonishment, found Joan's face staring out at him from under General Lambert's nightcap. 'In the name of God, Joan,' cried the astonished jailer, 'what makes you here?' The answer we can only imagine.

With a £100 reward on his head, Lambert lay low in a Republican safe house somewhere in the labyrinth of London's pre-Great Fire streets. As with the Elizabethan Catholics in the previous century, the Puritan Roundheads were now an unpopular minority, stubbornly clinging to their rigid beliefs against the prevailing Royalist reaction. But since the whole purpose of Lambert's escape had been a political one – to rally the scattered supporters of the 'good old cause' for one glorious last stand, he could not stay underground indefinitely. From his hiding place word went out for his old army comrades to rendezvous with him in the English Midlands, a conveniently central spot for rekindling the flickering embers of Republican resistance. And what better place, the romantic general decided, for a muster point, than the old battlefield of Edgehill?

The escarpment of Edgehill near Kineton in Warwickshire was crowded with ghosts. This was the place where, nearly two decades before, in October 1642, the first pitched battle of the Civil War had taken place, and freeborn Englishmen had flung down the gauntlet of revolt against a tyrannical King Charles I. So the summons went out. It was impossible to gather a substantial body of men without the government hearing about it, and Monck, effectively dictator of England as he awaited the return of the king, dispatched an old comrade to intercept Lambert before he reached the rendezvous.

Colonel Sir Richard Ingoldsby was a particularly piquant choice for the delicate task. For he was a regicide – one of the officers who had signed King Charles I's death warrant. As such, he feared for his future under the regime of the son of the king whose head he had helped cut off. Therefore Ingoldsby was anxious to ingratiate himself with the new masters by foiling his old friends.

By the time Ingoldsby's two regiments caught up with Lambert near Daventry, the general had been joined by six troops of horse under John Okey, an unreconstructed Republican diehard and regicide who had commanded the Roundhead dragoons at the battle of Naseby. Ingoldsby rode up and down the lines haranguing Lambert's men. Did they, he demanded, want to restart the Civil War? None did, and their drawn pistols gradually dipped towards the ground as they gave up the fight. There would be no repetition of Edgehill. As his men melted away, Lambert himself took off across the fields mounted on a Barbary stallion. But the galloping horse became bogged down in a ploughed meadow, and Lambert was overtaken and rearrested. The implacable Ingoldsby refused his old comrade's pleas to release him.

As they rode back towards London and the Tower, crowds gathered at Northampton to jeer the fallen hero. Their hoots led Lambert to recall a happier day in 1650, when he and Cromwell had ridden out of London together at the start of their victorious campaign in Scotland, to the cheers of a crowd. Naively, he had observed to Cromwell that he was glad they had the nation on their side. The cynical Oliver had replied, 'Do not trust to that; for these very persons would shout just as much if you and I were going to be hanged.' Since execution was now his likely fate, concluded Lambert, he had added the mantle of prophet to all Cromwell's other admired attributes.

In fact, John Lambert escaped execution, probably because he had not been a regicide. Ingoldsby, who had been, duly won forgiveness from the king for nipping the revolt in the bud. Returned to the Tower, Lambert was tried for treason and sentenced to perpetual imprisonment, serving the first part of his sentence at Guernsey's Castle Cornet in the Channel Islands. His wife Frances secured permission to join him at the forbidding fortress and he was given freedom to roam the castle grounds, which led to another – unsuccessful – escape attempt in 1670. Brought back to England, he was more closely confined in another island fortress, that of St Nicholas (now called Drake's Island) in Plymouth Sound.

Here Frances brought their ten children for Lambert was yet another fertile Tower escaper – to visit their father. But when his loyal wife died at Christmas 1676, Lambert's mind gave way, and the lonely prisoner lapsed into intermittent madness. He must have had lucid moments, however, for in 1683, after nearly a quarter of a century's confinement, Lambert was visited by the man responsible for his sentence – Charles II himself, along with his brother James, Duke of York. They are reported to have spent more than an hour chatting with the last of their father's Roundhead foes. The following year, still a prisoner, John Lambert found the ultimate release of death.

At first, in the reaction against the harshness of Cromwell's rule, Charles II carried all before him. But lively Protestant fears of the influence of French and Spanish Catholicism – Charles's brother and heir James and his queen, Catherine, were open Catholics, Charles himself a covert one – persisted. Such fears of a new royal tyranny, and a nostalgia for the political and religious radicalism of the 1640s and '50s coalesced into a powerful opposition who began to call themselves 'Whigs'. They had their first success in 1678–9 with the Popish Plot, a manifestation of widespread anti-Catholic paranoia, which saw several innocent Catholic peers executed and a serious attempt made to exclude James from the succession in favour of Charles's illegitimate Protestant son, James, Duke of Monmouth.

But the Popish Plot and the Exclusion Crisis passed when Charles and his court party – increasingly known as 'Tories' – turned the tables on the Whigs and engineered the exile of their chief, the Earl of Shaftesbury, after he had briefly tasted the Tower. Left leaderless, the Whig lords turned to conspiracy – or talking about it in their taverns and coffee-houses. But Charles, a canny and cynical political operator, trounced his Whig enemies by linking their harmless grumbling with a genuine – albeit botched – plot by Roundhead veterans to assassinate him and his brother in Hertfordshire on their return from horse racing at Newmarket. The smashing of this Rye House Plot, and the arrest of its instigators, gave Charles a perfect excuse to round up the Whig lords, hotheads who dreamed of deposing the monarchy and restoring an ideal republic.

The five Whig leaders, Lord Howard of Escrick, Algernon Sidney, Lord Russell, Lord Gerard and Forde, Lord Grey de Werke, were arrested and locked in the Tower. Another peer, Arthur Capel, the Earl of Essex, was a surprising recruit to the plotters' ranks, and provides a tragic and myste-rious coda to the death of his namesake father thirty years before. For this Arthur Capel was the same youth whom we last saw bidding a sad farewell to his father on the scaffold before the Cavalier's execution.

Capel junior had served Charles II as faithfully as his father had served the 'Merry Monarch's' father. He rose to be Lord Lieutenant of Ireland, sticking out among the crooked Restoration placemen for his honesty and efficiency. Fatally for him, however, he crossed the king's notoriously corrupt mistress, Barbara Villiers, Duchess of Cleveland, by refusing to sanction her land grab for Dublin's Phoenix Park. In revenge, she had him removed from his post. An embittered Essex, always a staunch Protestant, now joined the Whig opposition. Although not directly involved with the Rye House Plot, he was arrested in its wake and was cruelly – and doubtless deliberately – confined in the same room in the Tower between the Lieutenant's Lodgings and the Beauchamp Tower that his father had occupied.

Three days later, on 13 July 1683, King Charles and his brother James, Duke of York, visited the Tower for the first time in years. The ostensible purpose of the trip was to inspect some new ordnance, but the royal visit coincided with the confinement of the Whig lords in the fortress, and the real agenda was to gloat over the humbling of their enemies. After the visit, as the royal party were embarking on their barge, escorted by the Tower lieutenant, Captain Tom Cheek, a cry of 'Murder! Murder!' was heard from inside the fortress.

In his locked and blood-spattered room, the Earl of Essex was found dead – his throat slashed by a razor. The wound, inflicted with extraordinary violence, had severed both jugular veins, his windpipe and oesophagus, and extended as far back as his spine, nearly decapitating him as his father had been beheaded before him. The king professed to be distressed when he heard the news. He claimed that he would not have had Essex put to death with his fellow Whigs over the Rye House Plot because 'I owed him a life'. Charles was clearly still mindful of the services the elder Arthur Capel had rendered to his father and himself.

The Earl of Essex's death remains one of the Tower's most perplexing unsolved mysteries. Those who suspect murder have some compelling evidence: two children playing on Tower Green said they had seen a mysterious hand toss a bloody razor from the earl's window onto the grass, just after hearing cries and the sounds of a scuffle. The blade, still bloody and wet, had instantly, they added, been retrieved by a maid and returned to the earl's room. A soldier claimed that two mysterious strangers had been admitted to the lodgings just before the shouts of 'Murder!'. Moreover, the medical evidence was odd: could a razor, wielded by the victim himself, really have cut through the neck to the backbone, inflicting wounds so deep that 'an executioner with an axe could hardly have done more'?

Those believing that the earl committed suicide have also got a strong case: he was a moody, emotional man, much given to depression and introspection. The day before his death he had demanded a razor to pare his nails – a drastic instrument to accomplish such a routine task. Moreover, there was a motive: a peer who died before being executed for treason would escape the usual attainder, meaning the forfeiture of title, land and property. Did Essex act to save his family from penury? We will never know, but the day after his death an inquest jury brought in a speedy verdict of suicide. Despite the doubts, most historians have accepted that conclusion.

One Whig lord arrested with Essex, who also escaped the headsman's axe – albeit by an easier method than Essex's bloody razor – was Forde, Lord Grey de Werke. Lord Grey had the luck of the Devil; and he pushed it to the limit. Not only did he successfully carry out one of the most audacious escapes from the Tower, but returning to the fortress a second time years later, facing an even graver charge of treason, he managed to avoid the block yet again.

Grey was an opportunistic fellow. He appeared a typical wealthy Restoration rake, with a fine country seat at Uppark in Sussex. Beneath the foppish facade, however, beat a rebel heart: his grandfather was Henry Ireton, Cromwell's son-in-law and most trusted lieutenant, the hard man of the English revolution. Grey's first experience of the Tower had come in 1682, when he had been locked up there accused of eloping to France with his sister-in-law, the eighteen-year-old Lady Henrietta Berkeley. Disarmingly, he explained to a court – presided over by the notorious future 'Hanging Judge' George Jeffreys – that having married Lady Mary Berkeley, 'expecting a maidenhead . . . but not finding it, hee resolved to have one in the family, if any be left'.

Released after it was revealed that the lusty Lady Henrietta was herself secretly married to another man, Grey turned his energies from sexual to political intrigue. A prominent member of the Whig opposition, he tirelessly promoted the claims of his drinking and wenching crony, the Protestant Duke of Monmouth, to succeed his father Charles II as king. Intensely irritated, Charles added Grey's name to the list of Whig lords rounded up after the Rye House Plot. Grey was arrested by a king's messenger, Henry Denham. When Denham arrived at the Tower's gate with his prisoner, the hour was late and the gate was firmly shut. This presented Denham with a problem: Charles's orders specified that Grey had to be handed over to Tom Cheek, the Tower lieutenant, in person. Grey suggested that they should adjourn to one of the many taverns near the Tower in the local 'liberty' – a slum known as Petty Wales – and while away the hours in convivial style until the gates opened.

Prisoner and escort settled down in a riverside inn, with its clientele of soldiers, sailors and Tower warders, to carouse the night away. Denham drank deeply of the wine that Grey paid for, but his companion was unusually abstemious. Grey was already weighing up the chances of escape. As the night wore on, and more wine flowed, Denham grew flushed and fuddled. Grey, however, while affecting to join in the drunken merry-making, remained alert. Finally, Denham slumped on the table, snoring in sottish slumber.

This might have been Grey's chance to get away, but he hesitated. The inn was filled with the Tower's warders and officers, who would be unlikely to let this important political prisoner go. As dawn broke, the boom of a signal cannon, and the unmistakable clanking and crashing of the Tower's gates opening were clearly heard in the inn. Denham stirred, lurched to his feet, and the two men left the tavern to meet the morning. Quite casually, Grey strolled towards the gatehouse – the Middle Tower – with the stumbling, hungover Denham staggering along in his wake. Grey engaged the sentries on the gate in easy conversation: he was innocent, he protested, and he asked to see his old friend Tom Cheek, the lieutenant. He was not yet up, the guards told Grey, and in the meantime, he was admitted to the Tower to wait.

Grey and Denham passed through the forbidding gateway and crossed the stone bridge over the moat to the inner gatehouse, the Byward Tower, which at that early hour was deserted. Grey was at last alone with the hungover Denham. Here was his chance. Under the archway of the Byward Tower he knew that there was a passage – the Sally Port – to the right, leading directly to the wharf. This privy passage was for the convenience of important Tower visitors who wished to enter and leave discreetly. It was normally guarded, but at this early hour, it was not. Grey looked across at Denham. His escort was asleep on his feet. With a single step, Grey entered the dark passage and pushed the door at the end. By a miracle, it was open. In a moment he was on the wharf, and by another miracle, a wherry boat was already moored there, touting for trade.

Within seconds, Grey was on the river, and a few minutes later he was landing on the other side, at a tavern appropriately called the Pickled Herring. He disappeared into the crowds thronging the waking city and made his way towards Greenwich, where he begged and bribed his way on to a ship bound for Holland. Grey spent the next months among other English exiles in the Dutch republic, fruitlessly plotting to depose Charles. The king himself, when he heard how easily Grey had slipped his leash, was as enraged as his grandfather King James had been after William Seymour's bolt. The hapless Denham sobered up fast when instead of his prisoner he was thrown into the Tower, where he spent the next six months. Robert Lock, the boatman who had unwittingly ferried Grey away from the Tower, was flung into the Marshalsea jail – despite pleading that he had lost a leg serving the king as a soldier.

In 1685 Charles died, and was succeeded by his Catholic brother James II. Grey and the other English exiles in Holland had been joined the previous year by the Duke of Monmouth, a charming but weak chancer who had been persuaded that he could be England's Protestant king in place of his uncle James. By June 1685 the motley crew of around eighty malcontents were ready for their desperate throw of the dice. With Monmouth at their head, they sailed in three ships to Lyme in Dorset, and began the ill-starred rebellion that would end at Sedgemoor – the last pitched battle on England's soil. The command of Monmouth's 'cavalry' – a couple of hundred nags and shire horses – was given to Lord Grey.

The rebels trailed disconsolately around the West Country, gathering a small army of 6,000 peasant farmers and ploughboys. Grey's finest moment came at Wells Cathedral, when, single-handedly, he successfully defended the high altar against destruction by overzealous Protestant idolaters in his army. His role at Sedgemoor, when the professional royal army destroyed Monmouth's brave but ill-trained amateurs, was less glorious. His cavalry ran away, and he himself accompanied Monmouth in a precipitous flight on horseback, leaving their foot soldiers to be massacred by the victorious Royalists.

Lord Grey now made a belated return to the Tower – exactly two years after fleeing it. Arrested with Monmouth near Poole, he again escaped near-certain death, although on this occasion by more ignoble means. He turned king's evidence and testified against his fellow rebels – including his friend Monmouth, who was beheaded with an agonising half-dozen strokes of a blunt axe. Grey successfully bargained for his life, using a huge chunk – £40,000 – of his vast wealth as a bribe to dodge the block. There were rumours that he bore a grudge against Monmouth, the handsome duke having seduced Grey's wayward wife Mary. Grey survived to hail the Glorious Revolution of 1688 that succeeded where he and Monmouth had failed, in deposing James and ushering in the Protestant William of Orange. William made Grey an earl and he died in 1701 – a truly lucky man.

With the Whigs and Protestants once more firmly in the saddle after 1688, the role of romantic underdog rebels reverted to the Jacobites: those who charged their glasses to toast the 'king over the water' – the exiled James II – and his son, James Edward, and grandson Charles Edward, respectively the Old and Young Pretenders. Jacobite loyalty was strongest in Catholic northern England and the Scottish Highlands. When the last Stuart monarch, James II's Anglican daughter Anne, died childless in 1714, the Protestant succession – and thus the crown – went to her German cousins, the House of Hanover, in the unlovely person of King George I.

The Jacobites imagined that patriotic Britons would rather have one of their own – whatever his religion – on the throne, than this uncouth German. They forgot that James Edward, too, was practically a foreigner: since fleeing abroad with his parents as a newborn infant in 1688, he had never seen the land he aspired to rule. Nevertheless, the Scottish Jacobite plotters went ahead in 1715 with a fully fledged rising on James Edward's behalf.

The Scottish peer William Maxwell, 5th Earl of Nithsdale, was steeped in Stuart loyalty. Born in 1676, on coming of age Nithsdale had travelled to France to pledge allegiance to the exiled James II. While at James's court in St Germain, Nithsdale had met, wooed and in 1699 married, an equally fervent Jacobite – Winifred Herbert, daughter of the Marquess of Powys. The couple returned to the Nithsdale family estate at Terregles in Dumfries, and enjoyed sixteen years of quiet domestic life raising their five children before the Jacobite call to arms came in 1715.

After proclaiming the Old Pretender King James in the Scottish Borders, Nithsdale joined the English Jacobite army under Thomas Forster at Hexham in Northumberland. But the rebels were overwhelmed by King George's professional redcoats at the Battle of Preston, and Nithsdale and six fellow Jacobite peers surrendered and were brought to the Tower. Lady Nithsdale, still aged only thirty-six, received the news of her husband's capture just before Christmas 1715, and resolved to save her beloved. Pausing only to hide incriminating papers in the walls of her home, she and her maid, a Welsh girl named Evans, set off on the long journey south in the dead of winter.

The first obstacle facing the dauntless countess was the weather. The winter of 1715/16 was savage, and thick snow blanketed the roads. All communications with London were cut, and Lady Nithsdale was in an agony of ignorance. For all she knew, her husband had been tried and condemned already. As the roads were impassable for carriages, Winifred and Evans set off on horseback on the first stage of their 400-mile journey south. By Christmas Day, they had reached an inn near Newcastle. She had time to scribble a letter to her sister describing their ride though screaming gales and deep snowdrifts: 'Such a journey, I believe, was scarce ever made, considering the weather, but with God's help an earnest desire can achieve a great deal.'

At Newcastle, the two women boarded a stagecoach for York, 100 miles to the south. They hoped to be able to catch the regular mail coach to London, but when they reached York, a new blizzard had blocked the roads, and once again they took to horseback. Lady Nithsdale bought two hardy mounts and, without pausing to rest, they resumed the journey. A fortnight after setting out, the two brave riders finally arrived in London. Immensely relieved to hear that her husband was still alive – although about to be tried for high treason before the High Court of Parliament – Lady Nithsdale took rooms with a Jacobite sympathiser, a Mrs Mills, and set about preparing an appeal to the House of Lords against what she feared would be an inevitable death sentence.

Her fears were justified. The six Jacobite peers were condemned to pay the supreme penalty. Three were reprieved by King George but the others – an English peer Lord Derwentwater, and the two Scottish Lords Kenmure and Nithsdale – were told they would die in three weeks on 24 February. Desperately, Lady Nithsdale decided to petition the king in person to plead for her husband's life. Knowing she would never reach the monarch if her true identity was known, she disguised herself as a maidservant and arrived at the back door of St James's Palace. A woman as desperate and determined as she was found little difficulty in talking her way inside, and pretending to dust the furniture as she went, she made her way from room to room in search of the king.

She tracked him down to a small antechamber and, according to her own account, flung herself at his feet and blurted out in French – their common language, since the new German king of England could not speak English – that she was 'the unfortunate Countess of Nithsdale' come to plead for her husband's life. Startled by this unwelcome intrusion, the king tried to leave the room, but the distraught woman clung on to the tails of his coat, begging for mercy. The king stumbled out as best he could with Lady Nithsdale dragging behind him on her knees, still pleading for her lord's life. Two servants came to the king's rescue. One caught the countess round her waist, while the other prised her hands from the monarch's coat. The appeal petition that she had presented to Parliament pleading for mercy for the condemned man fell to the floor as she fainted away.

That night, Winifred visited her husband in the Tower to tell him of the failure of her mission. Nithsdale was held in a room off the Council Chamber in the Lieutenant's Lodgings (now called the Queen's House) – the room where Guy Fawkes had been interrogated a century before. Nithsdale took the news stoically, and began working on the speech he planned to deliver from the scaffold. His indomitable wife, however, had by no means given up. On her daily visits, she carefully scanned the Tower's geography. Having ruled out the traditional exit for Tower prisoners – out of the window and over the walls – she began to think of a better route. The Council Chamber adjoining her husband's room was always filled with people – warders, soldiers, officers and officials, the lieutenant's servants and their children – constantly coming and going. The place was a hubbub of noise. The prisoner awaiting death was almost out of sight and out of mind.

Lady Nithsdale came up with an escape plan fantastic, foolhardy even, but possibly, given a large slice of luck, with a sporting chance of success. Taking leave of her husband, she told Evans of her scheme. She meant to dress Nithsdale in women's clothes and smuggle him out of the room under the noses of the milling guards. She would dress him in mob cap and skirt, swathe him in a voluminous brown cloak, paint his face with her cosmetics – taking care to lighten his distinctive dark eyebrows and then take him out of the condemned cell, weeping and wailing as he went, with his head bowed and his hands held to his crying eyes. Such histrionics from Nithsdale's womenfolk would be quite understandable, given that he was due to die in a few short hours.

Time was pressing, and Lady Nithsdale swiftly recruited the helpers she needed to carry out her plan. Evans, as usual a tower of strength, had a friend, Miss Hilton, who agreed to play her part. Appropriately for the drama she was directing, Winifred's lodgings with Mrs Mills were in theatrical Drury Lane, and she added the landlady to her cast list. Miss Hilton was tall and thin; Mrs Mills equally tall – but stout. Lord Nithsdale was tall too, and Mrs Mills's riding cloak would fit him a treat, especially in the hours of winter darkness. A friend of Mrs Mills, a Mrs Morgan, also conveniently tall, was persuaded to join the cast. Finally, Mr Mills agreed to act as their coach driver. Naturally, the actors were all provided with the fake names of the characters they would play.

For a successful production, Lady Nithsdale needed convincing costumes. She sent Evans out to buy five identical hooded cloaks. The date was 23 February – tomorrow, unless her plan worked, her husband would die by the axe. Late that afternoon, as the short winter day faded, Lady Nithsdale, accompanied by Evans, Miss Hilton, Mrs Mills and Mrs Morgan, set out by coach to bid a final, fond farewell to the condemned man. Mrs Morgan, tallest and slimmest of the actors, put on two gowns, one over the other; then added two identical brown cloaks. The other women donned identical brown cloaks. Lady Nithsdale also carried her cosmetics bag and a bottle of brandy.

They arrived at the Tower, and parked their carriage at the gate with Mr Mills. The identically clad women went into the Tower and made their way through the Inner Ward where frozen snow was still piled in corners. They were let into the Lieutenant's Lodgings in the King's House, where Lady Nithsdale was told she could only take one companion at a time into her husband's room. Leaving Evans at the entrance, she went in first with Mrs Morgan. Once inside, Mrs Morgan slipped off her outer dress, and Lord Nithsdale struggled into the unfamiliar garb. Lady Nithsdale went to work with her make-up sticks and brushes on her husband's face. His dark eyebrows were lightened; his black stubble whitened; his pale cheeks rouged. Finally, a scarf was wrapped round his face, a maid's cap was set on his head, and the curls of a red wig – to simulate Mrs Mills's auburn hair – were carefully arranged.

Mrs Morgan left, lamenting loudly. She was replaced by Miss Hilton, who added her velvet riding cloak to Lord Nithsdale's ensemble. All the while, Lady Nithsdale was conversing in loud tones with her friends and visitors, saying that she was to re-present her petition to the king that night, and had every hope of obtaining a reprieve. She and Miss Hilton left the room and descended the stairs, and met Mrs Mills coming in. Lady Nithsdale returned with her to the cell. As they passed through the Council Chamber, the women put on a fine theatrical performance: keening and moaning, with much fluttering of handkerchiefs and loud blowing of noses. Slightly bemused by the comings and goings of these weeping women, and embarrassed at their distress, the guards glanced up and quickly returned to their card games. Once in Nithsdale's cell, Mrs Mills gave up her travelling cloak with its hood, before she too left the room. Playing his part gamely, Lord Nithsdale called after her, 'My dear Mrs Catherine [Mills's assumed name], pray go in all haste and send in my wife's waiting maid.'

The Nithsdales were left alone. Lady Nithsdale had never examined her husband's handsome features more closely. If he passed her scrutiny he might just pass the casual glances of the guards. Now the testing time had arrived. Taking a deep breath, she opened the door and ushered her husband into the Council Chamber, carefully shutting the door behind her. Boldly Nithsdale walked through the crowded room. His height was disguised by his bowed head under his hood. A muffler was wrapped around his mouth and a handkerchief hid the rest of his face. Softly, he sniffed and snuffled. His wife followed him. As they reached the end of the timbered room, a guard stepped forward. The Nithsdales' hearts missed a beat – but the sentry was only solicitously opening the door for the two unhappy 'ladies'. They left the room, and Lady Nithsdale said in a loud voice, 'For God's sake, Mrs Betty, make haste and fetch my maid.' Then she turned and returned alone to her husband's cell. Making sure not to trip over his skirts, Lord Nithsdale descended the stairs to join the faithful Evans. Together, lord and maid crossed the Inner Ward, went through the Byward and Middle Towers and got into the coach which Mr Mills was driving. He whipped up the horses and the coach crunched away across the snow.

Back in the cell, Lady Nithsdale put on a star solo performance. Throwing her voice like a trained ventriloquist, she carried on a loud conversation with herself playing the part of her husband. For up to half an hour, the bizarre conversation continued – the high female voice answered by Lord Nithsdale's deep masculine tones. Then she came out. Holding the door half-open, she spoke back into the empty room. She told her non-existent spouse to keep his head and hopes high. She was returning to the palace and had faith that she would come back with the king's reprieve. Until then, he should be of good heart and watch and pray. Then, slamming the door so hard that the latch on its string fell out of the lock, she begged the guards to be compassionate and not disturb her husband: he was praying hard and if her petition failed, he was facing his last night on earth.

Once again, Lady Winifred tripped through the crowded council room, followed by the sympathetic looks of the soldiers who saw only a distraught woman about to be brutally widowed. She descended the stairs, pausing to tell a servant coming in with candles not to disturb his lordship, and exited the Tower into the frosty February night. Within half an hour she had rejoined her husband in a nearby safe house. The next morning, they watched in horror from an attic window as Nithsdale's

Jacobite companions, Lords Kenmure and Derwentwater, paid the price for their rebellion as they were beheaded on Tower Hill. Lord Nithsdale had one person to thank that he had not shared their fate: his loving and resourceful wife.

After lying low for three days, the couple parted again. Nithsdale was taken to the household of the Stuart-sympathising Venetian ambassador, where he was once again put in disguise.

This time his role was to play one of the ambassador's footmen. A powdered wig and a tight gaudy uniform replaced the billlowing female robes, and Nithsdale safely left the country for Italy's sunnier climes. Lady Nithsdale had one more task to perform. By a circuitous route, she made her way back to the family seat and retrieved the papers she had hidden. Then she rejoined her husband in Rome. Neither would ever see their native land again. They lived on, poor but happy, until Nithsdale's death in 1744, aged sixty-eight.

Five years later, in 1749, the courageous Lady Nithsdale joined him. Both were finally brought back and buried in the Catholic family chapel of their relatives the Dukes of Norfolk at Arundel in Sussex. The Duchess of Norfolk still has the brown cloak used by Nithsdale in his dramatic escape. As for King George, he said of the lady who had clung so tightly to his coat-tails, that she had caused him more trouble than any other woman in Christendom. Later, he saw things differently. 'For a man in milord's situation,' he said of the escape, 'it was the very best thing he could have done.'

CHAPTER FOURTEEN

RESTORATION ROMPS

It is scarcely surprising that Henry III showed a more than casual interest in jewels and regal regalia. Not only did he incline to aesthetic things for their own sake, being of an artistic and religious rather than a martial nature; but his own personal interest in the Crown jewels – or the lack of them – was also intimately bound up with his earliest experiences. His father, King John – a rival with his son in the 'worst English king' stakes – famously 'lost' the Crown jewels in the Wash estuary. It was quite usual for medieval kings, constantly on the move around their kingdoms, to carry such royal regalia with them to impress their authority on local people with rich visual symbols wherever they went. Whether John's loss was due to incompetence or ill luck, there was literally precious little left when Henry, a nine-year-old child, was crowned in Gloucester after his father's death in 1216 – a simple gold circlet standing in for the missing crown.

It may have been his father's carelessness that caused Henry, in 1230, to be the first monarch to order that the core of the jewels – the crown, the orb and sceptre, symbols of a monarch's temporal power and spiritual authority – should be kept in the secure setting of the Tower when not required on the road. In doing so, he began the connection between the jewels and the Tower that endures to this day. However, in his own way, Henry was as careless with the jewels as his father had been. Permanently cash strapped – not least as a result of the costly work improving the Tower – he pawned the precious metals and sacred stones to a syndicate of French merchants. On Henry's death in 1272, they were hastily redeemed and returned to England, since they were needed for the coronation of his son and successor, Edward I.

It was Edward – like his father, a great augmenter of the Tower's defences and fortifications – who concentrated all the Crown jewels at the Tower, rather than just the basic royal toolkit of crown, orb and sceptre. Their previous home, since the time of Edward the Confessor, had been Westminster Abbey. But, after some of the treasures were stolen, Edward decided that the Tower was the safest place to house the whole collection. For good measure he sent the abbot and forty-eight monks from Westminster to the Tower too, as a punishment for not keeping his jewels safe.

After starting the Hundred Years' War, Edward I's grandson, Edward III, was forced to the humiliating necessity of pawning the jewels again to meet the considerable costs of the conflict. Since he was at war with France, the lucky recipients were a group of Flemish merchants. The jewels were again redeemed and returned to the Tower, only to be pawned yet once more by Richard II – another spendthrift monarch in the mould of Henry III. More patriotic, Henry V, the victor of Agincourt, pledged some of the jewels to the mayor and citizens of London for 10,000 marks – again to meet the costs of the Hundred Years' War which he had relaunched. His unhappy son, Henry VI, continued this practice of pledging the jewels against loans from merchants. (Ironically, the Wakefield Tower, where Henry was confined and murdered, became during the nineteenth century the place where the jewels were kept.)

By the reign of the first Stuart king, James I, the Tudors, a famously grasping dynasty, had not only ceased pawning the jewels, but had built the collection up into a treasury of great value housed in a supposedly 'secret Jewelhouse' built by Elizabeth I beside the White Tower. James personally signed an inventory of the jewels kept in an 'iron cheste' which included a coronet and circlet set with precious stones; a new richly jewelled coronet specially made for his queen, Anne of Denmark; no fewer than fifteen gold collars glowing with diamonds and other precious stones, and such costly trinkets as a purse inlaid with copper, a supposed 'long pece of unicorn horn', and other exotica obtained for Queen Elizabeth on their far-flung voyages by her sea dogs Francis Drake and Martin Frobisher.

Then, just as the Civil Wars of the 1640s brought ruination to human lives, so too they spelled disaster to the Crown jewels. First to go was the gold and silver plate used for ceremonial banquets. Smuggled from the Tower to Oxford, Charles I's wartime capital, at the outbreak of the war by Royalist sympathisers, the plate was melted down and sold to fill the Cavaliers' depleted war chests. The end of the Civil War left the whole nation impoverished, and the Parliamentary victors had no time for such fripperies as royal jewels and regalia. The decision was taken to remove the jewels from the Tower and break them up, melt them down for conversion to coinage, or sell them off.

The metal was converted into Cromwell's Commonwealth coinage at the Tower mint. But before consigning them to the furnace, a record was made of the treasure. Among the items destroyed were the imperial crown of 'massy gold' weighing seven pounds and six ounces, which was valued at £1,110; and the queen's crown, weighing about half the king's, which was valued at £338. Miscellaneous precious stones, including diamonds, rubies and sapphires, were together valued at £355; and there were assorted other items including two sceptres, a silver gilt rod, and the orb, or 'globe', which weighed one and a half pounds and was valued at £57. Also consigned to the furnace were two ancient Saxon crowns, reputedly once worn by King Alfred the Great and Queen Edith, which were brought from Westminster Abbey to the Tower and destroyed there. To their credit, some MPs protested against this wanton vandalism of such priceless ancient artefacts, but without success. The only items that survived from this massive meltdown 'bonfire of the vanities' were three swords, a solitary coronation anointing spoon, and a silver salt cellar once belonging to Elizabeth I which had been hidden by the monks at Westminster Abbey. Them and the Black Prince's ruby.

This magnificent blood-red stone, the size of a small chicken's egg – and actually, to be technically correct, a spinel rather than a ruby proper – has adorned the crowns of English monarchs since at least 1415, when it was worn by Henry V in his helmet at Agincourt. It first came into the Crown's possession when it was appropriated by another famous warrior prince of the Hundred Years' War with France – Edward III's eldest son, Edward the Black Prince. As with many famous jewels, there are several legends attached to this stone, some of them, befitting its colour, bloody ones. The legend of how the prince first acquired the stone is one such story. A chivalrous warrior equalling if not surpassing his famous father, the Black Prince won his spurs – and the Prince of Wales's feathers and motto 'Ich Dien' – on the battlefield of Crécy in 1346. Twenty years later, he was to win glory against France in his own right, capturing the French king after his triumph at Poitiers in 1356. Later still, in pursuit of an anti-French Spanish alliance, the prince journeyed to the heart of Old Castile in central Spain which was riven by civil war. Here he helped the province's king, the aptly named Pedro the Cruel, defeat his rebellious French-backed half-brother at the battle of Nájera in 1367.

Pedro's sadism disgusted the chivalrous English prince, and he sought to divest himself of this unwelcome friend. A genuine breakdown of his health gave him the excuse he needed to go, but Pedro was short of cash to pay the prince off for restoring him to his throne. Pedro had shown the prince his proudest possession – the bulbous, blood-red spinel. He had acquired the jewel, he bragged, by typically foul means. Originally it had been in the possession of Abu Said, a Moorish prince of Granada. Pedro had lured Abu Said to Seville, killed his servants, and then treacherously murdered his guest with his own hands, finding the stone in the dead man's clothes. Now the Black Prince demanded – and got – the stone as the price for his help.

But the bloodstained stone did not bring the prince good fortune. Never recovering his broken health, he died in 1376 before inheriting his father's throne. He left the spinel as his legacy. We next hear of the jewel at Agincourt, adorning the battle helmet of Henry V. At the height of the battle, in single combat with the Duc d'Alençon, Henry received a tremendous blow from d'Alençon's sword which dented the helmet. The jewel, however, survived, and may even have deflected d'Alençon's almost deadly blow. Reputedly worn by Richard III in his crown at another battle, Bosworth in 1485, it did not bring that murderous monarch the luck that Henry had enjoyed. The crown, with its spinel, as legend has it, rolled under a hawthorn bush just as Richard succumbed to his enemies and went down crying, 'Treason!' Retrieved by Lord Stanley, it was placed on the head of the new king, Henry VII, inaugurator of the Tudor dynasty.

The spinel continued to be the chief adornment of the crowns of England's kings and queens until the grand destruction of the Crown jewels under Oliver Cromwell's Commonwealth. When the great state crown itself was broken up, the spinel was saved and sold – for what was even then the derisory sum of £4 – to a secret Royalist sympathiser who carefully preserved it until the Restoration of Charles II in 1660. The spinel, too, was then proudly restored to its rightful place at the front centre of the king's state crown. This skilled job was the work of Charles's court jeweller, Sir Robert Vyner. To emphasise the continuity of monarchy, Vyner was told to make the new jewels as much like the destroyed originals as possible. Fortunately, detailed records survived in the Tower, enabling

Vyner to reconstruct the regalia. The work cost Charles the substantial sum of £32,000.

Money was always a problem for the Merry Monarch. He was generous with his promises to courtiers, supporters and mistresses; but the pensions that he lavished on so many were all too often in arrears – or never paid at all. The keeper of the restored Crown jewels during his reign, Sir Gilbert Talbot, was one of the favoured few who was exceptionally well remunerated for his duties. Allocated an annual salary of £50, Talbot had his own rent-free grace and favour apartment at the Tower, and the choice of rooms in other royal palaces too. He also received food amounting to 'fourteen double dishes per diem'. On top of all this he got a cut of £300 from the King's New Year's Gift money – a sort of tax on the nobility in the form of a cash 'gift' levied on the lords and paid to the king, that Talbot was responsible for collecting. He received another £300 annually in tips from foreign ambassadors to whom he presented gifts from the king. And as if all this was not enough to support a comfortable lifestyle, Talbot also creamed off a hefty £800 in sweeteners from the silversmiths and goldsmiths whom he favoured to execute royal commissions. The perks of his job also entitled Talbot to a closed cart for carrying his goods around; his own coronation robes; and the right to precede all the judges of the land in formal processions. As the cherry on his cake, Talbot alone had the singular honour of placing and removing Charles's crown on the king's head whenever he was required to wear it.

Gilbert Talbot's assistant keeper at the Tower, coincidentally named Talbot Edwards, was not nearly as well-off as his boss. Since Gilbert preferred the more commodious surroundings of Whitehall Palace to the Tower as his chief residence, it fell to Edwards to live permanently on site in the Tower. At the Restoration, the remade Crown jewels had been given a new home in the Martin Tower in the north-eastern corner of the fortress. Edwards and his wife and daughter literally lived over the shop – occupying the top floors of the tower immediately above the Jewel House, which was in a fortified basement vault. Edwards officially drew a state salary, but since he was lower down the pecking order than Gilbert Talbot, his wages were years in arrears – and since Edwards in 1671 was seventy-seven it appeared unlikely that he would ever see his money. He relied instead on the fees he charged visitors who came to see the jewels. He did not know it, but he was about to entertain the most singular visitor that the jewels would ever receive.

* * *

Thomas Blood, or 'Colonel' Blood as he is known to posterity (he constantly promoted himself and never actually rose above the rank of lieutenant), was not only the most celebrated jewel thief in history, but one of the most outlandish, outrageous and above all lucky rogues never to swing from a gibbet. His life story reads like a piece of far-fetched fiction from the pen of a Defoe or a Fielding, but it is well-documented reality.

Blood was born into a family of English Protestant settlers in County Meath, Ireland, in about 1618. His father – also named Thomas Blood – though a humble blacksmith, owned some 230 acres around Sarney, his notorious son's birthplace. The privileged position Protestants enjoyed is also reflected in the ironic fact that his son – an infamous outlaw if ever there was one – was appointed a magistrate at the tender age of twenty-one.

Soon afterwards, in 1641, the simmering tension between Catholic and Protestant communities exploded into violence when the Catholics rose in rebellion. Hundreds of Protestants were massacred; thousands more were driven from their homes to take shelter in the capital, Dublin, held for King Charles I by the moderate Anglican Protestant James Butler, Duke of Ormonde. English politics were also reaching boiling point. The Westminster Parliament was increasingly in opposition to King Charles I's high-handed attempts to impose his Anglo-Catholic, high church beliefs on the English Church and rule without parliamentary approval. In 1642 these strains led to the outbreak of the English Civil War.

Urgently needing troops to support his cause, Charles ordered Ormonde to reach a truce with the Irish rebels. Blood, a militant Protestant Nonconformist, switched support from king to Parliament. It also marked the beginning of a lifelong grudge that he held against Ormonde, whom he saw as a traitor to the Protestant cause. Blood came to England, joined the Parliamentary army, and married Mary, the daughter of a landed Lancashire family.

Blood settled into domestic life with Mary and their growing family. But Cromwell's death in 1658 changed everything for Blood. Bold and adventurous, he refused to accept the return of the monarchy. He was deeply involved in several Republican plots and risings – one aimed at seizing the Tower – in London in the 1660s, but, showing an extraordinary talent for escapology which would stand him in good stead throughout his life, managed to evade arrest.

Blood sank into the murky depths of London's political and criminal underworld. Under a variety of aliases, and in a bewildering array of disguises – the canonical robes of priests and minsters were his favourite costume – he flitted between ill-lit inns and basement cellars where spies, government provocateurs, religious maniacs, pimps, prostitutes and thieves mingled. In such a shady world it was difficult to tell a principled plotter from a treacherous rogue or government plant, but Blood took to it as to the manner born.

In July 1667, Blood executed an audacious coup. Hearing that one of his former co-conspirators, a Captain John Mason, who had been held in the Tower since the failure of an anti-government plot in 1663, was being transferred to York for trial and probably execution, he resolved to rescue him. Travelling north in Mason's party was one William Leving, a former rebel who had turned king's evidence, and was due to testify against Mason at his trial. Blood organised a daring ambush to save Mason and silence Leving for good. When the prisoners and their escort paused at an inn near Doncaster, Blood sprang his ambush. Despite falling from his horse three times, and sustaining a sword thrust through his arm, Blood won the fracas that followed, and managed to grab Mason from his guards' clutches and get clean away. In the confusion, Leving escaped; he lay low, only to be found poisoned in his jail cell in York a short time later, a killing probably arranged by the Duke of Buckingham – Blood's principal patron in the governing class.

Buckingham was also behind Blood's next audacious crime: the attempted abduction in 1570 of his old enemy, the Duke of Ormonde, who was ambushed by Blood's gang while driving in his carriage in the middle of London. Although the duke managed to escape his kidnappers, it was a very near thing. The outrageous Buckingham, a strong anti-Catholic, used Blood as a hitman to carry out crimes that he did not wish to sully his own hands with. The strong suspicion must be that Buckingham – who had himself survived four terms of imprisonment in the Tower – was also behind Blood's next, and even more sensational crime: the theft of the Crown jewels.

Sometime in the early spring of 1671, just weeks after the abortive abduction of Ormonde, Talbot Edwards, Assistant Keeper of the Jewels, received an unusual visitor at the Tower. The man was dressed as a clergyman of the Church of England, appeared to be about fifty years old, and had fierce, penetrating eyes above a hawkish Roman nose with a notable scar (a relic of Blood's rescue of John Mason). Although the cleric's appearance was slightly outlandish – he sported a long beard, a cassock and cloak, and a cap with 'ears' – Edwards, scenting a fee, was only too happy to show the reverend gentleman and the lady accompanying him – whom he introduced as his wife – the jewels in his care.

Edwards led the odd couple to the basement of the Martin Tower, unlocked the reinforced door, and let them into the vault where the jewels were kept behind a metal grille in a cupboard inside a recess in the thick walls. As Blood greedily feasted his eyes on the glittering regalia, his 'wife' – in reality a hired actress named Jenny Blaine – apparently overcome by the sight, proved her theatrical skills by staging a fainting fit, or in Edwards' words, complained of 'a qualm upon her stomack'. The old gentleman hurried away to fetch a reviving glass of water, leaving Blood to case the joint. Jenny, invited to rest in the Edwards family's apartment, made a rapid recovery. As she did so, Blood took the opportunity to strike up an intimacy with the assistant keeper and his wife – and returned a few days later, still in his clergyman's garb, with a gift of gloves as a token of appreciation for their kindness.

Blood now began an intensive campaign of 'grooming' the elderly couple and their unmarried daughter – a softening-up process for the crime he was planning. After several visits, the relationship had progressed far enough for Blood to advance a typically bold proposal. He had, he said, a very eligible nephew and he could not help noticing the wondrous beauty of the Edwardses' spinster daughter Elizabeth. Would it not be a fine thing, he asked, if the young people were joined in holy matrimony? And, naturally, he added, he would conduct the ceremony for the happy couple. The Edwardses were overwhelmed by this generous offer to take their daughter off their hands, particularly after Blood threw in the information that his nephew had a couple of hundred acres of good land in Ireland. A celebratory dinner was held in the Martin Tower to formalise the betrothal, at which the clergyman offered fervent prayers for the well-being of the royal family. Afterwards Edwards gave his guest a detailed tour of the Tower, and even sold him a pair of pistols that Blood had admired. Having thus neatly disarmed his 'mark' both literally and metaphorically, and thoroughly reconnoitred the scene of the coming crime, Blood departed to make final preparations for his heist.

He had arranged to bring his 'nephew' to meet the Edwardses at the

Martin Tower on 9 May 1671 – at seven in the morning – an hour when the Tower was unlikely to be crowded. He kept the appointment, accompanied by his criminal son, Thomas Blood junior, a professional highwayman, who was playing the part of the nephew under the alias 'Tom Hunt'. Also in the party were two regular members of Blood's gang, Robert Perrot, a fierce Baptist and former Parliamentarian trooper turned silk dyer, and Robert Halliwell, who was to act as lookout man. All were armed to the teeth with concealed pistols, stiletto daggers and swordsticks. A fourth member of the gang, William Smith, a Fifth Monarchist sect stalwart, remained outside the Tower walls as 'getaway driver' – he was holding their horses. Halliwell hung around outside the Martin Tower, trying not to look furtive, while the Bloods, *père et fils*, went inside with Perrot. Elizabeth Edwards, eager to see her fiancé, but shy of making a premature appearance, sent her maid to take a peek. The maid saw Halliwell at the door of the tower, assumed he was her mistress's intended, and returned to make her report.

Meanwhile, inside the Tower, after making the introductions, Blood suggested that while they awaited the arrival of Mrs Edwards and her daughter – still at their toilette in an upper room – Mr Edwards could show the jewels to the 'nephew' and Perrot. Once again thinking of his fee, the old man readily agreed, and led the Bloods and Perrot below. As soon as Edwards had unlocked the door and admitted the trio to the Jewel House, he was set upon as he bent to lock the door behind them. A cloak was thrown over his head, and a pre-fashioned gag – a plug of wood with an air hole drilled through it – was thrust into his mouth and secured with a leather thong. Immediately Edwards began to struggle frantically. His assailants told him that if he kept still his life would be spared. Undaunted, the brave old man continued to attempt to fight free of the cloak enveloping him. The ruthless Blood produced a wooden mallet and bludgeoned Edwards to the ground. But the keeper continued to kick, struggle and gurgle, and so Blood stabbed him in the stomach with a long stiletto knife.

Leaving Edwards for dead, the gang set about their task. Blood removed the metal grille and flattened the king's state crown with his mallet. This made it easier to carry it off in a bag he wore under his cassock. Young Blood started to saw the long sceptre in half with a file so he could carry it away; while Perrot hid the heavy orb in his breeches. The blows of Blood's mallet dislodged some of the jewels encrusting the crown, including the Black Prince's famous 'ruby'. As Blood scrabbled on the floor after the precious stones there was an unwelcome interruption.

It was exactly at this moment that the Edwardses' long-lost son, Wythe – who had been in Flanders fighting as a soldier for the last ten years – returned to witness his sister's betrothal. Edwards junior passed Halliwell at the door, identified himself, and went upstairs to greet his mother and sister. Halliwell hurried down to the Jewel House to let his companions in crime know what was afoot. With no time to complete the sawing in half of the sceptre, the jewel thieves hastily made off with only the crown and orb, leaving the rod lying on the floor.

As soon as they had gone, old Talbot Edwards, miraculously still alive, with a superhuman effort managed to spit his gag out and shout, 'Treason! Murder! The crown is stolen!' at the top of his voice. Hearing his cries, his daughter rushed downstairs to find her father in a pool of blood. She followed the thieves' trail across the courtyard between the Martin and White Towers and took up her father's cries, wailing, 'Treason! The crown is stolen!' Hearing his sister's shouts, young Wythe Edwards emerged from the Martin Tower, accompanied by a Captain Marcus Beckman, a military friend of his who had also been invited to witness Miss Edwards' betrothal. The fit young soldiers gave chase across the courtyard. Beckman, a Swedish-born military engineer and soldier of fortune, was already familiar with the Tower, having once been imprisoned there as a suspected spy.

In the short time the two soldiers took to catch up with the thieves, young Blood and Halliwell had passed through the Byward and Middle Towers, reached their horses and were about to mount and ride away. Blood himself, and Perrot, weighed down with their loot, had just passed under the archway of the Bloody Tower and turned right into Water Lane, heading towards the Byward Tower and the exit. Seeing them about to escape, Edwards and Beckman shouted to the Yeoman Warder manning the drawbridge over the moat between the Byward and Middle towers to stop the thieves. As he attempted to do so, Blood drew a pistol and fired, causing the warder – wisely but not heroically – to hit the deck. A second warder at the Middle Tower also let discretion play the better part of valour and allowed the two miscreants to escape. If Blood and Perrot had turned right up Tower Hill, they might have got clean away with their booty, but instead, closely pursued, they decided to try to lose themselves in the early-morning crowds thronging the riverside wharves.

They swerved sharp left and ran along the quays. But the two soldiers, younger and fitter men, were fast gaining on them. Blood resorted to the old ploy of yelling, 'Stop thief!' as he ran, pointing to his two pursuers. Momentarily fooled, some upstanding citizens laid hands on Edwards and Beckman, but the deception did not last long, and the chase continued. In the confusion, both Bloods and Perrot managed to reach their horses held by Smith at the Iron Gate and were in the act of mounting, when their persistent pursuers finally caught up with them. Blood fired the second of the pistols he was carrying at Beckman, but missed, and after a grim struggle, during which some of the jewels fell from his pockets, rolled off and were never seen again, both Blood and Perrot were subdued and arrested. The crown and orb – minus some missing stones – were repaired and restored to their rightful place. Blood's son, whose horse had collided with a cart and thrown him during his hasty escape, was also detained; and Halliwell was picked up later. As he was led away Blood was philosophical, remarking, 'It was a gallant deed, although it failed.'

Blood and his gang were imprisoned in – where else? – the Tower. They were held in the vaults beneath the White Tower – where prisoners had been tortured in Tudor times – to await the king's pleasure. Few doubted that their fate would be the traditional terrible death meted out to traitors of hanging, drawing and quartering. The theft of the Crown jewels was not just any old jewel robbery. Taking the jewels with their sacral, religious symbolism was akin to kidnapping the monarch himself. But, astonishingly, this was not the punishment that awaited the notorious Thomas Blood. In fact, the abortive and bloody raid on the jewels was to be but the beginning of another stage in Blood's amazing career. From being the Republican rebel and bold, buccaneering outlaw forever outwitting the state's agents, Blood became one such agent himself. How did this transformation from poacher to gamekeeper come about?

The motivation behind Blood's attempt to steal the jewels has been much debated. Though violent and ruthless, Blood was never a career criminal *per se* and despised his namesake son for being a common highwayman. Blood senior's crimes – from a plot to seize Dublin Castle to the attempted abduction of the Duke of Ormonde – were of a different order. They always had a political and/or religious motive. If his aim was financial gain it is likely that he would have used any monies obtained to further the cause of Republican Nonconformism. It has also been plausibly suggested that the raid was an 'inside job' organised with the knowledge and secret approval of the king himself, who – as ever – was chronically short of cash.

Charles's actions after the crime were certainly suspicious. Blood remained remarkably calm in captivity, maintaining that he would only make a complete confession to the king himself. Although Blood was brought to Charles in irons and closely questioned by a royal inquisition, consisting of Charles, his brother James, and their cousin Prince Rupert, he was never executed, nor even punished, beyond his few weeks' imprisonment in the Tower. Nor were any of his confederates. Even more astonishingly, Blood was actually *rewarded* by the king for his crime – receiving lands in his native Ireland, and a pension of £500 a year. Before bestowing this, the king laughingly asked Blood what he would do if granted mercy, and Blood, typically bold, replied, 'I would endeavour to deserve it, sire.' Cheekily, he added that Charles owed him his life, since in his Republican days, he had once stalked the king with a musket, intending to assassinate him. But, observing the king skinny-dipping in the Thames at Vauxhall, Blood, hiding in some nearby reeds, said he was so 'awe-struck' by the sight of his naked sovereign that he forebore to open fire.

Whatever his reasons – and they certainly do not bear much examination – Charles's lenient treatment of Blood astonished his contemporaries. The diarist John Evelyn was staggered to see the jewel thief sitting at the treasury table at a dinner to honour a party of French noblemen soon after the heist:

> Blood . . . that impudent bold fellow who had not long before attempted to steal the Imperial Crown itself out of the Tower . . . How came he to be pardoned, and even received into favour, not only after this, but several other exploits almost as daring both in Ireland and here, I could never come to understand . . . The only treason of this sort that was ever pardoned. The man had not only a daring but a villainous unmerciful look, a false countenance, but very well spoken and dangerously insinuating.

Whether Charles was moved merely by fellow feeling for a rascal like himself, or whether, more plausibly, Blood was acting as his agent when he raided the Tower, the fact is that Blood inexplicably escaped punishment and spent the rest of his murky life as a 'cut-out' link man between the government and his colleagues in the Nonconformist opposition. In stark contrast, the victim of the crime – brave old Talbot Edwards – was treated less than generously. Although he recovered from the stabbing and battering, he became very infirm and applied for a pension – which was initially refused. Grudgingly, the government eventually granted it shortly before Edwards died. Elizabeth Edwards did find a husband as a direct result of that dramatic May morning, but it was not young Thomas Blood. The man she married was the gallant Captain Beckman, who was promoted major for his courage in capturing Blood. The old rogue himself lived on until 1680 when he died, in bed, aged sixty-two. Someone in a very high place had clearly been protecting Blood – but who?

Just as an earlier Duke of Buckingham has often been accused of being the evil genius behind Richard III's crimes in the Tower, so Charles's childhood companion, and crony in lechery, George Villiers, 2nd Duke of Buckingham, has been long suspected as the *éminence grise* behind Blood. We have already seen that Buckingham was widely suspected as the originator of Blood's bold rescue of John Mason and his bid to kidnap Ormonde, against whom both he and Buckingham held grudges. Certainly, Ormonde's son Lord Ossory publicly accused Buckingham of the crime – a grave charge that Buckingham, tellingly, failed to answer.

As a convinced anti-Catholic, the Duke sympathised with Blood's Nonconformist religious stance, if not his Republican politics. Himself descended from royalty on his mother's side, and brought up with Charles as a member of the royal family after his namesake father's assassination, Buckingham had pretensions to succeed Charles's himself, and even on his deathbed referred to himself as 'a prince'. Finally, the course of his whole life shows that Buckingham was a killer quite capable of commissioning a grand larceny like the theft of the Crown jewels.

The archetypal Restoration rake, Buckingham's own extraordinary career encompassed no fewer than three separate spells in the Tower. Still a baby when his father, George Villiers, 1st Duke of Buckingham, the highly unpopular favourite of both James I and Charles I, was murdered in 1628, the younger Buckingham and his siblings were brought up practically as the adopted children of Charles I, and childhood companions of the king's own children. Buckingham was at Charles II's side at the battle of Worcester and, like his friend, made a daring escape abroad after their defeat. But he frequently fell out with Charles, and was more than ready to defy his royal friend and master.

Their first clash came in 1657 when Buckingham, having run out of cash in exile, despaired that the monarchy would ever be restored. He decided to desert Charles II in Holland and return to England to recover his vast estates, confiscated by Parliament after the Civil War. His lands in Yorkshire had been awarded to Lord General Thomas Fairfax, victorious commander of the New Model Army. Buckingham's plan was awesome in its simplicity: a notable ladies' man, he set about wooing Fairfax's only child, Mary, a plain girl of nineteen, in order to get back his family estates by marrying her. Buckingham's campaign scandalised both Royalists and Roundheads, but, astonishingly, it won over the people who mattered: the Fairfax family themselves. Mary fell head over heels for the rogue, breaking off her engagement to Lord Chesterfield in Buckingham's favour, while even her hardbitten old soldier father was melted by his charm – and possibly the snobbish appeal of making his only daughter a duchess.

In September 1657 Buckingham married Mary Fairfax. Cromwell was incandescent with rage – particularly as Buckingham had bragged that if he failed with the Fairfaxes he would set his cap at one of the Lord Protector's equally plain daughters! The duke was placed under house arrest in York House, his palatial London home in the Strand. Outraged at this insult to his family, Fairfax journeyed to London to plead his new son-in-law's case. Ironsided as ever, Cromwell retorted that Fairfax should have consulted his old friends before agreeing to such a scandalous match. A furious Fairfax stormed out of the gallery in Whitehall Palace where the interview was being conducted. It was the last time that the two old Roundheads would meet.

Though supposedly confined to his mansion, Buckingham soon charmed his jailers into letting him leave his house on excursions. Cromwell decided that a more rigorous incarceration was needed. After Buckingham was arrested travelling incognito in Kent, he was sent to the Tower. However, his first confinement in the fortress was not to last long. Within a few days, Cromwell died on 3 September 1658. When Buckingham heard the news, as he recalled later:

> . . . I was then close prisoner in the Tower, with a couple of guards lying always in my chamber and a sentinel at my door. I confess I was not a little delighted with the noise of the great guns, for I presently knew what

it meant, and if Oliver had lived for three days longer I had certainly been put to death.

The mournful boom of the cannon firing a tribute to the dead dictator did indeed sound a signal of freedom for the duke. Within days he was removed from the Tower to Windsor Castle, and the following February his father-in-law Lord Fairfax stood bail for him in the astronomical sum of £20,000. Pledging loyalty to Parliament, Buckingham was released by order of the House of Commons.

The duke's second spell in the Tower was of even shorter duration. It came after the Restoration of Charles II in 1660. The king had magnanimously forgiven his errant friend for making his peace with Parliament. Charles and Buckingham were both cynical chancers. Their friendship, though often ruptured, was just as frequently repaired. In December 1666, the ever-combustible Buckingham quarrelled with a fellow aristocrat, the Marquess of Dorchester, when he jostled him during a joint session of Parliament. In the ensuing altercation, Buckingham pulled off the Marquess's periwig, while Dorchester retaliated by tearing out a fistful of the duke's fair hair – of which he was inordinately proud. Such an affray was a rarity in the dignified House of Lords, and the two peers were both sent to the Tower for a cooling-off period. Within a week, however, both were freed after making a grovelling apology at the bar of Parliament.

Though made a member of Charles's cabinet known as the Cabal (from the initials of their names), Buckingham never settled into the role of elder statesman. Vexatious and vindictive, his favourite medium was hot water. (Although he had such an aversion to washing that his reputation as a stinker was as pungent as his moral turpitude.) He darkened the Tower's doors for a third time in June 1667 as a result of his own complex intrigues. Accused of necromancy and casting the king's horoscope, Buckingham may well have been innocent of the actual charges. But the whiff of sulphur clung to him. He sealed his fate by dodging the serjeant-at-arms sent to arrest him at his Northamptonshire country home, Althorp (later the childhood home and burial site of Diana, Princess of Wales), opting to go on the run.

Eventually, he threw himself on the king's mercy, gambling that the fit of rage in which the king had ordered Buckingham's arrest had probably passed. Buckingham was again ordered to the Tower. However, the manner of his entry suggests that he knew his stay within its walls would be as short as usual. He journeyed there by coach, accompanied by a group of hard-drinking cronies, and, as they passed through Bishopsgate, stopped for dinner and more alcoholic refreshment at the Sun Inn. A crowd gathered, and Buckingham played up to his public by bowing to his admiring audience from the tavern's balcony. Samuel Pepys recorded in his diary that the duke sent word ahead to the Tower apologising for his delayed arrival, and promising that he would be there as soon as he had dined. On 12 July 1667, Pepys also recorded the sequel to Buckingham's last Tower stay:

> The Duke of Buckingham was before the Council the other day, and there did carry it very submissively and pleasingly to the King . . .

Two days later Buckingham was freed.

A decade later, Pepys himself would have good cause to regret that Buckingham had got off so lightly. He had already experienced the duke's spite and the damage it could do. In 1668 he realised that Buckingham was targeting one of his own patrons on the Navy Board, Lord William Coventry, for destruction, noting that the duke 'will ruin Coventry if he can'. Buckingham had both a personal and a political grudge against Coventry. Politically, Buckingham opposed the succession of Charles's Catholic brother James, whose secretary and ally Coventry had been. Personally, Coventry had been on the Select Commission that had interrogated Buckingham during his most recent incarceration in the Tower. For taking part in this humiliating procedure, Buckingham would not forgive him.

Buckingham's method of attack was subtle. A patron of the Restoration stage, the duke turned playwright himself. In 1668 he wrote a comedy, *The Country Gentleman*, which mocked Coventry as a character called Sir Cautious Trouble-All, a fussy little bureaucrat who had invented a circular desk with a hole in the middle in which he could sit, turning this way and that to deal with the piles of paper surrounding him. Since Coventry had proudly invented just such a desk himself, and had shown it off to – among others – Pepys (who recorded it in his diary), the insult was obvious. Getting wind of the play while it was still in rehearsal, the offended official complained to Charles, who demanded the script from Buckingham. Artfully, the duke presented his play to the king – minus the scene in which Sir Cautious appeared. Finding the text innocuous, Charles told

Coventry to bother him no more. Enraged, Coventry next turned to Tom Killigrew, manager of the King's House Theatre where the play was about to open. He threatened that he would pay thugs to slit the nose of any actor daring to mock him on the stage. When this too failed to halt the production (Killigrew knew that Buckingham, with his underworld contacts like Blood, could far outdo Coventry in the matter of hiring hoodlums), Coventry challenged the duke to a duel.

This was a fantastically foolish move. Buckingham was one of the deadliest duellists in the land, and had recently killed Francis Talbot, the 11th Earl of Shrewsbury, in a duel, by running him through with a rapier. The earl had had the misfortune to be the cuckolded husband of Buckingham's long-term mistress, Anna, Countess of Shrewsbury, an open affair which scandalised even a Restoration court noted for its sexual loucheness. It was rumoured that the countess had held the horses while her lover had fought it out with her husband, and after the former had killed the latter, had joyously ridden off with the victor. Although Buckingham would doubtless have been happy to administer the same cold steel to Coventry, this scandal was still too recent for him to risk skewering a second peer. Instead he reported Coventry's challenge to the king.

Not only was duelling between privy councillors illegal, Charles had also specifically commanded Coventry to drop his complaints about the play. Furious at this direct defiance, the king had Coventry committed to the Tower. Coventry's friends were so appalled at the way he had been treated that they literally queued up to visit him there. One visitor was Pepys, who counted no fewer than sixty coaches drawn up outside the fortress, before going in to see his friend at his cell in the Brick Tower. They 'walked and talked . . . an hour alone, from one good thing to another'. The diarist well knew who was behind Coventry's persecution, commenting, 'The Duke of Buckingham will be so flushed.' Coventry's friends, including the king's brother James, succeeded in obtaining his release from the Tower. But although he remained an MP, his career was ruined. It was now dangerous for an ambitious man on the make like Pepys to be seen with Coventry – and he made an excuse to avoid accompanying the fallen statesman on one of their formerly habitual strolls through St James's Park. As for Buckingham's offending play, having served its malign purpose, it was refused a licence and not performed.

Like Coventry, Pepys had been one of the Duke of York's men since

James's appointment as Lord High Admiral to run the navy. But in the wake of the 1678 Popish Plot, associates of the duke were in danger of arrest, ruin and even death. Pepys knew that to incur the enmity of Buckingham was dangerous. But the rakish duke and he were on opposite sides of the growing political gulf dividing England. For, although not a Catholic himself, in the eyes of the Protestant Whigs, anyone as closely linked to the Duke of York as Pepys was guilty by association. As the diarist wrote to York, 'For, whether I will or no, a Papist I must be because favoured by your Royal Highness.' Now it was Pepys's turn to be devoured by wolves – and thrown into the Tower.

Pepys was familiar enough with both the benign and the malign aspects of the Tower before he joined the long list of its prisoners. As an ambitious young man taking his first steps in his civil service career he had curried favour with Lord Montagu, his boss in the Navy Office, by taking some of Montagu's ten children to visit the menagerie there.

In 1662 Pepys was back at the Tower on another mission for Montagu, now ennobled as the Earl of Sandwich. His mentor had received a report that Sir John Barkstead, Tower lieutenant under Cromwell, and a regicide, had buried thousands of pounds in gold coins (the alleged amount ranged between £7,000 and £50,000) in butter barrels inside the fortress when he realised that the political winds were shifting and he was about to lose his job. Barkstead had then fled into exile in Germany. But he was lured back to his doom by another former Cromwellian, Sir George Downing, England's ambassador in the Netherlands. To cement his credentials as a born-again Royalist, this reptilian individual – the man whose name is immortalised in the street where Britain's prime ministers reside, which he once owned – set a trap for Barkstead and two other exiled regicides, Colonel John Okey and Miles Corbet, and arrested them at their lodgings in Delft as they relaxed over beer and tobacco.

The betrayal of Downing was particularly repellent as he himself had served as chaplain in Okey's regiment during their Cromwellian days. The three regicides were shipped back to Britain, and held in the Tower before suffering hanging, drawing and quartering at Tyburn. Pepys saw them taken to their deaths and remarked that 'they all looked very cheerful' considering the circumstances. Pepys, who owed his early rise in the Admiralty to Downing's patronage, nevertheless called his former boss 'a perfidious rogue' and 'a low villain' for his triple abduction. Fearing that the funeral of the popular Okey would turn into a riot by Cromwellian sympathisers, King Charles broke his word to Okey's widow and refused to release the body to her for burial. Instead, his mutilated corpse was transported back to the Tower where it was secretly interred. Barkstead, a notably cruel persecutor of Royalist prisoners during his time running the Tower, was treated with even less respect. His head was spiked on a pole and mounted on St Thomas's Tower looking over the river.

Pepys's current boss, Lord Montagu, was himself a former Cromwellian loyalist who, like Downing, had accommodated himself to the new Royalist regime. Professing to believe the story of Barkstead's hidden gold – for Cromwell's lieutenant had received the substantial salary of £2,000 per annum as reward for his distasteful duties at the Tower – Montagu ordered Pepys to conduct a detailed search for the buried treasure, King Charles II, always short of cash, authorised the hunt on condition that he received a generous cut of any money found.

On 30 October 1661, six months after Barkstead's grisly end, Pepys presented himself to the Tower's constable and lieutenant, Sir John Robinson (who combined the two jobs with that of Lord Mayor of London), and began his quest. Wade and Evett, the two men whose story had sparked the search, took Pepys and his digging party, equipped with picks and shovels, to the vaulted basement of the Bell Tower, Sir Thomas More's grim prison. Here they started to dig in the earthen floor. Five hours of frantic excavation produced much sweat and cursing and a large heap of turned soil and stones – but no sign of gold. Frustrated, but undaunted, Pepys entrusted the Bell Tower's key to Robinson's deputy governor – 'Lord, what a young, simple, fantastic coxcomb,' as he characteristically described him in the diary – promising to return and continue the search.

Two days later, he was back. Three more hours of digging produced the same negative results as before. Pepys adjourned to the nearby Dolphin Tavern with Wade and Evett to question them more closely. They promised to bring their witness – a woman who claimed to have been Barkstead's mistress – to their next digging session. On Friday 7 November, a week after the gold rush had begun, Pepys and his gold-diggers made their third visit to the Bell Tower. Barkstead's supposed mistress – wearing a disguise to hide her modesty – appeared as promised and confirmed that this was where she had seen her lover burying his barrels. Thus encouraged, the gold-diggers went back to work, only pausing for lunch: 'Upon the head of a barrel [we] dined very merrily,' wrote Pepys. By the end of the day they were exhausted and had dug over the entire area of the Bell Tower's floor – to no avail. Pepys concluded philosophically, 'We were forced to give over our expectations, though I do believe there must be money hidden somewhere by him, or else he did delude this woman in hopes to oblige her to further serving him, which I am apt to believe.'

But the hunt was still not quite over. Wade and Evett reported to Pepys that Barkstead's mistress's memory had been at fault. The barrels were buried, she now remembered, not in the Bell Tower, but in Barkstead's former garden outside the Lieutenant's Lodgings. Although it was now December, and the earth was frozen solid, in an astonishing triumph of hope over experience, Pepys suppressed any doubts about the two con men's credibility, and once again returned to the Tower. This time, Pepys did not personally participate in the dig, contenting himself with watching from a window in the governor's house as workmen broke the ice-hard soil in the garden outside the Bloody Tower. Here, snugly sitting before a roaring fire with refreshments to hand, Pepys kept one eye on his chilly diggers and the other reading John Fletcher's play *A Wife for a Month*, which he loftily pronounced as containing 'no great wit or language'.

As the winter light failed, Pepys and the governor left their warm snug to check on the labourers' progress. Once again, they were disappointed. The four workmen, utterly exhausted, stood disconsolately around a gaping hole they had dug under the foundation of the garden wall: but of barrels of gold there was still no sign. At last, even the relentlessly optimistic Pepys gave up:

> I bade them give over, and so all our hopes ended . . . and so home and to bed, a little displeased with my wife, who, poor wretch, is troubled with her lonely life.

As for Barkstead's elusive treasure – even in the unlikely event of its ever having existed, it was never found. The Tower guards its secrets well.

The diarist's next recorded visit to the Tower came in 1666. On hearing of the outbreak of the Great Fire of London from his servants in the early hours of Sunday 2 September, it was to the Tower that Pepys hastened from his home in nearby Seething Lane to assess the extent of the conflagration. He climbed to a high window in a western turret of the White Tower, accompanied by the small son of his old acquaintance Sir John Robinson, the lieutenant, to make his observation. The blaze had already consumed a large number of streets near its seat in a baker's shop in Pudding Lane. The great mass of dense smoke and orange flame, and the homeless refugees displaced by the fire emerging on to Tower Hill with their salvaged belongings, so alarmed Pepys that he hired a boat and had himself rowed upstream past the inferno to Whitehall Palace to bring the king his first news of the fire that was consuming his capital.

The Great Fire posed a mortal danger to the Tower, despite its thick stone walls. The entire supply of the Royal Navy's gunpowder – at least half a million pounds of it – was kept in the White Tower in the Royal Armoury's arsenal. As a Navy Office mandarin, Pepys was acutely aware of the problem, and when, on the fourth day of the fire, the wind which had been fanning the flames shifted to the south, the danger became an imminent peril. Pepys's friend and fellow diarist John Evelyn spelled out what would have happened had the flames reached the Tower's magazine. The gigantic blast, he wrote, 'would undoubtedly have not only beaten down and destroyed all the [London] Bridge, but sunk and torn all the vessels in the river and rendered the demolition beyond all expression for several miles even about the country at many miles distance'. A modern authority on the seventeenth century, Professor Ronald Hutton, has said that if the Tower's magazine had gone up it would have been 'the greatest explosion in early modern history'.

A desperate effort therefore was begun to remove the powder from the fire's path. Royal Navy seamen, together with civilians press-ganged into helping them, staggered in and out of the Tower laden with heavy barrels of gunpowder which they loaded on to ships bound downriver to Woolwich and Greenwich. They sweated under their burdens, their task made desperately hazardous by smoke-darkened skies swirling with sparks from the fire – any one of which could have detonated a catastrophic blast. But the work went on until all the powder was taken out of harm's way.

Gunpowder was not the only precious commodity in the Tower which needed to be preserved from the hungry flames. Soon after the fire began its devastating course, London's goldsmiths and silversmiths started to arrive at the fortress gates bearing their money, metal and plate, seeking a place of safety for their wealth while the fire raged. A vast amount of treasure – worth some £1,200,000 – was taken into the Tower. No sooner was it safely stored, however, than the fire changed course as the easterly wind veered south and the smiths began to worry whether even the Tower would be safe. So once again, the treasure was moved: this time, like the gunpowder, it was hastily loaded on boats and taken upstream to the safety of Whitehall. The danger was real and close enough: Tower Street blazed, and the Dolphin Tavern, where Pepys had interrogated Wade and Evett, was burned down. When the great Elizabethan Custom House burst into flames, the conflagration was only 100 yards from the western walls of the Tower.

By this time, the authorities had realised that no conventional fire-fighting could stop the fire from engulfing the whole city in a ferocious blanket of flame. London's narrow medieval streets were easy prey for the flames to leap over, ravenously feeding on the timbers and thatch of the huddled houses, tinder dry after an exceptionally parched summer. At first, attempts were made to pull houses in the fire's path apart with billhooks, but when this method proved far too slow, orders went out to blow up buildings with gunpowder. This is what saved the Tower from a fiery death.

Using what gunpowder remained in the White Tower's armoury, sailors began to blow up the hovels along the Tower Ditch – the wretched street lining the Tower's western moat. Gunpowder was also used to demolish a wine shop and warehouse at the foot of Seething Lane, where Pepys lived and worked, narrowly saving the diarist's home along with the Navy Office. He had famously already taken the precaution of burying his most valued possessions, including a prized Parmesan cheese, in his garden. At the Tower itself, the cacophony of roaring flames, crackling and crashing timbers, and human voices raised in cries of fear, were joined by the roars and screeches of the terrified creatures in the menagerie. Maddened by the heat and smoke, abandoned by their keepers and frightened by the crump of the explosions, the elephant, lions, apes and bears mixed their fear into the bubbling cauldron of terror caused by the fire.

And then, almost as suddenly as it had arisen, the Great Fire burned itself out. Five days after the burning baker's oven sparked the catastrophe, the exhausted flames subsided and flickered out for lack of fuel. The walls of the Tower, smoke stains adding to the grime of centuries, looked out over a devastated city in which old St Paul's Cathedral, eighty-four lesser churches, forty-four livery company halls, the ancient Guildhall and Baynard's Castle – almost as old as the Tower itself – along with hundreds of mansions and thousands of lesser dwellings, had all been consumed in less than a week. But the Tower – as ever – had survived.

* * *

Pepys frequently visited the Tower in his leisure hours, as it was a short stroll from Seething Lane. In 1668, two years after the fire, and with London's reconstruction under the guidance of Sir Christopher Wren well under way, the fortress was the scene of one of the libidinous diarist's many flirtations. The actress Elizabeth Knipp, a star of the Restoration stage, had long been an object of Pepys's lust. Sometimes she permitted his familiarities, but often slapped his wandering hands away – which only served to increase his interest. He squired her around the Tower on at least two occasions, taking her to see the menagerie, and another time along with a group of her female friends, paying old Talbot Edwards to show them the Crown jewels. (The visit came four years before Blood's celebrated theft.) Pepys was duly impressed by the regalia on display, writing, 'The Crown and sceptres and rich plate, which I myself never saw before . . . indeed, is noble and I mightily pleased with it.'

In the decade that followed, Pepys continued his climb up the greasy pole of government service. Although he gave up keeping his famous diary in 1669, fearing that writing by flickering candlelight, coupled with his growing mountain of professional paperwork, was endangering his eyesight, his worldly success rolled on. In 1673 he reached the summit of his career when he was appointed Secretary of the Admiralty and became an MP. For a few short years Pepys was on the pinnacle – enjoying regular access to the king and the esteem of most of his peers. In 1678, though, he fell, struck down by the poisonous politics of the Popish Plot.

The plot originated in the fevered brain of Titus Oates, an Anglican clergyman disgraced for sodomy, who had then studied at Catholic seminaries in Europe where he had acquired a smattering of knowledge of the Jesuits, shock troops of the Catholic Counter-Reformation, before being expelled for his disreputable conduct. Returning to England, Oates's overactive imagination conceived a vast conspiracy hatched by the Jesuits to kill the king, murder all Protestants, and return the country to the rule of Rome. At a time when the memory of Bloody Mary's burnings and the Gunpowder Plot were still strong, such Protestant paranoia found a ready audience.

After interviewing Oates, the king, though immediately perceiving him to be a pathological liar, felt unable to resist the popular panic. On Oates's accusations many innocent Catholics were arrested and several hanged. And after Sir Edmund Berry Godfrey, a magistrate to whom Oates had sworn an affadavit detailing his allegations, was found mysteriously murdered, panic turned to hysteria. Powerful Protestant politicians, notably two fallen Protestant members of the Cabal, the Earl of Shaftesbury and the Duke of Buckingham, both of whom had spent spells inside the Tower as their power waned, rode the wave of the plot to strike down their enemies. Their main aim was to exclude Pepys's Catholic patron, James, Duke of York, from succeeding his brother on the throne. And when the duke was forced into exile at the height of the plot, Pepys was left defenceless.

Shaftesbury's Whigs amassed a small army of hostile witnesses willing to accuse Pepys. Chief among these was James Scott, an acquaintence of Blood's in the criminal underworld, and, like Blood, claiming the rank of colonel. Scott, another protégé of the villainous Buckingham, had all his friend's criminal ingenuity, with additional malice thrown in. A plausible con man who had once purchased Long Island on a fraudulent prospectus, Scott was paid by Buckingham to accuse Pepys of betraying English naval secrets to Catholic France. A Whig MP named William Harbord, who was after Pepys's Admiralty job, weighed in with the charge that 'Mr Pepys is an ill [i.e. evil] man, and I will prove him so' – while a disgruntled former servant of the diarist, John James, was prepared to swear that the employer who had fired him was a secret Papist.

On 20 May 1679, in the House of Commons, the deadly charges of 'Piracy, Popery and Treachery' were levelled at Pepys. Spluttering with indignation, Pepys rose to refute 'so many things cast at me at once, and all by surprise'. Despite his repeated denials, as someone accused of treason, he was committed to the custody of the serjeant-at-arms, forced to resign as admiralty secretary – and taken as a prisoner to the Tower. In this dire situation, Pepys kept a cool head. He sent his French brother-in-law, 'Balty' St Michel, across the Channel to find evidence to expose Scott as the liar and fraudster he was. As a person of power, wealth and influence, Pepys had unrestricted ability to send and receive mail from the Tower, and get visits from his friends – his fellow diarist John Evelyn being one. A month after he was incarcerated, Pepys was released from the Tower on bail – but it took a whole year before his name was cleared and he was restored to his office.

CHAPTER FIFTEEN

CIVIL WARS AND UNCIVIL PEACE

Samuel Pepys was a child of the Civil War. Born off Fleet Street in the heart of London, the gossipy diarist was already an adolescent when the conflict tore the nation apart. Though London – especially the city – remained a stronghold of Parliament throughout the struggle, and Royalist forces got no closer to the capital than the outlying western village of Turnham Green, the Tower played a central role in the unfolding drama.

Early in Charles I's reign, the growing Parliamentary opposition was led by Sir John Eliot, a Cornish Puritan and a disciple of Walter Ralegh's 'advanced' ideas for curbing monarchy and advancing Parliament. Eliot first tasted the Tower's hospitality in 1626, when he made a fiery speech attacking the late James I's favourite catamite, George Villiers, 1st Duke of Buckingham (father of Pepys's enemy, the 2nd Duke). Buckingham was the favourite of both James I and Charles I, whose aggressive and foolish foreign policy, aimed simultaneously against Spain and France, had led to repeated military disasters and vast expense.

Three years later Eliot was back in the Tower, this time accompanied by eight fellow Puritan MPs. Eliot was now aiming his attacks on Charles's promotion of the Anglo-Catholic 'Arminianism' of his Archbishop of Canterbury, William Laud – fated one day to grace the Tower too. During a stormy Commons debate, Eliot and a colleague forcibly held the speaker in his seat to prevent the sitting from being curtailed. Two days later, the unruly Parliamentarian was detained in the Bloody Tower, accused of 'stirring up sedition' – and this time he would not emerge alive.

Because Charles bitterly blamed Eliot for creating the climate of hatred against Buckingham that had led to the duke's assassination in Portsmouth the previous year (the assassin, a disgruntled ex-officer named John Felton, had also been imprisoned in the Bloody Tower before his execution), he was determined to detain the MP 'at his pleasure' – which, as it turned out, meant for ever. Charles's bitterness was doubtless exacerbated because he had been unable to torture the killer of his friend Buckingham. Threatened with the rack by Archbishop Laud, Felton had impudently retorted that torture was illegal under English law. Although this had never stopped anyone from being racked in the Tower before, Laud consulted the law books, found Felton was correct, and advised Charles not to proceed, as Buckingham had been so hated that torturing his assassin might provoke a riot, if not a revolution. Felton was hanged at Tyburn instead, and his rotting carcass was suspended in chains in Portsmouth near the scene of his crime.

The spirited Eliot was popular with his fellow politicians of all opinions: the forty correspondents he wrote to from the Tower included two men destined to die fighting on opposite sides in the coming Civil War; his fellow Puritan, John Hampden, to whom he entrusted the custody of his children; and a fellow Cornish aristocrat and Cavalier hero, Sir Bevil Grenville.

But King Charles's petty malevolence against the man who had dared to defy him was implacable. On top of his perpetual imprisonment, he fined Eliot £2,000. Never wealthy, Eliot responded sardonically that he had '. . . two cloaks, two suits, two pairs of boots and galoshes, and a few books . . . and if they could pick £2,000 out of that, much good might it do them'. Like his hero Ralegh before him, Eliot devoted himself to literary composition. Along with his voluminous correspondence, he wrote books advocating parliamentary sovereignty (*The Monarchy of Man* and *De Jure Melestatis: a Political Treatise of Government*); a philosophical defence of his own position (*An Apology for Socrates*); and a history of Charles's first Parliament – of which Eliot had been such an awkward Member. Sarcastically, Eliot reported to Hampden in 1630:

> I have no news to give you but the happiness of this place, which is so like a paradise that there is none to trouble us but ourselves . . . Amongst the other rarities of this sphere there is newly here exposed some part of the [Crown] Jewels to be seen, the font the Prince [the future Charles II] was christened in and such others.

Charles's response to Eliot's resolute defiance in 1631 was to withdraw the privilege of the liberty of the Tower, remove him from the Bloody Tower, where he had been able to take the air on the ramparts in the footsteps of

Walter Ralegh, and confine him to a damp, cold and dark cell. He was forbidden visits from his friends and even his family. Eliot complained:

> I am now where candlelight may be suffered, but scarce fire. None but my servant, hardly my sons, may have admittance to me; my friends I must desire for their own sakes to forbear coming to the Tower.

Eliot was persecuted by being constantly moved from cell to cell – ten times in all.

Under such wretched conditions, his health rapidly declined. A hacking cough proclaimed the onset of the tuberculosis that rapidly gained a fatal hold. At last, the proud man bent to petition Charles for the freedom to take fresh air for his failing lungs. Charles callously rejected the request on the grounds that the petition 'was not humble enough'. Realising that he was dying, his friends commissioned a portrait of Eliot painted in the Tower. Clad in a nightgown, with one hand on his hip and the other holding a book, he gazes out at the artist, defiant to the last. Eliot died in the Tower on 28 November 1632. The king's cruelty pursued him beyond the grave: rejecting his family's request that his body be released for burial in his beloved Cornwall, Charles spitefully ordered that he be interred in St Peter ad Vincula.

Sir John Eliot was the first martyr to the cause that would see the downfall of monarchy and the execution of the king who had persecuted him. His example inspired others – like his friend John Hampden, and the leader of the Puritans in Parliament, John Pym – to complete the work he had started and end royal absolutism. But there were many on the other side of the quarrel equally determined to fight, and if necessary, die, to uphold the Crown.

One such was Thomas Wentworth, a Yorkshire gentleman whom Charles would create Earl of Strafford for his efforts to bolster royal authority. Strafford began his career as a critic of royal absolutism, but in 1628, he decided that attacks on the king's authority had gone far enough, switched sides, and became an able – and ruthless – royal servant. 'Black Tom tyrant', as his enemies called the saturnine Wentworth, became King Charles's enforcer in his native Yorkshire, as president of the Royal Council of the North. Promoted to Lord Deputy in Ireland, his hard-line policy of 'Thorough', aimed at keeping down the restless Catholic majority, succeeded in containing a Catholic rebellion.

As Strafford brought the north and Ireland to heel, William Laud, Charles's peppery, red-faced little Archbishop of Canterbury, attempted to subject an increasingly Puritanical Church of England to an Anglo-Catholic Counter-Reformation. Laud's rigidly enforced policy, with its emphasis on restoring altars, ritual, vestments and other 'Popish' ways to the Anglican Church, drove many Puritans into exile. (This was the era when the *Mayflower* took the Pilgrim Fathers to America's shores.) Others, however, such as an obscure MP named Oliver Cromwell, resolved to stay and fight.

In April 1640 Charles finally ran out of cash. Two expensive and ill-advised attempts to force the Presbyterian Scots to adopt the English system of bishops had resulted in the so-called Bishops' Wars of 1639. But instead of tamely submitting to Charles's commands, the Scots had formed a 20,000-strong army to defend their religious and political liberties to the death. Charles found his own army inadequate for the task of subduing the Scots – some being armed only with bows and arrows. He was obliged to agree to a humiliating peace. Still worse, he was forced to summon the Parliament he had dispensed with for eleven years.

The MPs were in an ugly mood. Led by John Pym, they were determined to bring down the twin pillars of royal rule, temporal and spiritual, in the persons of Strafford and Laud. Strafford was summoned to London by Parliament, going, as he wrote to a friend, 'with more danger beset, I believe, than ever man went with out of Yorkshire; yet my heart is good and I find nothing cold within me'.

Pym had proclaimed that 'Stone-dead hath no fellow' and Strafford knew that before Parliament rose again either Pym or he would be no more. It was literally a duel to the death. Hearing that Pym planned to impeach him for high treason, Strafford planned to use a royal review of troops at the Tower as cover for a coup in which Pym and his friends would be arrested in the fortress and royal authority restored. But Pym had his spies at court, notably the beautiful intriguer Lucy Percy, Countess of Carlisle. Lady Carlisle, daughter of the 'Wizard Earl' of Northumberland, who had been imprisoned in the Tower along with Ralegh, had reputedly been the lover in succession of Strafford and Pym. After the Civil War, she swung round to Royalism once again – and was sent to the Tower as a suspected agent of Charles II, dying shortly after the 1660 Restoration.

Well aware from his mistress's reports of what Strafford intended, Pym struck first. On 10 November, the day that Strafford arrived in London from Yorkshire, he was impeached by the Lords for high treason. Strafford declared that he would 'look his accusers in the face' – and was promptly arrested. On 25 November he was taken to the Tower in a closed coach through jeering crowds. Ruthless and tyrannical he may have been, but Strafford was also brave. Inside the Tower, he marshalled his defence, confident that his accusers lacked the evidence to convict him. Pym had him confined to a suite of three rooms in the Lieutenant's Lodgings, and constantly watched. Strafford remained resolutely cheerful – going to daily services in the Tower's chapel, and taking exercise with the lieutenant, Sir William Balfour, seemingly oblivious to the hostile mobs who gathered daily outside the Tower's gates to howl for his head.

When he was brought by river to face his accusers in the House of Lords, the peers were shocked by Strafford's appearance. After just two cold winter months in the Tower the tall, dark earl was now a grey, stooping figure, shrunken and leaning on a stick. But his mind was as quick as ever, and he refuted the allegations against him with scorn. Given a fortnight to consider his reply to the twenty-eight charges, he was rowed back to the Tower from where he wrote confidently to his wife, telling her that there was 'nothing capital' in the charges. Trustingly, he added:

> I know at the worst His Majesty will pardon all, without hurting my fortune and then we shall be happy by God's grace. Therefore comfort yourself, for I trust these clouds will away and that we shall have fair weather afterwards.

But Strafford had reckoned without the weakness and duplicity of his royal master and without Pym's determination to destroy him. As he was rowed daily to Westminster for his eighteen-day trial, his ally Laud joined him in the Tower on 1 March. The cleric, nearing seventy, was, like Strafford, brought to the fortress in a closed coach through abusive crowds. He was lodged in the Bloody Tower. Strafford knew that his and Laud's roles were to act as fall guys for the sins of their king.

Although the Commons was overwhelmingly against him – Pym's supporters commanded a two-thirds majority – the Lords were more equivocal, and Strafford's skilled defence succeeded in refuting most of the charges against him. The key accusation was that Strafford had intended to use troops from Ireland not just against the Scots, but against the king's enemies in England, too. Since the sole 'proofs' of this rested on the suspect memory of a single man, Sir Henry Vane, Strafford was easily able to disprove it. Pym was now faced with the dire prospect of his enemy's acquittal.

In this desperate extremity Pym resorted to an equally desperate strategm: an Act of Attainder. By this medieval device, last used in the Wars of the Roses, no evidence needed to be proved against a person accused of treason. By Parliament simply passing the act, the accused could be lawfully executed and his estates forfeit. It was legalised murder, but Pym now put the attainder against Strafford before Parliament.

Back at the Tower, blissfully unaware of the deadly new threat, Strafford was cock-a-hoop at his apparent demolition of the case against him. He had even exchanged a significant smile across the courtroom with the king at the conclusion of the trial. Now, a witness reported, the earl 'walked up and down the Tower in high spirits, even singing songs of thanksgiving'. Charles wrote reassuringly, 'Upon the word of a king, you shall not suffer in life, honour or fortune.' Those words would come back to haunt both Strafford and the king.

The Commons rushed through the attainder, passing it by 204 votes to fifty-nine. It now remained for the Lords to accept or reject it, and for the king – who had just promised Strafford his protection – to sign it into law. Pressure on the Lords was intense. The fury of the London mob had been thoroughly aroused, and shops and businesses were abandoned as their owners surrounded Parliament, lustily yelling for Strafford's death. But as the Lords debated, another plot was revealed which sealed Strafford's fate.

In a typically maladroit move, Charles attempted another coup at the Tower designed to snatch Strafford from the jaws of death now closing upon him. The king first attempted to bribe the lieutenant, Sir William Balfour, with £20,000 to turn a blind eye to Strafford's escape. The fallen minister's faithful secretary, Guildford Slingsby, had chartered a ship which lay at Tilbury, ready to whisk Strafford abroad. To aid the escape, on 2 May a Captain Billingsby appeared at the Tower's main gate with a troop of 100 soldiers, demanding admittance in the king's name. The plotters, however, had reckoned without Balfour's staunch Scots Presbyterianism, which made loyalty to Parliament his priority. He turned Billingsby and his men away, refused the king's bribe and told Pym what was afoot.

The revelation of the Tower plot swung wavering lords behind the bill of attainder. Those who still hesitated were intimidated by the mob besieging Parliament, and many stayed away from the vital vote. When it came, the majority was wafer thin: just seven votes condemned Strafford to death. It was in vain that Charles had sent his eleven-year-old son, the future Charles II, to Parliament to make a personal plea for mercy. In vain too that he promised never to appoint Strafford to another office – 'not even a constable' if only his life was spared. The mob now transferred its attention from Westminster to Whitehall, and threatening crowds surrounded Charles's palace demanding that he sign the act that would take Strafford's life.

As the king wriggled like a worm on a hook, Strafford nobly took the decision for him. In an extraordinary letter of self-sacrifice from the Tower, he released the king from his promise to save his life in order to preserve the peace and stability of the realm:

> So now to set your Majesty's conscience at liberty, I do most humbly beseech your Majesty for prevention of evils which may happen by your Refusal to pass this Bill . . .

With this letter, Strafford laid his own neck upon the block.

If Charles had been a stronger man he would have ignored the letter and insisted on reprieving his most loyal and able servant. But he was not. And with the howls of the besieging mob ringing in his ears, and tears running down his face, he signed the bill. Self-pityingly he declared that 'my Lord of Strafford's condition is happier than mine', and when he himself faced the same fate eight bloodstained years later, he claimed that he was being justly punished as atonement for his sin in permitting Strafford's judicial killing. It is, however, doubtful whether even Charles could have saved Strafford from the fury of an aroused and vengeful populace. Lord Newport, a supposed Stuart sympathiser, whom the king had recently appointed constable of the Tower in the hope that he could somehow save Strafford, had, like Balfour, sniffed which way the political wind was blowing. Newport now sent a message to the palace that unless the king authorised Strafford's execution he would order it on his own authority. Coming on top of Strafford's own letter of renunciation, this finally pushed the king into signing away his faithful servant's life.

When the fatal tidings were brought to Strafford, despair and disillusion broke through his mask of resignation and he burst out with the biblical quotation, 'Put not your trust in princes, nor in the sons of men, for in them is no salvation.' When told the news in the nearby Bloody

Tower, Archbishop Laud was ever more bitter: Charles, he said, was a king who 'knew neither how to be, or to be made, great'. Strafford spent his last days in calm preparation for death. After settling his business affairs and writing consoling letters to his family, he made his spiritual peace with the help of Archbishop James Ussher, the Calvinist Primate of Ireland, most famous for having calculated the precise date of the Creation as 23 October 4004 BC. Ussher reported that Strafford had repented his sins and sought forgiveness from his many enemies and 'never was such a white soul returned to his maker'.

His soul may have been white, but Strafford was clad from head to toe in sombre black at eleven o'clock on 12 May when Lieutenant Balfour came to escort him to the scaffold. Passing beneath the Bloody Tower, Strafford paused to receive a final blessing from his old friend and ally, William Laud. Emotion overcame the old man, and having pronounced his blessing through his cell window, the cleric fell back in a dead faint. Strafford calmly walked on to meet his fate. So hated was 'Black Tom tyrant' that the huge open space of Tower Hill was completely filled with an exultant crowd of more than 100,000 who had come to see him die. Special stands had been erected to give paying punters a better view, and the Tower's battlements were lined with curious, exultant or sympathetic spectators. The mob was so immense that they were pressing against the gates of the Tower itself, and an alarmed Balfour, fearing a lynching, begged Strafford to leave the Tower as he had entered it – in a closed coach.

Strafford would have none of it and he replied:

> No, I dare look death in the face. And I hope the people too. I care not how I die, whether by the hand of the executioner, or by the madness and fury of the people. If that may give them better content it is all one to me.

The gates swung open and Strafford strode fearlessly up the hill, his fierce gaze reducing the hostile crowd to silence. From the scaffold itself he spoke an eloquent final message, doubting that the people's happiness could be purchased by the shedding of his blood. He tried to comfort his brother George, who was weeping helplessly:

> One stroke will make my wife husbandless, my dear children fatherless, my poor servants masterless, and separate me from my dear brother and all my friends. But let God be to you and them all in all.

Then, declaring that he cast off his doublet 'as cheerfully as ever I did when I went to bed', Strafford knelt at the block to receive his stroke. A roar of vengeful triumph arose as the executioner, Richard Brandon, lifted the severed head, still spurting blood. Horsemen at the edge of the crowd rode out through London's streets and the villages beyond the city waving their hats in glee and yelling, 'His head is off! His head is off!' The Royalist diarist John Evelyn was in the crowd to see 'the fatal stroke', which severed what he called 'the wisest head in England'. But Evelyn was in a minority. That May morning, England's monarchy had fallen to its lowest point in popular esteem, and Charles's ignoble offering up of the one man who could possibly have saved his tottering throne was a revelation. It showed to both his growing band of enemies and his diminishing group of friends his faithless – and fatal – weakness which would now lead his kingdom to civil war, and his own head to be lopped off with Strafford's – ironically by the same impartial headsman, Richard Brandon.

As the kingdom spiralled towards armed conflict, both sides manoeuvred for advantage. King Charles saw the Tower as the key to controlling London, and at Christmas 1641 dismissed Sir William Balfour, who had betrayed him over Strafford, and installed a swashbuckling Cavalier soldier, Sir Thomas Lunsford, in his place as lieutenant. Known to be 'fit for any wicked design', the ruthless Lunsford would have transformed the Tower into a citadel to overawe London, with its strong Parliamentary sympathy. The battle over his appointment became a power struggle that Parliament was determined not to lose. The Commons told the king that London's merchants would refuse to supply the Tower mint with bullion unless Lunsford was removed, thus halting the production of the nation's coinage at a stroke.

Crucially, Charles had failed to replace Lord Newport as constable, and Newport refused to accept Lunsford as his lieutenant. The king was forced to back down, and Lunsford became the lieutenant with the shortest time in office on record – just four days. It was not, however, the end of Lunsford's Tower connections. In 1645, after a brave and bloody career as a Royalist soldier in the Civil War, he was captured – and joined the hundreds of Royalists thronging the Tower as Parliament's prisoners of war. Lunsford stayed in the Tower until 1647 when he was released on condition that he emigrated to Virginia, where he died in 1656.

After Lunsford's dismissal, the king named another loyal soldier, Sir John Byron, to be lieutenant in Lunsford's place. But Byron – an ancestor of the great Romantic poet – lasted little longer than Lunsford. Parliament checked Charles by drafting in its own militia – the City Trained Bands, a volunteer force composed largely of London apprentices – to beef up the Tower's garrison. When Byron attempted to replace the Trained Bands with royal troops there was an armed clash – the first skirmish of the coming Civil War. Byron resigned in disgust, and Sir John Conyers, a Parliamentary loyalist, replaced him – from henceforth to the Restoration in 1660, the Tower remained firmly in Roundhead hands.

Charles left his capital in January 1642 after a bungled attempt to arrest John Pym and four of his closest Parliamentary associates. The king would only return to London as a prisoner. William Laud remained the Tower's most distinguished inmate through the first Civil War, which broke out in August 1642. The fussy old archbishop busied himself with preparing his own defence against his eventual trial, and interfering in the services at the Tower chapel, even forbidding marriages if he thought the couples concerned were unsuited. Laud had to witness the destruction of his life's work, as the Puritans, now in the ascendant, smashed his precious altar rails for firewood, and broke the stained glass decorating so many churches.

Laud's fate mirrored that of his friend Strafford. After John Pym's death from cancer, his chief tormentor was William Prynne, a Puritan preacher whom the archbishop had himself savagely persecuted in the days of his pomp for his 'heretical' pamphlets. Laud had had Prynne exposed in the pillory, had slit his nose, and ordered his ears cropped to bloody stumps, before finally branding his face with the letters 'SL' for 'Seditious Libeller'. In addition Prynne had been fined £5,000 and imprisoned in the Tower. Now the tables were well and truly turned and the mutilated Prynne had the power to take revenge on his persecutor. His first move, in 1643, was to appear at the Bloody Tower early one morning accompanied by a guard of musketeers, while Laud was still in bed. Prynne took away twenty-one bundles of papers which Laud had meticulously assembled to bolster his defence.

Despite the lack of documentation, the old man's phenomenal memory enabled him to put up a stout defence when he was finally tried in 1644. Like Strafford, he was rowed from the Tower to Westminster every day for his trial – except one particularly bitter January day when the river froze and he was driven through hooting crowds in a coach. Like Strafford before him, when the evidence failed to make a charge of treason stick,

Laud was convicted of trying to 'subvert religion and the laws of the realm' under a bill of attainder and condemned to death.

Laud was happy to die. His life's work lay in ruins, his country was convulsed by civil war, and the king he had served had been exposed as a man of straw. In his will, drawn up in the Tower, the archbishop wrote with feeling, 'I most willingly leave the world, being weary at the very heart at the vanities in it.' He slept soundly the night before his execution, on 10 January 1645, and preached a fine sermon from the scaffold on Tower Hill, predicting that God would bring him 'from the banks of the Red Sea into the Land of Promise'. As he knelt at the block, Laud saw between the planks of the scaffold's floor that members of the public had gathered directly beneath. He called for more sawdust to be scattered as he had 'no desire that his blood should fall on the heads of the people'. His last words as the axe was raised were, 'I am coming, O Lord, as fast as I can.'

William Prynne's subsequent history reflects the strange twists and turns in loyalty and fortune as the nation negotiated the switchback fortunes of civil war. Always a contrarian, Prynne sided with the Presbyterian members of Parliament who fell out with an increasingly radical army as the bitter war went on. Finally, Prynne was even reconciled to the Restoration of the monarchy under which he had been persecuted so relentlessly. After the return of Charles II in 1660, by a supreme irony, the man who had deprived Laud of the written records to mount his defence was himself made Keeper of the Records at the Tower by the new king.

Prynne found the records in a chaotic mess. They had been thrown into a room in the White Tower, and were lying scattered in heaps with no attempt at order. Prynne primly described the state in which he found them:

> I have been almost choked with the dust of neglected records interred in their own rubbish for sundry years in the White Tower; their rust eating out the tops of my gloves with their touch, and their dust rendering me, twice a day, as black as a chimney sweeper.

Somewhat surprisingly, Prynne proved an admirable historian of the Tower and his last decade was spent happily in the fortress where he had once suffered. The old polemicist was seen at work there by the gossipy antiquarian John Aubrey who described him among his now ordered papers, wearing:

... a long quilt cap, which came two or three inches over his eyes, which served him as an umbrella to defend his eyes from the light. About every two or three hours his man was to bring him a roll and a pot of ale to refocillate his wasted spirits. So he studied and drank, and munched some bread; this maintained him till night and then he made a good supper.

Prynne's experience of seeing the two sides of the Tower – as captive, and as custodian – was not unique in Civil War England. London's lord mayor, Sir Richard Gurney, the capital's leading Royalist and a former Tower lieutenant, was deprived of his office by Parliament and imprisoned in the fortress where he had once presided in pomp, only being freed as his death approached in 1647. The man Parliament installed as lord mayor in Gurney's place, a Puritan MP named Sir Isaac Pennington, was also made lieutenant of the Tower in place of Sir John Conyers. Pennington, in his turn, was deposed at the Restoration and imprisoned in his former workplace, where he soon died.

Nor was Prynne the only man to turn his coat politically in the wars. Two who followed him – or attempted to – in his erratic progress across the political spectrum were Sir John Hotham and his son, another John. The Hothams, scions of an old Yorkshire family, were early Parliamentary heroes, seizing their bastion, Hull, and denying the king entry to this vital port. Their action – in January 1642 – precipitated the Civil War, in which both fought for Parliament. However, the hotheaded younger Hotham fell out with his fellow Yorkshire Roundheads and persuaded his father to change sides. The Hothams were in the midst of negotiations to hand Hull over to the Royalists – in return for a hefty £20,000 bribe – when their treachery was discovered. They were arrested, brought to the Tower, and, on successive days, executed.

Another Parliamentary governor of another port – Plymouth in Devon – Sir Alexander Carew, suffered a fate similar to that of the Hothams. He too was originally a stout Parliamentarian. Refusing to vote against the attainder that killed Strafford, Carew replied, 'If I was sure to be the next man that should suffer upon the same scaffold with the same axe, I would give my consent to the passing of it.' Little did he know then that this would be exactly what happened to him. Entrusted by Parliament with holding Plymouth, a rare Roundhead outpost in the Royalist West Country, Carew opened negotiations with the Cavaliers to hand the port over. But he was betrayed by a servant and brought to the Tower from

Plymouth by sea. Here he was held for a year before – despite his wife's plea that he was insane – being executed on Tower Hill like Strafford before him. Ironically, his younger brother, who remained true to the Roundhead cause, was hanged, drawn and quartered as a regicide after the Restoration.

In the 1640s and 1650s, the Tower was crammed with more prisoners than at any time since the Elizabethan persecution of Catholic priests and plotters in the 1580s and 1590s. At first, most of the captives were Royalist prisoners of war and peers who could not accept the assault on hereditary privilege culminating in the first English republic. It is estimated that no fewer than one third of the entire House of Lords were imprisoned in the fortress during this period.

As well as peers, the Tower played host to a pair of precious poets during these troubled times. Edmund Waller combined the writing of classically restrained lyric verse with a successful Parliamentary career. A moderate man in an age of extremes, he was one of the delegates appointed by Parliament in 1643 to negotiate with Charles I on a possible compromise peace. The atmosphere in the Royalist capital, Oxford, seems to have influenced Waller, and on his return to London he became involved in a Cavalier conspiracy – named 'Waller's Plot' in his honour – to seize the Tower, liberate its Royalist prisoners and use it as a base to take over London for the king. The plot was betrayed and Waller was arrested. Fortunately for him, he was a distant cousin of Cromwell and still had friends among his fellow MPs, which – along with his abject betrayal of his co-conspirators – saved his life when he was tried for treason after spending several months as a prisoner in the fortress he had hoped to seize. Even so, he was forced to pay a fine of £10,000, and exiled – a sentence only remitted after he wrote a fawning poetic 'Panegyric' to Cromwell in 1655. After the Restoration, he wrote a similar grovelling verse tribute to Charles II, and when teased by the king that his verses in praise of Cromwell were of higher quality, Waller neatly replied, 'Sire, we poets succeed better in fiction than in truth.'

The Tower's other poet prisoner, Sir William Davenant, was a godson – and rumoured to be even a natural son – of Shakespeare, who often stayed at Davenant's birthplace, the Crown Inn, Oxford, en route between London and Stratford. Davenant certainly inherited some of the Bard's literary interests, if not his genius, and turned out a wide array of works, ranging from love lyrics to England's first opera libretto, *The Siege of Rhodes*. Appointed Poet Laureate by Charles I on the death of his mentor and collaborator Ben Jonson, Davenant fought bravely for the king's cause in the Civil War and went into exile in France with Charles II. Named as Lieutenant-Governor of Maryland, Davenant was crossing to the Americas with a cargo of white slaves for the colonies culled from French jails when he was captured in mid-Channel by a Parliamentary warship.

Imprisoned on the Isle of Wight, Davenant wrote a heroic verse epic, *Gondibert*, and had just published it when he was transferred to the Tower to await his trial. The poem included verses in praise of a woman John Aubrey calls 'a handsome black wench', who reputedly infected the libidinous poet with syphilis – causing him to lose his nose to the disease. He spent a year – 1651 – in the Tower before, like Waller before him, benefiting from the aid of a greater poet than himself, Cromwell's Latin secretary, John Milton, who successfully begged his boss for Davenant's release. Influential in the Restoration theatre that followed the Cromwellian ice age, Davenant was responsible for the revival of the plays of his godfather, Shakespeare, as well as staging his own works. He was buried in the Poets' Corner of Westminster Abbey.

After the Parliamentarians triumphed in 1645, simmering tensions between a Parliament dominated by Presbyterian sympathisers and an army leaning heavily towards radical Puritan 'independents' – a host of sects including Baptists, Anabaptists, Muggletonians and 'Fifth Monarchy Men' – burst into the open, and the Tower's already overcrowded cells stretched still further to accommodate more men whose views were at variance with the dominant faction.

In such conditions security at the Tower lapsed, and several notable escapes were made – including those of General Lambert and Lord Capel. The famous escape in drag of the Jacobite Lord Nithsdale was anticipated by another Scotsman, John Middleton, who had started as a distinguished Parliamentary soldier, defeating the great Royalist hero Montrose, but had switched support to Charles II after Charles I's execution. As Charles's military commander at the battle of Worcester, Middleton was defeated, wounded, captured and brought to the Tower. He soon escaped in women's clothes brought in by his wife, slipped across to France and rejoined Charles, who made him an earl after the Restoration.

Edward Massie was another Parliamentary hero turned Royalist whose career curiously parallels that of Middleton. Famed for his epic defence as governor of Gloucester against a Royalist siege conducted by Charles I himself, Massie later emerged as a moderate Presbyterian in the struggle against the extreme republicans. Disgusted by Charles's execution, Massie joined Charles II in exile, was wounded at Worcester, captured after the battle – and succeeded in escaping from the Tower by shinning up a chimney and crossing to France. Like Middleton, he was rewarded with lands and titles after the Restoration.

After Cromwell finally settled the Parliament versus army conflict in the latter's favour by dissolving both the Long Parliament that had sat since Pym's day and the Rump Parliament of leftovers after repeated purges, he established a military dictatorship called the Commonwealth, with himself as 'Lord Protector'. The remaining Royalist prisoners in the Tower were joined by various radicals and republicans – loosely known as 'Levellers' – whose leading spokesman was John Lilburne, dubbed 'Freeborn' John. Advocating ideas of social equality far in advance of their era, the Levellers became a major force in the New Model Army that had won the Civil War. But their radical proposals for regular Parliaments voted for by all adult males were seen as a dire threat to property and privilege by the army's 'Grandees': Generals Cromwell, Fairfax and Ireton.

The clash between the Grandees and the Levellers was at first conducted only with words – at the army debates at Putney and in the pamphlets churned out by Lilburne and the other Leveller leaders. Soon, however, the intoxicating Leveller doctrines led to army mutinies which were put down only with bloodshed. Parliament in 1649 decided that the Tower was the best place for Lilburne and the other chief Leveller agitators, William Walwyn, Richard Overton and Thomas Prince. It was not 'Freeborn' John's first experience of the Tower. He had been consigned there in 1647 for attacking his former Parliamentary army commander, the Earl of Manchester, for his lacklustre conduct of the war. Cromwell, who shared Lilburne's jaundiced opinion of the half-hearted Manchester's military ability, helped get him out; but Lilburne was such a habitually quarrelsome spirit (it was said that when he died 'John' would quarrel with 'Lilburne' about the best place to be buried) that he was soon biting the hand that had freed him, making himself one of the sharpest thorns in Cromwell's side.

The four Leveller leaders did not let their incarceration hinder their agitation. From the Tower they wrote and distributed a new pamphlet, *An Agreement of the Free people of England*. Lilburne was especially productive of pamphlets and polemics. It was said that even in the Tower it was 'impossible to separate him from ink', and words flew from his pen like sparks struck from a smithy. Eventually, Parliament banished him and Walwyn to the Netherlands, where the two ardent republicans found themselves conspiring with their fellow exiles from the Royalist camp. Returning incognito to England, Lilburne was arrested and sent back to the Tower in 1653. Freed yet again, he became a Quaker in 1655 and forsook a lifetime of noisy political activism for the quietist life.

If most Levellers were content to keep their opposition to Cromwell's regime to words, the same could not be said of those militant republicans who – like their Royalist opponents – actively sought the death of the dictator. Edward Sexby and Miles Sindercombe were two ex-Cromwellian soldiers who believed their former military chiefs had sold out the 'good old cause' of Roundhead republicanism. After the suppression of the Leveller-inspired army mutinies in 1649, both fled abroad and actively plotted Cromwell's death, issuing a pamphlet, *Killing No Murder*, justifying the assassination of tyrants.

In 1656 Sindercombe returned to England to put his theories into action. With a group of fellow malcontents, he rented two houses close to Whitehall Palace, from where they intended to shoot Cromwell with an arquebus. Finding that the crowded streets made it difficult to get a clear shot, the conspirators relocated to Hammersmith where they planned to kill Cromwell on his way to or from his favourite out-of-town residence, Hampton Court Palace, by shooting at him with a home-made infernal machine consisting of seven blunderbusses tied together. When Cromwell failed to show on the appointed day, Sindercombe's gang moved again – this time to Hyde Park where they hoped to shoot the Lord Protector while he was out riding. After they had broken the hinges to the park's gates for a quick getaway, Cromwell upset their plans by calling his would-be assassin, one John Cecil, over to discuss the imperfections of his horse.

In despair, the plotters changed their method of execution to arson. Infiltrating the ancient rooms and corridors of Whitehall Palace, Sindercombe hid in the palace's chapel and set it on fire, intending to incinerate Cromwell in his bed. By this time the regime was aware of the plot. Cromwell had his own efficient spymaster, John Thurloe, a man with the espionage genius of Francis Walsingham, whose network of agents across Europe monitored the rival exile communities of Royalists and republicans. Sindercombe was arrested before the fire had taken hold, and had his nose sliced off with a sword before he was subdued.

He and Cecil were taken to the Tower where Cecil saved his skin by agreeing to testify against his confederates. After failing in a bid to bribe his warders to let him go, Sindercombe cheated the executioner on the night before he was due to be beheaded by persuading his sister to slip him a draught of poison when she made an eve-of-execution visit to his cell to bid him farewell. Asking his guards to leave him alone while he said his final prayers, Sindercombe swallowed the poison and died. Despite this unorthodox exit, the law took its course, and his lifeless corpse was dragged up Tower Hill on a hurdle and solemnly interred with an iron-tipped stake marking the spot 'as an example of terror to all traitors for the time to come'.

The following year, Edward Sexby returned to pick up the threads of conspiracy left by his friend Sindercombe. But on his arrival he found that Thurloe's nets were so tight that any possibility of a successful assassination had vanished. Despondent, he decided to return to the Continent – only to be arrested as he boarded a ship bound for Flanders. Sexby, too, was detained in the Tower and harshly interrogated. His sufferings may have contributed to his death there from fever in January 1658 – just under eight months before the demise of his enemy Cromwell.

Cromwell disdained the Tower as a residence. Given its state of decay and the proximity of the many prisoners he sent there, this is scarcely surprising. He did, however, take an interest in the fortress. Indeed, he succeeded his rival General Fairfax as its constable, and made his mark on the place – albeit in a destructive way. Not only were the Crown jewels – which Cromwell considered worthless baubles – melted down and sold off, but the Lord Protector took the demolition ball to the Tower's physical fabric too. The now redundant Jewel House abutting the White Tower went. So did the old royal Palace to the south of the White Tower. The structure which had witnessed so many of the Tower's historic moments was unceremoniously torn down. Its stonework was left lying in untidy heaps until Charles II had them carted away. With it went the ancient

Coldharbour Tower and the nearby Wardrobe Tower, which had once housed the state's documents.

Like the Tower, the Lord Protecter left the realm in a state of chaos. His increasingly unpopular regime had alienated not only Royalists and republicans, but ordinary folk who wanted to enjoy the harmless pleasure of the theatre and Christmas without interference from an overbearing state. Cromwell's designated successor, his son Richard, proved far from a chip off the old block – being unable to unite the warring generals who held the real power.

Eventually one general, George Monck, emerged as literally the king-maker: the man who was instrumental in restoring Charles II. In his own changes of allegiance – Royalist, reluctant Roundhead, loyal Cromwellian, and back full circle to Royalism again – Monck epitomises the journey made by so many of his fellow Tower prisoners in the two troubled decades between 1640 and 1660. Born in 1608 to an impoverished West Country gentry family, Monck sought a military career. Europe, with the Thirty Years' War raging, offered plentiful opportunities to acquire practical military experience and Monck seized them with both hands.

As a mercenary soldier, Monck served in Spain, France and the Netherlands. When the Civil War broke out, he sided with the king, but was captured by an old soldiering friend, Thomas Fairfax, at Nantwich in 1644. At first Fairfax kept his captive in comfortable accommodation in Hull, hoping to persuade him to offer his talents to Parliament. But Monck stubbornly stayed loyal to the king, so sterner persuasion was decided upon: Monck was taken to the Tower, and told he would stay there unless or until he changed his allegiance.

Monck was confined in St Thomas's Tower. Apart from the rising damp from the river below, his chief problem was lack of cash. Prisoners were expected to pay for their accommodation – including extra food to augment the Tower's inadequate basic diet, laundry, writing materials and the necessary bribes to their warders. Although his elder brother Thomas sent him £50, the money was soon gone, and Monck was compelled to beg for more. Across the chasm of war, the king, from Oxford, despite his own desperate cash shortage, sent Monck a generous gift of £100 in gold coins. Perhaps Charles was remembering the way he had let down another loyal servant, Strafford, in his hour of need in the Tower. Or maybe the money was a reminder of where Monck's true loyalties should lie.

Monck remained in the Tower for two and a half years, steadfastly refusing his captors' threats and blandishments, and remaining true to his Royalist cause. To while away the weary hours, Monck wrote a textbook, *Observations upon Military and Political Affairs*. Though unpublished in his lifetime, the book remained an influential text for centuries. Monck had a modern military mind, emphasising the importance of good intelligence and a sound supply system. 'Intelligence is the most powerful means to undertake brave Designs and to avoid great ruines.' A good general should not be 'so prodigal of his Soldiers' blood as though men were made only to fill ditches and to be the woeful executioners of his rashness'. Such sensible compassion was new in warfare and marks Monck out as the very model of a modern major-general (a rank he had not yet in fact obtained).

Life in the Tower was not all endless frustration for George Monck, however. According to the garrulous antiquary John Aubrey, Monck found, if not true love, then a lifelong loyal partner in the fortress. His laundry, darning and sewing were attended to by a seamstress called Anne – or 'Nan' – Clarges, the twenty-five-year-old daughter of a blacksmith who lived and worked on the corner of London's Drury Lane and the Strand. Her father, John Clarges, had shod the horses of Monck's regiment. Nan had had a rough, tough city upbringing. Local women had once ganged up on her and shaved her pudenda for spreading reports that one of their husbands had been 'clappt' (afflicted with a venereal pox), and her tongue would get her into trouble later in life too.

Though reportedly unfamiliar with soap and water herself, Nan had somehow obtained the contract to supply clean linen to the Tower's more privileged prisoners. Aubrey says that, despite being married to an elderly man named Ratford, with whom she ran a glove and perfume shop in the city, the seamstress 'was kind to [Monck] in a double capacity' and became his mistress. Eventually, after her husband's death, Nan became pregnant by Monck. The news was broken to him by her brother, Thomas Clarges, on board ship after Monck had become an admiral in the first Anglo-Dutch naval war. On being told by Clarges that his sister had been 'brought to bed', Monck asked in alarm, 'Of what?' 'Of a son,' Clarges replied. 'Why, then,' responded Monck, 'she is my wife' – and married her.

The forceful Nan established such an ascendancy over her husband that the man who was said to be fearless on the battlefield was terrified of her cutting tongue. An ardent Royalist, she influenced the decisive part he played in bringing about the Restoration. Nan could never shake off her humble origins, however, and even after Charles II had made her husband

Duke of Albemarle in gratitude for restoring him to the throne, his home-spun duchess often embarrassed Monck with her plebeian language and rough-hewn ways. Her brother Tom rose on her petticoats, becoming a knight, a diplomat and a man of property after the Restoration; London's fashionable Clarges Street is named after him.

Meanwhile, as Monck expounded military theory inside the Tower, outside its walls the real war, without his participation, was going from bad to worse for the king's cause. After the king's decisive defeat at Naseby in June 1645, Monck reluctantly concluded that Charles's cause was irretriev-ably lost. It was time to make his peace with the victorious Parliamentarians. His chance came in April 1646 when Parliament agreed that captured Royalists could be released if they swore not to take up arms against Parliament again. Monck indicated that he was ready to take such an oath – although it seems that he never actually did so. In July he was freed to take a command in the English army battling the seemingly endless Catholic rebellion in Ireland. In doing so he demonstrated the sly political skills he would increasingly show. By fighting in Ireland he would be combating the king's enemies without directly helping the Roundhead 'rebels'.

Desperate to prove himself worthy to be the ideal commander whose qualities he had outlined in his *Observations*, Monck extricated himself from Ireland, like the Earl of Essex before him, by making an unauthorised peace treaty with the rebels. In 1650 he joined Cromwell in Scotland, and was Cromwell's chief lieutenant in his great victory over the Scots at Dunbar. The following year, Cromwell trusted the old Royalist enough to hand over command of Scotland to Monck, now a major-general. Monck completed the Cromwellian conquest of Scotland and remained there as governor. When Cromwell died, Monck put into practice his long-cherished plan of bringing back the Stuarts. Cautiously he moved his army south, peacefully disposing of the oppositon as he did so. Public opinion in the country, tired of the stifling Cromwellian dictatorship, hankered for a return of Royalist rule, and Monck had little difficulty in engineering the Restoration – sending diehard republicans like Lambert to languish in the Tower where he himself had once rotted.

CHAPTER SIXTEEN

IRON DUKES AND LUNATIC LORDS

George Monck's skilful managing of the return of the king reaped him rich rewards after Charles II returned in triumph to London on his thirtieth birthday in May 1660. The second son of a Devonshire squire ended as the Duke of Albemarle, Earl of Torrington, Baron Beauchamp and a Knight of the Garter. As well as his titles, Monck was given substantial lands by his grateful monarch, including (though he never visited them) the colonies of North and South Carolina in the ever-expanding Americas. But the general acclaim and relief which greeted the Restoration masked underlying tensions which had not gone away. The conflicts – Anglicanism versus Calvinist dissent and Roman Catholicism; the struggle between Royalist absolutism and awakening Parliamentary democracy; the competition between a landed aristocracy and gentry and a rising urban mercantile class – had not been solved by the Civil War and would continue to seed division for centuries to come.

A youthful victim of the continuing religious ferment thrown up by the Civil War was young William Penn, later the founder of Pennsylvania. Born in 1644, close to the Tower, to a wealthy city family in the midst of the first Civil War, Penn converted to Quakerism – one of the myriad sects thrown up from the maelstrom of English Protestantism, and considerably more militant than its modern descendant. The early Quakers, with their insistence on social equality and their disdain for priests and kings, were seen as a threat to order, and after writing an unlicensed pamphlet denouncing the established Anglican religion in 1668, young Penn was thrown into the Tower for blasphemy, where bishops and theologians visited the stubborn young firebrand in an effort to convince him of the error of his ways. They failed. 'The Tower is to me the worst argument in the world,' Penn told his interlocutors. 'My prison will be my grave before I will budge a jot.' Unknown to his principled son, Penn's father bought him out with a substantial bribe and he went to America to successfully seek better fortune.

The hopes of Protestant England were increasingly focused on the handsome figure of a very different James from the Catholic Duke of York. James Scott, Duke of Monmouth, was acknowledged by Charles II as the eldest of his bastard sons – although there is considerable doubt as to whether Charles was Monmouth's real father. Doubt also surrounds the status of Monmouth's mother, a Welshwoman named Lucy Walters, as notoriously promiscuous as Charles himself (she was dead of syphilis before she was thirty). The rumours that she married Charles in a secret ceremony in The Hague may well be true. Even if Monmouth privately did not believe the reports that his parents were lawfully wed, he certainly encouraged them.

Ambitious, and malleable to the machinations of more ruthless men, Monmouth was encouraged by the Protestant opposition to bid for the Crown – to the point where he became involved in the Rye House Plot to do away with his father and the uncle who stood in his way. After the plot's failure, Monmouth fled back to the Netherlands – and when Charles died in February 1685 and was succeeded by James, Monmouth claimed that his uncle had poisoned the king. In exile, he attracted a following of Protestant malcontents and assembled a trio of ships, landing at Lyme Regis in Dorset in June with a small group of eighty-two rebels to stake his claim to the throne.

Some 6,000 of the West Country's sturdy Protestant peasantry joined Monmouth's motley army, which defeated the local county militia in a couple of skirmishes as he moved inland into Somerset. Ominously, however, the aristocracy held aloof, and after the failure of a parallel Protestant revolt in Scotland, Monmouth retired into the Somerset Levels – a boggy marshland criss-crossed by deep drainage ditches known as 'Rhines'. Ominously, too, one of the greatest soldiers in history was now hot on his tail.

John Churchill, the future Duke of Marlborough, was an exact contemporary of Monmouth. From a family of West Country Cavaliers who had lost their fortune in the Civil Wars, Churchill, like Monmouth, had drawn King Charles's indulgent eye. As a poor young courtier, Churchill had shared with the king the favours of his most insatiable mistress, Barbara Villiers, Duchess of Cleveland. Charles had even caught the impoverished young blade naked in Barbara's bedchamber, but said he forgave him, 'for he only did it for his bread'. Churchill's soldiering ability had brought him the field command of the professional royal army now closing on Monmouth's ill-trained ploughboys, and though the nominal command was in the hands of a French-born veteran, Lord Feversham, the organising brain was Churchill's.

The royal army caught up with the duke outside Bridgewater on 2 July 1685. In the brief pitched battle that followed on Sedgemoor – the first of John Churchill's many victories – Monmouth's army was shattered. As his men fell or fled, the duke took horse and with his friend Lord Grey de Warke (as we have seen, a notable escaper from the Tower) made for the south coast. Separated from his friends and starving, Monmouth was caught a couple of days later sleeping in a ditch under an ash tree on the edge of the New Forest, his pockets filled with raw peas foraged from the field where he was hiding. Taken to a house in nearby Ringwood, the duke wrote the first of many abject pleas for mercy to his uncle King James.

Desperate to save his skin, Monmouth sought a personal interview with the uncle whom he had accused of murdering his father. He offered to betray his confederates, and swore that he would be the king's loyal subject in future. He wasted his breath. The cold-hearted James was set on destroying his nephew – and since he had been attainted for his treason, could do so legally without the tiresome formality of a trial. Hoping to gather information about Monmouth's fellow plotters, he granted Monmouth's request for a personal interview, but used it only to gloat at his nephew's humiliation.

Taken to see James in Whitehall Palace as soon as he arrived in London, his arms bound tightly behind his back with a silken cord, Monmouth lost what little dignity he retained. Throwing himself on the floor, he wept and begged for mercy – in vain. James wrote icily to his son-in-law William of Orange, ruler of the Netherlands, where Monmouth had sought refuge:

> The Duke of Monmouth seemed more concerned and desirous to live, and did not behave himself as well as I expected, nor as one ought to have expected from one who had taken upon him to be King. I have signed the warrant for his execution tomorrow.

Not for nothing did John Churchill compare James's heart to a marble mantelpiece. But little did the cold-hearted king think that William, the man to whom his sneering report was addressed, would, in three years, succeed where Monmouth had failed – and take James's throne after another invasion of the West Country launched from the Netherlands.

Monmouth was taken straight from the king to the Tower. His stay was brief. Within forty hours of him being rowed under Traitor's Gate on the evening of 13 July, he was dead. Poignantly, awaiting him were his wife and children, who had been rounded up as a precaution by the king when Monmouth had landed in England. The Monmouths' marriage had been a loveless match arranged in childhood by their parents. Nevertheless, he and his wife Anna produced seven children, of whom three survivors – James, eleven; Henry, eight; and Anne, five – received their father in the Tower. The couple had not met since Monmouth's flight into exile in 1683, and the duke's heart now belonged firmly to his mistress, Lady Henrietta Wentworth.

Anna reproached him for his passionate liaision with Henrietta, and for his recent rebellion. Monmouth dutifully expressed his contrition for the latter, but not for his love for Lady Wentworth. The painful interview with his family over, he appealed to a cousin of his wife, Colonel Scott, commander of the Tower's guard. Still hoping to save his life, the duke asked Scott to carry a secret letter to the king. Scott claimed that he had orders from James to remain with Monmouth until his execution, but suggested one of his captains as a substitute postman. This officer carried out his mission, but was intercepted by Robert Spencer, Earl of Sunderland, the king's Secretary of State.

Sunderland was a slippery trimmer who had first supported excluding James from the succession, before converting to Catholicism and becoming a fervent advocate of royal absolutism. He was, however, strongly suspected of having kept in touch with Monmouth in case his rebellion succeeded. Monmouth's letter may well have concerned this delicate subject. At all events, Sunderland confiscated it from Scott's captain, promising to give it to the king. Needless to say, it was never seen again and Monmouth's last slim hope of saving his life vanished with it. Sunderland, true to his turncoat form, secretly supported William of Orange's 'Glorious Revolution', deserting James and reconverting to Protestantism when he judged it safe to do so. He served William as ably as he had done his predecessor.

On St Swithin's Day, 15 July – the date on which a soothsayer had told him he would either die or go on to great things – Monmouth met a bevy of clerics in his cell. They implored him to renounce his impious love for Lady Wentworth, but Monmouth, recovering some shreds of spirit now that he had but two hours to live, firmly refused. In a last statement he affirmed that his father had told him that he had never married his mother – but declined to say whether he believed that to be the truth. He also declared that he died a 'martyr for the people' and a true son of the

Protestant faith, while expressing sorrow for 'the blood that was shed on his account'.

Monmouth dressed carefully for his final appearance in clean shirt and stockings, a sober grey suit lined with black, and a long black periwig. In an emotional and tearful farewell with his wife, he begged Anna's forgiveness for his infidelities and failings as a husband. He told his children, who clung weeping to him, to obey their mother – and the king. At 10 a.m. the doomed duke climbed into a coach for the short journey up Tower Hill. He was accompanied by Thomas Ken, the Bishop of Bath and Wells – ironically the churches whose stained-glass images and 'Popish' decor Monmouth's icono-clastic troops had trashed during their progress through the West Country. Ken, author of some of England's best-loved hymns, including 'All People That On Earth Do Dwell', struggled vainly to persuade the duke to repent of his 'sin' in rebelling. But Monmouth's mind was now on other things.

The black-draped scaffold was surrounded by a double row of armed guards. The king knew how popular the handsome 'Protestant Duke' was and was taking no chances. Monmouth climbed the steps nonchalantly, smiling and waving to the crowd, like an actor putting on a final command perform-ance. Catching his first sight of the executioner, a ruffian called Jack Ketch, Monmouth blanched. This was the man who had botched the beheading of his friend and fellow Rye House plotter Lord William Russell, taking three strokes to sever his head. 'Do your work well,' Monmouth told Ketch grimly, 'and do not use me as I hear you hacked my poor Lord Russell.'

A huge crowd, said by some to equal or exceed that which had watched Strafford die, had assembled to greet their hero. The prelates continued to pester him to make public penance for his rebellion, but Monmouth only responded that he was sorry for all his sins. His mind was still with his lover, declaring that what had passed between him and Lady Wentworth was innocent in the sight of God. He refused to make any further speeches and began to prepare for the ordeal ahead, removing his coat and ruff. He tipped Ketch with a generous six guineas, begging him to strike true; and doubt-fully felt the edge of the axe, wondering aloud if it was sharp enough.

Either it was blunt or Ketch, unnerved by the murmuring crowd and his own sympathy for Monmouth, again bungled the job. Refusing a blindfold, Monmouth knelt at the block having removed his wig and waistcoat. Ketch, visibly shaking, raised the heavy axe as the priests chanted around him. The first blow merely gashed the duke's neck, at which he raised his head and looked reproachfully at his killer. Ketch's second blow made a deeper gash – but still Monmouth's head remained attached to his shoulders, a movement of the legs the only sign of the agony he was enduring. As the crowd began to roar their disapproval, Ketch lost it. He flung the bloodied axe aside, crying, 'God damn me, I can do no more, my heart fails me. I cannot do it.' Mr Gostlin, the Sheriff of London, sternly ordered the headsman to pick up the axe, get a grip, and finish his bloody work. Three more blows were needed to kill Monmouth, but his head still dangled, obstinately adhering by a piece of skin, which Ketch was obliged to cut with a butcher's knife hanging at his belt. Never had an execution been more mangled, and Ketch was lucky to escape the scene with his life, such was the anger of the enraged crowd.

Monmouth's head, handsome and calm in death, despite his agonisingly protracted end, was placed alongside his body in a coffin and trundled back to the Tower; there to be sewn back on his neck and painted by the court artist Godfrey Kneller. After this macabre posthumous 'sitting' the much abused body of the duke was finally laid to rest beneath the flag-stones of St Peter ad Vincula.

Agonising as it was, Monmouth's end was more enviable than that of hundreds of his humbler followers, who were executed or transported as slaves to the colonies for their roles in his rebellion. King James appointed the merciless Lord Chief Justice, George Jeffreys, to conduct a purge through the West Country that became known as the 'Bloody Assize'. Jeffreys was a sadistic brute who took delight in his victims' sufferings. His apologists have pointed to the painful kidney disease that eventually killed him in the Tower as an excuse for the judge's obscene behaviour, but he was a vindictive bully by nature.

Jeffreys and his subordinate judges moved through the West Country towns like an avenging whirlwind, trying and sentencing those involved in Monmouth's rising with brutal dispatch. Wherever they went – Winchester, Salisbury, Dorchester, Exeter, Taunton and Wells – they left a trail of hanged and eviscerated bodies and unlucky wretches shuffling in chains towards a grim future as slaves in the New World. Jeffreys delighted in browbeating his victims from the bench, and even watched executions while enjoying his dinner. He sentenced some 333 souls to death – including the aged Lady Alice Lisle, who was condemned to be burned alive for merely harbouring two rebels overnight. Her sentence was commuted to beheading. Executioner Jack Ketch was able to wield his butcher's knife again as he carried out the full gruesome rite on the bodies of convicted traitors. At the end of the Bloody Assize, a grateful King James rewarded Jeffreys by making him Lord Chancellor.

The brutal repression that followed Monmouth's rising fatally increased James's unpopularity. And when in June 1688 the king's equally fervently Catholic Italian second wife, Mary of Modena, gave birth to a male heir, Prince James Edward, the growing opposition acted. The king already had two adult daughters by his first marriage: Mary, wife of William of Orange, the *stadtholder* or ruler of the Netherlands; and Anne, who was married to Prince George of Denmark but lived in London. Both women were fervent Protestants who deeply disapproved of their father's Catholicism. The birth of their infant half-brother persuaded them, and the powerful Whig lords, that James had to go. If he stayed, the prospect of a Catholic heir completing England's reconversion to Rome was inevitable – and intolerable. James brought his house tumbling down in the same month when he issued a so-called 'Declaration of Indulgence', removing the remaining discrimination against Catholics and Dissenters, and ordered it to be read from the pulpits of all Anglican churches. Seven Anglican bishops – headed by the Archbishop of Canterbury and including Thomas Ken – refused the order, and were sent to the Tower for their temerity.

For once, the whole range of Protestant opinion united behind the Anglican clerics. London was thick with crowds demonstrating their support, so they had to be brought to the Tower by boat to forestall a rescue attempt. Arriving at the Tower's wharf, people rushed forwards to touch the hems of their vestments, and the guards who admitted them to the fortress drank toasts to their health. Only the Tower's lieutenant, Sir Edward Hales, who had cynically followed the king's conversion to Catholicism to aid his career, treated the clerics – according to diarist John Evelyn, who visited them in the Tower – 'very surlily'. Even the Tower's chaplain, ordered to read the Declaration of Indulgence from his pulpit, refused – and was dismissed.

After a week, the bishops were brought to trial at Westminster Hall. They were triumphantly acquitted by a London jury and freed. The verdict, to the king's fury, was celebrated across the city with bonfires and triumphant Protestant parades. That night, another magnificent seven – a group of the kingdom's leading peers – wrote to William of Orange inviting him and his wife Mary, James's daughter, to cross from Holland to take the throne. William did not need to be asked twice. A cold, calculating man, he was actuated not so much by his Protestantism – still less by love of his wife and her English homeland – but by his Dutch patriotism. As in the time of Philip II of Spain, Dutch Protestantism was under siege from a militantly Catholic and expansionist power, Louis XIV's France. If England, with her large navy and newly professional army, could be brought into the war against France, the Netherlands would be saved. Despite the three naval wars they had fought under Cromwell and Charles II, England and Holland were natural allies: both maritime Protestant trading nations with a healthy tradition of religious toleration and dissent, and a common interest in opposing French domination of Europe.

On 5 November 1688 – the anniversary of the Catholic Gunpowder Plot – blown by a 'Protestant wind', William landed at Torbay in Devon. Unlike that of Monmouth and his motley band of malcontents, this was a professionally planned invasion – the first successful one since another William's 1066 conquest. Instead of Monmouth's pathetic three boats, William had a Dutch fleet of sixty ships and an international army of 15,000 soldiers hardened by years of fighting the French. Crucially, he also carried a printing press to turn out Protestant propaganda to an increasingly literate people. James, menaced by desertions even within his own family (his daughters joined the Williamite camp), moved sluggishly to Salisbury with a royal army, which, though it numbered 25,000, was of doubtful loyalty. While the king was prostrated by a severe nosebleed, his cause was irretrievably lost.

After an inconclusive council of war, John Churchill led a group of officers across the winter countryside to join William's army. He left behind a letter to the king justifying his desertion on the grounds that his conscience and religion came before obedience to the sovereign who had promoted him. A week later, Churchill was back in Salisbury with William's triumphant army and James had fled. As his regime collapsed, James made his way to Dover – only to be arrested and returned to London. Magnanimous in victory, William allowed him to escape again, this time successfully. James went to the court of his co-religionist Louis XIV in France and exile, where – apart from an unsuccessful attempt to recover his throne from Ireland – he remained for the rest of his life.

In London, Judge George Jeffreys was left marooned by his master's flight. Well aware of how deeply he was hated, Jeffreys knew that he could expect little mercy if he was caught. Trimming his bushy eyebrows, he disguised himself as a sailor, boarding a coal barge anchored in the Thames. However, the alcoholic judge could not resist slipping ashore for a last drink before sailing. Jeffreys adjourned to the Red Cow tavern in Wapping. Here, he was recognised by a former victim and a hostile crowd gathered. Fortunately for Jeffreys, he was taken into the custody of the London Trained Bands militia who took him, at his own request, terrified but unharmed – to the Tower. So desperate was Jeffreys to get into the safest fortress in London that he even offered to sign his own warrant of committal to the prison.

Although he was saved from the fury of the mob, the Tower did not provide a complete sanctuary from the people's vengeance. Jeffreys' visitors included several of those who had appeared in the dock before him. They roundly abused the fallen judge through the bars of his cell door, throwing rotten food and spitting at him as Jeffreys cowered in a corner. When a barrel of oysters arrived from an anonymous well-wisher, Jeffreys greedily seized on it as manna from heaven, proving that he still had friends. Alas! The gift was a cruel jest: when opened, all the oyster shells were empty and curled at the bottom of the barrel was a noose tied with a hangman's knot.

Allowed a plentiful supply of brandy, Jeffreys drank himself into a stupor, mawkishly telling anyone who would listen that in conducting the Bloody Assize, he had only been carrying out the king's orders. After four months in the Tower, Jeffreys, aged only forty-one, died of kidney disease aggravated by alcoholism. No one came forward to claim his hated body, so by a supreme irony, he was buried next to Monmouth's grave in St Peter ad Vincula. The venal Tower constable Sir Edward Hales, it is pleasant to record, also failed to escape into exile. He tried to sail for France disguised as King James's servant, but, like Jeffreys, was recognised, arrested and sent to the Tower – this time as a prisoner.

At first John Churchill did not profit from switching his allegiance. Sidelined under James for his stubborn Protestantism, he found himself cold-shouldered by William who did not trust a deserter and promoted his own Dutch lieutenants. The new King William III's distrust was well merited. Despite his desertion of James, Churchill was careful to keep lines open to the Jacobites. The Jacobites were dominant in Catholic Ireland and strong in Scotland and the north, too. The Tory party, having dominated government in the reigns of Charles II and James II, found themselves out in the cold, displaced by their Whig rivals who had summoned William. The Tories, too, looked longingly to 'the king over the water'. Once again the familiar divisions of the Wars of the Roses and the Civil Wars yawned open: the impoverished Catholic north and west stuck loyally to the old ways; the progressive, prosperous Protestant south and east welcomed the Williamite Revolution, and supported the coronation of William and Mary as the new joint monarchs.

The Tower filled with those who stayed loyal to the old regime. For the next half-century most of the fortress's political prisoners were Jacobites. Among the first were a trio of peers: Lord Preston, Lord Dartmouth and Henry Hyde, Earl of Clarendon. Preston, though a Protestant, was loyal to James and accepted money from Louis XIV to stir up Jacobite revolution in his native north. Jailed in the Tower, he was freed – only to be caught red-handed crossing the Channel with papers revealing the existence of a 20,000-strong French army at Cherbourg poised to invade. Condemned to death, Preston saved his skin by betraying his fellow conspirators, including Clarendon and Dartmouth.

Clarendon's loyalty to James was easily explained: as the brother of James's first wife, Anne Hyde, he was the exiled king's brother-in-law (although also the uncle of the new Queen Mary II, and her sister Princess Anne). Despite this relationship Queen Mary felt obliged to send her Jacobite uncle to the Tower after Preston's revelation of his treachery. The indulgent queen allowed Clarendon's wife to lodge with him, and he was visited by that assiduous Tower tourist John Evelyn. Finally, after many months he was freed, on condition that he remained on his country estates and conspired no more. Lord Dartmouth was less lucky. He was already familiar with the Tower when he arrived there as a prisoner, for he had been the fortress's constable under James. Dartmouth died of a stroke soon after arriving at his old home.

In May 1692, the Jacobites in the Tower were joined by John Churchill, now Lord Marlborough, the title of his eventual dukedom. Churchill landed in the Tower as the victim of a malicious forger. Robert Young, a skilled imitator of handwriting, had forged a letter demanding James's restoration signed by several high-ranking peers, along with the ex-Archbishop of Canterbury, William Sanford, who – despite having been sent to the Tower by James – had stayed steadfast and been dismissed for refusing to crown William and Mary at Westminster; and Bishop Sprat of Rochester. The final signature forged by Young had been that of John

Churchill, whose writing characteristically lacked dots (allegedly so the mean soldier could save on ink). Young's facsimile was so convincing that when shown the letter Churchill had failed to recognise it as a fake. Young persuaded a fellow crook named Blackhead to secrete his forgery among Bishop Sprat's papers. Failing to do this, Blackhead had merely left the incriminating document in a flowerpot in the bishop's house where it had been found by the authorities who had been tipped off by Young. An alarmed council took no chances. Despite the letter's dubious provenance, Churchill was arrested on the strength of it and taken to the Tower.

Churchill's main supporter was his feisty wife Sarah, a domineering beauty who had established an ascendancy over Princess Anne, the heiress to the throne. Anne, a dumpy, short-sighted woman depressed by her failure to produce a healthy heir despite multiple births and pregnancies, confided her woes to Sarah whom she called 'Mrs Freeman', while Sarah dubbed Anne 'Mrs Morley'. The tone of the relationship can be detected in Anne's girlish letters to her friend:

> I hear Lord Marlborough is sent to the Tower; and although I am certain they have nothing against him yet I was struck when I was told it, for methinks it is a dismal thing to be sent to that place . . . But let them do what they please, nothing shall ever vex me so I can have the satisfaction of seeing dear Mrs Freeman and I swear I would live on bread and water, between four walls, without repining. For as long as you continue kind, nothing can ever be a real mortification to your faithful Mrs Morley.

Sarah visited her husband daily in the Tower to keep his spirits up. After he had spent more than a month there, the council examined Young and Blackhead. The atmosphere of panic in which Marlborough had been arrested had abated after the French invasion fleet had been routed, and the council was prepared to look more critically at the rogues who had sought the great soldier's downfall. Blackhead collapsed under forceful questioning and admitted that Young had given him the document. On hearing that the accusation had broken down, Marlborough applied for a writ of Habeas Corpus and was released on bail. His return to Sarah was darkened, however, by the death of their two-year-old younger son, Charlie, who had passed away while his father had been in the Tower. Young was convicted of perjury and jailed. But after he escaped from the King's Bench prison his crimes caught up with him and he was hanged at Tyburn in 1698 for forging coins.

* * *

It was not the Churchill family's last brush with the fortress. Marlborough's brother George, who would head the Royal Navy while John was winning his famous victories over France on land, was also imprisoned in the Tower for taking bribes; while yet another brother, Charles, a soldier like John, became lieutenant of the Tower after Marlborough's great victory at Blenheim. That battle, and those that followed it – Ramillies, Oudenarde and Malplaquet – established Marlborough as the greatest general of his age, and put Britain (England and Scotland formally united in 1704) firmly on Europe's map as a superpower in the making. Small wonder that Sir Winston Churchill revered the ancestor who made his family's fortune.

The religious conflicts which had dominated the sixteenth and seventeenth centuries slowly gave way before the dawning Enlightenment to political and economic power struggles between nation states. One notable Tower prisoner who exemplified the new pragmatic age was Britain's first recognised prime minister, the Norfolk squire Sir Robert Walpole. Although Marlborough was a man of war and Walpole one of peace – seeing war as a waste of both men and money – the two men had other things in common. Both were Whigs. Both, too, in keeping with the acquisitive spirit of the age, were unprincipled and spectacularly corrupt, Walpole famously opining that 'every man has his price'. Walpole's peace policy kept England out of European wars for the long years of his premiership and his habit of taking bribes allowed him to build a fabulous stately home in his native Norfolk. It also brought him to the Tower.

Ironically for a peace-loving man, Walpole was serving as Secretary for War in 1712 when he was accused of corruption and embezzling government funds. His political enemies had him committed to the Tower. But Walpole continued to hold court from there, distributing his ill-gotten largesse in wining and dining visitors who could be influential in getting him out. The wily Walpole also forked out for tear-jerking propaganda – one pamphlet called him *The Jewel in the Tower* – portraying himself as a wronged innocent. Expelled from the house, his loyal Norfolk constituents returned him unopposed at the subsequent by-election. Even so, Walpole was kept in the Tower for six dreary months, during which time he wrote a history of Parliament, an institution he managed and manipulated more successfully than any politician since John Pym. On his release, he resumed his upwardly mobile political career as if nothing had happened.

*   *   *

The year after Queen Anne was succeeded by the German-speaking Hanoverian George I, the Jacobites launched the 1715 rising in favour of James II's son, James Edward, 'the Old Pretender', which led to the dramatic escape from the Tower of Lord Nithsdale. In 1745 came the much more serious rebellion of the Scottish clans in support of James Edward's son, Charles Edward, aka 'Bonnie Prince Charlie' or 'the Young Pretender'. The prince's Highland army took Edinburgh, marched south and reached Derby before a lack of English support caused it to turn tail for Scotland, where the Jacobites were crushed by the Hanoverians at Culloden in April 1746 – the last pitched battle on British soil.

After the rising's failure, as after the failure of the 1715 revolt, another clutch of Scottish Jacobite peers arrived at the Tower. One was the elderly Simon, Lord Lovat, chief of the Fraser clan, who, after a life devoted to selfish personal pleasure and domestic abuse (he had raped an aunt after his uncle's death before forcing her to marry him to acquire her husband's estate), had unwisely, aged over eighty, committed himself to Bonnie Prince Charlie's doomed cause. Found hiding in a hollow tree on an island after Culloden, the wicked but irrepressible old scoundrel attempted to shift the blame for his treason on to his son. He continued this heartless farce even after arriving at the Tower, telling the lieutenant, 'We can hang my eldest son and then my second son will be my heir and can marry your niece.'

Lovat's chutzpah is evident in the report of his trial by Robert Walpole's gossipy son Horace. Lovat told the lords that he would have broken out of the Tower if he were a younger man. Told that much younger men had been successfully held there he replied, 'Yes – but they were inexperienced. They had not broke out of as many gaols as I have.' (Lovat had indeed escaped from prison while in French exile.) On his way to his trial a woman thrust her head into Lovat's coach and taunted him with the words, 'You ugly old dog, don't you think you will have that frightful head cut off?' Lovat (whose admittedly unhandsome features were brilliantly etched by William Hogarth as he awaited trial) responded unabashed, 'You ugly old bitch, I believe I shall.'

He was right. Lovat was sentenced to be beheaded on Tower Hill. On 9 April 1747, a year after Culloden, the old man was taken by coach the short distance from the Tower and had to be helped up the steps of the scaffold. He did not die alone. A vast crowd had assembled to see his departure, and one of the crowded stands erected to give spectators a better view collapsed under their weight. Twenty people died. When told of the disaster, Lovat replied with characteristic callousness, 'The more who go, the better the sport.' Urged to hurry as he laboriously prepared to die, the old man grumbled, 'God save us! Why should there be such a bustle about taking off an old grey head, that needs cannot go up three steps without three bodies to support it?' Lovat was the last person to be beheaded on the hill where so many had died before him.

Lovat's three prime characteristics – murderous psychopathology, aristocratic eccentricity and physical ugliness – came together in a trio of famous Tower prisoners of the eighteenth century. The first, Laurence Shirley, 4th Earl Ferrers, was a sadistic rake whose violence and drunken womanising (he had a mistress, Mrs Clifford, and a parallel family of four children) did not delight his pretty young wife, who separated from him in 1758 after enduring six years of abuse. His excesses put his extensive Midlands estates in danger, and trustees were appointed to manage them. Ferrers resented any curb on his activities, and in January 1760 after summoning one of the trustees – an elderly steward named John Johnson – to an interview, he shot the old man dead.

Ferrers was detained in the Middle Tower while he was tried for murder before his fellow peers in the House of Lords. He entered a plea of insanity, but conducted his own defence so ably that he was found guilty and sentenced to be hanged. He was visited in the Tower by his aged aunt, Selina Hastings, Countess of Huntingdon, a patron of the early Methodist movement. But her earnest evangelising had no effect on the earl, whose only wish was for his mistress to come on a conjugal visit. The countess vetoed this as she would not let Ferrers 'die in adultery'.

The murderous earl was determined to make a fine exit. He spent his last night hearing one of his four warders read *Hamlet* and then, having paid all his bills as though the Tower were merely a tavern where he had been staying, he left on his final journey. Dressed in his wedding finery – a silver-edged coat, silk breeches, and white stockings with silver knee buckles – he departed for the gallows at Tyburn. The earl headed a parade more fit for a fair than an execution. Ferrers rode to his death in a fine carriage drawn by six horses, followed by his own hearse. Behind came his family and retainers attended by liveried servants and foot soldiers. Proceeding at a funereal pace through thronged streets, the macabre procession took almost three hours to reach the place of execution. Refused a final drink, Ferrers had to be content with puffing a pipe of tobacco. Lavish to the last, he gave the hangman a five-guinea tip. As a peer, Ferrers enjoyed the dubious privilege of being hanged with a silken cord rather than a rough hempen rope. He was the last lord to be hanged in Britain.

Three years after Ferrers went to his doom with such panache, a very different man became the hero of the London crowd – and such a danger to the established order that he was sent to the Tower. The radical MP John Wilkes, though spectacularly ugly, with cross eyes, snaggle teeth and a massive jaw, was a successful ladies' man who boasted that he could talk away his looks within minutes. A reprobate who cavorted with prostitutes dressed as nuns in the caves of the notorious Hellfire Club, Wilkes was nonetheless, as his slogan proclaimed, 'a Friend to Liberty'. He challenged the authority of king and aristocracy with a boldness not seen since the Levellers. When a typically outspoken assault on the royal government of King George III appeared in Wilkes's newspaper *The North Briton*, he and fifty of his followers were arrested. With typical defiance, Wilkes contested the legality of the warrant committing him to the Tower, cheekily suggesting that it should be re-addressed to his next-door neighbour: the Lord Chancellor and King George's favourite, Lord Bute. Rejecting this idea, the arresting officers dragged Wilkes away. But he was out of the Tower within a week to continue his rumbustious career – which culminated in him being elected Lord Mayor of London.

The third Tower prisoner to embody the half-crazed spirit of Lord Lovat was another Scots aristocrat, Lord George Gordon. Although the religious conflicts that had convulsed the realm for two centuries had diminished, anti-Catholicism was still a powerful force in the late eighteenth century, and Gordon, the president of the Protestant Association, led the charge against attempts to repeal discriminatory laws against Catholics. In June 1780, after Gordon presented a huge petition to Parliament objecting to any relaxation of anti-Papist laws, mob fury spilled into London's streets, giving the city its most horrific taste of mass violence since the Peasants' Revolt exactly four centuries before. Newgate and other jails were burned down by the rampaging crowds, releasing hundreds of criminals into the teeming streets; the Bank of England and the Royal Exchange were attacked; the house of the Lord Chief Justice, Lord Mansfield, was torched, and scores of rioters drowned in alcohol when the vats in a distillery they were looting burst. The rioters were only narrowly prevented from freeing the lions in the Tower menagerie to roam the streets and join the mayhem when the fortress's drawbridge was raised against them.

Thoroughly alarmed, the authorities called out the army – including the Tower's garrison – to restore order. Between 300 and 850 rioters were shot or executed, and Gordon was unceremoniously carted off to the Tower. Horace Walpole commented approvingly, 'The monster that conjured up this tempest is now manacled in the Tower.' Although charged with treason and kept a close prisoner without access to writing materials, there was no evidence that Gordon had directly incited the riots that bore his name. When the conditions of his confinement were relaxed, one of his visitors was the founder of Methodism, John Wesley, who recorded:

> I spent an hour with him at his apartment in the Tower. Our conversation turned upon Popery and religion. He seemed to be well acquainted with the Bible and had abundance of other books, enough to furnish a study.

Gordon was acquitted and freed after eight months in the Tower. He eventually abandoned the Protestant faith and converted to Judaism.

A distinguished American who came as a captive to the Tower at the same time as Gordon was held there was South Carolina's Henry Laurens, president of the Continental Congress that drew up the Declaration of Independence. Laurens was intercepted at sea by the Royal Navy en route to Holland to rally support for the United States in Europe's first fellow republic. On arrival at the fortress he was greeted by the Yeoman Warders with a rousing chorus of 'Yankee Doodle'. Laurens was detained in the Tower for a year, complaining constantly that his quarters were cramped and that he was inconvenienced by being continually guarded by soldiers with fixed bayonets. He strongly objected, too, to the Tower's practice of charging for its board and lodging, and refused outright to pay. He was sustained, however, by the support of many British sympathisers with America's cause who brought him food and other creature comforts in such quantities that he was able to distribute them to his guards. Ironically one of his visitors was his son who, despite the war, was being educated in England. In 1782 Laurens was exchanged for Lord Cornwallis, the British general whose surrender at Yorktown effectively ended the War of Independence. After his return to the US, Laurens was nicknamed 'Tower' Laurens.

* * *

The Gordon Riots were seen by many as a fearful precursor to the French Revolution, which broke out a decade later. Subsequently, Britain's two decades of continuous warfare with revolutionary and Napoleonic France left the country exhausted, impoverished and rife with the radical doctrines that had inspired the great upheaval across the Channel – many spread by discharged soldiers. One such was Arthur Thistlewood, the gaunt-faced leader of the Cato Street Conspiracy. Thistlewood was an inveterate plotter involved in one revolutionary enterprise after another. One such plan, hatched in 1816, was to seize the Tower and the Bank of England – the idea being that securing the financial and military centres of the capital would lead to a collapse of the established order and an English revolution. But the government's system of spies and agents provocateurs was as efficient as it had been in Walsingham and Thurloe's day, and Thistlewood found himself inside the Tower as he had planned – but as a prisoner.

In 1820, Thistlewood conceived a more deadly plan. He gathered a group of well-armed fellow fanatics with the aim of murdering the entire British cabinet as they sat at dinner. Thistlewood's right-hand man, Edwards, was, however, a government spy, and the plotters were surprised as they gathered above a stable in London's Cato Street to carry out their plan. Thistlewood fatally stabbed a Bow Street Runner (a prototype policeman) before he was subdued and taken to the Tower with seven of his co-conspirators. Thistlewood was honoured by being lodged in the Bloody Tower itself, while his fellow plotters were distributed among the Byward, Middle, Salt and St Thomas's Towers. In keeping with holding them in the same cells where Catholic conspirators had gone before, the Tory authorities dealt with the would-be revolutionaries in a ferociously Elizabethan manner: Thistlewood and his four closest confederates were hanged at Tyburn; the other two were transported for life. They met their deaths with courage, Thistlewood proclaiming:

> Albion is still in the chains of slavery. I quit it without regret. My only sorrow is that the soil should be a theatre for slaves, for cowards, for despots.

England still awaits the revolution that the Cato Street conspirators died to bring about.

The Duke of Wellington embodied the conservative values of tradition and stability that the conspirators had been assailing. In 1826, six years after the Cato Street conspirators had gone to their deaths, the Iron Duke, the man who had humbled the great Napoleon at Waterloo, and subsequently became Tory prime minister, was made constable of the Tower. His appointment marked the end of the Tower's position as the state's main political prison – though it would reprise the role in the two world wars – and its transformation into England's leading tourist attraction.

The duke, still furiously energetic and ruthlessly efficient, did not regard his role as merely symbolic. His first act was to transform the Yeoman Warders from patronised pensioners into proper servants of the state. Recruited from army NCOs, the 'Beefeaters' would in future be paid regular salaries and infused with an *esprit de corps* appropriate to the proud guardians of the kingdom's most prestigious fortress. As we have seen, the duke also presided over the closure of the outdated Tower menagerie and its transfer to the more spacious Regent's Park zoo. Finally, and most significantly, Wellington ordered that the paying public could be admitted to the Tower as tourists.

At first, tourists were only allowed into the keep of the White Tower, but as the reign of Queen Victoria opened in 1837, it became clear that to satisfy public curiosity other parts of the ancient complex would have to be shown as well. Public pressure for increased access became even more intense in 1840 with the publication of *The Tower of London*, a romantic novel by the popular author William Harrison Ainsworth. Although Ainsworth's fiction – focusing on the story of Lady Jane Grey – romanticised the Tower, and invented wholly imaginary features into the fortress such as a network of underground tunnels, it served to draw the attention of Londoners to a monument which over-familiarity had perhaps caused them to take for granted.

The process of gradually increasing public access, however, was disastrously disrupted on the night of 30 October 1841 when fire – probably caused by an overheating stove – broke out in the Bowyer Tower in the northern inner wall. The alarm was sounded and soon the nine appliances of the Tower's private firefighting service were on the scene. However, a shortage of water meant that only one engine could be used and the flames began to spread. To prevent a curious public from getting in, the Tower's gates were closed – which had the unintended consequence of delaying the arrival of the London Fire Brigade who had been summoned to assist.

By now, the conflagration had spread to the Grand Storehouse between the Bowyer and White Towers. The storehouse was used to house the armoury, the nation's premier collection of ancient and modern weaponry. The firefighters and the Tower's garrison only had time to remove some of the most valuable items when the building's roof collapsed at 11.20 p.m. Their focus now shifted to saving the Crown jewels housed in the Martin Tower. In the confusion the keys could not be found, and the cases housing the regalia had to be smashed and prised open with crowbars. Most of the smaller items had been safely passed through the tower's bars when the baptismal font became stuck. The Keeper of the Jewel House's clothes were smouldering by the time that the silver font was successfully prised free.

The Tower recovered from the fire with remarkable speed. The Bowyer Tower was rebuilt, and on the site of the storehouse, a new barrack block – named the Waterloo Barracks in Wellington's honour – was opened by the duke himself in 1845, seven years before his death – still in office as constable – in 1852. The duke had also commissioned the barracks' designer, the Gothic architect Anthony Salvin, to reverse centuries of decay, and restore the Tower to the approximate appearance it still bears today. Among other works, Salvin built a new Lanthorn Tower, replacing the old one which had been burned in another blaze in 1788 – but demolished the Flint Tower in the northern wall, which was so derelict that it was about to collapse. The duke also ordered the draining of the noisome and filthy moat – which he rightly considered a health hazard – revealing piles of oyster shells, along with human bones and Tudor bottles.

There was conflict between the duke – who naturally put the Tower's function as a military garrison first – and those who saw its potential as a tourist magnet. By the 1850s the American author Nathaniel Hawthorne gave a wide-eyed description of the first of two visits he made to the Tower as a paying punter. Though complaining of the speed with which the Yeoman Warder rushed him round, Hawthorne was shown the armoury – with Henry VIII's corpulent armour and flattering codpiece as its centre-piece; the execution block and axe; and the Crown jewels – and the tour culminated with tea and buns in the newly opened refreshment room before he exited over the newly drained moat. The Tower, with all its ghosts and secrets, had entered the tourist age.

CHAPTER SEVENTEEN

THE TOWER AT WAR

Apart from a bomb placed by Irish Fenians in the White Tower in 1885 (there was another planted by the Fenians' IRA successors almost a century later), the Tower of London, so soaked in blood for centuries, was barely touched by violence after the deaths of the Cato Street conspirators for the rest of the nineteenth century. A guide published in the Edwardian era tells us that public entry to the Tower was free on Mondays and Saturdays between ten and six o'clock. On other days the Tower was closed at four o'clock, and sixpence was charged to enter the White Tower and a second sixpence to visit the Crown jewels – then housed in the Wakefield Tower.

In 1914, this peaceful picture changed. As the First World War broke out, the Tower was transformed once more into its traditional roles of military fortress and state prison. Although it was almost 150 years since the last execution – that of Lord Lovat – had taken place at the Tower, once again, in the supposedly enlightened and humane early twentieth century, men would die for their crimes at the fortress.

The first decade of the new century had seen an outbreak of popular paranoia about German spies worming their way into the nation while England slept – or at least dozed. These fears were not wholly groundless: there were a number of German agents quietly collecting information about their future foe, particularly around the ports where England's Royal Navy docked. One such was a naval officer, Carl Hans Lody, who had been living in the neutral US and spoke good English. When the First World War broke out in 1914, Lody arrived under an American alias, Charles Inglis. He spent three weeks mooching around Edinburgh trying to get information about the fleet anchored at nearby Rosyth naval base. He passed on such snippets to his handler in neutral Sweden in coded letters which were nevertheless intercepted and read by the security service MI5. Lody even passed on the wild rumour that Russian troops had arrived in Britain in great numbers – identifiable by the snow on their boots.

Lody became aware that he was under suspicion and fled to Ireland. Arrested at a hotel in Killarney, he was tried by a court martial in London and condemned to death. The night before his execution he was transferred from Wellington Barracks near Buckingham Palace to the Tower. A long wooden shed had been set up before the war for the Tower's garrison to use as an indoor rifle range. The shed lay between the inner and outer western walls of the fortress between the Martin and Constable Towers. It was here that Carl Lody – and the ten spies who followed him during the war – died.

On the fateful date of 5 November 1914, a cold and wet evening, Lody was lodged in the guardroom of the Casemates, near the Tower's main entrance, for his last night on earth. Lody, a punctilious sailor, wrote his last letters: to the officer commanding Wellington Barracks, thanking him for his correct treatment during his confinement; and, movingly, to his family:

My Dear Ones, I have trusted in God and He has decided. My hour has come. And I must start on the journey through the Dark Valley like so many of my comrades in this terrible war of the Nations. May my life be offered as a humble sacrifice on the altar of the Fatherland. A hero's death on the battlefield is certainly finer, but such is not to be my lot, and I die here in the enemy's country silent and unknown, but the consciousness that I die in the service of the Fatherland makes death easy. The Supreme Court-Martial of London has sentenced me to death for Military Conspiracy. Tomorrow I shall be shot here in the Tower. I have had just judges, and I shall die as an officer, not as a spy. Farewell. God bless you. Hans.

Lody's last words about being an officer rather than a spy were echoed when he greeted the Assistant Provost-Marshal who came to fetch him from his cell. 'I suppose that you will not care to shake hands with a German spy?' 'No,' replied the soldier. 'But I will shake hands with a brave man.' Lody, upright and unafraid, was marched into the execution shed, seated in a wooden chair and blindfolded. The eight-man firing squad, from the 8th battalion of the elite Grenadier Guards, took aim and fired. The ten agents who followed Lody to death in the Tower during the war were of a lesser calibre. Mostly civilians, and often motivated by the hope of money rather than Lody's patriotism, they were quickly recognised and arrested.

A more distinguished and famous wartime resident was the Irish humanitarian and martyr (or traitor, depending on your viewpoint), Sir Roger Casement. Casement was the Ulster-born diplomat who before the war had ruined his health, but made his humanitarian reputation, by fearlessly exposing the brutal genocidal oppression practised by colonisers first in Africa's Belgian Congo, and later in the Putomayo region on the upper Amazon between Brazil and Peru. The reports into these outrages produced by Casement had shocked world opinion and led to reform. The Irishman was rewarded with a knighthood, and took early retirement, becoming ever more extreme in his Irish republican views.

The outbreak of war found him propagandising among the Irish community in America, whence he was sent to Germany in an attempt to persuade Irish prisoners of war serving in the British Army to fight with Germany for their country's freedom. Failing in this endeavour, a frustrated and depressed Casement was sent back to Ireland in 1916 on board a U-boat to either support or call off the planned Easter Rising against British rule, depending on the conditions he found on arrival. The dinghy which brought Casement and his companions ashore near Tralee on Ireland's west coast was swamped; half-drowned, he was rapidly arrested.

He was brought to London and taken to the Tower, where, like the German spies, he was confined in the guardroom of the Casemates. Treated as a traitor and turncoat by his guards, and denied visits from his London sympathisers, Casement's physical and mental condition dramatically deteriorated. He twice attempted suicide: once by ingesting curare, the South American paralysing poison which he had carried since the Putomayo; and once by swallowing nails he twisted from the walls of his cell. His guards were forbidden to speak to him, and he only discovered what had happened in Dublin when a Welsh guard, with sympathy for a fellow Celt, whispered the news that the Easter Rising had been bloodily suppressed.

Eventually, the Liberal prime minister, H. H. Asquith, was told of Casement's desperate state and ordered him to be moved to an ordinary prison. His solicitor, Gavan Duffy, later a Sinn Fein leader, saw him in the Tower and was unable to believe that the tattered scarecrow was the elegant man he had known before the war. The prisoner was filthy and covered in bites from the bugs infesting his cell. He was still dressed in the sea-soaked clothes he had worn when he came ashore. His beard was matted, his eyes bloodshot and sunken, and he seemed unable to speak or concentrate. Deprived of his braces lest he attempt to hang himself, he was forced to hold his trousers up. The last of the Tower's distinguished traitors, Casement's deplorable condition revived the very worst of its traditions.

Tried at the Old Bailey, Casement received the inevitable sentence of a traitor in wartime: death. His sympathisers attempted to win a reprieve on the grounds of Casement's pre-war humanitarian work. To counter the campaign, the government secretly circulated documents, the 'Black Diaries', revealing Casement's obsessive homosexuality — then regarded as a moral, as well as a criminal offence. He was hanged at London's Pentonville prison in August 1916, although his body was repatriated to Dublin in 1966. He walked to his execution, said the hangman, 'like a prince'.

Between the wars another, albeit less distinguished, traitor who worked for the Germans was detained at the Tower – much to the curiosity of the press, and the public who continued to flock to within a few feet of the guardroom in the Tower barracks where the prisoner was held. Norman Baillie-Stewart was a disgruntled army officer of the Seaforth Highlanders, who resented authority and was attracted by the new Nazi regime which had come to power in Germany in 1933. On holiday in Germany, he seems to have fallen for a honeytrap set by the Nazi secret services, became entangled with a German girl, and agreed to become a spy.

He was quickly detected. At the time, Britain was still anxious to appease Hitler and Baillie-Stewart was an embarrassment. It was too awkward to put him on public trial, so the authorities threw him into the Tower. Held in the Wellington barracks in a guardroom with slit windows, Baillie-Stewart's presence soon became known to the press who dubbed the anonymous prisoner 'the Officer in the Tower'. He was eventually court-martialled, after which it was felt that the simplest thing was to expel Baillie-Stewart from the army and let him return to Germany. He became a German citizen and broadcast propaganda over Berlin Radio during the war. It was Baillie-Stewart's posh voice, rather than the nasal tones of William Joyce, that first led a British journalist to dub him 'Lord

Haw-Haw' – a nickname soon bestowed on Joyce. Baillie-Stewart's German citizenship saved him from sharing Joyce's fate dangling from a rope after the war, and he died in a Dublin bar in 1966.

Like that other London landmark St Paul's Cathedral, the Tower survived the Blitz virtually unscathed. However, the fortress's most enduring and best-beloved tradition – its population of ravens – came close to extinction. No one knows when the ravens first arrived at the Tower, although this biggest member of the carrion crow family may originally have been attracted by the quantities of rotting human remains left in and around the fortress after executions. All except one of the Tower's dozen or so ravens were scorched or scared to death by the bombs. The sole survivor – a bird named Gyp – lived, maintaining the tradition that so long as ravens stay at the Tower, Britain will endure.

In the Second World War a single German agent, Josef Jacobs – who broke his ankle parachuting into a field in Cambridgeshire, and was soon captured – shared the fate of the eleven spies shot in the Tower in the First World War, thus becoming the last man to be executed in the Tower – to date. The Tower, however, played host to a rather more important parachutist than the sad figure of Jakobs. Rudolf Hess, Hitler's deputy Führer and faithful dog-like follower, arrived unexpectedly in wartime Britain, parachuting out of a clear sky over Scotland in May 1941. Hess, always an eccentric figure, was apparently trying to regain lost favour with the Führer by undertaking a one-man peace mission to Britain so Germany would not have to fight a war on two fronts when it invaded Russia the following month. He may have been lured across in a British Intelligence 'sting' which suggested that he would meet members of a secret 'peace party' favouring a compromise deal with Nazi Germany. Arrested on his arrival, Hess never tasted freedom again, and his first place of confinement when he was brought to London from Scotland was the Tower.

The beetle-browed Nazi leader arrived at the fortress in an anonymous ambulance and was put in the Lieutenant's Lodgings, the half-framed Tudor house where Lady Jane Grey and Guy Fawkes had been among those preceding him, and which Hess described as 'charming'. During his time at the Tower, Hess watched admiringly as the fortress garrison drilled to pipes and drum with a precision he praised as 'worthy of Prussians'. After four days, Hess was driven away – again by ambulance

– to the first of several safe houses in London and Wales where he would spend the rest of the war. Tried at Nuremberg, he was sentenced to prison for life – and stayed in Berlin's Spandau jail until the end of his days in 1987.

If Rudolf Hess was one of the Tower's most infamous prisoners, the pair of young toughs who spent a week in the guardhouse of the Wellington Barracks in 1952 were almost equally notorious. Identical twins Reggie and Ronnie Kray were the East End wide boys who became London's most notorious gangsters of the 1960s, building an empire in their native 'manor' based on murder and violence meted out without mercy to those who crossed them. The first of their many enemies was the Royal Fusiliers army garrison at the Tower, from which they absconded after assaulting a corporal on their first day as conscripts doing compulsory military National Service in the fortress.

Arrested at their mother's house, the twins were brought back to the Tower where they spent a week sleeping on the bare boards of the Wellington Barracks' punishment cell before absconding again. The boys, who had trained as boxers, were handy with their fists and soon made life too hot for even the army to hold them. After months of the same cat-and-mouse game of absconding followed by recapture, the Army gave them up as a bad job. In 1954 the Krays were freed to begin a very different career. The twins, in their brutal and violent ways, marked an appropriate full stop to the Tower's thousand years as the world's premier prison.

EPILOGUE

The words of an anonymous and tattered guidebook to the Tower, published at the dawn of the twentieth century, are as true today, when the old fortress is Britain's bustling, buzzing high-tech tourist trap, as when they were written a century ago:

There is no spot in the British Isles where the memories of the past cluster more thickly than around the old grey walls, the picturesque towers and the dark and gloomy chambers of the Tower of London. The Tower is one of the most notable historic monuments in existence. For seven centuries it occupied a foremost place in all the transactions that affected the welfare of the kingdom and the personal fortunes of its rulers. As we tour the Tower there pass before us in memory's sad review the shadowy figures of kings and queens, statesmen and warriors, prisoners, martyrs and those doomed to a cruel and bloody death. Every tower reminds us of a memorable deed, every chamber of a famous name. The great fortress is peopled once more with its victors and its victims; past times live again; history ceases to be a dull record; it becomes a living, moving tale; men and women of other ages are mere names no longer, they are clothed with flesh and blood; we witness their triumphs, we hear their prayers and sighs, we note their bearing in hours of trial, of exaltation and despair, and we see them in the dismal torture chamber or on the terrible scaffold with the glitter of the headsman's axe before their eyes. To know the story of the Tower of London is to be familiar with all the great actors in the drama of English history, for its ancient walls and weather-beaten stones are the links that bind generation to generation and age to age from the Norman conquest to the present day.

APPENDIX

THE TOWER'S GHOSTS

I thought long and hard about whether to include any material about the Tower's unauthorised spectral visitors in a factual work of history. However, on hearing from a staff member that the Tower's ghosts were the chief subject of enquiry by visiting tourists – and following the example of Alison Weir, who includes a substantial section on the posthumous appearances of Anne Boleyn at the conclusion of her superb study *The Lady in the Tower* – I decided that a few words on the subject would not go amiss.

I myself try to maintain an open mind on the existence or otherwise of supernatural phenomena, though I am increasingly inclined to believe that there is 'something' out there of which we have as yet imperfect and disputed knowledge and awareness. Of one thing, however, I am certain: that particular places that have been the scene of tragic, momentous and violent events carry a numinous 'charge' – and that no place in England, possibly nowhere else on earth, carries such a concentrated spirit of place as the Tower. In that sense, it is indeed a haunted and sacred spot. And I am convinced of one more thing: however sceptically we read these accounts, the people I refer to here were sure that they saw what they saw.

The first reported sighting of a ghost at the Tower came during the building of the outer curtain wall. Thomas Becket, the ill fated martyr archbishop murdered in his own cathedral at Canterbury, who had once supervised earlier works at the fortress, allegedly appeared to the labourers building the wall.

Another saint and martyr – certainly the most pious monarch in English history – was Henry VI, who in 1471 was murdered as he knelt in prayer in his tiny private offertory in the Wakefield Tower – at the behest of Edward IV, and quite probably by the hand of the future Richard III. Henry is supposed to haunt the scene of the crime each year on the anniversary of the assassination: 21/22 May.

The most famous victims of violence at the Tower, the 'little princes' King

Edward V and his brother Richard, Duke of York, who arrived at the Tower exactly twelve years after Henry departed it so violently, made frequent posthumous appearances in and around the Bloody Tower, both clad in white nightshirts and weeping softly. It is recorded that they shot arrows at targets in the Tower's garden, so they may well haunt the place – though they may equally well have been murdered in the White Tower where their skeletons were found in 1674.

Another longer-term resident of the Bloody Tower, Sir Walter Ralegh, has been reported to have been seen sitting at the desk in the study there which is furnished as it was in the time when he wrote his *History of the World*. Sir Walter's spirit has also been seen pacing the ramparts along Ralegh's Walk where he took his exercise adjacent to the tower. He is said to bear a strong resemblance to his portrait, which hangs in the Bloody Tower.

Several of the women executed within the Tower's precincts are said to revisit the scenes of their sufferings. The sightings of Anne Boleyn are so ubiquitous as to make even the most hardened sceptic wonder. They range from a spectral 'grey' or 'white' lady to an unseen presence in a room in the Queen's House which lowers the temperature and makes animals and children scared. Anne is said to be seen on occasion without her head, or else with a black hole in place of her face.

Perhaps the most extraordinary sighting of Henry VIII's second wife came in 1864, and led to the court martial of a soldier of the Tower's garrison. When an infantryman of the Sixtieth Rifles saw a white figure glide from the Queen's House, he challenged the headless apparition with a fixed bayonet, only to sense it gliding through him. After fainting in understandable terror, he was court-martialled for dereliction of duty, but was acquitted after other soldiers supported his story, and said they too had seen the ghost.

Other sightings of drifting white or blueish lights have been seen in locations such as the White Tower, St Peter's Chapel and the Martin Tower, the scene of an extraordinary haunting in October 1817, recounted by Edmund Lenthal Swifte. He had been appointed keeper of the Crown jewels in 1814 when they were still kept in the vault from where Thomas Blood had stolen them. Many years later, in September 1860, Swifte recounted his scary experience in the journal '*Notes & Queries*'. He said he had been sitting at supper one evening with his wife, sister-in-law, son and daughter when 'a cylindrical figure, like a glass tube' appeared in the room, hovering in the air. 'Its contents appeared to be a dense fluid, white and a pale azure, like to the gathering of a summer cloud and incessantly rolling and mingling within the cylinder.' Passing behind Swifte's wife, it paused over her right shoulder, at which she crouched down and cried, 'Oh

Christ, it has seized me!' Utterly horrified, Swifte seized a chair and struck at the apparition – at which it disappeared.

The oddest haunting at the Tower was not a human spectre but that of an animal, and it occurred in January 1816, a few months before Swifte saw the cylinder. A sentry patrolling the paved yard outside the Jewel House saw a bear cross the yard and descend a flight of steps. The sentry was so scared that he fell in a faint, and regained his consciousness only to blurt out his story before dying.

SELECT BIBLIOGRAPHY

TOWER HISTORIES CONSULTED

The earliest general study of the Tower and its history is *The History and Antiquities of the Tower of London: With Memoirs of Royal and Distinguished Persons* by John Bayley (1830, available from Kessenger Publishing). The end of the Victorian era saw two substantial two-volume histories published very close to each other. The first was *Her Majesty's Tower* by Hepworth Dixon (1900), swiftly followed by Lord Ronald Sutherland Gower's *The Tower of London* (1902). An excellent semi-official guidebook from the same period, *The Tower of London: An Illustrated Guide* by Charles Morley and William Stead junior (1900), is full of nuggets of interesting information. Major-General Sir George Younghusband, a member of the Tower's garrison, wrote a solid work, *The Tower of London from Within* (1918); while journalist Walter George Bell penned a more concise *The Tower of London* (1921, also available from Kessenger). There were few further histories published until R. J. Minney's wide-ranging and informative overview, *The Tower of London* (1970). The eccentric historian A. L. Rowse took his own sometimes outlandish take on the Tower in *The Tower of London in the History of the Nation* (1973). By contrast, the distinguished popular historian Derek Wilson's *The Tower 1078–1978* (1978) – published to mark the Tower's millennium – is serious and sensible, and the most recent general history of the fortress. The same year John Charlton of Her Majesty's Stationery Office edited *The Tower of London: Its Buildings and Institutions*

(HMSO 1978), incorporating invaluable information on the Tower's architecture gleaned from twenteeth-century excavations and investigation.

Populist modern books focusing on particular aspects of the Tower include: *The Tower of London: Cauldron of Britain's Past* by Plantagenet Somerset Fry (1990); *Tales from the Tower of London* (2004) by Daniel Diehl and Mark P. Donnolly; *Shot in the Tower* by Leonard Sellars (1997), on the executions there of German spies in the two world wars; and Daniel Hahn's *The Tower Menagerie* (2003), a bright and breezy history. Even breezier are the short books of G. 'Bud' Abbott, a retired Yeoman Warder with an encyclopaedic knowledge of his former workplace, deployed in his very readable *Tortures of the Tower of London*; *Great Escapes from the Tower of London*; *Ghosts of the Tower of London*; and *The Beefeaters of the Tower of London* (all published in the 1980s).

The Tower of London: The Official Illustrated History (2000) by the Tower's sometime official historians Edward Impey and Geoffrey Parnell is of course authoritative and packed with facts. In addition, the official guidebooks on the Tower published and regularly updated by Her Majesty's Stationery Office are invaluable; see also HMSO's *The Royal Mint: An Outline History* (1977).

SELECT BIBLIOGRAPHY

GENERAL WORKS CONSULTED

Chapter One: Beginnings

For William the Conqueror, his sons and successors, the conquest, Gundulf and the origins of the Tower I have relied on Robert Bartlett's *England under the Norman and Angevin Kings* (2000); and David C. Douglas's *William the Conqueror: The Norman Impact upon England* (1964). David Howarth's *1066: The Year of the Conquest* (1981); Frank McLynn's *1066: The Year of Three Battles* (1999); and Peter Rex's *1066: A New History of the Norman Conquest* (2009) were all also useful.

For Stephen, Matilda and Geoffrey de Mandeville see J. H. Round, *Geoffrey de Mandeville: A Study of the Anarchy* (1892); Jim Bradbury, *Stephen and Matilda: The Civil War of 1139–53* (2000); R. H. C. Davis, *King Stephen* (1977);

Marjorie Chibnell, *The Empress Matilda* (1991); and Nesta Pain, *Empress Matilda, England's Uncrowned Queen* (1978).

For Richard I, King John and William Longchamp, see John Gillingham, *Richard I* (1999); W. L. Warren, *King John* (1991); Ralph V. Turner, *King John, England's Evil King?* (2009); and Frank McLynn, *Lionheart and Lackland* (2006).

The Anglo-Saxon Chronicle and J. Stow's *Survey of London* (both online) have also been useful.

Chapter Two: The Menagerie and the Mint

For Henry III, Hubert de Burgh and Simon de Montfort see David Carpenter's *The Minority of Henry III* (1990) and *The Reign of Henry III* (1996); and Margaret Wade Labarge's *Simon de Montfort* (1962).

For the Tower's menagerie see E. T. Bennet's *The Tower Menagerie* (1829); and Daniel Hahn's more contemporary *The Tower Menagerie* (2003). For the impressions of a foreign visitor to the Elizabethan menagerie see *The Diary of Baron Waldstein* (trans. 1981). For Samuel Pepys's account of his visit see his *Diary*.

For the Royal Mint see J. Craig, *The Mint* (1953); C. E. Challis (ed.), *A New History of the Royal Mint* (1992); and for Isaac Newton's duel with Thomas Chaloner see *Newton and the Counterfeiter* by Thomas Levenson (2009).

Chapter Three: The Captives and the Kings

For Edward I, see Marc Morris's superb biography, *A Great and Terrible King: Edward I and the Forging of Britain* (2008). For William Wallace see Graeme Morton, *William Wallace* (2004) and Chris Brown, *William Wallace* (2005).

For Edward III see Ian Mortimer's *The Perfect King* (2006) – a near-perfect biography. For King Jean II of France see J. Devaisse, *Jean le Bon* (1985). For King James I of Scotland see Michael Brown's *James I* (1994).

Chapter Four: Plague and Peasants

For the Black Death, see Philip Ziegler, *The Black Death* (1969); William Naphy and Andrew Spicer, *The Black Death and the History of Plagues 1345–1730* (2000); John Kelly, *The Great Mortality* (2005); and Benedict Gummer, *The Scourging Angel: The Black Death in the British Isles* (2009).

For the Peasants' Revolt (and other popular risings) see the racy, learned and informative *The English Rebel* (2009) by David Horspool. *Summer of Blood: The Peasants' Revolt of 1381* by Dan Jones (2009) supersedes all previous accounts. For the remainder of the reign of Richard II see Nigel Saul's definitive biography, *Richard II* (1999). For an earlier view, see *Richard II* by Anthony Steel (1941).

For the mysterious death of Richard II (and other monarchs) see Dr Clifford Brewer's fascinating *The Death of Kings: A Medical History of the Kings and Queens of England* (2000) and Michael Evans's *The Death of Kings: Royal Deaths in Medieval England* (2003).

Chapter Five: Uneasy Heads

For Henry IV see Ian Mortimer's *The Fears of Henry IV* (2008); and for his son Henry V see *Agincourt: The King, the Campaign, the Battle* by Juliet Barker (2005).

The best and fullest biography of the tragic *Henry VI* is by Bertram Wolffe (1981); and for his feisty queen see Jock Haswell's *The Ardent Queen: Margaret of Anjou and the Lancastrian Heritage* (1976); or for a French perspective, Philippe Erlanger's *Margaret of Anjou, Queen of England* (1970). The fate of their dynasty is ably told by R. L. Storey in *The End of the House of Lancaster* (1966, 1986).

A detailed and excellent account of the collapse of royal authority under Henry VI and the early years of the Wars of the Roses is Alison Weir's *Lancaster and York* (1995). The wars themselves have generated a large and impressive recent literature. The following, all titled *The Wars of the Roses*, are warmly recommended: J. R. Lander (1965), Charles Ross (1976) and John Gillingham (1981) all set the wars in their political context; while Robin Neillands (1992), Anthony Goodman (2005) and Trevor Royle (2009) focus on the military aspects of the conflict. Desmond Seward (1995) concentrates colourfully and rivetingly on the leading personalities, bringing them to breathing life.

Chapter Six: Roses are Blood Red

Edward IV, the central and dominant figure of the wars, is dealt with in detail by Charles Ross in *Edward IV* (1976), the definitive life. His ally turned rival, *Warwick the Kingmaker*, has been equally fully and fairly treated by Michael

Hicks (1998). Edward's Queen, *Elizabeth Woodville*, that great survivor, has found a good biographer in David Baldwin (2002).

The villainous yet strangely appealing Richard III has attracted a larger literature than the wars themselves.

Highly recommended is the definitive life, *Richard III* by Michael Hicks (2000). While Desmond Seward's *Richard III: England's Black Legend* (1982) readably damns Richard with all this author's customary gusto.

Accounts of battles include *Barnet and Tewkesbury* by P. W. Hammond (1990); *The Battle of Bosworth* by Michael Bennett (1985); and *Bosworth 1485* by Michael K. Jones (2002). The biggest bloodbath of all is covered by A. W. Boardman in *The Battle of Towton* (1994) and by George Goodwin in *Fatal Colours: Towton, 1461, England's Most Brutal Battle* (2011).

Chapter Seven: The Princes, the Protector and the Pretenders

The Tower's most enduring mystery, the fate of the little princes, is considered at length by Elizabeth Jenkins in *The Princes in the Tower* (1978); and by A. J. Pollard in *Richard III and the Princes in the Tower* (1991); and is definitively solved with the finger of guilt pointing firmly at Richard by Alison Weir in her clear and concise indictment, also titled *The Princes in the Tower* (1992).

The unlikely accession of Henry Tudor to power as Henry VII is briefly narrated by Ralph A. Griffiths and Roger S. Thomas in *The Making of the Tudor Dynasty* (1985); while the two chief challenges to his rule, those of Lambert Simnel and Perkin Warbeck, are covered respectively by Michael Bennett in *Lambert Simnel and the Battle of Stoke* (1987) and Anne Wroe in *Perkin* (2003). The chief fomentor of Yorkist conspiracies against Henry, Margaret, Duchess of Burgundy, has been given her considerable due by Christine Weightman in *Margaret of York, Duchess of Burgundy 1446–1503* (1989), while Desmond Seward brings his usual brio to telling the story of the continuing Yorkist threat to the Tudors into the reign of Henry VIII in *The Last White Rose* (2010).

Chapter Eight: The King's Great Matter

There are numerous biographies of Henry VIII, of which the following can be safely and strongly recommended: *Henry VIII* by Francis Hackett (1929, 1949); and *Henry VIII* by J. J. Scarisbrick (1968).

We eagerly await the concluding volume of David Starkey's life which began with his study of the young Henry in *Henry: Virtuous Prince* (2008); meanwhile his *The Reign of Henry VIII: Personalities and Politics* (2002) is a good short introduction to the period.

Alison Weir's *Henry VIII, King and Court* and Derek Wilson's *In the Lion's Court* (both 2002) offer excellent accounts of the murderous and risky life at the top in Henry's England. The best biographies of the major figures at Henry's court are *Cranmer* by Diarmaid MacCulloch (1996), *Thomas Cromwell* by Robert Hutchinson (2007) and *Thomas More* by Richard Marius (1985).

Sharply contrasting views are offered of Anne Boleyn by her American biographers, Retha Warnicke whose *The Rise and Fall of Anne Boleyn* (1989) attributes her death to male fears of witchcraft and of an educated and outspoken woman, and Professor George Bernard whose *Anne Boleyn: Fatal Attractions* (2010) suggests that Anne was, after all, guilty of the adultery for which she died. Professor Eric Ives, Boleyn's major British biographer, in *The Life and Death of Anne Boleyn* (1986, reworked in 2004), by contrast attributes her downfall to wider politics: the diplomatic duels between England, Spain and France, and the clash between reformers and conservatives in the Church. Alison Weir, in *The Lady in the Tower: The Fall of Anne Boleyn* (2009), sensibly sifts the available evidence and comes to the conclusion that the traditional explanation for Anne's fall – chiefly her inability to produce a male heir and Henry's declining sexual interest – is broadly correct.

A fascinating speculative account of Anne's friend – and possibly more – the poet Thomas Wyatt, who suffered in the Tower like his father before him and his son after, is *Graven with Diamonds* by Nicola Shulman (2011). Among other nuggets, Shulman reveals that the poet's father, Henry Wyatt, who had been tortured at the Tower under Richard III with a horse's barnacle – a device for pinching and tearing the mouth – incorporated this instrument of torture into the family coat of arms.

Chapter Nine: The Henrician Terror

Geoffrey Moorhouse wrote the most accessible modern account of *The Pilgrimage of Grace* (2002); while for the clash between religious reformers and conservatives which marked the latter years of Henry's reign see *The Last Days of Henry VIII* by Robert Hutchinson (2005).

For the histories of the two rival dynasties, riven by religious, political and personal feuds – and who, like the Wyatts, both suffered in the Tower over three generations – see Robert Hutchinson's *House of Treason* (2009) on the Howards, and Derek Wilson's *The Uncrowned Kings of England* (2005) on the Dudleys.

For the execution of Catherine Howard see *The Six Wives of Henry VIII* (1991) by Alison Weir and *Jane Boleyn: The Infamous Lady Rochford* by Julia Fox (2007). For the execution of the Earl of Surrey see *Henry VIII's Last Victim* by Jessie Childs (2007).

Chapter Ten: Tudor Children

For Edward VI see *Edward VI: The Lost King of England* (2007) by Chris Skidmore. The Duke of Somerset still lacks his own biography, but for his rival John Dudley see *John Dudley, Duke of Northumberland* by David Loades (1996). For Lady Jane Grey see *Lady Jane Grey: Nine Days Queen* by Alison Plowden (2003) and *Lady Jane Grey: A Tudor Mystery* by Eric Ives (2009). For Mary I see Carolly Erickson's *Bloody Mary* (1978), Linda Porter's *Mary Tudor, First Tudor Queen* (2007) and Anna Whitelock's *Mary Tudor: England's First Queen* (2009).

For the Marian persecutions see *Bloody Mary's Martyrs: The Story of England's Terror* by Jasper Ridley (2001) and Eamon Duffy's fine *Fires of Faith* (2009).

For Elizabeth I see *Elizabeth I* by J. E. Neale (1954), *Elizabeth, Queen of England* by Neville Williams (1967), *Elizabeth: A Study in Power and Intellect* by Paul Johnson (1974), *Elizabeth I* by Anne Somerset (1991), *and Elizabeth the Queen* by Alison Weir (1999)

Chapter Eleven: Fallen Favourites

For Elizabeth and Robert Dudley see *Elizabeth and Leicester* by Milton Waldman (1946); and studies under the same title by Elizabeth Jenkins (1961) and Sarah Grist Wood (2007). See also *Sweet Robin: A Biography of Robert Dudley, Earl of Leicester 1553–1558* by Derek Wilson (1997) and *Death and the Virgin* by Chris Skidmore (2010) – an examination of the mysterious death of Dudley's wife Amy Robsart.

For Sir Walter and Bess Ralegh see *Sir Walter Ralegh* by Eric Ecclestone (1941), *That Great Lucifer* by Margaret Irwin (1960), *Sir Walter Ralegh* by Robert Lacey (1973) and *My Just Desire* by Anna Beer (2003). See also

Sir Walter Raleigh: Selected Prose and Poetry edited by Agnes M. C. Latham (1965) and *The Creature in the Map: Sir Walter Ralegh's Quest for El Dorado* (1996) by the always excellent Charles Nicholl.

For the Earls of Essex and Southampton see *Robert, Earl of Essex* by Robert Lacey (1971) and *Shakespeare and the Earl of Southampton* by G. P. V. Akrigg (1968). For James I – by my estimation England's most despicable monarch – see *The Cradle King* by Alan Stewart (2003).

Chapter Twelve: Papists, Plots and Poisons

For Catholic plots against Elizabeth I and the state's repressive response see *Danger to Elizabeth* by Alison Plowden (1971); Alice Hogge's *God's Secret Agents* (2005) gives a remarkably well-researched, detailed yet dispassionate account of the heroic and treasonous efforts of the undercover Jesuit missionary priests to keep the Catholic faith alive in Elizabethan England. Alan Haynes' *The Elizabethan Secret Services* (1992) is a densely detailed and equally well-researched investigation into the embryonic Elizabethan secret state. Charles Nicholls' engrossing and beautifully written *The Reckoning* (1992), though about the murder of the playwright Christopher Marlowe, opens out to present a convincing picture of the wilderness of mirrors in which Marlowe and other secret agents moved. For the austere manipulator of Marlowe and a myriad other players see Robert Hutchinson's life of Sir Francis Walsingham, *Elizabeth's Spymaster* (2006).

For the Gunpowder Plot see Antonia Fraser's fast-paced *The Gunpowder Plot: Terror and Faith in 1605* (1996). Though herself a Catholic, Lady Antonia is remarkably objective. Alan Haynes' *The Gunpowder Plot* (1994) deploys his expert knowledge of the subject; while James Travers' *Gunpowder: The Players Behind the Plot* (2005) uses documents from the National Archives to reveal the plotters' motivations.

For the Overbury case, see William McElwee's *The Murder of Sir Thomas Overbury* (1952), Beatrice White's *Cast of Ravens* (1965), Edward le Comte's *The Notorious Lady Essex* (1970), A. L. Rowse's *Simon Forman* (1974) and David Lindley's *The Trials of Frances Howard* (1993). Anne Somerset's *Unnatural Murder: Poison at the Court of James I* (1997) is the best and most recent account of this quintessential case of Jacobean cruelty, conspiracy and corruption.

Chapter Thirteen: Great Escapes

For Ranulf Flambard see Frank Barlow's *William Rufus* (1983).

For Roger Mortimer and Edward II see *The Greatest Traitor* by Ian Mortimer (2006).

For Sir John Oldcastle and the Lollards see *Actes and Monuments* – popularly known as *Foxe's Book of Martyrs* (online) by John Foxe, *Sir John Oldcastle* by W. T. Waugh (1905) and *Sir John Fastolf* by Stephen Cooper (2010).

For John Gerard see *God's Secret Agents* by Alice Hogge (op. cit., 2005) and Gerard's own *Autobiography of an Elizabethan*, translated from the Latin by Philip Caraman SJ (1956).

For Edmund Nevill, see G. Abbott's *Great Escapes from the Tower of London* (op. cit., 1982).

For William Seymour and Arbella Stuart see *Arbella Stuart: A Rival to the Queen* by David N. Durant (1978), *In the Shadow of the Throne: The Lady Arbella Stuart* by Ruth Norrington (2002) and *Arbella: England's Lost Queen* by Sarah Gristwood (2003).

For Lord Capel see *Lord Capel, First Baron Capel of Hadham* by Ronald Hutton (*DNB*, 2004).

For John Lambert, see *Cromwell's Generals* by Maurice Ashley (1954) and *John Lambert* by David Farr (2003).

For Lord Grey de Warke see *Sedgemoor 1685* (1985) by David Chandler and for Lord Nithsdale see *The Jacobites* by Daniel Szechi (1994).

Chapter Fourteen: Restoration Romps

The sparkling yet elusive and enigmatic personality and exciting and erotic life of Charles II has received more biographical attention than that of any other British king – with the possible exception of Henry VIII. Of the vast number of lives, these can be warmly recommended: Hesketh Pearson's *Charles II: His Life and Likeness* (1960), Maurice Ashley's *Charles II: King and Statesman* (1974), *Charles II* by Antonia Fraser (1979), *Charles II: Portrait of an Age* by Tony Palmer (1979), *Charles the Second* by Ronald Hutton (1989), *Charles II* by John Miller (1991) and *Royal Survivor* by Stephen Coote (1999).

For the Crown jewels see *The Jewel House* by George Younghusband (1921) and *Crown, Orb and Sceptre* by D. Hilliam (2003). For Thomas Blood see *Colonel Blood: The Man who Stole the Crown Jewels* by David C. Hanrahan (2003).

For Restoration politics and the radical underground see Alan Marshall, *Intelligence and Espionage in the Reign of Charles II* (1994) and *The Strange Death of Edmund Godfrey* (1999) by the same author. See also *The Popish Plot* by John Kenyon (1971).

For George Villiers, 2nd Duke of Buckingham, see *Charles II and the Duke of Buckingham* by David C. Hanrahan (2006).

For Samuel Pepys, naturally consult the incomparable *Diary* (op. cit) itself, and *Pepys: A Biography* by Richard Ollard (1999). *Samuel Pepys: The Unequalled Self* by Claire Tomalin (2002) is an indispensable life; and *The Plot Against Pepys (2007)* by James and Ben Long examines in minute detail the reasons behind his confinement in the Tower.

Chapter Fifteen: Civil Wars and Uncivil Peace

For Sir John Eliot see *The Life of Sir J. Eliot* by J. Forster (1864) and *Sir John Eliot* by Conrad Russell (*DNB*, 2004).

For Strafford see *Thomas Wentworth, First Earl of Strafford 1593–1641: A Revaluation* by C. V. Wedgwood (1961).

For Archbishop William Laud see *William Laud* by Anthony Milton (*DNB*, 2004).

For William Prynne see *William Prynne* by William Lamont (*DNB*, 2004).

For William Davenant, John Suckling, Edmund Waller and the Royalist plot to take the Tower see *Reprobates* by John Stubbs (2011).

For John Lilburne and the Levellers see *Freeborn John* by Pauline Gregg (1961, 1986).

For General Monck see *The Life of General George Monck: For King and Cromwell* by Peter Reese (2008).

Of the many biographies of Charles I and Oliver Cromwell, two are outstanding: *Charles I* by Pauline Gregg (1988) and *Cromwell: Our Chief of Men* (1973) by Antonia Fraser. Another woman historian C. V. Wedgwood's masterly overview of the Civil War, *The King's War* (1978), though dated, still repays reading. See also John Aubrey's charming *Brief Lives* (17th c. 1949) for vignettes of many of the players.

Chapter Sixteen: Iron Dukes and Lunatic Lords

For the Duke of Monmouth, see B. Bevan, *James, Duke of Monmouth* (1973) and J. N. P. Watson, *Captain-General and Rebel Chief* (1979).

For Judge George Jeffreys and the Bloody Assize see William Humphrey, *The Life of Judge Jeffreys* (1852, reissued 2006) and *The Bloody Assize* by I. G. Muddiman (1929).

For the Duke of Marlborough see Winston Churchill's monumental hagiography of his ancestor, *Marlborough: His Life and Times* (1929). For a more objective view see Richard Holmes, *Marlborough: England's Fragile Genius* (2008); or read Christopher Hibbert's gossipy and entertaining *The Marlboroughs* (2001) which gives the irrepressible Sarah her due too. Richard Holmes has also written the best modern biography of *Wellington: The Iron Duke* (2002).

The villainous Lord Lovat deserves – but sadly lacks – a biography. But *Bonnie Prince Charlie* (2003) by Frank McLynn is a reliable account of the rising which cost the old man his head.

For Lord George Gordon and the riots that bear his name see Christopher Hibbert's. *King Mob* (1958); and John Nicholson's *The Great Liberty Riot of 1780* (2008).

The Cato Street Conspiracy by John Stanhope (1962) is still the best and fullest account of the plot.

Chapter Seventeen: The Tower at War

Of the many biographies of Roger Casement, the best are *Roger Casement* (1974, 2002) by Brian Inglis and *Casement: The Flawed Hero* (1984) by Roger Sawyer.

The fullest and most convincing study of the Tower's other notorious short-stay wartime resident is *Rudolf Hess* (1994) by Peter Padfield.

The strange story of Norman Baillie-Stewart 'as told to' John Murdoch is related in *The Officer in the Tower* (1967).

Finally, details of the brief residence of possibly the last of the Tower's many infamous prisoners, the Kray twins, is told in *The Profession of Violence* by John Pearson (1972, 1984).

LIST OF ILLUSTRATION CREDITS

Musee de la Tapisserie, Bayeux, France / With special authorisation of the city of Bayeux Giraudon / The Bridgeman Art Library

Matthew Paris, Historia Anglorum. Ms. Royal 14, C.VII, fol.136, Credit: akg-images / British Library

Matthew Paris, Chronica mayora. Ms. 16, fol.IV. Parker Library, Cambridge / akg-images

P.124–1950.pt43 The Tyger: plate 43 from 'Songs of Innocence and of Experience' (copy R) c.1802–08 (etching, ink and w/c), Blake, William (1757-1827) / Fitzwilliam Museum, University of Cambridge, UK / The Bridgeman Art Library

King James I of England and VI of Scotland by Daniel Mytens, oil on canvas, 1621, 58½ in. x 39⅝ in. (1486 mm x 1006 mm). Purchased, 1860 / © National Portrait Gallery, London

Extraordinary and Fatal Combat, 1830 (coloured litho), English School, (19th century) / Guildhall Library, City of London / The Bridgeman Art Library

Royal Mint, Stamping Room from Ackermann's 'Microcosm of London', Rowlandson, T.(1756–1827) & Pugin, A.C.(1762–1832) / Guildhall Library, City of London / The Bridgeman Art Library

Jean Froissart, Chroniques de France, d'Angleterre, Vol. II. Ms. Royal 18, E.I, f. 165 v, akg-images / British Library

Private Collection / © Look and Learn / The Bridgeman Art Library

Royal Ms 16 F II, f.73: Tower of London and shipping, with Charles, Duke of Orleans seated in the Tower writing, from Poems of Charles Duke of Orleans, c.1500 (vellum), English School, (16th century) / British Library, London, UK / © British Library Board. All Rights Reserved / The Bridgeman Art Library

Edward V and the Duke of York in the Tower (Les Enfants d'Edouard) 1831 (oil on canvas) Delaroche, Hippolyte (Paul) (1797-1856) / © Wallace Collection, London, UK / The Bridgeman Art Library

Anne Boleyn (1507–36) in the Tower, detail, 1835 (oil on canvas), Cibot, Edouard (Francois Berthelemy Michel) (1799–1877) / Musee Rolin, Autun, France / The Bridgeman Art Library

Engraving. World History Archive / Credit: IAM / akg-images

British Museum / Mary Evans Picture Library

Mary Evans Picture Library

Sir Thomas Wyatt (c.1521–54) Attacking the Byward Tower (engraving) (b/w photo), Cruikshank, George (1792–1878) / Private Collection / The Bridgeman Art Library

Henry Wriothesley, 3rd Earl of Southampton (1573–1624), 1603 (oil on canvas), Critz, John de, the Elder (c.1552–1642)(attr. to) / Boughton House, Northamptonshire, UK / The Bridgeman Art Library

The Execution of Lady Jane Grey, 1833 (oil on canvas), Delaroche, Hippolyte (Paul) (1797–1856) / National Gallery, London, UK / The Bridgeman Art Library

Stapleton Historical Collection / © 2011. Photo Scala Florence/Heritage Images

F Nash / Mary Evans Picture Library

The Gunpowder Plot Conspirators, 1606 (engraving) (b&w photo), German School, (17th century) / Private Collection / The Bridgeman Art Library

Henry Percy, 9th Earl of Northumberland, wearing Chancellor's robes and the Garter Ribbon by Dyck, Sir Anthony van (1599–1641) (workshop of) Private Collection/ Photo © Bonhams, London, UK/ The Bridgeman Art Library

Dan Kitwood/PA Archive/Press Association Images

Frances, Countess of Somerset, studio of William Larkin, oil on panel, feigned oval, circa 1615, 22⅛ in. x 17¼ in. (575 mm x 438 mm). Purchased, 1922 / © National Portrait Gallery, London

The Tower of London, 1647 (engraving), Hollar, Wenceslaus (1607–77) / Private Collection / The Stapleton Collection / The Bridgeman Art Library

Copper engraving by G. Scott. From: James Caulfield, Portraits, memoirs and characters of remarkable persons . . ., London, 1813. C.152.b.9 volume II, opp.177, akg-images / British Library

Blood and his Accomplices Making their Escape after Stealing the Crown of Charles II, 1793 (engraving) (b&w photo), Simpson, T. (fl.1790–1815) / Private Collection / The Bridgeman Art Library

Photo by Tim Graham / Getty Images

Charles II (1630–85) c.1661–2. John Michael Wright. Purchased by Queen Victoria / The Royal Collection © 2011, Her Majesty Queen Elizabeth II

Unknown man, formerly known as James Scott, Duke of Monmouth and Buccleuch by Unknown artist, oil on canvas, 22¼ in. x 26¼ in. (565 mm x 667 mm). Purchased, 1910. Primary Collection

The Escape of Lord Nithsdale from the Tower, 1716, from 'Illustrations of English and Scottish History' Volume II (engraving) (see also 17890), Osborn, Emily Mary (1834–93) (after) / Private Collection / Ken Welsh / The Bridgeman Art Library

Portrait of Simon Fraser, Lord Lovat (c.1667–1747) 25 August 1746 (engraving) (b/w photo), Hogarth, William (1697–1764) / Private Collection / The Bridgeman Art Library

"Breaking into the Strong room, in the 'Jewel Tower' and Removal of the Regalia, on the night of the Fire, Oct 30 1841" etched by George Cruickshank, published in George Cruickshank's Omnibus, 1870. Steel engraving (originally published about 1841), 10.5 x 19.5 cms including title, plus margins. Image: Steve Bartrick, Antique Print Collection

Photo by Popperfoto / Getty Images

Photo by Topfoto.co.uk

Photo by Evening Standard / Getty Images

INDEX